Common Value Auctions and the Winner's Curse

Common Value Auctions and the Winner's Curse

*John H. Kagel and
Dan Levin*

PRINCETON UNIVERSITY PRESS

PRINCETON AND OXFORD

Library of Congress Cataloging-in-Publication Data

Kagel, John H. (John Henry), 1942–

Common value auctions and the winner's curse / John H. Kagel and Dan Levin.

p.   cm.

Includes bibliographical references and index.

ISBN 0-691-01667-4 (alk. paper)

1. Auctions. 2. Paradoxes. 3. Value. I. Levin, Dan, 1947– II. Title.

HF5476 .K27 2002

381'.17—dc21   2002072254

British Library Cataloging-in-Publication Data is available

This book has been composed in Times Roman
Printed on acid-free paper. ∞

www.pupress.princeton.edu

Printed in the United States of America

1 3 5 7 9 10 8 6 4 2

To Our Families

Harriette, Beth and Julie

Irit, Gilad and Shoshana

Contents

Preface

With various colleagues and students we have been studying common value auctions for well over fifteen years now. We have written a series of papers looking at different aspects of these auctions that have appeared in a number of journals. Having reached closure on a number of questions, we thought it might be nice to pull the papers together in one spot both for the convenience of interested readers and to make the connections between the papers clearer. We have also taken the opportunity to include some of the appendixes to the original material that wound up on the cutting room floor, and that we get requests for from time to time. As part of the exercise we have agreed to update the survey of experimental work on common value auctions which first appeared in the *Handbook of Experimental Economics* (1995), and to write briefly on the interrelationships between the papers, providing some retrospective thoughts on the work and some of the motivation for undertaking the different studies.

There are many people to acknowledge in a work of this sort. First and foremost are our many coauthors and students without whose collaboration the papers would have never been written. Also, the many referees and discussants of the papers at various conferences, and the referees for the book itself. While maybe not always liking what they had to say at the time, their input has been quite valuable. Funding for the experiments has been provided throughout by the SBS Division of the National Science Foundation. Significant research support has been provided at various times by the Sloan Foundation, the Russell Sage Foundation, Resource for the Future and the Energy Laboratory at the University of Houston. We could not have done the work without the research support. Jo Ducey provided valuable editorial support.

January 2001

Credits

Chapter 2: "First-Price Common Value Auctions: Bidder Behavior and the 'Winner's Curse,'" John H. Kagel, Dan Levin, Raymond C. Battalio, and Donald J. Meyer. Reprinted from *Economic Inquiry*, Vol. XXVII, April 1989, 241–258. Reprinted by permission of the Western Economic Association International.

Chapter 3: "The Winner's Curse and Public Information in Common Value Auctions," John H. Kagel and Dan Levin. Reprinted from *The American Economic Review*, Vol. 76, No. 5 (December 1986), 894–920. Reprinted with the permission of the American Economic Association. Addendum: "Benchmark Equilibrium for First-Price Auctions with Public Information," Colin M. Campbell, John H. Kagel, and Dan Levin, *The American Economic Review*, Vol. 89, No. 1 (March 1999), 329–334. Reprinted with the permission of the American Economic Association.

Chapter 4: Reprinted from *International Journal of Game Theory*, "Comparative Static Effects of Number of Bidders and Public Information on Behavior in Second-Price Common Value Auctions," John H. Kagel, Dan Levin, Ronald M. Harstad, Vol. 24 (1995), 293–319 with permission from Springer-Verlag GmbH.

Chapter 5: "Information Impact and Allocation Rules in Auctions with Affiliated Private Values: A Laboratory Study," John H. Kagel, Ronald M. Harstad, and Dan Levin, *Econometrica*, Vol. 55, No. 6 (November 1987), 1275–1304. Reprinted with the permission of The Econometric Society.

Chapter 6: "Revenue Effects and Information Processing in English Common Value Auctions," Dan Levin, John H. Kagel, and Jean-Francois Richard, *The American Economic Review*, Vol. 86, No. 3 (June 1996), 442–460. Reprinted with the permission of the American Economic Association.

Chapter 7: "Common Value Auctions with Insider Information," John H. Kagel and Dan Levin, *Econometrica*, Vol. 67, No. 5 (September 1999), 1219–1238. Reprinted with the permission of The Econometric Society.

Chapter 8: "Can the Seller Benefit from an Insider in Common-Value Auctions?" by Colin M. Campbell and Dan Levin, from *Journal of Economic Theory*, Vol. 91, 106–120, copyright © 2000 by Academic Press, reprinted by permission of the publisher.

Chapter 9: "Second-Price Auctions with Asymmetric Payoffs: An Experimental Investigation," Christopher Avery and John H. Kagel, *Journal of Economics &*

Management Strategy, Vol. 6, No. 3 (Fall 1997), 573–603. © 1997 by the Massachusetts Institute of Technology, reprinted by permission of the publisher.

Chapter 10: Reprinted from *Journal of Economic Behavior and Organization*, Vol. 25, Susan Garvin and John H. Kagel, "Learning in Common Value Auctions: Some Initial Observations," 351–372 (1994), with permission from Elsevier Science.

Chapter 11: Reprinted from *Economics Letters*, Vol. 49, John H. Kagel, "Cross-Game Learning: Experimental Evidence from First-Price and English Common Value Auctions," 163–170 (1995), with permission from Elsevier Science.

Chapter 12: "A Comparison of Naïve and Experienced Bidders in Common Value Offer Auctions: A Laboratory Analysis," Douglas Dyer, John H. Kagel, and Dan Levin, *The Economic Journal*, Vol. 99 (March 1989), 108–115. Reprinted by permission of Blackwell Publishers.

Chapter 13: Reprinted by permission, Douglas Dyer and John H. Kagel, "Bidding in Common Value Auctions: How the Commercial Construction Industry Corrects for the Winner's Curse," *Management Science*, Vol. 42, No. 10 (October 1996), 1463–1475. Copyright INFORMS, 901 Elkridge Landing Road, Suite 400, Linthicum, MD 21090 USA.

Common Value Auctions and the Winner's Curse

1

Bidding in Common-Value Auctions: A Survey of Experimental Research

John H. Kagel and Dan Levin[1]

Auctions are of considerable practical and theoretical importance.[1] In practical terms, the value of goods exchanged in auctions each year is huge. Governments routinely use auctions to purchase goods and services, to sell government assets, and to fund the national debt. Private-sector auctions are common as well, and of growing importance in areas such as deregulated utility markets, allocation of pollution rights, and the large variety of items now being sold via Internet auctions. Auctions are commonly employed when one party to the exchange (for example, the seller) is uncertain about the value that buyers place on the item. Auctions provide a mechanism, absent middlemen, to establish value in such situations. Auctions play a prominent role in the theory of exchange, as they remain one of the simplest and most familiar means of price determination in the absence of intermediate market makers. In addition, auctions serve as valuable illustrations, and one of the most prominent applications, of games of incomplete information, as bidders' private information is the main factor affecting strategic behavior (Wilson 1992).

Auctions have traditionally been classified as one of two types: private-value auctions, where bidders know the value of the item to themselves with certainty but there is uncertainty regarding other bidders' values, or common-value auctions, where the value of the item is the same to everyone, but different bidders have different estimates about the underlying value. Most (nonlaboratory) auctions have both private-value and common-value elements. There are also many different methods for auctioning items, with first-price sealed-bid auctions and open outcry English auctions being the most common institutions. In analyzing auctions, economists have focused on questions of economic efficiency (getting items into the hands of the highest-valued bidders), on maximizing sellers' revenue, and on how auctions aggregate information. The most developed branch of the literature deals with single-unit auctions, where a single item is sold to a number of competing bidders or a number of sellers compete for the right to supply a single item. Recent Federal government spectrum (airwave rights) auctions have exposed many gaps in economists' knowledge about auctions in which multiple units of closely related items are sold, and in which individual bidders demand more than a single unit of the commodity.

The chapters in this book all deal with single-unit common-value auctions. As noted, in a pure common-value auction, the ex post value of the item is the same to all bidders. What makes the auction interesting is that bidders do not know the value at the time they bid. Instead, they receive signal values that are correlated with the value of the item.[2] Mineral-rights auctions, particularly the Federal government's outer continental shelf (OCS) oil-lease auctions, are typically modeled as pure common-value auctions. There is a common-value element to most auctions. Bidders for an oil painting may purchase for their own pleasure, a private-value element, but they may also bid for investment and eventual resale, reflecting the common-value element.

There are no efficiency issues in pure common-value auctions, as all bidders place equal value on the item.[3] What has been of overriding concern to both theorists and practitioners is the revenue-raising effect of different auction institutions. A second key issue, one that provides much of the focus for the essays in this book, is the winner's curse, an *unpredicted* effect that was initially postulated on the basis of field data, and whose existence has often been hotly debated among economists.

The winner's curse story begins with Capen, Clapp, and Campbell (1971), three petroleum engineers who claimed that oil companies had suffered unexpectedly low rates of return in the 1960's and 1970's on OCS lease sales "year after year."[4] They argued that these low rates of return resulted from the fact that winning bidders ignored the informational consequences of winning. That is, bidders naively based their bids on the unconditional expected value of the item (their own estimates of value), which, although correct on average, ignores the fact that you only win when your estimate happens to be the highest (or one of the highest) of those competing for the item. But winning against a number of rivals following similar bidding strategies implies that your estimate is an overestimate of the value of the lease *conditional on the event of winning*. Unless this adverse selection effect is accounted for in formulating a bidding strategy, it will result in winning bids that produce below normal or even negative profits. The systematic failure to account for this adverse selection effect is commonly referred to as the winner's curse: you win, you lose money, and you curse.

(*Terminological aside*: Unfortunately, in discussions of the winner's curse, many economists, particularly theorists, use the term to refer to the difference between the expected value of the item conditional on the event of winning and the naive expectation [not conditional on the event of winning]. Further, their use of the term typically refers to the study of players who fully account for the winner's curse, rather than those who fall prey to it.)

The idea that oil companies suffered from a winner's curse in OCS lease sales was greeted with skepticism by many economists, as it implies that bidders repeatedly err, violating basic economic notions of rationality and contrary to equilibrium predictions.[5] An alternative and simpler explanation as to why oil companies might claim that they fell prey to a winner's curse lies in cartel theory, as responsiveness to the winner's curse claim could serve as a coordination device to get rivals to reduce their bids in future sales. Nevertheless, claims that bidders fell prey to the winner's curse have arisen in a number of field settings. In addition to the oil industry (Capen, Clapp, and Campbell 1971; Lorenz and Dougherty 1983, and references cited therein), claims have been made in auctions for book publication rights (Dessauer 1981), in professional baseball's free-agency market (Cassing and Douglas 1980; Blecherman and Camerer 1998), in corporate-takeover battles (Roll 1986), and in real-estate auctions (Ashenfelter and Genesore 1992).

It is exceedingly difficult to support claims of a winner's curse using field data because of reliability problems with the data and because alternative explanations for overbidding are often available. For example, Hendricks, Porter, and Boudreau (1987) found that in early OCS lease sales, average profits were negative in auctions with seven or more bidders. Hendricks et al. note that one possible explanation for this outcome is the increased severity of the adverse selection problem associated with more bidders. However, they note that the data could also be explained by bidder uncertainty regarding the number of firms competing on a given tract (their preferred explanation). That is, since most tracts received less than six bids, it seems likely that firms would expect this number or less. As a result, although firms might have fully accounted for the adverse selection effect based on the *expected* number of firms bidding on a tract, they would nevertheless be incorrect for tracts that attracted above-average numbers of bidders, and overbid on those tracts. (These results, along with other empirical studies of OCS oil-lease sales, are briefly reviewed in section 6.1 below.)

The ambiguity inherent in using field data, in conjunction with the controversial nature of claims regarding a winner's curse, provided the motivation for experimental studies of the winner's curse. Early laboratory experiments showed that inexperienced bidders are quite susceptible to the winner's curse (Bazerman and Samuelson 1983; Kagel and Levin 1986; Kagel, Levin, Battalio, and Meyer 1989). In fact, the winner's curse has been such a pervasive phenomenon in the laboratory that most of these initial experiments have focused on its robustness and the features of the environment that might attenuate its effects. Additional interest has focused on public-policy issues—the effects of public information regarding the value of the auctioned item and the effects of different auction institutions on sellers' revenue.

This survey begins with a brief analysis of the first experimental demonstration of the winner's curse (Bazerman and Samuelson 1983). This is followed by summaries of experiments investigating bidding in common-value auctions using an experimental design that we developed. These experiments also demonstrate the existence of a winner's curse even when allowing for extensive feedback and learning from past auction outcomes. They also address policy issues such as the effects of public information and different auction institutions (e.g., first-price sealed-bid auctions versus open outcry English auctions) on sellers' revenue. Experimental work on the winner's curse in other settings—in bilateral bargaining games with uncertainty, in "blind-bid" auctions, in two-sided auction markets with a lemon's problem, and in voting—are also reviewed. This is followed by reviews of experiments investigating whether and how bidders learn to overcome the winner's curse and a brief review of field data in relationship to findings from the experiments. The penultimate section of this survey summarizes the empirical findings from the experimental literature, and discusses several theoretical developments motivated by the experimental outcomes and the role this line of research has played in the successful sale of government airwave rights (the spectrum auctions). We conclude with an overview of the rest of the book.

1. An Initial Experiment Demonstrating the Winner's Curse

Bazerman and Samuelson (1983) conducted the first experiment demonstrating a winner's curse. Using M.B.A. students at Boston University, the experiment was conducted in class, with students participating in four first-price sealed-bid auctions. Bidders formed their own estimates of the value of each of four commodities—jars containing 800 pennies, 160 nickels, 200 large paper clips each worth 4¢, and 400 small paper clips each worth 2¢. Unknown to subjects, each jar had a value of $8.00. (Subjects bid on the value of the commodity, not on the commodity itself.) In addition to their bids, subjects provided their best estimate of the value of the commodities and a 90% confidence bound around these estimates. A prize of $2.00 was given for the closest estimate to the true value in each auction. Auction group size varied between four and twenty-six. The analysis focused on bidder uncertainty about the value of the commodity and the size of the bidding population.

The average value estimate across all four commodities was $5.13 ($2.87 below the true value). As the authors note, this underestimation should reduce the likelihood and magnitude of the winner's curse. In contrast to the mean estimate, the average winning bid was $10.01, resulting in an average loss to the winner of $2.01.[6] The average winning bid generated losses in over half of all the auctions.

Estimated bid functions, using individual bids as the unit of observation, showed that bids were positively, and significantly, related to individual estimates, so that bidders indeed faced an adverse selection problem, only winning when they had higher estimates of the value of the item. Bids were inversely related to the uncertainty associated with individual estimates, but this effect was small (other things equal, a $1.00 increase in the 90% confidence interval reduced bids by 3¢). Number of bidders had no significant effect on individual bids, although the sign was negative (but very small in absolute value).

In contrast, regressions employing the average winning bid showed that these bids were positively, and significantly, related to the winning bidder's estimate of uncertainty and to the number of bidders in the auction.[7] This suggests that winning bidders are substantially more aggressive than other bidders. Indeed, Bazerman and Samuelson note that average winning bids were sensitive to a handful of grossly inflated bids.

The results of this experiment show that the winner's curse is easy to observe. However, many economists would object to the fact that subjects had no prior experience with the problem and no feedback regarding the outcomes of their decisions between auctions, so that the results could be attributed to the mistakes of totally inexperienced bidders. The robustness of these results is even more suspect given their sensitivity to a handful of grossly inflated bids, which one might suppose would be eliminated as a result of bankruptcies or learning in response to losses incurred in earlier auctions. Common-value auction experiments conducted by Kagel and Levin and their associates explore these issues, along with a number of public-policy implications of the theory.

2. Sealed-Bid Auctions

Kagel and Levin and their associates conducted experiments in which bidders participated in a series of auctions with feedback regarding outcomes. Bidders were given starting cash balances from which losses were subtracted and profits were added. Bidders whose cash balances became negative were declared bankrupt and were no longer permitted to bid. Unlike the Bazerman and Samuelson experiment, Kagel and Levin (hereafter, KL) controlled the uncertainty associated with the value of the auctioned item rather than simply measuring it. They did this by conducting auctions in which the common value, x_0, was chosen randomly each period from a known uniform distribution with upper and lower bounds $[\underline{x}, \overline{x}]$. In auctions with a symmetric information structure, each bidder is provided with a private information signal, x, drawn from a uniform distribution on $[x_o - \varepsilon, x_o + \varepsilon]$, where ε is known. (Given this informational structure, private signals are affiliated in the sense of Milgrom and Weber 1982.) In first-price sealed-bid auctions, bids are ranked from highest to lowest with the high bidder paying the amount bid and earning profits equal to $x_o - b_1$, where b_1 is the highest bid. Losing bidders neither gain nor lose money.

In this design, the strategy of bidding max $[x - \varepsilon, \underline{x}]$, which we refer to as the risk-free strategy, fully protects a bidder from negative earnings since it is the lower-bound estimate of x_0. This lower-bound estimate for x_0 was computed for subjects along with an upper-bound estimate of x_0, (min $[x + \varepsilon, \overline{x}]$). Bidders were provided with illustrative distributions of signal values relative to x_o, and several dry runs were conducted before playing for cash. Following each auction period, bidders were provided with the complete set of bids, listed from highest to lowest, along with the corresponding signal values, the value of x_o and the earnings of the high bidder (subject identification numbers were, however, suppressed).

Surviving bidders were paid their end-of-experiment balances in cash. To hold the number of bidders fixed while controlling for bankruptcies, $m > n$ subjects were often recruited, with only n bidding at any given time (who bid in each period was determined randomly or by a fixed rotation rule). As bank-ruptcies occur, m shrinks, but (hopefully) remains greater than or equal to the target value n. Alternative solutions to the bankruptcy problem are discussed below.

2.1 Theoretical Considerations: First-Price Sealed-Bid Auctions

Wilson (1977) was the first to develop the Nash equilibrium solution for first-price common-value auctions, and Milgrom and Weber (1982) provide signifi-cant extensions and generalizations of the Wilson model. In the analysis that follows, we restrict our attention to signals in region 2, the interval $\underline{x} + \varepsilon \leq x \leq \bar{x} - \varepsilon$, where the bulk of the observations lie. (For data outside this interval, we direct the reader to chapters 3 and 6.) Within region 2, bidders have no endpoint information to help in calculating the expected value of the item.[8]

For risk-neutral bidders, the symmetric risk-neutral Nash equilibrium (RNNE) bid function $\gamma(x)$ is given by[9]

$$\gamma(x) = x - \varepsilon + h(x) \qquad (1)$$

$$\text{where } h(x) = \frac{2\varepsilon}{n + 1} \exp\left[-\frac{n}{2\varepsilon}[x - (\underline{x} + \varepsilon)]\right].$$

This equilibrium bid function combines strategic considerations similar to those involved in first-price private-value auctions, and item valuation considerations resulting from the bias in the signal value conditional on the event of winning. We deal with the latter first.

In common-value auctions, bidders usually win the item when they have the highest, or one of the highest, estimates of value. Define $E[x_o \mid X = x_{1n}]$ to be the expected value of the item conditional on having x_{1n}, the highest among n signal values. For signals in region 2,

$$E[x_o \mid X = x_{1n}] = x - [(n - 1)/(n + 1)]\,\varepsilon. \qquad (2)$$

This provides a convenient measure of the extent to which bidders suffer from the winner's curse, since in auctions in which the high signal holder always wins the item, as bidding above $E[x_o \mid X = x_{1n}]$ results in negative expected profit. Further, even with zero correlation between bids and signal values, if everyone else bids above $E[x_o \mid X = x_{1n}]$, bidding above $E[x_o \mid X = x_{1n}]$ re-sults in negative expected profit as well. As such, if the high signal holder frequently wins the auction, or a reasonably large number of rivals are bidding above $E[x_o \mid X = x_{1n}]$, bidding above $E[x_o \mid X = x_{1n}]$ is likely to earn nega-tive expected profit.

Recall that within region 2, $(x - \varepsilon)$ is the smallest possible value for x_o, and that x is the unconditional expected value of x_o (the expected value, *indepen-dent* of winning the item), so that the expected value, conditional on winning, must be between $(x - \varepsilon)$ and x. Thus, from equation (2) it is clear that the amount bids ought to be reduced relative to signal values (the "bid factor"), just to correct for the adverse selection effect from winning the auction, is quite large relative to the range of sensible corrections (ε): with $n = 4$, the bid factor is 60% of ε, and with $n = 7$, it is 75% of ε. Or put another way, for signals in region 2, the RNNE bid function is well approximated by $\gamma(x) = x - \varepsilon$ (the negative exponential term $h(x)$ in equation [1] approaches zero rapidly as x moves beyond $\underline{x} + \varepsilon$). Thus, the bid factor required just to break even, on average, represents 60% of the total bid factor with $n = 4$, and 75% with $n = 7$.[10] Equation (2) also makes it clear that the correction for the adverse selection effect is relatively large and increasing with increases in the number of bidders.

Strategic considerations account for the rest of the bid factor, $2\varepsilon/(n + 1)$. The strategic element results from the fact that if just correcting for the adverse selection effect, the winner would earn zero expected profits, which is not a very attractive outcome. As such, a bidder would find it profitable to lower her bid from this hypothetical benchmark (equation [2]), since zero expected gains are lost by doing so even if this causes her not to win the item, and strictly positive expected gains are awarded should she win the item with the lower price. The interplay of these strategic considerations between different bidders results in the additional discounting of bids relative to signal values beyond equation (2).

2.2 Some Initial Experimental Results: Inexperienced Bidders

Auctions with inexperienced bidders show a pervasive winner's curse that results in numerous bankruptcies. Table 1.1 provides illustrative data on this point. For the first nine auctions, profits averaged $-\$2.57$ compared to the RNNE prediction of \$1.90, with only 17% of all auctions having positive profits. Note, this is after bidders had participated in two to three dry runs, with feedback of signal values, x_o, and bids following each auction, so that the results cannot be attributed to a total lack of experience. The negative profits are not a simple matter of bad luck either, or a handful of grossly inflated bids, as 59% of all bids and 82% of the high bids were above $E[x_o \mid X = x_{1n}]$. Further, 41% of all subjects starting these auctions went bankrupt. In short, the winner's curse is a genuinely pervasive problem for inexperienced bidders. It is remarkably robust being reported under a variety of treatment conditions (Kagel et al., 1989; Lind and Plott 1991; Goeree and Offerman 2000) and for different subject populations, including professional bidders from the commercial construction industry (Dyer, Kagel, and Levin 1989, discussed in section 6.2 below).

2.3 Auctions with Moderately Experienced Bidders and the Effects of Public Information on Sellers' Revenue

Kagel and Levin (1986) report auctions for moderately experienced bidders (those who had participated in at least one prior first-price common-value auc-

TABLE 1.1
Profits and Bidding in First Nine Auctions for Inexperiences Bidders

Experiment	Percentage of Auctions with Positive Profits	Average Actual Profits (t-statistic)	Average Predicted Profits under RNNE $(S_m)^a$	Percentage of All Bids $b > E[x_o\|X = x_{1n}]$	Percentage of Auctions Won by High Signal Holder	Percentage of High Bids $b > E[x_o\|X = x_{1n}]$	Percentage of Subjects Going Bankrupt[b]
1	0.0	−4.83 (−3.62)**	.72 (.21)	63.4	55.6	100	50.0
2	33.3	−2.19 (−1.66)	2.18 (1.02)	51.9	33.3	88.9	16.7
3	11.1	−6.57 (−2.80)*	1.12 (1.19)	74.6	44.4	88.9	62.5
4	11.1	−2.26 (−3.04)**	.85 (.43)	41.8	55.6	55.6	16.7
5	33.3	−.84 (−1.00)	3.60 (1.29)	48.1	44.4	88.9	50.0

6	22.2	−2.65 (−1.53)	2.55 (1.17)	67.3	66.7	100	33.3
7	11.1	−2.04 (−2.75)*	.57 (.25)	58.5	88.9	66.7	50.0
8	11.1	−1.40 (−2.43)*	1.59 (.34)	51.9	55.6	55.6	16.7
9	44.4	.32 (.30)	2.37 (.76)	35.2	88.6	66.7	16.7
10	0.0	−2.78 (−3.65)**	3.53 (.74)	77.2	66.7	100	20.0
11	11.1	−3.05 (−3.53)**	1.82 (.29)	81.5	55.6	88.9	37.5
Average	17.2	−2.57	1.90	59.4	59.6	81.8	41.1

Source: Kagel, Levin, Battalio, and Meyer 1989.

$^{a}S_M$ = standard error of mean.

^{b}For all auctions.

*Statistically significant at the 5% level, 2-tailed test.

**Statistically significant at the 1% level, 2-tailed test.

TABLE 1.2
Profits and Bidding by Experiment and Number of Active Bidders: Private Information Conditions (profits measured in dollars)

Auction Series (no. of periods)	No. of Active Bidders	Average Actual Profit (t-statistical)[a]	Average Profit under RNNE (standard error of mean)	Percentage of Auctions Won by High Signal Holder	Percentage of High Bids $b_I > E[x_o|X = x_{In}]$
6 (31)	3–4	3.73 (2.70)*	9.51 (1.70)	67.7	22.6
2 (18)	4	4.61 (4.35)**	4.99 (1.03)	88.9	0.0
3 small (14)	4	7.53 (2.07)	6.51 (2.65)	78.6	14.3
7 small (19)	4	5.83 (3.35)**	8.56 (2.07)	63.2	10.5
8 small (23)	4	1.70 (1.56)	6.38 (1.21)	82.6	39.1
1 (18)	5	2.89 (3.14)**	5.19 (.86)	72.2	27.8
3 large (11)	5–7	−2.92 (−1.49)	3.64 (.62)	81.8	63.6
7 large (18)	6	1.89 (1.67)	4.70 (1.03)	72.2	22.2
4 (25)	6–7	−.23 (−.15)	4.78 (.92)	69.2	48.0
5 (26)	7	−.41 (−.44)	5.25 (1.03)	42.3	65.4
8 large (14)	7	−2.74 (−2.04)	5.03 (1.40)	78.6	71.4
Small-Market Average	3–4	4.32 (5.55)**	7.48 (0.77)	75.2	19.0
Large-Market Average	6–7	−0.54 (0.87)	4.82 (0.50)	62.9	53.9

Source: Kagel and Levin 1986.
[a]Tests null hypothesis that mean is different from 0.0.
*Significant at the 5% level, 2-tailed t-test.
**Significant at the 1% level, 2-tailed t-test.

tion experiment). Treatment variables of interest were the number of rival bidders and the effects of public information about x_o on revenue. Table 1.2 reports some of their results. For small groups (auctions with three to four bidders), the general pattern was one of positive profits averaging $4.32 per auction, which is significantly greater than zero, but still well below the RNNE prediction of $7.48 per auction. In contrast, for these same bidders, bidding in larger groups (auctions with six to seven bidders), profits averaged $-$0.54 per auction, compared to the RNNE prediction of $4.82.[11] Thus, the profit picture had improved substantially compared to that of the inexperienced bidders discussed in the previous section.

However, comparing large- and small-group auctions, actual profit decreased substantially more than profit opportunities as measured by the RNNE criteria. This implies that subjects were bidding more aggressively, rather than less aggressively, as the number of rivals increased, contrary to the RNNE prediction. This is confirmed in regressions using individual subject bids as the dependent variable. Higher individual bids in response to increased numbers of rivals is often considered to be the hallmark of a winner's curse. Thus, although bidders had adjusted reasonably well to the adverse selection problem in auctions with three to four bidders, in auctions with six to seven bidders, with its heightened adverse selection effect, the winner's curse reemerged as subjects confounded the heightened adverse selection effect by bidding more aggressively with more bidders. This result also suggests that the underlying learning process is context-specific rather than involving some sort of "theory absorption" that readily generalizes to new environments.[12]

Public information was provided to bidders in the form of announcing the lowest signal value, x_L. For the RNNE, public information about the value of the item raises expected revenue. The mechanism underlying this outcome works as follows: All bidders evaluate the additional public information assuming that their signal is the highest since, in equilibrium, they only win in this case. Evaluating additional information from this perspective, together with affiliation, induces all bidders other than the highest signal holder to, on average, revise their bids upward after an announcement of unbiased public information. This upward revision results from two factors:

1. Affiliation results in bidders without the highest signal systematically treating the public information as "good news." These bidders formulated their bids on the assumption that they held the highest private information signal and would win the auction. As such, with affiliation, the public information tells them that, on average, the expected value of the item is higher than they had anticipated (i.e., the private information signal they are holding is somewhat lower than expected, conditional on winning, for this particular auction), which leads them to increase their bids.

2. Bidders know that rivals with lower signal values are responding in this way. As such, other things equal, they will need to increase their bids in response to the anticipated increase in bids from lower signal holders.

The bidder with the highest signal is not, on average, subject to this first force. Thus, she does not, on average, revise her estimate of the true value. Nevertheless, she raises her bid in response to this second factor, the "domino" effect of bidders with lower signals raising their bids.[13]

These strategic considerations hold for a wide variety of public information signals (Milgrom and Weber 1982). There are, however, several methodological advantages to using x_L. First, the RNNE bid function can be readily solved for x_L, provided low signal holders are restricted to bidding x_L, so that the experimenter continues to have a benchmark model of fully rational behavior against which to compare actual bidding. Second, x_L provides a substantial dose of public information about x_o (it cuts expected profit in half), while still maintaining an interesting auction. As such it should have a substantial impact on prices, regardless of any inherent noise in behavior. Finally, the experimenter can always implement finer, more subtle probes of public information after seeing what happens with such a strong treatment effect.[14]

KL (1986) found that in auctions with a small number of bidders (three to four), public information resulted in statistically significant increases in revenue that averaged 38% of the RNNE model's prediction. However, in auctions with a larger number of bidders (six to seven), public information *reduced* average sellers' revenue by $1.79 per auction, compared to the RNNE model's prediction of an increase of $1.78. KL attribute this reduction in revenue to the presence of a relatively strong winner's curse in auctions with a large number of bidders. If bidders suffer from a winner's curse, the high bidder consistently overestimates the item's value, so that announcing x_L is likely to result in a downward revision of the most optimistic bidders' estimate. Thus, out of equilibrium, public information introduces a potentially powerful offset to the forces promoting increased bids discussed earlier, and will result in reduced revenue if the winner's curse is strong enough. This hypothesis is confirmed using data from auctions with six to seven bidders, which shows that the RNNE model's prediction of an increase in sellers' revenue is critically dependent on whether or not there was a winner's curse in the corresponding private information market.[15]

(*Methodological aside:* These experiments were conducted using a dual-market bidding procedure in which subjects first bid in a market with private information and then, before these bids were opened, bid again in a market with x_L announced. This maintains the *ceteris paribus* conditions under which the comparative static predictions of the theory are formulated. This procedure greatly facilitated understanding the basis for the breakdown in the model's predictions.)

KL relate this public information result to anomalous findings from OCS auctions. Mead, Moseidjord, and Sorensen (1983, 1984; hereafter MMS) compared rates of return on wildcat and drainage leases in early OCS auctions. A wildcat lease is one for which no positive drilling data are available, so that bidders have symmetric information. On a drainage lease, hydrocarbons have been located on an adjacent tract so that there is an asymmetric information structure, with companies who lease the adjacent tracts (neighbors) having superior information to other companies (non-neighbors). The anomaly reported by MMS is that *both* neighbors and non-neighbors earned a higher rate of return on drainage compared to wildcat leases. In other words, with the asymmetric information structure, even the less-informed bidders (non-neighbors) received a higher rate of return on drainage leases than on leases with a symmetric information structure (wildcat tracts). In contrast, a fundamental prediction for models with "insider information" is that less-informed bidders will earn smaller informational rents than they would in a corresponding symmetric information structure auction like the wildcat auctions (see section 3.2 and chapter 7 below). KL (1986) rationalize the MMS data by arguing that there is a considerable amount of public information associated with drainage tracts,[16] and the public information may have corrected for a winner's curse that depressed rates of return on wildcat tracts.[17] Although this is not the only possible explanation for the field data—the leading alternative explanation is that the lower rate of return on wildcat leases reflects the option value of the proprietary information that will be realized on neighbor tracts if hydrocarbons are found— the KL explanation has the virtue of parsimony and consistency with the experimental data.

KL also note that in markets with x_L announced, average profits were positive in all auction sessions and only slightly less than predicted on average. Further, there were no systematic differences in realized profits relative to predicted profits between auctions with small and large numbers of bidders. These two characteristics suggest that with the large dose of public information involved in announcing x_L, the winner's curse had been almost entirely eliminated.

2.4 Is the Winner's Curse a Laboratory Artifact? Limited Liability for Losses

Results of experiments are often subject to alternative explanations. These alternative explanations typically provide the motivation for subsequent experiments that further refine our understanding of behavior. This section deals with one such alternative explanation and the responses to it.

In the KL (1986) design, subjects enjoyed limited liability, as they could not lose more than their starting cash balances. Hansen and Lott (1991; hereafter HL) argued that the overly aggressive bidding reported in KL *may* have been a rational response to this limited liability rather than a result of the winner's curse. In a one-shot auction, if a bidder's cash balance is zero, so that he is not liable for *any* losses, it indeed pays to overbid relative to the Nash equilibrium bidding strategy proposed in section 2.1. With downside losses eliminated, the only constraint on more aggressive bidding is the opportunity cost of bidding more than is necessary to win the item. In exchange, higher bids increase the probability of winning the item and making positive profits. The net effect, in the case of zero or small cash balances, is an incentive to bid more than the Nash equilibrium prediction. HL's argument provides a possible alternative explanation to the overly aggressive bidding reported in KL 1986 and in Kagel et al. 1989.[18]

Initial responses to this limited-liability argument were twofold. First, KL (1991) reevaluated their data in light of HL's arguments, demonstrating that for almost all bidders cash balances were *always* large enough so that it *never* paid to deviate from the Nash equilibrium bidding strategy in a one-shot auction. Second, Lind and Plott (1991) replicated KL's experiment in a design that eliminated limited-liability problems, and reproduced KL's primary results. This provides experimental verification that limited-liability forces do not account for the overly aggressive bidding reported.

KL's design protects against limited-liability problems, since bidding $x - \varepsilon$ insures against all losses, and bidders have their own personal estimate of the maximum possible value of the item (min $[x + \varepsilon, \bar{x}]$). The latter implies that it is never rational, limited liability or not, to bid above this maximum possible value in a first-price auction. Further, cash balances only have to be a fraction of the maximum possible loss for the limited-liability argument to lose its force in a first price auction. For example, KL (1991) report simulations for auctions with four or seven bidders, with $\varepsilon = \$30$ and cash balances of $4.50 (which forty-eight out of the fifty bidders always had), for which unilateral deviations from the RNNE bid function were not profitable even when fully accounting for bidders' limited liability. Further, limited-liability arguments imply more aggressive bidding in auctions with fewer rather than greater numbers of bidders, just the opposite of what the data shows.[19] As such, overbidding in the KL experiment must be explained on some other grounds, such as the judgmental error underlying the winner's curse.[20]

Lind and Plott (1991; hereafter LP) replicated KL's results in auctions where bankruptcy problems were almost completely eliminated. One experimental treatment involved conducting private-value auctions where subjects were sure to make money simultaneously with the common-value auctions, thereby guaranteeing a steady cash inflow against which to charge any losses incurred in the common-value auctions. In addition, subjects agreed that if they ended the experiment with a negative cash balance, they would work losses off doing work-study type duties (photocopying, running departmental errands, etc.) at the prevailing market wage rate. A second treatment involved sellers' markets in which bidders tendered offers to sell an item of unknown value. Each bidder was given one item with the option to keep it and collect its value or to sell it. In this auction, all subjects earned positive profits, including the winner, but the winner could suffer an opportunity cost by selling the item for less than its true value.[21]

LP's results largely confirm those reported by KL and their associates. First, a winner's curse exists, and although the magnitude and frequency of losses decline with experience, it persists (see Table 1.3). Second, the winner's curse does not result from a few "irrational" bidders, but almost all agents experience the curse. Finally, LP test between alternative models of bidder behavior— comparing the RNNE bidding model with the naive bidding model offered in

TABLE 1.3

Frequency of Losses for Winning Bidders in the Lind and Plott Experiment, in dollars (Francs)

	Experiments				
	1. Buyers	2. Buyers	3. Sellers	4. Sellers	5. Sellers
Periods 1–10					
Number of periods of loss	8/10	8/10	5/10	6/10	5/10
Average profit per period	−7.90 (−7.90)	−8.31 (−8.31)	−0.075 (−29.80)	−0.048 (−48.20)	0.001 (1.10)
Average RNNE profit per period*	4.53 (4.53)	5.70 (5.70)	0.177 (70.96)	0.060 (60.44)	0.048 (68.71)
Periods 11–20					
Number of periods of loss	4/10	2/7	3/7	2/10	7/10
Average profit per period	4.57 (4.57)	3.12 (3.12)	0.053 (21.00)	0.032 (31.60)	−0.016 (−22.40)
Average RNNE profit per period*	18.47 (18.47)	13.58 (13.58)	0.212 (84.85)	0.048 (48.15)	0.037 (52.68)
Periods 21–30					
Number of periods of loss	—	—	—	3/10	5/10
Average profit per period	—	—	—	0.058 (58.40)	−0.004 (−6.10)
Average RNNE profit per period*	—	—	—	0.104 (104.02)	0.090 (128.91)
Periods 31–40					
Number of periods of loss	—	—	—	2/5	8/10
Average profit per period	—	—	—	0.063 (62.80)	−0.033 (−46.80)
Average RNNE profit per period*	—	—	—	0.065 (65.34)	0.024 (33.72)

Source: Lind and Plott 1991.

*The given RNNE equation is valid only for $\underline{x} + \varepsilon \leq X_i \leq \bar{x} - \varepsilon$. Some of the winners' signals were not in this range, so no predicted RNNE is possible. Therefore, this average includes only periods for which the RNNE predicted profit can be calculated.

KL. Since these models imply different sets of parameter restrictions on a common functional form, LP compute F-statistics comparing the sum of squared errors of the unrestricted model with the restricted model, using the F-statistic as a measure of the relative goodness of fit of the competing models. They find that neither model organizes the data, but that the RNNE provides a better fit. This last result, in conjunction with the negative average profits reported, indicates that there was partial, but incomplete, adjustment to the adverse selection forces in LP's auctions.

Cox, Dinkin, and Smith (1998; hereafter CDS) conducted auctions using KL's design in which, under one treatment, they reinitialized bidders' cash balances in each auction period, with balances large enough that subjects could not go bankrupt even if bidding well above their signal values. In contrast to this unlimited-liability treatment, their other treatments employed procedures where cash balances fluctuated, bidders could go bankrupt, and, in some treatments, bidders with negative cash balances were permitted to continue to bid.[22] Using data for all treatments and all levels of bidder experience, CDS find no significant differences in individual bid patterns in the unlimited-liability treatment, contrary to HL's argument. Further, restricting their analysis to experiments with experienced subjects, and dropping data from an entire experiment if even one subject adopted a pattern of high bids when having a negative cash balance, CDS find that the unlimited-liability treatment significantly *increased* individual bids, the exact opposite of HL's hypothesis. This seemingly bizarre outcome is, however, consistent with KL's (1991) argument that in a multiauction setting, where cash balances carry over from one auction to the next, there is a potentially powerful offset to any limited-liability forces present in a one-shot auction: overly aggressive bidding due to low cash balances may be offset by the risk that such bids will result in bankruptcy, thereby preventing participation in later auctions with their positive expected profit opportunities.[23]

2.5 Second-Price Sealed-Bid Auctions

LP are puzzled that even though there is a winner's curse in their first-price common-value auctions, the RNNE model provides the best fit to the data: "A major puzzle remains: of the models studied, the best is the risk-neutral Nash-equilibrium model, but that model predicts that the curse will not exist" (LP 1991, 344). They go on to comment that "part of the difficulty with further study stems from the lack of theory about [first price] common-value auctions with risk aversion. . . . If the effect of risk aversion is to raise the bidding function as it does in private [value] auctions, then risk-aversion . . . might resolve the puzzle; but, of course, this remains only a conjecture" (ibid.). Second-price auctions provide an ideal vehicle for exploring this conjecture.

In contrast to first-price auctions, the theory of risk-averse bidders is well understood in second-price auctions with both *symmetric* risk-averse bidders and with *asymmetric* risk-averse bidders.[24] Second-price sealed-bid auctions are similar to first-price auctions with one major difference: the price is determined by the second-highest (and not the winner's) bid. Matthews (1977) and Milgrom and Weber (1982) showed that the bid function $\gamma(x)$ implicitly defined by:

$$E[u(x_o - \gamma(x)) \mid X_i = x = Y_{1n}] \doteq 0 \qquad (3)$$

is the symmetric Nash equilibrium (symmetric in both risk preferences and strategy choices), where u(•) is a (common) concave utility function, x_i is the signal of bidder i, and Y_{1n} is the highest signal among $n - 1$ rival bidders.[25]

Under risk neutrality (RN), for signals in region 2, the bid function satisfying (3) is

$$\gamma^{RN}(x) = E\,[x_o \mid X_i = x = Y_{1n}] = x - \varepsilon(n - 2)/n, \qquad (4)$$

where $E\,[x_o \mid X_i = x = Y_{1n}]$ is bidder i's expected value of the item conditional on having the highest signal value and conditional on the next highest rival having the *same* signal value. $\gamma(x)$ (or $\gamma^{RN}(x)$) measures a bidder's *maximum willingness to pay* conditional on winning in a symmetric equilibrium. It is the maximum in that it leaves that bidder just indifferent between winning and paying that price or not winning. In cases where $X_i = x$ is the highest signal, $X_i = x \geq Y_{1n}$ so that the winning bid is greater than the expected value (utility) of the item (since $\gamma(x)$ or $\gamma^{RN}(x)$ condition on $X_i = x = Y_{1n}$). Nevertheless, the winning bidder earns positive expected profit since she is paying the maximum willingness to pay of the second-highest signal holder, which is lower than hers. Losing bidders would earn negative expected profit by raising their bid enough to win the item, since in this event the highest signal holder sets the price (her maximum willingness to pay), which is higher than the expected utility of a deviating loser, who holds a lower signal.

With risk aversion, and symmetry, the Nash equilibrium bid factor is even larger than in (4), resulting in even larger profits than under risk neutrality, as the maximum willingness to pay given that risk is involved is lower than that of a risk-neutral bidder.[26] Even if bidders do not have identical risk preferences, they will bid below (4), provided they are all risk-averse. This result even extends to auctions where the strategy profile is not an equilibrium (Harstad 1991; Kagel, Levin, and Harstad 1995). Corresponding predictions in first-price auctions require symmetric bidders and are conditional on risk attitudes and the underlying distribution of information at bidders' disposal. Further, the symmetric Nash equilibrium bidding model has the important comparative static prediction that individual bids must decrease with more rivals.[27] This last prediction is also robust to assumptions regarding risk preferences and applies to best-response profiles in addition to equilibrium bid functions (Harstad 1991; Kagel, Levin, and Harstad 1995).

Kagel, Levin, and Harstad (1995; hereafter KLH) investigated these comparative static predictions, along with the effects of public information on sellers' revenue. They used moderately experienced bidders that had all participated in at least one prior series of second-price common-value auctions.[28] Table 1.4 reports results from this experiment. As with the first-price auctions, there are

TABLE 1.4
Market Outcomes under Private Information Conditions: Second-Price Auctions

Session (no. of auctions)	No. of Active Bidders	Percentage of Auctions Won by High Signal Holder	Median Rank-Order Correlation Coefficient between Bids and Signals	Average Profit (standard, error mean)			Profit as a Percentage of RNNE
				Naive Bidding	Observed	RNNE	
5A (20)	4	70.0	.90	−3.49 (1.83)	3.34** (1.48)	5.49 (2.09)	60.8
6A (22)	4	90.9	.80	−2.71 (1.82)	5.42** (1.73)	6.68 (1.51)	81.1
6B (7)	5	42.9	.70	−5.86 (2.33)	3.24 (4.84)	7.61 (2.51)	42.6
1 (25)	5	40.0	.80	−5.69 (1.04)	1.11 (1.18)	3.45 (.93)	32.2
5B (12)	5–6	58.3	.76	−9.03 (3.22)	−5.84* (2.89)	6.19 (3.91)	−94.5
2 (20)	6–7	70.0	.84	−5.10 (1.01)	−1.01 (1.28)	4.23 (1.14)	−23.9
4 (25)	6–7	44.0	.86	−10.80 (1.16)	−.50 (1.19)	2.04 (.95)	−24.5
3 (23)	7	43.5	.79	−9.44 (1.40)	−3.06** (1.45)	4.72 (1.25)	−64.8

Source: Kagel, Levin, and Harstad 1995.
*Significantly different from zero at 10% level in 2-tailed t-test.
**Significantly different from zero at 5% level in 2-tailed t-test.

substantial differences in profits conditional on the number of active bidders. In auctions with four or five active bidders, profits are positive, averaging 52.8% of the profits predicted under the symmetric RNNE. Such outcomes are closer to the RNNE benchmark than to a naive bidding model, in which bidders take their signal values to be equal to the value of the item (i.e., bidding as if in a second-price private-value auction). Note, however, that contrary to LP's conjecture, in this case profits below the RNNE benchmark cannot be attributed to risk aversion. Further, as in the first-price auctions experiments, in auctions with six or seven active bidders, average profits were consistently negative, averaging −$2.15 per auction period, compared with predicted profits of $3.97 under the symmetric RNNE benchmark.

Using a fixed-effect regression model, and comparing auctions with four and five bidders to those with six and seven bidders, KLH find no response to increasing numbers of rivals. This directly contradicts the comparative static prediction of the Nash bidding model, regardless of the degree of asymmetry in bidders' risk preferences or in their bidding strategies. However, it is consistent with a naive bidding model in which bidders fail to account for the adverse selection effect inherent in winning the auction.

As in the first-price auction experiments, the effects of public information on sellers' revenue are studied through publicly announcing x_L, the lowest private information signal.[29] In auctions with four or five bidders, announcing x_L raises average revenue by about 16% of the symmetric RNNE model's prediction (however, this increase is not statistically significant at conventional levels). In contrast, in auctions with six or seven bidders, announcing x_L *reduces* average revenue by $4.00 per auction (which is significant at conventional levels), compared to a predicted *increase* of $1.80 per auction under the symmetric RNNE. As in the first-price auctions, the ability of public information to increase revenue is conditional on eliminating the worst effects of the winner's curse. In the presence of a strong winner's curse, announcement of x_L serves to offset the high signal holders' overly optimistic estimate of the value of the item, thereby reducing, rather than raising, sellers' revenue.

Avery and Kagel (1997; hereafter AK) study a second-price common-value auction in which x_o, the value of the item, is the *sum* of two independent random variables, x_1 and x_2. In this "shoebox" auction, two bidders each bid on the item, with one signal for each bidder. Signals are drawn from a common uniform distribution with support $[\underline{x}, \bar{x}]$. In the unique symmetric equilibrium of this auction, each bidder bids $b_i = 2x_i$, which is implied by equation (4). There is no ex post regret in this symmetric equilibrium, so that even after learning the results of the auction, no bidder wishes to change his bid: When $x > y$, the winner is guaranteed a profit (in equilibrium), since she earns $x + y$ and pays only $2y$. Further, the loser is guaranteed to lose money if he deviates and bids above $2x$, since he would pay $2x$ and earn only $x + y$. Thus, there is no scope for limited liability for losses to affect bidding in equilibrium. In contrast, in the KLH experiment, the random variation in x_o relative to bidders' signal values means that with limited liability for losses, bidders can bid above (4) hoping to get lucky, while being shielded from all, or part, of the negative expected consequences of such overly aggressive bidding. Further, since the equilibrium bid function with only two bidders depends only on bidder i's signal value (x_i), there is no scope for risk preferences to affect bidding. Thus, this experiment rules out, by design, risk aversion and limited liability for losses as possible explanations for deviations from equilibrium bidding.

AK report strong traces of the winner's curse in this setting, as bids are closer to the unconditional expected value of the item ($x_i + [\bar{x} + \underline{x}]/2$) than to the symmetric Nash equilibrium. Expected-value bidding is a classic example of the winner's curse here. In a world with expected-value bidders, anyone with a signal below the mean value $[\bar{x} + \underline{x}]/2$ cannot make a positive profit in any auction: if a bidder with a signal $x_i < [\bar{x} + \underline{x}]/2$ wins, it implies that $x_j \leq x_i$, so that i earns ($x_i + x_j$), and pays j's bid ($x_j + [\bar{x} + \underline{x}]/2$), so that i's profit is ($x_i - [\bar{x} + \underline{x}]/2$) < 0, a certain loss. In contrast, with expected-value bidding, bidders with signals greater than $[\bar{x} + \underline{x}]/2$ will make positive profits. Both inexperienced and once-experienced bidders earned negative profits in around two-thirds of all auctions won with signal values less than or equal to $[\bar{x} + \underline{x}]/2$.[30]

AK also investigate the effect of asymmetric payoffs on behavior in this environment. Consider the case where one of the two bidders is known to have a fixed extra payoff advantage, K, should she win the item. For example, in the FCC spectrum (airwave) auctions, it was well known that PacTel had a particular interest in acquiring licenses in Los Angeles and San Francisco (Cramton 1997). Theory suggests that in a second-price auction, (1) the advantaged bidder must win the auction with certainty in any Nash equilibrium, no matter how small K is, and (2) the disadvantaged bidder reduces her bid drastically in response to K, causing a large reduction in expected revenue compared to the symmetric payoff case (Bikhchandani 1988).[31] Essentially what the private-value advantage does is to destroy the symmetric equilibrium of the second-price auction. In the resulting asymmetric equilibrium, the private-value advantage has a "snowball" effect resulting in the advantaged bidder winning all the time, bidding too high for the disadvantaged bidder to try to unseat him. The second-price auction institution is crucial to this outcome—it does not emerge in a first-price auction—as the high bidder does not have to pay what he bids. In the experiment, the effect of the K value advantage on bids and prices was a proportional reduction in losing bids, not the explosive reduction anticipated by the theory. That is, the symmetric model continues to provide a reasonable approximation to behavior given the modest value of K employed ($1.00). This result has important potential public-policy implications, since there are typically some small asymmetries in auctions outside the laboratory, and these are often implemented using a second-price auction format (which includes open outcry, English auctions, close to the format employed in the FCC spectrum auctions). However, given that in virtually all experimental work, behavior is much closer to equilibrium predictions in open outcry, English auctions compared to sealed-bid auctions (Kagel, Harstad, and Levin 1987; Levin, Kagel, and Richard 1996; Kagel and Levin 1999), there is a clear need to explore asymmetries of this sort in English auctions and FCC multiple-round auctions before relying too heavily on the conclusion that small asymmetries do not matter very much in practice.

2.6 Group versus Individual Bids

Cox and Hayne (1998; hereafter CH) explore possible differences in bidding strategies between groups of bidders and individual bidders. The experiment is motivated by the fact that in many market settings, bids are made by groups of individuals in consultation with one another rather than by individuals acting on their own. Psychological research on group versus individual decision-making identifies classes of decision-making problems in which groups reduce judgmental errors to which individuals fall prey, but other types of problems where the opposite result holds (see the many references in CH). Further, it is not clear, a priori, into which of these two categories the winner's curse falls.

Using KL's experimental design, CH explore two different types of environment: one in which bidders in both the group and individual treatments receive one signal value, and a second in which they receive multiple signal values (each bidder in a group of five receives one independently drawn signal value, whereas in the individual treatment each bidder receives five independently drawn signals).[32] CH report that for inexperienced bidders, the winner's curse is alive and well regardless of treatment conditions. They also explore once- and twice-experienced bidders in some detail. In markets of size 7 (seven individual bidders or seven groups of five decision-makers) and 1 signal value, estimated bid functions in region 2 have slopes that are not significantly different from 1.0 with respect to their own signal value, and have bid factors (intercepts) that do not differ significantly from the minimum bid factor required to avoid the winner's curse. That is, neither individuals nor groups commit the winner's curse; both just about break even, failing to come anywhere close to earning the positive profits predicted in equilibrium. Although CH provide no direct comparisons of group and individual bid functions, differences in bid factors appear to be too small for there to be any statistically significant differences in bid patterns for the one signal case.[33]

In auctions with multiple signal values, estimated bid functions employ the midpoint of the winning bidders' signal values. However, this statistic ignores the information content inherent in the spread in signal values that bidders receive. The latter conveys considerable additional information not captured in using the midpoint of the signal values. To take an extreme example, suppose a bidder receives five signals. In one case, all five signals are the same, which is really no better than receiving one signal in identifying the expected value of the item. Alternatively, suppose that the midpoint of the five signals is the same as in the first case, but the spread between the maximum and minimum signal values is equal to 2ε. This set of signals identifies the value of the item precisely.

Thus, the underlying bid function CH estimate is incorrectly specified. Nevertheless, the results reported are suggestive, since slopes of the bid function with respect to this midpoint signal value are significantly less than 1 and the bid factors are consistently positive in sign. That is, in region 2, the estimated bid functions suggest that (1) with multiple signals, both groups and individuals bid less, other things equal, the higher the absolute signal value, which makes little sense (and has not been reported in previous studies of individual bidders receiving only one signal), and (2) there is no bid discount, on average, with lower signal values, in response to either residual item-valuation uncertainty or strategic considerations. Further, the positive bid factors are four to five times larger in the group bid functions, and significantly greater than zero for twice-experienced bidders, suggesting that groups handle the multiple signal value case much worse than individuals do. It will be interesting to see if these observations continue to hold up once there is a better specification for the benchmark bid function and, if so, to determine why groups mishandle the greater information content of the multiple signal case.

2.7 Summing Up

Even after allowing for some learning as a result of feedback regarding past auction outcomes, a strong winner's curse is reported for inexperienced bidders in sealed-bid common-value auctions. High bidders earn negative average profits and consistently bid above the expected value of the item conditional on having the high signal value. Further, this is not the result of a handful of overly aggressive bidders but applies rather broadly across the sample population. Similar results are reported in low-bid wins, supply auctions with both student subjects and professional bidders drawn from the commercial construction industry (Dyer, Kagel and Levin 1989; see section 6.2 below and chapter 11). Arguments that these results can be accounted for on the basis of limited liability for losses have been shown to be incorrect (KL 1991; LP 1991; CDS 1998; AK 1997).

In the absence of a winner's curse, public information tends to raise revenue, as the theory predicts. However, with a winner's curse, public information reduces revenue, as the additional information helps high bidders to correct for overly optimistic estimates of the item's worth. These results are found in both first- and second-price auctions. Increased numbers of bidders produce no change in bidding in second-price auctions, contrary to the robust Nash equilibrium prediction that bids will decrease. Second-price, "shoebox" auctions of the sort AK conducted also show classic traces of the winner's curse. Finally, there are no differences in bid patterns between individuals and groups when both receive one signal value, but the data suggest that groups bid more aggressively in the multiple-signal case.

We are still left with the puzzle expressed by Lind and Plott: although many experiments report a clear winner's curse (negative profits), comparing between the symmetric RNNE and totally naive bidding models offered in the literature, bidding is closer to the RNNE. Experiments in second-price auctions show that these differences between behavior and theory cannot be rationalized by risk aversion, as they can be in private-value auctions (see Kagel 1995a for a survey of private-value auction experiments). Rather, a more promising explanation appears to be that bidders are cursed to different degrees. That is, agents may make partial, but incomplete, adjustments for the adverse selection effect associated with common-value auctions, with the perfectly rational and perfectly naive bidding models being polar cases. (In a perfectly naive bidding model, all players treat their signals as if they are private values and go on to bid as if in a private-value auction; see KL 1986 and KLH 1995 for development of naive bidding models for first- and second-price auctions, respectively.) Depending on the extent to which players are "cursed," they may suffer losses, but bidding can, in fact, still be closer to the symmetric RNNE bidding model than to the totally naive bidding model.

Eyster and Rabin (2000) have recently formalized a model of this sort, employing the concept of a cursed equilibrium: each player correctly predicts the distribution of other players' actions, but underestimates the degree to which these actions are correlated with these other players' signals. The formalization offered has at least two nice characteristics. First, it provides a ready-made, intuitively plausible measure of the extent of the winner's curse that can be applied in a variety of settings. Among other things, this enables one to identify the degree to which bidders must be cursed for negative profits to emerge.[34] Second, analyzing the comparative static properties of the model, one can readily identify predictions that are robust to the presence or absence of a winner's curse, evenly for mildly cursed agents. This in turn can enable experimenters (and those who consume results of experiments) to identify the crucial comparative static treatments that will provide rigorous tests of the theory in its many, related applications.

3. English Auctions and First-Price Auctions with Insider Information

We have also studied bidding in English auctions and first-price auctions with insider information (one bidder knows the value of the item with certainty and this is common knowledge). These experiments were initially motivated by efforts to identify institutional structures that would eliminate, or mitigate, the winner's curse for inexperienced bidders. The experiments also investigate the comparative static properties of Nash equilibrium bidding models for very experienced bidders. In both institutional settings, the winner's curse is alive and well for inexperienced bidders, although it is clearly less severe in English than in first-price auctions. In contrast, comparative static predictions of the Nash equilibrium bidding model are largely satisfied for more experienced bidders. However, in the case of English auctions, the information-processing mechanism that the Nash bidding model specifies is not satisfied. Rather, bidders follow a relatively simple rule of thumb that results in almost identical prices and allocations as the Nash model's predictions for the distribution of signal values employed in the experiment. In the insider-information auctions, less-informed bidders (outsiders) have some proprietary information (i.e., the insider knows the value of the item with certainty, but does not know the outsiders' signals). This results in marked differences in predicted outcomes compared to the standard insider-information model in which the insider has a double informational advantage—she knows the value of the item and the signals the outsiders have (Wilson 1967; Weverbergh 1979; Engelbrecht-Wiggans, Milgrom, and Weber 1983; Hendricks, Porter, and Wilson 1994). Most notably, in our model the existence of an insider generates higher average revenue than in auctions with a symmetric information structure, a prediction that is satisfied in the data for experienced bidders. In contrast, in the double informational advantage model, the existence of an insider reduces average revenue.

3.1 English Auctions

Levin, Kagel, and Richard (1996; hereafter LKR) implemented an irrevocable-exit, ascending-price (English) auction. Prices start at x, the lowest possible value for x_o, and increase continuously. Bidders are counted as actively bidding until they drop out of the auction and are not permitted to reenter once they have dropped out.[35] The last bidder earns a profit equal to x_o less the price at which the last bidder dropped out. Bidders observe the prices at which their rivals drop out of the bidding. Auctions of this sort have been run in Japan (Milgrom and Weber 1982; also Cassady 1967). The irrevocable-exit procedure, in conjunction with the public posting of drop-out prices, insures that in equilibrium, bidders can infer their rivals' signal values from their drop-out prices.

For signals in region 2, in a symmetric RNNE, the bidder with the low signal value (x_L) drops out of the auction once the price reaches his signal value.[36] The price at which the low bidder drops out of the auction reveals his signal value to the remaining bidders. Thus, the public information, x_L, that was provided in KL (1986) exogenously is provided here endogenously (at least theoretically) by the first drop-out price. Given the uniform distribution of signal values around x_o, in a symmetric equilibrium, for any remaining bidder j $(x_L + x_j)/2$ provides a sufficient statistic for x_o *conditional* on x_j being the highest signal, so that drop-out prices other than x_L contain no additional information and should be ignored. This sufficient statistic is the equilibrium drop-out price for j (d_j) in the symmetric RNNE

$$d_j = (x_L + x_j)/2. \tag{5}$$

The logic underlying this symmetric equilibrium is similar to the symmetric equilibrium for the second-price auction, as each bidder's dynamic (price-dependent) drop-out price is equal to her maximum willingness to pay conditioned on all the information revealed by earlier drop-out prices, and on winning. Conditioning on winning implies that a bidder's signal is the highest in the sample. Since the first drop-out price reveals x_L, with a uniform distribution of signals the average of the lowest and the highest sample signals is a sufficient statistic for x_o. This holds regardless of any other signal values, and serves as the relevant maximum willingness-to-pay benchmark. As in the first-price and second-price auctions with x_L publicly announced, expected profit in the English auction is sharply reduced (by about half) compared to first- and second-price auctions with strictly private information (as long as $n > 2$). As such, in equilibrium, the English auction is predicted to significantly raise average sellers' revenue compared to first- and second-price sealed-bid auctions.

The key difference between the English auction and the sealed-bid auctions with x_L publicly announced is that in the English auction, information dissemination is endogenous, rather than exogenous. As such, higher signal holders must be able to recognize and process the relevant information, and low signal holders must recognize the futility of remaining active once the price exceeds their signal value. Thus, we would expect the information-dissemination process to be noisier than with x_L publicly announced. Nevertheless, if bidders are able to correctly recognize and incorporate the public information inherent in other bidders' drop-out prices, we would predict that (1) for inexperienced bidders, *contrary* to the Nash equilibrium bidding model's prediction, English auctions will reduce average sellers' revenue compared to first-price sealed-bid auctions, as losses will be sharply reduced, or even be eliminated, on average, in the English auctions, and (2) for more experienced bidders, where negative average profits have been largely eliminated in the sealed-bid auctions, the English auctions will raise average revenue, as the theory predicts. The second prediction is the standard, equilibrium prediction. The first prediction follows directly from our experience with first- and second-price auctions with x_L publicly announced.

Table 1.5 shows averages of predicted and actual changes in revenue between English and first-price auctions for inexperienced bidders, as well as averages of predicted and actual profit, with the results classified by number of bidders and ε (t-statistics are reported in parentheses).[37] Average revenue is predicted to be higher in the English auctions in all cases, for the set of signal values actually drawn, with significantly higher average revenue predicted for all values of ε with $n = 4$ and for ε = \$12 with $n = 7$.[38] However, for these inexperienced bidders, with the exception of $n = 4$ and ε = \$24, actual revenue is lower in the English auctions in all cases, with significantly lower average revenue for $n = 4$ and 7 with ε = \$6, and with the reduction in revenue barely missing statistical significance (at the 10% level) with $n = 7$ and ε = \$12. Further, the revenue increase with $n = 4$ and ε = \$24 is statistically insignificant, and is well below the predicted increase.

These perverse revenue effects in terms of Nash equilibrium bidding theory are associated with negative average profit in both the first-price and English auctions. The negative average profits reported in Table 5 indicate that inexperienced bidders suffered from a winner's curse in both auction institutions, but that the curse was relatively stronger in the first-price auctions. These results serve to generalize those reported for sealed-bid auctions with x_L publicly announced: given a relatively strong winner's curse in sealed-bid auctions, public information reduces rather than raises sellers' average revenue. The major differences between the present results and those with x_L publicly announced are (1) here public information is generated endogenously in the form of drop-out prices, and (2) average profits in the English auctions were negative, but with the exogenous release of public information they were positive. This last result suggests that information dissemination in the English auction is noisier than with x_L publicly announced.[39]

For more experienced bidders, English auctions are capable of raising aver-

TABLE 1.5

Inexperienced Bidders: Actual versus Theoretical Revenue Changes and Profit Levels in English versus First-Price Auctions (in dollars)

						n = 4				
	Average Change in Revenue: English Less First-Price (standard error)						Average Profit (standard error)			
				First-Price				English		
	Actual	Theoretical	Difference	Actual	Theoretical	No. of Auctions	Actual	Theoretical	No. of Auctions
$\varepsilon = \$6$	-1.54*	1.54**	-3.08**	-2.13	2.76	29	-0.58	1.23	28
	(0.72)	(0.49)	(0.71)	(0.52)	(0.38)		(0.50)	(0.30)	
$\varepsilon = \$12$	-0.54	2.76**	-3.30**	-1.32	5.01	41	-0.78	2.25	45
	(1.25)	(0.92)	(0.84)	(0.79)	(0.60)		(0.95)	(0.69)	
$\varepsilon = \$24$	1.09	8.10**	-7.01*	1.20	9.83	25	0.11	1.73	13
	(3.29)	(2.32)	(3.05)	(1.93)	(1.25)		(2.64)	(2.14)	

Source: Levin, Kagel, and Richard 1996.
*The null hypothesis that the value is greater than or equal to zero can be rejected at the 5% significance level.
**The null hypothesis that the value is greater than or equal to zero can be rejected at the 1% significance level.

age sellers' revenue, as the data in Table 1.6 demonstrate. With $n = 4$, actual revenue is higher in the English auctions for both values of ε, with a statistically significant increase for $\varepsilon = \$18$. However, for $n = 7$, there is essentially no difference in revenue between the first-price and English auctions. The significant increase in revenue in English auctions with $n = 4$ and $\varepsilon = \$18$ is associated with elimination of the worst effects of the winner's curse in the first-price auctions, as bidders earned a substantial share (more than 50%) of predicted profit. The importance of eliminating the winner's curse for the revenue-raising prediction of the theory to hold is reinforced by the absence of any revenue increase with $n = 7$, in conjunction with the relatively low share of expected profit (21%) that was earned in these first-price auctions.[40]

LKR develop an econometric model to characterize how bidders process information in the English auctions. As noted, the Nash bidding model predicts that bidders with higher signal values will average their own signal value with the first drop-out price observed, ignoring all intermediate drop-out prices. What LKR found, however, is that bidders placed weight on their own signal value and the immediate past drop-out price, ostensibly ignoring x_L and any earlier drop-out prices. Further, as more bidders dropped out, subjects placed less and less weight on their own signal value, and more weight on the last drop-out price. This pattern, although inconsistent with the Nash model, is consistent with bidders acting "as if" they were averaging their own signal value with the signal values underlying the drop-out prices of all earlier bidders (see chapter 6 for details). LKR explain the adoption of this signal-averaging rule in favor of the Nash rule by noting that (1) it is easy and quite natural to use, and

TABLE 1.5 (continued)

					n = 7			
Average Change in Revenue: English Less First-Price (standard error)			Average Profit (standard error)					
			First-Price			English		
Actual	Theoretical	Difference	Actual	Theoretical	No. of Auctions	Actual	Theoretical	No. of Auctions
−1.98*	0.10	−2.08*	−3.85	0.99	18	−1.87	0.89	18
(0.87)	(0.34)	(0.78)	(0.71)	(0.19)		(0.51)	(0.29)	
−1.95	1.08	−3.03**	−3.75	2.76	30	−1.80	1.68	43
(1.19)	(0.65)	(0.92)	(0.89)	(0.53)		(0.77)	(0.40)	
—	—	—	—	—	—	—	—	—
—	—	—	—	—	—	—	—	—

(2) it yields results quite similar to the Nash rule without requiring that bidders explicitly recognize the adverse selection effect of winning the auction and/or knowing anything about sufficient statistics. One unanswered question raised by this analysis is whether the signal-averaging rule would still be used with distribution functions where it leads to outcomes markedly different from the Nash equilibrium. In this case, bidders would have more opportunity to recognize and respond to the profit opportunities inherent in abandoning the signal-averaging rule.

3.2 Auctions with Insider Information

Kagel and Levin (1999) investigate bidding in first-price sealed-bid auctions with an asymmetric information structure (AIS). The asymmetry is introduced by choosing one bidder at random in each auction period—the insider (I)—to receive a private information signal x equal to x_o and to be told that $x = x_o$. Each of the other bidders, the outsiders (Os), receive a private information signal from a uniform distribution on $[x_o - \varepsilon, x_o + \varepsilon]$, as in the auctions with a symmetric information structure (SIS). The insider does *not* know the realizations of Os' private information signals. Os know that they are Os, that there is a single I who knows x_o, and the way that all other Os got their private signals.

Note that this information structure differs substantially from the "standard" insider information structure in which the insider has a double informational advantage—I knows x_o and Os only have access to public information about x_o (Engelbrecht-Wiggans, Milgrom, and Weber 1983; Hendricks and Porter 1988). In contrast, in our design, Os have some proprietary information, which permits

TABLE 1.6
Super-Experienced Bidders: Actual versus Theoretical Revenue Changes and Profit Levels in
English versus First-Price Auctions (in dollars)

	n = 4								
	Average Change in Revenue: *English Less First-Price* *(standard error)*			*Average Profit* *(standard error)*					
				First-Price			*English*		
	Actual	*Theoretical*	*Difference*	*Actual*	*Theoretical*	*No. of* *Auctions*	*Actual*	*Theoretical*	*No. of* *Auctions*
ε = $18	2.21*	3.96**	−1.75*	3.37	6.77	163	1.16	2.82	107
	(0.95)	(0.73)	(0.68)	(0.50)	(0.48)		(0.88)	(0.53)	
ε = $30	1.20	2.98	−1.78	8.45	11.27	31	7.25	8.29	33
	(3.10)	(2.30)	(2.19)	(1.28)	(1.34)		(2.76)	(1.93)	

Source: Levin, Kagel, and Richard 1996.
*The null hypothesis that the value is greater than or equal to zero can be rejected at the 5% significance level.
**The null hypothesis that the value is greater than or equal to zero can be rejected at the 1% significance level.

them to earn positive expected profit in equilibrium. In the double informational advantage model, Os earn zero expected profit in equilibrium.

This experimental design has a number of interesting comparative static predictions that contrast sharply with the double informational advantage model. First and foremost, the existence of an insider benefits the seller by increasing expected revenue relative to auctions with an SIS. In contrast, in the double informational advantage model, the existence of an insider *unambiguously reduces* sellers' expected revenue.[41] Second, increases in the number of Os result in Is bidding more aggressively in our model. In contrast, in the double informational advantage model, I's bidding strategy is unaffected by increases in the number of Os. Finally, both models imply that Is earn substantially larger expected profit than Os (zero profit for Os in the double informational advantage model) and that Is earn higher expected profit, conditional on winning, than in SIS auctions, although the predicted increase in profit is relatively small in our design.

KL (1999) conjecture that for inexperienced bidders, the existence of an insider might attenuate the winner's curse. Os in the AIS auctions who win against better-informed Is face a stronger adverse selection effect than in SIS auctions. However, it is entirely plausible that the need to hedge against the existence of an insider is more intuitive and transparent than the adverse selection problem resulting from winning against symmetrically informed rivals. Thus, at least for inexperienced bidders, having an insider may actually reduce the severity of the winner's curse. This would be true, for example, if Os view the situation as similar to a lemon's market (Akerlof 1970), where it seems reasonably clear that there is no rampant winner's curse (our culture warns us to beware of used-car salesmen).[42] On the other hand, inexperienced subjects

TABLE 1.6 (continued)

					n = 7			
Average Change in Revenue: English Less First-Price (standard error)			Average Profit (standard error)					
			First-Price			English		
Actual	Theoretical	Difference	Actual	Theoretical	No. of Auctions	Actual	Theoretical	No. of Auctions
−0.25*	2.85**	−3.10**	0.76	3.86	75	1.01	1.01	96
(0.86)	(0.61)	(0.59)	(0.65)	(0.50)		(0.56)	(0.37)	
—	—	—	—	—	—	—	—	—
—	—	—	—	—	—	—	—	—

may bid higher in order to make up for their informational disadvantage, thus exacerbating the winner's curse.

KL employ two alternative definitions of the winner's curse for Os in the AIS auctions. In the first definition, KL ignore I's bid, and note that Os can expect to earn negative profits just competing against other Os when $\gamma(x)$ is greater than

$$E[x_o \mid x_1^{n^o} = x] = x - \frac{n^o - 1}{n^o + 1} \varepsilon, \tag{6}$$

where n^o is the number of Os bidding. Further, if all Os bid according to equation (6), and Is employ their best response to these bids, then Os would earn average *losses* of more than $1.50 per auction, conditional on winning. As such, bidding above (6) provides a first, very conservative definition of the winner's curse. The second definition of the winner's curse accounts for Is best responding to Os' bids, and solves for the zero expected profit level for Os. Not surprisingly, this requires a somewhat larger bid factor (reduction of bids relative to private signals) than equation (2) requires for SIS auctions with equal numbers of total bidders.

Table 1.7 reports results for inexperienced bidders in these auctions. The data clearly indicate that the winner's curse is alive and well for inexperienced Os. Consider auctions with $\varepsilon = 6$, which were used to start each session. With $n = 4$, almost 60% of the high Os' bids were above the conservative measure of the winner's curse (equation [6]), so that these bids would have lost money, on average, just competing against other Os. Further, considering the behavior of both Is and Os (the second winner's curse measure), 94% of the high O bids were subject to the winner's curse. With $n = 7$, there is an even stronger adverse selection effect, with the result that the winner's curse was more pervasive: 100% of the high O bids and 85.2% of *all* O bids fell prey to the winner's curse, even with no accounting for Is' bids. The net result, in both cases, was

TABLE 1.7

Inexperienced Bidders: Auctions with Asymmetric Information Structure (AIS)

		Outsiders' Bids								Insiders' Bids	
				Frequency of Winner's Curse (raw data)							
				Against Outsiders Only		Against Outsiders and Insiders					
No. of Bidders	ε	Average Earnings Conditional on Winning (S_m)	Frequency of Outsiders Winning (raw data)	High Outsider Bid	All Bids	High Outsider Bid	All Bids	Average Bid Factor[a] (S_m)	Frequency High Outsider Bid from High Outsider Signal Holder (raw data)	Average Earnings Conditional on Winning (S_m)	Average Bid Factor (S_m)
4	$6	−1.68 (0.93)	70.6% (12/17)	58.8% (10/17)	39.2% (20/51)	94.1% (16/17)	70.6% (36/51)	1.16 (0.62)	52.9% (9/17)	0.71 (0.35)	1.46[b] (0.26)
	$12	−1.40 (0.50)*	65.2% (15/23)	39.1% (9/23)	23.2% (16/69)	65.2% (15/23)	47.8% (33/69)	6.00 (0.77)	73.9% (17/23)	2.74 (0.77)*	2.25 (0.35)
	$24	−6.56 (3.07)	71.4% (5/7)	28.6% (2/7)	14.3% (3/21)	85.7% (6/7)	57.1% (12/21)	11.61 (2.78)	100% (7/7)	5.05 (3.50)	5.09 (1.27)
7	$6	−3.68 (0.61)**	100% (9/9)	100% (9/9)	85.2% (46/54)	100% (9/9)	92.6% (50/54)	−0.61[c] (0.62)	66.7% (6/9)	—	1.09[b] (0.29)
	$12	−2.47 (1.03)*	78.9% (15/19)	89.5% (17/19)	68.4% (78/114)	89.5% (17/19)	79.8% (91/114)	4.85 (1.03)	73.7% (14/19)	1.93 (0.61)**	1.91[b] (0.33)

Source: Kagel and Levin 1999.

S_m = Standard error of the mean.

*Significantly different from zero at the 5% level, 2-tailed t-test.

**Significantly different from zero at the 1% level, 2-tailed t-test.

[a]High bids only.

[b]A single outlier bid less than $x_0 - ε$ was dropped.

[c]In this treatment high Os actually bid *above* their signal values, on average.

large negative profits for Os when they won ($-\$1.68$ per auction with $n = 4$; $-\$3.68$ with $n = 7$). Although somewhat diminished in frequency, a strong winner's curse is also reported for higher values of ε as Os continued to earn negative profits throughout, with at least 47% of all bids subject to the winner's curse for any value of ε (when accounting for both Is' and Os' bids). Finally, regressions comparing bid functions for inexperienced Os in AIS auctions versus inexperienced bidders in SIS auctions show no significant difference between the two treatments. Thus, contrary to KL's original conjecture, the introduction of an insider did not induce significantly less-aggressive bidding for inexperienced Os compared to SIS auctions.

Table 1.8 reports data for super-experienced bidders (subjects who had participated in at least two prior first-price sealed-bid auction sessions). For these bidders, the winner's curse has been largely eliminated, and the comparative static predictions of the theory are generally satisfied. Is earned significantly greater profits conditional on winning than did Os. For example, with $\varepsilon = \$18$ and $n = 7$, Os earned average profits of around $\$0.50$ per auction, conditional on winning. In contrast, Is earned around $\$3.25$ per auction, conditional on winning. Further, Os earned substantially lower profits than in corresponding SIS auctions, for which profits averaged around $\$2.25$ per auction. Also, as the theory predicts, Is increased their bids in the face of greater competition from more Os.

Last, but not least, as the theory predicts, auctions with insider information consistently raised average sellers' revenue compared to SIS auctions (Table 1.9). The intuition underlying this prediction for our model is as follows: The seller would be unambiguously worse off in the AIS auction relative to the SIS auction if Is in the AIS auction won *all* the time while bidding according to the prescribed (AIS) equilibrium. However, Is do not win all the time, and when Os win (with their equilibrium bid), they win with relatively high signal values, yielding more revenue than when Is win. Further, the existence of the insider helps to "protect" the seller's revenue compared to the SIS auction, when Os would have won with relatively low signal values since in this case I wins and pays more than O would have paid. The net result is higher revenue for the seller and reduced variance in seller's revenue (holding x_o constant) in the AIS auction compared to SIS auctions.[43]

The increase in revenue resulting from an insider in our model is counterintuitive for those whose intuition has been honed on the double informational advantage model. This reversal of the double informational advantage model's prediction rests critically on the fact that less-informed bidders have some proprietary information. Many "real world" cases are more realistically modeled with Os having some proprietary information and not just public information. In these circumstances, it may well be the case that the introduction of a single well-informed insider increases average sellers' revenue, and that both Is and Os earn economic rents. This potential for insider information to raise average sellers' revenue had not been explicitly recognized in the auction literature prior to this.[44]

TABLE 1.8

Super-Experienced Bidders: Auctions with Asymmetric Information Structure (AIS)

No. of Bidders	ε	Outsiders' Bids						Insiders' Bids	
		Average Earnings Conditional on Winning (S_m)	Frequency of Outsiders Winning (raw data)	Frequency of Winner's Curse against Outsiders and Insiders (raw data)		Average Bid Factor[a] (S_m)	Frequency High Outsider Bid from High Outsider Signal Holder (raw data)	Average Earnings Conditional on Winning (S_m)	Average Bid Factor (S_m)
				High Outsider Bid	All Bids				
4	$12	0.65 (0.43)	53.7% (29/54)	9.3% (5/54)	4.9% (8/162)	10.05 (0.23)	92.6% (50/54)	3.30 (0.23)**	3.60[c] (0.19)
	$18	0.87 (0.68)	63.3% (19/30)	3.3% (1/30)	1.1% (1/90)	15.29 (0.26)	93.3% (28/30)	4.13 (0.37)**	5.80[c] (0.50)
	$30	3.67 (2.32)	42.1% (8/19)	5.3% (1/19)	3.5% (2/57)	27.04 (0.65)	94.7% (18/19)	7.94 (0.69)**	8.24 (0.61)
7[b]	$18	0.52 (0.34)	64.5% (49/76)	22.4% (17/76)	17.2% (77/453)	15.86 (0.26)	86.8% (66/76)	3.24 (0.36)**	4.35 (0.26)
	$30	3.90 (3.07)	41.7% (5/12)	16.7% (2/12)	19.4% (14/72)	26.95 (0.85)	83.3% (10/12)	4.95 (0.80)**	5.98 (0.67)

Source: Kagel and Levin 1999.

S_m = Standard error of the mean.

[a]High bids only.

[b]Includes several auctions with $n = 6$.

[c]A single outlier bid less than $x_0 - \varepsilon$ was dropped.

*Significantly different from zero at the 5% level, 2-tailed *t*-test.

**Significantly different from zero at the 1% level, 2-tailed *t*-test.

TABLE 1.9

Change in Seller's Revenue: AIS versus SIS Auctions with Super-Experienced Bidders

	n = 4			n = 7		
ε	*Change in Revenue: AIS less SIS Auctions[a] (t-stat)[b]*	*Mean Profits (σ^2)* AIS	SIS	*Change in Revenue: AIS less SIS Auctions[a] (t-stat)[b]*	*Mean Profits (σ^2)* AIS	SIS
$18	1.759 (2.057)*	2.063 (8.561)	3.822 (49.972)	0.739 (1.573)**	1.492 (6.770)	2.231 (19.221)
$30	2.734 (1.097)	6.148 (24.334)	8.876 (59.731)	0.919 (0.425)	4.517 (17.978)	5.436 (15.839)

Source: Kagel and Levin 1999.

[a]Change in seller's revenue, normalized for variation in x_o, is bidder profits in SIS auctions less bidder profits in AIS auctions.

[b]t statistics calculated for populations with unknown and unequal variances (Guenther 1964). Auction period is unit of observation.

*Significantly different from zero at the 5% level, 1-tailed test.

**Significantly different from zero at the 1% level, 1-tailed test.

4. The Winner's Curse in Other Settings

The potential for a winner's curse is not limited to common-value auctions. This section reviews experiments dealing with three different market settings exhibiting varying degrees of a winner's curse: bilateral bargaining games, "blind-bid" auctions, and two-sided auctions where product quality is endogenously determined. Although inexperienced subjects suffer from a winner's curse in all three settings, the strength of the winner's curse varies considerably, being quite persistent in the bilateral bargaining game and being eliminated, after a few replications, when product quality is endogenously determined. This last outcome results from the strong incentive sellers have to dilute quality, which creates such a strong adverse selection effect that the market quickly unravels to the point that only "lemons" are sold, with buyers paying lemons' prices. Finally, we also consider recent work investigating incentives for strategic voting based on the "swing voter's curse."

4.1 The Winner's Curse in Bilateral Bargaining Games

Samuelson and Bazerman (1985; hereafter SB) explored the winner's curse in the following bilateral bargaining game: A buyer (the acquiring firm) knows that the target's value, V_S, is a random variable uniformly distributed in the interval [$0, $100]. The value of the target firm to the buyer, V_B, is $V_B = 1.5V_S$. A buyer does not know V_S at the time he bids, but a seller does and follows the dominant strategy of only accepting offers that are greater than or equal to her own known value $V_S = v_S$. Obviously, the buyer never wants to bid over \$100. Thus, consider someone who naively bids the ex ante expected value of \$50. For all v_S greater than or equal to \$50, this bid is never accepted. Rather, it is only accepted for v_S between \$0 and \$50, so that the expected value of V_S *conditional on winning the item* is \$25, or a value to the buyer of \$37.50, for a bid of \$50! This same logic applies to any positive bid between \$0 and \$100, so that *expected* profit to the buyer for any *accepted* bid is negative. Thus, the optimal bid is zero.

The original SB study consisted of a game where buyers bid one time only and the experimenter acted as the seller. Comparing games with and without monetary incentives, in both cases the overwhelming number of subjects (more than 90%) fell prey to the winner's curse, bidding positive amounts for the target firm.[45] The majority of subjects (59% with monetary incentives, 73% without) followed the naive strategy of bidding somewhere between the expected value of the target (\$50) and the expected value of the target in the hands of the acquiring firm (\$75), with most others bidding less. SB attribute the modest downward shift in the bid distribution under monetary incentives to risk aversion.[46]

Ball, Bazerman, and Carroll (1991; hereafter BBC) extended SB's design to allow for learning from repeated play. Each subject played a total of twenty trials, and players received feedback regarding the value of the company and how much money was made or lost following each trial. Players were given starting cash balances that were more than sufficient to cover any expected losses and were paid their net, end-of-experiment balance in cash. Figure 1.1 shows their results. There is virtually no downward adjustment in mean bids from the beginning to the end of the twenty trials, with bids over the first three trials averaging \$57 compared to \$55 over the last three trials. Only 7% of the subjects (five out of sixty-nine) learned to avoid the winner's curse, defined as bidding either \$0 or \$1.00 at some point and continuing to do so until the end of the experiment. Students with quantitative backgrounds (e.g., engineering degrees) did no better in avoiding the winner's curse than those with nonquantitative backgrounds (e.g., English degrees).

The BBC experiment, like the SB study, employed "realistic" instructions with subjects being told, "In the following exercise you will represent Company A (the acquirer), which is currently considering acquiring Company T (the target) by means of a tender offer" (BBC 1991, Appendix 1). Further, subjects were explicitly told that the target company was expected to accept any offer greater than or equal to its value, but that "acquiring a company is a neutral event—your performance will be judged only on the value of your assets at the end of this exercise" (BBC 1991, Appendix 1). Nevertheless, for many experimentalists (us included), embedding the game in a takeover context might be expected to generate overly aggressive bidding, as that would seem to be what this context calls for, particularly for MBAs. In response to this criticism, Ball (1991) has replicated the twenty-period design using value-free instructions and

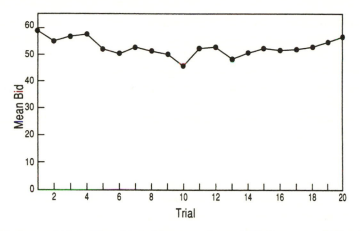

Figure 1.1. Average bids in bilateral bargaining game. *Source*: Ball, Bazerman, and Carroll 1991.

finds no difference in the outcome, as only 5% of the subjects (two out of thirty-seven) avoided the winner's curse.

Cifuentes and Sunder (1991) have independently replicated the BBC results using neutral instructions and forty trials in a session. In addition, under one treatment, V_S was distributed uniformly on the interval [\$10, \$100]. Since the value to the buyer is $1.5V_S$, this creates non-negative expected profit for bids between \$10 and \$30, with an optimal bid of \$19–\$20, generating an expected profit of \$0.28 per trial. Thus, a buyer does not have to totally withdraw from active bidding to avoid the winner's curse. This is important, since it might be argued that subjects bid positive amounts in the BBC design out of boredom.[47] Nevertheless, Cifuentes and Sunder found few subjects avoiding the winner's curse: only two out of thirteen learned to consistently bid \$0 with $v_S \in$ [\$0, \$100], and only 7% of all bids were between \$10 and \$30 for $v_S \in$ [\$10, \$100]. Overall, bids averaged well above the equilibrium prediction.

The Thrill of Winning—A "Loser's Curse"

One potential explanation for the winner's curse here, and in the auction experiments, is that subjects get extra utility from winning. Holt and Sherman (1994) employ a clever design to test this alternative explanation. The key insight is that a failure to perceive the correct conditional expected value does not necessarily cause the bid to be too high. Rather, with a change in the support from which the seller's values are drawn, naive bidding can result in bids that are too low, so that purchases are too infrequent, relative to the optimal bid. Holt and Sherman refer to this as the "loser's curse." For example, consider the case where the seller's values are uniform on the interval [\$50, \$100], with everything else the same as in the original SB experiment. Consider someone who now naively bids the expected value of the item, \$75. The distribution of seller's values conditional on this bid's acceptance is uniform on [\$50, \$75].

This translates into a range of buyer values distributed uniformly on [\$75, \$112.50], so that the bid, if accepted, yields positive expected profit of \$18.75, and winning 50% of the time on average, so that average earnings per auction are \$9.38. But an even higher bid, although yielding lower expected profit *conditional on winning,* would more than make up for this by winning more often. For example, a bid of \$100 yields expected profit conditional on winning of \$12.50 per auction. But now the bidder wins 100% of the time, for average earnings of \$12.50 per auction.

Holt and Sherman's experimental design employs two control conditions: a distribution of sellers' values that will produce the usual winner's curse, and a distribution for which naive and sophisticated bidding coincide. In addition, expected gains per auction for sophisticated bidding were positive and the same across all three treatments, with expected gains per auction for naive bidding also positive and the same for the winner's curse and loser's curse treatments. This rules out rival explanations for any differences observed based on incentives.[48] If the winner's curse is a result of extra utility from winning rather than a failure to account for the seller's acceptance rule, then underbidding will not materialize with the loser's curse treatment, or if underbidding does occur, it will be substantially weaker than overbidding in the winner's curse treatment. Results from the experiment show that average actual bids are remarkably close to the naive bid under all three treatments. As such, Holt and Sherman conclude that the extra utility from winning does not explain the winner's curse. Rather, it results from bidders' inability to correctly anticipate the adverse selection effect associated with winning the item.

4.2 The Winner's Curse in "Blind-Bid" Auctions

Consider the following extension of the bilateral bargaining game. Several buyers compete to purchase an item whose value V is common to all buyers and is uniformly distributed on some known interval. The seller receives no value from retaining the item and sells it in a first-price sealed-bid auction. Further, the seller, who knows the exact value of the item, has an option, prior to the sale, of *truthfully* revealing the value of the item or concealing it (in which case the item is said to be "blind bid"). Buyers have no information about the value of items other than what the seller provides them and the distribution of V.

If none of the sellers reveal the value of the item, buyers should bid the expected value, earning negative profits on low-valued items and positive profits on high-valued items. However, sellers have an incentive to reveal information on high-valued items in order to receive full value for these items. As such, buyers face an adverse selection problem for items that are blind bid. If buyers adjust to this adverse selection problem, the only (sequential) equilibrium is one in which the game completely unravels, with sellers revealing information on all but the lowest-valued items and being indifferent between revealing or concealing information on the low-valued items (Milgrom and Roberts

1986; Forsythe, Isaac, and Palfrey 1989). Failure to recognize this adverse se-lection problem results in a winner's curse, with buyers earning negative aver-age profits on the blind-bid items.

Forsythe, Isaac, and Palfrey (1989; hereafter FIP) investigate blind-bid auc-tions of this sort.[49] Each experimental session consisted of a series of auctions, so there was time for feedback and learning. Sellers were required to truthfully reveal the value of items that were not blind bid. Values of blind-bid items were publicly announced at the end of each auction.

FIP report clear evidence of a winner's curse in early auctions. First, there was an adverse selection problem as sellers started out revealing information on higher-valued items and blind-bidding lower-valued items.[50] Second, the win-ning bid was greater than the value of the item for 69% of all blind-bid items. This winner's curse was present in later auction periods as well, with buyers suffering losses on two-thirds of the blind-bid items. Finally, sellers took advan-tage of the winner's curse, as almost all low-valued items (96%) were blind bid (the theory predicts that sellers will be indifferent between blind-bidding or revealing information on these low-valued items).

FIP's primary focus is on the unraveling reported within each experimental session as fewer and fewer items were blind bid over time: 44.2% of all items in the first ten periods compared to 28.1% from period eleven on. In addition, the value of blind-bid items decreased monotonically over time, as did the prices paid for the items and the average losses on blind-bid items.[51] These results are illustrated in Figure 1.2, which shows the value of the blind-bid items and the amounts bid, by auction period, from two of FIP's markets.

These results lead FIP (p. 230) to conclude that "the practice of blind bidding causes no difficulties once an equilibrium is obtained. After sufficient market experience, sellers only blind bid low quality items, and buyers' bids indicate that they had adjusted their beliefs properly." In other words, most of the excess profit that sellers earned on low-valued items occurred in the initial auctions prior to the unraveling (equilibrium) outcome.

The relatively rapid reduction in bids and losses on blind-bid items stands in marked contrast to the persistence of the winner's curse in the takeover game (BBC 1991). What seems partly, if not entirely, responsible for these differ-ences is the role that sellers play. Buyers tend to adopt a naive strategy of bidding the expected value of items that are blind bid. As such, sellers can earn more on high-valued items by revealing their value since, absent the informa-tion revelation, they can expect to receive bids that are lower than the value of these items (and unsold items are worth nothing to the seller). This in turn creates an adverse selection problem for blind-bid items that buyers do not fully compensate for in their bidding, but that they adjust to by lowering their bids. But the lowering of bids on blind-bid items induces sellers to reveal informa-tion on even lower-quality items. As this process repeats itself, the market slowly unravels, with only the lowest-valued items being blind bid.

Note the important difference between this and the bilateral bargaining game. Here sellers have the opportunity and incentive to reveal information on higher-

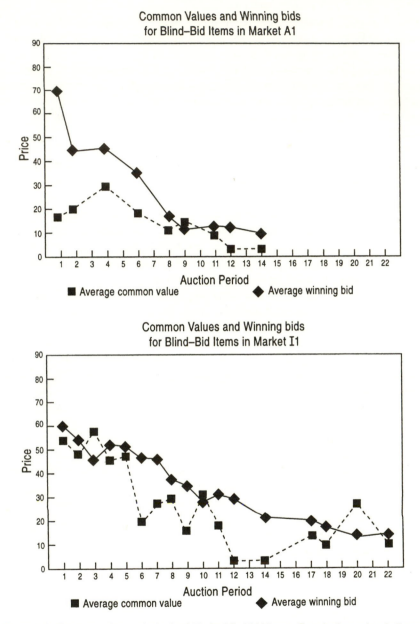

Figure 1.2. Common values and winning bids for blind bid items. Gaps in data points indicate that no items were blind bid that period. *Source*: Forsythe, Isaac, and Palfrey 1989.

valued items, which promotes the unraveling.[52] In the bilateral bargaining game, sellers do not have the opportunity to reveal information on any items sold. In the blind-bid auctions, the unraveling proceeds until, in equilibrium, only the lowest-quality items are blind bid, and buyers fully anticipate this. The winner's curse has been largely eliminated in this case because there is no longer an adverse selection problem; only low-quality items are blind bid. It is the winner's curse that *prevents* the instantaneous establishment of the equilibrium for this game, for without it, buyers would fully anticipate that only the worst items would be blind bid. In turn, this would provide sellers with no incentive to blind bid any items. As will be shown in the next section, a similar process is at work in markets where quality is endogenously determined.

The FIP experiment is representative of a broader class of voluntary disclosure experiments that have appeared primarily in the finance literature as a result of the informational asymmetry between the seller of a financial asset and potential buyers. Left unchecked, this asymmetry is predicted to lead to all but the lowest-quality assets being withdrawn from the market. Theoretical analysis suggests a number of institutional remedies that might help correct the problem, many of which are observed in practice, and a number of which have been subject to experimental investigation. For example, sellers can engage in costly signaling by retaining a larger-than-optimal share of the firm or by hiring outside auditors. (See Miller and Plott 1985 and Cadsby, Frank, and Maksimovic 1990 for signaling experiments along these lines.) Alternatively, firms can credibly communicate quality, as in the FIP experiment. (See King and Wallin 1991 and Forsythe, Lundholm, and Reitz 1999 for additional experiments along these lines.) In addition, firms can engage in noncredible disclosure—"cheap talk" (possibly nontruthful communication). (Forsythe et al. investigate this issue experimentally.) Remarkably, from a theoretical point of view, cheap talk significantly reduces the adverse selection problem in this experiment. Although most sellers in the experiment tout their products as higher quality than it is, and many buyers are taken in by the cheap talk, this is not entirely irrational, as over the last half of the experiment there remains a positive rank-order correlation between the minimum state in the seller's disclosure and the true state. Additional remedies for the adverse selection problem include warranties, guarantees, and sellers' reputations for honesty. The Lynch, Miller, Plott, and Porter experiment (1986, 1991), discussed in brief below, investigate the efficacy of these remedies.

4.3 Lemons and Ripoffs: The Winner's Curse in Markets with Quality Endogenously Determined

Lynch, Miller, Plott, and Porter (1986, 1991) study markets in which product quality is endogenously determined and cannot be observed by buyers prior to purchase (in all other experiments reviewed so far, value has been exogenously determined). Sellers chose between producing a high- or a low-quality product, with higher marginal costs for producing the high-quality product. It is common knowledge that it cost sellers more to produce "supers" (the high-quality product) than "regulars," with higher values to buyers from purchasing the high-quality product. Markets were organized as continuous double-auction markets.

In markets where there were no enforceable warranties and sellers' identities were anonymous, so that they could not develop reputations for product quality, there is a potential adverse selection problem present in which a market may not exist, or only the lowest-quality products ("lemons") are sold in the market (Akerlof 1970). In equilibrium, this lemons problem is fully anticipated so that the market collapses, and no one gets stuck with a "lemon" who does not fully anticipate it.[53] However, if agents suffer from a sufficiently strong winner's curse, the adverse selection problem will not be fully anticipated, resulting in losses for buyers as a result of paying premium prices for what turn out to be low-quality products (the winner's curse). These losses, in turn, will lead to adjustments in demand and to the market unraveling to the point that only low-quality products are sold. Indeed, this is the way a number of intermediate textbooks describe the evolution of these markets, and motivate the lemon's problem for markets with asymmetric information (see, for example, Pindyk and Rubinfeld 2001, 596–97).

The Lynch et al. experiment provides a good case study of unraveling along these lines. In the experiment, inexperienced buyers fall prey to the winner's curse in the first market period, as sellers almost always produce a low-quality product and buyers almost always pay prices greater than the value of these low-quality products. That is, buyers naively start out paying prices close to the average market value of regulars *and* supers. But sellers are primarily delivering regulars, resulting in buyers paying too much. These overpayments result in large losses, which, in conjunction with sellers' continued delivery of low-quality products, generate rapid adjustments on the buyers' part.[54] Prices converge close to the competitive equilibrium for markets delivering only regulars by the fourth period in virtually all markets.[55]

Lynch et al. also explore the effects of warranties and sellers' reputations for correcting the lemon's problem (warranties are effective, but reputation effects do not necessarily guarantee efficient market performance). However, the relevant points to note here are that even in this simplified setting, buyers initially fall prey to the winner's curse, and that sellers' behavior, almost always supplying low-quality products, appears to be largely responsible for the rapid elimination of the problem. However, like in the blind-bid auctions, the problem is eliminated because sellers wind up producing only low-quality products. This is recognized by even the slowest learners, so that with the adverse selection problem eliminated, there is no longer any basis for a winner's curse. As in the blind-bid auctions, it is the presence of a sufficiently strong winner's curse that *prevents* the market from unraveling to a competitive equilibrium for low-quality products right from the start.

4.4 The Swing Voter's Curse

One interesting recent extension of the winner's curse idea has been to voting. Elections play two roles in society. First, they provide a mechanism for deciding between alternatives when individuals disagree about the appropriate action. Second, they serve to aggregate information when individuals hold different information sets but would agree on the same action had they shared all information available to them. The winner's curse phenomenon applies with respect to this second class of voting problems, since in these circumstances a sophisticated voter should always vote "as if" her vote were pivotal to the outcome. In a general election, this may lead a sophisticated voter with a strict preference based on her private information to not vote, even with zero cost to voting (Feddersen and Pesendorfer 1996; hereafter FP). And it may lead a juror to vote to convict a defendant contrary to her own private information that the defendant is innocent (FP 1998, 1999).

Take the case of a criminal trial. The assumption is that all jurors agree that the defendant should be convicted if guilty and acquitted if innocent. However, jurors have different information regarding the guilt or innocence of the defendant.[56] Further, a verdict to convict requires unanimity, as it usually does in Anglo-Saxon criminal trials. Why would a juror vote to convict even though her information suggests that the defendant is innocent? For her vote to be pivotal, a juror must assume that all other jurors are voting to convict, since otherwise a vote of innocent does not matter. A sophisticated juror with an innocent signal would then try to correctly infer what information other jurors must have to make them vote guilty, and then decide how to vote based on this inference and on her own private information. The answer is that in certain circumstances, even if her information favors "innocent" but is less than definitive, she should vote to convict (FP 1998, 1999). By analogy to the winner's curse in auctions, FP label this the "swing voter's curse." Note that FP's use of the term "swing voter's curse" reflects the equilibrium outcome, not to the *failure* to vote strategically.

Under strategic voting, the information-aggregation properties of elections change. Strategic voting also changes the way that electoral rules trade off error probabilities. For example, under naive voting, a unanimity rule for conviction minimizes the probability of convicting an innocent defendant. In contrast, under strategic voting, a unanimity rule results in much higher probabilities of convicting innocent defendants than other rules. The intuition behind this result is that strategic voters compensate for the bias introduced by the voting rule and are more likely to vote to convict. As a result, even in a large jury, the probability of convicting an innocent defendant must stay bounded away from zero (FP 1998).[57]

Note that the informational structure assumed in the jury example is the same as in a pure common-value auction, where bidders would place exactly the same value on the object if they all had the same information. However, in practice, there is an important difference between a common-value auction and a jury, as well as a large number of other voting situations. In an auction, bidders with private information are competing against each other to win the object. In a jury, under the assumptions of the model that there are no disagreements regarding the appropriate action, no such conflict of interest exists. This has implications for the applicability of the ideas underlying the swing voter's curse, to which we shall return after reporting an experiment by Guarnaschelli, McKelvey, and Palfrey (2000; hereafter GMP) investigating the model.

The GMP experiment uses the analogy of a jury trial. In their experiment, the prior probability of a defendant being guilty or innocent is .5. For simplicity they assume that the threshold of reasonable doubt is .5 as well. This, of course, is *not* the case under the Anglo-American legal system with its "beyond a reasonable doubt" rule. It does, however, simplify the experimental design. It is implemented using a "generic" procedure (balls and bingo cages) to capture the underlying structure of the game. (The tradeoff between voting for a red bingo ball ["guilty"] when the true color is blue ["innocent"], or vice versa, is presumably 0.5; people do not have preferences, or meaning responses developed outside the lab, when choosing over bingo balls, which is not the case when choosing between guilt and innocence.) Each juror receives a private, independently drawn "signal" regarding the guilt or innocence of the defendant. This evidence takes on one of two values, guilty (g) or innocent (i). When the defendant is guilty, each juror independently observes a signal g with probability .7 or i with probability .3. When the defendant is innocent, each juror independently observes a signal i with probability .7 or g with probability .3. In each trial, subjects receive fifty cents if the *group* decision is correct, and five cents if it is incorrect. GMP compare majority voting with unanimity rules for three- and six-person juries.

The optimal voting rule in a jury with one member is to vote to convict if she observes g, and to acquit if observing i. This rule is optimal because the probability that the defendant is guilty (innocent) when receiving a guilty (innocent) signal is .7, which is above the threshold of reasonable doubt (.5). Using the same logic, it is also optimal in a jury requiring a simple majority to convict. However, this voting rule is "naive" in a jury requiring unanimity to convict. Consider, for example, a three-person jury under a unanimity rule. A juror observing i who votes to acquit will be pivotal only if the other two jurors vote to convict. Thus, she should condition her assessment of guilt or innocence on this additional information. It turns out that the symmetric Bayesian-Nash equilibrium for this game is for jurors observing g voting to convict and for jurors observing i to use a mixed strategy, voting to convict with a probability of 0.314. In the six-person jury, those jurors observing i vote to convict with probability 0.651, with jurors observing g always voting to convict. The net effect is that the predicted frequency of a jury verdict of guilty, *conditional on being innocent*, is 0.216 under a majority voting rule versus 0.140 under a unanimity rule with three jurors, compared to 0.070 under a majority rule and 0.186 under a unanimity rule with six jurors.

Table 1.10 reports the voting outcomes for the GMP experiment. The data provide some support for the strategic-voter model as the percentage voting to convict, given signal i, is increasing with the size of the jury under unanimity. Quantitatively, however, the model does not do so well. It is reasonably accurate for the three-person jury, as the percentage voting to convict (36.0%) is close to the predicted level (31.6%). However, for six-person juries, the percentage voting to convict (47.8%) is significantly below the predicted level (65.1%). This suggests some responsiveness to the swing voter's curse, but the quantitative results indicate far less than fully sophisticated voting.[58] Further

TABLE 1.10
Vote versus Signal: Proportion Voting to Convict

	Majority						Unanimous					
	n = 3			n = 6			n = 3			n = 6		
Signal	No. of Observations	Data	Nash	No. of Observations	Data	Nash	No. of Observations	Data	Nash	No. of Observations	Data	Nash
Innocent	157	.057	0.00	172	.209	0.00	186	.360	.316	186	.478	.651
Guilty	143	.972	1.00	188	.954	1.00	174	.954	1.00	174	.897	1.00

Source: Guarnaschelli, McKelvey, and Palfrey 2000.

evidence against fully sophisticated voting can be found in the increased frequency of voting guilty with signal i in going from three to six jurors reported under the control condition, majority voting, even though the theory predicts no increase in this case.[59]

These differences between individual juror behavior and theoretical predictions translate into major differences between theory and behavior at the jury level. Aggregate effects on jury accuracy are reported in Table 1.11. First, in the experimental data, under unanimity, the probability of voting to convict an innocent defendant goes down from 0.190 to 0.029 as the jury becomes larger ($t = 2.22$, $p < 0.05$ using a difference-of-proportion test). In contrast, the Nash theory predicts the opposite (an increase in the probability of convicting an innocent defendant from 0.14 to 0.19). Further, the error rate for six-person unanimous juries is lower than the error rate for majority juries (0.03 vs. 0.30) in the innocent state. This difference, which is significant at the 0.01 level, is counter to the strategic-voter model as well. For juries requiring majority votes, the error rate declines with larger juries in the guilty state, and with larger juries increases in the innocent state. The latter is consistent with the increased frequency of voting guilty with signal i in larger juries with majority voting, but is the exact opposite of what is predicted in the Nash equilibrium.

GMP provide possible explanations for these differences between the theory and their data. For one thing, they note that the idea of conditioning decisions on the event that one's vote is pivotal is a very subtle idea, so that consistency with the theory might be expected to increase over time. (They find some evidence to this effect for unanimous juries.[60]) They also note that, within the framework of the symmetric informative equilibrium on which they base their predictions, a low frequency of individual juror errors can result in large changes in the probability of erroneous judgments at the jury level. This effect is particularly pronounced for juries requiring unanimity.[61] In addition, looking at individual juror decisions, they find strong evidence for lack of symmetry in the juries requiring unanimous votes, with only 56% of the individual subjects "mixing" (voting to convict and acquit at least one time when receiving an innocent signal). The remaining subjects either always vote to acquit (25%) or always vote to convict (18%).[62] There are a lot of pure strategy asymmetric equilibria for these games, so the empirical restrictions of equilibrium theory are limited once one drops the assumption of symmetry.[63]

Finally, note that the discussion of equilibrium voting has all been within a framework in which jurors vote simultaneously, without deliberations. Once one accounts for deliberations in the form of a straw vote, there exist equilibria in which voters reveal their information in the straw vote, and then vote optimally based on the pooled information in the actual vote (Coughlan 1997); i.e., strategic voting is no longer an issue. If these equilibria hold, then decisions under majority rule will be identical to those under unanimity, thereby eliminating the unattractive aspects of unanimity. GMP include a unanimous jury-vote treatment, with a prior straw vote in their experiment. They find that the presence of a straw vote increased the accuracy of the jury outcomes in the guilty

TABLE 1.11

Jury Decision versus True State: Proportion of Incorrect Decisions

| | Majority | | | | | | Unanimous | | | | | |
| | n = 3 | | | n = 6 | | | n = 3 | | | n = 6 | | |
True State	No. of Observations	Data	Nash	No. of Observations	Data	Nash	No. of Observations	Data	Nash	No. of Observations	Data	Nash
Innocent	40	.175	.216	27	.296	.071	63	.190	.140	34	.029	.186
Guilty	60	.300	.216	33	.212	.256	57	.526	.499	26	.731	.485

Source: Guarnaschelli, McKelvey, and Palfrey 2000.

state, but there was essentially no effect in the innocent state. The key problems here appear to be that (1) subjects do not always vote sincerely in the straw poll, with false revelation of innocent signals occurring about twice as often as false revelation of guilty signals,[64] and (2) jurors base their votes on both the public information (the outcome of the straw poll) and their private information, and do not ignore the latter as they should under the Coughlan equilibrium.

The extension of the winner's curse idea to voting is a very nice intellectual contribution that uses asymmetric information and adverse selection to potentially explain important real-life observations. As FP (1999) note, research in this area has only just begun, so where it will eventually lead, and what its real-world implications will be, have yet to be fully sorted out. However, applications of this idea to date have yet to be fully convincing. For example, in juries, the whole idea of deliberation and straw polls is to permit pooling of information prior to voting. And as Coughlan (1997) notes, in this case strategic voting is no longer an issue. More generally, the possibility of strategic voting arises *only* when for some reason (legality, cost, or complexity) voters cannot aggregate their information, but must instead rely on their "raw" signals without any opportunity to sort out their relative reliability. Since in all purely informational voting games there are no tensions between agents regarding the desired outcome (as there is, for example, in auctions), communication is likely to occur, particularly if such exchanges are not too costly. As such, this is a case where cheap talk is credible and can help to facilitate information aggregation, which in turn can help eliminate the need for strategic voting.

4.5 Summing Up

In the bilateral bargaining game, buyers repeatedly suffer from a winner's curse as they fail to account for the adverse selection problem inherent in the seller's strategy of rejecting bids below the value of the item. It is clear at this point that bidder behavior reported in the original SB (1985) paper is robust, and remarkably resistant to the feedback associated with repeated losses. (Factors that promote learning in this environment, and in common-value auctions, are discussed in section 5 below.)

In both FIP's (1989) blind-bid auctions and Lynch et al.'s (1986, 1991) lemons markets there are potential adverse selection problems that are realized. Prior to unraveling, the winner's curse is alive and well in these experimental markets. However, once the market unravels, the winner's curse disappears. This outcome occurs not because buyers have achieved some sort of magical insight that helps them to overcome the winner's curse, but because the complete unraveling essentially eliminates the adverse selection problem that underlies the winner's curse. Sellers' short-run profit-maximizing behavior helps to promote the unraveling in both cases, an option not present in SB's bilateral bargaining game. Several questions remain to be explored in these markets. Will the history of unraveling serve to protect new entrants, or infrequent participants, in these markets from the strong winner's curse found in the start-up phase of the market? Will the answer to this question depend on the relative sizes of the experienced and inexperienced agents present in the market at a given point in time?

More recent work extends ideas about adverse selection and the winner's curse to voting models in which agents' preferences are based on information alone; i.e., they agree on the correct course of action but have different information regarding what is best. Applications of the model lead to a number of surprising results as pivotal voters may ignore their own signals and vote strategically instead. There have been only very limited experimental studies to date of the extent to which voters are able to avoid the "swing voter's curse." In light of the auction and bilateral bargaining game results, it is not surprising that these studies show only a limited ability of agents to avoid the swing voter's curse. Further, unlike high-stakes auctions, where one might expect to find highly motivated bidders with expert advisers who *might* help to overcome the winner's curse, many applications of the swing voter's curse involve ordinary people making decisions with no expert help and with few repetitions. In this case, experimental studies with the usual subject population (college students) is likely to involve a subject population that is as sophisticated as, or more sophisticated than, the general population the theory is intended to describe.

5. How Do Bidders Learn to Overcome the Winner's Curse?

This section is concerned with whether and how subjects learn to overcome the winner's curse in common-value auctions and bilateral bargaining experiments. Learning and adjustment processes are important phenomena in most experiments, and are of growing interest to both theorists and experimenters, since it is clear that equilibria do not emerge instantaneously in games. Rather, equilibrium play is likely to evolve gradually out of some sort of learning/adjustment process. To the extent that convergence to equilibrium is slow, as it often is, this out-of-equilibrium play may be more relevant in terms of its positive and normative implications than are equilibrium outcomes.

5.1 Bilateral Bargaining Games

BBC (1991) and Cifuentes and Sunder (1991) report virtually no adjustment to the winner's curse in repeated bilateral bargaining trials for inexperienced subjects (recall Figure 1.1). Indeed, the absence of any noticeable within-session adjustments in either of these studies is quite remarkable, at least to these reviewers. However, BBC do not stop at this, but go on to investigate possible mechanisms that will enhance learning: (1) buyers playing the role of sellers, and (2) more experience, with buyers returning for a second night of play.

To determine the effect of experience on the sellers' performance as buyers, BBC's subjects participated in two experimental sessions. The first session consisted of two parts: twenty trials in which subjects acted as buyers, followed by twenty trials in which they acted as sellers. In their role as sellers, subjects were told the value of the company they were trying to sell, were given an offer, and were asked to accept or reject it (offers were taken from a representative subject's behavior in an earlier experiment). Following each period, the computer calculated the seller's earnings for that period and the earnings of their imaginary buyer opponent. In the second experimental session, conducted several days later, subjects again played the role of buyers for twenty trials. As a control condition, another group of subjects acted as buyers in an initial experimental session (of twenty trials), returning as buyers for a second experimental session several days later.

When subjects acted as both buyers and sellers, the percentage of learners (defined as subjects bidding zero from any particular trial until the end of the experimental session) jumped from 9% (4 out of 44) to 37% (15 out of 41) between sessions 1 and 2 (a statistically significant increase). Further, the mean bid for the nonlearners changed from $51 to $34, indicating that these subjects had learned to reduce their chances of losing money in any given trial, and to reduce their losses conditional on the event of winning. Learning seems to have occurred between experimental sessions, or while playing as sellers, as there were virtually no adjustments over time within the second session.

BBC report some adjustments in the control group as well. The percentage of learners increased from 6% (2 of 34) to 12% (4 of 34), although this difference is not significant at conventional levels. Further, the mean bid of nonlearners dropped from $50 to $34, almost the same as the reduction reported for the nonlearners who had played as sellers. Here, too, almost all the learning took place between the two experimental sessions, with minimal adjustments within the second session.

The fact that playing as sellers dramatically affected buyers' behavior squares nicely with one's intuition. The role reversal from buyer to seller literally forces buyers to act out the behavior of sellers, which should promote incorporating the seller's decisions into their bids after the experience. In other words, to the extent that the winner's curse results from buyers' failure to account for the adverse selection problem inherent in the seller's decision rule, playing the role of seller promotes buyers' accounting for this fact.

(*Methodological aside:* Experimenters often employ role reversals in their designs in efforts to promote more rapid adjustments to equilibrium. The BBC experiment provides one of the few explicit tests of the efficacy of role reversals in promoting learning.)

5.2 Inexperienced Bidders in Sealed-Bid Auctions

In common-value auctions, there are two distinctly different vehicles for bids adjusting over time. First, there is the possibility of Darwinian "market learning" as bankruptcies drive out the more aggressive bidders, who then self-select out of returning for further experimental sessions. Second, there is the possibility for individual learning as subjects respond to repeated losses by bidding less. This can occur in one of two ways: (1) through direct responses to one's own losses, and (2) through observing losses of others, with enough information feedback provided to learn from others' mistakes. There is evidence that both these factors are at work in sealed-bid auctions.

In Lind and Plott (1991), both the number of bidders and the size of ε were held constant throughout. LP conclude that "the winner's curse persists with experience but the magnitude and frequency of losses decline with experience" (LP 1991, Conclusion 2). Clear evidence for this is found in Table 1.3, reported earlier. In Table 1.3 both loss frequencies and average profits are divided into ten-period quartiles for each experimental session. As can be seen, with the notable exception of session 5, both the frequency and magnitude of losses decrease after the first ten auctions.[65] To the extent that these adjustments are real rather than spurious, they must be the result of individual learning, as there were no bankruptcies in these sessions.[66]

Garvin and Kagel (1994; hereafter GK) identify substantial adjustments in bidding in first-price sealed-bid auctions between inexperienced and once-experienced bidders (subjects who have participated in one previous first-price auction series). Table 1.12 reports some of their results. For example, with $n = 4$, the winning bid is *greater* than $E[x_o \mid X = x_{1n}]$ in 75.6% of all auctions with inexperienced bidders compared to 34.8% with experienced bidders. Or, looking at the same behavior from a different point of view, for inexperienced subjects the average bid factor $(x - \gamma(x))$ for winning bidders was $4.42, well below what is required to avoid the winner's curse (a bid factor of $7.20 with $\varepsilon = \$12$), compared to an average bid factor of $7.44 for once-experienced bidders. This overly aggressive bidding translates into negative average profits for inexperienced bidders of $1.32 per auction and losses in more than 50% of all auctions, compared to positive average profits of $1.37 and positive profits in 58.4% of all auctions for once-experienced bidders.

GK identify two mechanisms behind these changes. First, a kind of market learning/self-selection effect is at work as bankrupt subjects were much less likely to return for the second auction series: 27% of bankrupt bidders (4 out of 15) returned, compared to 86% of the solvent bidders (32 out of 37).[67] Bankrupt bidders and others who declined invitations to return for additional experimental sessions bid more aggressively, on average, than did returning bidders.[68] Thus, there is a rather strong market-level learning, or self-selection effect, in the data.

Second, there were clear individual subject learning effects as well. Following losses, inexperienced bidders consistently increased their bid factor in the next auction period. GK refer to this as experiential learning. Further, subjects also bid less when they did not win the item but when the feedback from the auction showed that they would have lost money applying their bid factor to the winning bidder's signal value. GK refer to this as observational learning. In fact, under some conditions, this observational learning was almost as strong as

TABLE 1.12

Effects of Experience on Bidding in First-Price Common-Value Auctions ($\epsilon = \$12$)

n		Percentage of Auctions Won with x_1 (raw data)	High Bidders: Percentage of $b_1 > E[x_o|X = x_{1n}]$ (raw data)	All Bidders: Percentage of $b_1 > E[x_o|X = x_{1n}]$ (raw data)	Percentage of Auctions with Positive Profit (raw data)	Average Actual Profit (S_m)	Average Predicted RNNE Profit (S_m)	Average Discount[a] $= (x - b)$ (S_m)
4	Inexperienced	73.2 (30/41)	75.6 (31/41)	64.6 (106/164)	43.9 (18/41)	−1.32 (0.79)	5.01 (0.60)	4.60 (.685)
	Once-Experienced	66.3 (59/89)	34.8 (31/89)	29.5 (105/356)	58.4 (52/89)	1.37 (0.49)	4.32 (0.41)	8.07 (.359)
6 or 7	Inexperienced	56.7 (17/30)	76.7 (23/30)	58.2 (121/208)	30.0 (9/30)	−3.75 (0.89)	2.76 (0.53)	3.56 (0.97)
	Once-Experienced	47.4 (9/19)	68.4 (13/19)	33.8 (45/133)	31.6 (6/19)	−0.32 (0.56)	2.93 (0.54)	5.53 (1.10)

Source: Garvin and Kagel 1994.

S_m = Standard error of mean.

[a]Data for $x \geq \underline{x} + \epsilon$.

the response to actually losing money. Likewise, in cases where losing bidders would have made money had their bid factor won the item when applied to the high bidder's signal value, bids were higher in the next auction. Although these "hypothetical" gains tend to retard convergence to the RNNE, they were smaller and less frequent in magnitude than the hypothetical losses, so the net effect of both the observational and experiential learning was to move bids closer to the RNNE.

One noticeable difference between the common-value auction experiments and the bilateral bargaining experiments is the within-session adjustments to the winner's curse reported for inexperienced subjects: in the bilateral bargaining experiments, there is virtually no adjustment, while reasonably large reductions in bids are found in the auctions. It is interesting to conjecture as to the basis for these differences. BBC (1991) argue that there is a higher frequency of earning positive profits conditional on winning in the bargaining game (this happens one-third of the time with a naive bidding strategy) than in the auctions, so that the message, "bid less," comes through much more clearly in the auctions. Although this observation is true for the experiments reported in Kagel et al. (1989), it is not true in GK or LP, where inexperienced bidders earned positive profits in 30% or more of the auctions. So this explanation appears suspect. A second factor to consider is that actual losses are often considerably larger in the auctions—averaging between $-\$1.30$ and $-\$3.75$ in GK (Table 1.12) and around $-\$8.00$ in the first ten periods in LP—compared to $-\$0.06$ per period in BBC and Cifuentes and Sunder (experimental dollars were converted into cash at the rate of one cent to the dollar in the bilateral bargaining studies). Perhaps subjects are more sensitive to these larger losses.[69] Third, the observational learning reported by GK in common-value auctions is not available in the bilateral bargaining game, where bidders only get to see the outcome of their own choices.[70] Further studies are needed to carefully sort between these alternative explanations.

5.3 Super-Experienced Bidders in Sealed-Bid Auctions

Kagel and Richard (2001; hereafter KR) investigate bidding for super-experienced bidders—subjects who had participated in two or more prior auction sessions.[71] These super-experienced bidders had learned to overcome the worst effects of the winner's curse in first-price common-value auctions, rarely bidding above $E[x_o \mid x = x_{1n}]$, but still earned less than 50% of the Nash equilibrium profits (at a cost of between $2.50 and $3.50 per auction conditional on winning). KR set out to investigate the reason for the continued shortfall relative to the RNNE benchmark.

KR first looked at the bid function itself, which is quite complicated over the full support from which signals are drawn, to see if rules of thumb that boundedly rational bidders might employ were responsible for the earnings shortfall. They are not. Subjects employ sensible piecewise linear bid functions that differ systematically from the RNNE benchmark (they are far too flat to begin with and completely overlook the nonlinear elements of the Nash bid function). However, simulations with bidders restricted to employing these piecewise linear bid functions identify symmetric equilibria in which profits are equal to or *greater* than the RNNE benchmark. As such, bidders' inability to account for the complexities of the Nash bid function cannot account for the marked reduction in their earnings.

KR then looked at the intercepts of the bid function, which are quite heterogenous across bidders, and in the overwhelming majority of cases (90% of all bidders) are higher than the symmetric rule-of-thumb equilibria (RTE) identified. They conduct Monte Carlo simulations to determine if these overly aggressive bid factors might be the best response to rivals' overly aggressive bidding. This is not the case, as large sample estimates of best-response intercepts are remarkably robust relative to the observed heterogeneity in rivals' bid functions, averaging around $-\$18.00$ with $\varepsilon = \$18$. In other words, for bidders employing piecewise linear bid functions as subjects did, the best response to overly aggressive bidding by one's rivals, even when the latter do not commit the winner's curse, typically requires bidding close to the symmetric RTE benchmark (which in turn is close to the RNNE benchmark in most of region 2). Losses relative to large sample estimates of best-response intercepts average 20% and 44.3% with four and seven bidders, respectively. Thus, bidders still suffer from a winner's curse, albeit a much less pronounced and more subtle winner's curse than the negative average profits from which inexperienced bidders suffer (Kagel et al. 1989; Dyer, Kagel, and Levin 1989; LP 1991).

KR suggest two primary reasons for these continuing losses relative to the RNNE and RTE benchmarks. First, best responses are highly variable in small samples of the sort that individual bidders would have seen, sometimes pointing in the wrong direction (bid more aggressively) and sometimes implying overly passive bidding (bid below $x - \varepsilon$). At best, this makes best responding more problematic than the large-sample estimates suggest. At worst, it could lead bidders simply to ignore the information content inherent in the feedback once satisfactory (i.e., consistently positive) profit levels were achieved. Second, large-sample best responses require winning half as many auctions, on average, as were actually won. This might have posed two problems for bidders: the variability in the small-sample estimates makes identifying the optimal tradeoff difficult; and this is made all the harder, psychologically at least, by the fact that bidders are earning relatively large positive profits compared to their inexperienced selves. As a result, they may have been reluctant to deviate from a rule of thumb that had proved capable of generating acceptable profit levels in such a high-variance environment.

5.4 The Role of Information Feedback in Learning

The regressions reported in GK point to a clear role for observational learning in speeding up the adjustment process underlying elimination of the worst effects of the winner's curse. Armantier (1998) attacks this issue directly by comparing auctions in which bidders receive the complete feedback offered in GK after each auction (all bids and signal values, as well as the true value of the item) and auctions in which bidders receive minimal feedback (only the winning bidder gets to observe the true value of the item and profits earned; all others are only informed that they did not win the item). The latter provides the minimum information the winner needs to be able to verify her gains or losses from the auction.

Armantier's experiment shows quite clearly that full feedback enhances bidders' ability to avoid the winner's curse. As shown in Figure 1.3, the average bid factor reaches the minimum value required to avoid negative expected profits after the twentieth period with full feedback, compared to around the fortieth period with minimal feedback.[72] Moreover, after sixty periods, individual bids in the full feedback treatment were within a narrow band near the RNNE. In contrast, after sixty periods, bids in the minimal feedback treatment continued to oscillate in a large band well above the RNNE, with no indication of convergence to the RNNE. Armantier estimates and compares different learning models. He concludes that a continuous-reinforcement learning model, which incorporates observational learning and direction learning, explains the experimental data the best, outperforming belief-based learning models. The latter is not surprising since (rational) belief-based learning models predict no winner's curse, which is rampant in the data.

What is important in these results is further identification of the role of observational learning (full feedback regarding all bids and signal values) in speeding up elimination of the worst effects of the winner's curse. The data provide no support for the idea that the larger losses resulting from eliminating observational learning might "shock" bidders into overcoming the winner's curse more quickly (as GK conjectured might happen). Finally, the kind of feedback bidders typically get in field settings is intermediate between the full-feedback and minimal-feedback treatments, as bidders are usually informed of the distribution of bids but not the underlying signal values, and winning bidders only receive information regarding gains and losses after considerable delay. As such, it would be interesting to see if full disclosure of bids, but not signal values or information about profits earned (except to the winner), would result in an adjustment process that is closer to one or the other of these two extreme cases.

6. Comparing Results from Field Studies with Experiments

There are important tradeoffs in studying auctions using field data compared to experimental data. In an experiment, the researcher has full control of the auction structure so that, for example, a pure common-value or a pure private-value auction can be constructed and the private information signals/valuations underlying bids are known. Failure to control these factors can make interpretation of field data problematic, as most actual auctions contain important private- as

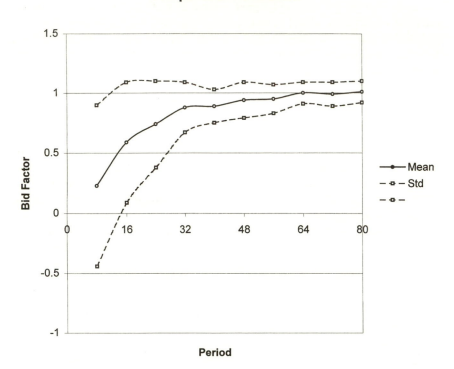

Figure 1.3. Evolution of the bid factor: (a) sample with feedback; (b) sample with no feedback.

well as common-value elements, and the investigator must construct proxies for the private information signals/valuations underlying bids. Laboratory control also permits quite precise and demanding tests of the theory and facilitates identifying the causal factors underlying the behavior reported (see, for example, the analysis of the effects of public information on sellers' revenue in KL 1986 and KLH 1995, and Holt and Sherman's [1994] loser's curse experiment). On the other hand, field data has the advantage that it involves experienced professionals, with substantially larger amounts of money at stake than in the typical auction experiment, which may result in fundamentally different behavior. Wilson (1992, 261–62) summarizes the differences between field studies and laboratory experiments nicely:

> Empirical [field] studies must contend with less complete data, and few controls in the auction environment are possible. On the other hand, they have the advantage that the data pertain to practical situations in which the stakes are often large and the participants are skilled and experienced.

Despite these differences, results from field studies and experiments are complementary in the sense that they both deal with the same phenomena, auction

Evolution of the Bid Factor
Sample with No Feed Back

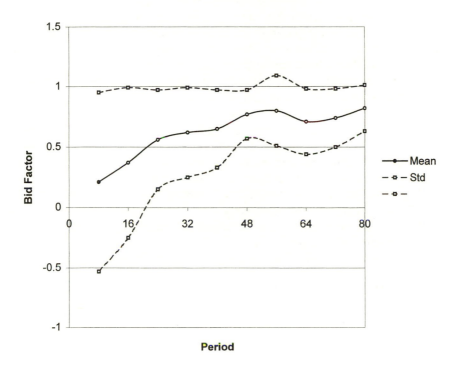

Period

behavior. As such, both similarities and differences in behavior need to be identified (and, in the case of differences, hopefully reconciled) in order to enhance
understanding. One purpose of this section is to make these comparisons.

A middle ground between field studies and experiments is to bring experienced professionals into the laboratory to participate in an experiment. Here,
one presumably has the best of both worlds, strict control over the structure of
the auction, and experienced professionals to behave in it. Dyer, Kagel, and
Levin (1989; hereafter DKL) did this in an experiment comparing the behavior
of student subjects with construction industry executives in a common-value
offer auction (bidding to be the low-cost supplier). Behavior was found to be
qualitatively similar, as both students and executives fell prey to the winner's
curse. This raises the puzzling issue of why presumably successful executives
from the construction industry, an industry in which the competitive bidding
process is often characterized as, essentially, a common-value auction, could do
so poorly in the laboratory. The second purpose of this section is to provide
summary results from a field study of the construction industry designed to
answer this question.[73]

6.1 Direct Comparisons between Laboratory and Field Data

One unsurprising prediction that has been confirmed using both field data and experimental data is that better-informed bidders make a higher rate of return than less-informed bidders (see Mead, Moseidjord, and Sorensen 1984, and Hendricks and Porter 1988, for field data results; Kagel and Levin 1999, chapter 7, for experimental results). In contrast, sightings of a winner's curse in early OCS wildcat leases have met with considerable controversy regarding how to interpret the outcomes reported.

Considerable fieldwork has been devoted to the study of outer continental shelf (OCS) oil-lease auctions in the Gulf of Mexico for the period 1954–69. Much of this research has focused on the existence of a winner's curse. In an initial study, Mead, Moseidjord, and Sorensen (1983; MMS) found after-tax rates of return to be somewhat less than average returns on equity for U.S. manufacturing corporations, concluding that "they [lessees] have historically received no risk premium and may have paid too much for the right to explore for and produce oil and gas on federal offshore lands" (1983, 42–43). MMS argue that these results provide qualified support for Capen, Clapp, and Campbell's position (1971) that oil companies fell prey to the winner's curse in these auctions. On the other hand, McAfee and McMillan (1987) argue that MMS's results overturn Capen, Clapp, and Campbell's claims. The difference in interpretation has to do with whether investors require a risk premium for investing in oil and gas leases. MMS argue that they do. McAfee and McMillan argue that they do not, given large oil companies' access to capital markets and a diversified portfolio of leases.

Hendricks, Porter, and Boudreau (1987; hereafter HPB) reexamined rates of return for OCS leases during the period 1954–69. Using somewhat different accounting procedures from MMS, one of their main conclusions is that average realized profits were negative for auctions with more than six bidders, a conclusion remarkably similar to that reported in KL (1986). However, as noted earlier, HPB argue that these negative profits can be explained by nonoptimal bidding strategies that fail to account for the winner's curse, or equally, by adverse selection effects in estimating the number of bidders. That is, since most tracts receive less than six bids, and assuming that firms expect this, ex post profits will be less on tracts receiving more bids. As a result, HPB conclude that overall, "the data are consistent with both the assumptions and predictions of [equilibrium bidding in] the [common-value] model," allowing for bidders' uncertainty about the number of active bidders on each tract. As Wilson (1992) points out, however, this conclusion is stronger than in previous studies, where mixed results regarding profitability are often reported (Gilley, Karels, and Leone 1986).

Given the inconclusive nature of rate-of-return studies for OCS leases, KL (1986) used the anomalous finding reported in MMS (1983; 1984) that rates of return were higher on *both* neighbor and non-neighbor tracts for drainage leases compared to wildcat leases to argue for a winner's curse in these early OCS auctions (see section 2.2 and chapter 3 for details of this argument, as well as alternative explanations that do not rely on the winner's curse).

A second anomalous result that has emerged from field studies, which might be more parsimoniously explained by appealing to a winner's curse, concerns U.S. timber-lease sales. These have been conducted using both English and first-price auctions. Using ordinary-least-squares regressions, Mead (1967) reports that first-price sealed-bid auctions had significantly higher prices than English auctions; that is, English auctions resulted in significantly lower average revenue. Further study by Hansen (1985; 1986), who noted a selection bias caused by the way the Forest Service chose which auction to use and corrected for it using a simultaneous equations model, found that although first-price auctions had slightly higher prices than English auctions, the difference was not statistically significant, so that revenue equivalence could not be rejected. The puzzling part about these results is that there are strong common-value elements to timber-lease sales that should, in theory, result in English auctions raising more revenue. McAfee and McMillan (1987, 727) note this puzzle and go on to add, "The puzzle could be resolved by appealing to risk aversion of the bidders, but this remains an open empirical question."

Results from LKR (1996; see section 3.1 and chapter 6) offer an alternative to risk aversion to resolve this anomaly. In auctions with inexperienced bidders who clearly suffered from the winner's curse, English auctions consistently yield less revenue than first-price auctions. Further, even in auctions where bidders earned positive profits, but still exhibited relatively strong traces of the winner's curse, as in auctions with once-experienced bidders and auctions with a large number of super-experienced bidders ($n = 7$), the two auctions yield roughly the same revenue. In other words, in auctions where bidders suffer from a winner's curse, earning substantially lower profits than predicted in first-price auctions, English auctions fail to raise more revenue. Of course, to use this mechanism to resolve the anomaly for the timber-lease sales requires postulating that bidders suffer from traces of the winner's curse, something many economists are loath to do. Nevertheless, this hypothesis is more consistent with the experimental data than the risk-aversion hypothesis.[74]

Blecherman and Camerer (1998; hereafter BC) take comparisons between field data and experiments one step further. They reexamine the issue of a winner's curse in major league baseball's free agency market (Cassing and Douglas 1980). Their study has two parts. First, they test for a winner's curse in the 1990 free-agent baseball market. This is done by econometrically estimating the marginal revenue product (MRP) of free agents compared to what these players' salaries were.[75] In equilibrium, absent a winner's curse, players' salaries should equal their MRP. To test for specification errors in their MRP estimates, BC repeat the exercise for re-signed players who did not declare, or were not eligible, for free agency. They argue that salaries for these players should equal estimated MRP if there is no systematic bias in the MRP estimates. Although this "control treatment" is far from perfect (players ineligible for free agency have limited bargaining power, which may result in salaries below MRP), it does provide a gross check on the statistical accuracy of their MRP estimates (a check not employed in earlier studies). BC's calculations show that for the thirty-two free agents in 1990, average MRP was $604,678 versus average salaries of $934,115, an average return of −35%. Further, twenty-five of the thirty-two free agents were paid more than their MRP. In contrast, non–free agents signed in the same year had average salaries of $712,023 with average MRP of $704,317.

BC go on to conduct an experiment designed to mimic baseball's free-agency market. They compile career statistics for ten fictional hitters (batting average, runs batted in, etc.), which are mapped into the MRPs (the common value) using the regressions estimated from the field data.[76] This leaves MRPs unknown prior to bidding, but gives subjects ("teams") data upon which to form their own estimates of MRP (which were solicited and recorded). Teams first selected which, if any, free agents they wanted to bid on so that the level of competition for individual players was determined endogenously. The number of teams competing for each free agent was announced, and then the teams bid.

Average profits were negative for most levels of competition for both inexperienced and experienced bidders. However, experienced bidders had higher earnings as (1) there was a reduction in the average number of players teams bid on from 45.2% of all free agents to 38.8%, and reduced competition reduces the severity of the winner's curse; and (2) there was a sharp increase in the frequency with which free agents attracted only one team, from 5.6% to 15.0% for experienced bidders. (With only one team bidding, minimum bids were entered, and teams invariably made relatively large, positive profits.) Further, there was an increase in the frequency with which free agents attracted only two or three teams bidding on them, from 28.4% to 43.8% of all bids. This reduction in teams bidding on a given player acts like tacit collusion, since equilibrium profit rises as the number of bidders falls. The extent to which these changes in bid patterns reflect teams explicitly shying away from more attractive players, as opposed to an overall reduction in the number of free agents on which teams bid, is not reported. There is a striking parallel between the reduced bidding competition in the lab and earlier convictions of team owners for conspiring not to bid on free agents in 1985–86. In the latter case, teams were convicted of explicit collusion. However, in the typical laboratory experiment, there is no real possibility of explicit collusion, only room for tacit collusion of the sort BC observed.

6.2 Differences in Structure between Laboratory and Field Auctions

Dyer and Kagel (1996) address the question of why experienced construction industry executives fell prey to the winner's curse in laboratory offer auctions in DKL (1989). They focus on two possibilities, which are not necessarily mutually exclusive. One is that the executives had learned a set of situation-specific rules of thumb that permit them to avoid the winner's curse in the field, but that could not be applied in the laboratory. The second is that the bidding environment created in the experiment, which is based on theoretical work, is not representative of the environment encountered in the construction industry.

Evidence supporting this first possibility emerges from interviews with contractors. In these interviews, it is clear that an important determinant of the risk associated with bidding a job involves the architect/owner. The architect/owner's reputation for admitting mistakes or ambiguities in construction plans, and willingness to implement functionally equivalent construction outcomes using alternative, and cheaper, construction techniques than originally specified, play an important role in the cost estimates assigned to specific job components, as well as the markup assigned to the total cost estimate.[77] In addition, firms tend to specialize in different types of construction projects. Experienced contractors pride themselves on their familiarity with building different types of structures (e.g., churches, schools, office buildings) and figure their estimates to lie within a rather narrow band of the true value. This familiarity is based on past experience. During one bidding session we attended, when doubts arose as to the cost estimate to assign to a particular component of the job, the bid team simply pulled up records from a recently completed job on a similar building designed by the same architect and filled in the missing numbers.[78] Needless to say, the contractors did not have these situation-specific rules to rely on when bidding in the laboratory.

Evidence that the construction industry differs in important ways from the one-shot auctions studied in the laboratory is shown in Table 1.13, which reports the distribution of bids on a particular job, measured in terms of deviations from the low winning bid. The first thing to note is that the lowest bid is some $30,000 *below the low winning bid*. This was the result of a bidding "error" that resulted in the original low bidder withdrawing his bid *without* a penalty after the bids were announced.[79] Standard auction theory does not account for such possibilities.[80] The second thing to note is the small difference between the winning low bid and the second lowest bid ("money left on the table"), less than 1% of the low bid. This difference is minuscule and indicative of the relatively small differences between the low bid and the second lowest bid characteristic of much of the industry, which averaged around 5% for the sample of jobs analyzed in Dyer and Kagel. By way of contrast, HPB (1987) report money left on the table from OCS leases averages around 50% of the winning bid.[81] This implies that there is much smaller scope for the winner's curse to express itself in the branch of the construction industry in which these executives worked. That is, private-value elements, such as the firm's overhead and the amount of idle resources anticipated, often play the decisive role in determining the low bidder in the construction industry, not the differences in bidder estimates of construction costs. As such, bidders would have been unprepared for the complete absence of private-value elements, and the large bid factor required to simply avoid negative expected profits in the experimental environment.

TABLE 1.13
Bids by Firm, Measured in Terms of Deviation from Low Winning Bid

Firm	Deviation for Low Bid (in dollars)	Deviaton as a Percentage of Low Bid
1	− 30,000[a]	− 0.71
2	0	0.00
3	32,000	0.75
4	64,000	1.50
5	74,600	1.75
6	87,679	2.06
7	90,000	2.12
8	105,000	2.47
9	142,000	3.33
10	144,000	3.38
11	155,000	3.64
12	166,000	3.90
13	183,000	4.30
14	564,000	13.25

Source: Kagel 1995a.
[a]Mistake in bid and let out of bid. Second high bidder got the job. Mean bid $4.38 million.

6.3 Summing Up

Unsurprising predictions of auction theory regarding higher profits for bidders with superior information in common-value auctions with insider information are confirmed in both field and laboratory studies. Reports of a winner's curse in early OCS oil-lease auctions have been hotly disputed. Anomalies identified in laboratory experiments have parallels in field data, but alternative explanations for the field data are available as well. Professional bidders from the construction industry fell prey to the winner's curse in a laboratory offer auction. Reasons suggested for this are that (1) learning tends to be situation-specific and the experiment stripped away many of the contextual clues the professionals employ in field settings, (2) the variance associated with the common-value element is small, much smaller than the variance in buyer estimates of cost employed in the experiment, so that bidders were unprepared for the strong adverse selection effect present in the experiment, and (3) there are repeated-play elements in the construction industry that help to mitigate the winner's curse and that were not present in the experiment.

7. Concluding Remarks

7.1 Summary of Empirical Findings from the Laboratory

Experimental studies of common-value auctions have been going on for more than fifteen years, paralleling the profession's interest in the theoretical and practical properties of these auctions. This research has established several facts about behavior relative to theory.

For inexperienced bidders, Nash equilibrium bidding theory does not predict well. Inexperienced bidders suffer from a winner's curse, earning negative average profits and going bankrupt in relatively large numbers. Overbidding here represents a fundamental breakdown in the theory, resulting in the reversal of a number of important comparative static predictions: bidding does not decrease in response to an increased number of bidders in second-price auctions as the theory predicts, and public information about the value of the item reduces, rather than raises, revenue in the presence of a winner's curse. This perverse effect of public information in the presence of a winner's curse extends to the endogenous release of public information in English clock auctions.

Experienced bidders in the lab eventually overcome the worst effects of the winner's curse, rarely bidding above the expected value of the item conditional on winning and earning positive average profits. Super-experienced bidders also satisfy key comparative static predictions of the theory: release of public information in sealed-bid auctions raises revenue, and English clock auctions raise more revenue than do sealed-bid auctions. Further, average revenue increases in an experimental design where the existence of an informed insider is predicted to raise revenue compared to auctions with symmetrically informed bidders. Nevertheless, these super-experienced bidders still earn well below equilibrium profits and, in the overwhelming majority of cases, are not best responding to rivals' bids.

It is worth noting that these very experienced bidders in the lab have learned how to overcome the worst effects of the winner's curse in an environment with strong information feedback, substantially stronger than is likely to be present in field settings. As such, learning might not proceed as quickly in field settings. Further, there are dynamics of interactions within organizations that may retard adjustment to the winner's curse. These include (1) payments of large salaries to petroleum geologists to estimate likely reserves, and the recognition that these estimates still have a very large variance and are not very precise, (2) transfers of personnel within the firm and between firms prior to receiving feedback about the profitability of bids, and (3) gaming that goes on within organizations.[82] Finally, even assuming that the winner's curse will be eliminated in the long run in field settings, it often takes some time before this happens, so this out-of-equilibrium behavior is important in its own right.

The winner's curse extends to other market settings as well, being particularly robust in bilateral bargaining games. However, blind-bid auctions and markets where quality is endogenously determined unravel rather quickly, largely eliminating the winner's curse through eliminating the adverse selection problem; i.e., after a few periods with only lemons being sold, there is no winner's curse to fall prey to! What these markets add that the auctions and bilateral bargaining games lack is the dynamic interaction between sellers pursuing their own self-interest and buyers who at least partially adjust to the adverse selection effects. The net effect is not a magical transformation of naive bidders into sophisticated ones, but a transformation of the environment into one with which even the most unsophisticated bidders are capable of dealing.

7.2 Theory Motivated by Experiments

Although many of the experiments reviewed here have been motivated by theoretical developments in the auction literature, experimental outcomes have also motivated new theoretical developments. This section briefly discusses three such cases.

Generalizing the Role of Insider Information in First-Price Common-Value Auctions

Our experiments with insider information (Kagel and Levin 1999) yielded the unanticipated result that the existence of a well-informed insider raised, rather than lowered, seller revenue compared to the standard symmetric information environment. This result was unanticipated relative to the standard comparisons made in the literature, namely between auctions with insider information compared to symmetric information auctions in which all bidders have *identical* information (i.e., all information is public). This result motivated Campbell and Levin (2000) to further investigate the role of insider information in first-price auctions compared to homogeneous information environments. To do this, they developed a simple two-bidder model of a pure first-price common-value auction in which V, the value of the auctioned item, takes on discrete values of 0 or 1, and each of two bidders receives information signals, X_1 and X_2, which take on values of 0 or 1 as well but are correlated with V (e.g., Probability $[X = 0 \mid V = 0] = \alpha \in [0.5, 1]$ and Probability $[X = 1 \mid V = 1] = \alpha \in [0.5, 1]$). For auctions with insider information, Campbell and Levin distinguish between the case where the insider knows both signals but does not know the signal of the outsider, and cases where she knows both signals as well as the outsider's signal (the double informational advantage case). Note that in both cases, the insider has the same sufficient statistic for V, which makes the outsider information just a grabbling of the insider's information. The only difference between the two cases is that in the first one, the insider is not certain about the signal that the outsider possesses. The existence of an insider with a double informational advantage results in higher expected revenue than the standard symmetric private information environment for all cases where private information signals are strictly affiliated (exclusive of the limiting cases where the two signals are either independent, $\alpha = \frac{1}{2}$, or perfectly correlated, $\alpha = 1$). The strict revenue dominance in this case validates Milgrom and Weber's (1982) result on the revenue-raising effects of increased bidder information in an environment with heterogeneous information, since the insider has increased information. Further, in cases where the insider has superior information, but does not know the outsider's information signal, the existence of an insider raises revenue compared to the standard symmetric private information environment in cases where private information signals are not too strongly affiliated. Campbell and

Levin also note that the "standard" result that the existence of an insider reduces revenue rests in part on the reference point against which the revenue comparison is made (an environment in which bidders have no private information). This paper also shows that the insight that the existence of an insider can raise revenue compared to the standard symmetric private information environment, first reported in Kagel and Levin (1999), is not peculiar to that experimental design.[83]

The Development of Dynamic Vickrey Auctions
for Multi-unit Demand Auctions

One of the most robust results from our experimental work is that bidding is closer to equilibrium play in ascending-price (clock) auctions compared to sealed-bid auctions: inexperienced bidders in English clock auctions suffer from a rather mild form of the winner's curse compared to inexperienced bidders in first- or second-price sealed-bid auctions (section 3.1 and chapter 6). More striking yet, in private-value auctions, where bidders have a dominant strategy of full demand revelation in both second-price sealed-bid auctions and English clock auctions, bidding is much closer to the dominant bidding strategy in the clock auctions (chapter 5).[84] We attribute the superior performance of the clock auction to its greater transparency, as bidders can typically use much simpler reasoning processes and/or calculations compared to sealed-bid auctions to "get it right" (or at least come closer to getting it right).

This, in turn, has provided the motivation for theorists to develop new institutional forms for conducting multiple-unit demand auctions, in which individual bidders demand more than a single unit of the commodity. These auctions are substantially more complicated than the single-unit demand auctions that have provided the focus of the research reported in this book. These complications arise out of the fact that there may be synergies between different units, so that the value of purchasing two or more units is greater than the sum of these units' stand-alone values. (This was generally acknowledged to be the case for the broadband Major Trader Area [MTA] auction of airwave [spectrum] licenses; Ausubel et al. 1997). Alternatively, these different units may serve as partial or complete substitutes for each other, in which case bidders may find it most profitable to reduce demand on some units in an effort to buy other units at a cheaper price. (This was generally acknowledged to be the case for the initial nationwide narrow-band spectrum license sales; Cramton 1995). One way around these complications, at least in some settings, is to employ a variant of the second-price sealed-bid auction (also known as a Vickrey auction). However, the rules and logic underlying the Vickrey auction are substantially more complicated in multi-unit demand auctions than they are in single-unit demand auctions. This, in conjunction with the fact that experiments have demonstrated the greater transparency of the English clock auction over its sealed-bid counterpart, has motivated some theorists to develop dynamic (clock auction) analogues to the multi-unit demand Vickrey auction (Ausubel 1997; Perry and Reny 2000). Finally, an initial experimental implementation of one such dynamic Vickrey auction shows it to perform quite well, and helps overcome the demand-reduction problem associated with simpler auction formats (Kagel and Levin, in press).

Auctions with Endogenous Participation

Common-value auction experiments involve losses and bankruptcy, particularly for inexperienced bidders. As a result, to satisfy the requirements of the theory, which assumes a fixed number of bidders, experimenters have had to devise ways of holding the number of bidders fixed: e.g., using substitute bidders (KL 1986) or designs where losses were not possible (AK 1997; LP 1991) or were made up for by earnings in private-value auctions (LP 1991). Others, for example Cox, Dinkin, and Smith (1998), have allowed the number of active bidders to be determined endogenously, providing a positive-income, "safe-haven" alternative to bidding in the auctions. With the safe-haven alternative, the average number of active bidders was well below the maximum possible number of bidders. With fewer active bidders, in most cases losses for auction participants were eliminated entirely, or almost entirely, although profits were still consistently below the level predicted under the RNNE, given the number of bidders actually participating in the auctions. CDS use these results to suggest that this is how the market cures the winner's curse. It is important to note, however, that this "cure" is similar to the cure reported in the blind-bid auctions and the lemon's market: with fewer bidders, there is a sharply reduced adverse selection problem. Even for totally naive bidders, in CDS's experimental design, a winner's curse only emerges in auctions with four or more bidders.[85]

In any event, it is hard when faced with these experimental observations not to wonder if, how, and why bidder participation is affected by the auction type and other elements of the auction environment. Thus, it is not surprising that the first researchers to publish *theoretical* papers, in major journals, on common-value auctions with endogenous entry were experimenters (Harstad 1990; Levin and Smith 1994).[86] In the Levin and Smith model, bidders are symmetrically informed ex ante, and incur identical "bid preparation" costs when they decide to enter the market. Bidders mix between entering (with bid preparation costs) and staying out. Consequently, the number of active bidders is a random variable with a binomial distribution whose parameters are determined by the auction environment. This is in contrast to previous independent private-value models with entry where the number of entrants is deterministic.

Smith and Levin (in press) have pursued the theoretical implications of their model experimentally, contrasting its predictions with the deterministic entry model. The data are much closer to the stochastic entry model than to the deterministic model. Since the experimental design employs a reduced-form version of the auction model, we omit the details, as they are only remotely related to our central interests. The stochastic entry model developed in Levin and Smith also serves as the theoretical underpinning to recent econometric research on auctions (Li 2000). So this line of research has come more than full circle: from experimental evidence to theory and back to experiments, and on to econometric modeling of auctions using field data.

7.3 Auction Theory and Experiments at Work: Airwave Rights Auctions

One of the most successful applications of economic theory and experiments has been the auctioning off of airwave (spectrum) rights for cellular phone use and paging devices. Led by the Federal Communications Commission (FCC), the U.S. government has conducted a number of sales to date raising a total of $23.9 billion and selling over 10,000 licenses between July 1994 and July 2000. Even more spectacular, in an auction ending in April 2000, the British government raised £22.5 billion ($35.53 billion) from the sale of "third-generation" mobile phone licenses. (These will enable users to surf the net, download e-mails, music, and high-quality pictures, and hold video conferences, all on the move.[87]) The sale in Great Britain, averaging more than £4 billion per license, contrasts with earlier sales of similar licenses where firms paid £40,000 per license. The latter were allocated via a "beauty contest": government experts considered the business plans submitted by contending companies and handed out licenses at a nominal price to the companies whose business plans seemed best. Sales via auctions promise not only to raise substantially more money than such administrative procedures, but also to allocate licenses to bidders who value them the most (as bidders are forced to "put their money where their mouth is"), thereby also improving economic efficiency.

Spectrum licenses typically involve both common-value and private-value elements. (Private-value elements arise because licenses are typically worth more to bidders who, for example, already have stationary phone service in place.) These sales, in the U.S. at least, also involve bidders who have the ability and interest to purchase multiple licenses. (In the third-generation license sale in Great Britain, bidders were limited to purchasing a single nationwide license.) Design of these auctions has involved both economic theory and economic experiments. The latter have served two functions: as a "wind tunnel" to test out the auction software, which implements a relatively complicated set of bidding rules (see, for example, Plott 1997), and as a test bed against which to compare theory with behavior. In the latter role, a central design element has been to use ascending-price auctions (with price feedback for bidders) both to minimize the presence of the winner's curse and to generate increased revenue in the absence of a winner's curse, central insights derived from the interaction between common-value auction theory and experiments:

> An ascending auction ought to remove another common problem with auctions, the "winner's curse." This strikes when a successful bidder discovers too late that his prize is not worth what he paid for it. Some critics of the scale of the bids seem to see the curse at work [in Britain's third-generation sales]. Yet the winner's curse is much likelier in sealed-bid auctions, where bidders lack an important piece of information about the value of the asset:

the valuations of other, perhaps better-informed, bidders. In an ascending auction, however, that information is clearly revealed. (*The Economist*, April 15, 2000, p. 36)

By allowing bidders to respond to each other's bids, [an ascending-price auction] diminishes the winner's curse: that is, the tendency for naive bidders to bid up the price beyond the license's actual value, or for shrewd bidders to bid cautiously to avoid overpaying. (McAfee and McMillan 1996, 161)

Successfully designed auctions take careful thinking based on theory, using experiments to verify and refine the theoretical insights, as different environments call for different auction designs (Klemperer 2000). One design does not fit all.

8. Overview of What Follows

The following chapters provide detailed accounts and supplementary material from our work in common-value auctions. Chapter 2 reports our first common-value auction experiment with inexperienced bidders, using a first-price sealed-bid design, as in the offshore oil-lease auctions that led petroleum geologists to first claim a winner's curse (Capen, Clapp, and Campbell 1971). Our prior beliefs were like much of the economics profession at the time: with real payoffs and feedback, we were not likely to observe a winner's curse for very long. This forecast could not have been more wrong. The winner's curse is quite robust in these data, being present for inexperienced bidders throughout, with the possible exception of when bankruptcies reduce the number of bidders to the point that the adverse selection problem has been essentially eliminated.

An appendix to this chapter reports unpublished data documenting the same outcome for inexperienced bidders in a second-price sealed-bid auction experiment carried out at about the same time. Instructions for both sets of experiments are provided as well. Both experiments were carried out with pencil and paper. Subsequent chapters also report data for inexperienced bidders under a number of different institutional arrangements.

Being unprepared for the persistence of the winner's curse, the experiments reported in chapter 2 do not incorporate the kinds of controls that one might wish for and that were incorporated into later studies. The primary problem here is that with bankruptcies, and our rule that subjects with negative cash balances can no longer bid, the number of bidders may be reduced unless measures are taken to control for this eventuality. With fewer bidders, we find less of an adverse selection problem and higher expected profits, so that surviving bidders do not necessarily have to adjust their bidding strategies to go from making losses to earning positive profits. The obvious way to correct for this problem is to employ reserve bidders, or to have more subjects than active bidders, with only a subset bidding at any point in time (for example, six sub-jects with only four out of the six bidding in any given auction period). Then, if one is lucky, the session can be completed holding the number of bidders con-stant throughout. This still leaves potential self-selection problems to deal with (those going bankrupt are likely to bid more aggressively), but it does control for the original problem. Subsequent experiments employed these kinds of controls.

Initial reactions in a number of quarters to the inexperienced subject data reported in chapter 2 essentially ran "So what? What do you expect from inex-perienced bidders?" We therefore employed once- and twice-experienced bid-ders to explore two key comparative static predictions of the theory: the effects of public information on sellers' revenue, and the effects of changes in the number of bidders on individual bidding.

Chapter 3 looks at these more experienced bidders in first-price sealed-bid auctions. With a small number of bidders (four), more experienced bidders earn positive average profits (although still well below what the theory predicts), indicating that they had overcome the worst effects of the winner's curse. How-ever, these same bidders, in auctions with more rivals (six or seven), again suffer from a winner's curse, earning negative profits on average. Bidders had, apparently, learned to adjust to the winner's curse with fewer rivals through a trial-and-error learning process, but had no deeper understanding of the adverse selection forces at work. This chapter also explores the effects of public infor-mation on bids and seller revenue. It provided our first insight that the release of public information about the value of the item could help bidders overcome the winner's curse, thereby reducing sellers' revenue, contrary to the theory's prediction. This chapter also makes a connection between the laboratory results and field data: profit calculations for early Outer Continental Shelf oil-lease sales showed that greater profits were earned on drainage compared to wildcat leases, even for "non-neighbor" firms (those *not* holding leases next to the drainage tracts), in apparent violation of the theory's prediction that more infor-mation about track value would reduce profits and raise revenue. However, these higher profits are consistent with our finding that public information is likely to raise bidders' profits, not lower them, in the presence of a winner's curse. Alternative explanations for this field data are reported in the chapter, along with our explanation.

An addendum to chapter 3 corrects a small error in that chapter regarding the theoretical benchmark calculations for auctions with public information. The addendum characterizes the correct theoretical benchmark and briefly rean-alyzes the data with respect to the correct benchmark. This reanalysis serves to strengthen the original conclusions reached in chapter 3 regarding the impact of public information.

Chapter 4 looks at the effects of public information on sellers' revenue and the effects of changes in the number of bidders on individual bidding in second-price sealed-bid auctions using more experienced bidders. Second-price sealed-bid auctions have more robust predictions than first-price sealed-bid auctions:

risk aversion has the unambiguous implication in second-price auctions that bids will be below the risk-neutral Nash equilibrium benchmark, and individual bids must decrease with increasing numbers of bidders. The disadvantage is that first-price auctions are far more common in practice, and bidders tend to have problems with second-price auctions (they systematically deviate from the dominant strategy even in simple private-value second-price auctions; see chapter 5). Nevertheless, the two chapters make a nice pair, with the results of one reinforcing the other.

The experiment in chapter 5 was motivated by the effects of public information reported in chapters 3 and 4. In chapters 3 and 4 we argue that the failure of public information to raise revenue as the theory predicts results from the existence of a winner's curse. Public information is also predicted to raise revenue in auctions with affiliated private values (the same mechanism is at work in both cases). But since bidders have private rather than common values, there is no scope for a winner's curse. The experiment in chapter 5 shows that public information reliably raises average revenue in this private-value setting, but not by as much as predicted. The latter results in part from individual bidding errors and in part from a tendency to bid above equilibrium to begin with. One unanticipated result of this experiment, repeated now in a number of different settings (see chapter 6 below), is the closer-to-equilibrium outcomes found in open-outcry (English) auctions compared to sealed-bid auctions.

Chapter 6 studies bidding in ascending-price, English auctions. This experiment represents a natural extension of the study of public information reported in chapters 3 and 4. Drop-out prices in English auctions reveal information about bidders' signal values (bidders with lower signal values tend to drop out first). Hence the initial question motivating this experiment: Does the endogenous release of public information affect bidding in the same way that the exogenous release of public information does? The quick and easy answer for inexperienced bidders was yes: with inexperienced bidders, English auctions reduce rather than raise average sellers' revenue compared to first-price auctions, as bidders use the information contained in rivals' drop-out prices to correct for the winner's curse. The answer for more experienced bidders was harder to come by. It was not until we had bidders experienced enough to take home a substantial share of equilibrium earnings in the first-price sealed-bid auctions that the English auctions raised average sellers' revenue.

However, chapter 6 contains more than the answer to this relatively simple question. Estimates of individual subject bid functions show that a simple and natural signal-averaging rule that does not require recognizing the adverse selection effect of winning the auction better characterizes the data than the Nash bid rule. Further, Monte Carlo simulations using the full-information maximum likelihood estimates of the signal-averaging rule provide a number of insights into behavior: (1) the relatively low percentage of (50–60%) of high signal holders winning the auctions is completely consistent with a symmetric bidding model with bidding errors of the magnitude observed, (2) "panic" dropouts observed during the auctions (bidders dropping out immediately after a rival has dropped, but prior to arrival of any new information) can be explained on the basis of bidding errors in conjunction with the English auctions format, and (3) an assumption of independent errors across successive rounds of bidding is more consistent with the data than an assumption of perfectly correlated errors. This last point is of some general importance, since it has sometimes been argued that subjects interacting across a number of trials within an experimental session create such strong interdependencies that one is effectively left with only one observation per experimental session. This argument implies highly correlated errors between trials (auctions), no less between successive rounds of a given auction.

Chapter 7 explores bidding in auctions with insider information. The original motivation for this experiment was to see if the existence of a perfectly informed insider might shock outsiders into overcoming the winner's curse faster. It does not, at least not in this setting. The chapter then goes on to explore the comparative static predictions of the theory for experienced bidders.

The experimental design employed in chapter 7 was motivated by a desire to maintain procedures as close as possible to those employed in auctions with a symmetric information structure. This resulted in a design that differed in important ways from the standard insider-information model employed in the literature. In the latter, the insider typically has a double informational advantage: she knows the value of the item with certainty and knows all the information that the outsiders have as well. In contrast, in our experiment, outsiders have some proprietary information (although the outsiders have less information than the insider, the insider does not know exactly what information the outsiders have). The latter seems more realistic in a number of settings. In addition, it yields a number of different predictions from the standard model. Most important, the existence of an insider can raise sellers' expected revenue compared to a symmetric information structure (and does so for our design). In the standard model, the existence of an insider unambiguously reduces expected revenue. Although failure to employ the "standard" model gave us fits in terms of solving for the Nash equilibrium, it led to several new theoretical insights that were satisfied in the data.

Chapter 8 shows the interaction between theory and experiments, exploring the possibility for revenue-raising effects of better-informed bidders first discovered in chapter 7. Developing a manageable benchmark model for comparing revenue in common-value auctions with symmetrically informed bidders, compared to auctions where one bidder is better informed, this chapter explores games in which the insider holds a double informational advantage as well as games in which the outsiders maintain some proprietary information. This chapter connects the revenue-raising effects of an insider to more general propositions regarding the revenue-raising effects of increased bidder information found in Milgrom and Weber (1982).

Chapter 9 explores bidding in second-price, "shoebox" auctions with both symmetric and asymmetric payoffs. In auctions with asymmetric payoffs, one of the bidders has a private-value advantage. This might happen, for example, if the item up for auction is complementary to other holdings of one of the bidders. Auctions with asymmetries of this sort are quite common outside the lab. For example, in the recent FCC airwave auctions, it was well known that certain bidders wanted to complement existing holdings (Cramton 1997). In both second-price and English auctions, these asymmetries are predicted to have an explosive effect on bidding, causing large reductions in the disadvantaged bidders' bids and a large reduction in expected revenue compared to the symmetric payoff case. In the experiment, the effect of the asymmetry on bids and prices is proportional rather than explosive. Although advantaged bidders are close to making best responses to disadvantaged bidders, the latter bid much more aggressively than in equilibrium. The chapter explores alternative explanations for this more aggressive bidding.

Chapters 10 and 11 explore learning and adjustment processes of inexperienced bidders. A large number of inexperienced bidders were recruited to participate in a series of sealed-bid auctions, with all subjects invited back for a second experimental session. All inexperienced-subject sessions had reserve bidders. Several sessions had two groups bidding at once, so that if too many bankruptcies occurred, the groups could be combined and the auctions could continue holding the number of active bidders constant.

Chapter 10 explores adjustments over time in first-price sealed-bid auctions. The data reveal (1) a market-adjustment effect, as the most aggressive bidders, and those going bankrupt, declined invitations to return more often than other bidders, and (2) learning on the part of surviving bidders. The market-adjustment effect, although quite pronounced in analyzing the data, was far from obvious at the time the experiment was conducted. Individual bidders are found to be responsive to their own losses (experiential leaning), as well as to losses that would have occurred had they applied their bidding strategy to the high bidder's signal value (observational learning).

Chapter 11 briefly explores cross-game learning. Experience in first-price auctions improves performance in English auctions, as the injunction to bid more conservatively than naive expectations warrant is well served in both auctions. In contrast, experience in English auctions has no transfer value for first-price auctions, as the informational crutch bidders learn to employ in English auctions (other bidders' drop-out prices) is not present in the first-price auctions.

One common criticism leveled at laboratory experiments is that the behavior of typical experimental subjects (college sophomores) is likely to be quite different from that of mature agents with field experience. Chapter 12 addresses this question directly by comparing the performance of student subjects ("naive" bidders) with that of experienced executives from the commercial construction industry. The somewhat surprising answer is that behavior is essentially the same in our experimental design, as both suffer from a severe winner's curse. Chapter 13 goes on to try and understand why this is the case through a series of interviews with industry executives and study of industry data. The chapter identifies essential differences between the field environment and the laboratory that account for the executives' success in the field and a winner's curse in the lab. These are (1) industry-specific mechanisms that enable contractors to escape the winner's curse even when they bid too low, (2) learned, industry-specific behaviors that enable experienced contractors to avoid the winner's curse in the first place, and (3) important private-value elements that underlie bidding in the field that were not present in the lab.

From the psychology literature on learning generalizability and expertise, it seems clear that it will typically *not* be the case that experienced professionals will perform any better in the lab than the typical student subject, unless the laboratory experiment is set up to *very* closely correspond to the field setting with which the executives are familiar. The problems with transfer from the field to the lab are twofold. First, transfer of learning across environments is very difficult in general unless people have been specifically trained to make such transfers. Further, the more settings differ from each other, the less likely there is to be positive learning transfer (transfer of knowledge that is helpful in the new situation; see the references cited in note 12 here. Second, expertise tends to be context-specific, so that experts outside a familiar context tend to perform no better than nonexperts. For example, in classic experiments involving chess pieces arranged as they might be in the course of an actual game, experts recalled the position of many more pieces than did novices. This greater recall was based not on greater memory capacity, but rather on the ability to organize groups of pieces into subpatterns that could then be recalled as a chunk (e.g., a castled king, a chain of pawns). As a result, when pieces were arranged on the board in random positions, experts were no longer able to recall the positions with any greater accuracy than the novices.[88] Economic experiments are usually aimed at studying basic principles of behavior. As such, they typically lack the specific contextual clues that trigger learned responses from field settings. Some flavor of these clues for the commercial construction industry are identified in chapters 12 and 13.

Notes

1. Research support from the Economics and Information, Science, and Technology divisions of NSF, the Sloan Foundation, and the Russell Sage Foundation are gratefully acknowledged. Special thanks to our colleagues, and especially our coauthors, who have taught us much. This is a revised and updated version of the second part of "Auctions: A Survey of Experimental Research," which appeared in J. H. Kagel and A. E. Roth, eds., *The Handbook of Experimental Economics* (Princeton: Princeton University Press, 1995). Unlike the earlier survey, the present one deals exclusively with common-value auctions and extensions of the winner's curse to other contexts.

2. Or, more technically, signals that are affiliated with the value of the item. See Milgrom and Weber 1982 for an excellent presentation, discussion, and analysis of the statistical properties of affiliated variables in the context of auctions.

3. However, once the seller uses a minimum bid requirement, and/or we consider entry to be determined endogenously, different auctions may induce different probabilities of an actual sale. Thus efficiency may become an issue (Levin and Smith 1994).

4. Unless, of course, one argues that Groucho Marx's statement, "I wouldn't want to belong to any club that would accept me as a member," is an earlier recognition of the winner's curse.

5. See, for example, the exchange between Cox and Isaac (1984, 1986) and Brown (1986).

6. Winning bidders paid these losses out of their own pockets, or from earnings in the other auctions.

7. Value estimates for winning bidders were excluded from this regression.

8. For example, with a signal $x < \underline{x} + \varepsilon$, the bidder knows that $x - \varepsilon$ is smaller than $\underline{x}$, and can use this additional endpoint information to compute more precisely the expected value of the item (e.g., $x_o \in (\underline{x}, x + \varepsilon)$, which is smaller than the interval $(x - \varepsilon, x + \varepsilon)$.

9. Derivation of the RNNE bid function can be found in an appendix to Levin, Kagel, and Richard 1996 and Kagel and Richard 2001, reproduced at the end of chapter 6 below. A symmetric Nash equilibrium is one in which all bidders use the same bidding strategy but actual bids are based on different private signals. An asymmetric Nash equilibrium is one in which different bidders employ different bidding strategies. Most equilibrium solutions assume symmetry, as (1) it seems a natural assumption for most settings, and (2) it is often difficult to solve for asymmetric equilibria.

10. For example, consider the following random draw of signal values (within region 2) for $x_o = \$300$, $\varepsilon = \$18$, and $n = 4$, where signals have been ranked from lowest to highest: $285.17, $293.47, $296.77, $312.31. The average of the signal values is $296.93, reasonably close to x_o, but the maximum signal is $312.31, some $12 above x_o. If we add three more signal values for $n = 7$ ($288.96, $308.84, $316.75), the average of the signal values is now $300.32, but the maximum increases to $316.75, so that the adverse selection effect conditional on winning with the high signal value is more extreme.

11. Averages here differ slightly from those reported in KL 1986 and Kagel 1995a, as the earlier calculations employed session averages as the unit of observation. Here, individual auction periods serve as the unit of observation so that sessions with more auctions are weighted more.

12. There is a whole body of psychological literature indicating the difficulty of learning generalizing across different contexts (see, for example, Gick and Holyoak 1980; Perkins and Salomon 1988; Salomon and Perkins 1989).

13. In the auction literature, the revenue-raising effect of public information is commonly treated as an implication of the "linkage principle" (Milgrom and Weber 1982). The linkage principle argues that because private signals are correlated (affiliated), the additional information creates tighter "links" due to the reduction in bidders' privacy, which in turn reduces their ability to collect rents based on their private information. Though elegant and appealing, we think that the intuition underlying the "domino" effect described above is more precise, more informative, and better describes the adjustment process than the "linkage principle."

14. KL 1986 did not restrict low signal holders to bidding x_L, failing to recognize that without this restriction there is no pure-strategy Nash equilibrium, but a much more complicated mixed-strategy equilibrium. The benchmark calculations in KL 1986 solved for the RNNE assuming that it was optimal for low signal holders to bid x_L. However, the correct benchmark yields an even higher increase in revenue from announcing x_L, so that the conclusions reached regarding public information receive even stronger support with the correct benchmark (see the addendum to chapter 3 below).

15. The role of the winner's curse in reversing this prediction motivated an experiment with affiliated private values. The release of public information about the underlying value should also raise revenue in this environment, but since each bidder knows her value prior to bidding, there can be no winner's curse to offset this effect (Kagel, Harstad, and Levin 1987; chapter 5). Public information raised average revenue in this case, but not by as much as the symmetric RNNE predicts, in part because of individual bidding errors, and in part because of a general tendency to bid above the RNNE in the private information markets.

16. See Cooper 1998 for discussion of the extensive spying that goes on between rival companies once drilling starts on a tract and the difficulties involved in keeping drilling results out of the hands of competitors.

17. A subsequent study of drainage-lease auctions by Hendricks and Porter (1988; hereafter HP), for this same time period, does not yield this anomalous result. Rather, HP (1988) report the more conventional outcome that non-neighbors (those with inferior information) bidding on drainage tracts earned lower rates of return than firms bidding on wildcat tracts. However, updating their analysis to include production data from the 1980's, and more reliable production estimates prior to 1980, HP (1992) obtain net rate-of-return estimates quite similar to MMS (1984): *both* neighbors and non-neighbors earned a higher rate of return on drainage leases than the rate of return on wildcat leases.

18. Zheng 1999 provides a more formal specification of the limited-liability argument and relates it to results from the C-block FCC spectrum auctions, which resulted in wholesale defaults on payments by winning bidders.

19. The greater the number of rivals, the lower the probability of winning as a result of more aggressive bidding, hence the less likely it is to pay to deviate from the Nash strategy even with limited liability. See also the calculations reported in Kagel and Richard (2001).

20. Statistical estimates of the effect of cash balances on bids has been relatively unsophisticated in these discussions. The problem is that cash balances are endogenously determined, so that ordinary least squares estimates of cash-balance effects, such as those reported in HL, are biased. Fixed-effect estimates, like those reported in KL 1991, go a long way toward correcting these biases, but stop far short of what could be done with a little imagination, namely, instrumental variables estimation and experimenter-induced exogenous variation in the cash balances. For work along these lines, see Ham, Kagel, and Lehrer 2000.

21. To keep costs down, the sellers' auctions were conducted in francs as opposed to dollars. The conversion rate from francs to dollars reduced the cost of the experiment, but reduced the marginal incentives for equilibrium behavior as well. There is no free lunch in designing experiments; gains on one dimension are usually offset by losses in other dimensions.

22. To control for costs, three out of the thirty auctions were randomly selected for payment at the end of the experiment, rather than paying in all auctions, as in their other treatments.

23. CDS also explore the effects of endogenous entry, in conjunction with a positive-income "safe haven" treatment (a positive return for not entering the auction) on eliminating the winner's curse. This is discussed briefly in section 7.2 below.

24. Symmetric risk-averse bidders all have the same risk preferences (the same von Neumann Morgenstern utility function). Asymmetric risk-averse bidders have different risk preferences.

25. Levin and Harstad (1986) showed that this function is the unique symmetric Nash

equilibrium. Recently, Pesendorfer and Swinkles (1997) provide a more rigorous and general proof of this result.

26. This can be demonstrated through a straightforward application of the proofs in Pratt 1964 (pp. 128–29) to the symmetric bid function in equation (3).

27. The intuition with respect to this strong result about the number of bidders is that as long as bidders rely on their private signal values to determine their bids (so that bid profiles are strictly increasing in x), then as the number of bidders increases, the expected value of the item conditional on winning decreases. And since this is a second-price auction, many of the strategic considerations that complicate the first-price auction are not present.

28. Results for bidders with no prior experience in second-price common-value auctions are as disastrous as those reported in Table 1 for inexperienced bidders in first-price auctions. These data are tabulated at the end of chapter 2 below.

29. In a second-price auction, unlike a first-price auction, announcing x_L induces the low signal holder to bid x_L in equilibrium.

30. For bidders with signal values above ($[\bar{x} + \underline{x}]/2$), bidding the naive expected value in place of the Nash equilibrium can produce a loser's curse: had the loser employed the Nash bid function, she could have increased both the probability of winning and her expected profits (see Holt and Sherman 1994; section 4.1 below).

31. This prediction depends heavily on there being only two bidders and one item for sale. With three bidders and two items for sale, and with only one of the bidders having a private information advantage, revenue reductions are much less pronounced (Bulow and Klemperer 1997).

32. Except for practice rounds, CH only report back the winning bid and profits earned by the winning bidder. The study of group versus individual bids can also be insightful for issues associated with joint bidding, where individual bidders form a bidding consortium and share information.

33. In all of these experiments, bidders were allowed to continue to bid even when they had negative cash balances. Bids of such groups/individuals are eliminated from the regression analysis when they have negative cash balances so as not to directly contaminate the analysis. But there may still be indirect contamination from the effects of these bids on rivals' bids. Part of the problem here is that having reserve bidders to replace bankruptcies and hold the number of bidders constant is substantially more difficult with group bidding than with individual bids.

34. Note also that with fully cursed agents, the Eyster and Rabin model does not always yield bid patterns that experimenters have suggested correspond to naive bidding (e.g., in the takeover game, section 4.1 below).

35. Prices started at x as any other price rule would have involved revealing information about x_o. Initially, the price increased every second with increments of $1.00. Once the first bidder dropped out, there was a brief pause, after which prices increased every three seconds with smaller price increments as fewer bidders remained.

36. As in the second-price auction, but not the first-price, it is an equilibrium for the bidders with x_L to bid (drop out at) x_L. The intuition is roughly as follows: Given symmetry, the low signal holder knows that those remaining in the auction have higher signal values. But the low signal holder can't profit from this additional information, since it is only revealed once the price is greater than these remaining signal values; i.e., the price is already greater than the expected value of the item to the low signal holder.

37. Common-value auctions involve pure surplus transfers, so that revenue differences are calculated as $[\pi_E - \pi_F]$, where π_E and π_F correspond to profits in English and

first-price auctions, respectively. In this way we have effectively normalized for sampling variability in X_o by subtracting it from the price.

38. t-tests are conducted for predicted revenue increases to measure the reliability of the prediction for the LKR sample data. One-tailed t-tests are used here, since the symmetric RNNE makes unambiguous predictions regarding revenue increases. Two-tailed t-tests are used for determining statistical significance of actual revenue changes, since in practice there are forces promoting lower revenues in English auctions, and we often observe this outcome.

39. To further investigate this question, we have conducted some additional sessions with inexperienced bidders in which x_L was publicly announced prior to bidding in the English auction. In auctions with six bidders and $\varepsilon = \$12$, average profits in the standard English auction (where x_L was not announced) were $-\$1.55$, with average profits in auctions with x_L announced of $\$1.56$ ($t = 1.46$, $d.f. = 30$, $p < .10$, one-tailed test; unpublished data).

40. This insight has public-policy implications (see section 7.3 below).

41. Although one can readily demonstrate that increased revenue is *not* a general characteristic of AIS auctions in which Os have some proprietary information, it is a natural element in our design and can be found in other AIS structures as well (Campbell and Levin 2000). See Kagel and Levin 1999 or Laskowski and Slonim 1999 for derivation of these comparative static predictions.

42. "Presentation format" effects of this sort have been found in a number of game-theoretic contexts (see, for example, Andreoni 1995 and Cooper, Garvin, and Kagel 1997).

43. In our design, the increase in revenue going from SIS to AIS varies with n, with revenue differences increasing starting from low n, reaching a maximum revenue differential for intermediate levels of n, and decreasing thereafter.

44. These results motivated Campbell and Levin (2000) to further investigate the role of insider information in first-price auctions compared to homogeneous information environments. This paper connects the revenue-raising effects of an insider to more general propositions regarding the revenue-raising effects of increased bidder information found in Milgrom and Weber 1982.

45. Subjects were MBA students drawn from managerial economics classes. In the case of monetary incentives, subjects were responsible for losses out of their own pockets. The decision to play in this case was voluntary, with about 85% of those eligible choosing to bid.

46. See Carroll, Bazerman, and Maury 1988 for a closely related study that uses a "talk aloud" protocol in an effort to better understand the cognitive processes underlying buyers' decisions.

47. SB (1985) had designs that addressed this issue as well, but used one-shot trials with no allowance for learning.

48. Differences in the expected value of the naive bid and the rational bid are very small—less than two cents. If anything, this might be expected to bias the results in favor of the thrill of winning, as the expected cost of deviating from the rational bid is quite small.

49. This analysis concentrates on the three pure common-value auction series. The other three auction series combine common- and private-value elements, which complicates any evaluation of the winner's curse.

50. The average value of blind-bid items in period 1 was 41.8¢, compared to an average value of 91.7¢ on items that were not blind bid.

51. Average losses on blind-bid items were 10¢ per item in the first ten periods, compared to 4¢ per item from period 11 on. Excluding the positive profits made on one very highly valued item that was blind bid out of seller's ignorance, or seller's error, mean profits averaged -6.6¢ with a standard error of the mean of 2.72, for period 11 on, so that buyers' profits on these blind-bid items were significantly below zero.

52. Note that if sellers could commit to blind bid all items all of the time, we would be back in the bilateral bargaining game. Thus, part of the explanation for the unraveling has to do with sellers' inability to commit to such a strategy, going for the short-run profits on higher-valued items that are not blind bid. This is somewhat reminiscent of the durably good monopoly outcome under the Coath (1972) conjecture.

53. Even low-quality products are of some value to some buyers. Everyone does not drive a Mercedes Benz or a Lexus.

54. This is a good experiment to incorporate into the classroom when covering asymmetric information and lemon's markets (see Bergstrom and Miller 2000).

55. Information about product quality was delivered privately to buyers after their purchases. Public delivery of product quality is likely to speed up the adjustment process.

56. These differences may come about because each juror has a different area of expertise that allows her to evaluate some of the evidence more effectively.

57. All of these predictions are developed within the framework of a symmetric "informative" equilibrium. As noted below, there are many asymmetric equilibria for these games, and these equilibria generally yield different qualitative predictions at both the individual and the aggregate (jury decision) level.

58. Eyster and Rabin (2000) show that even with partially sophisticated voters (those that are somewhat sensitive to the swing voter's curse), the percentage voting to convict, given an innocent signal, is increasing with the size of the jury under super-major rules.

59. This could represent a hysteresis effect, as subjects participated in four different treatment conditions in each experimental session, treatments involving unanimity rules as well as majority voting rules. There is no discussion of this result, or this possibility, in GMP.

60. This is small comfort for those hoping to apply the theory to field data, since people participate in juries at most only a few times in their life.

61. The authors show that a logit equilibrium, which generalizes the concept of Nash equilibrium to account for agents' errors (and agents accounting for other agents' errors), predicts that the probability of conviction goes to zero in large juries requiring unanimity. In contrast, the probability of jury error under majority voting goes to zero as the jury size increases.

62. This absence of mixed-strategy play at the individual subject level is not uncommon in experiments.

63. Ladha, Miller, and Oppenheimer (1996) also study strategic voting experimentally, focusing on information aggregation under majority voting rules in groups of three. They employ an experimental design in which it is not a Nash equilibrium for all voters to vote informatively. Rather, there are multiple Nash equilibria. In one of these, voters implicitly coordinate their actions, with two out of the three voting sincerely, and the third voting strategically, ignoring her private information (when it is less informative) because of the pivotal nature of her vote. This pivotal voting improves information aggregation so that group decisions are correct more often than if all voted sincerely. There are, however, other Nash equilibria in which a majority vote uninformatively, out of

concern for the strategic impact of their votes. This would, of course, reduce the accuracy of group votes compared to sincere voting (and might even reduce accuracy compared to basing decisions on an arbitrary individual's vote). In their experiment, five of eight groups exhibited the non-Nash profile in which each voter persisted in informative voting. The three remaining groups succeeded in coordinating on a single pivotal voter, thereby improving group accuracy over sincere voting. Note, however, that two of these three groups employed doctoral students.

64. No explanation is provided for this higher frequency of false revelation of innocent signals. This, too, could be the result of a hysteresis effect from the same subjects playing under both unanimity requirements and other voting requirements in the same experimental session.

65. A Z statistic comparing the first quartile with the second quartile shows a statistically significant reduction in the proportion of auctions with losses from 64% to 41% ($Z = 2.24$, $p < .05$).

66. The qualifier in this sentence rests on the fact that in the two buyer sessions reported in Table 3, there is a noticeable and unexplained increase in average predicted profits from playing the RNNE in the second quartile, which typically results in higher actual profits.

67. A *chi*-square test indicates that this difference is significant at better than the .01 level.

68. The relevance of this "market learning" process outside the laboratory is problematic. Entry conditions were closed in the experiment—subjects were recruited back exclusively from those who had participated in earlier auction sessions. In field settings, open entry conditions permit new firms to join the bidding. It is not clear if these new players must undergo their own self-selection process, similar to a group of inexperienced bidders, or if the presence of seasoned bidders would speed up the learning process. And it is not clear what the market impact would be in either case, since these new bidders would, presumably, make up a minority of active bidders.

69. LP conducted auctions with large monetary losses (the high-price auctions) and with small losses (the offer auctions, which use an artificial currency; see Table 3). Their results are not sufficiently clear-cut to reach a firm conclusion on this point. The threat of bankruptcy might also carry some embarrassment, which would heighten subjects' sensitivity to losses.

70. An exception to this is Foreman and Murnighan (1996; hereafter FM), who compared different types of feedback. They report a general inability to avoid the winner's curse even with repeated experience and considerable information about others' outcomes both in the bilateral bargaining game and in a common-value auction design similar to KL. However, FM did not employ financial incentives, which might be expected to accelerate learning. On the other hand, FM's subjects participated in fewer auctions (16) than in GK or LP. So the questions posed here are still unanswered.

71. For auctions with $n = 7$, all subjects had participated in at least four prior sealed-bid auction sessions (with at least two prior sessions with seven bidders). For $n = 4$, all subjects had participated in two prior sealed-bid auction sessions with $n = 7$. Experience with the same or more bidders is important, since KL (1986) suggest that prior experience with small groups does not prepare bidders for auctions with larger groups. Also, experience does not generalize easily from English auctions to sealed-bid auctions, although the reverse experience does generalize rather well (Kagel 1995b).

72. Subjects participated in two experimental sessions of forty auctions each, taking

place one week apart. Each experimental session had two markets with six bidders, with subjects randomly rematched into different groups of size 6 in each auction. There were standbys to replace bankruptcies as well.

73. Yet another approach is to conduct semi-controlled experiments auctioning real goods over the Internet or in other semi-controlled settings (see Lucking-Reiley 1998).

74. See Rothkopf and Englebrecht-Wiggans (1993) for an alternative explanation of this anomaly, as well as work by Athey and Levin (1998) and Baldwin, Marshall, and Richard (1997) dealing with U.S. timber-lease sales.

75. MRP is the additional contribution to the teams' revenue attributed to these star players.

76. Unlike KL's auctions, but like BS and BBC, this experiment does not employ abstract labeling, but is conducted within the context of baseball's free-agency market.

77. In the experiment, one of the executives jokingly inquired, "Who is the architect associated with this job?"

78. It is our understanding that different oil companies specialize in different geological formations so that they can better apply accumulated past knowledge to interpret seismic records.

79. For publicly owned projects, there are laws explicitly recognizing the possibility of "arithmetic" errors in bids, permitting the contractor to withdraw a bid without a penalty. What constitutes an arithmetic error is often loosely interpreted. In this case, the low bidder used a plumbing subcontractor's bid that the subcontractor withdrew. However, the subcontractor was unable to reach all general contractors, the original low bidder included, in time to adjust their bids. What is clear in the construction industry is that no one wants a builder, or a subcontractor, working for them who is terribly unhappy with their bid, as this affects the speed, quality, and "headaches" associated with the construction. Owners who require that such bids be honored are likely to suffer from a winner's curse of their own. In OCS bidding, where the winner's curse expresses itself in terms of an inflated bonus bid, there are no corresponding considerations, since the bonus bid is a sunk cost.

80. The ability to withdraw bids without a penalty opens up additional strategic possibilities. However, in field settings, owners and contractors are involved in a game with two-sided reputations, so that too-frequent withdrawal of bids may result in being left off future invited bid lists.

81. There are fewer bidders on average for OCS leases (3.5 versus 7.5 in the construction data). Limiting analysis of the construction data to jobs with four bidders or less results in auctions with an average of 3.4 bidders and average money left on the table of 6.7% (with a standard error of 8.8%) (Dyer and Kagel 1996).

82. For example, a friend of ours in Houston was a geologist for a major oil company. He told us that there was such a broad range of legitimate value estimates for most tracts that when the bidding department started reducing bids relative to value estimates to the point that they were winning very few auctions, the geologists simply raised their estimates (geologists love to drill, and failure to win tracts means they can't drill).

83. Also see Laskowski and Slonim 1999 for analysis of revenue-raising effects of insider information in a limiting case of Kagel and Levin's experimental design, but one in which the insider does not possess perfect information regarding the true value of the item.

84. In private-value auctions, bidders know their own value for the item but are uncertain about their rivals' values, knowing only the distribution from which these values were drawn. Second-price sealed-bid auctions and English clock auctions are theo-

retically isomorphic in this setting. The existence of a Nash equilibrium supported by dominant bidding strategies in these auctions is a much stronger solution concept than the Nash equilibrium underlying the benchmark calculations in the common-value auctions. (See chapter 5 for details.)

85. This does not seem to us to be a cure to the winner's curse or the judgmental errors underlying it. It is like declaring the elimination of a disease once an epidemic has killed everyone.

86. See also Hausch 1988.

87. Not all auction sales have been as successful as these two (see McMillan 1994 for characterization of some early disasters in New Zealand and Australia). Some more recent sales have not worked out so well either, because of limited competition and/or alleged collusion among bidders (Klemperer 2000).

88. See Glaser 1990 and Zeitz and Glaser 1994 for summaries of the many differences between experts and novices identified to date.

References

Akerlof, G. 1970. "The Market for Lemons: Qualitative Uncertainty and the Market Mechanism." *Quarterly Journal of Economics* 89:488–500.

Andreoni, J. 1995. "Warm-Glow versus Cold-Prickle: The Effects of Positive and Negative Framing on Cooperation in Experiments" *Quarterly Journal of Economics* 110:1–22.

Armantier, O. 1998. "Learning Models and the Influence of Environment on Behavior." Mimeograph, University of Pittsburgh, Pittsburgh, Pa.

Ashenfelter, O., and D. Genesore. 1992. "Testing for Price Anomalies in Real Estate Auctions." *American Economic Review: Papers and Proceedings* 82:501–5.

Athey, S., and J. Levin. 1998. "Information and Competition in U.S. Forest Service Timber Auctions." Mimeograph, Massachusetts Institute of Technology, Cambridge, Mass.

Ausubel, L. M. 1997. "An Efficient Ascending-Bid Auction for Multiple Objects." Mimeograph, University of Maryland, College Park.

Ausubel, L. M., P. Cramton, P. R. McAfee, and J. McMillan. 1997. "Synergies in Wireless Telephony: Evidence from the Broadband PCS Auctions," *Journal of Economics and Management Strategy* 6:497–528.

Avery, C., and J. H. Kagel (AK). 1997. "Second-Price Auctions with Asymmetric Payoffs: An Experimental Investigation." *Journal of Economics and Management Strategy* 6:573–604.

Baldwin, L., R. Marshall, and J. F. Richard. 1997. "Bidder Collusion in U.S. Forest Service Timber Sales." *Journal of Political Economy* 105:657–99.

Ball, S. B. 1991. "Experimental Evidence on the Winner's Curse in Negotiations." Ph.D. dissertation, Northwestern University, Evanston, Ill.

Ball, S. B., M. H. Bazerman, and J. S. Carroll (BBC). 1991. "An Evaluation of Learning in the Bilateral Winner's Curse." *Organizational Behavior and Human Decision Processes* 48:1–22.

Bazerman, M. H., and W. F. Samuelson (BS). 1983. "I Won the Auction But Don't Want the Prize." *Journal of Conflict Resolution* 27:618–34.

Bergstrom, T. C., and J. H. Miller. 2000. *Experiments with Economic Principles*. 2d ed. New York: McGraw-Hill.

Bikhchandani, S. 1988. "Reputations in Repeated Second-Price Auctions." *Journal of Economic Theory* 46:97–119.

Bikhchandani, S., and J. G. Riley. 1991. "Equilibria in Open Common Value Auctions." *Journal of Economic Theory* 53:101–30.

Blecherman, B., and C. F. Camerer (BC). 1998. "Is There a Winner's Curse in the Market for Baseball Players?" Mimeograph, Brooklyn Polytechnic University, Brooklyn, N.Y.

Brown, K. C. 1986. "In Search of the Winner's Curse: Comment." *Economic Inquiry* 24:513–16.

Bulow, J., and P. Klemperer. 1997. "The Winner's Curse and the Failure of the Law of Demand." Mimeograph, Stanford University, Palo Alto, Calif.

Cadsby, C., M. Frank, and V. Maksimovic. 1990. "Pooling, Separating, and Semiseparating Equilibria in Financial Markets: Some Experimental Evidence." *Review of Financial Studies* 3: 341–67.

Campbell, C., and D. Levin. 2000. "Can the Seller Benefit from an Insider in Common Value Auctions?" *Journal of Economic Theory* 91:106–20.

Capen, E. C., R. V. Clapp, and W. M. Campbell. 1971. "Competitive Bidding in High-Risk Situations." *Journal of Petroleum Technology* 23:641–53.

Carroll, J. S., M. H. Bazerman, and R. Maury. 1988. "Negotiator Cognitions: A Descriptive Approach to Negotiators' Understanding of Their Opponents." *Organizational Behavior and Human Decision Processes* 41:352–70.

Cassady, R. 1967. *Auctions and Auctioneering*. Berkeley and Los Angeles: University of California Press.

Cassing, J., and R. W. Douglas. 1980. "Implications of the Auction Mechanism in Baseball's Free Agent Draft." *Southern Economic Journal* 47:110–21.

Cifuentes, L. A., and S. Sunder. 1991. "Some Further Evidence of the Winner's Curse." Mimeographed, Carnegie Mellon University, Pittsburgh, Pa.

Coath, R. H. 1972. "Durability and Monopoly." *Journal of Law and Economics* 15: 143–49.

Cooper, C. 1998. "Oil Firms Still Rely on Corporate Spies to Be Well-Informed." *Wall Street Journal*, Dec. 7:1, 23.

Cooper, D., S. Garvin, and J. Kagel. 1997. "Adaptive Learning versus Equilibrium Refinements in an Entry Limit Pricing Game." *RAND Journal of Economics* 28:662–83.

Coughlan, P. 1997. "In Defense of Unanimous Jury Verdicts: Communication, Mistrials, and Sincerity." Mimeograph, California Institute of Technology, Pasadena.

Cox, J. C., S. H. Dinkin, and V. L. Smith (CDS). 1998. "Endogenous Entry and Exit in Common Value Auctions." Mimeograph, University of Arizona, Tucson.

Cox, J. C., and S. C. Hayne (CH). 1998. "Group versus Individual Decision-Making in Strategic Market Games." Mimeograph, University of Arizona, Tucson.

Cox, J. C., and R. M. Isaac. 1984. "In Search of the Winner's Curse." *Economic Inquiry* 22:579–92.

———. 1986. "In Search of the Winner's Curse: Reply." *Economic Inquiry* 24:517–20.

Cramton, P. 1995. "Money Out of Thin Air: The Nationwide Narrowband PCS Auctions." *Journal of Economics and Management Strategy* 4:267–343.

———. 1997. "The FCC Spectrum Auctions: An Early Assessment." *Journal of Economics and Management Strategy* 6:425–30.

Dessauer, J. P. 1981. *Book Publishing*. New York: Bowker.

Dyer, D., and J. H. Kagel. 1996. "Bidding in Common Value Auctions: How the Commercial Construction Industry Corrects for the Winner's Curse." *Management Science* 42:1463–75.

Dyer, D., J. H. Kagel, and D. Levin (DKL). 1989. "A Comparison of Naive and Experienced Bidders in Common Value Offer Auctions: A Laboratory Analysis." *Economic Journal* 99:108–15.

Engelbrecht-Wiggans, R., P. R. Milgrom, and R. J. Weber. 1983. "Competitive Bidding and Proprietary Information" *Journal of Mathematical Economics* 11:161–69.

Eyster, E., and M. Rabin. 2000. "Cursed Equilibrium." Mimeograph, University of California at Berkeley, Berkeley.

Feddersen, T., and W. Pesendorfer (FP). 1996. "The Swing Voter's Curse." *American Economic Review* 86: 408–24.

———. 1998. "Convicting the Innocent: The Inferiority of Unanimous Jury Verdicts under Strategic Voting." *American Political Science Review* 92:23–36.

———. 1999. "Elections, Information Aggregation, and Strategic Voting." *Proceedings of the National Academy of Science* 96:10572–74.

Foreman, P., and J. K. Murnighan (FM). 1996. "Learning to Avoid the Winner's Curse." *Organizational Behavior and Human Decision Processes* 67:170–80.

Forsythe, R., and R. M. Isaac, and T. R. Palfrey (FIP). 1989. "Theories and Tests of 'Blind Bidding' in Sealed-Bid Auctions." *RAND Journal of Economics* 20:214–38.

Forsythe, R., R. Lundholm, and T. Reitz. 1999. "Cheap Talk, Fraud, and Adverse Selection in Financial Markets: Some Experimental Evidence." *The Review of Financial Studies* 12: 481–518.

Garvin, S., and J. H. Kagel (GK). 1994. "Learning in Common Value Auctions: Some Initial Observations." *Journal of Economic Behavior and Organization* 25:351–72.

Gick, M. L., and K. J. Holyoak. 1980. "Analogical Problem Solving." *Cognitive Psychology* 12:306–55.

Gilley, O.W., G. V. Karels, and R. P. Leone. 1986. "Uncertainty, Experience and the 'Winner's Curse' in OCS Lease Bidding" *Management Science* 32:673–82.

Glaser, R. 1990. "Expertise." In *The Blackwell Dictionary of Cognitive Psychology*, ed. M. W. Eysenck, A. Ellis, and E. B. Hunt. Oxford: Blackwell.

Goeree, J. K., and T. Offerman. 2000. "Efficiency in Auctions with Private and Common Values: An Experimental Study." Mimeograph, University of Virginia, Charlottesville.

Guarnaschelli, S., R. D. McKelvey, and T. R. Palfrey (GMP). 2000. "An Experimental Study of Jury Rules." Mimoegraph, California Institute of Technology, Pasadena.

Guenther, W. C. 1964. *Analysis of Variance.* Englewood Cliffs, N.J.: Prentice-Hall.

Ham, J., J. H. Kagel, and S. Lehrer. 2000. "Randomization, Endogeniety, and Laboratory Experiments." Mimeograph, Ohio State University, Columbus.

Hansen, R. G. 1985. "Empirical Testing of Auction Theory," *American Economic Review* 75:156–59.

———. 1986. "Sealed-Bid versus Open Auctions: The Evidence." *Economic Inquiry* 24:125–42.

Hansen, R. G., and J. R. Lott, Jr. (HL). 1991. "The Winner's Curse and Public Information in Common Value Auctions: Comment." *American Economic Review* 81:347–61.

Harstad, R. M. 1990. "Alternative Common Value Auction Procedures: Revenue Comparisons with Free Entry." *Journal of Political Economy* 98:421–29.

———. 1991. "Asymmetric Bidding in Second-Price, Common-Value Auctions." *Economic Letters* 35:249–52.

Hausch, D. B. 1988. "A Common Value Auction Model with Endogenous Entry and Information Acquisition." Mimeograph, University of Wisconsin, Madison.

Hendricks, K., and R. H. Porter (HP). 1988. "An Empirical Study of an Auction with Asymmetric Information." *American Economic Review* 76:865–83.

————. 1992. "Bidding Behavior in OCS Drainage Auctions: Theory and Evidence." Paper presented at the 1992 European Economics Association meetings.

Hendricks, K., R. H. Porter, and B. Boudreau (HPB). 1987. "Information, Returns, and Bidding Behavior in OCS Auctions: 1954–1969." *The Journal of Industrial Economics* 35:517–42.

Hendricks, K., R. H. Porter, and C. A. Wilson. 1994. "Auctions for Oil and Gas Leases with an Informed Bidder and a Random Reservation Price." *Econometrica* 62:1415–44.

Holt, C. A. Jr., and R. Sherman. 1994. "The Loser's Curse and Bidder's Bias." *American Economic Review* 84:642–52.

Kagel, J. H. 1995a. "Auctions: A Survey of Experimental Research." In *The Handbook of Experimental Economics*, ed. J. H. Kagel and A. E. Roth. Princeton: Princeton University Press.

————. 1995b. "Cross-Game Learning: Experimental Evidence from First-Price and English Common Value Auctions." *Economic Letters* 49:163–70.

Kagel, J. H., R. M. Harstad, and D. Levin. 1987. "Information Impact and Allocation Rules in Auctions with Affiliated Private Values: A Laboratory Study." *Econometrica* 55:1275–1304.

Kagel, J. H., and D. Levin (KL). 1986. "The Winner's Curse and Public Information in Common Value Auctions." *American Economic Review* 76:894–920.

————. 1991. "The Winner's Curse and Public Information in Common Value Auctions: Reply." *American Economic Review* 81:362–69.

————. 1999. "Common Value Auctions with Insider Information." *Econometrica.* 67:1219–38.

————. In press. "Behavior in Multi-Unit Demand Auctions: Experiments with Uniform Price and Dynamic Vickrey Auctions." *Econometrica.*

Kagel, J. H., D. Levin, R. Battalio, and D. J. Meyer. 1989. "First-Price Common Value Auctions: Bidder Behavior and the Winner's Curse." *Economic Inquiry* 27:241–58.

Kagel, J. H., D. Levin, and R. M. Harstad (KLH). 1995. "Comparative Static Effects of Number of Bidders and Public Information on Behavior in Second-Price Common Value Auctions." *International Journal of Game Theory* 24:293–319.

Kagel, J. H., and J. F. Richard (KR). 2001. "Super-Experienced Bidders in First-Price Common Value Auctions: Rules of Thumb, Nash Equilibrium Bidding and the Winner's Curse." *Review of Economics and Statistics* 83:408–19.

King, R. R., and D. E. Wallin. 1991. "Voluntary Disclosures When Seller's Level of Information Is Unknown." *Journal of Accounting Research* 29:96–108.

Klemperer, P. 2000. "What Really Matters in Auction Design." Mimeograph, Nuffield College, Oxford University, Oxford.

Ladha, K., G. Miller, and J. Oppenheimer. 1996. "Information Aggregation by Majority Rule: Theory and Experiments." Mimeograph, Olin School of Business, Washington University, St. Louis, Mo.

Laskowski, M. C., and R. L. Slonim. 1999. "An Asymmetric Solution for Sealed Bid Common-Value Auctions with Bidders Having Asymmetric Information." *Games and Economic Behavior* 28:238–55.

Levin, D., and R. Harstad. 1986. "Symmetric Bidding in Second Price Common Value Auctions." *Economics Letters* 20:315–19.

Levin, D., J. H. Kagel, and J. F. Richard (LKR). 1996. "Revenue Effects and Information Processing in English Common Value Auctions." *American Economic Review* 86:442–60.

Levin, D., and J. L. Smith. 1994. "Equilibrium in Auctions with Entry." *American Economic Review* 84:585–99.

Li, T. 2000. "Econometrics of First-Price Auctions with Entry and Binding Reservation Prices." Mimeograph, Indiana University, Bloomington.

Lind, B., and C. R. Plott (LP). 1991. "The Winner's Curse: Experiments with Buyers and with Sellers." *American Economic Review* 81:335–46.

Lorenz, J., and E. L. Dougherty. 1983. "Bonus Bidding and Bottom Lines: Federal Offshore Oil and Gas." SPE 12024, 58th Annual Fall Technical Conference.

Lucking-Reiley, D. 1998. "Tests of Revenue Equivalence in Internet Auctions." Mimeograph, Vanderbilt University, Nashville, Tenn.

Lynch, M., R. M. Miller, C. R. Plott, and R. Porter. 1986. "Product Quality, Consumer Information and 'Lemons' in Experimental Markets." In *Empirical Approaches to Consumer Protection Economics*, ed. P. M. Ippolito and D. T. Scheffman, pp. 251–306. Washington, D.C.: FTC Bureau of Economics.

———. 1991. "Product Quality, Informational Efficiency, and Regulations in Experimental Markets." In *Research in Experimental Economics*, ed. R. Mark Isaac, p. 4. Greenwich, Conn.: JAI Press.

Matthews, S. A. 1977. "Information Acquisition in Competitive Bidding Processes." Mimeograph, California Institute of Technology, Pasadena.

McAfee, R. P., and J. McMillan. 1987. "Auctions and Bidding." *Journal of Economic Literature* 25:699–738.

———. 1996. "Analyzing the Airwaves Auction." *Journal of Economic Perspectives* 10:159–76.

McMillan, J. 1994. "Selling Spectrum Rights." *Journal of Economic Perspectives* 8:145–62.

Mead, W. J. 1967. "Natural Resource Disposal Policy: Oral Auction versus Sealed Bids." *Natural Resources Journal* 7:195–224.

Mead, W. J., A. Moseidjord, and P. E. Sorensen (MMS). 1983. "The Rate of Return Earned by Leases under Cash Bonus Bidding in OCS Oil and Gas Leases." *Energy Journal* 4:37–52.

———. 1984. "Competitive Bidding under Asymmetrical Information: Behavior and Performance in Gulf of Mexico Drainage Lease Sales, 1954–1969." *Review of Economics and Statistics* 66:505–8.

Milgrom, P., and J. Roberts. 1986. "Relying on the Information of Interested Parties." *RAND Journal of Economics* 17:18–22.

Milgrom, P., and R. J. Weber. 1982. "A Theory of Auctions and Competitive Bidding." *Econometrica* 50:1485–527.

Miller, R. M., and C. R. Plott. 1985. "Product Quality Signaling in Experimental Markets." *Econometrica* 53:837–72.

Perkins, D. N. and G. Salomon. 1988. "Teaching for Transfer." *Educational Leadership* 46:22–32.

Perry, M., and P. Reny. 2000. "An Efficient Ascending Multi-Unit Auction." Mimeograph, University of Chicago, Chicago, Ill.

Pesendorfer, W., and J. M. Swinkles. 1997. "The Loser's Curse and Information Aggregation in Common Value Auctions." *Econometrica* 65:1247–82.

Pindyk, R. S., and D. L. Rubinfeld. 2001. *Microeconomics*. 5th ed. Upper Saddle River, N.J.: Prentice-Hall.

Plott, C. 1997. "Laboratory Experimental Test Beds: Application to the PCS Auction." *Journal of Economics and Management Strategy* 6:605–38.

Pratt, J. W. 1964. "Risk Aversion in the Small and in the Large." *Econometrica* 32:122–36.

Roll, R. 1986. "The Hubris Hypothesis of Corporate Takeovers." *Journal of Business* 59:197–216.

Rothkopf, M. H., and R. Engelbrecht-Wiggans. 1993. "Misapplications Reviews: Getting the Model Right—The Case of Competitive Bidding." *Interfaces* 23:99–106.

Salomon, G., and D. N. Perkins. 1989. "Rocky Roads to Transfer: Rethinking Mechanisms of a Neglected Phenomenon." *Education Psychologist* 24:113–42.

Samuelson, W. F., and M. H. Bazerman (SB). 1985. "The Winner's Curse in Bilateral Negotiations." In *Research in Experimental Economics*, vol. 3, ed. V. L. Smith. Greenwich, Conn.: JAI Press.

Smith, J. L., and D. Levin. In press. "Entry Coordination, Market Thickness, and Social Welfare: An Experimental Investigation." *International Journal of Game Theory*.

Weverbergh, M. 1979. "Competitive Bidding with Asymmetric Information Reanalyzed." *Management Science* 25:291–94.

Wilson, R. 1967. "Competitive Bidding with Asymmetric Information." *Management Science* 13:816–20.

———. 1977. "A Bidding Model of Perfect Competition." *Review of Economic Studies* 44:511–18.

———. 1992. "Strategic Analysis of Auctions." In *Handbook of Game Theory with Economic Applications*, vol. 1, ed. R. J. Aumann and S. Hart. Amsterdam: Elsevier Science Publishers.

Zeitz, C., and R. Glaser. 1994. "Expert Level of Understanding." In *The International Encyclopedia of Education*, 2nd ed., ed. T. Husen and T. N. Postelthwaite. Oxford: Pergamon Press.

Zheng, C. Z. 1999. "High Bids and Broke Winners." Mimeograph, University of Minnesota, Minneapolis.

2

First-Price Common-Value Auctions: Bidder Behavior and the "Winner's Curse"

*John H. Kagel, Dan Levin,
Raymond C. Battalio, and
Donald J. Meyer*

1. Introduction

Numerous occurrences of the winner's curse have been reported in bidding for items of uncertain value, resulting in below normal or even negative average profits for bidders. The winner's curse results from bidders' failure to account for the adverse selection problem inherent in winning auctions for items of uncertain value. Capen, Clapp, and Campbell [1971] claim that the winner's curse resulted in low profits for oil companies in the 1960s in bidding on off-shore oil and gas leases. Regarding corporate takeovers and mergers, Roll [1986] proposes a hubris hypothesis: acquiring firms generally fall prey to the winner's curse, paying too much on average for their targets. He claims that from the samples he has observed, the hubris hypothesis explains merger data as well as tax factors, synergy, or inefficient target management. Cassing and Douglas [1980] find that many baseball players in the free agency market have been over-paid on account of the winner's curse, and Dessauer [1981] reports a similar finding of overbidding in auctions for book publishing rights. Based on these occurrences, it appears that many agents are not fully cognizant of the intricacies involved with bidding on alternatives that have uncertain worth.

The winner's curse results from the fact that although bidders may hold unbiased estimates of the auctioned item's value, this estimate can be overly optimistic given that participants' bids are influenced by their estimates of value. In other words, the winner's curse results from an adverse selection problem that bidders fail to account for fully in submitting their bids. The existence of a winner's curse implies a breakdown of rational expectations on the bidder's part (as discussed by Milgrom [1981]) and identifies a market that is out of equilibrium.

A winner's curse need not result from bidding on items with uncertain value provided proper adjustments are made. One adjustment to the adverse selection problem is to deflate the expected value of the item (and hence the bid) *before* any action is taken. For example, Cox and Isaac [1984] show that agents who maximize expected utility will revise their expectations downward and submit bids that are strictly less than the expected value conditional on the event of winning. When agents behave in this fashion, a winner's curse does not result in the sense of bidders paying more on *average* than the items are worth.

This paper focuses on scaled-bid auctions for objects of uncertain value, a market institution for which theoretical predictions and empirical evidence concerning a winner's curse are mixed. Current theoretical development excludes the possibility of bidders paying more on average than the items are worth; yet some empirical evidence in the sale of oil tracts, as seen in Capen, Clapp, and Campbell [1971], Lohrenz and Dougherty [1983], and Mead, Moseidjord, and Sorenson [1983], suggests that the winner's curse may be present. A series of experiments is designed and conducted in order to answer the following empirical research questions: Does the winner's curse exist in this auction framework; and if it does, what is its duration, its relation to agent experience in the market, and its breadth of impact across agents?

The paper is organized in the following manner. The structure of the auctions is given in section 2. Section 3 contains a definition of the winner's curse and defines the risk-neutral Nash equilibrium for the auction market. Experimental results are presented in section 4 and a summary and conclusions are given in section 5.

2. Structure of the Auctions

Each experiment consisted of a series of auction periods in which a single unit of a commodity was awarded to the high bidder using a first-price sealed-bid procedure. The high bidder earned a profit equal to the value of the item less his bid; all other bidders earned zero profits. The value of the item, V, was not known at the time bids were placed.

V was drawn randomly from a uniform distribution on (V_L, V_H). Each bidder received a private information signal, s_i, randomly drawn from a uniform distribution on $(V - \varepsilon, V + \varepsilon)$. V_L, V_H, ε, and the underlying distributions were common knowledge. Given s_i, ε, V_L, and V_H, the maximum and minimum possible values for the item were min $(s_i + \varepsilon, V_H)$ and max $(s_i - e, V_L)$ respectively. In experiments 4 to 11 these bounds were computed for each subject and reported along with s_i.

Examples of the signal values relative to a given V were provided and discussed. Subjects were told that "over a sufficiently long series of auctions, the difference between your private information signal and the value of the commodity will average out to zero (or very close to it); but for a given auction, your private information signal can be above or below the value of the item. That's the nature of the random selection process generating the signals."

After all bids were tendered, V was announced, subjects' profits were calculated, and balances were updated. In experiments 1 and 4 to 9, the top three bids were posted. All bids were posted in experiments 2, 3, 10, and 11, with the private information signals posted, together with the bids in 10 and 11.

To cover the possibility of losses, subjects were given starting balances of $8.00 in experiments 1 to 9 and $10.00 in 10 and 11. Positive profits were added to this balance, and losses subtracted from it. If a balance dropped to zero or less, a subject was no longer permitted to bid, was paid his $4.00 participation fee, and was free to leave the experiment. (At the start of each auction period subjects were notified of the number of bidders remaining in the market.) Auction survivors were paid their end-of-experiment balance plus their participation fee in cash.

Since elements of the winner's curse were anticipated, starting balances were set so that (i) a subject could commit at least one gross overbid,[1] learn from his mistake, and still have a large enough balance to continue safely in the auction; and (ii) a conservative bidder who was shut out from winning by overly aggressive counterparts would earn a reasonable rate of return for participating in the experiment. The balance levels employed were successful on both counts, as losses averaged less than $3.00 in the early auction periods, and the majority of subjects were eager to participate in additional auctions.

Each of the experiments started with either two or three dry runs in which outcomes did not count toward players' final earnings. The analysis of the data begins with the first market period involving cash payoffs.[2] Table 2.1 summarizes the experimental treatment conditions.

3. Theoretical Considerations and the Winner's Curse

The equilibrium bidding concept of choice in much of the recent literature is that of a symmetric risk-neutral Nash equilibrium (hereafter SRNNE), as found in Wilson [1977] and Milgrom and Weber [1982]. Restricting the analysis to signal values in the interval $V_L + \varepsilon \leq s_i \leq V_H - \varepsilon$ yields the SRNNE bid function

$$b(s_i) - s_i - \varepsilon + Y \tag{1}$$

where $Y = (2\varepsilon/N + 1) \exp \{- (N/2\varepsilon) [s_i - (V_L + \varepsilon)]\}$ and N equals the number of bidders. Y contains a negative exponential which rapidly becomes negligible as s_i increases beyond $V_L + \varepsilon$.[3] Ignoring the exponential term in the bid function expected profit for the high bidder is positive and equal to $2\varepsilon/N + 1$.

In a symmetric Nash equilibrium, bidders properly account for the adverse selection involved in winning the auction and discount their bids accordingly. A proper response requires agents to deflate $E(V \mid s_i)$, the expected value of the

TABLE 2.1
Experimental Conditions

Experiment	Subject Population (number starting experiment)	Market Period	ε	V_L	V_H
1	U. of Houston	1–5	$5	$10	$30
	Undergraduates	6–13	$10	$20	$60
	(10)				
2	U. of Houston	1–5	$5	$10	$30
	MBA Students	6–10	$10	$20	$60
	(6)	11–18	$15	$20	$80
3	U. of Houston	1–3	$5	$10	$30
	MBA Students	4–8, 15–20	$10	$20	$60
	(8)	9–14	$15	$20	$80
4&5	Texas A&M	1–6	$5	$15	$100
	Undergraduates	7–18	$12	$15	$100
	(6)				
6&7	Texas A&M	1–6	$5	$15	$100
	Undergraduates	7–20	$12	$15	$100
	(6)				
8&9	Texas A&M	1–6	$5	$15	$100
	Undergraduates	7–16	$12	$15	$100
	(6)				
10	U. of Houston	1–6	$6	$25	$225
	Law Students	7–16, 23–25	$12	$25	$225
	(5)	17–22	$18	$25	$225
11	U. of Houston	1–6	$6	$25	$225
	Undergraduates	7–16	$12	$25	$225
	(8)[a]	17–26	$24	$25	$225

[a]This experiment employed six bidders with two "substitutes" to replace bankruptcies. All subjects had participated in a first-price private value auction.

item conditional on the player's private information signal. This naive expectation does not adjust for the adverse selection problem. Instead, agents must focus on $E(V \mid S_i = s_1)$, the expected value of the item conditional on having the *highest* signal value among all other signals. As noted by Cox and Isaac [1984], agents can avoid the winner's curse by entering bids that are strictly less than the posterior expected value, $E(V \mid S_i = s_1)$.[4]

One can find a number of alternative definitions of the winner's curse in the literature, as illustrated by Cox and Isaac [1984]. This paper uses the following: An auction market exhibits a winner's curse wherever (i) there is a strong positive rank-order correlation between bids (b_i) and private information signals (s_i), and (ii) individual bids exceed $E(V \mid S_i = s_1)$. This definition is designed to characterize the mechanism underlying the market outcomes; namely, that the winner's curse results from an adverse selection problem in that (1) bidders generally win the auction when they hold the highest, or one of the highest, signals, and (ii) they fail to account for this fact in formulating their bids.

Condition (i) of this definition will hold for the Nash equilibrium bidding model as well as for the winner's curse, and simply guarantees the existence of an adverse selection. Bidding in excess of $E(V \mid S_i = s_1)$ provides a readily measurable indication of subjects' failure to deflate the item's expected value accurately. A perfect rank-order correlation coefficient between bids and signals in conjunction with only the high bidder bidding in excess of $E(V \mid S_i = s_1)$, is sufficient to insure negative profits. Further, even with zero correlation between bids and signals, all subjects bidding in excess of $E(V \mid S_i = s_1)$ is sufficient to insure negative average profits. As such, a reasonably high positive rank-order correlation between bids and signals, together with a reasonably large number of agents bidding in excess of $E(V \mid S_i = s_1)$, is likely to generate ex ante negative expected profits for the high bidder in the auction.

It has been argued that since losses were limited to cash balances, rational agents would bid more aggressively than the SRNNE bid function. Although there are cases where limited liability can induce rational agents to accept gambles they would otherwise reject, for this particular experimental design limited liability for losses should have a negligible effect on rational bidders. A bid of $s_i - \varepsilon$ is close to the SRNNE and insures bidders against any possibility of losses. Consequently, a bidder deciding whether or not to bid δ more than the SRNNE is fully liable for losses provided δ is less than or equal to his cash value.[5] If a rational response to rival behavior is defined as a bid somewhere between the SRNNE bid (equation (1)) and $E(V \mid S_i = s_1)$, then starting cash balances were over five times larger than the maximum expected loss associated with such a bid.[6]

With time and losses, cash balances can diminish to the point where limited liability may impact on rational bidding.[7] However, with bankruptcy limited liability may impact on rational bidding bidders must exit the auction, losing potential profit opportunities in later auction periods. This may promote lower bidding with low cash balances. We test for the net impact of these two opposing forces in reporting the experimental results.

4. Experimental Results

4.1 Market Outcomes

Data from experiments 2, 4, 5, and 10 provide representative time series of market outcomes. Each of the four figures shows the actual profits earned for each market period (cross marks) along with the profits that would have been earned if everyone had bid according to the SRNNE model (closed circles). At the top of each figure the rank-order correlation coefficient is shown between the bids and signals by market period.

Experiment 2

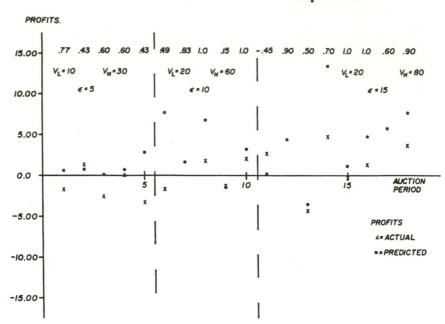

Experiment 4

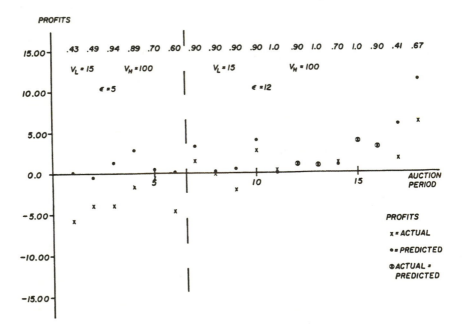

Figure 2.1.

Experiment 5

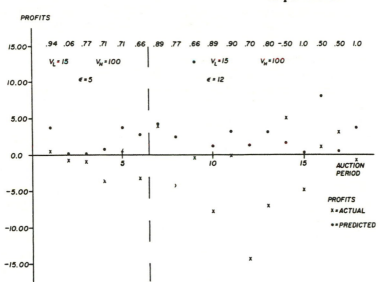

Experiment 10

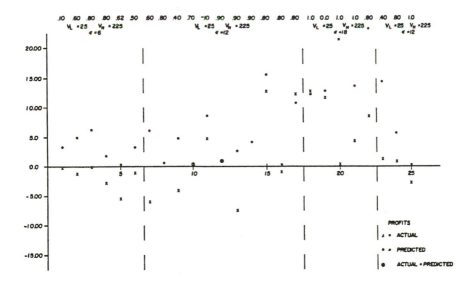

With the sole exception of experiment 9, high bidders earn negative average profits in the early auction periods. The full extent of these losses is captured in Table 2.2 where profits earned in the first nine auction periods are reported (the experiments lasted an average of seventeen to eighteen periods, not including trial runs). Negative profits were earned in approximately 80% of these periods, with losses averaging $2.57 per period, compared to positive expected profits of $1.90 per period that would have been earned under the SRNNE model.[8] The t-statistics shown in Table 2.2 indicate that the hypothesis of nonnegative profits can be rejected at the 5 percent significance level in seven of the eleven experiments. Treating the eleven experiments as independent repeated trials and combining the t-test outcomes as discussed in Maddala [1977, 47–48], the hypothesis of zero or positive profits is soundly rejected ($\chi^2 = 83.9$. 22d.f., $p < 001$).

Examining rank-order correlation coefficients between bids and signals for these periods shows that the correlation coefficient exceeded .5 in about 80 percent of all auction periods. Further, approximately 60% of all bids exceeded $E(V \mid S_i = s_1)$. These two statistics indicate that the losses observed are rooted in an adverse selection process resulting in bidder failure to discount bids sufficiently. Similar conclusions are reached on the basis of the frequency with which the high signal holder won the auction, approximately 60% of all cases, in conjunction with the frequency with which the high bidder's bid exceeded $E(V \mid S_i = s_1)$, almost 82% of all auction periods! Note finally that the more complete information conditions of experiments 10 and 11, where individual bids were posted together with signal values in all periods, did nothing to attenuate the overly aggressive bidding. Thus the results cannot be attributed to bidder ignorance of rivals' strategies relative to their signal values. The winner's curse seems to be alive and well and present in our early auction market period![9]

To capture the effects of experience on market outcomes, Table 2.3 brings together data for the last five auction periods for the experiments. Player earnings clearly improved with experience, as positive profits were earned in 57.4% of the last five auction periods (compared to 17.2% in the first nine auction periods). Positive average profits were earned in eight of eleven experiments, averaging $0.49 per auction period across experiments. Thus, the null hypothesis of zero or nonnegative profits can no longer be rejected.

While the profit data indicate that the worst effects of the winner's curse had been eliminated, strong traces still remained as 74.1% of all auctions were won by the highest signal holder, indicating strong adverse selection forces at work; while in 35.2% of all auctions the high bid exceeded $E(V \mid S_i = s_1)$, indicating a failure to account for the adverse selection problem. While this represents a sharp reduction in the frequency with which the highest bid exceeded $E(V \mid S_i = s_1)$, (compared to the first nine auction periods), it is still a sizable percentage. Although average profits were positive, they were only 10.2% of profits predicted under the SRNNE. Further, in only two of eleven experiments profits amounted to 50% or more of the profit opportunities as measured by the

SRNNE standard. This poor profit performance relative to the SRNNE standard is directly attributable to the winner's curse, given the relative frequency with which the winning bid exceeded $E(V \mid S_i = s_1)$.[10]

4.2 Individual Bidding Behavior over Time

Learning

Tables 2.2 and 2.3 indicate quite clearly that learning takes place at the market level as average profits turn from negative to positive and there is a sharp reduction in the frequency with which the high bid exceeds $E(V \mid S_i = s_1)$. Given the closed entry conditions of the experiments, a number of different scenarios could underlie this result. First, the survivors, those players who remained solvent and were bidding in the last five market periods, began bidding just like those who went bankrupt. Only they were lucky in the sense that they received relatively low signal values and did not win very often. With time, these players learned to bid more conservatively and/or simply profited from the reduced competition resulting from bankruptcies of others. Alternatively, the survivors may have simply bid more conservatively to start with relative to their signal values. In this polar case improved market performance results strictly from those bidding in excess of $E(V \mid S_i = s_1)$ suffering losses and eventually dropping out of the market. As a consequence, those who began bidding below $E(V \mid S_i = s_1)$ come to dominate market outcomes. Actual market outcomes may, of course, result from a combination of these forces.

Table 2.4 provides data relevant to evaluating these alternatives. The first two columns compare survivor bidding behavior over the first three auction periods with their bidding behavior in the last five market periods. The last column of Table IV shows bidding behavior of bankruptcies over the first three market periods. The number of bidders remained approximately constant over the first three periods as the losses that occurred then were generally not large enough to cause a significant number of bankruptcies.

Table 2.4 shows that on average survivors began bidding in excess of $E(V \mid S_i = s_1)$, as 63.5% of all survivor bids exceeded this value in the first three market periods. The implication is that a majority of survivor bids in the first three periods would have resulted in negative profits had they been unlucky enough to receive relatively high signal values! In this respect, the winner's curse is present in early auction periods even for survivors.

There appears to be considerable individual learning over time, however, as by the last five auction periods only 23.5% of the survivor bids exceeded $E(V \mid S_i = s_1)$. It is possible, of course, that survivor learning is exaggerated to the extent that the number of bidders was reduced from bankruptcies (recall from note 9 that $E(V \mid S_i = s_1)$ is decreasing in N). Experiment 11 affords some limited evidence on this point as the number of bidders was held constant at six for seventeen auction periods via the use of substitute bidders replacing bankruptcies. Looking at the bids of the four survivors who started bidding in

TABLE 2.2
Profits and Bidding in First Nine Auction Periods

Experiment	Percentage of Auctions with Positive Profits	Average Actual Profits (t-statistic)	Average Predicted Profits under SRNNE (S_M)[a]	Percentage of All Bids $b_i > E(V \mid S_i = s_1)$	Percentage of Auctions Won by High Signal Holder	Percentage of High Bids $b_i > E(V \mid S_i = s_1)$	Percentage of Subjects Going Bankrupt[b]
1	0.0	−4.83 (−3.62)**	.72 (.21)	63.4	55.6	100.0	50.0
2	33.3	−2.19 (−1.66)	2.18 (1.02)	51.9	33.3	88.9	16.7
3	11.1	−6.57 (−2.80)*	1.12 (1.19)	74.6	44.4	88.9	62.5
4	11.1	−2.26 (−3.04)**	.85 (.43)	41.8	55.6	55.6	16.7
5	33.3	−.84 (−1.00)	3.60 (1.29)	48.1	44.4	88.9	50.0

6	22.2	−2.65 (−1.53)	2.55 (1.17)	67.3	66.7	100.0	33.3
7	11.1	−2.04 (−2.75)*	.57 (.25)	58.5	88.9	66.7	50.0
8	11.1	−1.40 (−2.43)*	1.59 (.34)	51.9	55.6	55.6	16.7
9	44.4	.32 (.30)	2.37 (.76)	35.2	88.6	66.7	16.7
10	0.0	−2.78 (−3.65)**	3.53 (.74)	77.2	66.7	100.0	20.0
11	11.1	−3.05 (−3.53)**	1.82 (.29)	81.5	55.6	88.9	37.5
Average[c]	17.2	−2.57	1.90	59.4	59.6	81.8	41.1

[a]S_M = standard error of mean.
[b]Percentage over all market periods in experiment.
[c]Weighted by number of auctions in each experiment.
*Statistically significant at the 5% level, 2-tailed test.
**Statistically significant at the 1% level, 2-tailed test.

TABLE 2.3

Profits and Bidding in Last Five Auction Periods

Experiment	Percentage of Auctions with Positive Profits	Average Actual Profits (t-statistic)	Average Predicted Profits under SRNNE $(S_M)^a$	Profits as a Percentage of the SRNNE	Percentage of All Bids $b_i > E(V \mid S_i = s_1)$	Percentage of Auctions Won by High Signal Holder	Percentage of High Bids $b_1 > E(V \mid S_i = s_1)$
1	0.0	−1.82 (−2.54)	5.15 (1.11)	−35.3	45.0	75.0	100.0
2	60.0	1.51 (1.16)	6.59 (2.04)	22.9	32.0	80.0	40.0
3	60.0	1.74 (1.02)	3.16 (2.75)	55.1	6.7	80.0	20.0
4	100.0	3.08 (3.55)	4.94 (1.77)	62.3	32.0	80.0	40.0
5	60.0	.77 (.45)	2.79 (1.46)	27.6	13.3	60.0	20.0

6	40.0	.22 (.08)	3.39 (1.86)	6.5	14.3	80.0	20.0
7	80.0	1.29 (1.01)	3.15 (1.15)	41.0	16.7	60.0	20.0
8	40.0	−4.12 (−1.42)	1.87 (1.32)	−220.3	38.5	60.0	60.0
9	40.0	−1.52 (−.47)	3.45 (2.19)	−44.1	32.1	80.0	60.0
10	80.0	2.62 (1.38)	11.64 (3.99)	22.5	50.0	100.0	60.0
11	60.0	1.17 (.64)	6.99 (.76)	16.7	16.0	60.0	40.0
Average[b]	57.4	.49	4.82	10.2	28.2	74.1	35.2

[a]S_M = standard error of mean.
[b]Weighted by number of auctions in each experiment.

TABLE 2.4

Bidding Relative to Signal Values Survivors with and without Experience and
Survivors versus Bankruptcies

	Percentage of Bids		
	Bidding by Survivors		Bidding by Bankruptcies
Bid Relative to Signal Values	Periods One to Three	Last Five Periods	Periods One to Three
$b(S_i > E(V \mid s_i)$	11.7	4.4	35.6
$E(V \mid S_i = s_1) < b(s_i) < E(V \mid s_i)$	51.8	19.1	39.7
RNNE Bid$< b(s_i) < E(V \mid S_i = s_1)$	18.3	43.1	9.6
$b(s_i) <$ RNNE Bid	18.2	33.4	15.1

period one, 83% of all bids exceed $E(V \mid S_i = s_1)$ in the first three auction periods and only 10% of all bids exceed $E(V \mid S_i = s_1)$ in periods thirteen to seventeen, not unlike the general learning effects reported in Table 2.4. The less aggressive bidding behavior on the part of survivors in terms of the $E(V \mid S_i = s_1)$ benchmark cannot, in this case be attributed to a reduction in the number of bidders.

Comparing bankruptcies with survivors shows that while only 11.7 percent of survivors bid in excess of the naive expectation $E(V \mid S_i = s_1)$ in the first three market periods, some 35.6% of nonsurvivor bids exceeded this expectation. Pooling the first two bid categories, 75.3% of the nonsurvivor bids exceeded $E(V \mid S_i = s_1)$, compared to only 63.5% for the survivor bids. Thus, subjects going bankrupt tended to set themselves up for losses more frequently than survivors, and the losses for the subjects going bankrupt were generally larger.

Cash Balance Effect

With time and losses, cash balances diminish to the point where limited liability for losses may induce overly aggressive bidding. Alternatively, low cash balances may induce less aggressive bidding, since with bankruptcy bidders must exit the auction, losing potential profit opportunities in later auction periods. To determine the net effects of these two forces, individual subject bid functions were estimated for all signal values in the interval $(V_L + \varepsilon, V_H - \varepsilon)$ using the following specification:

$$b_{it} = \alpha_0 + \alpha_1 s_{it} + \alpha_2 \varepsilon_t + \alpha_3 N_t + \alpha_4 balance_{it} \qquad (2)$$

where s_{it} and $balance_{it}$ are bidder i's private information signal and cash balance at the beginning of period t, and ε_t and N_t are the value of ε and the number of bidders in period t. Bid functions were estimated separately for each experiment using a fixed-effects regression model, and for each individual sub-

TABLE 2.5
Effects of Cash Balances on Bidding: Coefficient Value for Cash Balance Variable in
Bid Function

Experiment	Fixed Effects Model Estimated Coefficient Value (standard error)	Individual Subject Regressions[a] Sign of Coefficient (number of bidders significantly different from zero at 10% level)	
		Negative	Positive
1	−.10 (.50)	1	3 (2)
2	.64** (.24)	1	4
3	.01 (.09)	1	1
4	.09 (.13)	2	4 (1)
5	.26 (.27)	3 (1)	2 (1)
6	−.02 (.08)	1 (1)	4 (1)
7	.32* (.17)	1	4 (2)
8	1.38** (.47)	2 (1)	3 (2)
9	.37** (.10)	2 (1)	4 (2)
10	.06 (.07)	2 (1)	3 (2)
11	−.04 (.05)	3	4 (2)

[a]Coefficient estimates could not be obtained for all subjects.
*Significantly different from zero at 10% level.
**Significantly different from zero at 5% level.

ject. Estimated coefficient values for the cash balance variable from each experiment are shown in Table 2.5, along with the number of subjects having positive or negative cash balance coefficients.

A positive coefficient value indicates that subjects were bidding less aggressively (lower) with smaller cash balances, while a negative coefficient indicates
more aggressive (higher) bids with smaller balances. The fixed-effects regres-

sion coefficients are positive in eight of eleven experiments and are significantly different from zero in four of these eight cases. Of the three experiments generating negative coefficient estimates, none are different from zero at conventional significance levels.

This general pattern of less aggressive bidding with lower cash balances is found in the individual subject regressions as well. Close to two-thirds of the fifty-five subjects have positive coefficients, indicating that they bid less aggressively with lower cash balances. In fifteen out of these thirty-six cases, bidding was significantly lower with lower cash balances. In contrast, only five subjects had negative coefficient estimates that were different from zero at the 10% significance level or better.[11]

Although the results of the regressions indicate that lower cash balances generally resulted in lower bids, it is not clear that this reflects a cash balance effect. It could be that it took real losses (hence lower cash balances) for bidders to perceive that they had to bid less aggressively relative to signal values to earn positive profits.[12]

This alternative interpretation is supported by two facts. First, ten of the fifteen subjects whose cash balance coefficients were significantly positive never had their balances drop below the $4.00 level, so that they were always in a relatively secure operating position. Second, Dyer [1987] conducted a series of common-value offer auctions with inexperienced bidders using procedures similar to ours. In two experiments bidders had starting cash balances of $10.00, while in a third experiment, with virtually identical procedures, they had starting balances of $20.00. He reports no significant differences in individual subject bid functions across experiments. Definitive sorting out of cash balance effects from learning effects will require more experiments with exogenous variation in cash balances.

5. Summary and Conclusions

This study shows a strong initial winner's curse as subjects earned negative profits and consistently bid in excess of $E(V \mid S_i = s_1)$. Both survivor (in 63.5 percent of the auctions) and bankruptcies (in 75.3% of the auctions) bid in excess of $E(V \mid S_i = s_1)$ in the first three auction periods. As such, survivorship, is at least in part dependent on being lucky enough *not* to receive high valuation signals in the early rounds, and it is clear that the market outcomes are not dependent on the aberrant behavior of a few individuals. Further, the winner's curse is unaffected by the posting of subjects' signal values along with their bids.

With experience the winner's curse is attenuated as bidders earned modest positive profits, and the majority of bids were less than $E(V \mid S_i = s_1)$ over the last five auction periods. Performance is relatively stable in the sense that few bankruptcies occurred as well. These adjustments in market outcomes are in part attributable to bankruptcy of the most aggressive bidders, and in part a result of survivors learning to bid less aggressively. Nevertheless there are still strong traces of the winner's curse as profits realized are only 10 percent of the profit opportunities as defined by the SRNNE, and a sizable minority of bids still exceeded $E(V \mid S_i = s_1)$.

Kagel and Levin [1986] report results from a series of first-price common value auction experiments in which all subjects were *experienced* in that they had previously participated in one or more common value auction experiments. These results indicate that with small numbers of competitors (three or four) bidder performance improved to the point where subjects consistently earned profits closer to the SRNNE level than to the zero or negative profit levels associated with the winner's curse. Previous participation in a common value auction environment clearly reduces the impact of the winner's curse in this case. Nevertheless, increases in the number of bidders (to six or seven) resulted in reemergence of the winner's curse with bidders earning negative average profits and consistently bidding in excess of $E(V \mid S_i = s_1)$. The continued dominance of strategic forces promoting increased bidding in the presence of increased numbers of rivals for these experienced bidders is indicative of the strength of the forces underlying the winner's curse. Further, a comparison of responses of these experienced bidders with bidders in early Outer Continental Shelf (OCS) lease sales shows bidding patterns in response to the release of public information which are similar and interpretable well only in the context of a winner's curse.

Clearly, the winner's curse issue must be separated into a theoretical question and an empirical question, as discussed by Cox and Isaac (1986). While current theoretical development generally indicates that no "rational" agent will commit the winner's curse, a significant amount of empirical evidence indicates that many agents do. The empirical existence of the winner's curse involves an agent's inability to account for the adverse selection problem inherent in competitive bidding on the basis of unbiased estimates of the item's value, causing him to tender bids that are overly optimistic conditional on the event of winning. This adverse selection problem is not unique to common value auctions but is likely to occur whenever market alternatives are uncertain and there is competition for the item. The findings of a winner's curse in experimental common value auction markets are consistent with similar reports in many other markets where the item up for bid has an uncertain, common value element.

Appendix: Inexperienced Bidders in Second-Price Common Value Auctions

We conducted a second, parallel series of second-price common value auctions with inexperienced bidders along with the initial series of first-price auctions reported in Kagel et al. (1989). These yielded essentially the same results—a strong winner's curse. We never published this data (there is not a great deal of demand by economics journals for such negative results). The following two tables report key parts of the data.

A total of five inexperienced subject sessions were conducted using the same procedures as described in Kagel, Levin, and Harstad (1995) (Chapter 4). Four out of the five started with six active bidders (at least three of the sessions employed one or more substitutes in order to maintain a constant number of active bidders as long as possible). Data are reported for these four sessions, with the analysis in Table 2.A2 limited to auctions with six active bidders. There were six active bidders throughout in Table 2.A1.

Table 2.A1 is designed to match Table 2.A2 in Kagel et al. (1989). Table 2.A2 provides additional data. All data were collected in collaboration with Dan Levin and Ron Harstad.

TABLE 2.A1

Second-Price Auctions: Profits and Bidding in First Nine Auctions for Inexperienced Bidders

Experiment	Percentage of Auctions with Positive Profits	Average Actual Profits (t-statistics)	Average Predicted Profit (S_m)	Percentage of All Bids	Percentage of Auctions Won by High Signal Holder	Percentage of Auctions Price Set by Second Highest Signal Holder	Percentage of High Bids
1	44.4	−1.73 (1.51)	1.70 (1.04)	90.7	22.2	22.2	100.0
2	22.2	−2.67 (2.71)*	2.26 (0.89)	83.3	33.3	22.2	100.0
3	11.1	−2.72 (−2.54)*	3.52 (1.20)	94.4	55.6	55.6	100.0
4	33.3	−1.35 (−0.65)	1.71 (0.96)	63.0	55.6	33.3	100.0
Average	27.8	−2.12	2.30	82.9	41.7	33.3	100.0

S_m = standard error of mean.

*Significantly different from zero at the 5% level, two-tailed test.

Note: Six active bidders in all auctions.

TABLE 2.A2
Actual and Predicted Profits as ε Changed: Inexperienced Bidders in
Second-Price Auctions

ε (number of auctions)	Actual Profits (S_m)	Predicted Profit (S_m)
6	−2.04**	1.90
(22)	(0.52)	(0.40)
12	−2.99**	2.70
(31)	(0.93)	(0.78)
18	0.74	8.26
(12)	(1.96)	(2.11)

S_m = standard error of the mean.
**Significantly different from zero at the 1% level, 2-tailed test.

Notes

This research was partially supported by grants from the Energy Laboratory and the Center for Public Policy at the University of Houston, the Technology and Society Research Division of the Texas Engineering Experiment Station, the Information Science and Economics Divisions of the National Science Foundation, and the Sloan Foundation program in behavioral economics. Tom Saal, Doug Dyer, and Susan Saroia provided able research assistance. Paul Milgrom and Ron Harstad provided helpful comments on an earlier draft, as did our referees.

1. Bids were restricted to be nonnegative and less than or equal to $s_i + ε$. The latter restriction was explained on the grounds that bidding in excess of $s_i + ε$ would insure losses. The full set of instructions are available from the authors.

2. In the second half of experiments 1 to 9 subjects bid simultaneously in two independent common value auctions. Analysis of behavior in this second set of auctions is reported in the working paper by Kagel, Levin, Battalio, and Meyer [1984].

3. This bid function and the corresponding bid function outside the interval $(V_L + ε, V_H − ε)$ are explicitly derived in our working paper, available upon request. Also see Kagel and Levin [1986], footnote 8.

4. This is provided that rivals are bidding their signal values or less.

5. The exponential term Y on the right hand-side of (1) is ignored, as it quickly goes to zero.

6. For example, in the A&M experiments with $N = 6$ and $ε = \$5.00$, the difference between (1) and $E(V \mid S_t = s_1)$ is \$1.43 (since $E(V \mid S_i = s_1) = s_i − (N − 1)ε/(N + 1))$, which is substantially less than the beginning cash balance of \$8.00.

7. By definition of a Nash equilibrium, increasing bids above the equilibrium bid function reduces expected profit. Consequently, for those signal values for which the SRNNE bid function is effectively $s_i − ε$, even in cases where subjects have *zero cash balances*, it is "irrational" for risk-neutral bidders to deviate from the Nash norm. The intuition here is straightforward. There are positive expected profits for all bidders at the Nash equilibrium. For one bidder to bid higher than Nash involves the following: (1) it

improves the chance of winning, while any possible losses map to zero due to limited liability and zero cash balances; *but* (2) deviations from the best response implies a reduction in ex ante expected profits. This second force is simply stronger than the first when the Nash bid is $s_i - \varepsilon$.

8. Bankruptcies occurred after the first nine auction periods in experiments 5, 7, 8, 9, 10, and 11 so that all losses reported here are real. If "paper" losses are omitted (i.e., losses in excess of cash balances) in those experiments with bankruptcies in the first nine periods, average losses were $4.20 (1). $1.78 (2), $4.02 (3), $1.91 (4), and $1.93 (6), where the number after the loss figure corresponds to the experiment in question. Average real losses across all experiments were $2.15 per auction period. Collectively, bidders turned back $212.57 of the starting balances we had given them.

Under the rules of the game, high bidders could have done much worse than the losses reported in Table II, generating average losses of over $12.00 per period if they had consistently bid $\min(s_i + \varepsilon, V_H)$. Thus, we can reject the hypothesis that the high bidders had simply adopted a win-at-any-cost strategy, or had simply decided to settle for their participation fee and were trying to minimize the time cost of obtaining it.

9. This is a particularly strong finding given that bidding $\max s_i - \varepsilon, V_L$ insured them against losses and yields positive average profits as long as others bid $b(s_i) \leq s_j$, a bidding profile that was commonly satisfied.

10. First-price private value auction experiments such as those reported by Cox, Roberson and Smith (1982) typically report profits well below the risk-neutral Nash equilibrium prediction, a result which can be attributed to risk aversion on the bidder's part. There are several reasons that the low profit levels here are not attributed to similar forces. First, realized profits are a much smaller percentage of risk-neutral predicted profits than in private value auctions. Second, theoretically, comparable degrees of risk aversion are likely to promote bidding much closer to the risk-neutral model's predictions here than in private value auctions. This is because risk aversion in relationship to item valuation considerations imposes a downward pressure on bids that is completely absent in private value auctions, where individual bidders know the value of the item (to themselves) with certainty, In fact, if the latter force is sufficiently strong, bidders will never bid above min $(V_L, S_i - \varepsilon)$ here, which would result in larger profits than predicted under the SRNNE.

11. An alternative specification including a time trend variable on the right-hand side of (2) yields virtually the same results as those reported.

12. Negative coefficient values cannot be interpreted unambiguously either. Suppose a bidder starts out bidding aggressively but is lucky enough to receive low signal values, so that he does not suffer losses. Observing the fate of others suffering losses and bankruptcies, he determines that he must bid lower. Lower bidding coincides with more favorable signal values, so that he wins and his cash balance increases. Something of this sort may well have actually occurred since of the five subjects with significant negative coefficients, minimum cash balances were $2.76, $6.06, $7.99 and $8.00 (for two bidders). In only one of these cases had balances dropped to the point where limited liability for losses could plausibly account for the more aggressive bidding.

References

Capen, E. C., R. V. Clapp, and W. M. Campbell. "Competitive Bidding in High-Risk Situations." *Journal of Petroleum Technology*, June 1971, 641–53.

Cassing, J. and R. W. Douglas. "Implications of the Auction Mechanism in Baseball's Free Agent Draft." *Southern Economic Journal*, July 1990, 110–21.

Cox, J. C. and R. M. Isaac. "In Search of the Winner's Curse." *Economic Inquiry*, October 1984, 579–92.

———. "In Search of the Winner's Curse: Reply." *Economic Inquiry*, July 1986, 517–20.

Cox, J. C., B. Roberson, and V. L. Smith. "Theory and Behavior of Single Object Auctions," in *Research in Experimental Economics* Vol. 2, edited by V. L. Smith. Greenwich: JAI Press, 1982.

Dessauer, J. P. *Book Publishing*. New York: Bowker, 1981.

Dyer, Douglas. "Experimental Studies of Bidding in Auctions." Ph.D. dissertation. University of Houston, 1987.

Kagel, J. H. and D. Levin. "The Winner's Curse and Public Information in Common Value Auctions." *American Economic Review*, December 1986, 894–920.

Kagel, J. H., D. Levin, R. C. Battalio, and D. J. Meyer. "First-Price, Sealed Bid, Common Value Auctions: Some Initial Experimental Results." Center for Public Policy Discussion Paper 84–1, 1984.

Lohrenz, J. and E. L. Dougherty. "Bonus Bidding and Bottom Lines: Federal Offshore Oil and Gas." Society of Petroleum Engineers 12024. Fifty-eighth Annual Fall Technical Conference, October 1983.

Maddala, G. S. *Econometrics*. New York: McGraw-Hill, 1977.

Mead, W. J., A. Moseidjord, and P. E. Sorenson. "The Rate of Return Earned by Lessees Under Cash Bonus Bidding for OCS Oil and Gas Leases." *Energy Journal*, October 1983, 37–52.

Milgrom. P. R. "Rational Expectations, Information Acquisition and Competition Bidding." *Econometrica*, July 1981, 921–43.

Milgrom, P. R. and R. J. Weber. "A Theory of Auctions and Competitive Bidding." *Econometrica*, September 1982, 1089–1122.

Roll, R. "The Hubris Hypothesis of Corporate Takeovers." *Journal or Business*. April 1986, 197–216.

Wilson, R. B. "A Bidding Model of Perfect Competition." *Review of Economic Studies*, October 1977, 511–18.

3

The Winner's Curse and Public Information in Common Value Auctions

John H. Kagel and Dan Levin

Common value auctions constitute a market setting in which participants may be particularly susceptible to judgment failures that affect market outcomes. In a common value auction, the value of the auctioned item is the same to all bidders. What makes the auction interesting is that bidders are unaware of the value of the item at the time the bids are placed. Mineral lease auctions, particularly the federal government's outer continental shelf (OCS) oil lease auctions, are common value auctions. There is a common value element to most auctions. Bidders for all oil painting may purchase for their own pleasure, a private value element, but they may also bid for investment and eventual resale, reflecting an uncertain common value element.

Judgmental failures in common value auctions are known as the "winner's curse." Assume that all bidders obtain unbiased estimates of an item's value and that bids are an increasing function of these estimates. The high bidder then tends to be the one with the most optimistic estimate of the item's value. Unless this adverse-selection problem is accounted for in the bidding process, it will result in winning bids that produce below normal or even negative profits. The systematic failure to account for this adverse selection problem is referred to as the "winner's curse."

Oil companies claim they fell prey to the winner's curse in early OCS lease sales (E. C. Capen, R. V. Clapp and W. M. Campbell, 1971; John Lorenz and E. L. Dougherty, 1983; and references cited there-in). Similar claims have been made in auctions for book publication rights (John Dessauer, 1981) in professional baseball's free agency market (James Cassing and Richard Douglas, 1980) and in corporate takeover battles (Richard Roll, 1986). Economists typically treat such claims with caution as they imply that bidders repeatedly err, in violation of basic notions of economic rationality. This caution is justified given the inherent problems in interpreting field data, self-serving motives of many of the claimants, and the general absence of conventional statistical tests documenting these claims. However, common value auction experiments using financially motivated, but inexperienced, subjects demonstrate a strong and nearly ubiquitous winner's curse which continues to significantly depress profits after as many as 15–20 auction periods (Kagel et al., 1986).

It is one thing to find that inexperienced bidders commit a winner's curse. It is another to find that experienced bidders do the same. Here we report the results of common value auction experiments with experienced subjects, survivors of one or more initial series of experiments. With continued experience, bidders' judgment improve. In auctions involving a limited number of competitors (3–4 bidders), average profits are consistently positive and closer to the Nash equilibrium bidding outcome than to the winner's curse hypothesis: behavior consistent with traditional notions of the effects of repeated exposure to market conditions, in conjunction with profit incentives and survival pressures. However, learning is situationally specific as bids are found to be an increasing function of the number of rivals faced, in clear violation of risk-neutral Nash equilibrium bidding theory under our design. This contributes to a reemergence of the winner's curse, with bankruptcies and negative profits, in auctions with large numbers (6–7) of bidders.

Just as Nash equilibrium bidding theory predicts, experimental manipulations providing public information reducing uncertainty about item value reliably result in higher winning bids and increased seller's revenues in the absence of a winner's curse. However, in the presence of a winner's curse, this same public information generates lower average winning bids and reduced seller's revenues. The differential response to public information conditional on the presence or absence of a winner's curse has practical implications which have largely gone unrecognized in the literature.

The paper is organized as follows. Section 1. describes the structure of the experiments. Section 2. characterizes the Nash equilibrium bidding strategies for the auction, provides a formal definition of the winner's curse, and states the research hypotheses that guided our investigations. The results of the experiments are reported and discussed in Section 3. Section 4. extends the analysis to field settings where our experimental results help explain a puzzling outcome of OCS lease sales: namely, that public information reducing item uncertainty increased bidder's profits, just as observed in our laboratory experiments in the presence of a winner's curse. A concluding section summarizes our research results and poses questions for further research.

1. Structure of the Auctions

1.1 Basic Auction Structure

Subjects were recruited for two-hour sessions consisting of a series of auction periods. In each auction period, a single unit of a commodity was sold to the high bidder at the high-bid price, with bidders submitting sealed bids for the item (a first-price, sealed-bid procedure). The high bidder earned profits equal to the value of the item less the amount bid; other bidders earned zero profits for that auction period.

In each auction period, the value of the item, x_0, was drawn randomly from a uniform distribution on the interval $[\underline{x}, \bar{x}]$. Subjects submitted bids without knowing the value of x_0. Private information signals, x_i, were distributed prior to bidding. The x_i were randomly drawn from a uniform distribution centered on x_0 with upper bound $x_0 + \varepsilon$ and lower bound $x_0 - \varepsilon$. As such, the x_i constitute unbiased estimates of the value of x_0 (or could be used to compute unbiased estimates in conjunction with the endpoint values $\underline{x}, \bar{x}$). Given x_i, ε, and the endpoint values, each bidder could compute an upper and lower bound on the value of x_0; these were min $\{x_i + \varepsilon, \bar{x}\}$ and max $\{x_i - \varepsilon, \underline{x}\}$, respectively. The bounds associated with a given x_i were computed and reported along with the x_i.

The distribution underlying the signal values, the value of ε, and the interval $[\underline{x}, \bar{x}]$ were common knowledge. The value of ε varied across auctions (see Table 3.1). All changes in ε were announced and posted. With signal values drawn independently relative to x_0, they satisfy the criteria of strict positive affiliation (Paul Milgrom and Robert Weber, 1982) which, roughly speaking, requires that large values for a given signal make it more likely that rivals signal values, and x_0, are large rather than small.

Bids were restricted to be nonnegative and rounded to the nearest penny. After all bids were collected, they were posted on the blackboard in descending order next to the corresponding signal values, x_0 was announced, subjects' profits were calculated, and balances were updated.[1] Earnings of the high bidder were also announced, but his/her identity was not. The x_0 values and the associated signal values were all determined randomly strictly according to the process described to the subjects.

To cover the possibility of losses, subjects were given starting balances of $8.00 in auction series 1–2, and $10.00 in series 3–8. Profits and losses were added to this balance. If a subject's balance went negative, he was no longer permitted to bid; he was paid the $4.00 participation fee and free to leave the experiment. The auction survivors were paid their end of experiment balance in cash, along with their participation fee.[2]

Given the information structure and uncertainty inherent in common value auctions, negative profits will occasionally be realized even if the market immediately locks into the risk-neutral Nash equilibrium outcome. The starting capital balance served to account for this possibility, and to impose clear opportunity costs on overly aggressive bidding. Balances were set so that: (i) subjects could commit at least one gross bidding error, learn from their mistake, and still have a large enough balance to actively participate in the auctions, and (ii) conservative bidders who were shut out from winning by overly aggressive counterparts would earn a reasonable return for participating.

TABLE 3.1
Experimental Conditions[a]

Auction Series	Subject Population (no. starting exp.)	Market Period	ε	$\underline{x}$	$\bar{x}$	Public Information[b] (market periods)	Number Active Bidders (market periods)	Experience
1	Texas A&M Undergraduates (5)	1–18	$12	$15	$100	Random signal (10–18)	5(1–18)	First-price common value
2	Texas A&M Undergraduates (4)	1–18	$12	$15	$100	Random signal (10–18)	4(1–18)	First-price common value
3	U. Houston Graduate/Senior Undergraduates (7)	1–8 9–17, 24–25 18–23	$12 $18 $30	$25	$225	Low signal (12–25)	7(1–4) 6(5–6) 5(7–11) 4(12–25)	Second-price common value, some first-price common value
4	U. Houston Graduate/Senior Undergraduates (8)	1–6 7–14 15–25	$12 $18 $30	$25	$225	Low signal (8–25)	7(1–10) 6(11–25)	Second-price common value, some first-price common value

5	U. Houston Graduate/Senior Undergraduates (9)	1–9 10–15, 24–26 16–23	$12 $18 $30	$25	$225	Low signal (7–26)	7(1–26) 7(1–26)	First- and Second-price common value
6	U. Houston Graduate/Senior Undergraduates (4)	1–5 6–16, 28–31 17–21 22–27	$12 $18 $24 $30	$25	$225	Low signal (9–31)	4(1–11) 4(1–11) 3(12–31)	First- and Second-price common value
7	U. Houston Graduate/Senior Undergraduates (6)	1–5 6–13, 26–32 33–37 14–25	$12 $18 $24 $30	$25	$225	Low signal (9–32)	4(1–19) 6(20–37)	First- and Second-price common value
8	U. Houston Graduate/Senior Undergraduates (7)	1–6 7–16 17–23	$12 $18 $30	$30	$500	None	4(1–23)[c] 7(10–23)	First-price common value, some private value

[a] Starting balances were $8 in experiments 1 and 2, $10 in all others.

[b] Profits were earned in markets with both public and private information in experiments 1 and 2; in only one market in experiments 3–8. The market paying profits was determined by a coin flip in experiments 3–8.

[c] Period 10 on involved a bidding in two markets with four subjects bidding first in a "small" market and all seven subjects bidding in a "large" market.

1.2 Auctions with Public Information

Approximately one-third of the way through auction series 1–7, we introduced bidding in two separate auction markets simultaneously. Bidding in the first auction market continued as before under private information conditions. After these bids were collected, but before they were posted, we introduced a public information signal and asked subjects to bid again. (Subjects retained their original private information signals; no new private information signals were distributed.) We employed two types of public information signals. In series 1 and 2, we randomly drew an additional signal, x_i, from the interval $[x_0 - \varepsilon, x_0 + \varepsilon]$, and posted it. In series 3–7, the lowest of the private information signals distributed, x_L, was posted. Bidders were always accurately informed of whether the public information signal was random or the lowest private information signal.

Profits were paid (or losses incurred) in only one of the two auction markets, determined on the basis of a coin flip after all bids were collected.[3] Subjects were told that they were under no obligation to submit the same or different bids in the two markets, but should bid in a way they thought would "maximize profits." All bids from both markets were posted along with the corresponding private information signals.

The dual market bidding procedure, involving the same set of bidders with the same item value and the same set of private information signals, has the advantage of directly controlling for between subject variability and extraneous variability resulting from variations in item value and private information signals. Some critics have mistakenly concluded that the procedure involves a "Portfolio" problem so that the optional bid in one market affects bids in the other market. This conclusion is unwarranted, however. There is no way that bids in the private information market can be used to hedge bids in the public information market any more than bids in the private information market in period t can be used to hedge bids in the private information market in period $t + 1$. In analyzing each member of a set of auctions, $t = 1, 2, \ldots, T$, as a single-shot auction (which we do below), we are assuming that the utility function is intertemporally separable in profits from the auction, $U = \Sigma_{t=1}^{T} u(\Pi_t)$. Similarly we are assuming separability in bidding between the dual markets. The breakdown of the separability assumption in either case (for example, $U = u(\Sigma_{t=1}^{T} \Pi_t)$) has comparable implications, namely no effect in the case of risk-neutral bidders, while risk-averse bidders will tend to be less risk averse than under separable preferences, as they can rely on the law of large numbers to smooth the variance in profits across auctions.

Of course, it is another matter entirely whether bidders actually bid as if their preferences are separable between the dual markets or over time. Experiments 1 and 2 explicitly tested for separability, holding ε constant throughout and having a relatively large number of private information auctions (9) before introducing dual markets. Regression analysis using dummy variables showed no systematic response to bids in the private information market under the dual market procedure.[4] Similar tests, conducted in a related series of first-price auctions, showed no systematic effects in going from private information markets only to dual markets with public information, and from dual markets to markets with public information only (Kagel, Ronald Harstad, and Levin, 1986). Bid patterns over time are presented in reporting our results.

1.3 Varying Numbers of Bidders

A number of tactics were employed to study the effects of varying the number of bidders. Auction series 1–6 used a between-groups design with different series having different numbers of active bidders. In pursuit of this objective, series 4 and 5 had more subjects than active bidders, in order to control for bankruptcies, with a simple rotation rule to determine which subjects would be active in any given auction period.[5] Variations in the number of active bidders in these series (see the eighth column in Table 3.1) resulted from bankruptcies.

Auction series 7 and 8 involved planned variations in the number of active bidders. Series 7 employed a crossover design, starting with four active bidders rotating among a set of six total bidders. In auction period 20, the rotation procedure ceased, and all six bidders were active in the remaining auction periods. Auction series 8 employed a within-subjects design, starting out with four active bidders rotating between seven total bidders. In auction period 10, dual market bidding procedures similar to those used to study the effects of public information were introduced; only numbers of active bidders varied between markets.[6] We refer to the different market sizes here as series 7 and 8 small, and 7 and 8 large. Auction series 3 involved a large unplanned variation in number of active bidders due to bankruptcies in early auction periods. Our analysis distinguishes between these early auction periods with five or more active bidders (series 3 large), and the later periods with four active bidders (series 3 small), as market outcomes were distinctly different between the two situations.

1.4 The Experience Factor

All auctions employed experienced subjects. In series 1 and 2, all subjects had been in one earlier first-price common value auction series using similar design parameters (see Kagel et al., 1986, auction series 4–6). These earlier auctions all began with six active bidders, but as a result of bankruptcies ended with three to five bidders. Recruitment into these experiments was restricted to subjects who had not gone bankrupt in the initial auction series.

Auction series 3–8 are numbered in chronological order as they involved a common core of subjects, recruited in varying combinations, in the different series. Thirteen of the 15 bidders in series 3 and 4 had participated in an earlier series of second-price common value auction experiments with similar design parameters. (The distinguishing characteristic of these second-price auctions was that the high bidders earned the item and paid the second-highest bid price.) Most of these subjects had been in two or more second-price series, at least one of which involved six to seven active bidders throughout. The two remaining subjects had been in a first-price common value series involving five to six active bidders throughout (Kagel et al., 1986, auction series 11). Seven of the nine subjects in series 5 were recruited from series 3 and 4, with the remaining two having extensive second-price experience. All six bidders in series 7 had been in both auction series 3 and 5, or 4 and 5. Three of the four bidders in series 6 had been in series 4, with the fourth bidder having been in series 3 and 5. Series 8 was conducted several months after the others and involved three veterans of series 7, 2 from series 6, and two bidders with experience in first-price auctions with positively affiliated private values (Kagel, Harstad, and Levin). Several subjects in this series had gone bankrupt in their initial common value auction series, but were included provided the bankruptcy occurred after a fair number of auction periods (15 or more periods was the rule of thumb employed).[7] Subjects were recruited into later series in this sequence without regard to performance earlier in the sequence.

2. Theoretical Considerations

2.1 Private Information Conditions

1. The Nash Equilibrium

The most common equilibrium bidding model in the economic's literature is that of a noncooperative Nash equilibrium with risk-neutral bidders (here-after RNNE). Robert Wilson (1977) was the first to develop a Nash equilibrium solution for first-price common value auctions, while Milgrom and Weber provide some significant extensions and generalization of the Wilson model.

We restrict our analysis in the text to signals in the interval

$$\underline{x} + \varepsilon \le x_i \le \bar{x} - \varepsilon. \tag{1}$$

The optimal bid function in this interval is, of course, affected by the bid function in the interval $x_i < \underline{x} + \varepsilon$, which in turn is affected by the added information associated with the end-point value, $\underline{x}$.[8] Assuming risk neutrality on bidder's part, the Nash equilibrium bid function for signals in (1) is

$$b(x_i) = x_i - \varepsilon + Y, \tag{2}$$

where $Y = [2\varepsilon/(N + 1)]\exp[-(N/2\varepsilon)(x_i - (\underline{x} + \varepsilon))]$ and N stands for the number of active bidders in the market. Y contains a negative exponential, and diminishes rapidly as x_i moves beyond $\underline{x} + \varepsilon$.

Under (2), expected profits for the high bidder are

$$E\,[\Pi \mid W] = 2\varepsilon/(N + 1) - Y. \tag{3}$$

In addition, the model predicts that the high signal holder always wins the auction. This follows directly from the assumption that all bidders use the same bid function, the only difference being their private information, x_i, regarding the value of the item.[9]

Accounting for risk aversion on bidder's part complicates the model's predictions, as equilibrium bids can be to either side of the RNNE prediction, depending upon the form of the utility function and the degree of risk aversion assumed. We do not pursue these extensions here, as they appear secondary to understanding the experiments' outcomes.[10] Note that under the RNNE there is no winner's curse as bidders fully account for the adverse-selection problem in determining their bids. The RNNE bidding model provides a convenient benchmark against which to compare the experiments' outcomes.

2. Judgmental Failures: The Winner's Curse

In common value auctions, bidders usually win the item when they have the highest, or one of the highest, estimates of value. Under these conditions an unbiased estimate of value, $E[x_0 \mid x_i)$, is biased as

$$E[x_0 \mid x_i] > E[x_0 \mid X_i = x_1] \qquad \text{for } N > 1$$

where $E[x_0 \mid X_i = x_1]$ is the expected value conditional on having the highest private information signal. Assuming that the highest signal holder always wins the auction and risk neutrality, or risk aversion, bids in excess of $E[x_0 \mid X_i = x_1]$ will insure negative profits on average, and can only result from failure to recognize the adverse-selection problem inherent in winning the auction. Since we have no reason to assume risk loving, and the highest signal holder usually wins the auction, bids in excess of $E[x_0 \mid X_i = x_1]$ will be attributed to such judgmental failures, and will be referred to as the winner's curse.[11]

For signal values in the interval (1),

$$E[x_0 \mid x_i] = x_i; \tag{4}$$

$$E[x_0 \mid X_i = x_1] = x_i - \varepsilon(N - 1)/(N + 1). \tag{5}$$

Avoiding the winner's curse requires considerable discounting of bids relative to signal values.[12] Further, the size of the discount is an increasing function of both N and ε.

In first-price sealed-bid auctions, strategic considerations generally dictate discounting of bids relative to the expected value of the item. Strategic discounting results strictly from known dispersion in rivals' values. It is informative to compare the bid function (2), and the size of the discount in (5), with strategic discounting based on the dispersion in the x_i values. Suppose that bidders completely ignore the adverse-selection problem inherent in the auction, employing (4) to compute the expected value of the item: they act as if they are in an auction with positively affiliated private values, where the x_i represents the value of the item to bidder i, and values are independently distributed over the interval (1). Under risk neutrality, the bid function here is[13]

$$b^s(x_i) = x_i - (2\varepsilon/N) + (Y/N), \tag{6}$$

where the expression Y is the same as in (2) above.

Comparing equation (5) with (6) shows that strategic discounting produces a winner's curse whenever $N > 3$. Further, strategic considerations (6), item valuation considerations (5), and the RNNE bid function (2) all call for greater discounting of bids relative to signal values with increases in ε.[14] Since evidence from private value auctions shows bidders to be sensitive to the strategic considerations inherent in these auctions (James Cox, et al.; our 1985 paper), we expect bidders to be sensitive to variations in ε.

However, with increasing numbers of bidders, equations (2), (5), and (6) give conflicting directions. Differentiation of (6) shows that strategic considerations require higher bids in the presence of more rivals as signal values are more congested. Item valuation considerations as expressed in (5) require less aggressive bidding as the adverse-selection problem becomes more severe. The net effect of these two forces, expressed in the RNNE bid function, is for bids to remain constant or decrease in the presence of more rivals.[15] This conflict between item valuation and strategic considerations suggests that structural variations in numbers of bidders is critical to determining whether experienced bidders learn to avoid the winner's curse in small groups out of a trial and error survival process that is situationally specific, as opposed to "understanding" the adverse-selection problem as it applies to new situations. If the survival process results in generalized learning (one interpretation of optimality via survival arguments in economics), behavior in both large and small groups should show comparable deviations from the RNNE reference point.[16] However, in the absence of generalized learning, behavior is likely to be markedly different, to the extent that the winner's curse, having been largely or entirely eliminated in small groups, will reemerge with increases in group size.

2.2 Effects of Public Information

1. The Nash Equilibrium

Extensions of the common value auction model show that public information reducing item valuation uncertainty will increase average seller's revenues (reduce bidder's profits) under the RNNE (Milgrom and Weber). This holds even though public information signals of the sort employed here, x_p, will, on average, be below the maximum private information signal, x_1. The economic forces at work here are roughly as follows: On average,

$$E[x_0 \mid X_i = x_1] = E[x_0 \mid X_i = x_1, X_p]$$

for the bidder actually holding the highest private information signal, x_1. (All symmetric, noncooperative Nash equilibria involve agents bidding as if $x_i = x_1$, since their bid only "counts" when this presumption is satisfied.) However, due to the affiliation of the signal values, for bidders whose private information signals $x_i < x_1$, the public information signal will, *ex post*, raise the average expected value of the item. This will induce an upward revision of these bids, which in turn puts pressure on the bidder with the highest private information signal, x_1, to bid more out of strategic considerations.

As an experimental device, the use of the low private information signal, x_L, as the public information signal has several advantages. First, the RNNE bid function with public information is readily solved analytically with x_L. Second, x_L provides a substantial amount of information concerning the location of x_0, and the signal values rivals are likely to have. For signals in the interval (1),

$$E[x_0 \mid X_i = x_1, X_p = x_L] = (x_L + x_i)/2 \qquad (7)$$

provides a sufficient statistic for the value of x_0 given the set of private information signals distributed, under the presumption that $x_i = x_1$. From (7), it is clear that announcing x_L should reduce the average spread in beliefs about the underlying value of the item between any two bidders by one-half. Under private information conditions, a similar reduction in beliefs would require halving ε, as this halves the average spread between any two private information signals (as well as the spread in expected values under (5)). Thus, announcing x_L induces strong competitive pressures on the high bidder and translates into relatively large increases in seller's revenues, or reduced bidder's profits (see equation (9) below), while still maintaining an interesting auction.

The RNNE bid function with, public information, x_L, and private information signals in the interval (1) is[17]

$$b(x_i, x_L) = x_L + \left[\frac{N-2}{N-1} \right]$$

$$\times \left[\frac{x_i + x_L}{2} - x_L \right] \qquad (8)$$

$$= \frac{N}{2(N-1)} x_L + \frac{(N-2)}{2(N-1)} x_i.$$

Expected profits are substantially diluted, being

$$E[\Pi \mid W, X_L] = \varepsilon/(N+1). \qquad (9)$$

This is a little more than one-half of the expected profits under private information conditions (3).

With risk aversion we cannot unambiguously determine whether public information will increase or decrease average seller's revenues (Milgrom and Weber). The impact depends upon the particular form of the utility function assumed, the degree of risk aversion displayed, and the extent to which public information dilutes private information differences. Nevertheless, we would anticipate that under most plausible scenarios, the relatively large dilution of private information differentials inherent in releasing x_L, would cause seller's revenues to increase, or at least not to decrease.

2. Judgmental Failures: The Winner's Curse

The judgmental error underlying the winner's curse consists of the high bidder's systematic overestimation of the item's value. To the extent that the magnitude of these judgmental errors decreases as the uncertainty concerning the value of the item decreases, public information will result in a downward revision in the most optimistic bidder's valuation of the item. This introduces a potentially powerful offset to any strategic forces tending to raise bids.[18] This effect is well illustrated through extending the notion of strategic discounting to auctions with public information, and comparing the resultant discount function with (6).

Under strategic discounting, we continue to assume that bidders employ naive expectations to determine the value of the item, to the point that they ignore the positional information inherent in announcing x_L, and act as if they are in a private value auction. For x_i and x_L in the interval (1), a naive expectation of x_0 is the same as (7):

$$E[x_0 \mid x_i, x_L] = (x_i + x_L)/2. \tag{10}$$

Consequently, under risk neutrality, the strategic discount function and the RNNE bid function (8) coincide here. Note that this follows directly from the fact that the naive (10) and sophisticated expectations (7) coincide. In markets with private information, the two bid functions differ as the expectations differ.

Comparing (6) with (8), $b^s(x_i) > b(x_i, x_L)$ on average for all $N \geq 3$. In auctions where bidders employ naive expectations, but strategic discounting, announcing x_L will result in *reductions* in average seller's revenues (increases in average bidder's profits) with 3 or more bidders. Finally, given that previous experimental studies indicate sensitivity to the strategic implications inherent in auction markets, and the coincidence of the strategic bid function with the RNNE bid function, the RNNE model should provide a fairly good predictor of market performance with x_L announced, irrespective of its predictive adequacy in comparable markets with private information only.

2.3 Summary of Research Questions of Primary Interest

We conclude this section by summarizing the research questions of primary interest in the form of hypotheses to be tested.

Hypothesis 1. *Under private information conditions market outcomes for experienced bidders are observationally indistinguishable from the RNNE as* (i) *the high signal holder usually wins the auction, and* (ii) *prices do not deviate substantially or systematically from the RNNE prediction.*

Hypothesis 2. *Announcing x_L, the lowest private information signal, raises average seller's revenues by the average amount predicted under the RNNE model.*

Hypothesis 3. *Under private information conditions, experienced bidders avoid the winner's curse as average profits are closer to the RNNE level than the zero/negative profits predicted under the winner's curse.*

Hypothesis 4. *Public information raises average seller's revenue.*

Hypothesis 5. *Hypotheses 3 and 4 apply uniformly to experiments with small and large numbers of bidders.*

Hypothesis 6. *Bidders are sensitive to the strategic implications of the auctions so that when the strategic discounting model and the RNNE model coincide, the RNNE model provides a reasonable characterization of the data.*

Hypotheses 1 and 2 involve strong predictions, which if satisfied would imply satisfaction of all the other hypotheses as well. Hypotheses 3–5 involve weaker predictions which may be satisfied even though Hypotheses 1 and 2, strictly interpreted, fail. Nevertheless confirmation of these weaker predictions would indicate that the RNNE model provided a reasonable "ballpark" characterization of behavior in general: that for experienced bidders, at least, the repeated nature of market decision processes in conjunction with survival pressures and profit opportunities, eliminate the judgmental failures underlying the winner's curse. Further, conditional on the confirmation of Hypotheses 3–5, one of the key policy implications of the theory, the revenue-enhancing effects of public information, would be reasonably accurate as well.

Finally, Hypothesis 6 captures the notion that bidders in private value auction experiments have been shown to be sensitive to the strategic implications inherent in these auctions. Hence, we would expect the RNNE model to perform well here when its predictions coincide with strategic discounting. If Hypothesis 6 is satisfied, but Hypotheses 1–5 are not, we have indirect evidence that it is the judgmental errors underlying the winner's curse that are responsible for the breakdown in the model's performance.

3. Experimental Results

3.1 Bidding Patterns with Private Information

Figures 3.1–3.5 provide representative data for market outcomes over time. The rank of the high bidder's signal value is shown at the top of each figure: 1 for the highest signal value, 2 for the second highest, etc. Closed triangles show the difference between $E[x_0 \mid X_i = x_1]$ for the high bidder and the high bid. A negative (positive) value here indicates that the high bid exceeded (fell below) $E[x_0 \mid X_i = x_1]$, implying negative (positive) expected profits should the high signal holder win the auction. Cross marks show actual profits earned, with closed circles showing profits predicted under the RNNE: cross marks below (above) closed circles indicate that the actual bid exceeded (was less than) the RNNE prediction and by how much. Eyeballing the data, there appears to be

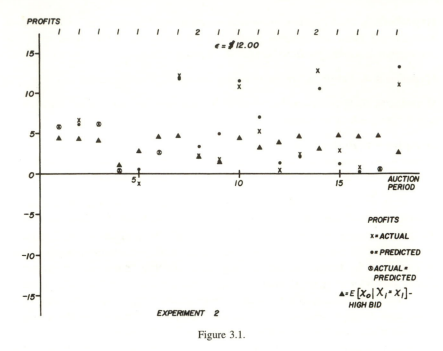

Figure 3.1.

little systematic variation in bids over time, within a given auction series, independent of variations in N and ε.

Table 3.2 provides summary statistics of auction outcomes.[19] Columns 4–6 show, respectively, actual profits earned, profits predicted under the RNNE, and profits earned as a percentage of the RNNE prediction. For comparative purposes, column 3 shows profits predicted under the strategic discounting formulation (profits predicted using the bid function 6, assuming that the highest signal holder always won the auction). The last two columns report the average frequency with which the high signal holder won the item, and the frequency with which the high bid exceeded $E[x_0 \mid X_i = x_1]$.

The auction series were ordered by the number of active bidders, beginning with the small group experiments, as we kept drawing the same conclusion: there were substantial differences in the ability of the RNNE bidding model to provide a ballpark characterization of the data in auctions involving small numbers (3–4) of bidders compared to those with large numbers (6–7) of bidders. In auction series that began with small numbers of bidders, one can observe bankruptcies (series 6) and some bidding in excess of $E[x_0 \mid X_i = x_1]$. There was at least one large group series where average profits were positive and bidding was generally below $E[x_0 \mid X_i = x_1]$ (series 7 large). However, the general pattern was one of positive average profits in small groups which, while well below the RNNE criteria, were clearly closer to the RNNE prediction than the zero/negative profit levels of the winner's curse: profits averaged across experiments with 3–4 bidders were $4.68 per auction period, about 65.1 per-

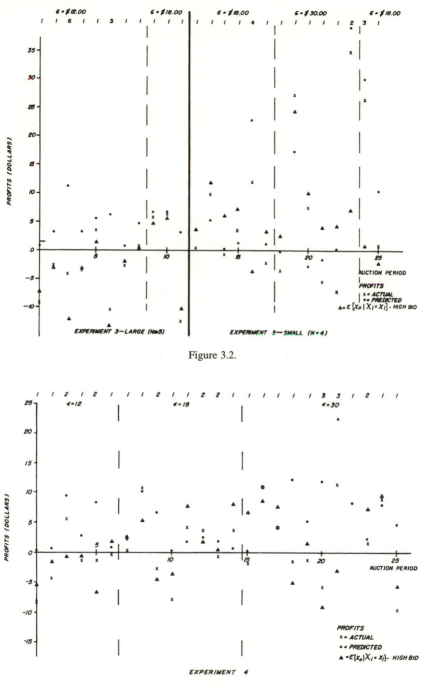

Figure 3.2.

Figure 3.3.

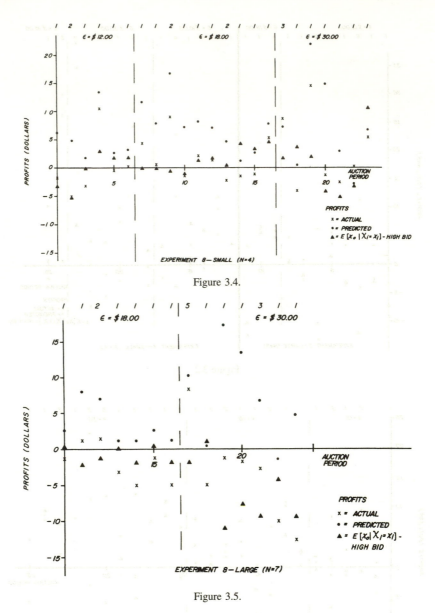

Figure 3.4.

Figure 3.5.

cent of the RNNE models prediction of $7.19 per auction period.[20] In contrast, auctions involving 6–7 bidders had average actual profits of $-$8.88 per auction period. While this is substantially better than profits predicted under strategic discounting, $-$8.89, indicating considerable adjustment to the adverse-selection problem, these adjustments were far from complete, as profit levels were negative, closer to the winner's curse prediction than the RNNE prediction of $4.68 per auction period. Further, comparing large and small group auctions, actual profits decreased substantially more than profit opportunities as measured by the RNNE criteria. The latter profit criteria dropped by $2.51 per auction period, while actual profits fell by $5.56. Thus, in going from small to large groups, profit performance deteriorated above and beyond that predicted under the RNNE.

In both small and large groups, the bidder with the high private information signal generally won. Averaging across auction series, the percentages were 76.6 and 68.9 percent for small and large groups, respectively. Thus, the adverse-selection mechanism hypothesized to underly the winner's curse was present for both group sizes. The high bid, b_1, was below $E[x_0 \mid X_i = x_1]$ in 82.7 percent of all auctions involving small number of bidders, but was below this value in only 46.2 percent of those auctions involving large numbers. The judgmental errors underlying the winner's curse were largely absent in small groups, but were quite prevalent in larger groups.[21]

Table 3.3 shows the relationship between profits and ε where the averages are computed over auction periods. We continue to distinguish between auctions involving small (3–4) and large (6–7) numbers of bidders, and pool the data for $\varepsilon = 24$ and $\varepsilon = 30$ as there were relatively few observations at $\varepsilon = 24$. In auctions involving small numbers of bidders, actual profits increased with increases in ε and constituted a relatively stable fraction of the profits predicted under the RNNE. With large numbers of bidders (6–7), average losses decreased with increases in ε, with positive average profits earned at $\varepsilon = 24$–30. Reduced losses with ε increasing implies that bids were reduced proportionately more relative to signal values. A stable proportionate discount in terms of ε would have resulted in larger absolute dollar losses as ε increased.[22] Instead, subjects took advantage of the increased profit opportunities inherent in the increased value of ε.

We used multiple regression analysis to summarize and quantify the influences on bidding in the private value auctions, Using an error components model, and restricting our analysis to signal values in the interval (1), Table 3.4 shows the results of two alternative bid function specifications.[23] The first regression involves a generalized version of the bid function (2), allowing for a nonzero intercept and including numbers of bidders as a right-hand side variable. Under this specification, both the intercept coefficient and the coefficient associated with the variable Y in (2) were not significantly different from zero. The second regression drops these two terms. Under both specifications, the x_i critically influences bids with an estimated coefficient value close to 1.0, as implied under the RNNE bid function and under strategic bidding. Further, bidders were clearly sensitive to changes in ε, so that we can soundly reject any naive bidding models which postulate a constant, fixed discount relative to x_i. On the other hand, the coefficient on ε is significantly below unity, and this contradicts the RNNE bid function. These results parallel those from private value auctions, where increases in the distribution of underlying values resulted in lower bids, but these bids were not reduced as much as predicted under the risk neutrality hypothesis (Kagel, Harstad, and Levin). Finally, the aggressive

TABLE 3.2

Profits and Bidding by Experiment and Number of Active Bidders: Private Information Conditions (Profits measured in dollars)

Auction Series (No. of Periods)	No. of Active Bidders	Average Profits with Strategic Discounting (standard error of mean)	Average Actual Profits (t-statistics)[a]	Average Profits under RNNE (standard error of mean)	Profits as a Percentage of RNNE Prediction	Percentage of Auctions Won by High Signal Holder	Percentage of High Bids $b_1 > E[x_0|X_i = X_1]$
6 (31)	3–4	3.25 (1.51)	3.73 (2.70)[b]	9.51 (1.70)	39.2	67.7	22.6
2 (18)	4	–.75 (1.07)	4.61 (4.35)[c]	4.99 (1.03)	92.6	88.9	0.0
3 small (14)	4	–3.82 (2.40)	7.53 (2.07)	6.51 (2.65)	115.7	78.6	14.3
7 small (19)	4	–.12 (1.56)	5.83 (3.35)[c]	8.56 (2.07)	68.1	63.2	10.5
8 small (23)	4	–2.24 (1.05)	1.70 (1.56)	6.38 (1.21)	26.6	84.6	39.1

1 (18)	5	−1.90 (.85)	2.89 (3.14)[c]	5.19 (.86)	55.7	72.2	27.8
3 large (11)	5–7	−5.19 (.55)	−2.92 (−1.49)	3.65 (.62)	−80.5	81.8	63.6
7 large (18)	6	−10.11 (.96)	1.89 (1.67)	4.70 (1.03)	40.2	72.2	22.2
4 (25)	6–7	−10.03 (1.05)	−.23 (−.15)	4.78 (.92)	−4.8	69.2	46.2
5 (26)	7	−8.07 (1.04)	−.41 (−.44)	5.25 (1.03)	−7.8	42.3	65.4
8 large (14)	7	−11.04 (1.35)	−2.74 (−2.04)	5.03 (1.40)	−54.8	78.6	71.4

[a]Tests null hypothesis that mean is different from 0.0.
[b]Significant at 5% level. 2-tailed t-test.
[c]Significant at 1% level, 2-tailed t-test.

TABLE 3.3
Profits and Bidding under Varying Levels of ε (All profits in dollars)

No. of Bidders	ε	Average Profits with Strategic Discounting (standard error of mean)	Average Actual Profits (t-statistics)[a]	Average Profits under RNNE[b] (standard error of mean)	Profits as a Percentage of the RNNE Prediction
3–4	12	−1.24 (.69)	2.60 (1.74)	4.52 (1.44)	57.5
	18	−.24 (1.03)	3.98 (3.71)[d]	7.20 (1.05)	55.4
	24/30	.60 (1.94)	6.75 (3.33)[d]	11.22 (2.06)	60.2
6–7	12	−3.68 (.54)	−1.86 (−2.21)[c]	3.46 (.56)	−53.8
	18	−8.51 (.52)	−.95 (−1.00)	3.19 (.51)	−29.8
	24/30	−12.31 (.89)	.60 (.51)	7.12 (.94)	8.4

[a]Tests null hypothesis that mean is different from 0.0.
[b]Based on sample of signal values drawn.
[c]Significant at 5% level, 2-tailed t-test.
[d]Significant at 1% level, 2-tailed t-test.

forces associated with increased numbers of bidders win out over the item valuation influences, as we find a statistically significant, positive coefficient associated with N under both specifications. The increased aggressiveness of individual bids with increases in N is in direct contradiction to the predictions of the RNNE bidding model. It adds to the dilution of bidders profits associated with increased N predicted under the RNNE, with the net result a persistent winner's curse with $N = 6$ or 7.

Learning patterns over time are not explored in detail here. The interested reader should consult Kagel et al. (1996) where individual learning patterns of inexperienced bidders are analyzed. The data reported there show considerable learning on survivors part, as most start out bidding in excess of $E[x_0 \mid X_i = x_1]$. Comparing the results here with end-of-experiment performance for these inexperienced bidders shows continued learning as well: averaging over the last 5 periods of 5 auction series of 3–4 inexperienced bidders shows 28 percent of all high bids in excess of $E[x_0 \mid X_i = x_1]$ (compared to 17.3 percent here) with profits averaging 27.5 percent of the RNNE prediction (compared to 65.1 percent here).[24] It is important to note, however, that the learning resulting in the strong performance of the RNNE model in small groups appears to be situa-

TABLE 3.4
Error Components Estimates of Bid Function in Private Information Markets[a]

$b(x_i) = -4.30$	$+ 1.00x_i$	$- .73\varepsilon$	
(3.36)	(.002)	(.03)	
	$+ .70N$	$- .02Y$	$R^2 = .99$
	(.16)	(.14)	$\sigma_\eta = 4.94$
$b(x_i) = 1.00x_i$	$- .74\varepsilon$	$+ .65N$	$R^2 = .99$
(.002)	(.03)	(.15)	$\sigma_\eta = 4.94$

[a]Standard errors are shown in parentheses.

tionally specific, and does not provide the "understanding" to respond appropriately to increased numbers of rivals (see Table 4), or to avoid the winner's curse in large group auctions.

3.2 Effects of Public Information on Seller's Revenues

Table 3.5 shows the actual effects of announcing x_L on average revenues and the predicted effects under both the RNNE and the strategic discounting models. As in Table 3.2, we have ordered the results by number of active bidders.

Averaging across the three auction series with small numbers of bidders, x_L raises revenues an average of $2.75 per auction period. Pooling auction periods, a t-test shows this to be statistically significant ($t = 2.41$, $p < .02$, 1-tailed test), although well below the RNNE prediction of a $6.30 increase in revenues. Public information reduced revenues in series 3, the auction series which came closest to the RNNE model's predictions under private information conditions. Nevertheless, this seems like an anomaly rather than the norm, since under all other conditions where the winner's curse was weak or nonexistent, as it was in series 6 and series 7 small and large, revealing the low information signal, x_L, raised seller's revenues (also see the discussion that follows).

Averaging across auctions with large numbers of bidders, public information *reduced* seller's revenues $1.79 per auction period. A t-test based on pooled observations indicates that this decrease is statistically significant ($t = -1.48$, $p < .08$, 1-tailed test). While the reduced revenues are well below the predictions of the strategic discounting model, they are opposite in sign and magnitude to the RNNE model which calls for a $1.78 *increase* in revenue.

A within-auction series analysis reinforces the importance of the winner's curse in determining whether public information raises or lowers revenues. The first two columns of Table 3.6 show the effects of announcing x_L conditional on the presence or absence of a winner's curse in large group auctions, for those auction periods where the RNNE model predicts an increase. A *chi*-square test shows the winner's curse to significantly affect the validity of the RNNE model's prediction ($\chi^2 = 4.25$, $p < .05$). The third column of the table shows

TABLE 3.5
Effects of Public Information on Seller's Revenues (All revenue figures in dollars)

Auction Series (No. of Periods)	No. of Active Bidders	Actual (t-statistic)[a]	Predicted (standard error of mean) RNNE Model	Predicted (standard error of mean) Strategic Discounting
6 (23)	3–4	4.38 (2.71)[b]	7.62 (1.54)	1.38 (1.41)
3 small (14)	4	−2.71 (−.99)	3.83 (2.05)	−6.51 (1.58)
7 small (11)	4	6.58 (2.79)[b]	7.46 (1.74)	−3.46 (1.52)
7 large (18)	6	.22 (.15)	1.64 (.87)	−13.16 (1.26)
4 (18)	6–7	−3.20 (−1.36)	1.25 (.82)	−15.75 (1.07)
5 (20)	7	−2.40 (−1.83)	2.43 (.86)	−12.34 (1.30)

[a]Tests null hypothesis that mean is 0.0.
[b]Significant at 5% level, 2-tailed t-test.

the effects on revenue in the absence of a winner's curse in the small group auctions. The pattern here is much the same as found in auctions with 6–7 bidders in the absence of a winner's curse ($\chi^2 = .086$).[25]

In the two auction series where public information consisted of posting an additional, randomly drawn, private information signal, public information raised revenues $.27 per auction (an average increase of −$.80 in experiment 1 and $1.33 in experiment 2). Note that neither of these series exhibited significant traces of the winner's curse under private information conditions. In contrast, in an earlier series of experiments involving inexperienced subjects, revealing a random public information signal consistently *reduced* revenues, in this case by an average of $2.95 per auction (Kagel et al., 1984). In two of these four auction series, average profits were negative under private information conditions, while in 3 of the 4, the high bid exceeded $E[x_0 \mid X_1 = x_1]$ in 40 percent or more of the auctions. These results serve to reinforce the hypothesis that an absence of a winner's curse is a necessary condition for public information to raise average revenues.

Table 3.7 reports market outcomes relative to the RNNE model's predictions with x_L announced. Average actual profits were positive in all experiments. While there is considerable variation in profits relative to the RNNE model's

TABLE 3.6
Effects of the Winner's Curse on Revenue Raising Effects of Public Information[a]

	Number of Periods in Auction		
	Large Numbers (6–7)		Small Numbers[b] (3–4)
Change in Seller's Revenues	Winner's Curse	No Winner's Curse	No Winner's Curse
Increase	6	12	29
Decrease	11	5	10

[a]Auction market periods where RNNE predicted an increase in seller's revenues. Winner's curse defined in terms of high bid in private information market in excess of $E[x_0 \mid X_i = X_1]$.

[b]Winner's curse present in three auction periods where RNNE predicts increase in seller's revenues. Hence omitted.

predictions across auction series (especially series 3 and 6), on average profits were only slightly less than predicted ($3.20 actual vs. $3.41 predicted). Further, unlike private information conditions, there were no systematic differences in realized profits relative to predictions as the number of active bidders varied. These results, at the market level at least, are consistent with our earlier sugges-

TABLE 3.7
Profits and Bidding with Public Information (x_L) (all profits in dollars)

Auction Series (no. of periods)	No. of Bidders	Average Actual Profits (t-statistic)[a]	Average Profits under RNNE (standard error of mean)	Profits as a Percentage of RNNE Prediction	Percentage of Auctions Won by High Signal Holder
6 (23)	3–4	.15 (.08)	2.96 (1.60)	5.1	30.4
3 small (14)	4	10.24 (3.33)[c]	2.68 (2.03)	382.0	21.4
7 small (11)	4	2.07 (.86)	4.54 (2.00)	45.6	18.2
7 large (18)	6	1.67 (1.56)	3.06 (.62)	54.6	27.8
4 (18)	6–7	3.43 (2.24)[b]	4.14 (1.04)	82.9	44.4
5 (20)	7	1.64 (1.62)	3.06 (.86)	53.6	35.0

[a]Tests null hypothesis that mean is 0.0.
[b]Significant at 5% level, 2-tailed t-test.
[c]Significant at 1% level, 2-tailed t-test.

TABLE 3.8

Error Components Estimates of Bid Function in Markets with x_L Announced

$b(x_i, x_L) =$	$-.95$	$+ .24x_i$	$- .07x_i^*$	$+ .72x_L$	$+ .12x_L^*$	$+ .14_\varepsilon$	$+ .08N$	$R^2 = .98$
	(6.2)	(.05)	(.06)	(.05)	(.06)	(.07)	(.70)	$\sigma_\eta = 7.39$
$b(x_i, x_L) =$		$.24x_i$	$- .07x_i^*$	$+ .72x_L$	$+ .12x_L^*$	$+ .14_\varepsilon$		$R^2 = .98$
		(.05)	(.05)	(.05)	(.06)	(.06)		$\sigma_\eta = 7.37$

Note: $x_i^* = x_i$ if $N = 6$ or 7, $x_i^* = 0$ otherwise; $x_L^* = x_L$ if $N = 6$ or 7, $x_L = 0$ otherwise.
Standard errors are shown in parentheses.

tion that the RNNE model would provide a more accurate characterization of performance with x_L announced, compared with private information conditions.

More detailed analysis of the data, however, shows that more is at work here than simple strategic discounting with all bidders employing identical bid functions. With x_L announced, there is almost a complete breakdown of the prediction that the bidder with the highest private information signal wins the auction. In these experiments the high private information signal holder won only 29.5 percent of all auctions. This is only modestly above what one would expect if chance factors alone determined whether the high private signal holder won, an expected frequency of 21.8 percent.

Detailed examination of the data shows a handful of bidders (20.0 percent) winning a disproportionately large number (57.7 percent) of the auctions with x_L announced. This handful of bidders did quite well as a group, earning average profits of $2.79 per auction period won, as compared to $2.89 for all other bidders. A distinguishing characteristic of these bidders is that they were relatively more aggressive than their rivals under private information conditions (ranking bids as a fraction of signal values consistently placed them in the top half of all bidders). The increased aggressiveness of this handful of bidders in the public information markets (they won only 15.1 percent of all private information auctions in which they did not have the highest private information signal, compared to 54.7 percent of the corresponding public information auctions) is directly attributable to the sharp reduction in beliefs about the underlying value of item inherent in announcing x_L. This reduction in the effective dispersion of information concerning x_0 permitted differences in risk attitudes and information processing capacities to play an increased role in the outcomes of auctions with public information.[26]

Table 3.8 reports the results of statistical estimates of individual bid functions with x_L announced. Recall from (8) that the parameters associated with the variables x_L and x_i are a function of the number of bidders present. The specifications in Table 3.8 employ different slope coefficients for these variables in small group ($N = 3 - 4$) and large group ($N = 6 - 7$) cases. With $N = 3 - 4$, the estimated slope coefficients for public and private information, are close to the theoretical bid function prediction (with $N = 4$, these are .67 and .33 for public and private information, respectively). With $N = 6 - 7$, more weight is attached to public rather than private information, in contrast to the theoretical bid function prediction (with $N = 7$, predicted weights are .58 and .42, respectively). Further, ε has a modest positive, statistically significant, effect on bids, contrary to the predictions of both the RNNE and strategic discounting models, in which x_L and x_i capture all the information necessary (recall equation (8)).

3.3 Summary of Experimental Outcomes of Primary Interest

The data permit us to reach clear conclusions regarding the research hypotheses of primary interest specified in Section 2.3. With respect to Hypotheses 1 and 2, we reject the strong form of the RNNE bidding model, irrespective of the number of rivals in the market or whether the market involves private or public information. Bidding consistently exceeded the RNNE prediction in private information markets, was highly variable relative to the RNNE reference point in markets with public information, and x_L failed to raise revenues by the predicted amount, even in markets without a winner's curse. The weak form of the RNNE model consistently outperformed the winner's curse and the strategic discounting model in markets with small numbers of rivals, consistent with Hypotheses 3 and 4. However this ballpark characterization of the data failed on both counts in markets with large numbers of rivals, leading us to reject Hypothesis 5. Finally, bidders were sensitive to the strategic implications of the auctions, responding correctly to variations in e and coming close, on average, to the RNNE model's prediction with x_L announced. This confirms Hypothesis 6, which in turn suggests that the rejection of Hypotheses 1–5, particularly the rejection of Hypothesis 5, follows from the judgmental errors underlying the winner's curse.

4. Toward Generalizability: But Is This How the Real World Operates?

A common criticism of experimental research in economics is that behavior in the laboratory is unlikely to be representative of field behavior. This criticism increases, as well it should, with the degree to which laboratory behavior deviates from accepted economic theory and common understanding of what constitutes "rational" economic behavior. Critics argue that auction market subjects, MBA students and senior undergraduates, are inherently less sophisticated, and clearly less experienced, than executives in the relevant industry, that experimental subjects do not have as much time to think and respond to events as industry executives, and that they lack the assistance of expert advisors that many industries have, to cite some of the prominent criticisms we have encountered. One can rebut these arguments on grounds that the experimental designs drastically simplify the decision-making structure, thereby obviating the need for expert advisors and reducing time requirements to make sensible decisions.

Further, experimental subjects receive substantially more feedback, with shorter delays, regarding the outcomes of their decisions, so that the feedback loops that promote learning and adjustment over time are substantially stronger for experimental subjects compared to industry executives. (This is particularly true in the case of OCS lease sales where executives know that returns on investment will only be revealed years after bids have been accepted, and the responsible parties might well be in different positions within the company, or moved to a rival firm.)

Logical arguments can only go so far in debates of this sort. The question posed here is, what do the relevant data outside the laboratory look like compared to laboratory-generated data? Is the same model capable of organizing behavior in both settings? Do the field data obviously contradict the laboratory data?

The remainder of this section examines these issues in the context of the U.S. government's outer continental shelf lease sales. Note that our objective here is not to definitively test between competing explanations using field data. If we thought the field data had this kind of potential, there would be no need to resort to laboratory experiments in the first place (see Vernon Smith, 1982, and Charles Plott, 1982, for general discussions of the problems involved in using field data to test between models of market behavior and the advantages of laboratory experiments). Rather, our objective is to show that a reasonable analysis of the available data does not falsify the hypothesis that similar economic processes are at work in both settings. If this can be done, the burden of proof rests on those who would argue that the results don't generalize to demonstrate that their arguments are correct.

The concept of a winner's curse arose from petroleum geologists analysis of OCS bidding patterns and industry based calculation of rates of return from winning lease sales (Capen et al.; Lorenz and Dougherty). In a more recent analysis, Walter Mead, Asbjorn Moseidjord, and Philip Sorensen (1983) found after-tax rates of return on all OCS leases in the Gulf of Mexico issued from 1954 to 1969 to be less than average returns on equity for U.S. manufacturing corporations. Mead et al. view lease purchases as high risk investments and conclude that ". . . they (lessees) have historically received no risk premium and may have paid too much for the right to explore for and produce oil and gas on federal offshore lands" (1983, pp. 42–43).[27] In light of the effects of public information on bidder's profits reported here, a second element of Mead et al.'s (1983) calculations, namely rate of return *differentials* between drainage and wildcat leases, provides important corroborating evidence for the argument that lessees probably paid "too much" in these early OCS lease sales. The remainder of this section details this argument.[28]

A wildcat lease involves a tract for which there are no drilling data available that would indicate potential productivity. When a hydrocarbon reservoir has been located on a wildcat tract that is expected to extend into adjacent unleased acreage, the adjacent tract is defined by the U.S. Geological Service (USGS) as a drainage tract. Considerably more information is available regarding the economic potential of drainage than wildcat tracts. This information has both public and private components. An important public information component is that drainage tracts are unlikely to be dry, thereby significantly reducing the uncertainty (relative to wildcat tracts) that hydrocarbons will be found. However, developers of the wildcat tract (called neighbors) are likely to have superior private information relative to non-neighbors regarding the quantity of oil likely to be found, oil pressures, and other significant seismic information.[29]

If the information available on drainage leases were purely public, it should, according to Nash equilibrium bidding theory, raise average seller's revenues, hence reducing bidder's profits (recall Section 2).[30] If the information were purely private, under Nash equilibrium bidding theory it would increase the rate of return for insiders (neighbors) relative to outsiders (nonneighbors), *and* reduce the average rate of return for non-neighbors below what would be earned in the absence of insider information (Wilson, 1975a, b; M. Weverbergh, 1979). If the added information on drainage leases contains both public and private information elements, rates of return for neighbors should be greater than for nonneighbors, but with nonneighbor returns definitely less than in the absence of the additional information (both the public and private information components push in this direction for nonneighbors).

What Mead et al. found were higher rates of return on drainage compared to wildcat leases for *both* neighbors (88.6 percent higher) *and* nonneighbors (56.2 percent higher). Further, nonneighbors won 43.2 percent of all drainage leases. While the higher rate of return for neighbors compared with nonneighbors can be explained by the presence of insider information (the explanation Mead et al. offer, 1983, 1984), the substantially higher rates of return for nonneighbors remains puzzling within the context of Nash equilibrium bidding theory. However, the higher rate of return for *both* neighbors and nonneighbors on drainage leases is perfectly consistent with our experimental findings, given the existence of a winner's curse in bidding on wildcat leases. According to this explanation, the additional information available from neighbor tracts served to correct for the overly optimistic estimate of lease value recorded in the average winning bids on wildcat tracts, thereby raising average profits for both neighbors and nonneighbors alike. In this respect, the OCS lease data parallel our experimental results with public information in the presence of a winner's curse.

What alternative explanations are available to explain *both* nonneighbors and neighbors rates of return being higher on drainage leases? Mead et al. suggest two alternatives. First, one might argue that the lower rate of return on wildcat leases reflects the option value of the private information consequent on discovering hydrocarbons. The higher rate of return of neighbors over nonneighbors on the drainage leases certainly suggests that neighbors had valuable proprietary information, the prospect of which would depress the value of the wildcat leases. However, returns to this proprietary information were far from certain to be realized, while the differential overall rate of return on leases in the Gulf, counting wildcats alone vs. counting wildcats plus drainage leases, was small, amounting to 7 percent of the wildcat rate of return (Mead et al., 1983). Thus the revealed value of the option is small and is unlikely to fully account for the depressed rate of return on wildcats relative to nonneighbors. Second, one can argue that the existence of insider information (and its common knowledge) scared off nonneighbors so that they did not bid, or bid very little, relative to lease value. Consequently, when nonneighbors won, since they bid quite low, they obtained higher rates of return as well. However, the frequency with which nonneighbors won drainage leases seems inconsistent with this argument.[31] To be sure, the average number of bids on drainage leases was less than on wildcats (2.88 vs. 3.33), but the data suggest only a modest 6.4 percent decline in the rate of return in going from leases with 2 bids to leases with 3–4 bids (Mead et al., 1983; 1994).[32]

Note that we do not dispute Mead et al.'s (1994) argument that neighbors had proprietary information leading to higher rates of return on drainage leases than wildcats, or on drainage leases relative to nonneighbors. What we are claiming is that this proprietary information does not fully account for the substantially higher rates of return on drainage leases over wildcat leases for *both* neighbors and nonneighbors alike. Rather this element of the data is more readily explained by the public information component of the drainage lease designation, in conjunction with a winner's curse on wildcat leases. This explanation has the virtue of parsimony and consistency with the experimental results reported here.[33]

Our analysis of field data has been limited to 1954–69, prior to the publication of Capen et al.'s article alerting the industry to the presence of a winner's curse, and suggesting ways to avoid it. Many would argue that adjustments in bidding in the 1970's, partly in response to Capen et al.'s article and related publications, has eliminated the winner's curse in OCS lease sales, although opinions are not unanimous on the subject (see Lorenz and Dougherty, for example). We know of no rate-of-return studies on drainage vs. wildcat leases for the 1970's similar to Mead et al.'s for the 1960's that might help resolve the issue. We do know that at times there are significant discrepancies between cognitive understanding of the "right" thing to do and actual behavior. For mineral rights auctions, this involves firms recognizing and admitting that their geologists' estimates of value (and their economists' estimates of future price) have a significant error component, and that in the absence of insider information are unlikely to be better (on average) than their rivals. Such an admission is no small matter when paying substantial salaries to these professionals. As such we reserve judgment for the moment on the issue of a continuing winner's curse in OCS sales. Even assuming elimination of a winner's curse in more recent OCS lease sales does not affect our argument here, however: the available data outside the laboratory are consistent with data inside it in the absence of extensive efforts to alert bidders to the presence of a winner's curse.

5. Conclusions

Our experiments provide an empirical example of a market where individual judgment errors significantly alter market outcomes. Bidders in common value auctions, as in other auctions, are sensitive to the strategic opportunities inherent in the auction process. However, when strategic considerations and adverse-selection forces resulting from uncertainty about the value of the item conflict, behavior falls to conform, in important ways, with the requirements of Nash equilibrium bidding strategies.

Although we reject the general applicability of Nash equilibrium bidding models, market outcomes come closer to the risk-neutral Nash equilibrium model's predictions than to the winner's curse in auctions with small numbers (3–4) of bidders. In addition, there is considerable adjustment to the adverse-selection problem with large numbers (6–7) of bidders. However, these adjustments are far from complete, as profit levels are consistently negative, in conformity with the winner's curse. The existence of a winner's curse in large groups, in conjunction with the positive effect of the number of bidders on the size of individual bids, indicates that avoidance of the winner's curse in small groups is specific to the situation, and does not carry over to auctions with larger numbers of bidders. Bidders have learned to avoid the winner's curse in small groups out of a trial and error survival process, as opposed to "understanding" the adverse-selection problem as it applies to new situations.

Accounting for judgmental errors in these markets has some practical policy implications in terms of whether sellers choose to obtain and release information narrowing down the value of the auctioned item. In the absence of judgmental errors, this information clearly enhances seller's revenues, as Nash equilibrium bidding theory predicts. In the presence of judgmental errors, however, such information will almost surely reduce average revenues, a factor ignored to date in the literature.

Given sufficient experience and feedback regarding the outcomes of their decisions, we have no doubt that our experimental subjects, as well as most bidders in "real world" settings, would eventually learn to avoid the winner's curse in any particular set of circumstances. The winner's curse is a disequilibrium phenomenon that will correct itself given sufficient time and the right kind of information feedback.[34] Clearly the attenuation of the feedback loop between a decision and determining the outcomes of that decision, as is commonly the case in outer continental shelf lease sales and a number of other settings, serves to perpetuate the phenomena. Further, comparative evaluations of management performance in terms of money "left on the table" (the difference between the high bid and the second high bid) can do little to arrest the problem since the winner's curse is ubiquitous and applies fairly uniformly across individuals at early stages of the learning process (Kagel et al., 1986). Finally, to the extent that market participants feel that they have an inside edge, and better judgmental abilities than their rivals, the winner's curse is bound to be difficult to eliminate.

Apart from the important task of replicating our experiments, a number of interesting research questions remain to be explored. Since avoidance of the winner's curse involves a learning process, exactly what mechanisms, if any, insure market memory of past mistakes? To what extent do new entrants learn from experience compared to learning from observation or formal education? Do inexperienced bidders learn more quickly in markets dominated by experienced bidders? What are the dynamics of markets characterized by continual entry of new "suckers" who must learn from personal experience, and do we observe these dynamics in field environments?

Notes

Financial support was received from the Information Science and Technology Division and the Economics Division of NSF the Energy Laboratory and the Center for Public Policy of the University of Houston-University Park. Ray Battalio, Don Meyer, and Carl Kogut ran auction series 1 and 2; Ron Harstad and Doug Dyer assisted in series 3–8. Doug Dyer and Susan Garvin provided valuable research assistance. This paper has benefited from discussion with Badi Baltagi, Ron Harstad, Mark Isaac, Asbjord Moseidjord, Jim Smith, and Philip Sorensen, the comments of Daniel Friedman, Robert Wilson, two referees, and participants in seminars at the University of Houston. Texas A&M University and the University of Indiana. An earlier version of this paper was presented at the 1985 Winter Econometric Society meetings. We alone are responsible for errors and omissions.

1. In auction series 1 and 2, the top three bids were posted, and the signal values underlying the bids were not revealed.

2. Series 1 and 2 had a $3 participation fee. Many subjects in series 3–7 had signed a contract to participate in 3 different auction series, for which they were paid a single participation fee of $25 at the end of the last series.

3. Once again, series 1 and 2 involved an exception to these procedures as profits and losses were computed and paid in both the public and private information markets.

4. The bid function had the form $b_{it} = \alpha_0 + \alpha_1 x_{it} + \alpha_2 Y_{it}$ as suggested by equation (2), where α_i were constants to be estimated (ε was constant in these auctions). The function was fit to individual subject data for signals in the interval (1), and a dummy variable added to account for simultaneous bidding in two auctions. Combining independent t-tests on the dummy variable coefficient using the z statistic suggested in Ben Winer (1971, p. 50), we were unable to identify any systematic effects associated with simultaneous bidding ($z = .124$).

5. For example, with 9 subjects and 7 active bidders, in period 1, subjects 1–7 were active; in period 2, subjects 2–8 were active, etc. Inactive subjects received signals and bid, but these bids were discarded (the latter was common knowledge).

6. Using a single set of private information signals and a single true value, x_0, 4 subjects first bid in a small market. Then, before these bids were opened, all 7 subjects bid in a large market. The 4 subjects in the small market continued to be determined through rotation, and bids only counted in one of the two markets using a coin flip rule. Raymond Battalio, Carl Kogut, and Donald Meyer (1983) report tests of the separability assumption underlying the dual market technique in private value auctions with varying numbers of bidders. They found no systematic biases associated with the dual market technique.

7. In a private value auction, bidders know their value for the item with certainty, but only the distribution of their rivals' values. Under the first-price rule, the high bidder

wins the item and earns profits equal to his private value less the bid price; others cam zero profits.

8. For $x_i < \underline{x} + \varepsilon$, the RNNE bid function is

$$b(x_i) = \underline{x} + (x_i + \varepsilon - \underline{x})/(N + 1)$$

and yields zero expected profits. This equilibrium bid function is obtained from Wilson (1977) under the initial condition $b(x_i) = \underline{x}$ for $x_i = \underline{x} - \varepsilon$. The initial condition for the bid function in (2) exploits continuity in the bid function at the junction point $x_i = \underline{x} + \varepsilon$. For $x_i > \bar{x} - \varepsilon$, the optimal bid function defies analytic solution. For observations in this interval, we employ the bid function (2) in comparing performance with the RNNE model. This tends to overstate the RNNE bid, hence underestimate the discrepancy between actual and predicted bids. Since the bias is small, and favors the null hypothesis, correcting for it will not change the conclusions reached. These bid functions are explicitly derived in Kagel et al. (1984).

9. The model can be generalized to account for both private value and common value elements (see Wilson, 1981, for example). In this case, the high signal holder does not always win the item, even assuming identical bidding strategies. Undoubtedly, actual auction sales, even OCS lease sales, contain both private and common value elements. Developments in Section 3 suggest that the Nash equilibrium model must be generalized to account for individual differences in risk attitudes and/or information-processing capacities, as well as simple random errors on bidder's part. Developing and testing such a model lies beyond the scope of the present paper.

10. Milgrom and Weber, section 8, and Steven Matthews (1986) develop some results for risk-averse bidders.

11. Results from private value auction experiments generally support an assumption of risk neutrality or risk aversion (James Cox, Bruce Roberson, and Vernon Smith, 1982; Kagel, Harstad, and Levin).

12. The size of the discount seems remarkably large, particularly for larger N's. To get an idea of the adverse-selection bias involved here, compared to alternative distributions, we normalize it in terms of the standard error of the underlying distribution. For x_i in (1) the standard error of the uniform distributions is $\sigma = 2\varepsilon / \sqrt{12}$. From (5), knowing that your estimate is the maximum of N such estimates, means that it is biased upwards by the amount $\sqrt{12}(N - 1)\sigma/2(N + 1)$. For $N = 2 - 8$, the resulting bias is quite similar to what would be found if the x_i were normally distributed around x_0.

13. Kagel, Harstad, and Levin experimentally investigate first-price sealed bid auctions with positively affiliated private values, where private values were generated using exactly the same procedures generating the x_i values here. Equation (6) corresponds to the bid function developed there. Note, these private value experiments show bids commonly in excess of (6) with $N = 6$.

14. In addition, an increase in ε increases the variance associated with the naive expectation (4). Thus to the extent that bidders are generally risk averse and bid more cautiously in the face of increased risk, but are poor Bayesians so that they continue to employ the naive expectation (4), they will respond correctly (at least directionally) to changing ε.

15. Differentiation of (2) with respect to N shows the Y term to require lower bids in the presence of more rivals.

16. An earlier reader of this paper argued that optimality by survival arguments implied "correct" responses under all possible states of the world, as survivors had experienced all relevant states and had learned to adapt to them. While acknowledging the

validity of this interpretation, it seems to rob the survival argument of empirical content as: 1) the survival process would never be complete as real economies are repeatedly subject to changing conditions and changes in the set of agents, and 2) there would be no role left for economic theory in terms of understanding behavioral processes or in predicting responses to novel economic conditions.

17. For x_i in the interval (1), the RNNE equilibrium bid function is obtained under the initial condition that $b(x_L) - x_L$ Note that ε is not explicitly represented in (8). However, the average difference $(x_i + x_L)/2 - x_L$ depends directly on ε.

18. Note that unbiased random errors, even if they do not result in high bids in excess of $E[x_0 \mid x_i = x_1]$, will not cancel out here in terms of their effects on seller's revenues. This results from the auction selection mechanism whereby market outcomes overrepresent bids with upward biases, resulting in average bids in excess of the RNNE. Consequently, if public information reduces the magnitude of these item valuation errors, public information will still result in a downward revision of the market price, which offsets the strategic forces promoting increased revenues. High bids in excess of $E[x_0 \mid x_i = x_1]$ can constitute an extreme form of these errors and/or a systematic tendency, on at least some bidder's part, to overestimate the item's value.

19. Our computations include all auctions under dual market procedures, regardless of whether bidders actually made profits (or losses) as a consequence of our coin flip procedure. Since the coin flip was made after bids from both markets had been accepted, its outcome should not affect decisions. Experiments involving experienced, as opposed to super-experienced, subjects had one or more dry runs with no money at stake. These auction periods are *not* included in the analysis.

20. Averages reported here and elsewhere in the text are simple, unweighted averages across experiments, unless noted otherwise. All RNNE profit calculations are exact, based on the bid function in (2) and fn. 8.

21. The adverse-selection discount identifying the winner's curse fails to account for the high signal holder not always winning the item. Bidders should have been responsive to this and used a smaller adverse-selection discount based on actual frequencies with which different ranked signal holders won. Since over 90 percent of all auctions were won by the first- or second-highest signal holder, $E[x_0 \mid x_i = x_2]$ serves as a reasonable *upper* bound on the relevant discount. Using this measure, less than 1 percent of all small group auctions had a winner's curse, while 28.7 percent of all large group auctions did. Our conclusion regarding the differential frequency of the winner's curse in large and small groups is unaffected, although the overall frequency is reduced substantially.

22. Recall that $E[x_0 \mid x_i = x_1]$ is decreasing in ε.

23. An error components specification was employed, with error term

$$\eta_{it} = u_i + \upsilon_{it} \qquad i = 1, \ldots, N; \qquad t = 1, \ldots, T;$$

where u_i is a subject-specific error term, assumed constant subject across auction series, and υ_{it} is an auction period error term. Standard assumptions were employed: $u_i \sim (0, \sigma_u^2)$ and $\upsilon_{it} \sim (0, \sigma_\upsilon^2)$ where u_{it} and υ_{it} are independent among each other and among themselves. Badi Baltagi's (1986) weighted least squares computational procedure was used to invert the variance-covariance matrix. A fixed-effects error specification generated similar coefficient estimates and standard errors. Permitting the u_i to vary with subject participation in different auction series yields similar estimates except for the variable N, which increases in value with no loss in statistical significance.

24. There are no large group end-of-experiment data from the inexperienced subject

experiments to compare with the results reported here, as bankruptcies precluded keeping groups of 6–7 bidders intact for very long.

25. Results similar to these have been found in a companion series of 6 second-price common value auction experiments.

26. However, these bidders were unable to overcome the inherent disadvantage of holding only public information, as their average profits did not deviate significantly from zero in cases where they held the low private information signal.

27. There is some argument as to whether investors require risk premiums for investing in oil and gas leases. A number of writers suggest that risk-averse bidders would require a premium relative to investing in alternative activities. Others, one of our referees included, argue that large oil companies with access to capital markets and having a diversified portfolio of leases would not be expected to earn risk premiums.

28. Our analysis is not concerned with absolute rates of return, or absolute present discounted value calculations, for OCS sales compared to other industries. Rather, we are concerned exclusively with *differences* in rate of return between drainage and wildcat leases. Differential rate calculations within an industry, by the same research team, should be relatively more robust to the empirical problems encountered in obtaining such measure than comparisons across industries by different research groups.

29. Only drainage leases have neighbors, namely those responsible for the development of the neighboring wildcat tract.

30. All leases had the same royalty rate and were allocated on the basis of a first-price cash bonus bid. Drainage leases were spread throughout the Gulf so that each lease is likely to represent an independent pool of oil (Asbjorn Moseidjord, personal communication). The revenue-raising (profit-reducing) effects of public information in the RNNE model are expectations based on samples of independent observations (Milgrom and Weber). Hence, the drainage lease sample satisfies the assumptions of the model.

31. Under Nash equilibrium bidding theory, it is not perfectly clear what ought to happen to the frequency with which the informationally disadvantaged will win auctions. We suspect that this depends critically on the underlying distributions of item value and private information signals, and the nature of the insider information. However, all formal Nash equilibrium bidding models developed to date have the less informed earning lower profits than under symmetric information conditions (Wilson, 1975a,b; Weverbergh).

32. Numbers of bidders in field environments is endogenous, depending in part on perceived lease value, rather than exogenous, as commonly treated in the auction market literature (and as one can arrange for in the laboratory). As such it is far from clear why, in theory, rates of return should vary systematically with numbers of bidders in field environments, unless again we postulate the existence of a winner's curse that is exaggerated with increased numbers of bidders.

33. Drainage tracts have sharply reduced exploration costs as there are substantially fewer dry holes drilled per lease than on wildcats. Further, there are reduced production costs as a consequence of existing investments on neighbor leases and possibilities of joint production. In efforts to reconcile Mead et al.'s (1983) estimates of higher rates of return on drainage leases with their own estimates that prior drilling raised seller's revenues in the Gulf, Jeffrey Leitzinger and Joseph Stiglitz (1984) argue that developers capture at least some of the rent associated with reduced production costs on drainage leases. No explanation is offered for how this can plausibly account for the full differential rate of return between wildcat and drainage leases. Nor why, since these savings are public knowledge and contain a strong common value element, traditional motions of rent capture in competitive markets should fail. (Reduced production costs are in large

measure available to both neighbors and nonneighbors as a consequence of the federal government's ability to force unitization, and the strong effects of these enforcement powers on voluntary unitization of tracts; see Gary Liebcap and Steven Wiggins, 1985). An alternative explanation is that Mead et al.'s rate of return estimates are incorrect. However, there are equally strong, if not stronger, reasons to suppose that Leitzinger and Stiglitz's estimates of information externalities, which are based on the size of the bonus bid on drainage compared with wildcat leases, are highly exaggerated, as the public information component associated with the drainage lease designation is systematically biased towards raising the expected value of these leases.

34. Auction series 7 large clearly indicates this as it involved super-experienced subjects all of whom had been in at least two previous large group series.

References

Baltagi, Badi H., "Pooling Cross-Sections with Unequal Time-Series Lengths," *Economics Letters*, 1986, *18*, 133–36.

Battalio, Raymond C., Kogut, Carl and Meyer, Donald J., "Individual and Market Bidding Behavior in a Vickery First Price Auction: Varying Market Size and Information," paper presented at Econometric Society Winter Meetings, 1983.

Capen, E. C., Clapp, R. V. and Campbell, W. M., "Competitive Bidding in High-Risk Situations," *Journal of Petroleum Technology*, June 1971, *23*, 641–53.

Cassing, James and Douglas, Richard W., "Implications of the Auction Mechanism in Baseball's Free Agent Draft," *Southern Economic Journal*, July 1980, *47*, 110–21.

Cox, James C., Roberson, Bruce and Smith, Vernon L., "Theory and Behavior of Single Object Auctions," in V. L. Smith, ed., *Research in Experimental Economics*, Vol. 2, Greenwich: JAI Press, 1982.

Dessauer, John P., *Book Publishing*, New York: Bowker, 1981.

Kagel, John H. et al., "First-Price, Sealed-Bid, Common Value Auctions: Some Initial Experimental Results," Center for Public Policy Discussion Paper 84–1, University of Houston, 1984.

———, "First Price Common Value Auctions: Bidder Behavior and the 'Winner's Curse'," mimeo., University of Houston, 1986.

Kagel, John H., Harstad, Ronald M. and Levin, Dan, "Information Impact and Allocation Rules in Auctions with Affiliated Private Values: A Laboratory Study," mimeo., University of Houston, 1986.

——— and Levin, Dan, "Individual Bidder Behavior in First-Price Private Value Auctions," *Economics Letters*, 1985, *19*, 125–28.

Leitzinger, Jeffrey J. and Stiglitz, Joseph E., "In formation Externalities in Oil and Gas Leasing," *Contemporary Policy Issues*, March 1984, *5*, 44–57.

Libecap, Gary D. and Wiggins, Steven N., "The Influence of Private Failure on Regulation: The Case of Oil Field Unitization," *Journal of Political Economy*, August 1985, *93*, 690–714.

Lorenz, John and Dougherty, E. L., "Bonus Bidding and Bottom Lines: Federal Offshore Oil and Gas," SPE 12024, 58th Annual Fall Technical Conference, October 1983.

Matthews, Steven A., "Comparing Auctions for Risk Averse Buyers. A Buyer's Point of View," *Econometrica*, forthcoming 1986.

Mead, Walter, J., Moseidjord, Asbjorn and Sorensen, Philip R., "The Rate of Return Earned by Leases Under Cash Bonus Bidding in OCS Oil and Gas Leases," *Energy Journal*, October 1983, *4*, 37–52.

————, "Competitive Bidding Under Asymmetrical information: Behavior and Performance in Gulf of Mexico Drainage Lease Sales, 1959–1969," *Review of Economics and Statistics*, August 1984, *66*, 505–08.

Milgrom, Paul R. and Weber, Robert J., "A Theory of Auctions and Competitive Bidding," *Econometrica*, September 1982, *50*, 1089–122.

Plott, Charles R., "Industrial Organization Theory and Experimental Economics," *Journal of Economic Literature*, December 1982, *20*, 1485–527.

Roll, Richard, "The Hubris Hypothesis of Corporate Takeovers," *Journal of Business*, April 1986, *59*, 197–216.

Smith, Vernon L., "Microeconomic Systems as an Experimental Science," *American Economic Review*, December 1982, *72*, 923–55.

Weverbergh, M., "Competitive Bidding With Asymmetric Information Reanalyzed," *Management Science*, March 1979, *25*, 291–94.

Wilson, Robert, (1975a) "Comment on David Hughart, informational Assymetry, Bidding Strategies and the Marketing of Offshore Petroleum Leases," mimeo., Stanford University, 1975.

————, (1975b) "On the Incentive for Information Acquistion in Competitive Bidding with Asymmetrical Information," mimeo., Stanford University, 1975.

————, "A Bidding Model of Perfect Competition," *Review of Economic Studies*, October 1977, *44*, 511–18.

————, "The Basic Model of Competitive Bidding," mimeo., Stanford University, 1981.

Winer, Ben J., *Statistical Principles in Experimental Design*, 2nd ed., New York: McGraw-Hill, 1971.

Addendum

This Appendix verifies that the bid functions described in the text of the Reply constitute an equilibrium, and that it is the unique equilibrium in which informed bidders use symmetric, monotonic bidding strategies. To prove equilibrium, we show in turn that the bidder receiving signal x_L, a typical informed bidder receiving a signal $x \in [x_L + [n/(n-1)]\varepsilon, x_L + 2\varepsilon]$, and a typical informed bidder receiving a signal $x \in [x_L, x_L + [n/(n-1)]\varepsilon]$, are each using best replies.

First, consider the bidder receiving signal x_L. Because x_0 is distributed uniformly and each x_i is distributed uniformly conditional on x_0, the expected value of x_0 conditional on all the signals is simply the arithmetic average of the lowest and highest signals, $(x_H + x_L)/2$. This means that for each bidder, all relevant uncertainty about x_0 can be summarized by that bidder's posterior on x_H. So to check optimality for the bidder receiving signal x_L, we must derive the posterior $f(x_H \mid x_L)$. Conditional on x_0 each of the n signals is an independent draw from a uniform distribution on $[x_0 - \varepsilon, x_0 + \varepsilon]$, so using the properties of order statistics we have

$$f(x_H, x_L \mid x_0) = n(n-1)\left(\frac{x_H - x_L}{2\varepsilon}\right)^{n-2}\left(\frac{1}{2\varepsilon}\right)^2.$$

Also by the property of order statistics, we have that $f(x_L \mid x_o) = (n/2\varepsilon)[(x_0 + \varepsilon - x_L)/2\varepsilon]^{n-1}$, yielding

$$f(x_H \mid x_0, x_L) = \frac{n(n-1)\left(\dfrac{x_H - x_L}{2\varepsilon}\right)^{n-2}\left(\dfrac{1}{2\varepsilon}\right)^2}{\dfrac{n}{2\varepsilon}\left(\dfrac{x_0 + \varepsilon - x_L}{2\varepsilon}\right)^{n-1}}.$$

Since x_0 is distributed uniformly, Bayes' rule yields that $f(x_0 \mid x_L) = f(x_L \mid x_0) = (n/2\varepsilon)[(x_0 + \varepsilon - x_L)/2\varepsilon]^{n-1}$, so $f(x_H \mid x_L)$ is given by

$$\int_{x_H - \varepsilon}^{x_L + \varepsilon} n(n-1)\left(\frac{x_H - x_L}{2\varepsilon}\right)^{n-2}\left(\frac{1}{2\varepsilon}\right)^2$$

$$dx_0 = n(n-1)\left(\frac{x_H - x_L}{2\varepsilon}\right)^{n-2}\left(\frac{1}{2\varepsilon}\right)^2 (2\varepsilon - (x_H - x_L)).$$

We now use the derived $f(x_H \mid x_L)$ to show that when informed bidders use the function $b_I(\cdot)$ in the text, the bidder receiving signal x_L earns zero expected profit by submitting any bid in the support of bids used by informed bidders. Suppose the bidder receiving signal x_L bids $b_I(\hat{x})$, and that all informed types $x \in [x_L, \hat{x}]$ use $b_I(\cdot)$. Then the expected payoff to this uninformed bidder is

$$\int_{x_L}^{\hat{x}}\left(\frac{x_H + x_L}{2} - b_I(\hat{x})\right) n(n-1)\left(\frac{x_H + x_L}{2\varepsilon}\right)^{n-2}\left(\frac{1}{2\varepsilon}\right)^2 (2\varepsilon - (x_H - x_L)) \, dx_H$$

$$= \left(\frac{\hat{x} + x_L}{2} - b_I(\hat{x})\right)\left(n\left(\frac{\hat{x} - x_L}{2\varepsilon}\right)^{n-1} - (n-1)\left(\frac{\hat{x} - x_L}{2\varepsilon}\right)^n\right)$$

$$- \frac{1}{2}\int_{x_L}^{\hat{x}}\left(n\left(\frac{x_H - x_L}{2\varepsilon}\right)^{n-1} - (n-1)\left(\frac{x_H - x_L}{2\varepsilon}\right)^n\right) dx_H$$

$$= \left(\frac{\hat{x} + x_L}{2} - b_I(\hat{x})\right)\left(n\left(\frac{\hat{x} - x_L}{2\varepsilon}\right)^{n-1} - (n-1)\left(\frac{\hat{x} - x_L}{2\varepsilon}\right)^n\right)$$

$$- \frac{1}{2}\left(2\varepsilon\left(\frac{\hat{x} - x_L}{2\varepsilon}\right)^n - \frac{2\varepsilon(n-1)}{n+1}\left(\frac{\hat{x} - x_L}{2\varepsilon}\right)^{n+1}\right).$$

Substitution of $b_I(\hat{x})$ from the text reveals that this expression is zero for all $\hat{x}$. Thus, the bidder receiving signal x_L is indifferent over all bids in this range.

To show optimality for the uninformed bidder, it now suffices to show that $b_{II}(x) \geq b_I(x)$ for all $x \in [x_L + [n/(n - 1)]\varepsilon, x_L + 2\varepsilon]$; if so, then this bidder cannot earn positive profit by bidding in the support of bids used by informed types in this range. As stated in the text, it is the case that $b_I(x_L + [n/(n - 1)]\varepsilon) = b_{II}(x_L + [n/(n - 1)]\varepsilon)$. Furthermore, we have that

$$b_I(x) - b_{II}(x) = b_I(x) - \left[x_L + \frac{n - 2}{n - 1}\frac{x - x_L}{2}\right]$$

$$- \frac{\left[b_I\left(x_L + \frac{n}{n - 1}\varepsilon\right) - \left(x_L + \frac{n - 2}{n - 1}\frac{n\varepsilon}{2(n - 1)}\right)\right]\left(\frac{n}{n - 1}\varepsilon\right)^{n - 2}}{(x - x_L)^{n - 2}}.$$

This has the same sign as

$$(x - x_L)^{n - 2}\left[b_I(x) - \left(x_L + \frac{n - 2}{n - 1}\frac{x - x_L}{2}\right)\right]$$

$$- \left(\frac{n}{n - 1}\varepsilon\right)^{n - 2}\left[b_I\left(x_L + \frac{n}{n - 1}\varepsilon\right) - \left(x_L + \frac{n - 2}{n - 1}\frac{n\varepsilon}{2(n - 1)}\right)\right].$$

Thus, the proof would be completed if it could be shown that the function $(x - x_L)^{n - 2}[b_I(x) - [x_L + (n - 2)/(n - 1)(x - x_L/2)]]$ were nonincreasing for $x \in [x_L + [n/(n - 1)]\varepsilon, x_L + 2\varepsilon]$. The derivative of this function is

$$(n - 2)(x - x_L)^{n - 3}\left[b_I(x) - \left(x_L + \frac{n - 2}{n - 1}\frac{x - x_L}{2}\right)\right]$$

$$+ (x - x_L)^{n - 2}\left(b_I'(x) - \frac{n - 2}{2(n - 1)}\right).$$

which has the same sign as

$$\left(\frac{4\varepsilon}{n - 1} - \frac{2(x - x_L)}{2}\right)^2\left[\frac{n - 2}{x - x_L}\left[b_I(x) - \left(x_L + \frac{n - 2}{n - 1}\frac{x - x_L}{2}\right)\right]\right]$$

$$+ \left(b_I'(x) - \frac{n - 2}{2(n - 1)}\right)\right].$$

Plugging in $b_I(x)$ and $b_I'(x)$ yields a quadratic expression, whose coefficient for x^2 is negative; the quadratic expression is positive when evaluated at $x = x_L$ but negative at $x = x_L + [n/(n - 1)]\varepsilon$ for $n \geq 3$, which is the only case of interest [for $n = 2$ the lone informed bidder only uses $b_I(\cdot)$]. This guarantees that it is negative for all $x \geq x_L + [n/(n - 1)]$, completing the proof of optimality for the uninformed bidder.

We now turn to whether an informed bidder receiving signal $x \in [x_L +$

$[n/(n-1)]\varepsilon, x_L + 2\varepsilon]$ is playing a best reply. To do so, it will be valuable to derive the posterior of such a bidder on the highest signal received by the other $n-2$ informed bidders, which we will call y_H. Conditional on x_0, the joint distribution of x_L, y_H, and x is $f(y_H, x_L, x \mid x_0) = (n-1)(n-2)(y_H - x_L/2\varepsilon)^{n-3}(1/2\varepsilon)^3$. Using Bayes' rule yields that

$$f(y_H \mid x_0, x_L, x) = \frac{(n-1)(n-2)\left(\dfrac{y_H - x_L}{2\varepsilon}\right)^{n-3}\left(\dfrac{1}{2\varepsilon}\right)^3}{\dfrac{n-1}{(2\varepsilon)^2}\left(\dfrac{x_0 + \varepsilon - x_L}{2\varepsilon}\right)^{n-2}}.$$

In addition, we have that

$$f(x_0 \mid x_L, x) = \frac{\dfrac{n-1}{(2\varepsilon)^2}\left(\dfrac{x_0 + \varepsilon - x_L}{2\varepsilon}\right)^{n-2}}{\dfrac{1}{2\varepsilon}\left(1 - \left(\dfrac{x - x_L}{2\varepsilon}\right)^{n-1}\right)}.$$

This allows integration to yield

$$f(y_H \mid x_L, x) = \frac{(n-1)(n-2)\left(\dfrac{y_H - x_L}{2\varepsilon}\right)^{n-3}\left(\dfrac{1}{2\varepsilon}\right)^3 (2\varepsilon - (x - x_L))}{\dfrac{1}{2\varepsilon}\left(1 - \left(\dfrac{x - x_L}{2\varepsilon}\right)^{n-1}\right)}.$$

Note that if an informed bidder receiving signal $x \in [x_L + [n/(n-1)]\varepsilon, x_L + 2\varepsilon]$ uses the proposed equilibrium strategy, he will always beat the uninformed bidder. Therefore, to check whether he is using a best reply it is sufficient to check that the standard differential equation defining a symmetric first-price equilibrium bid function is satisfied. This differential equation is

$$\frac{(n-1)(n-2)\left(\dfrac{x - x_L}{2\varepsilon}\right)^{n-3}\left(\dfrac{1}{2\varepsilon}\right)^3 (2\varepsilon - (x - x_L))}{\dfrac{1}{2\varepsilon}\left(1 - \left(\dfrac{x - x_L}{1\varepsilon}\right)^{n-1}\right)}\left(\dfrac{x + x_L}{2} - b_{II}(x)\right)$$

$$- \frac{(n-1)\left(\dfrac{x - x_L}{2\varepsilon}\right)^{n-2}\left(\dfrac{1}{2\varepsilon}\right)^2 (2\varepsilon - (x - x_L))}{\dfrac{1}{2\varepsilon}\left(1 - \left(\dfrac{x - x_L}{2\varepsilon}\right)^{n-1}\right)} b'_{II}(x) = 0$$

for all $x \in [x_L + [n/(n-1)]\varepsilon, x_L + 2\varepsilon]$. Substitution of $b_{II}(x)$ reveals that this equation is satisfied for all such x, proving optimality for these types of informed bidder.

Finally, it must be shown that an informed bidder receiving signal $x \in [x_L, x_L + [n/(n-1)]\varepsilon]$ is using a best reply by bidding $b_I(x)$. Note that such a bidder faces a positive probability of losing to the uninformed bidder if he bids according to the proposed equilibrium. Letting $F(x)$ denote the probability that the uninformed bidder bids less than or equal to $b(x)$, the appropriate first-order condition for optimality, given below, must be modified to account for this probability:

$$
F'(x) \frac{(n-1)\left(\dfrac{x - x_L}{2\varepsilon}\right)^{n-2}\left(\dfrac{1}{2\varepsilon}\right)^2 (2\varepsilon - (x - x_L))}{\dfrac{1}{2\varepsilon}\left(1 - \left(\dfrac{x - x_L}{2\varepsilon}\right)^{n-1}\right)}\left(\dfrac{x - x_L}{2} - b_I(x)\right)
$$

$$
+ F(x)\left[\frac{(n-1)(n-2)\left(\dfrac{x - x_L}{2\varepsilon}\right)^{n-3}\left(\dfrac{1}{2\varepsilon}\right)^3 (2\varepsilon - (x - x_L))}{\dfrac{1}{2\varepsilon}\left(1 - \left(\dfrac{x - x_L}{2\varepsilon}\right)^{n-1}\right)}\left(\dfrac{x - x_L}{2} - b_I(x)\right)\right.
$$

$$
\left. - \frac{(n-1)\left(\dfrac{x - x_L}{2\varepsilon}\right)^{n-2}\left(\dfrac{1}{2\varepsilon}\right)^2 (2\varepsilon - (x - x_L))}{\dfrac{1}{2\varepsilon}\left(1 - \left(\dfrac{x - x_L}{2\varepsilon}\right)^{n-1}\right)} b_I'(x)\right] = 0
$$

for all $x \in [x_L, x_L + [n/(n-1)]\varepsilon]$. Substitution of $F(x)$ and $b_I(x)$ from the text reveals that this condition is satisfied for all such x, proving optimality for these types.

Having established equilibrium, we now show that it is unique in the class of strategy profiles in which the informed bidders use a symmetric bidding function that is monotonic in the signal received. Consider first whether it is possible that there is some range of informed types whom the uninformed bidder bids higher than with probability one. All such types never win the item and earn zero profit in such a strategy profile, and for such a profile to be an equilibrium it would have to be the case that these types cannot earn a positive expected profit by submitting a bid that wins with positive probability. Now consider the lowest bid over which the uninformed bidder randomizes. This bid only wins when all informed bidders are types that never win. However, if a bidder with the highest type among those who never submit winning bids (say type x) cannot earn a positive profit by submitting a potentially winning bid, then the uninformed bidder must necessarily earn a strictly negative profit by submitting a bid that only beats types less than or equal to x, since the highest signal is a sufficient statistic for doing inference on x_0 and the highest signal is less than x whenever the uninformed bidder wins with this lowest bid. Thus, in any equilibrium the lowest bid the uninformed bidder ever submits must be the same as the bid of an informed bidder who receives signal x_L. But since this type of informed bidder always loses, such a bid earns zero expected profit; since mixing in equilibrium implies indifference over the strategies that are randomized over, the uninformed bidder must earn zero profit in equilibrium.

Consider bid function $b_I(\cdot)$ in the text. As shown above, if all informed bidders used this bid function the uninformed bidder would earn zero expected profit by submitting any bid between x_L and $x_L + [n/(n-1)]\varepsilon$. Since by the above argument the uninformed bidder must earn zero profit in equilibrium, the symmetric bid function used by the informed bidders must not take values less than $b_I(\cdot)$ for any range of x, or else bids will exist that would yield a positive expected profit for the uninformed bidder. Furthermore, if the symmetric bid function takes values strictly higher than $b_I(\cdot)$ for some range $(x', \bar{x})$, then the uninformed bidder must not make a bid in the range of bids made by these types, as such a bid yields a strictly negative payoff to the uninformed bidder.

We now argue that the support of the uninformed bidder's randomization must be bids in $[x_L, b_I(x^*)]$. Suppose we take as a candidate bid function for the informed a function that coincides with $b_I(\cdot)$ for arguments in $[x_L, x']$ for some $x' \in [x_L, x_L + 2\varepsilon)$, and suppose additionally that the uninformed bidder does not submit bids in the range $[b_I(x'), b_I(x' + \delta))$ for some $\delta > 0$. Using the same differential equation that was used to show optimality for informed bidders of type $x \in [x_L + [n/(n-1)]\varepsilon, x_L + 2\varepsilon]$, it can be verified that the only candidate for a symmetric equilibrium bid function for the informed bidders entails that types $x \in [x', x' + \delta)$ use the bid function

$$b_{II}(x \mid x') = x_L + \frac{n-2}{n-1}\frac{x - x_L}{2} + \frac{b_I(x') - \left[x_L + \frac{n-2}{n-1}\frac{x' - x_L}{2}\right]}{\left(\dfrac{x - x_L}{x' - x_L}\right)^{n-2}}.$$

This is the only candidate because it is the only possible symmetric best response for these types given that informed types in $[x_L, x']$ use $b_I(\cdot)$ and that the uninformed bidder does not submit bids in $[b_I(x'), b_I(x' + \delta))$. However, from the previous argument, to be part of an equilibrium this new function cannot take on values less than $b_I(\cdot)$ for arguments in $[x', x' + \delta)$. Thus, the right-hand derivative of $b_{II}(\cdot \mid x')$ when evaluated at x' cannot he strictly less than the derivative of $b_I(\cdot)$ when evaluated at x'. It can be verified that this condition holds only for $x' \geq x_L + [n/(n-1)]\varepsilon$. Thus, any symmetric equilibrium bid function for the informed bidders must coincide with $b_I(\cdot)$ for signals in $[x_L, x_L + [n/(n-1)]\varepsilon]$.

Consider now whether it is possible that the uninformed bidder submits bids greater than $b_I(x_L + [n/(n-1)]\varepsilon)$ as part of his randomization. Suppose the uninformed bidder makes bids in some range $(\underline{b}, \bar{b})$, with $\underline{b} \geq b_I(x_L + [n/(n-1)]\varepsilon)$. Obviously, if no informed bidders bid more than $\underline{b}$ under their symmetric strategy, this cannot be a best response for the uninformed bidder. Therefore, suppose some informed bidders also bid in the range $(\underline{b}, \bar{b})$. These informed bidders have an incentive to raise their bids above those given by b_{II} $(\cdot \mid x_L + [n/(n-1)]\varepsilon)$, because raising one's bid now has the extra positive effect of increasing the likelihood of beating the uninformed bidder. However it is already the case that $b_{II}(x \mid x_L + [n/(n-1)]\varepsilon) > b_I(x)$ for all $x > x_L + [n/(n-1)]\varepsilon$, so under a best response for the informed bidders the uninformed bidder would earn a negative expected profit by submitting any bid greater than $b_I(x_L + [n/(n-1)]\varepsilon)$. Thus, the only possible candidate for a symmetric, monotonic equilibrium bid function for the informed bidders is $b^*(x)$ described in the text.

$b^*(\cdot)$ ensures that the uninformed bidder earns zero expected profit by making any bid less than or equal to $b^*(x_L + [n/(n-1)]\varepsilon)$, and negative expected profit by making any bid greater than this, and that informed bidders with types $x \geq x_L + [n/(n-1)]\varepsilon$ are using a best reply provided the uninformed bidder never bids more than $b^*(x_L + [n/(n-1)]\varepsilon)$. All that remains to complete the description of the equilibrium is to construct a mixed strategy for the uninformed bidder over bids in $[x_L, b^*(x_L + [n/(n-1)]\varepsilon)]$ ensuring that informed bidders of types $x < x_L + [n/(n-1)]\varepsilon$ are also playing best responses. Letting $F(x)$ denote the probability that the uninformed bidder submits a bid less than or equal to the bid used by informed type x in a candidate mixed strategy, the particular $F(x)$ described in the text is the unique distribution that rationalizes $b_I(\cdot)$ as a best response for types with low signals, in that it is the unique distribution function satisfying the differential equation shown previously that ensures optimality for these informed types.

References

Cox, James C.; Dinkin, Samuel H. and Smith, Vernon L. "The Winner's Curse and Public Information in Common Value Auctions: Comment." *American Economic Review*, March 1999, *89*(1), pp. 319–24.

Engelhrecht-Wiggans, Richard; Milgrom, Paul R. and Weber, Robert J. "Competitive Bidding and Proprietary Information." *Journal of Mathematical Economics*, April 1983, *11*, pp. 161–69.

Harstad, Ronald M. and Levin, Dan. "A Class of Dominance Solvable Common Value Auctions." *Review of Economic Studies*, July 1985, *52*(3), pp. 525–28.

Kagel, John H. "Auctions: A Survey of Experimental Research," in John H. Kagel and Alvin E. Roth, eds., *Handbook of experimental economics*. Princeton, NJ: Princeton University Press, 1995, pp. 501–85.

Kagel, John H. and Levin, Dan. "The Winner's Curse and Public Information in Common Value Auctions." *American Economic Review*, December 1986, *76*(5), pp. 894–920.

Kagel, John H.; Levin, Dan and Harstad, Ronald M. "Comparative Static Effects of Number of Bidders and Public Information on Behavior in Second-Price Common Value Auctions." *International Journal of Game Theory*, 1995, *24*(3), pp. 293–319.

Kagel, John H. and Richard, Jean-Francois. "Super-Experienced Bidders in First-Price Common Value Auctions: Rules-of-Thumb, Nash Equilibrium Bidding and the Winner's Curse." Mimeo, University of Pittsburgh, May 1997.

Levin, Dan; Kagel, John H. and Richard, JeanFrancois. "Revenue Effects and Information Processing in English Common Value Auctions." *American Economic Review*, June 1996, *86*(3), pp. 442–60.

Milgrom, Paul M. and Weber, Robert J. "A Theory of Auctions and Competitive Bidding." *Econometrica*, September 1982, *50*(5), pp. 1089–122.

4

Comparative Static Effects of Number of Bidders and Public Information on Behavior in Second-Price Common Value Auctions

John H. Kagel, Dan Levin, and Ronald M. Harstad

1. Introduction

In common value auctions the value of the item is the same for all bidders. Before bidding, each of the N bidders privately observes an informative signal (or estimate) which is a random variable affiliated with the value. Affiliation means that a higher estimate for one bidder makes higher estimates for rivals and a higher asset value more likely. Mineral rights auctions, such as outer continental shelf (OCS) leases, are often characterized as common-value auctions; here the signals represent different bidders' pre-sale estimates of lease value. Any auction of a potentially resalable asset involves a common-value element.

In common value auctions, bidders face an adverse selection problem, as the high bidder is likely to have the highest estimate of the item's value. Unless this adverse selection problem is accounted for in bidding, the high bidder may suffer from a "winner's curse," winning the item but making below normal profits. Bidders in early outer continental shelf (OCS) oil lease auctions are often thought to have suffered from a winner's curse (Capen, Clapp and Campbell, 1971; Mead, Moseidjord, and Sorensen, 1983; Gilley, Carrols and Leone, 1986).[1] Inexperienced bidders in first-price laboratory auction markets suffer from a winner's curse as well, earning negative average profits (Kagel et al., 1989; Lind and Plott, 1991; Garvin and Kagel, in press). Experienced bidders in first-price laboratory auction markets overcome the winner's curse with relatively few bidders, but succumb again when exposed to the heightened adverse selection forces associated with larger numbers of bidders (Kagel and Levin, 1996). "Sophisticated" bidders drawn from the commercial construction industry behave no differently than student subjects in laboratory auction markets (Dyer, Kagel and Levin, 1989).

In spite of these outcomes, Lind and Plott (1991, p. 344) note, "A major puzzle remains: of the models studied, the best is the risk-neutral Nash-equilibrium model, but that model predicts that the curse will not exist." They go on to comment that "Part of the difficulty with further study stems from the lack of theory about (first-price) common value auctions with risk aversion. . . . If the effect of risk aversion is to raise the bidding function as it does in private auctions, then risk-aversion . . . might resolve the puzzle; but, of course, this remains only a conjecture" (Lind and Plott, 1991, p. 344). There is also a lack of theory regarding the effect of asymmetries in bidders risk preferences in first-price common value auctions, which makes it even more difficult to unambiguously analyze real life bidding patterns in these auctions.

From this perspective second-price auctions provide an ideal vehicle to explore bidding in common value auctions. In a second-price auction, the high bidder obtains the item for a price equal to the second-highest bid. Although rarely observed in field environments (Cassady, 1967), second-price auctions permit us to observe item valuation behavior while avoiding many of the strategic issues that complicate the more commonly encountered first-price institution. In contrast to first-price auctions, behavior of risk averse bidders is well understood in second-price auctions with both *symmetric* risk averse bidders and with *asymmetric* risk averse bidders. Our experiment shows a strong winner's curse even with full accounting for the potential effects of risk aversion on bidding. More importantly, the existence of robust comparative static predictions in second-price auctions allows us to better understand the mechanism(s) underlying this failure of Nash equilibrium bidding theory.

Experienced bidders in auctions with 4 or 5 bidders exhibit substantial positive profits which are reasonably close to the risk neutral Nash benchmark. However, in auctions with 6 or 7 bidders, the same subjects earn negative average profits, as they clearly suffer from a winner's curse. There is no way to rationalize these negative average profits in terms of a Nash equilibria, whether it involves symmetric or asymmetric bidding. However, to simply reject the theory at this point seems a bit harsh and leaves us with no clear understanding of the mechanism(s) underlying these results. Perhaps bidders are simply miscalibrated relative to the Nash point predictions, so that they satisfy the comparative static predictions of the theory? Perhaps they are still learning, so while moving in the right direction relative to the theory they have yet to achieve the equilibrium outcome? Perhaps the overbidding can be explained by a utility for winning the auction? None of these factors can explain our data.

Overly aggressive bidding in second-price common value auctions cannot be rationalized in terms of bidders' risk aversion. Rather best responses are less aggressive for risk averse than for risk neutral bidders. Further, individual bidders fail to reduce their bids in response to increased numbers of bidders, a comparative static implication of the theory which holds for both risk averse symmetric and asymmetric Nash equilibria, and even extends to auctions where the strategy profile is not an equilibrium (corresponding predictions in first-price auctions require symmetry and are conditional on risk attitudes and the underlying distribution of information at bidder's disposal). This provides rather incontrovertible evidence that bidders fail to appreciate the adverse selection forces inherent in common value auctions.

Public information is predicted to rise average revenue in second-price auctions, both in symmetric and asymmetric constant absolute risk averse Nash equilibria (no such extensions of Nash bidding theory are available for risk averse bidders in first-price auctions). However, public information is predicted to *reduce* revenue in the presence of a strong winner's curse, a prediction which is consistent with the results of our experiment. Not only does this result have public policy implications, but it also rules out overly aggressive bidding on account of a utility of winning the auction, as the utility of winning should be unaffected by the presence or absence of public information. Finally, assuming symmetry and risk aversion (of any sort), we are able to derive predictions regarding individual bidder response to the type of public information provided in our second-price auctions, which provides insight into whether bidders have accounted for the information implied by the event of winning (no comparable predictions have been obtained for a first-price institution). Although the value of this prediction is mitigated somewhat by the extent of the asymmetry reported in bidding, these data still provide insight into why the revenue-raising mechanism of second-price auctions fails, and the proposition demonstrated may prove useful to those who choose to replicate our results or to test the theory with even more experienced bidders.

The robustness of the predictions of second-price auction theory to assumptions regarding bidders' risk references and the outcomes of our experiment demonstrate that risk aversion cannot account for overly aggressive bidding in common value auctions. Rather, since the implications of Nash equilibrium bidding theory apply to a far wider variety of circumstances than in first-price auctions, there is far less scope to rationalize the failure of the theory under second-price rules. In addition, the failure of the comparative static implications of the model with respect to increasing numbers of bidders provides rather clear evidence that bidders fail to account for the adverse selection forces inherent in common value auctions, which failure is at the heart of the winner's curse. In this context, the positive average profits observed in auctions with 4 or 5 bidders may be attributed to the reduced adverse selection forces associated with reduced N and to survivorship principles— experience with losses teaches bidders to bid less in these auctions without necessarily understanding the adverse selection forces at work.

The structure of the paper is as follows. In section II we describe our experimental procedures. Section III characterizes the Nash equilibrium bidding strategy and offers a naive bidding model with its contrasting implications. The results of the experiments are reported in section IV. The concluding section summarizes our results.

2. Structure of the Auctions

2.1 Basic Auction Structure

Subjects were recruited for two-hour sessions consisting of a series of auction periods. In each period a single item was sold to the high bidder at a price equal to the second highest bid, with bidders submitting sealed bids for the item (a second-price, sealed bid procedure). The high bidder earned a profit equal to the value of the item less the second highest bid; other bidders earned zero profit for that auction period.

In each auction period the value of the item, x_0, was drawn randomly from a uniform distribution of the interval $[\underline{x}, \overline{x}] = [\$25, \$225]$. Subjects submitted bids without knowing the realization x_0. Private information signals, x_i, were distributed prior to bidding. The x_i were randomly drawn from a uniform distribution with upper bound $x_0 + \varepsilon$ and lower bound $x_0 - \varepsilon$. As such the x_i constitute unbiased estimates of the value of x_0 (or could be used with the end point values $\underline{x}, \overline{x}$ to compute unbiased estimates). Along with x_i each bidder received an upper and a lower bound on the value of x_0; these were min $\{x_i + \varepsilon, \overline{x}\}$ and max $\{x_i - \varepsilon, \underline{x}\}$, respectively. The distribution underlying the signal values, the value of ε, and the interval $[\underline{x}, \overline{x}]$ were common knowledge. The value of ε varied across auctions (see Table 4.1); all changes in ε were announced and posted.

After all bids were collected, they were posted on the blackboard in descending order next to the corresponding signal values, x_0 was announced, the high bidder's profit was announced (but not his/her indentity), and balances were updated. Bids were restricted to be non-negative and rounded to the nearest penny.

Given the information structure and uncertainty inherent in common value auctions, negative profits would occasionally be realized even if the market were immediately to lock into the Nash equilibrium outcome. To cover this possibility, and to impose clear opportunity costs on overly aggressive bidding, subjects were given starting balances of $10.00. Profits and losses were added to this balance. If a subject's balance went negative he was no longer permitted to bid and was paid his $4.00 participation fee. Auction survivors were paid their end-of-experiment balances and participation fees in cash.

2.2 Auctions with Public Information

After several auction periods we introduced bidding in two separate auction markets during each period. Bidding in the first auction market continued as before (called private information conditions). After these bids were collected, but before they were posted, we publicly announced the lowest of the private information signals distributed, x_L, and asked subjects to bid again. (Subjects retained their original private information signals; no new private information signals were distributed.)

TABLE 4.1
Experimental Treatment Conditions

Session (number starting session)	Market Period	ε	Periods with Public Information (market periods)	Number of Active Bidders
1(5)	1–18	$12	10–25	5(1–25)
	19–25	$24		
2(7)	1–13	$12	9–20	7(1–10)
	14–20	$18		6(11–20)
3(9)	1–8	$12	9–23	7(1–23)
	9–14	$18		
	15–23	$30		
4(7)	1–7	$12	12–25	7(1–21)
	8–15, 21–25	$18		6(22–25)
	16–20	$30		
5(6)	1–5	$12	9–32	4(1–20)
	6–14, 27–32	$18		6(21–26)
	15–26	$30		5(27–32)
6(5)	1–5	$12	9–29	4(1–20, 28–29)
	6–14, 25–29	$18		5(21–27)
	15–24	$30		

Profits were paid (or losses incurred) in only one of the two auction markets, determined on the basis of a coin flip after all bids were collected. Subjects were told that they were under no obligation to submit the same or different bids in the two markets, but should bid in a way they thought would "maximize profits." All bids from both markets were posted along with the corresponding private information signals.

Observing the same subjects bidding in dual markets directly controls for between-subject variability and extraneous variability resulting from fluctuations in item valuations and private information signals. The dual market procedure creates two strategic choices which are theoretically separate, and subjects treat them as separate in a number of bidding contexts.[2]

2.3 Subject Experience and Varying Numbers of Bidders

The sessions are numbered in chronological order as they involved a common core of subjects, 17 in all, recruited in varying combinations (no two sessions involved exactly the same set of subjects and group composition varied unpredictably between sessions). All were MBA students or senior economics majors at the University of Houston. Each subject in session 1–3 had participated in at least one earlier session of second-price common-value auctions; 5

of 9 subjects in session 3 took part in session 1 or 2.[3] Session 4 recruited back from this same subject pool, while recruiting two new subjects with experience in a parallel series of first-price common-value auction experiments. All of the subjects in sessions 5 and 6 had participated in one or more of sessions 1–4.

This sequence was designed to study performance in 7-bidder auctions during sessions 2, 3 and 4. Sessions 5 and 6 were designed to have 20 auctions with 4 active bidders, rotating participation among seven subjects, and then to follow with 7-bidder auctions. Recruitment imperfections and bankruptcies created a slightly different pattern. Only 6 bidders survived auction series 2 and 4, while increasing the number of bidders led to a bankruptcy in both sessions 5 and 6. Below, we refer to 4-bidder auctions in these last two sessions as sessions 5A and 6A, and to auctions with more bidders as 5B and 6B.

3. Theoretical Considerations

The bulk of realizations of private information signals lie in the interval

$$\underline{x} + \varepsilon < x_i < \bar{x} - \varepsilon. \tag{1}$$

Any signal satisfying (1) is unbiased:

$$E[x_0 \mid X_i = x] = x. \tag{2}$$

We restrict our theoretical analysis in the text to the realizations satisfying (1).[4]

In what follows we establish two benchmark models against which to evaluate the experimental results. A naive bidding model and the risk neutral symmetric Nash equilibrium bidding model (RNSNE for short). The naive bidding model represents an extreme form of naivete, while the RNSNE bidding model represents a very demanding form of rational play. We formulate these contrasting models as benchmarks against which to evaluate the outcomes reported and not because we believe that either one will exactly characterize behavior. We put much greater weight on the contrasting *directional* implications of the two models in response to increasing numbers of rivals and to the release of public information. Responses to these comparative static tests of the theory provide, in our opinion, a clearer test of whether or not subjects are sensitive to the contrasting item valuation forces underlying the two formulations.

3.1 Naive Bidding under Private Information Conditions:
A Model of the Winner's Curse

The notion of a winner's curse expressed in the petroleum engineering literature (Capen, Clapp and Campbell, 1971; Lorenz and Dougherty, 1983) differs from game-theoretic models by a failure when formulating bids to fully account for the information implied by the event of winning. In what follows we specify an extreme version of this judgmental failure: bidders take *no* account of any information implied by winning, using only the private information signal x_i to estimate x_0, as in (2). A risk neutral bidder is willing to pay up to the expected value of the item, so that given the second-price bid rule, he has a dominant strategy of bidding (2) (Vickrey, 1961). In other words, naive bidders act as if they are in a private value auction, only they are bidding on a lottery with expected value (2). With all bidders using (2), expected profit, conditional on winning, is $\varepsilon(3 - N)/(N + 1)$ which is negative whenever $N < 3$. Note, we do not advocate (2) as a sensible bidding strategy, but are simply trying to develop implications of strategies using the naive expectation (2).

With risk aversion, naive bidders who are expected utility maximizers are only willing to pay up to the certainty equivalent of the lottery. As such a risk averse bidder employing (2) would bid below his signal value. Nevertheless, bids are likely to still be well above the Nash equilibrium bid function (equation 4 below).

Naive bidders do not react to changes in the number of bidders since the expectation, (2), is independent of the number of bidders. That is, this extreme form of the winner's curse, because it takes no account of the adverse selection problem inherent in winning the auction, predicts an individual bid function that is not sensitive to the number of bidders. Further, since it is a dominant strategy for risk averse naive bidders to bid the certainty equivalent of the item, this insensitivity to numbers of bidders applies irrespective of risk preferences or asymmetry in these preferences.

3.2 Nash Equilibrium Bidding under Private Information Conditions

Game-theoretic papers on second-price common-value auctions outline a model and proceed to characterize the symmetric Nash equilibrium, symmetric in both risk tolerances and strategy choices. Matthews (1977) and Milgrom and Weber (1982) showed that the function $b(x)$ defined by

$$E[U(x_0 - b(x)) \mid X_i = Y_i = x] = 0 \qquad (3)$$

where x_i is the signal of bidder i and y_i is the highest signal among $N - 1$ rival bidders, is a symmetric Nash equilibrium. Levin and Harstad (1986) showed that this function is the unique symmetric Nash equilibrium. Further, following a result in Bikhchandani and Riley (1991), as extended in Harstad (1991), if there are more then 3 bidders, the symmetric equilibrium is the only locally nondegenerate risk neutral Nash equilibrium in increasing bid strategies.[5]

Under risk neutrality the bid function satisfying (3) is

$$E[X_0 \mid X_i = Y_i = x] = x - \varepsilon(N - 2)/N. \qquad (4)$$

This bid function discounts bids well below signal values, unlike the naive bidding model.[6] Expected profit when all bidders employ (4) is $2\varepsilon(N - 1)/[N(N + 1)]$, which is positive, in marked contrast to the naive bidding model. As in the naive bidding model, the RNSNE predicts that the high signal holder always wins the auction. This follows directly from the assumption that all bidders have identical bid functions, the only difference being their private information, x_i, regarding the value of the item.

Risk averse symmetric Nash equilibrium bidders will be below (4) resulting in even larger profits than under risk neutrality. This effect of risk aversion follows from the fact that the equilibrium bid function (3) is a simple expectation. This can be demonstrated through a straightforward application of the proofs, in Pratt (1964, pp. 128–129) to the symmetric bid function in (3).

The symmetric Nash equilibrium bidding model has the important comparative static prediction that individual bids must decrease with more rivals. This holds for *all* symmetric Nash equilibrium bidding formulations in second-price auctions irrespective of the form of the utility function. This follows from the fact that bidding in second-price auctions is based on a conditional expected value calculation, such as (3), which decreases with more bidders, independent of risk attitudes.[7]

Harstad (1991, Proposition 2) extends the comparative static implications of increased numbers of rivals to asymmetric bidding models when the source of asymmetry is differences in bidders risk preferences. That is, for a given set of asymmetric equilibrium bidding strategies that results in strictly increasing, locally nondegenerate bid profiles, reductions in the number of bidders results in increased bidding, provided that any given rivals' bid is equally likely not to be submitted; i.e., the identity of the bidders who have dropped out of the auction is not known prior to bidding (bidder identity reveals the risk profile of those who have dropped out of the bidding, which is likely to affect the remaining bidders' strategies). This proposition even extends to auctions in which the strategy profile is not an equilibrium. That is, as long as bidding strategies involve strictly increasing, nondegenerate bid profiles, a best response to an equally likely reduction in the number of bidders involves an increase in one's own bid, whether or not these bidding strategies satisfy the more demanding requirements of a Nash equilbrium.[8]

3.3 Naive Bidding under Public Information Conditions

The winner's curse results from systematic overestimation of x_0 by the high bidder as he fails to account for the adverse selection problem inherent in winning the auction. Under these conditions, the release of public information, particularly information that substantially reduces uncertainty about x_0, is likely to result in a downward revision in the expected value of the item for a high signal holder, resulting in a lower bid and reduced average revenue for sellers.

To continue modeling an extreme case, suppose bidder i takes proper (Bayesian) account of the announced lowest signal, x_L, but makes no inferences about others signals compared to his, conditional on the event of winning. His estimate of the value of the item becomes

$$E[x_0 \mid X_i = x, X_L = x_L] = x_L + \frac{N - 2}{N} \varepsilon \qquad (5)$$

$$+ \frac{\theta^{N-1}}{1 - \theta^{N-1}} \frac{N-1}{N} (x_L + 2\varepsilon - x)$$

where $0 < \theta = \dfrac{x - x_L}{2\varepsilon} \le 1$.[9] Under second-price rules, risk-neutral bidders using this estimate would adopt (5) as their bid function (using the same dominant strategy argument developed earlier).

Figure 4.1A illustrates the impact of announcing x_L on individual bids, as predicted by the naive bidding model. The bid function, under private information conditions, which takes no account of rivals' lower signals, (2), and the corresponding function under public information conditions, (5), calls for any bidder holding a signal above the value labeled $C_w(x_L)$ to reduce his bid upon learning x_L. On average, $C_w(x_L)$ occurs just below x_0, so that given the distribution of signal values, the naive bidding model predicts that the second-highest bidder will reduce his bid with x_L announced most of the time (over 82% frequency for $N = 4$, over 97% for $N = 7$).[10] Further, if all bidders employed (5), the dramatic reduction in bidding resulting from public information would restore a slight expected profit in auctions with 4 active bidders ($\varepsilon/25$), but would still result in (modest) expected losses for auctions with 7 active bidders.

For market outcomes the implications of the symmetric, risk neutral, naive bidding model are clear. Making x_L common knowledge will reduce expected revenue (increase bidders' expected profit). As will be shown, this is in marked contrast to the prediction of the Nash equilibrium bidding model.

Extensions of the naive bidding model to account for risk aversion yield more ambiguous results. Consider a naive bidder whose signal value is above x_0. Now, in addition to reducing the expected value of the item, there is reduced uncertainty about the value of the item. This reduced uncertainty will tend to result in bids that are closer to the expected value of the item. Thus, there are two opposing forces at work: the surprise value of x_L which promotes lower bidding and the reduction in uncertainty which promotes higher bidding. Assuming constant absolute risk aversion, which we argue for below, the net effect depends on the extent of bidders' risk aversion. As long as bidders are not too risk averse (a coefficient of constant absolute risk aversion of .10 or less) numerical calculations based on the expected location of the price setters signal show that the net effect of public information will be a lower bid (over the range of ε values employed). These two opposing forces are also at work in a naive bidding model in which bidders have asymmetric risk preferences.

3.4 Nash Equilibrium Bidding under Public Information Conditions

Extensions of the common value auction model show that releasing public information, additional information that is affiliated with the variables of the model, will increase average revenue (reduce bidders' expected profits) under the RNSNE (Milgrom and Weber, 1982). Announcing the lowest of the private information signals drawn, x_L, sharply reduces uncertainty concerning x_0, thereby

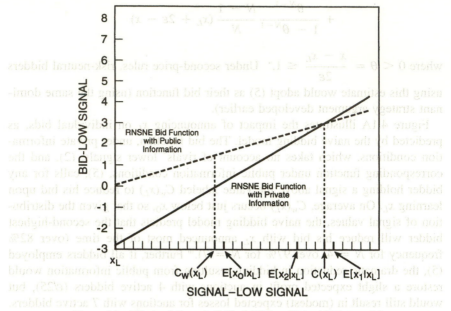

Figure 4.1a. Effects of X_L on individual bidding: Naive bidding model.

markedly increasing average revenue. This occurs even though these announcements do not, on average, alter the expected value of the item for the high signal holder as

$$E[x_0 \mid X_i = x_1] = E[E[x_0 \mid X_i = x_1, X_L] \mid X_i = x_1]$$

However, with affiliation, the announcement of x_L increases the *ex post* expected value of the item for the second highest, and lower value, signal holders; they are surprised on average, and raise their bids. Since the second highest bid constitutes the sale price, average revenue increases.

In the RNSNE each bidder acts as if his signal value is higher than his rivals'. Under the uniform distribution, this assumption and the announcement of the lowest signal provide a bidder with a sufficient statistic for the aggregate information possessed by all bidders: the average of x_i and x_L. Bidding $(x_i + x_L)/2$ is the dominance solvable outcome of the game.[11]

Under the dominance solvable solution, announcing x_L nearly halves bidders' expected profit to $\varepsilon/(N + 1)$. Further, any bidder for whom

$$X_i = x < x_L + 2\varepsilon(N - 2)/N = : C(x_L) \tag{6}$$

will increase his bid following announcement of x_L. Remarkably, for our distributional parameters, this characterization does not depend on risk neutrality.

Proposition. For any concave utility function, any bidder i with $X_i = x < C(x_L)$, x in the interval (1), raises his bid with x_L publicly announced, in the symmetric Nash equilibrium. (A proof is in the appendix.)

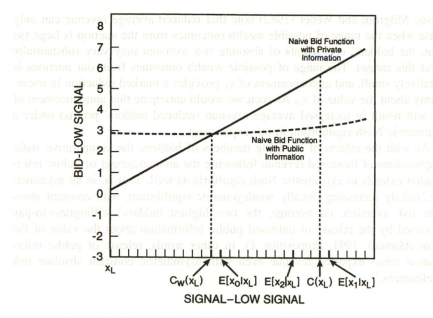

Figure 4.1b. Effects of X_L on individual bidding: RNSNE bidding model.

Figure 4.1B illustrates the impact of announcing x_L on individual bids under the RNSNE. The bid function under private information conditions, (4), intersects the bid function with public information at $C(x_L)$, which lies beyond the expected location of the second-highest signal. The second-highest signal holder will find $x_i < C(x_L)$ over 65% of the time. This results in substantially greater relative frequency of increased bidding on the part of the second highest bidder than in the naive bidding model. Further, as the Proposition indicates, this frequency is not diminished by risk aversion in the symmetric Nash equilibrium.

Comparing Figures 4.1A and 4.1B we find important differences in predicted changes in bidding patterns for all individual bidders under the naive bidding model compared to the symmetric Nash formulation. Both models predict increasing bids, following the announcement of x_L, for signal holders in the interval $x_L < x_i < C_w(x_L)$. Further, for $x_i > C(x_L)$, the naive bidding model predicts reduced bidding, while the Nash equilibrium bidding model permits higher or lower bidding, depending upon bidders' qui risk attitudes. However, for signal values in the interval $C_w(x_L) < x_i < C(x_L)$, the naive bidding model predicts decreased bidding, while the Nash model requires increased bidding. This provides a basis for distinguishing between the two models at the level of individual bidding behavior.

Although as shown, in a symmetric equilibrium we can predict individual responses to public information by risk-averse bidders, it takes constant absolute risk aversion on bidders' part to insure that public information will raise average revenues in a second-price auction (Milgrom and Weber, 1982). On this basis, Milgrom and Weber (1982) note that reduced average revenue can only arise when the range of possible wealth outcomes from the auction is large (so that. the bidders' coefficients of absolute risk aversion may vary substantially over this range). The range of possible wealth outcomes from our auctions is relatively small, and announcement of x_L provides a marked reduction in uncertainty about the value of x_0. As such we would anticipate that announcement of x_L will result in increased average revenue (reduced bidders' profits) under a symmetric Nash equilibrium in our experiment.

As with the effects of changing numbers of bidders, the comparative static implications of increased revenue following the announcement of public information extends to asymmetric Nash equilibria as well. That is, in an asymmetric, strictly increasing, locally nondegenerate equilibrium, with constant absolute risk aversion, on average, the two highest bidders' willingness-to-pay is raised by the release of unbiased public information about the value of the item (Harstad, 1991, Proposition 1). In other words, release of public information raises expected revenue even with asymmetric constant absolute risk preferences.[12]

4. Experimental Results

4.1 Bidding Patterns with Private Information

Table 4.2 provides summary statistics of auction outcomes, where sessions are ordered by number of active bidders (shown in column 2).[13] Columns 3 and 4 show the frequency with which the high signal holder won the auction, and the median rank-order correlation coefficient between bids and signals for each auction series. Data here are relevant to evaluating the extent to which an adverse selection problem existed, conditional on the event of winning the auction. Mean profit predicted under the naive bidding model, reported in column 5, serves to identify maximum expected losses, with bidders suffering from an extreme form of the winner's curse. Columns 6–8 compare actual profit earned and profit predicted under the RNSNE.

Looking at columns 3 and 4 in Table 4.2 we see that although the high signal holders fell well short of winning all auctions, as any symmetric bidding model predicts, they won 57.8% of them, significantly more than would be expected on the basis of chance factors alone. Further, the median rank order correlation coefficient between bids and signals within each auction period consistently exceeded .70, again well beyond what would be expected on the basis of chance. These two results indicate that conditional on the event of winning, a bidder's signal was a biased estimate of the item's value. Further, the high positive rank order correlations between bids and signal values strongly supports the assumption of local nondegeneracy.

Profit reports in Table 4.2 show substantial differences conditional on the number of active bidders. In auction series with four or five active bidders,

TABLE 4.2
Market Outcomes under Private Information Conditions

Session (no. auctions)	No. of Active Bidders	Percentage of Auctions Won by High Signal Holder	Median Rank-Order Correlation Coefficient between Bids and Signals	Average Profit (standard error mean)			Profit as a Percentage of RNSNE
				Naive Bidding	Observed	RNSNE	
5A (20)	4	70.0	.90	-3.49 (1.83)	3.34** (1.48)	5.49 (2.09)	60.8
6A (22)	4	90.9	.80	-2.71 (1.82)	5.42** (1.73)	6.68 (1.51)	81.1
6B (7)	5	42.9	.70	-5.86 (2.33)	3.24 (4.84)	7.61 (2.51)	42.6
1 (25)	5	40.0	.80	-5.69 (1.04)	1.11 (1.18)	3.45 (.93)	32.2
5B (12)	5-6	58.3	.76	-9.03 (3.22)	-5.84* (2.89)	6.19 (3.91)	-94.5
2 (20)	6-7	70.0	.84	-5.10 (1.01)	-1.01 (1.28)	4.23 (1.14)	-23.9
4 (25)	6-7	44.0	.86	-10.80 (1.16)	-.50 (1.19)	2.04 (.95)	-24.5
3 (23)	7	43.5	.79	-9.44 (1.40)	-3.06** (1.45)	4.72 (1.25)	-64.8

*Significantly different from zero at 10% level in 2-tailed t-test.
**Significantly different from zero at 5% level in 2-tailed t-test.

profits were consistently positive, averaging $2.78 per auction period overall, 52.8% of profits predicted unter the RNSNE.[14] Here profits are consistently closer to the predictions of the benchmark RNSNE model then the naive bidding model. In contrast, in auction series with six or seven active bidders, average profits were consistently negative, averaging $-$2.15 per auction period, compared with predicted profits of $3.97 per period under the RNSNE. Here the naive bidding model predicts an average loss of $8.88, so bidders had made some adjustments to the adverse selection problem, but these were clearly inadequate to avoid losses (profits are almost equidistant between the two benchmark models). One obvious reason for the decrease in profits between small and large groups is that expected profits have decreased for the benchmark RNSNE. As such it is worthwhile pointing out that average profit decreased $4.93 per auction, substantially more than the decline predicted by the RNSNE, $1.29 per auction.

Table 4.3 shows the relationship between profits and e. We continue to distinguish between auctions with small (4–5) and large (6–7) numbers of bidders, and the few observations at $\varepsilon = 24 are pooled with $\varepsilon = 30 observations. In auctions involving 4–5 bidders, observed mean profit increases with ε. However, with 6–7 active bidders, observed losses increase with increases in ε, with the largest losses earned at $\varepsilon = $24–30$. Although increasing e increases profit opportunities in these auctions, it also involves increased opportunity for losses in cases where bidders fall prey to the winner's curse.[15]

Table 4.4 provides evidence on the effect of increasing numbers of bidders on individual bidding using fixed effect regression models (so that each subject has their own intercept term). The first specification is suggested by the RNSNE bid function (4), as the response to changing ε is conditional on the number of active bidders. Specification 2 differs only by adding an intercept shift parameter for increasing numbers of bidders. Both fixed effects estimates restrict the subject dummy coefficients to sum to zero, so that the negative intercept values reported represent a small fixed markdown component to bids.

Under both specifications, the x_i critically influence bids, with an estimated coefficient value of 1.0. Further, the coefficient on ε is negative, and statistically significant, under both specifications. However, it is substantially smaller in absolute value than the RNSNE equilibrium prediction: with $N = 4$ and 5, the RNSNE model predicts coefficient values of $-$.50 and $-$.60, compared to the estimated value of $-$.33, differences which are statistically significant as well. Finally, under both specifications there is essentially no response to increasing numbers of rivals as the coefficient values for these variables are all small in size, and nowhere close to being statistically significant at conventional levels. Thus, individual bidders generally fail to reduce their bids in the presence of the increased adverse selection problem resulting from more rivals, consistent with the naive bidding model.

Though the results in Table 4.4 are indicative of overall bidding patterns, the following two restrictive assumptions underlie the analysis, (1) we impose the same bidding function on all subjects and (2) we employ questionable assump-

TABLE 4.3
Profits and Bidding under Varying Levels of ε (all profits in dollars)

| No. of Bidders | ε | Average Profits (standard error mean) | | | Profits as a Percentage of the RNSNE Prediction |
		Naive Bidding	Observed	RNSNE	
	12	−3.49	1.73*	3.01	57.5
		(.70)	(.92)	(.69)	
4–5	18	−2.07	3.09**	7.00	44.1
		(1.05)	(1.39)	(.99)	
	24/30	−8.49	3.66*	5.80	63.1
		(2.01)	(2.15)	(2.14)	
	12	−5.15	−.97	3.12	−31.1
		(.56)	(.72)	(.60)	
6–7	18	−9.29	−1.60	2.95	−54.2
		(1.22)	(−1.51)	(1.21)	
	24/30	−13.55	−4.53**	6.49	−69.8
		(2.20)	(−2.14)	(2.27)	

*Significantly different from zero at 10% level, 2-tailed t-test.
**Significantly different from zero at 5% level, 2-tailed t-test.

tions regarding independence of observations between auction periods. We address the first issue by running individual subject regressions. Recall that the Nash model prediction about lower bids with increased numbers of bidders extends to asymmetric bidding models (where the source of asymmetry is differences in bidders risk preferences) and to auctions in which the strategy profile is not an equilibrium. Hence, we should see *each* individual subject reducing their bids with increased numbers of rivals.

But this still leaves open the question of independence of observations between auction periods. Fitting individual subject bid functions (like those in Table 4) to the data *within* each experimental session typically shows an absence of serial correlation (as measured by the Durbin-Watson statistic). This is consistent with independence of observations within a given experimental session. However, fitting individual subject bid functions *across* experimental sessions and examining the residuals, we typically find experimental session effects. That is, the residuals all tend to be positive in one experimental session and negative in another, indicating experimental session effects. There are two equally plausible reasons for these effects: (i) subjects are responding to the bidding patterns of others in their group and/or (ii) there is learning across experimental sessions (for which we have strong evidence, at least in first-price common value auctions; see Garvin and Kagel, in press).[16] Although we cannot sort out between these alternatives on this data set, introducing dummy vari-

TABLE 4.4
Fixed Effects Model Estimates of Individual Subject Bid Function in Private
Information Markets

	Model	
	1	*2*
Variable	*Coefficient Estimates (standard error)*	
Intercept	−1.69*	−1.30
	(.874)	(1.21)
x_i	1.00**	1.00**
	(.005)	(.005)
ε	−.33**	−.35**
	(.037)	(.056)
DEPS	−.01	.03
	(.025)	(.071)
D	—	−.68
		(1.45)
R^2	.98	.98

D = 0 if N = 4 or 5, D = 1 otherwise.
DEPS = 0 if N = 4 or 5, DEPS = ε otherwise.
1. Restricted to signals in the interval (1).
*Significantly different from zero at 10% level.
**Significantly different from zero at 5% level.

ables (intercept shifts) into the regressions to capture these experimental session effects results in reasonably well behaved residuals.

After correction for these experimental session effects, we are left with 11 subjects for which we can identify N effects using either the first or second bid functions specified in Table 4.4. (We fit model 2 to the data wherever we could. However, for about half the subjects the experimental session dummy variables meant that we could not identify the dummy variable D in model 2. In these cases we fit model 1 to the data.) On the basis of these regressions we classified subjects as bidding higher, lower or the same across values of N. In determining whether or not subjects bid higher or lower (as opposed to the same) we employed a .20 significance level; i.e., in model 2 the F-statistic associated with the dummy variable D and DEPS had to be significantly different from 1.0 at the .20 level or better, while in model 1 the t-statistic associated with the DEPS variable had to be significantly different from 0 at the .20 level (two-tailed t-test).[17] Further, in cases where the signs of the D and DEPS dummy variables differed (indicating that the effect of N varied with ε), we counted a subject as not changing their bid if there where ε values for which the net effect was zero (2 subjects fall into this category). Using these rules, we classify 2 subjects as bidding less with increased N (as Nash equilibrium bidding theory requires), 3 subjects as bidding more with increased N (in direct contradiction to the Nash model's predictions), and 6 as not changing their bids (in contradiction to the Nash model, but consistent with the naive bidding model). That is, only 2 of 11 subjects were bidding consistent with the Nash model's predictions.

Assuming that these directional responses to increases in N are independent across subjects (a point we will return to in the concluding section of the paper), and that our subject population represents a random draw from the population as a whole, the proportion of the parent population we might expect to bid consistent with the Nash model's predictions (using a 95% confidence interval) may be as low as 3% or as high as 56%. In other words, we might expect as many as 97%, but no fewer than 44%, of the parent population to bid the same or to increase their bids as N increases, which is inconsistent with the Nash model's predictions. We conclude that a substantial part of the parent population is unlikely to take account of the heightened adverse selection problem inherent in auctions with more bidders, which failure underlies the winner's curse.[18]

4.2 Effects of Public Information on Revenue

Table 4.5 shows the actual effects of announcing x_L on revenue, and the predicted effects under the RNSNE. The ability of public information to raise revenue appears to be conditional on the number of active bidders in the auction, and by association, on the presence or absence of a strong winner's curse (losses) under private information conditions. Pooling data from auctions with four or five active bidders, x_L raises revenue an average of \$.25 per auction period, which is not significantly different from zero ($t = .21$), and amounts to 16.1% of the RNSNE model's prediction.

In contrast, in auctions with 6 or 7 active bidders, announcing x_L *reduces* revenue an average of \$3.98 per auction period, compared to the Nash equilibrium prediction that revenue will *increase* by \$1.91 per period. Further, a t-test shows the decrease in revenue here to be statistically significant ($t = -3.43$, significant at better than the .01 level).

There is no theoretical reason why increasing numbers of bidders should, by itself, result in x_L lowering rather then raising revenue. However, increasing numbers of bidders does exacerbate the adverse selection problem resulting in negative average profits (a winner's curse) under private information conditions. As the naive bidding model suggests, under these circumstances the release of public information may help correct for the overly optimistic estimate of the item's value held by the high bidder. Individual bidders' responses to x_L support this conclusion, and suggest that residual traces of the winner's curse were responsible for x_L not raising revenue nearly as much as predicted under the RNSNE bidding model with $N = 4$–5.

Table 4.6 reports individual bidders' responses to the release of public information. Responses have been categorized as increasing, decreasing, or not

TABLE 4.5
Effects of Public Information on Revenue

Session (no. auctions)	No. of Active Bidders	Average Change in Revenue	
		Actual (standard error)	RNSNE Prediction (standard error)
5A (12)	4	−.05 (3.09)	1.50 (1.85)
6A (14)	4	−1.12 (3.02)	.33 (1.09)
6B (7)	5	2.06 (3.37)	2.24 (.67)
1 (16)	5	.35 (1.40)	1.71 (1.11)
5B (12)	5–6	−5.91 (3.61)	2.56 (1.51)
2 (12)	6–7	−2.37 (1.80)	1.98 (.88)
4 (14)	6–7	−1.25 (1.52)	.91 (.81)
3 (15)	7	−4.02** (1.86)	2.52 (.78)

**Significantly different from zero at 5% level in 2-tailed t-test.

changing with the announcement of x_L, separated into regions by distance between the bidder's signal and the lowest signal. In region (i), $x_i < C_w(x_L)$, both the naive and the symmetric Nash equilibrium bidding models predict that individual bids will increase with announcement of x_L. In region (iii), $x_i > C(x_L)$, both the naive model and the RNSNE model predict that individual bids will decrease with announcement of x_L (no general prediction can be made here under Nash allowing for risk aversion). However, in region (ii), $C_w(x_L) < x_i < C(x_L)$, the naive model calls for bids to decrease with announcement of x_L, while the symmetric Nash model calls for bids to increase (even with risk aversion).

For signals in region (i), bidders generally responded in the appropriate direction, with 89.5% of all bids increasing for $N = 4-5$ and 79% increasing for $N = 6-7$. For signals in region (111), most bids decreased as expected; 80.4% of all bids for $N = 4-5$ and 81% of all bids for $N = 6-7$. Finally, for signals in region (ii), where the symmetric naive and Nash models offer different predictions, we find a higher frequency of bids decreasing then increasing: 45.8% decreasing with $N = 4-5$, compared to 40.7% increasing; 57% decreasing for $N = 6-7$, compared to 30.1% increasing.

TABLE 4.6
Changes in Individual Bids Following Release of Public Information

Number of Bidders	Private Information Signal Categories (total no. signals in category)	Change in Bids (in percentages)		
		Increase	Decrease	No Change
	(i) $x_i \leq C_w(x_L)$ (114)	89.5	3.5	7.0
4–5	(ii) $C_w(x_L) < x_i < C(x_L)$ (59)	40.7	45.8	13.6
	(iii) $x_i \geq C(x_L)$ (46)	8.7	80.4	10.9
	(i) $x_l \leq C_w(x_L)$ (138)	79.0	10.9	10.1
6–7	(ii) $C_w(x_L) < x_i < C(x_L)$ (93)	30.1	57.0	12.9
	(iii) $x_i \geq C(x_L)$ (42)	16.7	81.0	2.4

The relatively high frequency with which individual bids decrease, or do not change, for signal values in category (ii) goes a long way towards explaining why public information did not raise revenue as much as predicted under the RNSNE bidding model with small numbers of rivals, and resulted in decreased revenue with larger numbers of bidders. The second highest signal occurs in region (i) less than 18% of the time for $N = 4$, dropping rapidly to less than 3% for $N = 7$; it occurs in region (iii) a little over 30% of the time (the frequency here is insensitive to N). The mechanism for public information to raise revenue under the Nash formulation depends critically on the fact that the second highest signal holder increases his bid in region (ii) when x_L is announced. But the frequency with which individual bids decrease, or remain constant, in this category indicates that this mechanism is simply not working well in these auctions, irrespective of the number of participants.[19] Finally, the consistency of changes in individually bids with the naive model's predictions provides further evidence that overly aggressive bidding is rooted in the failure to recognize the adverse selection problem conditional on winning the auction.

Table 4.7 reports market outcomes under public information conditions, Mean actual profit was positive in 7 of the 8 auction series, averaging 47.6% of profit predicted under the RNSNE ($1.57 per period actual vs $3.30 predicted). Although profits varied considerably across auction periods relative to the RNSNE model's predictions, unlike private information conditions they did not differ substantially conditional on the number of bidders present: with $N = 4$–5 average profits were 51.7% of predicted ($1.93 per period actual vs $3.73 predicted), and with $N = 6$–7 profits were 41.2% of predicted ($1.15 actual vs

TABLE 4.7
Market Outcomes under Public Information Conditions

Session (no. auctions)	No. of Active Bidders	Percentage of Auctions Won by High Signal Holder	Median Rank-Order Correlation Coefficient between Bids and Signals	Average Profit (standard error mean)			Profit as a Percentage of RNSNE
				Naive Bidding	Observed	RNSNE	
5A (12)	4	50.0	.40	.76 (2.03)	2.69 (2.14)	4.88 (2.22)	55.1
6A (14)	4	28.6	.30	2.93 (1.55)	6.41** (2.25)	5.87 (1.53)	109.2
6B (7)	5	14.3	−.20	1.64 (1.80)	1.17 (3.03)	5.38 (2.11)	21.7
1 (16)	5	25.0	.30	−1.85 (1.11)	0.02 (1.50)	1.39 (.79)	1.4
5B (12)	5–6	16.7	.31	−.68 (2.22)	0.07 (2.43)	3.62 (2.40)	1.9
2 (12)	6–7	25.0	.14	0.01 (1.05)	1.54 (1.17)	2.90 (1.23)	53.1
4 (14)	6–7	42.9	.36	−.92 (1.02)	1.21 (1.53)	1.61 (1.06)	75.2
3 (15)	7	40.0	.56	−1.34 (1.25)	−0.43 (1.59)	2.33 (1.38)	−18.5

**Significantly different from zero at 5% level in 2-tailed test.

$2.79 predicted). That is, unlike private information conditions, the actual reduction in profits is proportional to the predicted reduction so that the strong winner's curse present with large numbers of bidders under private information conditions has been eliminated.

Finally, as columns 3 and 4 of Table 4.7 show, both the frequency with which the high signal holder won these auctions, and the median rank order correlation coefficient between bids and signals, have deteriorated substantially relative to private information conditions (recall Table 4.2). However, both are still greater then one would expect on the basis of chance factors alone, so that the adverse selection problem is still present, but with substantially reduced intensity.[20] The reduced correlation between bids and signals under public information conditions can readily be accounted for by the fact that announcement of x_L substantially reduced the diversity of expectations regarding x_0, relative to private information conditions. This permits any underlying differences in aggressiveness, risk attitudes, or information processing capacities, to play an increased role in auction outcomes.

5. Summary and Conclusions

We have reported a series of second-price common value auctions with experienced bidders. Auctions with four or five bidders exhibit substantial positive profits with outcomes closer to the benchmark RNSNE then the naive bidding model. In contrast, in auctions with six or seven bidders, there is some adjustment to the adverse selection forces, as profits exceed the naive bidding model's prediction, but subjects, consistently earn negative profits, as they suffer from a winner's curse.

The comparative static tests of the Nash equilibrium bidding model, which are theoretically quite robust and more revealing of the underlying behavioral process in second-price auctions, indicate strong elements of a winner's curse. The individual bid function does not change with varying number of rivals, consistent with the naive bidding model, and in direct contradiction to the Nash equilibrium bidding formulation. This provides rather striking evidence that losses in auctions with six or seven bidders do not result from simple miscalculations, but from a failure to appreciate the adverse selection forces inherent in common value auctions. Announcing public information results in a less-than-significant increase in average revenue for auctions with four or five bidders, but a large *decrease* in revenue for auctions with six or seven bidders. Further, the pattern of individual bidders' responses to public information suggests a failure to account reliably for the information implied by the event of winning. Finally, bidders are sensitive to the changes in ε, which is consistent with the Nash model and is inconsistent with risk neutral naive bidders. But this outcome is consistent with risk averse, naive bidders.

One potentially troublesome problem with our experimental design is the use of a single set of 17 subjects, in different combinations, in the different experimental sessions (11 out of 17 participated in more than one session). This experimental design was, motivated by the desire to provide subjects with maximum experience with the task at hand and to compare the effects of bidding in auctions with different numbers of bidders. But the design does raise questions about the independence of observations both within and across experimental sessions. That is, aside from any individual subject learning effects that might be present, are we justified in treating each auction period within a given experimental session as an independent observation? If we cannot treat each auction period as independent can we treat each experimental session as an independent observation or does the fact that subjects often played in more than one game with some of the same people mean that we really only have one observation?

There are two potential reasons for lack of independence in a small group experiment of this sort. First, the repeated interactions of individuals within an experimental session creates the potential for super game effects in which players may achieve outcomes that are not equilibria in single shot games. In the context of our experiment, these additional equilibria would typically involve subjects achieving some sort of collusive outcome (tacit or otherwise) resulting in higher profits than the single-shot RNNE. As such we can safely rule out these supergame effects as subjects consistently earned negative profits in auctions with six or seven bidders. The second possibility, which is very real and consistent with game theoretic reasoning, is that the outcomes of the game (whether or not they involve equilibrium behavior or best responses to others' actions) reflect the composition of the group within a given experimental session. From this perspective we would have to rule out independence of observations between auction periods within a given experimental session (i.e., seeing negative profits in 9 out of 12 auction periods in experimental session 5 with $N = 5$ or 6, as we did, is not the same as seeing negative average profits in 9 out of 12 different experimental sessions with different groups of subjects). Moreover, the experimental sessions are not completely independent since there was some overlap of participants between sessions. However, if one is willing to make the assumption that subjects have stable bid functions which are reflected by our regressions, we can treat the 11 subjects for whom we could identify N effects in their individual subject bid functions as independent draws from some parent population, as we evaluate these effects after controlling for individual session effects.[21] And these data are most damaging to Nash bidding theory, indicating that between 44% and 97% of the parent population will not consistently decrease their bids when N increases, thereby committing the winner's curse. Of course, it is still possible that the outcomes we observe are peculiar to the particular history of play our subjects experienced. So in this respect our results require replication.

The results here closely parallel those of earlier reports of bidding in first-price common value auctions (Kagel and Levin, 1986; Dyer, Kagel and Levin, 1989; Kagel et al., 1989). The distinguishing characteristics of the present study is that in conducting it in a second-price auction institution the testable implications of Nash equilibrium bidding theory apply to a far wider variety of circumstances then in first-price auctions. As such there is far less scope to rationalize the failure of Nash equilibrium bidding theory under the second-price rules.

One noticeable difference between bidding in second and first-price common value auctions is the frequency with which high signal holders win the auctions: 70.3% of all auctions were won by the high signal holders in first-price auctions (Kagel and Levin, 1986) compared to 57.8% here. In comparison, in auctions with affiliated private values, 90.4% of all first-price auctions were won by the high value holder compared to 73.4% of second-price auctions (Kagel, Harstad and Levin, 1987). Thus, there is a reduction in the frequency with high signal holders win the auction in going from private to common value auctions as well as in going from first-price to second-price auctions. One possible explanation for the reduced frequency of winning in common value auctions is that the item valuation component makes these auctions substantially more complex than private value auctions. As such there is more scope for individual subject bidding errors to express themselves, or for any inherent variability in players' ability to process information to affect bids. With respect to differences in the frequency with which high signal holders win under first and second-price rules, we conjecture that it is the increased flatness in bidders' payoff functions that is partly responsible for the differences observed. With a flatter payoff function, there are reduced monetary costs to deviating from the optimal bidding strategy. As such, any inherent variability in bidders behavior is less constrained in second-price auctions as the relative cost of deviating from the optimal bidding strategy has been reduced.

Appendix

This appendix proves the proposition in the text. It starts by providing a few known results on symmetric second-price auctions and proceeds, by proving a lemma used in the proof of the proposition.

Matthews (1977) and Milgrom and Weber (1982) showed that the function $b(x)$ defined by $E[u(x_0 - b(x)) \mid X_i = Y_i = x] = 0$, where X_i is the signal of bidder i and Y_i is the highest signal among the $N - 1$ rival bidders, is a symmetric Nash equilibrium (SNE). Levin and Harstad (1986), showed that this function is the unique SNE. With public information in the form of x_L, the lowest private signal received by the participating bidders, the unique SNE becomes $B(x, x_L)$ defined by $E[u(x_0 - B(x, x_L)) \mid X_i = Y_i = x, X_L = x_L] = 0$.

Consider the distributions functions $F(x_0 \mid X_i = Y_i = x)$ and $G(x_0 \mid X_i = Y_i = x, x_L = x_L(x))$ where x_L is restricted to the interval (1) (i.e. $\underline{x} + \varepsilon \leq x_L \leq \bar{x} - \varepsilon$) and where $x_L(x)$ is defined by

$$E[x_0 \mid X_i = Y_i = x] = E[x_0 \mid X_i = Y_i = x, X_L = x_L(x)]. \quad \text{(A.1)}$$

In the interval (1), $E[x_0 \mid X_i = Y_i = x] = x - \varepsilon[(N - 2)/N]$ and $E[x_0 \mid X_i = Y_i = x, X_L = x_L(x)] = (x + x_L)/2$. Thus,

$$x_L(x) = x - 2\varepsilon(N - 2)/N \quad \text{and} \quad dx_L(x)/dx = 1. \quad \text{(A.2)}$$

Let $C(x_L)$ be the inverse of $x_L(x)$ thus,

$$C(x_L) = x_L + 2\varepsilon(N - 2)/N. \tag{A.3}$$

Lemma: $F[x_0 \mid X_i = Y_i = x]$ is a Mean Preserving Spread (MPS) of $G[x_0 \mid X_i = Y_i = x, X_L = x_L(x)]$.

Proof: The way we define $x_L(x)$ in (A.1) assures that F and G have the same mean in interval (1).

$$F[x_0 \mid X_i = Y_i = x] = \begin{cases} 0 & x_0 \leq x - \varepsilon \\ 1 - [(x + \varepsilon - x_0)/2\varepsilon]^{N-1} & x - \varepsilon < x_0 < x + \varepsilon \\ 1 & x + \varepsilon \leq x_0 \end{cases}$$

$G[x_0 \mid X_i = Y_i = x, X_L = x_L(x)] =$

$$\begin{cases} 0 & x_0 \leq x - \varepsilon \\ (x_0 + \varepsilon - x)N/4\varepsilon & x - \varepsilon < x_0 < x - \varepsilon(N - 4)/N \\ 1 & x - \varepsilon(N - 4)/N \leq x_0 \end{cases}$$

Define $S(x_0 \mid x) =: F[x_0 \mid X_i = Y_i = x] - G[x_0 \mid X_i = Y_i = x, X_L = x_L(x)]$.

$S(x_0 \mid x) =$

$$\begin{cases} 0 & \text{if } x_0 \in D_1 =: [\underline{x} + \varepsilon, x - \varepsilon] \\ 1 - [(x + \varepsilon - x_0)/2\varepsilon]^{N-1} - (x_0 + \varepsilon - x)N/4\varepsilon & \text{if } x_0 \in D_2 =: [x - \varepsilon, x - \varepsilon(N - 4)/N] \\ - [(x + \varepsilon - x_0)/2\varepsilon]^{N-1} & \text{if } x_0 \in D_3 =: [x - \varepsilon(N - 4)/N, x + \varepsilon] \\ 0 & \text{if } x_0 \in D_4 =: [x + \varepsilon, \bar{x} - \varepsilon]. \end{cases}$$

It is easy to verify that S is a continuous function in x_0 and that $\int dS(x_0 \mid x) = 0$ on supp $[x_0 \mid x]$. (This will establish that F and G are indeed mean preserving.) $S = 0$ if $x_0 \in D_1 \cup D_4$ and $S < 0$ if $x_0 \in D_3$. Thus to show that S satisfies the *Integral Condition* for MPS, it is sufficient to show that there exist $\xi \in D_2$ such that $S \gtrless 0$ as $x_0 \gtrless \xi$, $x_0 \in D_2$. $S(x - \varepsilon \mid x) = 0$, i.e. S is zero on the left boundary of D_2 but strictly increases there since

$$\lim_{\substack{x_0 \to x - \varepsilon \\ x_0 > x - \varepsilon}} \partial S/\partial x_0 = (N - 2)/4\varepsilon > 0.$$

S is concave in x_0 on D_2 ($\partial^2 S/\partial x_0^2 < 0$ if $x_0 \in D_2$), and negative on the right boundary of D_2. ($S(x - \varepsilon(N - 4)/4 \mid x) = -[(N - 2)/N]^{N-1} < 0$). These facts in conjunction with the continuity of S establish our proof.

Proof of the Proposition in the Text: Let $X_L = x_L$ be the public information revealed. $0 = E[u(x_0 - b(C(x_L))) \mid X_i = Y_i = C(x_L)] < E[u(x_0 - b(C(x_L))) \mid X_i = Y_i = C(x_L), X_L = x_L]$. The equality follows the definition of $b(x)$, the inequality is due to the fact (established in the lemma) that the distribution F is a MPS of G and u is a concave function. The inequality and the definition of $B(x, x_L)$ imply that $B(C(x_L), x_L) > b(C(x_L))$. If $x < C(x_L)$ then by (A.2) $x_L(x) < x_L$. Thus for such x we have $B(x, x_L) > B(x, x_L(x)) > b(x)$ where the first inequality is due to affiliation which implies monotonicity of these bidding functions (see Milgrom and Weber, 1982), and the second inequality is due to the result established just above. We showed that $x < C(x_L)$ implies $B(x, x_L) > b(x)$.

Notes

Financial support was received from the Information Science and Technology Division and the Economics Division of the National Science Foundation, the Russell Sage Foundation, the Sloan Foundation's Program in Behavioral Economics, the Energy Laboratory and the Center for Public Policy of the University of Houston Doug Dyer. Susan Garvin and Steve Kerman provided valuable research assistance We thank the referees for particularly helpful comments that underlie the current version of the paper. An earlier version of this paper circulated under the title "Judgement, Evaluation and Information Processing in Second-Price Common Value Auctions."

1. This conclusion is, of course, not without its critics. See Wilson (1992) for an evenhanded review of the results from field data.

2. The Nash equilibrium model used to provide a game-theoretic prediction in a single unit auction presumes a von Neumann-Morganstern expected utility function. The independence axiom thus assumed, and the coin flip, make the optimal strategy in either market unaffected by the other. Battalio, Kogut and Meyer (1990), Kagel and Levin (1986) and Kagel, Harstad, and Levin (1987) report no systematic behavioral differences under dual market as compared to single market procedures.

3. We do not report outcomes of 5 sessions involving a total of 29 inexperienced subjects. The inexperienced-subject sessions followed procedures of section II(a) above, one beginning with 5 bidders, the others with 6. Any subject acquiring experience in those sessions (arbitrarily defined as having completed at least 15 auction periods without going bankrupt), was eligible to be recruited for the sessions reported here. Once recruited, subjects were invited back for later sessions without regard to earlier performance.

4. The x_0 values and the associated signal values were all determined randomly, strictly according to the process described to the subjects. As such a sizable number, but small fraction, of signal values lie outside the interval (1). In cases where we can extend the theoretical analysis to cover such observations (for example, equilibrium bidding; see note 5) these data are included in the analysis along with observations in the interval (1).

5. An equilibrium is locally nondegenerate when the probability of any given bidder winning the auction is positive for all bidders.

6. For $x_i < \underline{x} + \varepsilon$, the RNSNE bid function is $\underline{x} + [x_i - (\underline{x} - \varepsilon)]/N$. For $x_i > \bar{x} - \varepsilon$, the RNSNE bid function is $x_i - \varepsilon(N - 2)/N - (\bar{x} + \varepsilon - x_i)(N - 1)\theta(x)^{N-1}/\{(1 - \theta(x)^{N-1})N\}$ where $\theta(x) = (x_i + \varepsilon - \bar{x})/2\varepsilon$.

7. More formally, this comparative static prediction is an unstated consequence of Theorem 5 in Milgrom and Weber (1982) applied to the symmetric bid function (3). Since (3) depends only on monotonicity of the utility function and not on risk attitudes (Levin and Harstad, 1986), the result applies to both risk averse and risk loving bidders. No comparable general result holds for first price auctions; for the distributional parameters employed here and in Kagel and Levin (1986), the risk neutral first-price Nash equilibrium bid function falls with increased numbers of bidders, but this comparative static property is not invariant to risk attitudes.

8. A caveat is in order here. We have not been able to prove that there is a unique asymmetric equilibrium as a consequence of asymmetric risk preferences. Consequently

there *may* be multiple asymmetric equilibria (we have not been able to demonstrate that such equilibria exist either). Harstad's proposition does not apply across two such increasing, locally nondegenerate asymmetric equilibria.

9. This equation assumes x strictly exceeds x_L, so that public information reveals a rival's signal. The expectation is discontinuously higher for the lowest signal holder.

10. Frequency calculations for the location of $X_i = x_2$ here, and elsewhere in the text, are from a numerical simulation using 1000 sets of signal values for each value of N.

11. If a single outcome remains after finite iterations of deleting dominated strategies, the game is dominance solvable (Moulin [1979]). The argument here parallels Harstad and Levin [1985]: given the underlying distribution of signal values, with symmetry and risk neutrality any bidder is willing to bid at least as aggressively as $(x_i + x_L)/2$ independent of rivals' behavior, but no more aggressively than this against rivals bidding at least $(x_i + x_L)/2$.

12. The caveat of note 8 holds here as well.

13. Our computations include all auctions under dual market procedures, whether or not bidders actually made profits (or losses) as a consequence of our coin flip rule. Since the coin flip was made after bids from both markets had been submitted, its outcome should not affect decisions. Dry run auctions with no money at stake, used at the beginning of a session to refresh bidders' memories, are not included in the analysis. Within a given series of auctions, there appears to be little systematic variation in bids over time, notwithstanding variations in N and ε.

14. Note that a risk-averse equilibrium model would predict higher profits. The possibility that observed profit levels result from risk-loving may be discounted; subjects drawn from the same population for first-price, affiliated private value auctions exhibit no signs of risk loving in a setting free of item value estimation complexities (Kagel, Harstad, and Levin, 1987).

15. Limited-liability for losses sets up the possibility that players will bid more aggressively then under the one-shot Nash equilibrium as potential losses are truncated. However, initial cash balances were such that bidders were fully liable for all losses relative to the RNSNE prediction except with $N = 4$ and $\varepsilon = \$30$ (as the data indicates loses and gains do not vary systematically over time or with e and the average cash balance of the 6 bidders who went bankrupt was $7.56 at the time of bankruptcy). Further, other things equal, limited-liability for losses is more of a problem with $N = 4$ then with $N = 6$ or 7, as the Nash model calls for reduced bidding with increased numbers of bidders (whereas the data shows positive profits with $N = 4$ and losses with $N = 6$ or 7, the exact opposite of the pattern implied by a limited-liability argument). See Hansen and Lott (1991), Lind and Plott (1991), and Kagel and Levin (1991) for further discussion of limited-liability issues in the context of first-price common value auctions.

16. Another possibility is "super game" effects as the repeated interactions might allow subjects to obtain outcomes that could not be achieved in a one-shot game. However, as noted in the concluding section of the paper these super game effects are not consistent with the profit levels observed.

17. The choice of significance level here is fairly arbitrary. Using the standard .05 or .10 level seems too severe since the theory makes no predictions regarding the variance in bidders' responses to changes in N. However, using a more common significance level does little to alter the classifications; e.g., using a 5% significance level, we classify 2 subjects as bidding less with increased N, 2 subjects as bidding more, and 7 as no change.

18. We have a good check on the robustness of these results. In session 5 (when

subjects had maximum experience), we employed a cross-over design with subjects first bidding in games with $N = 4$ and then in games with $N = 6$ (observations are limited to $\varepsilon = \$30$ since a bankruptcy reduced N after several periods with $N = 6$). Limiting the analysis to signals, in the interval (1) and computing the average discount factor $(x - b(x)$ where $b(x)$ is the bid associated with signal value x) for $N = 4$ versus $N = 6$ we obtain the following results:

Subject	Average $x - b(x)$ $N = 4$	Average $x - b(x)$ $N = 6$	t-statistic[a] (prob t = 0)	Degrees of Freedom
1	.1	−12.7	1.76 (.13)	6
2	15.7	23.7	−2.13 (.09)	5
3	−3.7	−2.2	−.86 (.42)	7
4	16.8	17.5	−.64 (.54)	6
5	10.1	9.4	.62 (.56)	5
6	12.6	5.7	2.41 (.05)	7

[a]Difference between $x - b(x)$ with $N = 4$ less $N = 6$.

Using the .20 significance rule to identify a change in discount rates (as in the text), 1 subject (S2) decreases her bid going from $N = 4$ to 6 (has a higher discount with $N = 6$ than with $N = 4$), 2 subjects increase their bids (S1 & S6), and 3 do not change their bids as N changes.

19. Similar results are reported for individual subjects for signals in region (ii), where the symmetric and Nash models offer different predictions: With $N = 4$ or 5, 56% of the subjects (5 out of 9) decrease their bids or do not change their bids 50% of the time or more following the release of public information (contrary to the symmetric Nash model's predictions). With $N = 6$ or 7, 80% of the subjects (8 out of 10) do the same.

20. Pooling data across auction series, chance factors alone would account for 18% of all auctions being won by the high private information signal holder, compared to the high signal holder winning 30% of all auctions. The difference is significant at better than the 1% level using a binomial test statistic.

21. As noted, examination of the residuals from individual subject regressions support this argument, after the adjustment for experimental session effects. Also, unlike some games coordination games), in our auction individual subject's best response to an increase in N does not depend on what others' responses are to these increases, provided certain mild regularity conditions are satisfied.

References

Battalio RC, Kogut C, Meyer J (1990) The effect of varying number of bidders in first price private values auctions: An application of a dual market bidding technique. In:

Green L, Kagel J, Advances in Behavioral Economics, Ablex Publishing: Norwood NJ 95–125.

Bikhchandani S, Riley JG (1991) Equilibria in open common value auctions. Journal of Economic Theory 53: 101–130.

Capen EC, Clapp RW, Campbell WM (1971) Competitive bidding in high-risk situations. Journal of Petroleum Technology 23: 641–653.

Cassady R Jr (1967) Auctions and auctioneering. Un California Press, Los Angeles Ca.

Dyer D, Kagel JH, Levin D (1989) A comparison of naive and experienced bidders in common value offer auctions: A laboratory analysis. Economic Journal 99: 108–115.

Garvin S, Kagel JH (in press) Learning in common value auctions: Some initial observations. Journal of Economic Behavior and Organization.

Gilley OW, Karels GV, Leone RP (1986) Uncertainty, experience and the 'winner's curse' in OCS lease bidding. Management Science 32: 673–682.

Hansen RG, Lott JR Jr (1991) The winner's curse and public information in common value auctions: Comment American Economic Review 91: 347–361.

Harstad RM (1991) Asymmetric bidding in second-price, common-value auctions. Economic Letters 35: 249–252.

Harstad R, Levin D (1985) A class of dominance solvable common value auctions. Review of Economic Studies 52: 525–528.

Kagel JH, Levin D (1986) The winner's curse and public information in common value auctions. American Economic Review 76: 994–920.

Kagel JH, Levin D, Battalio RC, Meyer DJ (1989) First-Price, sealed-bid common value auctions: Bidder behavior and the 'winner's curse'. Economic Inquiry 27: 241–259.

Kagel JH, Levin D (1991) The winner's curse and public information in common value auctions: Reply American Economic Review 81: 362–369.

Kagel JH, Harstad RM, Levin D (1987) Information impact and allocation rules in auctions with affiliated private values: A laboratory study. Econometrica 55: 1275–1304.

Levin D, Harstad R (1986) Symmetric bidding in second price common value auctions. Economics Letters 20: 315–319.

Lind B, Plott CR (1991) The winner's curse: Experiments with buyers and with sellers. American Economic Review 81: 335–346.

Lorenz J, Dougherty EL (1983) Bonus bidding and bottom lines: Federal offshore oil and gas. SPE 12024, 58th Ann Fall Tech Conf.

Matthews S (1977) Information acquisition in competitive bidding processes. Mimeographed, California Institute of Technology, Pasadena, CA.

Mead W, Moseidjord A, Sorensen PE (1983) The rate of return earned by leases under cash bonus bidding in OCS oil and gas leases. Energy Journal 4: 37–52.

Milgrom PR (1981) Rational expectations, information acquisition and competitive bidding. Econometrica 49: 921–943.

Milgrom PR (1985) Auction theory. Cowles Foundation Discussion paper, Yale University.

Milgrom PR, Weber RJ (1982) A theory of auctions and competitive bidding. Econometrica 50: 1099–1122.

Moulin H (1979) Dominance solvable voting scheme. Econometrica 47: 1337–1352.

Pratt JW (1964) Risk aversion in the small and in the large. Econometrica 32: 122–136.

Vickrey W (1961) Counterspeculation, auctions, and competitive sealed tenders. Journal of Finance 16: 8–37.

Wilson R (1992) Strategic analysis of auctions. In: Aumann RJ, Hart S (Eds) Handbook of Game Theory with Economic Applications Vol 1. Amsterdam, Elsevier Science Publishers 227–280.

5

Information Impact and Allocation Rules in Auctions with Affiliated Private Values: A Laboratory Study

—

John H. Kagel, Ronald M. Harstad, and Dan Levin

1. Introduction

A series of auction experiments are reported in which a single indivisible item is auctioned off among six bidders under different information conditions and using different allocation rules. The induced valuations are private and satisfy the criterion of strict positive affiliation (Milgrom and Weber, 1982). With private values each bidder has perfect information concerning the value of the object at auction for him/herself; with affiliation, a higher value of the item for one bidder makes higher values for other bidders more likely. A simple example of an auction with affiliated private values would be a charity fundraiser of consumer perishables, where an item unusually appealing to you is typically more appealing to other bidders as well.

Milgrom and Weber (1982) provide general characterizations of auctions with affiliated variables. Our experiments afford a test of three important implications of these auctions: (i) In a first-price sealed bid auction,[1] public information about rivals' values announced prior to bidding increases expected revenue, in risk-neutral symmetric equilibrium. (ii) An English auction[2] attains higher expected revenue than a first-price auction, again evaluated at the risk-neutral symmetric Nash equilibrium in the first-price auction, and the dominant strategy equilibrium in the English auction. (iii) A second-price auction[3] results in the same dominant strategy outcome as an English institution, with the same expected revenue advantage over a first-price auction. In conducting these tests, we specify alternative ad hoc (rule of thumb) bidding models and their implications for the experimental manipulations employed. In this way we can compare Nash equilibrium bidding models with specific alternative rival formulations, rather than merely test whether the data satisfy point predictions of the Nash formulation.

In the first-price auction experiments, Nash equilibrium bidding theory organizes the data better than either of two ad hoc bidding models, embodying simple or sophisticated discounting behavior. A simple fixed discount rule fails to account for the fact that bids decrease with increases in the interval from which private values are drawn. Large doses of public information raise average revenue, but the resulting revenue increases are lower and considerably less reliable than predicted under the risk-neutral symmetric Nash equilibrium. Observed increases in revenue, and adjustments in individual bids resulting from release of public information, correspond more closely to the predictions of a risk averse Nash equilibrium bidding model than to a sophisticated ad hoc discounting rule. The failure of public information to raise average revenue as much as predicted under risk neutrality might largely be accounted for by risk aversion. However, individual bid patterns and variability in revenue increases are attributable to a sizable frequency of individual bidding errors (relative to Nash theory) in responding to the release of public information.

Nash equilibrium bidding theory precisely organizes English auction outcomes after a brief initial learning period. The dominant strategy equilibrium does not organize second-price auction outcomes nearly as well, as market prices persistently exceed predicted prices. Overbidding in second-price auctions involves bidding errors, relative to theory, of a somewhat different nature than those associated with the release of public information in first-price auctions. The difference between English and second-price auction outcomes appears attributable to differential information flows inherent in the structure of the two institutions. Revenue-raising effects of these two auction institutions, relative to a first-price auction, are examined in light of observed bidding patterns.

The paper is organized as follows. Section 2 characterizes the experimental procedures. Section 3 specifies the ad hoc bidding models, the Nash equilibrium bidding models and the differential predictions of the models given our experimental design. The results of the experiments are reported in Section 4. The concluding section summarizes our results.

2. Structure of the Auctions

2.1 First-Price Auctions

2.1.a Private Information Conditions

Each experiment had several auction periods with 6 subjects bidding for a single unit of a commodity under a first-price, sealed-bid procedure.[4] Subjects' valuations of the item were determined randomly each period according to procedures described below. In each auction the high bidder earned profit equal to his/her value of the item less the high bid; other subjects earned zero profit.

Subjects were told that their private values (x_i) would be determined according to a two step procedure. First, a random number (x_0) would be drawn from a uniform distribution on $[\underline{x}, \overline{x}] = [\$25.00, \$125.00]$. Once x_0 was determined, private values x_1 through x_6, one for each bidder, were randomly drawn from a uniform distribution centered on x_0 with upper bound $x_0 + \varepsilon$ and lower bound $x_0 - \varepsilon$ (all ε are measured in dollars). Subject i, if he or she wins the auction has a price redeemable in the amount x_i. Since subject i is told the value of x_i at the outset, he/she has perfect information about the value of the object at auction to him/herself. Moreover, the level of ε was posted and announced prior to each auction period. Subjects were not told the value of x_0 under these conditions (which we refer to as the private information conditions). Private values are independently drawn relative to x_0, yet are strictly positively affiliated, as bidders' private values are positively correlated relative to the set of possible valuations.

Bids were restricted to be nonnegative and rounded to the nearest penny. After all bids were collected, they were posted on the blackboard in descending order and the high bid noted. Thus subjects had full information about each others' bids, but not about private values underlying bids. The level of ε varied under these private information conditions (see Table 5.1).

2.1.b Public Information Conditions

Approximately half way through each experiment subjects began bidding in two separate auction markets simultaneously. Bidding in the first auction market continued as before under private information conditions. After these bids were collected, but before they were posted, we introduced a public information signal and asked subjects to bid again, with the same private values. We employed two types of public information. In experiments designated x_+ in Table 5.1 (experiments 6 and 7), the public information consisted of randomly drawing an additional private value, which we refer to as x_+, from the same interval as subjects' private values were drawn, and posting it on the blackboard. In experiments designated x_0 in Table 5.1 (1–5), public information consisted of posting x_0 on the blackboard, along with lower and upper bounds of the interval from which private values were drawn, $[x_0 - \varepsilon, x_0 + \varepsilon]$.

Subjects were told that we would only pay profits to the high bidder in one of the two auction markets to be determined by a coin flip *after* bids under *both* information conditions had been collected. Subjects were told that they were under no obligation to submit the same or different bids in the two markets but should bid in a way they thought would "generate greatest profits." All bids from both markets were posted in descending order, side by side.

This dual market bidding procedure, involving the same set of bidders with the same item value and the same set of private information signals, has the advantage of directly controlling for between subject variability and extraneous variability resulting from variations in item value and private information signals.[5] Some critics have argued that under the dual market procedure, the optimal

TABLE 5.1
Design Parameters[a]

| Experiment | Auction Periods ε | | | Dual Market Periods with Public Information |
	$6	$12	$24	
First-Price Auction Experiments x_0 Design				
1&2	1–5	6–16, 25–26	17–24	12–26
3&4	1–5	6–16, 24–25	17–23	12–25
5	—	1–14	15–28	10–28 (public information only periods 25–28)
x_+ Design				
6	1–6	7–16	17–24	12–24
7	1–6	7–18, 26–27	19–25	13–27
English Auction Experiments				
8	1–5	6–10	—	
9	1–5	6–12	13–15	
Second-Price Auction Experiments				
10	1–5	6–15, 23–27	16–22, 28–30	
11[b]	1–6	7–16, 25–28	17–24, 29–31	

[a] Experiments 1–3, 6, 8, and 9 had one dry run with no monetary payoffs. Experiments 7 and 10 had two dry runs. Experiments 4 and 5 had no dry runs.
[b] From period 23 on there were only 5 bidders (see Section 4.2.a below).

bid in one market will affect bids in the other market. However, under the expected utility hypothesis, which underlies our analysis of the first-price auctions, and using the coin flip rule to determine which market to pay in, this conclusion is unwarranted irrespective of the form of the utility function: the optimal strategy in the private information market is unaffected by bids in the public information market, and vice versa.[6]

Of course, it is another matter entirely whether the dual market procedure actually affects bids. The tactic of beginning each experiment with a number of auction periods with private information only, before introducing the dual market bidding procedure, and of ending experiment 5 with bidding in the public information market only, permit us to test for these effects. Using individual subject data, a fixed-effects regression model was fit to each experiment. The sign of a single dummy variable, which distinguished auction periods with dual markets, was found to vary between experiments, but did not differ significantly from zero except in experiment 7 (using independent t tests and a 5 per cent significance level).[7] Detailed examination of experiment 7 showed that one bidder markedly reduced his bidding, relative to valuations received, with the introduction of the dual market procedure, effectively withdrawing from the auction. This one bidder was equally passive in the public information market, however, effectively withdrawing from the bidding process there as well. Thus our analysis of the effects of public information remains internally consistent even for this experiment, albeit for an auction market with effectively 5 rather than 6 bidders.

2.2 Second-Price/English Auctions

The second-price and English auction procedures were designed to match as closely as possible the first-price auction experiments with private information. Private values were determined using the same procedures as the first price auctions. Subjects knew ε but not the value of x_0 at the time they bid.

Under the second-price auction rules the high bidder won the item and paid the second-high-bid price. All bids were posted in descending order, the high bid noted, and profits of the high bidder computed and posted. Bids were restricted to be nonnegative and rounded to the nearest penny.

The English auction experiments used an ascending clock procedure whereby the price of the item increased at small fixed increments and bidders had to signal their intention to drop out of the bidding. Once withdrawn, bidders could not reenter the auction for that market period. The number of active bidders in the auction was publicly stated at all times, with the last bidder receiving the item at the price when the next-to-last bidder dropped out of the bidding.[8]

The start point for the clock was set at the largest multiple of $(\bar{x}, \underline{x})/4$ which was below $x_0 - \varepsilon$. Price increments decreased with the number of active bidders: once two bidders were left, price increments were fixed at 5¢ for $\varepsilon = \$6$, 10¢ for $\varepsilon = \$12$, and 20¢ for $\varepsilon = \$24$. In cases where the last two bidders dropped out on the same increment, a coin toss was used to determine who earned the item.[9] Bids were not posted here, but the prices where rivals dropped were announced as they occurred. Profits of the high bidder were computed and posted on the blackboard at the end of each auction period.

2.3 Subjects

Subjects were drawn primarily from MBA classes in first-price auction experiments 1, 2, 6, and 7 and both second-price auction experiments; and from senior undergraduate economics classes in first-price experiments 3 and 4 and the two English auctions. Experiment 5, conducted last in the first-price auction series, involved experienced subjects who had participated in one earlier first-price auction experiment.

Subjects were paid profits in cash at the end of the experiment plus a $4.00 participation fee.

3. Theoretical Predictions

3.1 First-Price Auctions

In a first-price auction, it is clear that bidders should bid below their private resale values. The relevant question is how far below these values to bid (how much to "discount") and what are the operating principles underlying these bids. We consider four different models of bidding behavior here. Two are ad hoc models in which bidders are specified as adopting (more or less) sensible bidding/discount rules. In contrast to Nash equilibrium bidding models, there is no explicit consideration of whether the rule adopted is the best response to rivals' behavior, although the second model discussed is based on sensible considerations, concerning rivals' behavior. One might justify bidding schemes of this sort with reference to stringent informational requirements inherent in calculating a best response to rivals' behavior. Certainly, the ad hoc models provide an interesting contrast to the two Nash equilibrium bidding models considered: a risk-neutral symmetric Nash equilibrium bidding model (RNSNE hereafter) and a risk-averse symmetric Nash equilibrium bidding solution (RASNE hereafter). Our analysis focuses on the models' predictions regarding responses to variations in ε and the release of public information.

3.1.a Naive Markdown Bidding

The simplest ad hoc bidding model is one in which subjects merely discount their private values in linear fashion:

$$b(x) = \alpha_0 + \alpha_1 x \qquad (1)$$

where $\alpha_0 \leq 0$ and $0 < \alpha_1 \leq 1$. Such simple markdown bidders are insensitive to strategic implications of varying ε and to informational content of announcing x_+ or x_0. While not advocated, this model represents a null hypothesis against which to evaluate predictions of more sophisticated bidding theories.

3.1.b Sophisticated Markdown Bidding

Consider a bidder who is aware of rudimentary strategic implications inherent in the auction, such as effects of varying ε on the closeness of potential rivals' values to his. Furthermore, this bidder bids as if he holds the highest private value conditional on his subjective evaluation of the potential distribution of rivals' private values, and discounts his bid accordingly:

$$b(x) = x - \alpha \left[\frac{x - \tilde{E}(x_0 - \varepsilon)}{N} \right] = \tilde{E}(x_0 - \varepsilon)$$

$$+ \frac{N - \alpha}{N} [x - \tilde{E}(x_0 - \varepsilon)] \qquad (2)$$

where $\tilde{E}(x_0 - \varepsilon)$ is the subjective expected value of $x_0 - \varepsilon$, α is a discount factor restricted to $\alpha > 0$, and N is the number of bidders. Restricting our analysis to values in the range

$$\underline{x} + \varepsilon \leq x \leq \bar{x} - \varepsilon, \tag{3}$$

there are two interesting cases to consider, depending on how the bidder estimates the lowest possible value, $x_0 - \varepsilon$, from his private information.

First consider the bidder whose subjective expectation matches the objective assessment presuming he has drawn the highest of the N private values (denoted $x = x_1$):[10]

$$E[x_0 - \varepsilon \mid x = x_1] = x - \frac{N}{N+1} 2\varepsilon. \tag{4}$$

This results in the bid function

$$b(x) = x - \alpha\left(\frac{2\varepsilon}{N+1}\right). \tag{5}$$

Over most of the range (3), this entails bidding more than the RNSNE (equation 8 below) when $\alpha \leq 1$. Further the predicted response to announcement of public information, x_0 (which is the case we will concentrate on in our analysis) is for individual bidders to increase (decrease) their bids whenever $x_0 - \varepsilon$ is greater (smaller) than (4). Unlike the RNSNE bidding model, however, public information would leave expected revenue unaltered. This follows directly from the ad hoc nature of the discount rule which, while it takes account of number of bidders and ε, does not consider the best response to rivals' behavior.

The second case to consider here is one in which

$$\tilde{E}[x_0 - \varepsilon] = x - \varepsilon. \tag{6}$$

Equation (6) is a naive expectation which ignores the fact that when bidder i wins the auction he/she has the highest (or one of the highest) private resale values. This is a manifestation of a winner's curse effect, a behavioral phenomena commonly cited in the context of common value auctions (Capen, Clapp, and Campbell, 1971; Kagel and Levin, 1986; Milgrom and Weber, 1982), but relevant here as well. Employing (6) in (2),

$$b(x) = x - \alpha\left(\frac{\varepsilon}{N}\right) \tag{7}$$

which involves bidding considerably in excess of RNSNE under private information conditions even with $\alpha = 1$. More importantly, with the announcement of x_0, individual bidders will only increase their bids when $x_0 > x$ and will reduce them whenever $x_0 < x$. Since on average $x_0 < x_1$, public information will reduce expected revenue.

3.1.c Nash Equilibrium Bidding with Risk Neutrality

Theoretical models of auctions have focused upon characterizing risk-neutral symmetric Nash equilibrium.[11] This section presents specification of equilibria in Milgrom and Weber (1982) and Vickrey (1961) for the design parameters employed in our experiments. Restricting our analysis to values in the range (3), under private information conditions, the risk-neutral equilibrium has every bidder employing the function:[12]

$$b(x) = x - \frac{2\varepsilon}{N} + \frac{Y}{N} \tag{8}$$

where

$$Y = \frac{2\varepsilon}{(N+1)} e^{-(N/2\varepsilon)[x-(\underline{x}+\varepsilon)]};$$

Y contains a negative exponential, and becomes negligible rapidly as x moves beyond $\underline{x} + \varepsilon$. Thus, expected profit to the high bidder under the RNSNE are approximately equal to $2\varepsilon/N$.

Milgrom and Weber (1982) demonstrate that revealing public information raises expected revenue in RNSNE. In their model, public information is an additional variable affiliated with values; this is the treatment in x_+ experiments. The x_0 experiments go further, providing maximal public information about the distribution of values—announcing, in effect, an infinite number of additional private valuations, x_+.

Disaggregating revenue enhancement into predictions of individual behavior is particularly tractable for the x_0 design. With x_0 known, the auction is exactly the independent private values model of Vickrey (1961), with the equilibrium bid function

$$b(x, x_0) = x_0 - \varepsilon + \frac{N-1}{N}[x - (x_0 - \varepsilon)] \tag{9}$$

for all x, x_0. Under the RNSNE bidding model, revealing x_0 raises individual bids unless x is extremely near $x_0 + \varepsilon$. As in the ad hoc model with rational expectations (4), the high bidder is not surprised on average by the announcement of x_0. Nevertheless, he/she raises their bid out of strategic considerations arising from the effect of x_0 on rivals' bids.

3.1.d Nash Equilibrium Bidding with Risk Aversion

If bidders' evaluations of uncertain profits associated with different bids are not summarized by the mathematical expectation, a model of risk-averse bidding can be explored. A symmetric formulation is to have each bidder maximize $E[u(\Pi)]$, where Π is the profit earned in any single auction, 0 if not high bidder, $u(0) = 0$, and u is concave. The introduction of risk aversion will result in bidding in excess of the RNSNE under private information conditions as bidders trade off lower expected profits for a higher probability of winning the auction (given rivals' bidding strategies).

A particularly tractable special case here is when u exhibits constant relative risk aversion (CRRA):

$$\frac{-\Pi u''(\Pi)}{u'(\Pi)} = r \quad \text{for all } \Pi \geq 0. \text{[13]}$$ (10)

If the coefficient of relative risk aversion were the same constant for all participants, the equilibrium bid function over range (3) would be

$$b(x, r) = x - \frac{2\varepsilon(1 - r)}{N} + \frac{Y_r}{N}$$ (11)

where

$$Y_r = \frac{(1 - r)^2 2\varepsilon}{(N + 1 - r)N} e^{[-N[x - (\underline{x} + \varepsilon)]/2\varepsilon(1 - r)]}$$

and Y_r becomes negligible rapidly as x moves beyond $\underline{x} + \varepsilon$. Note that (11) degenerates to (8) when $r = 0$ and (11) is greater than (8) for all $0 < r \leq 1$.

With risk aversion, effects of public information on expected revenue depend upon the nature of the utility function and the degree of risk aversion displayed. However, effects on individual bidding depend upon the following striking feature of the x_0 design.

Proposition. *For any concave $u(\Pi)$, over range (3), in a Risk-Average Symmetric Nash Equilibrium (RASNE) all bidders with private values $x < C(x_0)$ raise their bids with public information, where*

$$C(x_0) = x_0 + \frac{N - 2}{N} \varepsilon.$$ (12)

Proof: See Appendix.

On average, the highest value is $x_0 + \varepsilon(N - 1)/(N + 1)$, just above $C(x_0)$. Thus, the Proposition predicts that under a RASNE public information will raise individual bids over virtually the same range of private values that it would under sophisticated markdown bidding with rational expectations (4). Effects of x_0 on bids when values exceed $C(x_0)$, and on expected revenue, depend on the utility function and the degree of risk aversion shown. For example, under CRRA the lower the degree of risk aversion displayed (the closer r is to 0), the wider the interval beyond $C(x_0)$ for which bidders will increase their bids in response to x_0. Further, while revenue enhancing effects of announcing x_0 are sharply reduced in the presence of risk aversion, it is only under extremely high degrees of risk aversion ($r < 0.8$) that x_0 will fail to raise revenues (cf. Figure 5.1). We conjecture that these twin characteristics of the CRRA solution hold for a fairly wide range of concave utility functions, $u(\Pi)$.

The x_+ design experiments are not nearly as rich as the x_0 design in terms of

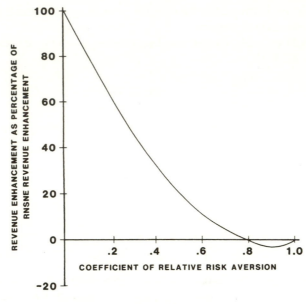

Figure 5.1.

our ability to analyze the impact of public information. Public information must increase revenues, on average, for risk-neutral bidders under our design (Milgrom and Weber, 1982).

3.2 Second-Price/English Auctions

Vickrey (1961) established that the bid function

$$b = x \tag{13}$$

is a dominant strategy in both second-price and English auctions, irrespective of attitudes toward risk. Further, Milgrom and Weber (1982) have shown that with strict affiliation between private valuation, as in our experimental design, under the dominant bidding strategy, second-price and English auction institutions will raise expected revenue relative to a first-price auction under the RNSNE. However given an RASNE, or some ad hoc rule resulting in bidding in excess of the RNSNE, and/or deviations from the dominant strategy, it becomes an empirical question as to which institution will raise the most revenue.

   In developing ad hoc bidding models for the second-price/English auction institutions, it is clear that there is no injunction, in terms of elementary survival requirements, against bids in excess of private values. With the high bidder paying the second-highest-bid price, bidding in excess of (13), and winning, does not assure losses as it would in a first-price auction. Indeed, consideration of the elementary economic/perceptual forces at work in second-price/English auctions suggests that bids are unlikely to fall below private values: bidding below (13) does nothing to improve profits conditional on winning, and only reduces the chances of making any money. Bidding in excess of (13) has the potential attraction of increasing the probability of winning, with no clear effect on profits given the second-price bid rule. The irrationality of bidding in (modest) excess of (13) only becomes apparent once the question is posed of what is the gain relative to bidding (13)? It may not be natural for bidders to pose this question under second-price and/or English auction procedures. Hence, our intuition suggested that deviations from the dominant bidding strategy would, if anything, result in bids in excess of private values's.[14]

This last prediction appears to fly directly in the face of previous experimental research on single unit, independent private value auctions which show mean prices at or below the dominant strategy price under both second-price and English auction institutions (Coppinger, Smith, and Titus, 1980; Cox, Roberson, and Smith, 1982). However, in these earlier private value auction experiments subjects were *not permitted* to bid in excess of their private values. In our second-price/English auction experiments there were no binding ceilings on bids.

4. Experimental Results

4.1 First-Price Auctions

4.1.a Bidding with Private Information Only

Figures 5.2–5.5 graph high market bids over time, in terms of deviations from the RNSNE model's predictions, for the odd-numbered experiments. Table 5.2 reports mean deviations from the RNSNE model's predictions for different levels of ε for all experiments. High bids lie scattered about, or slightly below, the RNSNE when $\varepsilon = \$6$, but tend to be well above the RNSNE prediction with $\varepsilon = \$12$ and even further above the RNSNE when $\varepsilon = \$24$. The pooled t statistic for the $\varepsilon = \$6$ condition shows that we can reject the risk-neutral equilibrium hypothesis at the 10 per cent significance level, in favor of risk loving when $\varepsilon = \$6$. If subjects' adjusting to experimental conditions argues for throwing out the first three auction periods, high bids still average 100 below RNSNE when $\varepsilon = \$6$, failing to reject the null hypothesis of risk neutral behavior.

Table 5.3 shows the effects of ε on profits realized.[15] Under the RNSNE hypothesis, expected profits per auction are approximately $2.00, $4.00, and $8.00 with $\varepsilon = \$6$, 12, and 24 respectively. Table 5.3 shows actual profits tending to increase as ε increases, but by much less than predicted under the RNSNE. With the notable exception of experiment 6, the increase in bids in going from $\varepsilon = \$6$ to 12 is sufficient to wipe out virtually all the increase in expected profit. In going from $\varepsilon = \$12$ to 24, profits increase by $1.00 or more in all experiments except 3 and 4. Increases here are inconsistent with the naive markdown bidding model which permits no adjustments in the face of changing ε levels.[16]

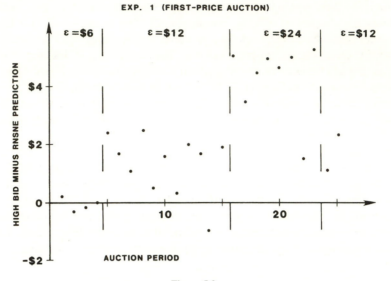

Figure 5.2.

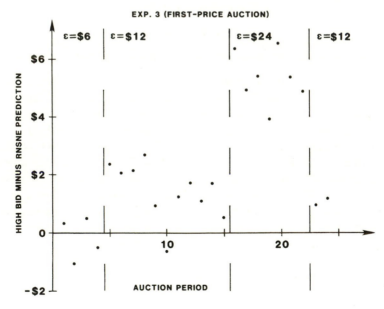

Figure 5.3.

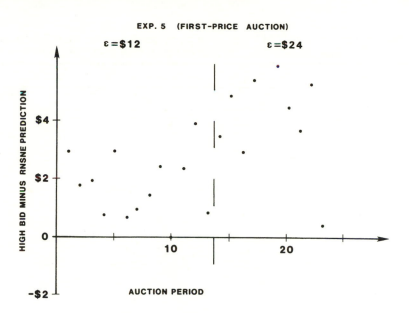

Figure 5.4.

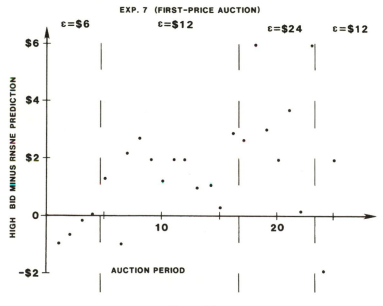

Figure 5.5.

TABLE 5.2
Differences between Actual Bid Prices and Risk-Neutral Symmetric Nash Equilibrium
Bid Prices: Mean Values with Standard Deviations in Parentheses[a]

Experiment	$6	$12	$24
		ε	
x_0 Design			
1	−.12	1.33	4.10
	(.21)	(1.01)	(1.25)
2	−.67	1.49	2.23
	(.71)	(1.43)	(2.84)
3	−.21	1.38	5.48
	(.74)	(.92)	(.93)
4	−.42	1.68	5.01
	(1.28)	(.56)	(1.75)
5	—	1.83	3.49
		(1.15)	(2.51)
x_+ Design			
6	.09	.736	.172
	(.71)	(1.52)	(4.11)
7	−.49	1.21	3.32
	(.47)	(1.36)	(2.12)
Average	−.29	1.40	3.34
[t statistics][b]	[−1.92]	[11.5]	[10.02]

[a]Data for all periods with monetary incentives. Actual bids less predicted bid under RNSNE (cf. equation (8) and note 13 for bid functions employed in RNSNE and calculations). All values in dollars.
[b]Test of null hypothesis that mean deviation is zero.

Both the sophisticated markdown model and the RASNE bidding model are capable of explaining the bidding in excess of the RNSNE with $\varepsilon = \$12$ and $\$24$. Both models would require modification, however, to account for bidding at the RNSNE with $\varepsilon = \$6$. The markdown coefficient, α, would have to vary with ε. To support the Nash equilibrium bidding model the utility function, $u(\Pi)$, would have to exhibit increasing relative risk aversion in gains from an individual auction period.[17]

4.1.b Effects of Public Information

Table 5.4 shows the effects on revenue of public information in the x_0 experiments. The first three columns show the actual average increase in revenue at

TABLE 5.3
Effects of ε on Profits (standard deviations in parentheses)

| Experiment | Actual Profits[a] | | | Actual Profits as a Percentage of Risk-Neutral Nash Equilibrium Prediction[b] | | |
	ε			ε		
	$6	$12	$24	$6	$12	$24
x_0 Design						
1	2.12	2.48	3.57	106.0	62.3	45.0
	(.21)	(.96)	(1.01)			
2	2.40	2.20	4.80	120.0	56.8	62.7
	(.75)	(1.45)	(2.52)			
3	2.18	2.27	2.40	109.0	57.9	30.2
	(.70)	(.84)	(.99)			
4	1.89	2.08	2.26	94.5	53.5	29.8
	(.64)	(.64)	(1.16)			
5	—	1.97	4.01	—	50.5	51.7
		(1.06)	(2.70)			
x_+ Design						
6	1.46	3.26	6.73	73.0	81.5	88.6
	(.56)	(1.53)	(3.73)			
7	2.30	2.30	3.54	115.0	57.8	46.4
	(.48)	(1.66)	(1.89)			
Average	2.03	2.33	3.97	101.7	59.3	51.5
(standard deviation)	(.58)	(1.31)	(2.28)			

[a]Profit calculations based on what high bidder would have earned if paying off in this market in each auction. All values in dollars.
[b]Predicted profits under RNSNE based on bid functions in equation (8) and note 13.

the different ε levels. The last three columns show the predicted increase in revenue under the RNSNE hypothesis for the x_0 design experiments. There is an average increase in revenue in the x_0 experiments of 22¢ per auction, which is about 30 per cent of the increase predicted under the RNSNE hypothesis. Changes in revenue are quite variable across auctions (more so than equilibrium predictions), with most of the increase being accounted for by experiment 2. Experience appears to have little impact upon failure to observe RNSNE predictions; revenue actually decreased 35¢ per period in experiment 5, the only one of the five x_0 experiments where revenue decreased and the only one to employ experienced subjects. While the 22¢ per auction average increase in revenue is not significantly different from zero, it is more in line with predictions

TABLE 5.4

Effects of Public Information on Revenue in x_0-Design Experiments: Mean Values with
Standard Deviation in Parentheses

	Realized Change in Revenues[a]			Predicted Increase in Revenues[a,b]		
	ε			ε		
Experiment	$12	$24	Combined	$12	$24	Combined
x_0, Design	−.21	.18	.00	.67	.65	.66
	(1.57)	(1.92)	(1.71)	(.66)	(1.00)	(.83)
2	.01	2.51	1.34	.43	1.05	.76
	(1.65)	(3.36)	(2.92)	(.46)	(.90)	(.78)
3	.34	−.26	.04	.44	.92	.68
	(1.29)	(1.48)	(1.37)	(.37)	(1.30)	(.95)
4	.63	−.57	.03	.39	.91	.65
	(.50)	(1.43)	(1.20)	(.19)	(1.47)	(1.04)
5	−.86	−.10	−.35	.30	.81	.64
	(.84)	(1.64)	(1.44)	(.34)	(1.37)	(1.14)
Average	.03	.37	.22	.45	.86	.68
[t statistic][c]	[.14]	[1.11]	[1.03]			

[a]High bid under public information less high bid under private information conditions. All values
in dollars.
[b]From RNSNE formula, for sample of high values actually drawn.
[c]Test of null hypothesis that mean deviation is zero.

of the RASNE bidding model than either of the sophisticated discount models,
as these predict no change, or a decrease in revenue, depending upon whether
expectations are rational (4) or naive (6).

Table 5.5 shows how individual subjects altered their bids upon release of
public information in the x_0 design experiments. The first column deals with
cases where $x < x_0$. Bids were raised 66.8 per cent of the time here. In most
cases where $x < x_0$, if subjects did not raise their bids in response to x_0, they
didn't change them at all, so that bids decreased in this case less than 6% of the
time.

With the exception of the naive markdown bidding model, all the models
considered dictate raising bids when $x < x_0$, even under naive expectations (6)
concerning the level of x_0. A partial explanation for the frequency of unchanged
bids here undoubtedly lies in subjective transactions costs associated with revis-
ing bids, one of our subjects remarked that in cases where $x < x_0$ he didn't
bother to change his bid as he didn't see much change of winning the particular
auction. With six bidders, his observation regarding the possibility of winning
is quite accurate. There is a corresponding tendency for low value holders to
"throw away" bids in independent private values auctions (Cox, Roberson, and

TABLE 5.5
Effects of Public Information on Individual Bids[a]

Bids	Private Value Relative to x_0		
	$x < x_0$	$x_0 \le x \le C(x_0)$	$x > C(x_0)$
$b(x, x_0) > b(x)$	66.8%	67.0%	38.2%
$b(x, x_0) = b(x)$	27.3%	17.0%	18.2%
$b(x, x_0) < b(x)$	5.9%	16.0%	43.6%
	100%	100%	100%
Total Number of Bids	187	106	55

$$C(x_0) = x_0 + \frac{N-2}{N}\varepsilon$$

[a]Each entry is the percentage of the values drawn, relative to x_0, as in the column heading, for which the subject responded as in the row heading. Only data in range (3) are reported.

Smith, 1982; Cox, Smith, and Walker, 1985). Such behavior makes economic sense, once one accounts for subjective costs of calculating a more meaningful bid under the circumstances.

Both the sophisticated discount model with rational expectations and the RASNE bidding model dictate that bidders with private values in the range

$$x_0 \le x \le C(x_0) \tag{14}$$

will increase their bids on release of public information. The middle column in Table 5.5 reports behavior in these cases. In 67% of all such cases bids increased with public information, well above the frequency expected by chance factors alone. When bids in range (14) did not increase, about half the time they decreased, while half the time they remained constant. The 16% of bids which were lower represents a marked increase relative to when $x < x_0$. Further, arguments for holding bids constant here on the grounds of subjective transactions costs, in conjunction with a low probability of winning the auction, are on substantially weaker footing than comparable arguments in cases where $x < x_0$. As such we would argue that the 33% of all bids in range (14) which do not increase, represent clear violations of the sophisticated discount model with rational expectations, as well as the RNSNE and RASNE models.

Note that our interpretation of violations of Nash equilibrium bidding theory here depends critically on all bidders having identical risk attitudes, as this was central to proving the proposition in Section 3.1.c. Without assuming symmetry, no method remains to isolate a critical value below which announcing x_0 must raise bids. Since we did not control for bidders' risk preferences, and there undoubtedly were some differences in risk attitudes across bidders, the increased bidding here might be attributable to a breakdown in our symmetry assumption, and is not necessarily inconsistent with Nash behavior. On the other hand, the interval over which bids are required to increase, $x < C(x_0)$, is quite conservative, as our proposition applies to any concave utility function. As such, we interpret the increased frequency with which bids decreased in response to public information in the range (14), as resulting in large part from subjective expectation's of x_0 being less than fully rational (4), as well as failures to act on the strategic implications of public information.

The third column of Table 5.5 shows what happens to bids in cases where $x < C(x_0)$. The RASNE model calls for increasing or decreasing bids here, depending upon the degree of subjects' risk aversion and the location of private values in the interval $[C(x_0), x_0 + \varepsilon]$. Since six bidders are sufficient for $C(x_0)$ to approximate the expected location of the high value, the sophisticated discount model with rational expectations calls for almost all bidders reducing their bids here. Instead, a sizable portion increase their bids, contrary to the prediction of that model.[18]

Results in Table 5.5, in conjunction with the average increase in revenue reported in Table 5.4, suggest that the Nash equilibrium bidding model, with risk aversion, does a better job of organizing the data than either the naive or sophisticated discount models with or without rational expectations. The RASNE bidding model, however, falls far short of providing a complete characterization of the data: the bids in range (14) (the middle column of Table 5.5) suggest a sizable proportion of individuals whose subjective expectations deviate from fully rational expectations, and/or who fail to act on strategic implications of public information. To obtain some sense of the relative role of risk aversion vs. bidders' errors on the revenue raising effects of public information, we consider a symmetric constant relative risk aversion bidding model (CRRA).

With public information announced, the bid function under CRRA is

$$b(x, x_0) = x_0 - \varepsilon + \frac{N-1}{N-r}[x - (x_0 - \varepsilon)] \tag{15}$$

which can be used to estimate the coefficient of relative risk aversion from the data.[19] This estimate yields a prediction of the level of revenue enhancement due to public information. The results of this exercise are reported in Table 5.6. Comparing the predicted impact on revenue in Table 5.6 with the risk-neutral predictions in Table 5.4 shows that the revenue-enhancing effects of public information are sharply curtailed on the basis of the degree of risk aversion observed. In fact there is slight difference, averaged across all auction periods, between the average predicted revenue increase of 15¢ per auction period under the CRRA bidding model and the observed increase of 22¢ per auction.

Table 5.5 identified errors in individual bidder behavior in terms of failure to increase bids appropriately in the presence of public information. Undoubtedly some of the increases in bids reported in Table 5.5, and/or the magnitude of the increase in bids, involved errors in assessing and acting on strategic implications of public information as well. The results in Table 5.6 suggest that in this

TABLE 5.6

Effects of Public Information on Revenue under the Hypothesis of Constant Relative
Risk Aversion

Experiment x_0 Design	Estimated Value of r	Predicted Impact on Revenue[a]	Actual Impact on Revenue[b]
1	.45	.14	.00
2	.46	.22	1.34
3	.51	.11	.04
4	.64	.06	.03
5	.38	.20	−.35
Average[c]	.49	.15	.22

[a]For sample of high private values drawn in the experiment. All values in dollars.
[b]From Table 5.4. All values in dollars.
[c]Average revenue impacts weighted by number of auctions in each experiment.

case these errors tend to cancel out: sometimes they reduce revenue enhancing possibilities of public information, but at other times they improve these possibilities.

Public information in the form of x_0 corresponds to an infinite number of announcements of an additional private valuation x_+, and resolves all uncertainty regarding the possible distribution of rivals' valuations. Given that the average response to this maximal dose of public information was relatively small, and quite variable, one would anticipate that responses to public announcement of a single private value in the x_+ design experiments would be even less reliable. Table 5.7 reports these results. Across the two experiments, public information reduces average revenue, although these results are not statistically significant. Moreover, the standard deviation of the change in revenue within these experiments tends to be larger than in the x_0-design experiments.

Table 5.8 shows the effects of public information on efficiency in the auctions. The efficiency index is defined as

$$E_t = 100[W_t - (x_0 - \varepsilon)] \div [V_t - (x_0 - \varepsilon)]$$

where W_t is the winning bidder's value, V_t the highest of the 6 values drawn[20] these are the same in a Pareto-efficient ($E_t = 100$) outcome. Otherwise, unrealized gains from exchange remain. Efficiency is not an issue in the theoretical models which analyze symmetric equilibria, thereby assuming Pareto efficiency. Symmetry of α parameters in (1) and (2) would yield Pareto-efficient predictions from the ad hoc bidding models, so equilibrium forces are not the source of efficient outcomes.

An asymmetric Nash equilibrium could generate inefficient outcomes from asymmetric risk preferences. This still does not make efficiency an issue, as public information serves no role to overcome risk asymmetries.

Table 5.8 shows, nonetheless, that announcing x_0 raises efficiency. Assymetries in information processing must be the source of these efficiency gains:

TABLE 5.7
Effects of Public Information on Revenue in x_+-Design Experiments: Mean Values
with Standard Deviations in Parentheses

Experiment x_+ Design	Realized Change in Revenue[a]		
	ε		
	12	24	Combined
6	−1.15 (1.06)	1.50 (6.70)	.48 (5.32)
7	−1.05 (3.55)	−1.43 (1.94)	−1.22 (2.82)
Average [t statistic][b]	−1.08 [−1.34]	.13 [.09]	−.43 [−.55]

[a]High bid under public information less high bid under private information. All values in dollars.
[b]Test of null hypothesis that mean deviation is zero.

announcing x_0 must disproportionately assist some bidders to avoid the perceptual errors associated with (6) above. The small dose of public information in x_+ experiments reduces efficiency. This suggests a differential impact conditional on the type of public information announced, and corresponds to our priors: there is more room for error, relative to theory, in assessing and acting on public information in x_+ as compared to x_0 designs.

TABLE 5.8
Effects of Public Information on Efficiency

Experiment	Private Information Only[a]		Public and Private Information	
	Percentage of Auctions Pareto Efficient	Mean Efficiency Index	Percentage of Auctions Pareto Efficient	Mean Efficiency Index
x_0 Design				
1	73.3	98.78	93.3	99.91
2	73.3	98.44	86.7	98.93
3	92.9	99.92	100.0	100.00
4	85.7	99.47	85.7	99.47
5	86.7	99.60	86.7	99.60
x_+ Design				
6	84.6	99.29	84.6	97.36
7	80.0	98.51	66.7	95.29

[a]Data reported for dual bidding procedure auctions only.

4.2 Second-Price/English Auctions

4.2.a Bid Patterns Over Time

Figures 5.6–5.9 graph market prices over time in terms of deviations from the dominant strategy price. Examination of the figures shows clear differences in bidding patterns between the English auction and second-price sealed bid auctions. Under the English institution (Figures 5.6–5.7) prices were quite close to the predicted dominant strategy. In 76% of all auction periods the difference between actual and predicted prices was less than or equal to the clock increment for that period. Experiment 8 shows a brief run up in prices, relative to the dominant strategy price, in early auction periods. But this occurrence was followed by collapse back to predicted prices, which then persisted. In experiment 9 the market price was $2.00 in excess of the dominant strategy price in the initial dry run, collapsed to within 25¢ of the predicted price in the first auction period with monetary payoffs, and did not deviate again after that. Thus, both experiments suggest an initial learning period with prices in excess of dominant strategy prices, followed by a steady state at the predicted equilibrium price.

Under the second-price auction institution average market prices were well in excess of the predicted dominant strategy price for all values of ε (cf. Table 5.9). In 80% of all auction periods, market prices exceeded the dominant strategy price by more than the minimal increments employed in the English clock auctions. Moreover, no obvious tendency for prices to converge to the dominant bid price over time was observed.

This persistent excess of market price above the dominant strategy price stands in marked contrast to reports of second-price sealed bid auctions with independent private values (Coppinger, Smith, and Titus, 1980; Cox, Roberson, and Smith, 1982). Results from those experiments show average market price consistently below the dominant strategy price, with varying significance levels dependent on the number of active bidders. The key institutional feature responsible for these different outcomes is, we believe, that those earlier second-price auction experiments did not permit bidding in excess of private valuations. As noted earlier, our second-price experiments had no such restriction, in anticipation that ad hoc forces could induce bidding in excess of private values, at least in the initial auction market periods.[21] Whatever the ultimate explanation of these differences, the fact remains that: (i) permitting bidding in excess of private values seems essential to testing the prediction that market prices will equal (or converge to) the dominant strategy price, and (ii) when such bidding is allowed, average market prices uniformly exceed the dominant strategy price, and there is no tendency for these price differences to be eliminated over time.[22]

Bidding in excess of x in the second-price auctions would have to be labeled as a clear mistake, since bidding x is a dominant strategy irrespective of risk attitudes. Bidding in excess of x is likely based on the illusion that it improves the probability of winning with no real cost to the bidder as the second-high-bid

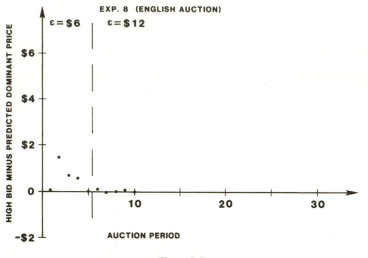

Figure 5.6.

price is paid.[23] The degree of overbidding observed was sustainable in the sense that average expected profits were positive at all values of ε (average expected profits under the dominant bidding strategy are $2\varepsilon/(N + 1)$). To the extent that more precise conformity with dominant strategy bidding results from learning through observation, or from real reinforcement effects, these forces are weak under the sealed bid procedures. First, the idea that bidding modestly in excess of x only increases the chances of winning the auction when you don't want to win is far from obvious under the sealed bid procedure. Second, the real costs of such overbidding are weak as well. For symmetric bid functions of the sort

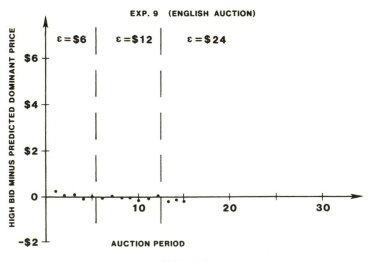

Figure 5.7.

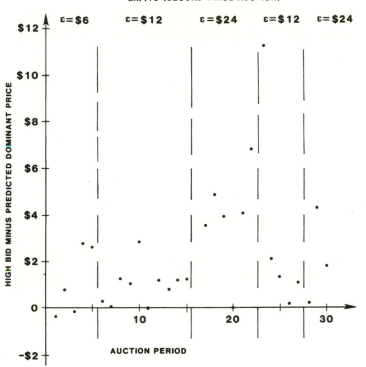

Figure 5.8.

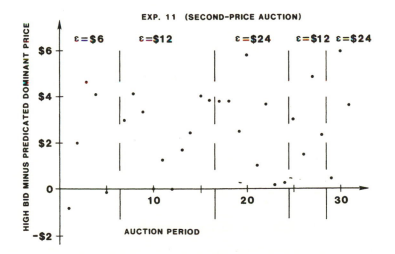

Figure 5.9.

TABLE 5.9
Differences between Actual Bid Price and Dominant Strategy Price in Second-Price
Auctions: Mean Values with Standard Deviation in Parenthesis[a]

	ε		
Experiment	$6	$12	$24
10	1.16	1.76	2.70
	(1.50)	(2.72)	(2.81)
11	1.14	2.40	2.86
	(3.04)	(1.43)	(2.10)
Average	1.15	2.07	2.78
[t test][b]	[1.62]	[5.10]	[5.32]

[a]Actual bid less predicted bid under dominant strategy. All values in dollars.
[b]Test of null hypothesis that mean deviation is zero.

$x + k\varepsilon$ with k equal to the average overbid per auction for $\varepsilon = \$12$ and $\varepsilon = \$24$, reported in Table 5.9, the probability of losing money conditional on winning the auction averages .36, with the overall probability of losing money averaging .06. These punishment probabilities are weak, given that bidders start with the illusion that bids in excess of x increase the probability of winning without materially affecting the price paid, and the majority of the time the auction outcomes support this supposition. Finally, the obvious question arises as to why we don't observe bidding even further in excess of private values than reported in Table 5.9. We can only presume that bidders were responding, to some extent, to the forces underlying the dominant strategy: with more substantial overbidding, the likelihood of winning when you don't want to win increases substantially.

The structure of the English clock auctions makes it particularly clear to bidders that they don't want to bid above their private values.[24] Once the clock price exceeds a bidder's value, it is clear that competing further to win necessarily involves losing money. Even then, some early overbidding is observed, only to collapse immediately after negative profits (losses) resulted (or would have resulted in the case of experiment 9). The "real time" nature of the English auction is ideal for producing observational learning, learning without experiencing the punishing effects of actually losing money consequent on bidding in excess of x. This enhanced capacity of the English clock institution to produce observational learning distinguishes it most clearly, on a behavioral level, from the second-price institution.[25]

4.2.b. Effects of Auction Institution on Revenue

With risk aversion in first-price auctions, and deviations from the dominant bidding strategy in second-price auctions, the enhanced revenue raising possibilities of English/second-price auction institutions relative to a first-price auction

TABLE 5.10

Effects on Revenue of Alternative Auction Institutions: Mean Differences with Standard Deviations in Parentheses

ε	Predicted[a] Second-Price/English Less First Price	Actual	
		English Less First-Price[b]	Second-Price Less First-Price[c]
6	.69	.98	2.13
	(1.10)	(1.26)	(1.66)
12	.08	−1.33	.74
	(3.46)	(3.64)	(3.34)
24	.42	−2.98	−.20
	(5.84)	(6.37)	(5.58)

[a]Calculated from sample of private values drawn in experiments 1–7 assuming a RNSNE in first-price auctions and the dominant bidding strategy in second-price/English auctions. All values in dollars.

[b]Calculated from experiments 1–7 assuming the dominant bidding strategy in English auctions less observed high bid in first-price auctions with private information. All value in dollars.

[c]Mean difference between actual bids and dominant strategy bids in experiments 10 and 11 less mean difference in actual first-price bids and dominant strategy second-price bids in experiments 1–7. All values in dollars.

need no longer hold (Milgrom and Weber, 1982); it becomes an empirical question which institution is likely to raise the most revenue. To contrast English and first-price auctions we compared average prices in our first-price auction experiments (experiments 1–7) with predicted prices under the English auction's dominant bidding strategy in these same experiments. If we accept the conclusion that, with learning, market prices converge to the dominant strategy price in English auctions, then this comparison is relevant to steady state behavior once learning has been effected in the English auctions.

The second column of Table 5.10 reports the results of this comparison. The first column compares, theoretically, revenue between the two institutions (assuming risk neutrality) for the same series of auctions. Consistent with Milgrom and Weber's proposition, under risk neutrality and Nash equilibrium bidding, an English auction would have raised more revenue than a first-price auction for all levels of ε. However, the risk attitudes of our bidders are such that with $\varepsilon = \$6$ an English auction would have raised revenues somewhat more sharply than predicted under risk neutrality. This follows directly from the dominant bidding strategy, in conjunction with observed bidding slightly below the RNSNE in first-price auctions. With $\varepsilon = \$12$ or $\$24$ though, the first-price institution would have raised substantially more revenues, due to bidding in excess of the RNSNE in these auctions.

The last column of Table 5.10 compares the revenue-raising effects of our second-price sealed bid auctions with the first-price auctions. To control for price differences between auctions, we have computed these revenue-raising effects on the basis of differences between actual and predicted second-price outcomes in both sets of experiments. Risk attitudes of our bidders and deviations from the dominant strategy are such that with $\varepsilon = \$6$ the second-price institution would have raised substantially more revenue than the first-price institution. With $\varepsilon = \$12$ or $\$24$, the overbidding relative to the RNSNE in first-price auctions tends to be offset by bidding in excess of the dominant strategy in second-price auctions. The net effect is a modest increase in revenue for second-price over first-price with $\varepsilon = \$12$, and a modest decrease with $\varepsilon = \$24$. Neither of these differences is statistically significant.

We do not maintain that there is any exact analogue between our experimental auction markets and field settings, rather that the basic economic forces at work in the laboratory are likely to be observed in the field as well.[26] If this is the case then the general conclusions that can be reached on the basis of Table 5.10 are: (i) The revenue-raising possibilities inherent in English/second-price auction institutions, relative to a first-price institution, with positively affiliated private values, are severely compromised by the potential for risk-averse bidding, and (ii) this compromise is more severe under the English auction institution, as it induces closer conformity to dominant strategy bidding.

5. Summary and Conclusions

A series of auction experiments were conducted in which a single-indivisible commodity was auctioned off among six bidders with positively affiliated private values under a variety of allocation rules. Under a first-price sealed-bid allocation rule the Nash equilibrium bidding theory outperformed two ad hoc bidding models involving both simple and sophisticated discount rules. Large doses of public information raised revenue, but these increases were lower on average and considerably less reliable than predicted. Lower average revenues may largely be attributable to risk aversion. Variability in revenue raised results from a sizable frequency of persistent individual bidding errors (relative to theory) in response to release of public information.

The dominant strategy equilibrium accurately organized English auction outcomes after a brief learning period. The dominant strategy equilibrium does not organize second-price auction outcomes, as bids consistently exceeded private values. The breakdown of the isomorphism between English and second-price institutions on a behavioral level can be attributed to differential information flows inherent in the structure of the two auctions.

Evaluating results across auction institutions and experimental manipulations indicates that bidders are sensitive to the strategic implications underlying private value auctions, and captured in Nash equilibrium bidding theory. Although we cannot definitively rule out the sophisticated discounting model in first-price auctions, the effects of public information on average revenue, and the directional changes in individual bids, come closer to the predictions of the RASNE. Further, there is much closer correspondence between Nash equilibrium bidding theory, and behavior, in first-price private value auctions then in first-price common value auctions (Kagel and Levin, 1986).

Ad hoc reasoning in second-price and English auctions call for overbidding, or underbidding, relative to the dominant strategy. These predictions are falsified in English auctions. Although we observe persistent overbidding in second-price auctions, clear economic forces are at work limiting the size of the overbid. Unlike deviations from theoretical predictions in first-price auctions, second-price bidding errors cannot be explained by references to asymmetric, risk-averse or disequilibrium behavior. Second-price errors are not robust, however, since a thoretically transparent treatment, the English auction, eliminates them.

Appendix A

The risk-averse symmetric Nash equilibrium can be characterized as follows:

$$b'(x_i) = [N/(x_i + \varepsilon - \underline{x})]u[x_i - b(x_i)]/u'[x_i - b(x_i)], \text{ if } x_i \in (\underline{x} - \varepsilon, \underline{x} + \varepsilon] \tag{A1}$$

and

$$b'(x_i) = (N/2\varepsilon)u[x_i - b(x_i)]/u'[x_i - b(x_i)], \text{ if } x_i \in [\underline{x} + \varepsilon, \bar{x} - \varepsilon], \tag{A2}$$

with initial condition

$$b_1(\underline{x} - \varepsilon) = \underline{x} - \varepsilon \tag{A3}$$

and continuity at $x_i = \underline{x} + \varepsilon$. With public information x_0 announced, the RASNE satisfies

$$\partial b/\partial x_i|_{(x_i, x_0)} = \left(\frac{N-1}{x_i + \varepsilon - x_0}\right)\left(\frac{u[x_i - b(x_i, x_0)]}{u'[x_i - b(x_i, x_0)]}\right) \tag{A4}$$

with

$$b(x_0 - \varepsilon, x_0) = x_0 - \varepsilon. \tag{A5}$$

These characterizations follow from Theorem 14 in Milgrom and Weber (1982); derivations are omitted. For $x_i > \underline{x} - \varepsilon$, the bid $\hat{b} = (x_i + \underline{x} - \varepsilon)/2$ yields positive expected utility, so the best response must satisfy $b(x) < x$ on $(\underline{x} + \varepsilon, \bar{x} - \varepsilon]$.

Let $C(x_0) = x_0 + \varepsilon(N - 2)/N$. Note that $C(x_0) > x_0$ for $N \geqslant 3$.

Proposition. *If $\underline{x} + \varepsilon \leqslant x_i \leqslant \bar{x} - \varepsilon$, for any, x_0, any, $u(\cdot)$, $x_i < C(x_0)$ implies $b(x_i) < b(x_i, x_0)$, i.e., a signal below the critical value $C(x_0)$ is associated in Nash equilibrium with a higher bid under public information.*

Proof. As noted above, $b(x_0 - \varepsilon) < x_0 - \varepsilon = b(x_0 - \varepsilon, x_0)$. By (A2) and (A4);

$$\partial b(x_i, x_0)/\partial x_i - b'(x_i) = \left(\frac{N-1}{x_i + \varepsilon - x_0}\right)\left(\frac{u}{u'}\right)\Bigg|_{x_i - b(x_i, x_0)}$$

$$-\left(\frac{N}{2\varepsilon}\right)\left(\frac{u}{u'}\right)\Bigg|_{x_i - b(x_i)}. \tag{A6}$$

Under the assumption that $b(x_i) = b(x_i, x_0)$, (A6) becomes:

$$\partial b(x_i, x_0)/\partial x_i - b'(x_i) = \left[\frac{N-1}{x_i + \varepsilon - x_0} - \frac{N}{2\varepsilon}\right]\left(\frac{u}{u'}\right)\Bigg|_{x_i - b(x_i)}$$

$$> \left[\frac{N-1}{C(x_0) + \varepsilon - x_0} - \frac{N}{2\varepsilon}\right]\left(\frac{u}{u'}\right)\Bigg|_{x_i - b(x_i)} = 0$$

where the inequality results from substituting the larger $C(x_0)$ for x_i in the denominator.

Thus, $b(x_i, x_0)$ starts out above $b(x_i)$ at $x_i = x_0 - \varepsilon$, and assuming the two curves intersect before $x_i = C(x_0)$ yields the contradictory inference that $b(x_i, x_0)$ crosses $b(x_i)$ from below.   Q.E.D.

Appendix B: Derivation of Risk Neutral Nash Bid Function*

Deriving the symmetric Nash equilibrium. There are three regions:

Region I: $s \in [V_L - \varepsilon, V_L + \varepsilon]$. The support of V given $s \equiv \Sigma V(s) = [V_L, s + \varepsilon]$.

The differential equation from the maximization problem is

$$\begin{cases} b_I'(s) + \beta(s)b_I(s) - \beta(s) \cdot s = 0, & \text{with initial condition} \\ b_I(V_L - \varepsilon) = V_L - \varepsilon \dots (E(\pi) = 0), & \text{where} \\ \beta(s) = N/(s - (V_L - \varepsilon)). \end{cases} \tag{A.1}$$

$$\text{Solution } b_I(s) = V_L - \varepsilon + \frac{N}{N+1}[s - (V_L - \varepsilon)]. \tag{A.2}$$

Region II: $s \in [V_L + \varepsilon, V_H - \varepsilon]$, $\Sigma V(s) = [s - \varepsilon, s + \varepsilon]$.

The differential equation is

$$\begin{cases} b_{II}'(s) + \alpha b_{II}(s) - \alpha s = 0, & \text{with initial condition} \\ b_{II}(V_L + \varepsilon) = b_I(V_L + \varepsilon), & \text{where } \alpha = N/2\varepsilon. \end{cases} \tag{A.3}$$

$$\text{Solution } b_{II}(s) = s - \alpha + \frac{\alpha}{N+1} \cdot e^{-\alpha(s-(V_L+\varepsilon))}. \tag{A.4}$$

Note the fact that $b_{II}(V_L + \varepsilon) = b_I(V_L + \varepsilon)$ makes via (A.1) and (A.3) $b_I'(V_L + \varepsilon^-) = b_{II}'(V_L + \varepsilon^+)$; i.e., at the junction point, bidding is not just continuous but also has continuous "slope."

*From working paper/notes underlying Kagel, Harstad, and Levin (1987).

Region III: $s \in [V_H - \varepsilon, V_H + \varepsilon]$ $\Sigma\, V(s) = [s - \varepsilon, V_H]$;

The differential equation is

$$
\begin{cases}
b'_{III}(s) + k(s)b_{III}(s) - k(s) \cdot s = 0 & \text{with initial conditions} \\[2mm]
b_{III}(V_H - \varepsilon) = b_{II}(V_H + \varepsilon) = V_H - \varepsilon - \alpha + \dfrac{\alpha}{N+1} \cdot e^{-\alpha(V_H - V_L - 2\varepsilon)},
\end{cases}
\tag{5}
$$

where $\quad k(s) = \dfrac{N}{2\varepsilon} \cdot \dfrac{1 - (\theta(s))^{N-1}}{1 - (\theta(s))^N}$

and $\quad 0 \le \theta(s) := \dfrac{s + \varepsilon - V_H}{2\varepsilon} \le 1.$

Remarks: There is no explicit solution to (5). The explicit solution will not be nice as a result of the way k(s) depends on N.

Notes

Financial support essential to conducting this research was received from the Information Science and Technology Division and the Economics Division of the National Science Foundation, the Alfred P. Sloan Foundation, the Energy Laboratory, and the Center of Public Policy of the University of Houston—University Park. Douglas Dyer provided valuable research support throughout. Paul Milgrom directed our attention to the relevance of studying effects of public information on revenue in first-price, affiliated private value auctions. Charles Plott, David Kreps, and the referees provided valuable comments on earlier drafts of the paper, which was originally presented at the 1984 Winter Econometric Society Meetings. The instructions used in the experiments are available from the authors.

1. Bidders submit scaled bids, with the high bidder obtaining the item and paying the amount bid.

2. The announced price increases regularly, with the last remaining bidder obtaining the item at the price where the next-to-last bidder dropped out of competition.

3. Bidders submit scaled bids, with the high bidder obtaining the item at a price equal to the second-highest bid.

4. Antecedent first-price, private-value auction experiments with independent private values (Cox, Roberson and Smith, 1982) indicated that, with 6 bidders and 1 unit, players were clearly noncooperative.

5. This tends to improve the power of tests of the effects of releasing public information, as it permits a within, rather than between, group analysis of variance. In testing market level predictions, comparable improvements in power can be obtained using a paired experiment design, where the same set of private values are distributed under different informational/institutional arrangements to different groups in different experiments (Cox, Roberson, and Smith (1982) effectively employ this procedure). The dual market procedure clearly affords more power than the paired experiment design with respect to tests of individual subject behavior, such as the Proposition in Section 3.1.d. In this case the paired experiment design would require accounting for variations in individual

bid functions, as different subjects are almost bound to receive different private valuations across experiments.

6. The case for treating each member of a series of auctions, $t = 1, 2, \ldots, n$ as a single shot auction (which we do) may be less compelling. If a subject's utility function over the net profits in an experiment exhibits constant absolute risk aversion (CARA), then utility of profits in individual auctions is multiplicatively separable, and yields a CARA function of the same degree in each auction period. Alternatively, there is some empirical evidence (Kahneman and Tversky, 1979), that people evaluate gambles in terms of deviations from the current status quo so that gambles in each auction period are independent of outcomes in other periods.

7. The fixed-effects regression model employed was suggested by the bid function (8) in the text (cf., p. 1283). Individual subject bids in each auction period served as the dependent variable, with right-hand-side variables including individual subject private values, the variable Y/N in equation (8), dummy variables for changes in ε, dummy variables for private values above and below the interval in equation (3), and subject-by-variable interaction terms for all of the above. A single dummy variable, taking the value of 1 under dual market conditions, was employed to test for any systematic effects. Coefficient values (with associated t statistics) for experiments 1–6 were: 0.00 (0.0), $-.30$ (-1.06), .90 (1.67), .26 (.56), $-.37$ (-1.36), $-.51$ (-1.08). Under the hypothesis that the mean value for the t statistic in the sample population is z,

$$z = \frac{\Sigma t_i}{\sqrt{\Sigma[f_i/(f_i - 2)]}}$$

where f_j is the degrees of freedom associated with t_j, has a sampling distribution which is approximately normal (0, 1) (Winer, 1971). Using this statistic, we are unable to reject the null hypothesis of no systematic change in private information auction bids under the dual market procedure ($z = -.21$). A similar simple fixed effects regression model (suggested by the bid function (9) in the text) was used to test for dual market effects on bidding in the public information market in experiment 5. The dummy variable coefficient here was $-.72$ with a t statistic of 1.53, which is not statistically significant.

8. Cassady (1967) refers to this procedure as an English clock auction. Milgrom and Weber (1982) refer to it as a "Japanese" English auction, quite distinct from the Japanese auction institution specified in Cassady (1967). Experiment 8 had bidders holding little paddles up for others to see as long as they remained active. Experiment 9 used a row of lights behind the subjects with the experimenters announcing the number of active players as bidders dropped.

9. The probability that the bids of the two highest resale value holders would be tied, using these increments and assuming the dominant bidding strategy was followed, is .0125.

10. This calculation is derived from Bayes' formula with the posterior support

$$\Sigma[x_0 - \varepsilon \mid x = x_1] = [x - 2\varepsilon, x].$$

11. Beginning with Vickrey (1961), continuing with Milgrom and Weber (1982) and most references cited there.

12. When x_i is outside $[\underline{x} + \varepsilon, \bar{x} - \varepsilon]$, the conditional distribution generating $x_j, j \neq i$ is no longer symmetric about x_i, which alters equilibrium bidding. For $x_i < \underline{x} + \varepsilon$, substitute the function

$$B(x) = \underline{x} + \left(\frac{N}{N+1} \right)(x - \underline{x})$$

where $\underline{x} = \underline{\underline{x}} - \varepsilon$. The differential equation characterizing equilibrium is not readily solved for x when $x > \bar{x} - \varepsilon$. We employed the bid function (8) in its place. This introduces a small upward bias in our estimates of RNSNE bids for these observations. An Appendix deriving these RNSNE bid functions is available from the authors.

13. The bid function is normalized so that $u(0) = 0$. Consequently $r = 1$ corresponds to infinite risk aversion in this setting. CRRA is not consistent with CARA, one of the potential justifications for treating each member in the series of auctions as a single shot auction. However, the CRRA assumption can be consistent with the single shot assumption as it applies to deviations in income from the current status quo.

14. In anticipation of this, subjects in these experiments were given \$5.00 starting capital balance to which profits were added and losses subtracted. In cases where the capital balance dropped to zero or less, subjects were no longer permitted to bid. To insure maintaining 6 active bidders in the face of potential brankruptcies, we enrolled 7–8 subjects in these experiments, with a rotation rule used to determine the 6 active bidders in each market period.

15. Standard deviations in Table III differ slightly from corresponding numbers in Table II, because Table II's construction contrasted the high bid with the RNSNE prediction based upon the high value. Table III subtracts the high bid from the high bidder's value.

16. Formal tests for effects of ε on bidder behavior were restricted to private values within the range (3) for which the term Y/N in (8) was at most \$0.10. The following linear bid function was fit separately to each experiment using a fixed-effects regression model:

$$b_t = \alpha_0 + \alpha_1 x_t + \alpha_2 \varepsilon_t$$

where t refers to the auction period, and each subject's bid in that period generated an observation comingled with other subjects' bids. The coefficient α_2 was negative in all seven regressions, statistically significant at $p < 0.01$ for experiments 1, 2, 5–7.

17. Alternatively we might assume that subjects have biases in their subjective evaluations of the distribution of rivals' private values which depend systematically on ε. However, at present, we have no independent means to distinguish this explanation from that offered in the text. As such we lump the deviations under the headings of risk aversion. Undoubtedly the true explanation lies somewhere between.

18. The frequency with which bids increase in the interval $x > C(x_0)$ is clearly greater than one would expect under the sophisticated markdown bidding model, as it predicts no increase in bidding here. Further, if we assume that there is an irreducible "error" rate in bidding of 6 per cent (the frequency with which bids decrease in the interval $x < x_0$), the frequency with which bids increase still exceeds what one would expect under the sophisticated discount model. That is, assuming a binomial distribution where there is a 6 per cent average chance of bids increasing, there is virtually no chance of observing 21 out of 55 bids increasing in the interval $x < C(x_0)$, which is what we observed.

19. There are clear specification errors involved in assuming CRRA here. It is nevertheless a readily tractable alternative to the RNSNE model for our purposes. Estimates of r were ere obtained using OLS procedures, individual subject data from each experiment, and the estimating equation

$$b_t^* = \alpha x_t^* + e_t$$

where in terms of equation (15) in the text $b_i^* = b(x, x_0) - x_0 + \varepsilon$, $x_i^* = [x - (x_0 - \varepsilon)]$, and e, is a random error term. Estimates of r obtained from a are biased, but consistent. Note however that our estimates are based on relatively large sample sizes.

20. Subtracting $x_0 - \varepsilon$ in numerator and denominator makes his formula correspond to the efficiency measure in Cox, Roberson, and Smith (1982).

21. It is unlikely that positive affiliation is responsible for these differences. We have conducted one second-price experiment with independent private values which showed average market prices in excess of the predicted dominant strategy price. Further, recently published nondiscriminatory, multiple unit sealed bid auctions with independent private values, where the dominant strategy is to bid one's value, show a substantial (and persistent) percentage of all bids in excess of private values (Cox, Smith, and Walker, 1985).

22. Note that our first-price auction market procedures did *not permit* bidding in excess of private valuations. In light of our second-price results this restriction may be subject to criticism. It does not appear, however, to invalidate our first-price results or comparisons across auction institutions: (i) Persistent bidding in excess of private values in first-price auctions will soon be extinguished as it *must* result in losses in the event of winning. In contrast, modest bidding in excess of private values in second-price auctions does not generally result in losses when winning the auction. Indeed, we conjecture (see the text) that it is the general absence of such feedback that sustains the behavior. (ii) Battalio, Meyer, and Ormiston (1985) have recently completed a series of first-price private value auctions with no binding ceiling on bids. In 5 experiments involving 45 inexperienced bidders, they observed a total of 4 subjects bidding in excess of their values. All such bids occurred in early auction periods and resulted in immediate bankruptcy for 3 of the 4 subjects. Our rationalization for employing a bid ceiling in first-price auctions was that bidding in excess of private values here was likely to involve clear confuision regarding procedures on a subject's part, and that the prohibition provided a convenient vehicle for clarifying procedures, (hereby speeding tip the learning process. The results of Battalio, et al. support this interpretation.

23. In this respect, bidding in excess of x here undoubtedly shares some motivational base with overbidding relative to the RNSNE, in the first-price auctions. In a first-price auction, however, subjects are clearly cognizant of the fact that increased bids reduced profits conditional on winning the auction. The results for the second-price auctions surely support our earlier suggestion (see footnote 18) that some of what we label risk aversion in the first-price auctions may well result from systematic biases in subjective estimates of the distribution of rivals' private valuations. The source of these biases and their effects on bidding in the first-price auctions, is far from clear, and the development of consistent models incorporating such effects lies well beyond the scope of the present paper.

24. Under our design, the dominant bidding strategy in both second-price and English auctions rests on first-degree stochastic dominance arguments, rather than the stronger requirements of expected utility theory. Karni and Safra (1986) show that in second-price and English auction institutions, where the object being sold is a lottery that assigns objectively known (non-degenerate) probabilities to a given set of money prizes, it is possible for a non-expected-utility maximizer to deviate rationally from the dominant strategy in the second-price auction, while adhering to it under the English clock institution. The non-expected-utility formulations used to obtain these results imply first degree stochastic dominance. Hence, the Karni and Safra formulation cannot be used to explain our results.

25. Independent private value auction experiments in Cox, Roberson, and Smith (1982) fail to observe a behavioral isomorphism between the first-price and Dutch auction institutions which theory predicts. Here too the "real time" auction (the Dutch auction) produces lower bid prices than the sealed bid institution. Whether these differences result from the same behavioral mechanisms as those underlying the differences reported here is an open question at this point.

26. See Kagel and Levin (1986) for some striking evidence on parallels between laboratory and field auction outcomes in cases where the laboratory observations are squarely at odds with Nash equilibrium predictions.

References

Battalio, R. C., D. J. Meyer, and M. B. Ormiston (1985): "First Price Auctions, Bid Preparation Costs and Endogenous Market Size," mimeographed, Texas A&M University.

Capen, E. C., R. V. Clapp, and W. W. Campbell (1971): "Competitive Bidding in High-Risk Situations," *Journal of Petroleum Technology*, 23, 641–653.

Cassady, R., Jr. (1967): *Auctions and Auctioneering.* Berkeley: University of California Press.

Coppinger, V. M., V. L. Smith, and J. A. Titus (1980): "Incentives and Behavior in English, Dutch and Sealed-Bid Auctions," *Economic Inquiry*, 18, 1–22.

Cox, J. C., B. Roberson, and V. L. Smith (1982): "Theory and Behavior of Single Object Auctions," in *Research in Experimental Economics*, Vol. 2, ed. by V. L. Smith. Greenwich, Conn.: JAI Press.

Cox, J. C., V. L. Smith, and J. M. Walker (1985): "Expected Revenue in Discriminative and Uniform Price Scaled Bid Auctions," in *Research in Experimental Economics*, Vol. 3, ed. by V. L. Smith. Greenwich, Conn.: JAI Press.

Kagel, J. H., and D. Levin (1986): "The Winner's Curse and Public Information in Common Value Auctions," *American Economic Review*, 76, 894–920.

Kahneman, D., and A. Tversky (1979): "Prospect Theory: An Analysis of Decision Under Risk," *Econometrica*, 47, 263–291.

Karni, E., and Z. Safra (1986): "Revelations in Auctions and the Structure of Preferences," Working Papers in Economics, Johns Hopkins University.

Milgrom, P. R., and R. J. Weber (1982): "A Theory of Auctions and Competitive Bidding," *Econometrica*, 50, 1099–1122.

Vickrey, W. (1961): "Counterspeculation, Auctions, and Competitive Sealed Tenders," *Journal of Finance*, 16, 8–27.

Winer, B. J. (1971): *Statistical Principles in Experimental Design*, 2nd ed. New York: McGraw-Hill.

6

Revenue Effects and Information Processing in English Common Value Auctions

—

Dan Levin, John H. Kagel, and Jean-Francois Richard

In a common value auction, the value of the item is the same to all bidders, but unknown at the time they bid. Rather, bidders have private information correlated with the unknown value. Mineral lease auctions are usually modeled as pure common value auctions, but there is a common value component to most auctions.

Economic theory predicts that the choice of institution for a common value auction will affect expected revenue. In particular, with symmetric, risk-neutral Nash equilibrium (RNNE) bidding, English auctions are predicted to raise more revenue than first-price, sealed bid auctions. This happens because both the pricing rule (the high bidder wins the item at the second highest bid price) and the "public" information disseminated during bidding (lower bidders' drop-out prices reveal their estimates of the value of the item) increase expected revenue (Paul R. Milgrom and Robert J. Weber, 1992).[1] Nash equilibrium bidding theory also makes precise predictions about how bidders combine this endogenously released and noisy public information with their private information in English auctions. This paper compares the information processing mechanism underlying the Nash model with an alternative, very sensible, signal-averaging rule that suggests itself.

The first part of the paper is concerned with the revenue-raising predictions of Nash equilibrium bidding theory. We find that, contrary to the theory, English auctions reduce rather than raise revenue for inexperienced bidders. These bidders suffer severely from the winner's curse in first-price auctions, bidding substantially above the Nash equilibrium prediction. They use the "public information" inherent in other bidders' drop-out prices to (largely) overcome the winner's curse in English auctions. The net effect is a reduction in revenue. In contrast, more experienced bidders have learned to overcome the worst effects of the winner's curse in first-price auctions, so that there is scope for the public information inherent in bidders' drop-out prices to increase revenue, as the theory predicts.

The second part of the paper develops an econometric model to explore how bidders combine endogenously released and noisy public information with their private information in the English auctions. Two versions of the model are specified: one uses ordinary least squares (OLS) and observed drop-out prices to analyze bidding round by round. The other uses a full-information, censored bidding model which corrects for potential biases inherent in the OLS estimates and applies all the information at our disposal (including the drop-out prices implicit in continuing to bid when others have dropped out). Both specifications indicate that a rule in which bidders act as if they are averaging their own signal value and the signal values underlying the dropout prices of all earlier bidders, characterizes behavior better than the Nash rule, irrespective of bidders' experience. Simulations using maximum likelihood estimates of the full information signal-averaging model show that it can quantitatively account for a number of data characteristics not directly employed in the maximum likelihood estimates (most importantly, the frequency of "panic" dropouts). These simulations also show that the relatively low percentage (50–60 percent) of high signal holders winning the auctions is completely consistent with a symmetric bidding model, given the bidding errors actually observed.

With symmetry, under our design both the signal-averaging rule and the Nash rule provide unbiased estimates of the expected value of the item conditional on winning, and the same average prices and profits. In principle, the averaging model permits profitable, unilateral deviations by high-valued signal holders who employ a "signal-jamming" strategy. The averaging rule continues to be employed, however, since it is substantially more natural to apply than the Nash rule and profitable deviations are difficult to detect, given the complexity of the environment.

The paper is organized as follows: Section 1 outlines our experimental procedures. The theoretical underpinnings of the analysis are developed in Section 2. Forces promoting as well as inhibiting revenue raising in English compared to first-price auctions are discussed, along with their observable implications. Section 3 reports the experimental results. Section 4 briefly compares our results to the limited field data examining the revenue raising effects of English auctions. Section 5 concludes with a summary of the main results.

1. Structure of the Auctions

Each experimental session consisted of a series of auction periods in which a single unit of a commodity was awarded to (be high bidder. The value of the item, x_o, was unknown at the time bids were submitted. In each auction period x_o

was drawn randomly from a uniform distribution on $[\underline{x}, \bar{x}]$. Each bidder received his own private information signal, x, randomly drawn from a uniform distribution on $[x_o - \varepsilon, x_o + \varepsilon]$. The number of bidders (n), the value of ε, and the distributions underlying both x_o and x were common knowledge.

In first-price auctions each bidder submitted a single, sealed bid with the high bidder earning a profit equal to the value of the item less the price bid. The English auctions used an ascending clock to set price, with price starting at $\underline{x}$ and increasing continuously. Bidders decided when to drop out of the auction and could not reenter once they had left (an irrevocable exit auction).[2] The last bidder earned a profit equal to x_o less the price at which the next-to-last bidder dropped out. Posted on each bidder's screen was the current price of the item and the number of bidders remaining in the auction (with *no* information regarding bidders' identity). Bidders who did not win the item earned zero profit for that auction period.

At the end of each auction period, all bids were posted from highest to lowest along with the corresponding signal values (bidder identification numbers were suppressed) and the value of x_o. Profits (or losses) were calculated for the winning bidder and were reported to all bidders, and cash balances were updated.

To cover the possibility of losses bidders were given starting capital balances of at least $10.00. Losses were subtracted from this balance and profits added to it. Subjects were told that if their balance went to zero or less they would no longer be allowed to bid. Bidders were paid their end of session balances in cash, along with a $4 or $5 participation fee.

Bidding was studied under two different values of n (4 and 7), five different values of ε (6, 12, 19, 24, and 30) and with three different levels of bidder experience (inexperienced, once experienced, and super-experienced). Super-experienced bidders are defined as having been in at least two previous first-price auction series. Experimental sessions using both first-price and English auctions had bidders first participate in a series of first-price (English) auctions, followed by bidding in a series of English (first-price) auctions, followed (sometimes) by an additional cross-over back to first-price (English) auctions.[3] Table 6.1 cross-classifies the experimental sessions by subjects' experience level, the number of active bidders, and by auction institution.

Subjects were primarily senior undergraduate economics majors and MBA students at the University of Houston (treatments 1–8 and 10) and the University of Pittsburgh (treatment 9). To cover the possibility of bankruptcies there were typically (up to three) extra bidders in each experimental session, with the active bidders in each auction period determined either randomly or through a rotation rule. For experienced subject sessions all bidders were invited back, with the exception of treatment 10 where the few bidders who went bankrupt early in both previous sessions were not invited back.[4] Each experimental session lasted approximately two hours and had a minimum of 20 auction periods.

TABLE 6.1
Treatment Conditions

Treatment Condition	Experience	Number of Bidders	Number of Experimental Sessions	Auction Type
1	None	4	4	English
2	None	4	5	First-price
3	Experienced (from 1)	4	3	English and first-price
4	Experienced (from 2)	4	4	First-price
5	None	7	3	English
6[a]	None	7	3	First-price
7	Experienced (from 5)	7	2	English
8	Experienced (from 6)	7	2	First-price
9	Super-experienced first-price	4	8	English and first-price
10[a]	Super-experienced first-price (from 4 and 8)	7	7	English and first-price

[a]Includes a few periods with $n = 6$. Earlier work shows that pooling $n = 6$ and 7 is justified (Kagel and Levin, 1986; Kagel et al., 1995).

2. Theoretical Considerations

2.1 Factors Promoting Revenue Raising in English Auctions

With symmetric risk-neutral Nash equilibrium bidding (RNNE), English auctions are predicted to raise more revenue than first-price auctions. In what follows we apply the theory to our design. The basic theoretical results underlying this analysis are developed in Robert Wilson (1977), Milgrom (1979a, b), and Milgrom and Weber (1982).

1. First-Price Auctions

For first-price auctions the RNNE bid function $\gamma(x)$ is given by

$$\gamma(x) = \underline{x} + \frac{1}{n+1}(x - \underline{x} + \varepsilon), \tag{1a}$$

$$\underline{x} - \varepsilon \leq x \leq \underline{x} + \varepsilon$$

$$\gamma(x) = x - \varepsilon + h(x), \tag{1b}$$

$$\underline{x} + \varepsilon \leq x \leq \bar{x} - \varepsilon \text{ where}$$

$$h(x) = \frac{2\varepsilon}{n+1}$$

$$\times \exp\left[-\frac{n}{2\varepsilon}[x - (\underline{x} + \varepsilon)]\right],$$

$$(\bar{x} - 2\varepsilon) + \frac{n-1}{n}(x - \bar{x} + \varepsilon) \tag{1c)^5}$$

$$\leq \gamma(x) \leq x - \varepsilon,$$

$$\bar{x} - \varepsilon \leq x < \bar{x} + \varepsilon.$$

Bidding in first-price auctions combines strategic considerations, similar to those involved in first-price private value auctions, and item valuation considerations. The latter involves recognizing that although x is an unbiased estimate of x_o, winning with it implies that it is the highest of the n signals and, therefore, must be used as a first-order statistic rather than an unbiased estimate of x_o. Failure to account for this adverse-selection effect is commonly referred to as the winner's curse. Both forces, strategic and item valuation, promote bidding below x, with the strategic forces reinforcing efforts to avoid the winner's curse.

Under (1a–c) expected profit for the high bidder is bounded from below and above as follows:

$$E_F^L[\pi] = \frac{2\varepsilon}{n+1} \tag{2a}$$

$$-\left[\frac{4\varepsilon^2}{\bar{x} - \underline{x}}\right]\left[\frac{3n+2}{n(n+1)(n+2)}\right]$$

$$E_F^u[\pi] = E_F^L[\pi] + \left[\frac{2\varepsilon^2}{\bar{x} - \underline{x}}\right]\left[\frac{1}{n+2}\right]. \tag{2b}$$

For the values of n (4 and 7), ε (6, 12, 18, 24, 30) and $[\underline{x}, \bar{x}]$ (50–250) employed, the lower bound of expected profit lies between -17 to -2 percent of $2\varepsilon/(n-1)$ and the upper bound lies between -5 to $+2$ percent of $2\varepsilon/(n+1)$.

2. English Auctions

Milgrom and Weber (1982) offer a symmetric RNNE for the irrevocable exit English auction. When there are three or more bidders, however, the prices at which earlier bidders drop out of the auction convey information to those who continue to bid. The irrevocable exit English auction, with its continuous display of prices and number of active bidders makes this price information unambiguously clear to other bidders.[6]

Let $x_1 < x_2 < ... < x_n$ denote the ordered private signals and $d_1 < d_2 < ... < d_{n-1}$ the sequential drop-out prices (ties occur with zero probability, lower case letters represent actual values and, when appropriate, caps denote the corresponding random variables). Let I_j denote the auction conveyed information available to a bidder who is active in round j (the round advances when an additional bidder drop, out), so that $I_1 = 0$ and $I_j = (d_1, \dots, d_{j-1})$. Let $\gamma(x; I_j)$ denote the round j reservation bid of an active bidder with private information signal x. The γ_j's which are obtained below are strictly monotone in x, given I_j. It follows that $d_j = \gamma(x_j; I_j)$ and that there is a one-to-one (recursive) correspondence between I_j and $(x_1, \dots, x_{j-1})$. Following Milgrom and Weber (1992), γ_j is given by

$$\gamma_j(x; I_j) = E(x_o \mid \xi_j(x; I_j)] \tag{3}$$

where $\xi_1(x; I_1)$ denotes the event $X_i = x$ for all i and for $j: 2 \to n - 1$; $\xi_j(x; I_j)$ represents the event $X_i = x_i$ for $i < j$ and $X_i = x$ for $i \geq j$. In other words, bidders form their reservation bids on the basis of earlier bidders' drop-out prices and their own signal value, assuming that all remaining bidders have the same signal value that they do. Active bidders infer whatever they can from the quitting prices of bidders who are no longer active. With affiliated signal values, the result is that each bidder remains active until the price rises to the point where the bidder is just indifferent between winning and losing at that price (Milgrom and Weber, 1982).[7]

Given the uniform distributions from which x_o and x are drawn, conditional on ξ_1, x_o is uniformly distributed on the interval $[a(x), b(x)]$ where $a(x) = \max(\underline{x}, x - \varepsilon)$ and $b(x) - \min(\overline{x}, x + \varepsilon)$; conditional on ξ_j, x_o is uniformly distributed on the interval $[a(x), b(x_1)]$. It follows that

$$d_j = \frac{a(x_j) + b(x_1)}{2}. \tag{4}$$

If $\underline{x} + \varepsilon < x_1 < x_n < \overline{x} - \varepsilon$ (referred to as region 2 in the following discussion) then

$$d_j = \frac{(x_1) + (x_j)}{2}. \tag{5}$$

Note that in equilibrium, conditional on the event of winning, for bidder j the pair $[a(x_j), b(x_1)]$ is a sufficient statistic for x_o. That is, in the equilibrium of our design, the bidder with the lowest signal value determines his dropout price strictly on the basis of his own signal value. Later bidders determine their drop-out prices based strictly on their own signal value and the first bidder's drop-out price, that is, bidders ignore the information contained in intermediate round drop-out prices.

The expected profit for the high bidder in the English auctions is

$$E_E[\pi] = \frac{\varepsilon}{n + 1}$$

$$- \left[\frac{4\varepsilon^2}{\overline{x} - \underline{x}} \right] \left[\frac{1}{(n + 1)(n + 2)} \right], \tag{6}$$

which is close to *half* the expected profit from winning in first-price sealed bid auctions. Lower profit, of course, translates into higher prices, so that with symmetry and risk neutrality, the English auction is within ± 10 percent of *doubling* expected revenue (after normalizing for the value of x_o) under our design.[8]

2.2 Forces Inhibiting Revenue Raising in English Auctions

There are three principal reasons why English auctions may raise less revenue than first-price auctions or why the revenue increases might be smaller than predicted: the existence of asymmetric equilibria in English auctions (even with risk-neutral bidders), risk aversion, and the winner's curse. We consider each of these factors briefly.

1. Asymmetric Equilibria

Bikhchandani and Riley (1991) prove that when $n \geq 3$ there exist a continuum of asymmetric equilibria in irrevocable exit English auctions. The idea underlying these asymmetric equilibria is as follows: there exist a continuum of asymmetric equilibria in second-price auctions with *two* bidders where one bidder bids higher and the second bidder bids lower than in the symmetric equilibrium (Milgrom, 1981). There does not exist a completely convincing way to rule out these "strange" equilibria, as Milgrom characterizes them (they are all perfect). These asymmetric equilibria apply to the irrevocable exit auction with $n \geq 3$ bidders since it reduces to a second-price auction with only two bidders, once $n - 2$ bidders have dropped out. Under certain regularity conditions, which are satisfied in our design, expected revenue in these asymmetric equilibria are lower than in the symmetric equilibrium (Bikhchandani and Riley, 1991 Proposition 3 and Corollary 1). Hence, the possibility for a revenue reversal relative to first-price auctions.[9]

2. Risk Aversion

The effects of risk aversion in first-price common value auctions are, in general, ambiguous, as there are two opposing forces at work: with positive expected profit, strategic considerations promote bidding above the RNNE, just as in first-price, private value auctions (Milton Harris and Arthur Raviv, 1981; Charles A. Holt, 1980; Riley and William F. Samuelson, 1981). However, unlike private value auctions, in equilibrium there exists the possibility of negative profits which, other things equal, promotes lower bidding for risk averse bidders.

In contrast, there is no ambiguity about the role of risk aversion in English auctions, as average prices must be reduced in auctions with symmetric risk averse bidders. This results from the fact that the reservation bids (4) correspond to simple expectations, so that with risk aversion these are replaced by their certainty equivalents, which are less than the simple expectations. This may reduce bids sufficiently to offset the revenue raising possibilities of the English auction, although we would doubt that this could happen, given the size of the payoffs involved and the strong revenue raising possibilities inherent in our design. Nevertheless, to use risk aversion to help explain any revenue raising shortfalls, prices must be lower, hence average profits must be higher, than predicted under the symmetric RNNE in the English auctions.[10]

3. The Winner's Curse

Failure to account for the adverse-selection effect associated with winning a common value auction is called the winner's curse. The winner's curse is likely to result in substantially higher bidding, relative to the RNNE, in first-price auctions, but much less overbidding in English auctions. The reason is that in English auctions drop-out prices of bidders reveal information regarding their signal values. If this information is not too distorted, it can alert higher valued signal holders to the fact that they have formed overly optimistic estimates of x_o, which will help attenuate overbidding. No such help is available in first-price auctions since they involve scaled bids. In this scenario, prices are substantially higher than predicted in first-price auctions and relatively closer to their predicted value in English auctions, hence the possibility for revenue reversals or reductions in revenue relative to those predicted.

There is precedent for this outcome from experimental studies of first- and second-price sealed bid auctions with public information (Kagel and Levin, 1986; Kagel et al., 1995). In these auctions, public information consisted of announcing x_1 (the lowest signal value). This is exactly the same information that is supposed to be revealed by the low signal holders' drop-out price in English auctions. In cases where bidders suffered from a clear winner's curse with only private information, announcing x_1 *lowered* revenue, *contrary* to the Nash prediction. It is another question entirely whether English auctions are capable of generating the same effect, as now information regarding x_1 is generated *endogenously* which (i) may degrade the quality of the information and (ii) may be more difficult for bidders to interpret, since they must now deduce that the low bidder's drop-out price is reflective of the underlying signal value.

3. Experimental Results

3.1 Revenue Effects of English Auctions

a. Inexperienced Bidders

Table 6.2 shows average changes in the auctioneer's revenue between English and first-price auctions, as well as the winner's average profit in both types of auctions.[11] "Actual" figures are arithmetic means (and their standard deviations) obtained from the data while "theoretical" values are produced by computing equilibrium bids corresponding to actual signals and the realized value of x_0.

TABLE 6.2

Inexperienced Bidders: Actual versus Theoretical Revenue Changes and Profit Levels

| | Average Change in Revenue: English Less First-Price | | | Average Profit | | | |
| | | | | First-Price | | English | |
ε	Actual (1)	Theoretical (2)	Difference (3)	Actual (4)	Theoretical (5)	Actual (6)	Theoretical (7)
$6	−1.54	1.54	−3.08	−2.13	2.76	−0.58	1.23
	(0.72)*	(0.49)	(0.71)*	(0.52)*	(0.38)	(0.50)	(0.30)
				[29]		[28]	
$12	−0.54	2.76	−3.30	−1.32	5.01	−0.78	2.25
	(1.25)	(0.92)	(0.84)*	(0.79)[a]	(0.60)	(0.95)	(0.69)
				[41]		[45]	
$24	1.09	8.10	−7.01	1.20	9.83	0.11	1.73
	(3.29)	(2.32)	(3.05)*	(1.93)	(1.25)	(2.64)	(2.14)
				[25]		[13]	

Notes: All values are reported in dollars. Bracketed terms are the number of auction periods. Standard errors are given in parentheses. ND stands for no data.

*The null hypothesis that the value is greater than or equal to zero can be rejected at the 5% significance level.

[a]The null hypothesis that the value is greater than or equal to zero can be rejected at the 10% significance level.

The null hypothesis of interest is that the actual revenue changes reported in columns (1) and (8) are nonnegative. However, with the exception of $n = 4$ and $\varepsilon = \$24$, actual revenue changes are all negative and are significantly less than zero (at the 5-percent level) in two cases. Further, as indicated in columns (3) and (10), actual revenue changes are significantly lower than theoretical revenue changes in all five cases. Thus, for inexperienced bidders, in all cases there is less of a revenue increase than the theory predicts, and in four out of five cases average revenue is actually lower under English compared to first-price auctions, so that the theory does not even get the directional prediction right.

Average winner's profits are reported in columns (4) to (8) and (11) to (14) and provide the explanation for the "perverse" revenue effects just reported: inexperienced bidders suffer from a winner's curse in both English and first-price auctions, but the curse is relatively stronger in first-price auctions. The revenue results in Table 6.2 cannot be explained on the basis of risk aversion or the existence of asymmetric equilibria in the English auctions, since actual profits are always below predicted RNNE profits in the English auctions.[12]

This perverse revenue effect is, however, consistent with earlier experimental work in which revenue was *reduced* following the announcement of x_1 in first- and second-price sealed bid auctions when bidders suffered from a winner's

TABLE 6.2 (continued)

			n = 7			
Average Change in Revenue:			*Average Profit*			
English Less First-Price			*First-Price*		*English*	
Actual (8)	*Theoretical* (9)	*Difference* (10)	*Actual* (11)	*Theoretical* (12)	*Actual* (13)	*Theoretical* (14)
−1.98 (0.87)*	0.10 (0.34)	−2.08 (0.78)*	−3.85 (0.71)* [18]	0.99 (0.19)	−1.87 (0.51)* [18]	0.89 (0.29)
−1.95 (1.19)[a]	1.08 (0.65)	−3.03 (0.92)*	−3.75 (0.89)* [30]	2.76 (0.53)	−1.80 (0.77)* [43]	1.68 (0.40)
		ND	ND			

curse (Kagel and Levin, 1986; Kagel et al., 1995). There is one important difference, however, between these earlier results and those reported here. With x_1 publicly announced, average profit was positive. In contrast, average profit here is negative for all n and ε (with the exception of $n = 4$ and $\varepsilon = \$24$). This suggests that information dissemination in the English auction is noisier relative to when x_1 is publicly announced.

b. One-Time Experienced and Super-Experienced Bidders

Tables 6.3 and 6.4 report average changes in the auctioneer's revenue between English and first price auctions, as well as the winner's average profit in both types of auctions for one-time experienced and super-experienced bidders. In all cases English auctions fail to increase revenue as much as the theory predicts (column (3) in Table 6.3 and columns (3) and (10) in Table 6.4). However, the qualitative implications of the theory are generally correct, as the actual revenue changes are all essentially nonnegative, and are significantly greater than zero in two cases.

For the one-time experienced bidders, average revenue is higher under the English auction rules for both $n = 4$ and 7 (with the increased revenue being significantly greater than zero at the 10% level with $n = 4$). The increased revenue from the English auctions is, in both cases, associated with considerably higher average profit in the first-price auctions than for completely Inexperienced bidders (holding ε constant), as the worst effects of the winner's curse have been eliminated.

For super-experienced bidders, with $n = 4$, actual revenue is higher in the

TABLE 6.3
One-Time-Experienced Bidders: Actual versus Theoretical Revenue Changes and Profit Levels

| | Average Change in Revenue: English Less First-Price | | | Average Profit | | | |
| | | | | First-Price | | English | |
	Actual (1)	Theoretical (2)	Difference (3)	Actual (4)	Theoretical (5)	Actual (6)	Theoretical (7)
n = 4	1.62	2.72	−1.10	1.37	4.32	−.25	1.60
ε = $12	(0.89)	(0.65)	(0.63)[a]	(0.49)	(0.41)	(0.80)	(0.45)
					[89]		[49]
n = 7	0.31	0.68	−0.37	−0.32	2.93	−0.63	2.25
ε = $12	(1.02)	(0.69)	(0.96)	(0.56)	(0.54)	(0.71)	(0.43)
					[19]		[32]

Notes: All values reported in dollars. Bracketed terms are the number of auction periods. Standard errors are given in parentheses.
[a]The null hypothesis that the value is greater than or equal to zero can be rejected at the 10% significance level.

English auctions for both values of ε, with a statistically significant increase (at the 5% level) for $\varepsilon = \$18$. However, for $n = 7$, there is essentially no difference in revenue between the first-price and English auctions. The significant increase in revenue in English auctions with $n = 4$ and $\varepsilon = \$18$ is, once again, associated with elimination of the worst effects of the winner's curse in

TABLE 6.4
Super-Experienced Bidders: Actual versus Theoretical Revenue Changes and Profit Levels

	n = 4						
	Average Change in Revenue: English Less First-Price			Average Profit			
				First-Price		English	
ε	Actual (1)	Theoretical (2)	Difference (3)	Actual (4)	Theoretical (5)	Actual (6)	Theoretical (7)
$18	2.21	3.96	−1.75	3.37	6.77	1.16	2.82
	(0.95)	(0.73)	(0.68)*	(0.50)	(0.48)	(0.88)	(0.53)
					[163]		[107]
$30	1.20	2.98	−1.78	8.45	11.27	7.25	8.29
	(3.10)	(2.30)	(2.19)	(1.28)	(1.34)	(2.76)	(1.93)
					[31]		[33]

Notes: All values reported in dollars. Bracketed terms are the number of auction periods. Standard errors are given in parentheses. ND stands for no data.
*The null hypothesis that the value is greater than or equal to zero can be rejected at the 5% significance level.

first-price auctions, as bidders earned a substantial share (more than 50%) of predicted profit. The importance of eliminating the winner's curse for the revenue raising prediction of the theory to hold is reinforced by the absence of any revenue increase with $n = 7$, in conjunction with the relatively low share (21%) of the profits that could have been earned in these first-price auctions.

The increased revenue in English auctions with experienced bidders who have largely overcome the winner's curse is consistent with earlier experimental work in which revenue was increased following the announcement of x_1 in first- and second-price sealed bid auctions when there was no winner's curse (as reported here, in these earlier experiments actual revenue increases were always lower than the theory predicts; Kagel and Levin [1986], Kagel et al. [1995]).[13] The important difference between the two sets of results is that in the English auctions the "public information" is generated endogenously so that (i) this information is noisier and (ii) bidders must figure out for themselves that lower bidders' drop-out prices have important informational content. Finally, since average actual profits are consistently at or below theoretical profits in the English auctions, the failure to raise as much revenue as the theory predicts cannot be attributed to risk aversion, but is more than likely due to residual traces of the winner's curse, which tends to be stronger in the sealed bid auctions.

3.2 Bidding Behavior in English Auctions

This section explores the behavioral process underlying bidding in English auctions. We ask what kind of information do bidders rely on in the English auctions. Is it their own signal value and the first drop-out price as the theory

TABLE 6.4 (continued)

n = 7						
Average Change in Revenue: English Less First-Price			Average Profit			
			First-Price		English	
Actual (8)	Theoretical (9)	Difference (10)	Actual (11)	Theoretical (12)	Actual (13)	Theoretical (14)
−0.25 (0.86)	2.85 (0.61)	−3.10 (0.59)*	0.76 (0.65)	3.86 (0.50) [75]	1.01 (0.56)	1.01 (0.37) [96]
ND			ND		ND	

predicts or is there some other behavioral process at work? If it is some other process, what is it and how does it work?

In developing an econometric model of the bidding process in English auctions we first introduce some notation. Three indices will be used: i for bidders ($i: 1 \rightarrow n$); j for bidding rounds ($j: 1 \rightarrow n - 1$) and k for auctions ($k: 1 \rightarrow K$). Without loss of generality, we can index bidders within each auction according to the order in which they drop out (so that the actual identity of bidder i varies across auctions). The relevant variables are:

γ_{ijk}: the reservation bid of bidder i in round j of auction k (with $i \geq j$, in line with our indexing rule);

d_{jk}: the drop out price in round j of auction k;

x_{ik}: the private signal of bidder i in auction k.

The information set available to bidder i in round j ($j \leq i$) of auction k consists of his private signal x_{ik} and, for $j > 1$, the drop-out prices of previous rounds $\{d_{sk}; s: 1 \rightarrow j - 1\}$. Hence, under an overall linearity assumption, our baseline model for reservation bids is given by

$$\gamma_{i1k} = \alpha_1 + \beta_1 x_{ik} + \varepsilon_{i1k}$$

(7)

$$(i: 1 \rightarrow n, k: 1 \rightarrow K)$$

$$\gamma_{ijk} = \alpha_j + \beta_j x_{ik} + \sum_{s=1}^{j-1} \delta_{js} d_{sk} + \varepsilon_{ijk}$$

(8)

$$(i: j \rightarrow n; j: 2 \rightarrow n - 1; k: 1 \rightarrow K).$$

We also assume that the ε_{ijk}'s are distributed independently of each other with zero means and variances $\sigma_j^2 = \text{var}(\varepsilon_{ijk})$. The assumption of mutual independence of the ε's could be relaxed in a number of ways that would not affect the consistency of our estimates, but only their efficiency. However, one assumption which is critical for the consistency of our estimates is independence of the ε's "across equations," that is, for different values of j. We will provide empirical verification of this assumption later.

In order to avoid technical complications, we only consider auctions with draws in region 2 ($\underline{x} + \varepsilon < x_1 < x_n < \bar{x} + \varepsilon$). It follows that the RNNE bidding model imposes the following restrictions on the parameters of the system of equations in (7) and (8)

$$\alpha_1 = 0 \quad \beta_1 = 1.0$$

(9)

$$\alpha_j = 0, \quad \beta_j = \delta_{j1} = 0.5, \quad \delta_{js} = 0$$

(10)

$$(j: 1 \rightarrow n - 1; 1 < s < j).$$

Weaker versions of these restrictions, as well as alternative hypotheses, will be considered in the course of our analysis.

The econometric analysis is complicated by the fact that the sole observables
are

$$\gamma_{ijk} = d_{jk} \ (j: 1 \rightarrow n - 1; \ k: 1 \rightarrow K). \tag{11}$$

All other γ's are "censored"; that is, for those bidders who do not drop out in
round j we only have categorical information regarding γ_{ijk} (the censoring process is characterized in full in subsection B2 below). Our problem is complicated by the fact that a Full Information Maximum Likelihood (FIML) search
on an unconstrained parameter set consisting of all the coefficients in equations
(7) and (8)—in all $3n + (1/2)(n - 1)(n - 2)$ coefficients—is neither practical nor likely to be numerically reliable. Some form of simpler pretest analysis
is required. Ordinary least squares (OLS) estimation based on the equalities in
formula (11) are computationally attractive in this respect. But OLS estimates
suffer from potential bias since conditional on γ_{ijk} being the lowest order statistic, the residuals ε_{ijk} have negative expectations and are potentially correlated
with the x's. However, Monte Carlo (MC) simulations based on the FIML estimates show that the most significant biases are in the intercepts and variances
(these are downward biased), which are essentially nuisance parameters, and
the OLS estimates of the β's and the δ's (and of constrained versions thereof)
provide a remarkably reliable picture of the salient features of the sampling
process.[14]

a. An OLS Pretest Analysis

Considering only the identities in formula (11) and substituting them into equations (7) and (8), we obtain the following system of equations for the observable drop-out bids

$$d_{1k} = \alpha_1 + \beta_1 x_{1k} + \varepsilon_{11k} \tag{12}$$

$$d_{jk} = \alpha_j + \beta_j x_{jk} + \sum_{s=1}^{j-1} \delta_{js} d_{sk} + \varepsilon_{ijk} \tag{13}$$

$$(j: 2 \rightarrow n - 1).$$

Note that this system is triangular in the dropout bids. In particular, the covari-
ance matrix of the residuals is diagonal since the ε's are assumed to be independent of each other for different j's. Hence, individual equation OLS estimators
do not suffer from (additional) simultaneity biases.

Tables 6.5 and 6.6 report the results of these regressions, where we have
pooled data from auctions with similar levels of bidder experience. Also shown
are F test statistics for the null hypothesis that the restrictions implied by the
symmetric RNNE model apply. The β's and the δ's being our primary coefficients of interest, we only report "conventional" F test statistics, whereby the
constant α_j are left unconstrained.[15] Two forms of the Nash hypothesis are
considered: (i) the *weak* Nash hypothesis which assumes that $\delta_{js} = 0$ for all

TABLE 6.5
Effect of Own Signal and Other Bidders' Drop-Out Prices on Bids ($n = 4$)

Bidder Experience	Dependent Variable	Coefficient Estimates[a]				Nash Test Statistics[b]		Signal-Averaging Test Statistics[b]		Adjusted R^2
		Intercept (α_j)	x_{ik} (β_j)	d_{1k} (δ_{j1})	d_{2k} (δ_{j2})	Weak[c]	Strong[d]	Weak[c]	Strong[f]	
Super-Experienced	d_{1k}	1.16 (3.60)	0.99 (0.03)**			NA	0.11	NA	0.11	0.915
	d_{2k}	2.81 (1.00)**	0.19 (0.03)**	0.80 (0.03)**		NA	62.1 (0.01)	NA	62.1 (0.01)	0.993
	d_{3k}	1.23 (0.94)	0.17 (0.03)**	0.07 (0.07)	0.76 (0.08)**	85.1 (0.01)	63.2 (0.01)	0.97	17.9 (0.01)	0.995
One-Time Experienced	d_{1k}	−0.62 (2.83)	1.01 (0.02)**			NA	0.19	NA	0.19	0.987
	d_{2k}	2.04 (1.06)	0.22 (0.06)**	0.77 (0.06)**		NA	12.1 (0.01)	NA	12.1 (0.01)	0.998
	d_{3k}	0.07 (1.11)	0.21 (0.04)**	−0.24 (0.13)	1.04 (0.13)**	60.4 (0.01)	29.1 (0.01)	3.43 (0.07)	4.56 (0.01)	0.998
Inexperienced	d_{1k}	0.66 (1.96)	1.00 (0.01)**			NA	0	NA	0	0.987
	d_{2k}	−0.11 (0.79)	0.19 (0.04)**	0.82 (0.04)**		NA	39.9 (0.01)	NA	39.9 (0.01)	0.998
	d_{3k}	0.37 (0.63)	0.25 (0.03)**	0.04 (0.08)	0.72 (0.08)**	71.5 (0.01)	38.4 (0.01)	0.22	3.34 (0.02)	0.999

Notes: Data analysis restricted to x_{1k} in the interval $\underline{x} + \varepsilon, \bar{x} - \varepsilon$. NA stands for not applicable.

**Significantly different from zero at the 1% level.

[a]Standard errors are given in parentheses.

[b]Probability $F = 1$ in parentheses.

[c]Tests the null hypothesis that $\delta_{js} = 0$ for all $s > 1$.

[d]Tests the null hypothesis that $\beta_j = \delta_{j1} = 0.50$ and $\delta_{js} = 0$ for all $s > 1$.

Tests the null hypothesis that $\delta_{js} = 0$ for all $s < j - 1$

$j > s > 1$; and (ii), the *strong* Nash hypothesis which assumes in *addition* that $\beta_j = \delta_{j1} = 0.50$.[16] The system of equations (12) and (13) being recursive, the F test statistics are evaluated for each equation individually.

We focus first on super-experienced bidders, those bidders who, according to the profit data reported, come closest to the symmetric RNNE model's predictions. For each round where a weak Nash test can be made (round 3 and higher), we overwhelmingly reject the Nash model's prediction that bidders ignore drop-out prices beyond the first round. In fact, looking at the coefficient estimates, from round 3 on, the lowest bidder's drop-out price is virtually ignored as the coefficient estimates for δ_1 are all essentially zero. Instead, bidders place weight on their own signal value and the drop-out price of the bidder who dropped out just before them (the drop-out price is round $j - 1$). Further, looking at auctions with $n = 7$, there is a general tendency for bidders who drop out later in the auction to put relatively less weight on their own signal value and more weight on the drop-out price in the preceding round. That is, for $j > 1$, bidders essentially appear to have adopted a (symmetric) rule of the form

$$\gamma_{ijk} = \lambda_j x_{ik} + \mu_j d_{j-1,k} \tag{14}$$

where the λ_j's decrease and the μ_j's increase as j increases. This same pattern characterizes the drop-out prices of inexperienced and once experienced bidders as well.

The obvious question is, what kind of information processing rule does (14) represent and is it sensible in the context of our English auctions? A little exploration immediately produces the following (quite plausible) scenario: assume bidders were not aware of all the subtleties of the RNNE model and, in particular, of the fact that the (joint) use of the sufficient statistic underlying the Nash formulation would protect them against the adverse selection problem which is inherent in common values auctions.[17] Consider the problem of choosing a reservation bid γ_{ijk} for bidder i who has reached round j (in auction k). If he or she knew the private signals of all the bidders who dropped out in earlier rounds, but was unaware of the adverse selection problem and the associated sufficient statistic underlying the uniform distribution, then it would be quite natural to average the signal values revealed to this point, along with their own signal value, and to use this to determine their reservation bid

$$\gamma_{ijk} = \frac{1}{j}\left(x_{ik} + \sum_{s=1}^{j-1} x_{sk}\right) \tag{15}$$

for $i \geq j > 1$.

In fact, bidders do not know their rival's *individual* private signals. However, assuming symmetric behavior by all participants according to rule (15), they can infer by recursion that

TABLE 6.6
Effect of Own Signal and Other Bidders Drop-Out Prices on Bids ($n = 7$)

Bidder Experience	Dependent Variable	Intercept (α_j)	x_{jk} (β_j)	d_{1k} (δ_{j1})	d_{2k} (δ_{j2})	d_{3k} (δ_{j3})	d_{4k} (δ_{j4})	d_{5k} (δ_{j5})	Nash Test Statistics[b] Weak[c]	Nash Test Statistics[b] Strong[d]	Signal-Averaging Test Statistics[b] Weak[c]	Signal-Averaging Test Statistics[b] Strong[f]	Adjusted R^2
Super-Experienced	d_{1k}	−4.21 (2.92)	0.97 (0.02)**						NA	2.84 (0.10)	NA	2.84 (0.10)	0.971
	d_{2k}	−0.18 (2.23)	0.45 (0.06)**	0.56 (0.07)**					NA	0.51	NA	0.51	0.984
	d_{3k}	1.14 (1.56)	0.36 (0.05)**	0.15 (0.07)*	0.49 (0.08)**				35.9 (0.01)	12.7 (0.01)	4.96 (0.03)	1.74 (0.17)	0.992
	d_{4k}	0.26 (1.08)	0.18 (0.03)**	0.01 (0.04)	0.09 (0.07)	0.73 (0.06)**			195.0 (0.01)	103.3 (0.01)	1.54 (0.22)	2.71 (0.04)	0.997
	d_{5k}	1.99 (0.76)*	0.10 (0.02)**	0.04 (0.03)	0.03 (0.05)	−0.08 (0.07)	0.91 (0.07)**		198.2 (0.01)	119.7 (0.01)	1.41 (0.25)	5.42 (0.01)	0.998
	d_{6k}	1.43 (0.98)	0.19 (0.03)**	−0.01 (0.04)	0.09 (0.06)	−0.02 (0.09)	0.00 (0.16)	0.75 (0.15)**	105.4 (0.01)	70.8 (0.01)	0.77	0.78	0.998
One-Time Experienced	d_{1k}	−2.22 (4.89)	1.00 (0.03)**						NA	0.0	NA	0.0	0.962
	d_{2k}	0.89 (2.30)	0.16 (0.06)*	0.85 (0.06)**					NA	15.4 (0.01)	NA	15.4 (0.01)	0.992
	d_{3k}	3.08 (2.85)	0.19 (0.08)*	0.09 (0.18)	0.71 (0.20)**				13.0 (0.01)	7.01 (0.01)	0.26	1.16 (0.34)	0.999

d_{4k}	−0.73 (0.96)	0.06 (0.04)	−0.01 (0.06)	−0.06 (0.07)	1.01 (0.06)**		221.3 (0.01)	114.0 (0.01)	0.88	10.7 (0.01)	0.999
d_{5k}	2.95 (1.43)*	0.20 (0.04)**	0.18 (0.09)	−0.14 (0.12)	−0.37 (0.29)	1.12 (0.26)**	42.9 (0.01)	28.3 (0.01)	1.69 (0.19)	1.47 (0.23)	0.997
Inexperienced											
d_{1k}	−3.39 (3.10)	1.03 (0.02)**					NA (0.01)	2.13 (0.15)	NA	2.13 (0.15)	0.979
d_{2k}	2.68 (1.16)*	0.32	0.67 (0.05)**				NA (0.01)	5.18 (0.01)	NA	5.18 (0.01)	0.997
d_{3k}	1.62 (1.00)	0.15 (0.05)**	0.04 (0.09)	0.81 (0.12)**			48.4 (0.01)	18.5 (0.01)	0.20	4.42 (0.01)	0.998
d_{4k}	1.37 (0.78)	0.08 (0.04)*	0.03 (0.07)	−0.18 (0.13)	1.06 (0.12)**		85.9 (0.01)	45.8 (0.01)	1.00	4.64 (0.01)	0.999
d_{5k}	1.30 (0.49)*	0.07	0.09	0.17	0.20 (0.13)	0.80 (0.10)**	159.9 (0.01)	113.4 (0.01)	2.04 (0.12)	12.0 (0.01)	1.00
d_{6k}	0.44 (0.49)	0.08 (0.03)**	0.02 (0.04)	0.00 (0.08)	−0.01 (0.11)	−0.38 (0.15)*	90.3 (0.01)	61.9 (0.01)	2.43 (0.06)	3.58 (0.01)	1.00
						1.29 (0.15)**					

Notes: Data analysis restricted to x_{1k} in the interval $\bar{x} + \varepsilon,\ \bar{x} - \varepsilon$. NA stands for not applicable.

*Significantly different from zero at the 5% level.

**Significantly different from zero at the 1% level.

[a]Standard errors are given in parentheses.

[b]Probability $F = 1$ in parentheses.

[c]Tests the null hypothesis that $\delta_{js} = 0$ for all $s > 1$.

[d]Tests the null hypothesis that $\beta_j = \delta_{j1} = 0.50$ and $\delta_{js} = 0$ for all $s > 1$.

[e]Tests the null hypothesis that $\delta_{js} = 0$ for all $s < j - 1$.

[f]Tests the null hypothesis that $\beta_j = 1/j;\ \delta_{jj-1} = 1 - (1/j)$, and $\delta_{js} = 0$ for all $s < j - 1$.

$$d_{j-1,k} = \gamma_{j-1,j-1,k} = \frac{1}{j-1} \sum_{s=1}^{j-1} x_{sk} \qquad (16)$$

for $j > 1$.

Substitution of that partial sum in the right-hand side of equation (15) produces a rule of the form given in equation (14) where

$$\lambda_j = \frac{1}{j}, \quad \mu_j = \frac{j-1}{j} = 1 - \lambda_j \qquad (17)$$

which we will refer to as the (symmetric) signal averaging rule. The signal averaging rule offers a number of key advantages to the players. First and foremost, it helps them to overcome the winner's curse by processing the information offered by the bid sequence. Second, it does not actually require deducing signals from bids and averaging them along with one's own signal (a process that is neither transparent or easy to do given the rapidity with which prices increased in our auctions), since it strictly relies on readily observable data that is quite natural to employ (one's own private signal and the latest drop-out price). Third, it is efficient in that except for bidding errors, players are eliminated in ascending order of their private signals. Fourth, it provides the winning bidder with an unbiased and robust estimator of x_o. Finally, given the uniform distribution of signal values, within region 2 *average* profits and prices are the same under the signal averaging and Nash bidding rules, as is round by round bidding. As such, as discussed in Section 5 below, it would take an exceptionally sophisticated player to take advantage of signal-averaging opponents. In many ways the signal-averaging rule constitutes a very sensible (symmetric) rule of thumb and it is remarkable to find it emerging as a natural strategy for bidders at all levels of experience.

The F statistics reported in Tables 6.5 and 6.6 under the heading "averaging rule" test two versions of the averaging model: (i) a weak signal-averaging hypothesis which assumes that $\delta_{js} = 0$ for all $1 \le s < j - 1$ in (14), and (ii) a strong signal-averaging hypothesis which assumes in *addition* that $\beta_j = 1/j$ and $\delta_{j,j-1} = 1 - \beta_j$.

Again, we start by focusing on super-experienced bidders, those who come closest to the predicted RNNE profits. With the exception of round 3 with $n = 6$ or 7, the weak signal-averaging test fails to be rejected at conventional significance levels for all $j > 2$. The strong test fails to be rejected at $p < 0.05$ in 6 of 10 rounds (when the strong hypothesis is rejected, particularly with $n = 4$, subjects put more weight on $d_{j-1,k}$ than (17) allows).[18] Looking at all the data, a similar pattern emerges. The weak signal-averaging hypothesis can be rejected at the 5% significance level in only 1 of 15 rounds in total. The strong hypothesis is consistently rejected in auctions with $n = 4$ and for inexperienced bidders with $n = 7$, but it fares considerably better, being rejected at a 5-percent significance level in 4 of 10 cases with $n = 7$ for super-experienced and onetime experienced bidders.[19]

The results reported in Tables 6.5 and 6.6 are robust to a number of alternative specifications. We obtain the same qualitative, and virtually the same quantitative, results using a fixed effects regression model specification, with subject dummy variables serving as the fixed effect. Interestingly, for super-experienced bidders the dummy variables are *not* significant at the 5-percent level in any auction round, although these dummy variables do achieve statistical significance in close to half the auction rounds for inexperienced and once experienced bidders. The results reported are also robust to controlling for different values of ε by restricting the analysis to auction periods with same value of ε.

In summary, our OLS pretest analysis appears to have produced a superior alternative to the Nash model. Bidders do not rely exclusively on their own signal value and the lowest bidder's drop-out price. Rather, behavior appears to be better characterized by a model in which bidders implicitly average their own signal value with the signal values implicit in all earlier bidder's drop-out prices.

One final point in concluding this section. Using the OLS estimators, we calculated the sample residual correlations across equations to test the assumption of independence of the residual ε's across equations (that is, for different j's). Among the 108 correlations that were computed, only one was significantly different from zero at the 10% level (with none significantly different from zero at the 5% level). This result strongly supports the assumption of independence across equations, which is essential to the consistency of the FIML censored estimators discussed next.

b. Full Information Analysis

When a player continues to bid after someone has dropped out of an auction, this bidder reveals that his reservation value is greater then the observed drop-out price; that is, $\gamma_{ijk} > d_{jk}$. Further, in a model which permits bidding errors, there are times immediately after a bidder has dropped out that a remaining bidder, on reevaluating his drop-out price in light of the new information, may wish that he had dropped out at the same time or even earlier than the bidder who just dropped out. The obvious response of such a bidder is to drop out immediately before the price has had a chance to increase.[20] We refer to such exits as panic drop outs. For these bidders, $\gamma_{ijk} \le d_{j-1,k}$ is less than the observed d_{jk} for that round. A FIML censored bidding model incorporates the additional information about reservation bids associated with both these cases and corrects for the potential bias associated with our OLS estimates.

In developing these estimates we reformulate the decision problem as one of choosing among two rival point hypotheses—the Nash and the signal-averaging models. Estimation was done under two different assumptions regarding the error structure (ε_{ijk}) in equations (7) and (8): (1) The errors for individual i are independent across successive rounds (j) of each auction, and (2) The errors for individual i are perfectly correlated across rounds.[21] Under both specifications the signal-averaging model outperforms the Nash model over *all* six data sets having (i) smaller standard errors and (ii) larger maximum likelihood values.[22]

Further, the variance dominance of the signal-averaging model is consistently greater in auctions with $n = 7$ than with $n = 4$, which is as it should be, since the difference between the two formulations increases with n.

c. The Effect of Bidding Errors on Other Observable Quantities

Table 6.7 reports the percentage of auctions won for the highest and second highest signal holders, average profits of these bidders when they win, and the percentage of panic dropouts for all six data sets. Also shown are the results of MC simulations based on the censored FIML estimated bid functions, assuming independent error draws across successive rounds of bidding. The simulated profit data "truncates" drop-out bids so that in cases where the ε_{ijk} drawn results in a panic dropout, we treat this bidder as dropping out at the previous price. Table 6.7 provides a number of insights:

(i) In the MC simulations, the existence of *stochastic* bidding errors in conjunction with *independent* error draws implies that with signal averaging the high signal holders will win the auction around 55 percent when $n = 4$ and around 35 percent when $n = 7$. These are dramatically lower than the 100 percent winning percentage implied by homogeneous bidding without bidding errors. These predicted frequencies are remarkably accurate for $n = 4$ and, for $n = 7$, lie within the 95 percent confidence interval or just below it (super-experienced subjects).[23] Thus, what appears to be a breakdown in the symmetry assumption of the model is quite consistent with symmetry in conjunction with stochastic bidding errors.

(ii) The simulated frequencies of panic dropouts lie within the 95-percent confidence interval of the realized data for the signal-averaging model with independent errors in all cases. In contrast, the simulated frequency of panic dropouts assuming perfectly correlated error terms across successive rounds of each auction are considerably smaller than the realized frequencies. For example, with super-experienced bidders and $n = 7$, the FIML estimates for the signal-averaging model yield a panic drop-out rate of 3.4 percent, which is far too low to provide a reasonable characterization of the data.

(iii) The simulated profit data for the signal-averaging model are well below the realized data for super-experienced bidders with both $n = 4$ and 7. The simulated profit data are quite sensitive, however, to the intercept value employed, and these coefficients are subject to reasonably large standard errors (see Table 1 of an appendix available from the authors). For example, for super-experienced bidders with $n = 7$, reducing the intercept value by one unit generates positive profits of $1.91 in the averaging model simulation when the high signal holder wins.

Accounting for the way in which constant terms accumulate across rounds within a given auction, expected profits would be significantly larger—by as much as $5 to $10—if the intercepts of the FIML bid functions were set to zero

TABLE 6.7
Comparison of Actual Data with Full Information Signal-Averaging Model Simulations

| | | Actual Data | | | | | Simulations | | | | |
| | | Percentage Wins by Signal Rank | | Average Profit by Signal Rank | | Percentage Panic Drops | Percentage Wins by Signal Rank | | Average Profit by Signal Rank | | Percentage Panic Drops |
n	Experience	2nd High	High	2nd High	High		2nd High	High	2nd High	High	
4	Super-Experienced	28.4 (5.01)	56.8 (5.50)	-0.96 (1.95)	2.20 (1.28)	ND[a]	28.7 (0.04)	55.4 (0.05)	-2.75 (0.01)	-1.01 (0.01)	15.1 (0.04)
	One-Time Experienced	26.8 (6.92)	56.1 (7.75)	1.39 (1.16)	-0.28 (1.17)	15.5 (3.26)	28.6 (0.04)	56.3 (0.05)	-1.66 (0.01)	-0.46 (0.01)	14.8 (0.04)
	Inexperienced	27.5 (7.06)	60.0 (7.75)	-0.66 (1.60)	-0.12 (0.98)	10.8 (2.84)	28.4 (0.04)	57.2 (0.05)	-0.97 (0.01)	0.23 (0.01)	15.3 (0.04)
7	Super-Experienced	17.4 (4.56)	57.9 (5.94)	-0.76 (1.25)	2.22 (0.48)	23.7 (2.09)	25.3 (0.04)	35.5 (0.05)	-1.61 (0.01)	-1.02 (0.01)	25.5 (0.04)
	One-Time Experienced	24.0 (8.54)	48.0 (9.99)	-0.62 (1.50)	-0.27 (1.49)	32.1 (3.67)	24.4 (0.04)	33.1 (0.05)	-1.63 (0.01)	-1.28 (0.01)	26.6 (0.04)
	Inexperienced	37.1 (8.17)	37.1 (8.17)	-3.14 (1.64)	-0.76 (0.92)	26.7 (3.05)	25.7 (0.04)	36.6 (0.05)	-3.34 (0.01)	-2.91 (0.01)	21.1 (0.04)

Notes: Standard errors reported in parentheses.
[a] ND stands for no data. See note 20.

in the simulations. These are considerably larger than expected profits with error free bidding. This finding indicates that bidding errors, if unaccounted for, bias downward estimates of x_o and raise expected profits. However, the significant positive intercepts for the estimated bid functions suggest that bidders have become aware of this bias, and compensate for it by adjusting the intercepts of their bidding rules, thereby preserving their intrinsic "simplicity."

4. Relationship to Field Data

Comparisons of revenue raising effects of English auctions using field data have been largely confined to U.S. government timber lease sales. Using OLS regressions, Walter J. Mead (1967) reports that first-price sealed bid auctions had significantly higher prices than English auctions; that is, English auctions resulted in significantly lower average revenue. Further study by Hansen (1985, 1986), who noted a selection bias caused by the way the forest service chose which auction to use, and corrected for it using a simultaneous equations model, found that although first-price auctions had slightly higher prices than English auctions, the difference was not statistically significant, so that revenue equivalence could not be rejected. The puzzling part about these results is that there are strong common value elements to timber lease sales which should, in theory, result in English auctions raising more revenue. R. Preston McAfee and McMillan (1987 p. 727) note this puzzle and go on to add, "The puzzle could be resolved by appealing to risk aversion of the bidders, but this remains an open empirical question."

Results from our common auction experiments offer an alternative resolution to this anomaly. In auctions with inexperienced bidders who clearly suffered from the winner's curse, English auctions consistently yield less revenue than first-price auctions (recall Table 2). Further, even in auctions where bidders earned positive profits, but still exhibited relatively strong traces of the winner's curse, as in auctions with one-time experienced and super-experienced bidders with $n = 7$, the two auctions yield roughly the same revenue. In other words, in auctions where bidders suffer from strong traces of the winner's curse, English auctions fail to raise more revenue. Of course, to use this mechanism to resolve the anomaly for the timber lease sales requires postulating that bidders suffer from a winner's curse, something many economists are loath to do. Nevertheless, this hypothesis is more consistent. with the experimental data than the risk-aversion hypothesis.[24]

5. Summary and Conclusions

Irrevocable exit English auctions are capable of raising average revenue compared to first-price, scaled bid auctions as symmetric RNNE bidding theory suggests. A necessary condition for this outcome is for bidders to have largely overcome the winner's curse in sealed bid auctions. Otherwise average revenue

in first-price auctions is substantially higher than predicted and the public information released in the English auctions serves primarily to correct for the winner's curse. These results replicate earlier experimental results concerning the
release of public information in first- and second-price sealed bid auctions
(Kagel and Levin, 1986; Kagel et al., 1995). The important difference between
the two cases is that public information is endogenous and noisy in English
auctions and exogenous and precise in the sealed bid auctions. Hence, there was
no prior assurance that these earlier results would generalize.

In English auctions, later bidders employ earlier bidders' drop-out prices in
determining what to bid, as Nash bidding theory suggests. However, the information processing mechanism is quite different from what Nash bidding theory
predicts, involving a signal-averaging rule that, under our design, with symmetry, yields the same average prices and profits as the symmetric RNNE. We
attribute the adoption of the signal-averaging rule to the fact that (i) it is easy
and quite natural to use and (ii) it yields results quite similar to the Nash model
without requiring that bidders explicitly recognize the adverse selection effect
of winning the auction. The latter seems essential to explain the data since
inexperienced and onetime experienced bidders use the same rule, while bidders with comparable experience in first-price, sealed bid auctions suffer from a
strong winner's curse.

The econometric model used to test between the signal-averaging and Nash
bidding models provides strong support for the averaging model. Both OLS
estimates using only observed drop-out prices and censored FIML estimates
show that the averaging model provides a remarkably accurate characterization
of the data. MC simulations based on the censored estimates of the signal-
averaging model accurately predict the frequency of panic dropouts and the
frequency with which the highest and second-highest signal holders win the
auction. These same simulations show that the relatively low percentage (50–
60 percent) of high-signal holders winning the auctions is fully consistent with
a symmetric bidding model, given the bidding errors actually observed.

Although the symmetric signal-averaging rule yields the same drop-out
prices, on average, hence the same expected profit for the high bidder as the
RNNE, it is not a Nash equilibrium. With $n \geq 4$, given that all other bidders
follow the averaging rule, when the second-highest signal holder determines he
has an above average signal value, he can unilaterally deviate by "hiding" his
signal value and not dropping out. In doing so, he induces the highest-signal
holder, who is forming his drop-out price according to the averaging rule, to
drop out at an expected value that is *below* the true value. Thus, such a unilateral deviation will, on average, be profitable. In contrast, under the Nash rule,
this "signal-jamming" strategy, except by the lowest-signal holder, will not affect the drop-out prices of the other bidders (and hiding by the lowest-signal
holder only causes other bidders to drop out at an expected value that is *above*
the true value, so that it does not constitute a profitable deviation).

One might ask, of course, why this signal-jamming strategy does not destroy
the signal-averaging strategy, to which there are several possible answers. The
most likely one is that the signal-jamming option (i) is not transparent and (ii)

given the noise in applying the signal-averaging strategy and the noise inherent in the realizations of expected values, it is very unlikely to be discovered.

Arguably, there is no way that our subjects could hit on the Nash bidding strategy since they were not trained to recognize sufficient statistics. On the other hand, averaging the lowest drop-out price with one's own signal value seems simpler and easier to do then tracking all the signal values and implicitly averaging them. The key point, however, is that bidders do make use of the public information inherent in other bidders' drop-out prices, as Nash equilibrium bidding theory predicts. The results of both rules are quite similar, on average, under our design. This raises an interesting topic for future research: will the signal-averaging rule still have drawing power for distribution functions when it leads to markedly different outcomes relative to Nash equilibrium bidding.

Appendix A:
Derivation of Equilibrium Bid Functions

1. Preliminaries

Let X_0 and $X_1 \leq X_2 \ldots \leq X_n$ denote the value of the item and the n-ordered private signals, respectively. their joint density function is given by

$$f(x_0, x_1, \ldots, x_n) = n! \, [(2\varepsilon)^n \cdot (\bar{x} - \underline{x})]^{-1} \qquad (A.1)$$

for $\underline{x} \leq x_0 \leq \bar{x}$ and $x_0 - \varepsilon \leq x_1 \leq \ldots \leq x_n \leq x_0 + \varepsilon$. It follows that

$$f(x_0 \, (x_1, \ldots, x_n) = [b(x_1) - a(x_n)]^{-1}, \text{ for } a(x_n) \leq x_0 \leq b(x_1) \qquad (A.2)$$

where $a(x) = \text{Max}(\underline{x}, x - \varepsilon)$ and $b(x) = \text{Min}(\bar{x}, x + \varepsilon)$. The expected value of x_0 given $(x_1, \ldots, x_n)$ is

$$E(X_o \mid X_1, \ldots, X_n) = \frac{1}{2} [a(X_n) + b(X_1)]. \qquad (A.3)$$

The unconditional density function x_i is given by

$$f_i(x) = n[(2\varepsilon)^n \cdot (\bar{x} - \underline{x})]^{-1} \cdot \binom{n-1}{n-i} \cdot \int_{a(x)}^{b(x)} (x_0 + \varepsilon - x)^{n-i} \, dx_0. \qquad (A.4)$$

The bounds of integration are $a(x) = x - \varepsilon$ and $b(x) = x + \varepsilon$, except that (1) if $x < \underline{x} + \varepsilon$, then $a(x) = \underline{x}$; and (2) if $x > \bar{x} - \varepsilon$, then $b(x) = \bar{x}$.

2. English Auctions

Following, for example, Milgram and Weber (1982), a symmetric RNNE bidding strategy for rounds $j : 2 \rightarrow N - 1$ is given by

$$d_j(x) = E(X_0 \mid X_i = x_i, i < j; X_i = x, i \geq j) = \frac{1}{2}[a(x) + b(x_1)]. \quad (A.5)$$

Hence the winner's expected profit is given by

$$\Pi_E = \frac{1}{2}\{(\underline{x} + \bar{x}) - E[a(X_{n-1}) + b(X_1)]\}, \quad (A.6)$$

where the relevant densities for X_1 and $X_{(n-1)}$ are given in equation (A.4). Conceptually straightforward though somewhat tedious piecewise integration produces the result in equation (6).

3. First-Price Auctions

Let $\rho(.)$ denote the RNNE bid function. Consider a bidder with private signal $\underline{x}$ and bidding $\rho(y)$. Expected payoff is given by

$$P(y, x) = [(2\varepsilon)^{n-1}(b(x) - a(x))]^{-1} \int_{a(x)}^{b(x)} [x_0 - \rho(y)](y - x_0 + \varepsilon)^{n-1} dx_0.$$

$$(A.7)$$

Incentive compatibility requires that

$$\left.\frac{dP(y, x)}{dy}\right|_{y=x} = 0. \quad (A.8)$$

The form of the resulting differential equation depends upon the ex of the bounds of integration in equation (A.7) and we have

$$\rho'(x) \cdot (x - \underline{x} + \varepsilon) + n\rho(x) - [x + \varepsilon + (n - 1)]\underline{x} = 0, x < \underline{x} + \varepsilon, \quad (A.9)$$

$$\rho'(x) \cdot 2\varepsilon + n\rho(x) + [(n - 2)\varepsilon - nx] = 0, \underline{x} + \varepsilon < x < \bar{x} - \varepsilon, \quad (A.10)$$

$$\rho'(x) + n\rho(x) \cdot p(x) + [(n - 1) - n(x + \varepsilon) \cdot p(x)] = 0, x > \bar{x} - \varepsilon, (A.11)$$

where

$$p(x) = \frac{(2\varepsilon)^{n-1} - (x - \bar{x} + \varepsilon)^{n-1}}{(2\varepsilon)^n - (x - \bar{x} + \varepsilon)^n}. \quad (A.12)$$

Initial conditions are given by $\rho(\underline{x} - \varepsilon) = \underline{x}$, together with continuity requirements for $x = \underline{x} + \varepsilon$ and $x = \bar{x} - \varepsilon$. Solutions for equations (A.9) and (A.10) are straightforward and are given by equations (1.a) and (1.b), respectively.

We could not find an analytical solution to equation (A.11). Since $h(\bar{x} - \varepsilon)$ turns cout to be negligible for all experimental setups under consideration, condition is given by $\rho(\bar{x} - \varepsilon) = \bar{x} - 2\varepsilon$. We were able to bracket the solution to equation (A.11) by a pair of linear functions of the form

$$\tilde{\rho}(x; \theta) = (\bar{x} - 2\varepsilon) + (1 - \theta)(x - \bar{x} + \varepsilon). \quad (A.13)$$

By substitution into equation (A.8), we find that

$$\tilde{\rho}\ (x;\ 0) \leq \rho(x) \leq \tilde{\rho}\ (x;\frac{1}{n}\ ). \tag{A.14}$$

Expected payoff is given by $\frac{1}{2}\ (\underline{x} + \bar{x}) - E[\rho(x_n)]$ and can be bracketed accordingly. Another round-off conceptually straightforward though analytically tedious piecewise integration produces the lower and upper bounds which are given in equations (2.1) and (2.6), respectively.

Appendix B:
Full Information Maximum Likelihood Bid Functions

1. The Basic Econometric Model

To avoid the complications that would result from reinterpreting our two competing models as composite "non-nested" hypotheses, we reformulate the decision problem as one of choosing among two rival point hypotheses. Let Γ_{ijk} denote the averaging rule used by the bidders. We restrict our attention to rules of the form

$$\Gamma_{i1k} = x_{ik}; \qquad \Gamma_{ijk} = \lambda_j X_{ik} + \mu_j d_{j-1,k} + \nu_j d_{1k}, \qquad \text{for } j\text{:}2 \to n - 1 \tag{A.1}$$

Let $\rho = \{(\lambda_j, \mu_j, \nu_j); j\text{:}2 \to n - 1\}$. The two competing *point* hypotheses are

$$Nash\text{: } \rho = \left\{\left(\frac{1}{2}, 0, \frac{1}{2}\right)\right\}^{n-2} \tag{A.2}$$

$$Signal\ Averaging\text{: } \rho = \left\{\left(\frac{1}{j}, \frac{j-1}{j}, 0\right); j\text{: } 2 \to n - 1\right\}. \tag{A.3}$$

The linear system in equations (7) and (8) of the text is now reinterpreted in the following way:

$$\gamma_{ijk} = a + b\Gamma_{ijk} + \varepsilon_{ijk}, \varepsilon_{ijk} \sim N(0, \sigma_j^2). \tag{A.4}$$

The coefficients a and b are assumed to be constant across successive rounds of bidding since all the action is meant to be captured by the averaging rule Γ_{ijk}. For later ease of reference let

$$e_{ijk} = d_{jk} - (a + b\Gamma_{ijk}). \tag{A.5}$$

For bidders who drop out in round j there are two cases to consider. First, "regular" drop-outs: The clock is restarted at $d_{j-1,k}$, it runs for one or more ticks and bidder j eventually drops out. It follows that $d_{jk} = \gamma_{jjk}$ or, equivalently, $\varepsilon_{jjk} = e_{jjk}$, where e_{jjk} was defined in (A.5). Second, "panic" drop-outs:

The clock is restarted at $d_{j-1,k}$ and bidder j drops out "instantly" (before the clock has had a chance to tick up). Panic drop-outs are interpreted as observing $d_{j-1,k}$, processing the new piece of information, and drawing an independent error term ε_{jjk} such that γ_{jjk} is *less* than or equal to $d_{j-1,k}$. Consequently, they drop out as soon as possible, to the effect that $d_{jk} = d_{j-1,k}$, so that $\varepsilon_{jjk} \leq e_{jjk}$.

For bidders who do *not* drop out in round j we have $\gamma_{ijk} > d_{jk}$ and $\varepsilon_{ijk} > e_{ijk}$.

Let $D = (d_{jk})$ denote the $(n-1) \times K$ matrix of drop-out prices. Let $\theta = (a,b,\{\sigma_j^2; j: 1 \rightarrow n\})$ denote the vector of parameters (other than those already included in ρ).

The binary indicator variable τ_{jk} is defined as follows: (1) regular drop-out: $\tau_{jk} = 1$ and (2) panic drop-out: $\tau_{jk} = 1$

The full information ("censored" likelihood function is now given by

$$L(\theta,\rho;D) = \prod_{k=1}^{K} \prod_{j=1}^{n-1} \left\{ \left[\frac{1}{\sigma_j} \phi\left(\frac{\theta_{ijk}}{\sigma_j}\right) \right]^{\tau_{jk}} \cdot \left[\Phi\left(\frac{\theta_{ijk}}{\sigma_j}\right) \right]^{1-\tau_{jk}} \right.$$

(A.6)

$$\left. \cdot \prod_{i=j+1}^{n} \left[1 - \Phi\left(\frac{\theta_{ijk}}{\sigma_j}\right) \right] \right\}$$

where the functions $\phi(.)$ and $\Phi(.)$, respectively, denote the density and the distribution functions associated with the standardized normal distribution.

2. Residual Variance Ratios

A second round of "pretest" OLS estimation was conducted in order to produce "guesstimates" of the residual variance ratios ("weights") across auction periods, $w_j = \sigma_j^2/\sigma_1^2$, for $j:2 \rightarrow n-1$. The "guess" component of the pretest procedure follows from the theory: The Nash specification implies that bidders should not revise there reservation bids after the second round, since subsequent rounds provide them with no new, relevant information. In contrast, under the signal-averaging model, bidders are implicitly averaging the private signals of all earlier bidders as they drop out.[1] Therefore the following sets of weights appear to be quite sensible from a theory viewpoint:

$$Nash: \omega_N = \left(1, \frac{1}{2}, \ldots, \frac{1}{2}\right)$$

(A.7)

$$Naive: \omega_n = \left(1, \frac{1}{2}, \ldots, \frac{1}{n}\right).$$

(A.8)

Equation (A.4) was estimated by OLS on all drop-out bids ($d_{jk} = \gamma_{ijk}$). The OLS estimates of $\hat{\sigma}_j^2$ are fully consistent with these "prior" values. Under the Nash specification, the variances $\hat{\sigma}_j^2$ are relatively constant for $j > 1$ and do not significantly differ from half of $\hat{\sigma}_j^2$. In contrast, under the averaging alternative, the variances $\hat{\sigma}_j^2$ decrease from one round to the next and are quite close to being inversely proportional to j.

Thus, the weights in (A.7) and (A.8) are sensible and supported by the data, and were incorporated into the two point hypotheses.

3. Censored Model Results

The parameters which remain to be estimated are (a, b, σ_1^2). The FIML estimates are obtained by maximization of the logarithm of the concentrated likelihood function (A.6). the results are found in Table A.1.[2]

Several remarks are in order. First, comparison of the estimated standard errors indicates that the signal-averaging modell fits the data significantly better than the Nash model does (recall that the estimated standard errors in Table A.1 are all *first round* standad errors; in round $j > 1$, the residual standard errors of the Nash model are divided by $\sqrt{2}$, while those of the averaging model are divided by $\sqrt{j}$). Second, calculation of (classical) type I and type II error probabilities for log likelihood differences is not trivial here since the Nash and the averaging models are "non-nested" relative to each other. However, the two models are perfectly "well-balanced" relative to each other. In particular, the Γ_{ijk}'s under both models are consistent estimates of a *common* quantity and both models have the same number of unknown coefficients. Hence, we suggest using a "critical" value of zero for the log likelihood differences. On this basis the signal-averaging model outperforms the Nash model for *all* the data sets.[3] Finally, high bidders appear to have formed remarkably close estimates of x_0 (accounting for the fact that the averaging model performs best and that in this case $\sigma_j^2 = \sigma_1^2/j$)).

4. Ex-Post Validation of Pretest Procedures

Our concern here is whether censoring biases might have invalidated the outcome of the OLS pretests reported in Tables 5 and 6. We generate MC bids according to the sampling process defined in equation (A.4) for both the Nash and the signal-averaging hypotheses. For the most part, $a = 5.0$, $b = 1.0$, and σ_1 is varried from 0.0 to 10.0 with $n = 7$ (see the parameter estimates for super-experienced bidders with $n = 7$ in Table A.1). Using the MC data, pretest OLS estimates are computed.[4]

(1). All intercept and variance estimates are significantly downward biased as a result of censoring. The magnitude of this bias is monotonic in σ_1.

(2). Under the signal-averaging model, the OLS estimates of all δ_j's that are equal to zero in equation (13) of the text are strictly unbiased (all plims are less than 0.02 in absolute value). Further, the only bias in the estimates of β_j and $\delta_{j,j-1}$

TABLE 6.A1

Comparison of Signal-Averaging and Nash Bidding Models: Full Information Analysis[a]

n	Experience	Nash Model				Signal-Averaging Model				Number of Auctions
		a	b	σ_1	Logl	a	b	σ_1	Logl	
4	Super-Experienced	6.11 (1.09)	1.00 (.009)	9.64 (0.41)	−993.0	5.41 (0.98)	1.00 (.008)	9.44 (0.40)	−977.7	81
	Once-Experienced	2.43 (1.04)	1.01 (.007)	6.26 (0.34)	−415.2	1.94 (0.93)	1.01 (.006)	6.07 (0.27)	−408.9	41
	Inexperienced	3.08 (1.06)	1.01 (.007)	5.76 (0.33)	−401.5	2.90 (0.97)	1.00 (.006)	5.72 (0.32)	−398.6	40
7	Super-Experienced	6.45 (1.22)	1.01 (.008)	12.48 (0.42)	−1612.2	5.00 (0.82)	1.00 (.005)	11.44 (0.38)	−1550.8	69
	Once-Experienced	5.86 (0.74)	1.01 (.006)	9.38 (0.43)	−575.4	4.01 (1.31)	1.00 (.008)	8.90 (0.50)	−571.7	27
	Inexperienced	5.92 (0.92)	1.00 (.006)	7.17 (.032)	−735.1	3.87 (0.69)	1.00 (.005)	7.09 (0.28)	−732.3	35

[a]Data analysis restricted to X_{1k} in the interval $\underline{X} + \varepsilon$, $\overline{X} - \varepsilon$.

Standard errors are in parentheses.

$\varepsilon = \$18$ for super-experienced $n = 4$ and 7; $\varepsilon = \$12$ otherwise.

is a tendency for $\hat{\delta}_{j,j-1}$ to be slightly upward biased and for $\hat{\beta}_j$ to be downward biased. But their plims add up to within 1–2% of 1.0. This overall pattern is apparent in Tables 5 and 6 and is captured in the semi-strong test of the signal-averaging model reported in note 18 of the text.

(3). Under the Nash model the OLS estimates of $\hat{\beta}_j$, $\hat{\delta}_{j,1}$, and $\hat{\delta}_{j,j-1}$ have non-zero plims, which sum essentially to 1.0 (all other $\hat{\delta}_j$'s are essentially equal to zero). Thus, there is a definte and quite significant upward bias (up to 0.6) for $\hat{\delta}_{j,1-1}$, with the coefficients for $\hat{\beta}_j$ and $\hat{\delta}_{j,1}$ downward biased, but clearly significantly different from zero.

In short, the picture that emerges from Table 5 and 6, which unequivocally points in the direction of the signal-averaging model, is fully vindicated.

We also examined the validity of the "pretest" estimates for the weights of the variances across auction rounds. All individual variance estimates are downward biased. The biases are monotonic functions of the underlying σ_j's, so that the weight estimates themselves are downward biased. Nevertheless, the overall pattern of weights found in the pretest is clearly recognizable. For example, under the Nash model with $\sigma_1 = 10.0$, the plims of the OLS estimates of the $\hat{w}_j^2$'s for $j \geq 2$ are all equal to 0.22 (within 1%) and, therefore, essentially equal. Under the signal-averaging model, the plims of the weights exhibit a characteristic declining pattern which, however, tails off a little quicker than the true weights.

Notes

Research support from the Economics Division and Information, Science and Technology Division of the National Science Foundation and the Energy Laboratory at the University of Houston are gratefully acknowledged. The paper has benefited from discussions, with Kemal Gular, John Hain, Ron Harstad and Jim Smith, the comments of two referees, and the many comments received when presenting earlier versions of the paper. Able research assistance was provided by Susan Garvin. Special thanks to Wei Lo for his tireless efforts with difficult maximum likelihood estimation programs. Correspondence regarding appendixes and data should be addressed to the second author.

1. These theoretical considerations played an important role in the design of recent U.S. government spectrum auctions (John McMillan, 1994; Peter C. Cramton, 1994). Although the underlying structure of the spectrum auctions is substantially more complicated than existing auction models, results from extant auction theory and related empirical work guided their design. The results of this paper are intended to add to this underlying knowledge.

2. Prices started at $\underline{x}$ as any other price rule would have involved revealing information about x_o. Initially, the price increased every second with increments of $1.00. Once the first bidder dropped out there was a brief pause after which prices increased every three seconds with smaller price increments as fewer bidders remained. With only 2 bidders remaining the price increments were $0.05 With $\varepsilon = $6.00, $0.10 with $\varepsilon = $12.00 and $0.20 for $\varepsilon > $12.00. There were no additional pauses as more bidders dropped out. A single stroke on any key was required to drop out.

3. Detailed specification of treatment conditions along with the raw data from the experiment are available from the authors on request.

4. Susan Garvin and Kagel (1994) provide evidence that in scaled-bid common value auctions returning bidders self-select with subjects who went bankrupt significantly less likely to return and with bidders who did not return bidding more aggressively than those who did return in the initial series of auctions.

5. Assuming $h(\bar{x} - \varepsilon)$ is negligible, which it is for the parameter values employed. An appendix outlining the derivation of the bid functions along with the expected profit functions is available from the authors on request.

6. Milgrom and Weber argue that the more loosely structured English auctions encountered in practice are best approximated by the irrevocable exit auction. Sushil Bikhchandani and John G. Riley (1991) disagree, arguing that they are better approximated by a second-price sealed bid auction as information revelation only occurs in English auctions despite the best efforts of the bidders. It's obviously beyond the scope of this paper to try and settle this issue (however, see Kagel et al. [1995] for an experimental investigation of bidding in second-price, common value auctions). The spectrum auctions contained an irrevocable exit element since, during the final stage, bidders generally had to remain active (be the current high bidder or put in a bid that exceeded the current high bid by the specified increment) on the number of licenses for which they wished to remain eligible.

7. In equilibrium, lower-valued signal holders cannot profit from the information of higher valued signal holders since this information is only revealed after the, latter have dropped out, at which point price is greater than the expected value of the item. The theory assumes a continuous price clock, which is not practical. With the discrete time clock employed, d_j is set at the nearest tick of the clock to (3).

8. Bikhchandani and Riley (1991) show that the expected profit of the symmetric RNNE is unique even though the reservation price functions (4) are not unique for $j < n - 1$. The problem is this. Although the low-signal holder never wants to drop out above (4), in a symmetric RNNE he is indifferent between dropping out at (4) or below it (since he never wins in equilibrium). Thus, bidders other than the two highest-signal holders may use alternative drop-out rules. We do not consider these alternative symmetric equilibria for several reasons: (i) they are not robust to the possibility that other signal holders may err by dropping out sooner than predicted by (4), (ii) they involve an implausible degree of coordination between bidders, and (iii) there is no evidence that alternative equilibria of this sort are present in our data.

9. Although, Bikhchandani and Riley (1991) note that symmetrically informed bidders are most likely to behave symmetrically, one might still see the emergence of such equilibria. No comparable asymmetric equilibria have been established for risk neutral bidders, in first-price auctions.

10. We do not consider risk loving as the evidence from the experimental literature indicates risk-neutral or risk-averse, bidding (see Kagel [1995] for a review of the literature).

11. Common value auctions involve pure surplus transfers so that revenue differences are calculated as: $[\pi_E - \pi_E]$ where π_E and π_E correspond to profits in English and first-price auctions, respectively. In this way we have effectively normalized for sampling variability in x_o by subtracting x_o from the price. For $x > \bar{x} - \varepsilon$ in first-price auctions we use the upper bound of the bid function in (1c) to compute predicted profit. Exact bid functions are used throughout in computing predicted profit for the English auctions.

12. Limited liability for losses establishes the possibility of more aggressive bidding

than predicted under the one-shot Nash equilibrium as potential losses are truncated (Robert G. Hansen and John R. Lott, 1991). However, the use of sizable starting cash balances controls for limited-liability problems and has been shown, as a practical matter, to eliminate the problem in first-price auctions (Kagel and Levin, 1991; Barry Lind and Charles R. Plott, 1991).

13. There is a potential artifactual explanation for the higher revenue in English auctions with super-experienced bidders. Since all of their experience was in first-price auctions it may be argued that the higher revenue in English auctions simply results from a lack of experience with English auctions, which results in larger errors and residual traces of the winner's curse than in the more familiar first-price auctions. However, as the data in Table 4 shows, realized profit as a percentage of predicted RNNE profit is roughly the same or greater in the English compared to first-price auctions. Further, comparing revenue effects over time for super-experienced bidders shows the same pattern as Table 4, albeit with some fluctuations in the size of the revenue differences (two auction sessions were conducted each week, for four weeks with $n = 4$ and for two weeks with $n = 7$, with subjects returning once a week in various combinations).

14. An appendix detailing the FIML estimates along with the MC simulations reported is available from the authors on request.

15. MC simulations show that the OLS estimates of the α's are essentially uninterpretable: on the one hand they suffer from a downward censoring bias. On the other hand the existence of bidding "errors" biases downward bidders' own estimates of x_o. Bidders appear to *raise* their intercepts in (12) and (13) to compensate for this bias. Which effect dominates is likely to vary from one round to another.

16. The weak Nash model tests are valid tests of the alternative symmetric RNNE described in footnote 8. The strong Nash model tests are not. Note, the F statistics reported have different degrees of freedom so that simply comparing F values between the weak and strong tests is not meaningful.

17. There is an adverse selection problem: for super-experienced bidders the high signal holder won the auction 57.1 and 53.1 percent of the time with $n = 4$ and $n = 6$ or 7, respectively. Further, the high signal holder and the second-highest signal holder won the auction 85.0 and 70.8 percent of the time with $n = 4$ and $n = 6$ or 7, respectively. See subsection B3 below for more discussion of these apparent deviations from symmetric bidding.

18. The FIML estimates show that the OLS estimates of the residual variances are downward biased (by as much as 50 percent in the first two rounds). Hence, actual p-levels are larger than those reported in Tables 5 and 6, to the effect that the signal-averaging hypothesis fares even better.

19. There is a natural "semi-strong" test for the signal-averaging model: $\delta_{js} = 0$ for $1 < s < j - 1$ and $\beta_j + \delta_{j,j-1} = 1.0$ in (13). This semi-strong test does nearly as well as the weak test: with $n = 4$, it is rejected using a 5-percent significance level in only one round (in this case involving inexperienced bidders) and with $n = 6$ or 7 it fails to be rejected in any round for all three data sets. The biases inherent in the OLS estimates indicate that this is a more reliable test of the signal-averaging rule than the "strong" test reported.

20. The computer program running the experiment had a built in delay of 10 seconds following the first dropout. After that the clock continued to increase rapidly at about 1 tick every 1–2 seconds. Bidders could tell immediately after someone had dropped out by the sound of that bidder hitting their terminal key and were able to respond before the clock could tick up. Our data files report these bidders as having dropped at the same

price as the previous bidder while correctly ordering these "simultaneous" dropouts with respect to the order in which they dropped. Both our hardware and software were updated for the $n = 4$ auctions with super-experienced bidders. For these auctions we recorded these panic dropouts as having dropped out at the next programmed tick of the clock, so that for this data set we cannot distinguish between panic dropouts and bidders who chose to remain active for one more tick of the clock.

21. Both specifications employ restrictions on the residual variance ratios ("weights") across auction periods which were suggested on both theoretical and empirical grounds.

22. For example, under the independent error specification, the log likelihood differences were 15.3 with $n = 4$ and 61.4 with $n = 7$ for super-experienced subjects (for which we have the most data).

23. Part of the explanation for the super-experienced $n = 7$ case may have to do with our simulations assuming a normal distribution for the error term, whereas the actual error distribution in this case deviates significantly from the normal distribution, with a higher frequency of early dropouts than the normal distribution implies. In contrast, for the $n = 4$ cases, a null hypothesis of normal errors fails to be rejected at conventional significance levels in all cases.

24. See Michael H. Rothkopf and Richard Englebrecht-Wiggans (1993) for an alternative explanation of this anomaly.

Appendix B Notes

1. In this formulation bidders ignore the strategic implications of the fact that their competitors also acquire new information as bidding proceeds and hence also have error terms with diminishing variances. This, in fact, appears to be the case.

2. The intercept and variance in (A.4) vary with the value of ε used in establishing private information signals. Hence, our estimates are restricted to auctions with the same value of ε (the value of ε in each data set with the most auction periods).

3. For a Bayesian argument supporting this choice, see our working paper.

4. A "large" number of simulations are conducted for each set of parameters (say 10,000 or 100,000). The large number of replications insures that the numbers obtained are accurate MC estimates of the actual probability limits of the statistic under scrutiny. For parameter estimates in particular, comparison with the MC "true value" of a parameter produces an immediate estimate of (asymptotic) bias.

References

Bikhchandani, Sushil and Riley, John G. "Equilibria in Open Common Value Auctions." *Journal of Economic Theory*, February 1991, *53*(1), pp. 101–30.

Cramton, Peter C. "Money Out of Thin Air: The Nationwide Narrowband PCS Auction." Mimeo, University of Maryland, 1994.

Garvin, Susan and Kagel, John H. "Learning in Common Value Auctions: Some Initial Observations." *Journal of Economic Behavior and Organization*, December 1994, *25*(3), pp. 351–72.

Hansen, Robert G. "Empirical Testing of Auction Theory." *American Economic Review*, May 1985, *75*(2), pp. 156–59.

————. "Sealed-Bid Versus Open Auctions: The Evidence." *Economic Inquiry*, January 1986, *24*(1), pp. 125–42.

Hansen, Robert G. and Lott, John R., Jr. "The Winner's Curse and Public Information in Common Value Auctions: Comment." *American Economic Review*, March 1991, *81*(1), pp. 347–61.

Harris, Milton and Raviv, Arthur. "Allocation Mechanisms and the Design of Auctions." *Econometrica*, November 1981, *49*(6), pp. 1477–99.

Holt, Charles A. "Competitive Bidding for Contracts under Alternative Auction Procedures." *Journal of Political Economy*, June 1980, *88*(3), pp. 433–45.

Kagel, John H. "Auctions: A Survey of Experimental Research," in John H. Kagel and Alvin E. Roth, eds., *The handbook of experimental economics*. Princeton: Princeton University Press, 1995, pp. 501–86.

Kagel, John H. and Levin, Dan. "The Winner's Curse and Public Information in Common Value Auctions." *American Economic Review*, December 1996, *76*(5), pp. 894–920.

————. "The Winner's Curse and Public Information in Common Value Auctions: Reply." *American Economic Review*, March 1991, *81*(1), pp. 362–69.

Kagel, John H.; Levin, Dan and Harstad, Ronald M. "Comparative Static Effects of Number of Bidders and Public Information on Behavior in Second-Price Common Value Auctions." *International Journal of Game Theory*, 1995, *24*(3), pp. 293–319.

Lind, Barry and Plott, Charles R. "The Winner's Curse: Experiments with Buyers and with Sellers." *American Economic Review*, March 1991, *81*(1), pp. 335–46.

McAfee, R. Preston and McMillan, John. "Auctions and Bidding." *Journal of Economic Literature*, June 1987, *25*(2), pp. 699–738.

McMillan, John. "Selling Spectrum Rights." *Journal of Economic Perspectives*, Summer 1994, *8*(3), pp, 145–62.

Mead, Walter J. "Natural Resource Disposal Policy: Oral Auction Versus Scaled Bids." *Natural Resources Journal*, April 1967, *7*(2), pp. 195–224.

Milgrom, Paul R. *The structure of information in competitive bidding*. New York: Garland Publishing, 1979a.

————. "A Convergence Theorem for Competitive Bidding with Differential Information." *Econometrica*, May 1979b, *49*(3), pp. 679–88.

————. "Rational Expectations, Information Acquisition and Competitive Bidding." *Econometrica*, July 1981, *49*(4), pp. 921–43.

Milgrom, Paul R. and Weber, Robert J. "A Theory of Auctions and Competitive Bidding." *Econometrica*, September 1982, *50*(5), pp. 1089–122.

Riley, John G. and Samuelson, William F. "Optimal Auctions." *American Economic Review*, June 1981, *71*(3), pp. 381–92.

Rothkopf, Michael H. and Engelbrecht-Wiggans, Richard. "Misapplications Reviews: Getting the Model Right—The Case of Competitive Bidding." *Interfaces*, May—June 1993, *23*(3), pp. 99–106.

Wilson, Robert. "A Bidding Model of Perfect Competition." *Review of Economic Studies*, October 1977, *44*(3), pp. 511–18.

7

Common Value Auctions with Insider Information

John H. Kagel and Dan Levin

This chapter investigates bidding in first-price, sealed bid common value auctions with an asymmetric information structure (AIS). Two types of AIS auctions have been analyzed in the literature. In both cases a single insider (I) has superior (often exact) information about the value of the item. In one case I's have a double informational advantage; they are better informed, and less informed bidders (outsiders; O's) only have access to *public* information. In this case, O's employ mixed strategies earning zero expected profits in equilibrium (Wilson (1967), Weverberg (1979), Englebrecht-Wiggans, Milgrom, and Weber (1983), Hendricks, Porter, and Wilson (1994)). In the second case, I's do not have access to the private information O's have, which provides O's with positive expected profits in equilibrium (Wilson (1985), Hausch (1987)).

The AIS auction studied here corresponds to the second category. The primary motivation for this was to maintain comparability with the vast amount of "baseline" data on auctions with a symmetric information structure (SIS).[1] I's were provided with a signal equal to the true value of the item, while O's received *private* information signals distributed around the true value as in previous SIS experiments. This design yields a number of interesting comparative static predictions that differ in important ways from the double informational advantage model. First, and foremost, for the parameter values employed, AIS auctions increase expected revenue relative to SIS auctions. In contrast, in the double informational advantage model, the insider *always* reduces the seller's expected revenue.[2] Further, unlike the double informational advantage model, O's earn informational rents, albeit, substantially smaller rents than in corresponding SIS auctions. Increases in the number of O's result in I's bidding higher in our model. In contrast, in the double informational advantage model, I's bidding strategy is unaffected by increases in the number of O's. Finally, both models imply that, conditional on winning, I's expected profits are larger than O's and larger than in SIS auctions.

Our experimental design also permits us to investigate possible ways in which the winner's curse is attenuated or eliminated in field settings. Inexperienced bidders in SIS auctions are subject to a strong winner's curse, consistently bidding above the expected value of the item conditional on winning and earning large negative average profits (Kagel, Levin, Battalio, and Meyer (1989), Dyer, Kagel, and Levin (1989), Lind and Plott (1991). Such losses clearly characterize markets that are out of equilibrium. In field settings with a common value element, one or more agents are often better informed than others. Although this will typically create a stronger adverse selection effect than in a SIS setting, it is entirely plausible that the need to hedge against a known insider is more intuitive and transparent than the need to correct for winning against equally well informed rivals. Thus, having an insider may actually reduce the severity of the winner's curse for inexperienced bidders. This would be true, for example, if O's view the situation as being closer in structure to a lemon's market (see Akerlof (1970)), where it seems reasonably clear there is no rampant winner's curse (our culture warns us to beware of used car salesmen).[3] On the other hand, inexperienced subjects may bid higher, rather than lower, in order to make up for their informational disadvantage, thus exacerbating the winner's curse.

Our main experimental results are: Super-experienced bidders, who have learned to overcome the worst effects of the winner's curse, generally satisfy the comparative static predictions of the theory. In contrast, for inexperienced O's the winner's curse is alive and well in AIS auctions as bids are consistently above expected value conditional on winning the item. More importantly, the introduction of an insider does not result in significantly lower bidding than in SIS auctions. However, the theoretical prediction that I's earn larger profits conditional on winning than O's do holds (superior information is valuable outside of equilibrium). Finally, I's adjustments to past outcomes are generally consistent with Selten and Buchta's (1994) "directional learning theory," with some important differences in the quantitative pattern of the adjustment process relative to previously reported results.

1. Structure of the Auctions

Each experimental session consisted of a series of auctions in which a single unit of a commodity was awarded to the high bidder in a first-price sealed bid auction. The value of the item, x_o, was unknown at the time bids were submitted. In each auction period, x_o was drawn randomly from a uniform distribution on $[\underline{x}, \bar{x}]$.

In SIS auctions, each bidder received his own private information signal, x, drawn iid from a uniform distribution on $[x_o - \varepsilon, x_o + \varepsilon]$. In AIS auctions one bidder—the insider—chosen at random in each auction, received private information signal $x = x_o$ and was told $x = x_o$. Each of the other bidders, the O's, received a private information signal as in the SIS auctions. I's did not know the realizations of O's signals. O's knew they were O's, that there was a single I who knew x_o, and the way that other O's got their signals (but not their realizations). The total number of bidders (n) and the values of ε and $[\underline{x}, \overline{x}]$ were publicly posted prior to each auction.

At the end of each auction all bids were posted from highest to lowest along with the corresponding signal values (bidders identification numbers were suppressed) and the value of x_o. In AIS auctions, the value of ε associated with each bidder's private information signal was also reported so that bidders could readily identify I's bid. Profits were calculated for the high bidder and reported to all bidders.

To cover the possibility of losses, bidders were given starting capital balances of $10.00. Losses were subtracted from this balance and profits added to it. If a subject's balance became nonpositive, they were no longer allowed to bid. To hold n constant, while dealing with the possibility of bankruptcies, there were typically several extra bidders in each session, with the active bidders in each auction determined randomly or through a rotation rule, Bidder identification numbers were suppressed throughout, so subjects did not know who they were competing against in any given auction.[4] Bidders were paid their end of session balances in cash, along with a $4 or $5 participation fee.

All inexperienced sessions began with $\varepsilon = \$6$ and progressed to higher values of ε. Each of these sessions employed a minimum of two "dry runs" to familiarize subjects with the procedures and the consequences of bidding too much. The instructions pointed out that, given x, ε, and the endpoint values, subjects had their own upper and lower bound estimates for x_o ($\min\{x + \varepsilon, \overline{x}\}$; $\max\{x - \varepsilon, \underline{x}\}$), which were reported to them along with x. Thus, under both information conditions, imperfectly informed bidders always had a "safe haven" strategy of bidding $\max\{x - \varepsilon, \underline{x}\}$, which completely protected them from losses.

Bidding was studied under two different values of n (4 and 7), five different values of ε (6, 12, 18, 24, and 30), and two different levels of bidder experience (inexperienced and super-experienced). Super-experienced bidders are defined as having been in at least two previous SIS or AIS first-price auction series. Table 7.1 cross-classifies experimental sessions by subjects' experience, the number of active bidders, and information structure.

Subjects were primarily senior undergraduate economics majors and MBA students at the University of Houston and the University of Pittsburgh. In establishing a pool of super-experienced bidders, all bidders were invited back, with the exception of the few bidders who went bankrupt early on in both of the first two auction sessions. Each experimental session lasted approximately two hours and had a minimum of 20 auctions.

2. Theoretical Considerations

Our focus here and throughout the data analysis is on $x_o \in [\underline{x} + 2\varepsilon, \overline{x} - 2\varepsilon]$ (referred to as region 2) for which we have clear bounds on behavior in the AIS auctions.

TABLE 7.1
Treatment Conditions

Condition	Experience[a]	Number of Bidders	Number of Experimental Sessions	Information Structure
1	None	4	2	Asymmetric
2	Super-Experienced	4	4	Asymmetric
3[b]	None	4	5	Symmetric
4[c]	Super-Experienced	4	8	Symmetric
5	None	7	2	Asymmetric
6[d,e]	Super-Experienced	7	8	Asymmetric and Symmetric
7[b,d]	None	7	5	Symmetric

[a]In super-experienced bidder sessions all bidders had participated in two or more first-price sealed bid auction sessions with equal numbers of bidders.

[b]Data have been previously reported in Garvin and Kagel (1994).

[c]Data have been partially reported in Levin, Kagel, and Richard (1996).

[d]Includes some periods with $n = 6$. Earlier work shows that pooling $n = 6$ and 7 is justified (Kagel and Levin (1986); Kagel, Levin, and Harstad (1995)).

[e]In 7 of 8 sessions; both SIS and AIS auctions were conducted using the same subjects.
Min$(\bar{x} - \underline{x}) = \$200$; Max$(\bar{x} - \underline{x}) = \$330$.

2.1 The Winner's Curse

For SIS auctions, we define a bidder as falling prey to the winner's curse when her bid is so high that it yields negative expected profits conditional on having the highest signal value, i.e., bids greater than

$$E[x_o \mid x = x_1^n] = x - \frac{n-1}{n+1}\,\varepsilon, \tag{1}$$

where x_1^n is the highest of the n private signals. In auctions where x_1^n always wins the item, bidding above (1) insures negative expected profit. In auctions where symmetry is not satisfied, but all bidders bid above (1), negative expected profits are insured as well. One or both of these initial conditions is reasonably well satisfied in our data so that bidding above (1) serves as a good *ex ante* indicator of a winner's curse.

For AIS auctions, O's bidding above

$$E[x_o \mid x = x_1^{n^o}] = x - \frac{n^o - 1}{n^o + 1}\,\varepsilon \tag{2}$$

(where n^o is the number of O's bidding) can expect to earn negative profits just competing against other O's. Further, if all O's bid according to (2), and I's employ their best response to these bids then, conditional on winning, O's would earn average *losses* of over $1.50 per auction. As such, bidding above

(2) provides a first, very conservative, definition of the winner's curse. A second definition of the winner's curse which accounts for I's best responding to O's bids is developed below.

2.2 Auctions with Symmetric Information Structure (SIS)

In SIS auctions the symmetric risk neutral Nash equilibrium (RNNE) bid function $\gamma(x)$ in region 2 is given by[5]

$$\gamma(x) = x - \varepsilon + g(x), \qquad \underline{x} + \varepsilon \leq x \leq \bar{x} - \varepsilon, \tag{3}$$

where

$$g(x) = \frac{2\varepsilon}{n + 1} \exp\left[-\frac{n}{2\varepsilon}[x - (\underline{x} + \varepsilon)]\right].$$

Equilibrium bidding combines strategic considerations similar to those involved in first-price private value auctions and item valuation considerations. The latter involves anticipating the adverse selection effect associated with winning. Both factors promote bidding below x in region 2, with expected profit for the high bidder approximately equal to $2\varepsilon/(n + 1)$.

2.3 Auctions with Asymmetric Information Structure (AIS)

Let $b(x)$ and $B(x_o)$ be the bid functions for O's and I's, respectively, and define $h(B)$ and $H(B)$ to be their inverse. When both $h(B)$ and $H(B)$ are in region 2, bidding in AIS auctions yields the following system of differential equations, where we assume symmetry among the O's:

$$h'(B) - \frac{h(B) + \varepsilon - H(B)}{n^o[H(B) - B]} = 0, \tag{4a}$$

$$[H'(B) - h'(B)][H(B) - B]\Theta^{n^o - 1} + [h'(B) - 1]\frac{2\varepsilon}{n^o}(1 - \Theta^{n^o}) \tag{4b}$$

$$+ h'(B)[h(B) - (B + \varepsilon)] = 0,$$

where

$$0 \leq \Theta \equiv \frac{h(B) + \varepsilon - H(B)}{2\varepsilon} \leq 1,$$

and H' and h' represent the first derivatives of the inverse bid functions. This system of differential equations defies analytical solution under the initial condition that the lowest possible bid is $\underline{x}$ (namely, $h(\underline{x}) = \underline{x} - \varepsilon$ and $H(\underline{x}) = \underline{x}$).[6] Numerical solution of this system of differential equations is nontrivial since the slopes of both I's and O's bid functions approach zero in a neighborhood around $\underline{x}$ (see Marshall, et al. (1994); these zero slopes mean that the solution to

(4a–b) need not be unique). Instead, we use an alternative approach based on boundedly rational bidding strategies which, as it winds up, provides a good approximation to the Nash equilibrium in region 2.

Assume that because O's are boundedly rational, their bids in region 2 are restricted to a bidding strategy of the form

$$b(x) = x - \beta \varepsilon, \qquad 0 < \beta \leq 1. \tag{5a}$$

Inspecting (4a), I's best response to this bidding strategy is

$$B(x_o) = x_o - \alpha(\beta)\varepsilon = x_o - [(1 + \beta)/n]\varepsilon. \tag{5b}$$

We will refer to this pair of bid functions as a β-discount bid factor (β-DBF), as it involves O's and I's discounting their bids, relative to their signal values, by the bid factors $\beta \varepsilon$ and $\alpha \varepsilon$.

In the special case where $\beta = 1$, (5a–b) become

$$b(x) = x - \varepsilon, \tag{6a}$$

$$B(x_o) = x_o - \frac{2\varepsilon}{n}. \tag{6b}$$

Note that (6a–b) satisfy the necessary conditions, (4a–b), for equilibrium in region 2. That is, (6a–b) constitute an equilibrium in region 2 in cases where O's, because of bounded rationality (e.g., limited computational abilities), are restricted to employing the bid function (5a). Also note that Laskowski and Slonim (in press) show that the unique pair of Nash equilibrium bid functions satisfying (4a–b) converges to (6a–b) as region 2 becomes larger and larger.[7] Further, examination of bidding in region 2, for both inexperienced and experienced O's, shows that equation (5a) provides a remarkably good fit to the data, yielding R^2 values of .99 or better and with coefficient estimates for x always within one standard deviation of 1.00 (see Tables III and V below).[8]

Finally, we can establish a second, tighter definition of the winner's curse that accounts for I's best responding to O's bids. This involves calculating the values of β_0 and α_0 (where $\alpha_0 = [1 + \beta_0]/n$) for equations (5a–b) that result in zero expected profit for O's. These are: for $n = 4$, $\alpha_0 = .421$ and $\beta_0 = .690$ and for $n = 7$, $\alpha_0 = .261$ and $\beta_0 = .825$. One can show that if O's employ a bid factor $\beta < \beta_0$, and I's best respond, O's would earn negative expected profits. These β_0 values are larger than the bid factors required to avoid the winner's curse in SIS auctions with the same total number of bidders.

Equilibrium under β-DBF has several interesting comparative static predictions:

1. As n increases from 4 to 7, I's must employ larger bid factors, while O's, bid factors remain unchanged.[9]

2. I's earn higher expected profits, conditional on winning, than O's do. For example, with $n = 4$ and $\varepsilon = \$18$, O's expected profit, conditional on winning, is $\$4.07$. For I's, it is $\$9.00$.[10]

3. Expected profits, conditional on winning, are substantially lower for O's in AIS than in corresponding SIS auctions. For example, with $n = 4$ and $\varepsilon = \$18$, these average around \$7.20 in the SIS auctions versus \$4.07 in the AIS auctions.[11]

4. I's earn higher expected profits, conditional on winning, than in corresponding SIS auctions. However, the expected differences here are smaller than the differences reported in (2) and (3) above. For example, with $\varepsilon = \$18$ and $n = 4$, the expected difference is \$1.80 versus expected differences of \$4.93 between I's and O's in (2) and of \$3.13 between SIS auctions and O's in (3).

5. Seller's expected revenue is *higher* in AIS than in corresponding SIS auctions for both $n = 4$ and 7. For example, with $n = 4$ and $\varepsilon = \$18$ seller's expected revenue in AIS auctions is $x_o - \$6.16$ compared to $x_o - \$7.20$ in SIS auctions. With $n = 7$ and $\varepsilon = \$18$ these values are $x_o - \$3.40$ in AIS compared to $x_o - \$4.50$ in SIS auctions. Note, sellers would be unambiguously better off in SIS compared to AIS auctions if I's won *all* the time. However, in our AIS auctions, the seller gains additional revenue because when O's win, they only win with relatively high signals, which yields more revenue than when I's win. These higher revenues more than offset the lower revenues when I's win (see Kagel and Levin (1998), for details of this argument).

Finally, with β-DBF bid functions, assuming that O's avoid the winner's curse and β in (5a) is no greater than 1.00, predictions 1–5 hold even if play does not converge to equilibrium.[12] Thus, the comparative static predictions 1–5 are quite robust.

3. Experimental Results

3.1 Auctions with Inexperienced Bidders

Table 7.2 presents summary statistics for inexperienced bidders for both AIS auctions and SIS auctions (top and bottom part of Table II, respectively). For inexperienced subjects within session experience covaries systematically with ε, as all sessions started with 6 to 8 auctions with $\varepsilon = \$6$ and then switched to $\varepsilon = \$12$. Thus, differences between different values of ε may reflect within session learning and/or bankruptcy and elimination of the most aggressive bidders. In what follows we first address the question of whether an insider helps inexperienced bidders to overcome, or at least attenuate, the winner's curse relative to SIS auctions. We then examine which, if any, of the predictions of the β-DBF bidding model hold for inexperienced bidders.

First, looking at the top of Table 7.2 (part A) we see that the winner's curse is alive and well. Consider auctions with $\varepsilon = \$6$, which were used to start each session. With $n = 4$, almost 60% of the high O's bids were above our first measure of the winner's curse (equation 2), so that these bids would have lost money, on average, just competing against other O's. Further, 94% of the high

TABLE 7.2
Inexperienced Bidders

A: Auctions with Asymmetric Information Structure (AIS)

				Outsiders' Bids						Insiders' Bids	
				Frequency of Winner's Curse (raw data)							
				Against Outsiders Only		Against Outsiders and Insiders					
Number of Bidders	ε	Average Earnings Conditional on Winning (S$_m$)	Frequency of Winning (raw data)	High Outsider Bid	All Bids	High Outsider Bid	All Bids	Average Bid Factor[a] (S$_m$)	Frequency High Outsider Bid from High Outsider Signal Holder (raw data)	Average Earnings Conditional on Winning (S$_m$)	Average Bid Factor (S$_m$)
4	6	−1.68 (0.93)	70.6% (12/17)	58.8% (10/17)	39.2% (20/51)	94.1% (16/17)	70.6% (36/51)	1.16 (0.62)	52.9% (9/17)	0.71 (0.35)	1.46[b] (0.26)
	12	−1.40 (0.50)*	65.2% (15/23)	39.1% (9/23)	23.2% (16/69)	65.2% (15/23)	47.8% (33/69)	6.00 (0.77)	73.9% (17/23)	2.74 (0.77)*	2.25 (0.35)
	24	−6.56 (3.07)	71.4% (5/7)	28.6% (2/7)	14.3% (3/21)	85.7% (6/7)	57.1% (12/21)	11.61 (2.78)	100% (7/7)	5.05 (3.50)	5.09 (1.27)
7	6	−3.68 (0.61)**	100% (9/9)	100% (9/9)	85.2% (46/54)	100% (9/9)	92.6% (50/54)	−0.61[c] (0.62)	66.7% (6/9)	— —	1.09[b] (0.29)
	12	−2.47 (1.03)*	78.9% (15/19)	89.5% (17/19)	69.7% (78/112)	89.5% (17/19)	79.8% (91/114)	4.85 (1.03)	73.7% (14/19)	1.93 (0.61)**	1.91[b] (0.33)

B: Auctions with Symmetric Information Structure (SIS)

Number of Bidders	ε	Average Earnings Conditional on Winning (S_m)	Frequency of Winner's Curse (raw data)		Average Bid Factor[a] (S_m)	Frequency High Bid from High Signal Holder (raw data)
			High Bidders	All Bidders		
4	6	−2.40 (0.55)**	88.4% (23/26)	70.2% (73/104)	0.13 (0.51)	57.7% (15/26)
	12	−1.10 (0.85)	74.3% (26/35)	66.4% (93/140)	5.02 (0.63)	80.0% (28/35)
	24	0.25 (1.84)	38.9% (7/18)	37.5% (27/72)	12.98 (2.20)	72.2% (13/18)
7	6	−3.63 (0.57)**	84.9% (28/33)	68.4% (158/231)	0.56 (0.48)	57.6% (19/33)
	12	−2.27 (0.69)**	72.1% (44/61)	43.5% (185/425)	5.06 (0.62)	60.7% (37/61)

Notes: S_m standard error of the mean; *significantly different from 0 at the 5% level, 2-tailed test; **significantly different from 0 at the 1% level, 2-tailed test.

[a] High bids only.

[b] A single outlier bid less than $x_o − ε$ was dropped.

[c] In this treatment high O's actually bid *above* their signal values, on average.

O bids were subject to a winner's curse under our second, tighter measure of the winner's curse. With $n = 7$, the adverse selection effect is stronger and the winner's curse was more pervasive: 100% of the high O bids and 85.2% of *all* O bids fell prey to the winner's curse just considering competition with other O's (equation 2). The net result was large negative profits for O's when they won ($-\$1.68$ per auction with $n = 4$; $-\$3.68$ with $n = 7$). Although somewhat diminished in frequency, a strong winner's curse is also reported for higher values of ε as O's continued to earn negative profits throughout, with at least 47% of all bids subject to the winner's curse, by the tighter measure, for any value of ε.

Comparing the bidding of O's in the AIS auctions (Table 7.2A) to bidding in SIS auctions (Table 7.2B), the raw data suggests a more extreme winner's curse in AIS auctions with $n = 7$, but just the opposite result with $n = 4$. Rather than belabor the raw data, we go directly to Table 7.3, which compares estimated bid functions between SIS and AIS auctions.[13] Dummy variables are used to capture the response to changes in ε since it is clear that bid factors do not change proportionately with ε.

Looking at O's bid functions, with the exception of the $n = 4$, $\varepsilon = \$24$ treatment, the bid factors are too small to avoid the winner's curse.[14] More relevant, however, are differences in bid factors between AIS and SIS auctions. These are found in the regressions pooling data for O's and SIS auctions, with the *DASY*EPS* dummies testing for differences in the bid factors for different values of ε. For $n = 4$, the *DASY*EPS6* and *DASP*EPS12* dummies are both negative, but neither coefficient is, by itself, significantly different from zero, and a test of the null hypothesis that all three coefficients arc zero cannot be rejected either ($\chi^2 = 0.68$, d.f. $= 3$). For $n = 7$, both *DASY*EPS* dummies are positive, but here, too, neither dummy is significantly different from zero by itself, and a test of the null hypothesis that both coefficients are zero cannot be rejected ($\chi^2 = 0.59$, d.f. $= 2$). As such, we conclude that, contrary to our initial conjecture, the existence of an insider did not induce significantly less aggressive bidding for inexperienced O's.

Raw data for inexperienced I's is shown in the right-hand most columns of Table 7.2A, with estimated bid functions reported in the right-hand most columns of Table 7.3. Note, first, that the functional form of I's bid function is consistent with equation (5b), indicating that they are close to best responding to O's.[15] However, I's employed a significantly smaller bid factor than the one employed in our tighter winner's curse measure, so that O's actually faced an even stronger adverse selection problem, and higher incidence of the winner's curse, than our second tighter measure implies.[16] I's smaller bid factors were, however, consistent with the overly aggressive bidding by O's, although I's did deviate marginally from best responses. The latter resulted in average losses with $\varepsilon = \$12$ (for which we have the most data) of 3.6¢ per auction with $n = 4$ and 4.9¢ with $n = 7$.[17]

The right-hand most column in Table 7.3 tests for differences in I's bid factors in auctions with $n = 4$ versus $n = 7$. Both of the *DN*EPS* dummies are

TABLE 7.3
Estimated Bid Functions: Inexperienced Bidders (standard errors of estimates in parentheses)

Variable	Outsiders & SIS				Variable	Insiders		
	n = 4		n = 7			n = 4	n = 7	n = 4 & 7
	O's	O's & SIS	O's	O's & SIS				
x	1.001	1.003	1.000	0.998	x_o	0.995	0.988	0.997
	(0.004)	(0.002)	(0.007)	(0.002)		(0.003)	(0.007)	(0.002)
EPS6	−2.672	−2.791	−2.031	−2.102	EPS6	−0.673	−0.268	−1.042
	(0.826)**	(0.744)**	(0.943)*	(0.527)**		(0.599)	(1.323)	(0.724)
DEPS12	−4.249	−3.816	−4.807	−5.102	DEPS12	−0.724	−1.064	−0.760
	(0.675)**	(0.518)**	(0.484)**	(0.287)**		(0.521)	(0.552)+	(0.495)
DEPS24	−13.707	−14.052	—	—	DEPS24	−3.429	—	−3.519
	(0.939)**	(0.614)**				(0.720)**		(0.673)**
DASY*EPS6	—	−0.161	—	0.215	DN*EPS6	—	—	−0.103
		(0.997)		(0.834)				(0.993)
DASY*EPS12	—	−0.633	—	0.537	DN*DPS12	—	—	−0.365
		(0.936)		(0.761)				(0.896)
DASY*EPS24	—	0.099	—	—				
		(1.217)						
R^2	.998	.997	.991	.998	R^2	.999	.995	.999
Number of Observations	141	461	168	810	Number of Observations	46	27	73
Number of Subjects	13	50	16	60	Number of Subjects	12	9	21

Notes: +significantly different from zero at $p < .10$ level, 2-tailed test; *significantly different from zero at $p < .05$ level, 2-tailed test; **significantly different from zero at $p < .01$ level, 2-tailed test. EPS6 = intercept of bid function. DEPS12 = 1 if EPS = 12; 0 otherwise. DEPS24 = 1 if EPS = 24 or 30; 0 otherwise. DASY = 1 if AIS auction; 0 if SIS auction. DN = 1 if n = 7; 0 if n = 4.

TABLE 7.4

Change in Seller's Revenue: AIS vs. SIS Auctions with Inexperienced Bidders
(in dollars)

	n = 4			n = 7		
ε	Change in Revenue: AIS − SIS Auctions[a] (t stat)[b]	Mean Profits (σ^2) AIS	SIS	Change in Revenue: AIS − SIS Auctions[a] (t stat)[b]	Mean Profits (σ^2) AIS	SIS
$6	− 1.425	− 0.975	− 2.400	0.045	− 3.680	− 3.635
	(− 1.588)	(8.474)	(7.995)	(0.054)	(3.386)	(10.616)
$12	− 1.098	− 0.005	− 1.130	− 0.715	− 1.550	− 2.265
	(− 1.063)	(7.879)	(25.331)	(0.622)	(16.128)	(28.846)
$24	3.503	− 3.257	.246	—	—	—
	(1.060)	(67.716)	(61.256)			

[a]Change in seller's revenue, normalized for variation in x_o, is bidder profits in SIS auctions less bidder profits in AIS auctions.

[b]t statistics calculated for populations with unknown and unequal variances (Guenther (1964)). Auction period is unit of observation.

negative, indicating somewhat larger bid factors with $n = 4$ than $n = 7$, contrary to the theory's prediction. However, neither coefficient is statistically significant by itself, and they are not significant in combination. This lack of responsiveness may well reflect the fact that both O's and I's had yet to converge to any sort of sustainable equilibrium.[18]

Table 7.4 reports the change in seller's revenue, normalized for variation in x_o, between AIS and SIS auctions. In three of five cases seller's revenue is *lower* in AIS compared to SIS auctions, *contrary* to the β-DBF model's prediction. Of the two remaining cases, there is essentially no change in revenue for $n = 7$ and $\varepsilon = \$6$, and the increase in revenue for $n = 4$, $\varepsilon = \$24$ is not significant at conventional levels.[19] This failure of the model's prediction can be directly attributed to the winner's curse. Recall that seller's revenue, normalized for variation in x_o, is simply the converse of bidder's profits. The relatively strong winner's curse for inexperienced bidders in both AIS and SIS auctions results in approximately the same negative average profits, conditional on winning. However, when I's win an item they earn positive profits. The net effect is an overall reduction in seller's revenue in AIS compared to SIS auctions.[20]

3.2 Super-Experienced Bidders

Table 7.5 reports data for super-experienced bidders. Looking at the top half of Table 7.5 (part A), the data for AIS auctions, the negative average earnings for inexperienced O's have been replaced by positive average earnings. Further, using our tighter definition of the winner's curse, it has been reduced to the point that it hardly exists in auctions with $n = 4$ and has been reduced substantially, compared to inexperienced bidders, with $n = 7$. (We have dropped our looser winner's curse measure, equation (2), since these numbers were less than 1% with $n = 4$ and less than 6% with $n = 7$ for all values of ε.) This sharp reduction in the winner's curse is the result of more aggressive bidders declining invitations to return for additional sessions, and less aggressive bidding by those who did return. Further, no new, inexperienced, bidders were permitted to enter the auctions, as might occur in field settings.

Table 7.6 reports estimated bid functions for super-experienced bidders.[21] O's bid factors were more than enough to avoid the winner's curse (accounting for I's bids) in all cases: for $n = 4$, estimated versus required bid factors are $10.46 versus $8.28 ($\varepsilon = 12), $15.93 versus $12.42 ($\varepsilon = 18), and $27.24 versus $20.70 ($\varepsilon = 30); for $n = 7$ the corresponding values are $16.01 versus $14.85 ($\varepsilon = 18) and $26.58 versus $24.75 ($\varepsilon = 30). Further, comparing O's bids with bids in SIS auctions, for $n = 4$, O's bid less as both $DASY*EPS$ dummies are significantly below zero at the .05 level. In contrast, for $n = 7$, there are no significant differences in O's bids versus bids in SIS auctions. Larger bid factors for O's than in SIS auctions with $n = 4$ may well be the result of I's bid factors being far smaller than what best response dictates (see below). Note, however, that in both cases O's were not best responding to I's bids, or to overly aggressive bids of other O's, as this calls for bidding close to $x - \varepsilon$. However, the opportunity cost of an individual O's failure to best respond was relatively small, averaging less than 10¢ per auction, in large measure because no individual O stood much of a chance of winning.[22]

Looking at Table 7.5 again, consistent with one of the most basic equilibrium predictions, conditional on winning, I's earned significantly greater profits than O's did for all values of ε and n (these differences are statistically significant in 4 of 5 cases).[23] I's profits, conditional on winning, were larger than in SIS auctions for both $n = 4$ and $n = 7$ with $\varepsilon = 18, treatments for which we have the most data, with significantly higher profits for I's in the $n = 7$ case ($t = 1.99$, d.f. $= 88$, $p < .05$, 1-tailed test).[24] However, average profits for I's were lower (but not significantly so), compared to profits in SIS auctions for $\varepsilon = 30. I's failure to earn consistently higher profits, conditional on winning, than in SIS auctions may be partially accounted for by that fact that under our design these differences are relatively small.

Turning to Table 7.6, for $n = 4$, I's bid factors were consistently smaller than the best (risk neutral) response to Os' bids. These opportunity costs averaged 54.7¢ per auction with $\varepsilon = 18 and 59.1¢ per auction with $\varepsilon = 12 (18.3% and 30.4% of best response earnings).[25] Notably, for the parameter set for which we have the most data, and with which our super-experienced subjects had the most experience $n = 7$ and $\varepsilon = 18), there is essentially no difference between best response and actual bidding, with average opportunity costs of 2.7¢ per auction (just under 2% of best response earnings).[26] Unfor-

TABLE 7.5
Super-Experienced Bidders

A: Auctions with Asymmetric Information Structure (AIS)

Number of Bidders	ε	Outsiders' Bids						Insiders' Bids	
		Average Earnings Conditional on Winning (S_m)	Frequency of Winning (raw data)	Frequency of Winner's Curse: against Outsiders and Insiders (raw data)		Average Bid Factor[a] (S_m)	Frequency High Outsider Bid from High Outsider Signal Holder (raw data)	Average Earnings Conditional on Winning (S_m)	Average Bid Factor (S_m)
				High Outsider Bid	All Bids				
4	12	0.65 (0.43)	53.7% (29/54)	9.3% (5/54)	4.9% (8/162)	10.05 (0.23)	92.6% (50/54)	3.30 (0.23)**	3.60[c] (0.19)
	18	0.87 (0.68)	63.3% (19/30)	3.3% (1/30)	1.1% (1/90)	15.29 (0.26)	93.3% (28/30)	4.13 (0.37)**	5.80[c] (0.50)
	30	3.67 (2.32)	42.1% (8/19)	5.3% (1/19)	3.5% (2/57)	27.04 (0.65)	94.7% (18/19)	7.94 (0.69)**	8.24 (0.61)
7[b]	18	0.52 (0.34)	64.5% (49/76)	22.4% (17/76)	17.2% (77/453)	15.86 (0.26)	86.8% (66/76)	3.24 (0.36)**	4.35 (0.26)
	30	3.90 (3.07)	41.7% (5/12)	16.7% (2/12)	19.4% (14/72)	26.95 (0.85)	83.3% (10/12)	4.95 (0.80)**	5.98 (0.67)

B: Auctions with Symmetric Information Structure (SIS)

Number of Bidders	ε	Average Earnings Conditional on Winning (S_m)	Frequency of Winner's Curse (raw data)		Average Bid Factor[a] (S_m)	Frequency High Bid from High Signal Holder (raw data)
			High Bidders	All Bidders		
4	18	3.82 (0.67)**	20.5% (23/112)	10.9% (49/448)	13.56 (0.40)	87.5% (98/112)
	30	8.88 (2.22)**	0% (0/12)	0% (0/48)	25.27 (1.07)	91.7% (11/12)
7	18	2.23 (0.36)**	13.0% (19/146)	6.1% (61/1007)	14.98 (0.32)	82.9% (121/146)
	30	5.44 (1.78)*	20.0% (1/5)	8.6% (3/35)	26.85 (2.03)	80.0% (4/5)

Notes: S_m standard error of the mean; *significantly different from 0 at the 5% level; 2-tailed t-test; **significantly different from 0 at the 1% level, 2-tailed t-test.

[a]High bids only.

[b]Includes several auctions with $n = 6$.

[c]A single outlier bid less than $x_o - \varepsilon$ was dropped.

TABLE 7.6

Estimated Functions: Super-Experienced Bidders (standard errors of estimates in parentheses)

	Outsiders and SIS Auctions					Insiders		
	n = 4		n = 7			n = 4	n = 7	n = 4 & 7
Variable	Outsiders	Outsiders & SIS	Outsiders	Outsiders & SIS	Variable			
x	1.001 (0.001)	1.001 (0.001)	1.000 (0.001)	1.000 (0.001)	x_o	0.994 (0.003)	1.000 (0.003)	0.996 (0.002)
EPS18	−15.933 (0.360)**	−14.973 (0.357)**	−16.025 (0.331)**	−15.625 (0.333)**	EPS18	−4.466 (0.746)**	−4.007 (0.711)**	−4.920 (0.655)**
DEPS30	−11.307 (0.231)**	−10.869 (0.373)**	−10.563 (0.247)**	−11.330 (0.266)**	DEPS30	−2.648 (0.613)**	−1.740 (0.727)*	−2.634 (0.611)**
DEPS12	5.470 (0.188)**	4.302 (0.562)**	—	—	DEPS12	2.193 (0.470)**	—	2.161 (0.469)**
DASY*EPS18	—	−1.165 (0.590)*	—	−0.332 (0.437)	DN*EPS18	—	—	1.587 (0.589)**
DASY*EPS30	—	−1.584 (0.672)*	—	0.425 (0.557)	DN*EPS30	—	—	2.454 (0.864)**
R^2	.999	.999	.999	.999	R^2	.999	.999	.999
Number of Observations	309	805	523	1562	Number of Observations	101	88	189
Number of Subjects	24	67	60	114	Number of Subjects	23	50	73

Notes: [+]significantly different from zero at $p < .10$ level, 2-tailed test; *significantly different from zero at $p < .05$ level, 2-tailed test; **significantly different from zero at $p < .01$ level, 2-tailed test. EPS18 = intercept of bid function. DEPS30 = 1 if EPS = 30; 0 otherwise. DEPS12 = 1 if EPS = 12; 0 otherwise. DASY = 1 if AIS auction; 0 if SIS auction. DN = 1 if n = 6 or 7; 0 if n = 4.

TABLE 7.7

Change in Seller's Revenue: AIS vs. SIS Auctions with Super-Experienced Bidders

	n = 4			n = 7		
	Change in Revenue: AIS − SIS Auctions[a]	Mean Profits (σ^2)		Change in Revenue: AIS − SIS Auctions[a]	Mean Profits (σ^2)	
ε	(t stat)[b]	AIS	SIS	(t stat)[b]	AIS	SIS
$18	1.759	2.063	3.822	0.739	1.492	2.231
	(2.057)*	(8.561)	(49.972)	(1.573)+	(6.770)	(19.221)
$30	2.734	6.148	8.876	0.919	4.517	5.436
	(1.097)	(24.334)	(59.731)	(0.425)	(17.978)	(15.839)

[a]Change in seller's revenue, normalized for variation in x_o, is bidder profits in SIS auctions less bidder profits in AIS auctions.

[b]t statistics calculated for populations with unknown and unequal variances (Guenther (1964)). Auction period is unit of observation.

*Significantly different from 0 at $p < .05$, 1-tailed test; +significantly different from 0 at $p < .10$, 1-tailed test.

tunately, we cannot determine whether this superior performance is a function of greater experience or a matter of chance.[27]

The comparative static prediction regarding I's response to increased numbers of rivals is satisfied as well. Looking at the raw data in the right-hand most column of Table 7.5, I's average bid factor is smaller for $n = 7$ versus $n = 4$ for both values of ε. This is consistent with the regression results reported in the right-hand most column of Table 7.6, which show the coefficients for both DN*EPS dummies to be positive and significantly different from zero at $p < .01$. In our design, I's are, effectively, participating in a first-price private value auction. There is an extensive experimental literature demonstrating that subjects in first-price private value auctions increase their bids when faced with more rivals, as the theory predicts (Kagel and Levin (1993), Kagel (1995)). This strategic sensitivity extends to I's bidding in AIS common value auctions.

Table 7.7 reports average revenue in AIS versus SIS auctions. In all four cases average revenue is higher in the AIS auctions, with these differences statistically significant for both $n = 4$ and 7 when $\varepsilon = $18 (for which we have the most data). Thus, this prediction of the theory is satisfied with experienced bidders who have generally learned, to avoid the winner's curse.

3.3 Learning and Adjustments in Insider's Bids over Time

This section examines adjustments in I's bids over time in relation to Selten and Buchta's (1994) (SB) "direction learning" theory, first applied to bidding in private value auctions.[28] Within direction learning theory players are assumed to be boundedly rational and to respond "sensibly" to the direct reinforcement effects of their bids in the previous auction period. As applied to our auctions, direction learning theory predicts: (a) If I wins, her bid factor will increase in reaction to money left on the table, (b) if she loses and O's winning bid is, below x_o, so that there is a lost profit opportunity, I's bid factor will decrease in the next period, and (c) if I loses and O's winning bid is above x_o, so that there was no opportunity to earn a profit (the outpriced case), there will be no systematic effect on I's bid in the next auction period.[29] We anticipate, as earlier studies have found (SB and Cason and Friedman (1997)), that (b) dominates (a), promoting higher bids over time. Finally, there is no formal consideration within direction learning theory for threshold effects; e.g., when I wins but her bid is only slightly above (say less than 5 cents) the next highest bidder, she might well feel "Wow, that was too close" and decide to *reduce* her bid factor in the next period. Threshold effects of this sort seem eminently reasonable for case (a), so we test for them as well.[30]

Table 7.8 reports I's qualitative responses for these three cases.[31] For super-experienced bidders changes in I's bid factors are completely consistent with directional learning theory: I's winning and leaving money on the table increased their bid factor 69% of the time with $n = 7$ ($p < .05$), 69% of the time with $n = 4$ ($p < .01$).[32] In contrast, after a lost profit opportunity, bid factors decreased 61% of the time with $n = 7$ ($p = .11$), 64% of the time with $n = 4$ ($p < .01$). However, the average absolute size of these responses was approximately equal (see the last column in Table 7.8) so that in both cases, unlike the results reported in SB and Cason and Friedman (1997) (CF), there was no systematic tendency to respond more strongly to lost earning opportunities than to money left on the table.

For auctions with $n = 4$, data from sessions leading up to I's super-experienced status are reported in the bottom panel of Table 7.8. Like the super-experienced bidders, I's increased their bid factor following winning (68%, $p < .10$) and decreased it following a lost profit opportunity (59%, $p = .20$). However, unlike the super-experienced bidders, but like the results reported in SB and CF, the reaction to lost profit opportunities was substantially stronger than to money left on the table (the net effect of these changes being an average reduction in the bid factor of 5% per auction). Since our super-experienced bidders had substantially more experience than the subjects in SB and CS, this suggests that with experience subjects become attuned to the more subtle strategic implications of winning and paying more than is necessary to win.

Testing for threshold effects in case (a), we regressed the change in I's bid factor between periods t and $t - 1$ against the amount of money left on the table in period $t - 1$. Direction learning theory implies a positive slope coefficient for the variable "money left on the table," with the existence of the predicted threshold effect indicated by a negative intercept value. There is no evidence for a threshold effect as (i) the regressions for experienced bidders have very low R^2 values (less than .05) and (ii) in all cases the intercept values, although not significantly different from zero, have the wrong sign.

TABLE 7.8

Effect of Past Outcomes on Change in Insiders' Bids

| | | Change in I's Bid Factor: Period t − 1 to t[a] | | | |
		Decrease	Increase	No Change	Average Change
Bidder Experience	*Outcome in Period* t − 1	*Decrease*	*Increase*	*No Change*	*Average Change*
Super-Experienced Bidders: $n = 7$	I wins: ("Money left on the table")	11	23	1	0.059
	I loses and O bids below x_o (lost profit opportunity)	25	16	2	−0.049
	I loses and O bids above x_o (outpriced valuation)	11	6	1	−0.041
	I wins: ("Money left on the table")	17	37	2	0.206
Super-Experienced Bidders: $n = 4$	I loses and O bids below x_o (lost profit opportunity)	21	12	2	−0.315
	I loses and O bids above x_o (outpriced valuation)	10	10	0	0.007
	I wins: ("Money left on the table")	9	17	0	0.058
Less-Experienced Bidders: $n = 4$	I loses and O bids below x_o (lost profit opportunity)	20	14	1	−0.165
	I loses and O bids above x_o (outpriced valuation)	16	21	1	−0.006

[a]Bid factor is computed as $[x − b(x)] / \varepsilon$.

4. Summary and Conclusions

We examined bidding in asymmetric information structure (AIS) auctions and compared it to bidding in symmetric information structure (SIS) common value auctions. In the AIS auctions a single insider (I) knows the value of the item with certainty, and outsiders (O's) are provided proprietary information affiliated with the value of the item. The existence of a perfectly informed insider did not significantly reduce the frequency or intensity of the winner's curse for inexperienced bidders compared to SIS auctions. Further, the only comparative static prediction of the AIS model consistently satisfied for these inexperienced bidders was that I's earned greater profits than O's. In contrast, super-experienced O's learn to overcome the worst effects of the winner's curse, generally bidding below the expected value conditional on winning. In this case the comparative static predictions of the theory are generally satisfied: (i) I's earn greater profits conditional on winning than O's do, (ii) with increased numbers of O's, I's bid more aggressively, (iii) O's earn positive average profits, but these are substantially less than earnings in SIS auctions, and (iv) AIS auctions *increase* seller's revenue compared to SIS auctions.

The predicted increase in seller's revenue in AIS auctions seems, at first blush, to be counterintuitive. This prediction of the model rests critically on the fact that in our experimental design less informed bidders have some proprietary information. Although this is not a sufficient condition for AIS auctions to raise revenue compared to SIS auctions, it clearly is a necessary condition. In contrast, models that start with bidders having only public information predict that the introduction of an insider will unambiguously reduce seller's average revenue. In many cases a model in which O's have some proprietary information is more realistic than one in which they only have public information. In these circumstances, it may well be the case, as in our experiment, that the introduction of an insider increases seller's revenue, and that both I's and O's earn economic rents. This potential for insider information to raise average seller's revenue has not been explicitly recognized in the auction literature prior to this.

Appendix
Increases in Expected Revenue in Auctions with Insider Information

This brief appendix clarifies the basis for the predicted increase in seller's revenue in AIS compared to Sis auctions in our experimental design, as well as the economic rents that O's earn in equilibrium: Denote by $SR(x_0; n, \varepsilon)$ and $AR(x_0; n, \varepsilon)$ the seller's average revenue in SIS and AIS auctions where x_0 denotes the true value of the item and n the total number of bidders:

$$SR(x_0; n, \varepsilon) \approx x_0 - 2\varepsilon/(n + 1) = [x_0 - 2\varepsilon/n] + [2\varepsilon/n(n + 1)],$$

and the lower bound bid functions in (3-a, 3-b) yield

$$AR(x_0; n, \varepsilon) = [x_0 - 2\varepsilon/n] + [(2\varepsilon/n)\pi^n],$$

where $\pi = [(n - 1)/n]$ is the probability that the insider wins against one outsider.[1] Recall that with a total of n bidders, $((n - 1)$ O's), the insider bids $[x_0 - 2\varepsilon/n]$, which is equal to average revenue in an SIS auction with $(n - 1)$ bidders. Thus, we can use $[x_0 - 2\varepsilon/n]$ as a benchmark to evaluate the different forces at work in the two auctions. In an SIS auction, the seller earns additional revenue of $[2\varepsilon/n(n + 1)]$ relative to $[x_0 - 2\varepsilon/n]$. This increment is the result of having n, rather than $(n - 1)$, bidders. Thus, the seller would be unambiguously better off in an SIS auction relative to an AIS auction if I's in the AIS auction won *all* the time. However, in an AIS auction the seller has additional revenue of $[(2\varepsilon/n)\pi^n]$, resulting from the fact that I's do not win all the time, and that when O's win they win with relatively high signal realizations, yielding more revenue than when I's win. These higher revenues when O's win more than offset the lower revenues (relative to SIS) when I's win. Higher revenue when O's win are a result of I's "protecting" the seller when O's have low signals relative to x_0, since in this case the insider wins and the seller earns at least $[x_0 - 2\varepsilon/n]$. As a result, when O's win, they have, from the seller's point of view, "good" (high) signals relative to x_0. This also implies that the variance in average bidder profits will be lower in AIS compared to SIS auctions. Finally, the increase in revenue going from SIS to AIS varies with n, with revenue differences increasing starting from low n, reaching a maximum revenue differential for intermediate levels of n, and decreasing thereafter; for example, with $n = 3$, $[AR - SR] = .031\varepsilon$; with $n = 4$ and 7, as in our design, the revenue differences are $.058\varepsilon$ and $.061\varepsilon$; and when $n = 20$, the difference is $.031\varepsilon$ once again.

As the intuition makes clear, there is nothing pathological in our experimental design that accounts for this revenue-raising effect of the AIS. To the contrary, the intuition suggests that the revenue-raising effects of AIS auctions apply to a far broader class of distributions than the one employed here (see, for example, Campbell and Levin, 1997). From this it is clear that revenue-raising predictions based on AIS in which the insider has a double informational advantage do not generalize to AIS auctions in which O's have some proprietary information.

Finally, note that, unlike the double informational advantage model, in our model O's earn positive economic rents in equilibrium. This is interesting in its own right since I's hold a sufficient statistic for x_0 (they know its value). Thus, using the language of Milgrom and Weber (1982), O's private information is a garbling of I's private information. In second-price common value auctions, bidders with only garbled information earn zero expected profits in equilibrium (Milgrom and Weber, 1982), just as O's do in a first-price auction where I's have a double informational advantage. Unfortunately, this coincidence may be misleading, as our AIS model demonstrates, since once O's have private information, even if it is just a garbling of I's private information, they earn positive economic rents in a first-price common value auction. This is due to the fact that in a first-price auction I's can only benefit from their superior information by bidding below x_0, which permits O's to earn positive economic rents.

Notes

Research was partially supported by grants from the Economics Division and Information Science and Technology Division of the National Science Foundation, Earlier versions of this paper were presented at the ESA meetings in Tucson, the CREED conference on experimental economics in Amsterdam, and the Barcelona conference on Auctions, Theory and Empirics. We thank participants at these meetings and the referees and editor of this journal for helpful comments. We alone are responsible for any errors.

1. AIS common value auctions have been used to analyze oil and gas drainage lease auctions. Arguably, as in our design, less informed bidders in drainage lease auctions have some proprietary information as they have conducted their own seismic readings and their own analysis of the data, conclusions of which are not available to the insider.

2. Note that increased seller's revenue is *not* a general characteristic of AIS auctions in which O's maintain some proprietary information. However, it is true for the parameter values of our experiment and in other cases as well (see Kagel and Levin (1998) and Campbell and Levin (1997)).

3. "Presentation format" effects of this sort have been found in a number of game theoretic contexts. See, for example, Andreoni (1995), Cooper, Garvin, and Kagel (1997), and Schotter, Weigelt, and Wilson (1994).

4. These procedures were maintained with super-experienced bidders, thereby preserving some degree of independence between auctions within a given experimental session.

5. Derivation of the RNNE bid function over the entire support can be found in an appendix to Levin, Kagel, and Richard (1996).

6. Note that for $\underline{x} - \varepsilon \le x \le \underline{x} + \varepsilon$ equation (4b) changes, but 4a remains unchanged.

7. O's bid function, (5a), corresponds to Laskowski and Slonim's assumption of a translation invariant bid function.

8. Further, Kagel and Richard (1998) show that for SIS auctions a piecewise linear bid function, with a single piece (5a) for region 2, provides a far better fit to the data than does the Nash bid function (bidders totally ignore $g(x)$).

9. Wilson's (1985) model, which is closest in structure to ours, yields similar results for Γ's.

10. Positive economic rents for O's result from the private nature of their information.

11. For SIS auctions we assume x_o is in region 2 and employ the approximation that profits, conditional tin winning, are equal to $2\varepsilon/(n + 1)$.

12. See our working paper (Kagel and Levin (1998)) for details. The single exception is that we cannot bound O's bid factor.

13. Random effects error specifications were employed in all cases, with subject as the random error component.

14. Estimated bid factors and minimum bid factors needed to avoid the winner's curse (accounting for Γ's bids) are as follows: $n = 4$, $\varepsilon = \$6$ (2.67 vs. 4.14; $p < .04$), $\varepsilon = \$12$ (6.92 vs. 8.28; $p < .07$), $\varepsilon = \$24$ (16.38 vs. 16.56); $n = 7$, $\varepsilon = \$6$ (2.03 vs. 4.95; $p < .01$), $\varepsilon = \$12$ (6.84 vs. 9.90; $p < .01$) (1-tailed significance levels reported).

15. R^2 values of .99 or better and coefficient estimates for x_o always within two standard deviations of 1.00, both here and for experienced bidders as well.

16. Γ's estimated bid factors versus best response values associated with O's earning zero expected profits are; $n = 4$, $\varepsilon = \$6$ (0.67 vs. 2.53, $p < .01$), $\varepsilon = \$12$ (1.39 vs. 5.05, $p < .01$), $\varepsilon = \$24$ (4.10 vs. 10.10, $p < .01$); $n = 7$, $\varepsilon = \$6$ (0.27 vs. 1.57, $p < .17$), $\varepsilon = \$12$ (1.33 vs. 3.13, $p < .07$) (1-tailed tests for estimated probabilities being significantly below predicted values).

17. Expected losses are calculated on the basis of estimated bid factors. Given O's estimated bid factor we can compute, analytically, Γ's best response bid factor and Γ's expected profits. Given Γ's and O's estimated bid factors, we compute, analytically, actual expected earnings. The difference between these two earnings measures constitute expected losses. These procedures are consistent with those of Fudenberg and Levine (1997) for estimating deviations from best responses in normal form, complete information games.

18. Given the obvious failure to converge to equilibrium, one might question why we have not broken up the data analysis, considering early versus later auctions separately. However, differences between early versus later auctions coincide with changes in ε, and our data analysis already distinguishes between different values of ε.

19. The reader may also notice the substantially larger variance in mean profits in SIS compared to AIS auctions. Our working paper (Kagel and Levin (1998)) shows that this is a derivative implication of our AIS model that is closely related to the propensity to raise seller's revenue compared to SIS auctions.

20. The winner's curse also results in reversals of the SIS model's prediction regarding the ability of public information to raise seller's revenue (Kagel and Levin (1986)) and English auctions to raise revenue compared to first-price auctions (Levin, Kagel, and Richard (1996)). There are different mechanisms at work in these cases compared to the present case, but what they have in common is that a key comparative static prediction of the theory fails in the presence of the winner's curse.

21. Regressions testing for differences in bid functions between early versus late auctions within a given experimental session, holding ε constant, show no systematic differences in bidding by either I's or O's. Thus, there were no systematic, statistically significant adjustments in bidding within these sessions.

22. Opportunity costs were relatively large in percentage terms, averaging close to 30% of best response earnings. Opportunity costs for O's were calculated using estimated bid factors from Table VI and running Monte Carlo (MC) simulations in which a single O unilaterally adjusts his bid factor.

23. For $n = 4$: $\varepsilon = \$12$, $t = 5.20$, $p < .01$, $\varepsilon = \$18$, $t = 3.45$, $p < .01$, $\varepsilon = \$30$, $t = 1.76$, $p < .10$; for $n = 7$: $\varepsilon = \$18$, $t = 5.15$, $p < .01$, $\varepsilon = \$30$, $t = 0.33$ (1-tailed t tests in all cases). Auction period is the unit of observation in each case.

24. t statistic calculated for populations with unknown and unequal variances (Guenther (1964)).

25. Our expected cost measures implicitly assume that all O's use the same bid factor (see footnote 18 above). Further analysis shows that these cost estimates are robust to the observed heterogeneity in O's bid factors.

26. I's estimated bid factor is 4.01 versus a best response bid factor of 4.70 ($Z = 1.20$, $p > .10$).

27. However, these results are not unlike those found in private value auctions, in which bidding above the RNNE is substantially greater, in both absolute and percentage terms, as the number of bidders decreases (Kagel, Harstad, and Levin (1987)).

28. Adjustment processes in SIS auctions have been discussed extensively elsewhere (Garvin and Kagel (1994); Kagel and Richard (1998)). O's adjustments no doubt follow a similar pattern.

29. Whether or not (c) is integral to SB's model or is a result of the limited information feedback subjects had in their experiment (they only learned the market price) is an open question. Garvin and Kagel (1994) report strong observational learning effects as subjects increased their bid factors substantially following auctions in which they would have lost money applying their bid factor to the high bidder's signal value. This is inconsistent with (c).

30. SB eliminate no change responses in evaluating their directional learning model. These responses may capture some of these threshold effects. We see no motive for a similar threshold effect in case (b).

31. Since I is determined randomly in each auction, our analysis is based on changes in bid factors (normalized for any changes in ε) between different individuals across adjacent auction periods. An alternative analysis, based on the same individual across nonadjacent auction periods yields similar results, but fewer observations.

32. No change outcomes are excluded from these percentages. Probabilities calculated test the null hypothesis of no systematic change in the bid factor versus a change whose sign is consistent with directional learning theory.

Appendix Note

1. Thus, π^{n-1} is the probability that the insider wins. Note that π^{n-1} is strictly decreasing in n but bound by $1/e = 0.368$.

References

Akerlof, George (1970): "The Market for Lemons: Qualitative Uncertainty and the Market Mechanism," *Quarterly Journal of Economics*, 89, 488–500.

Andreoni, James (1995): "Warm-Glow versus Cold-Prickle: The Effects of Positive and Negative Framing on Cooperation in Experiments," *Quarterly Journal of Economics*, 110, 1–22.

Campbell, Colin, and Dan Levin (1997): "Can the Seller Benefit from an Insider in Common Value Auctions?" Mimeographed, Ohio State University.

Cason, Timothy N., and Daniel Friedman (1997): "Price Formation in Single Call Markets," *Econometrica*, 65, 311–346.

Cooper, David J., Susan Garvin, and John H. Kagel (1997): "Adaptive Learning vs. Equilibrium Refinements in an Entry Limit Pricing Game," *RAND Journal of Economics*, 28, 662–683.

Dyer, Douglas, John H. Kagel, and Dan Levin (1998): "A Comparison of Naive and Experienced Bidders in Common Value Offer Auctions: A Laboratory Analysis," *Economic Journal*, 99, 108–115.

Engelbrecht-Wiggans, Richard, Paul R. Milgrom, and Robert J. Weber (1983). "Competitive Bidding and Proprietary Information," *Journal of Mathematical Economics*, 11, 161–169.

Fudenberg, Drew, and David K. Levine (1997): "Measuring Players Losses in Experimental Games," *Quarterly Journal of Economics*, 112, 507–536.

Garvin, Susan, and Rain H. Kagel (1994): "Learning in Common Value Auctions: Some Initial Observations," *Journal of Economic Behavior and Organization*, 25, 351–372.

Guenther, William C. (1964): *Analysis of Variance*. Englewood Cliffs, N.J.: Prentice-Hall.

Hausch, Donald B. (1987): "An Asymmetric Common Value Auction Model," *RAND Journal of Economics*, 18, 611–621.

Hendricks, Kenneth, Robert H. Porter, and Charles A. Wilson (1994): "Auctions for Oil and Gas Leases with an Informed Bidder and a Random Reservation Price," *Econometrica*, 62, 1415–1444.

Kagel, John H. (1995): "Auctions: A Survey of Experimental Research," in *The Handbook of Experimental Economics*, ed. by J. H. Kagel and A. E. Roth. Princeton: Princeton University Press.

Kagel, John H., Ronald M. Harstad, and Dan Levin (1987): "Information Impact and Allocation Rules in Auctions with Affiliated Private Values: A Laboratory Study," *Econometrica*, 55, 1275–1304.

Kagel, John H., and D. Levin (1986): "The Winner's Curse and Public Information in Common Value Auctions," *American Economic Review*, 76, 894–920.

———. (1993): "Independent Private Value Auctions: Bidder Behavior in First-, Second- and Third-Price Auctions with Varying Numbers of Bidders," *Economic Journal*, 103, 868–880.

————. (1998): "Common Value Auctions with Insider Information," Mimeographed, University of Pittsburgh.

Kagel, John H., D. Levin, R. Battalio, and D. J. Meyer (1989): "First-Price Common Value Auctions: Bidder Behavior and the Winner's Curse," *Economic Inquiry*, 27, 241–258.

Kagel, John H., D. Levin, and R. M. Harstad (1995): "Comparative Static Effects of Number of Bidders and Public Information in Second-Price Common Value Auctions," *International Journal of Game Theory*, 24, 293–319.

Kagel, John H., and J. F. Richard (1998): "Super-experienced Bidders in First-price Common Value Auction,: Rules-of-thumb, Nash Equilibrium Bidding and the Winner's Curse," Mimeographed, University of Pittsburgh.

Laskowski, M. C., and R. L. Slonim (in press): "An Asymmetric Solution for Sealed Bid Common-Value Auctions with Bidders Having Asymmetric Information," *Games and Economic Behavior* (in press).

Levin, D., John H. Kagel, and J. F. Richard (1996): "Revenue Effects and Information Processing in English Common Value Auctions," *American Economic Review*, 86, 442–460.

Lind, B., and C. R. Plott (1991): "The Winner's Curse: Experiments with Buyers and with Sellers," *American Economic Review*, 81, 335–346.

Marshall, Robert C., Michael J. Meurer, Jean-Francois Richard, and Walter Stromquist (1994): "Numerical Analysis of Asymmetric First Price Auctions," *Games and Economic Behavior*, 7, 193–220.

Milgrom, Paul R., and Robert J. Weber (1982): "A Theory of Auctions and Competitive Bidding," *Econometrica*, 50, 1089–1122.

Schotter, A., K. Weigelt, and C. Wilson (1995): "A Laboratory Investigation of Multiperson Rationality and Presentation Effects," *Games and Economic Behavior*, 8, 164–212.

Selten, Reinhard, and Joachim Buchta (1994): "Experimental Sealed Bid First Price Auctions with Directly Observed Bid Functions," Discussion Paper No. B-270, University of Bonn.

Weverbergh, M. (1979): "Competitive Bidding with Asymmetric Information Reanalyzed," *Management Science*, 25, 291–294.

Wilson, Robert (1967): "Competitive Bidding with Asymmetric Information," *Management Science*, 13, 816–820.

————. (1985): "Analytical Foundations of Pricing Strategy-Trading Procedures," Mimeographed, Stanford University.

8

Can the Seller Benefit from an Insider in Common-Value Auctions?

Colin M. Campbell and Dan Levin

1. Introduction

Models of auctions in which bidders are ex-ante homogeneous with respect to their private information have given economic theory great predictive mileage. These models have been applied with success to environments of both private and common bidder values, with major results concerning the revenue-raising properties of different auction rules being derived in, for instance, Myerson [10] and Riley and Samuelson [11] for the private values case, and Milgrom and Weber [9] for the general affiliated values case. Important results for environments in which bidders are ex-ante heterogeneous have been harder to discover, as the problem of characterizing equilibrium bidding behavior is much less tractable than under the homogeneity assumption. While some predictions are robust to heterogeneity, such as bidding behavior in second-price auctions and the optimality of second price auctions with individualized reserve prices in the independent private values case, the effects of heterogeneity on revenues for first-price auctions and common value auctions are largely undetermined.

The best-known effort to consider these effects is a model in which one bidder has private information (possibly imperfect) about the common value of the object being auctioned, while all other bidders have no private information (Wilson [13]; Weverbergh [12]; Engelbrecht-Wiggans, Milgrom, and Weber [3]; Milgrom and Weber [8]; Hendricks and Porter [4]; Hendricks, Porter, and Wilson [5]). This benchmark delivers the unambiguous result that in a first-price auction the seller's expected revenue is strictly less than the expected revenue in the corresponding first-price auction in which the informed bidder is instead also uninformed. The intuition for this result is quite straightforward when one considers the equilibrium when all bidders are symmetrically uninformed: every bidder bids the expected value of the object, allowing the seller to extract full expected surplus from the bidders. When there is an informed bidder, this bidder must earn a positive informational rent that necessarily reduces the seller's expected revenue one-for-one, since in a pure common value auction the bidders' expected rents and the expected revenue sum identically to the expected value of the object.

Our goal is to make a broader investigation of the role of information in first-price common-value auctions with heterogeneous bidders. As in the previous literature, we are particularly interested in the notion of an "inside" bidder who has information that is in some concrete sense superior to that of other bidders. The benchmark model described above yields one conclusion about the effect of the presence of an "insider" on revenues; does this conclusion hold for other comparisons that are made across homogeneous and heterogeneous information structures? In answering this question, we will point out what we believe to be the driving forces behind revenues and bidder rents in our environment. These forces are essentially the same ones that explain the revenue-ranking results of Milgrom and Weber [9] for homogeneous environments. In particular, if one environment can be interpreted as resulting from the release of public information into another environment, then the former environment will yield greater expected revenue for the seller in our setup. This obtains because when bidders' private information is affiliated, the public release of a signal makes their information less private, prompting stronger competition. This is the so-called "linkage effect." In our model, these factors swamp any others that may make bidder heterogeneity per se beneficial or detrimental to the seller relative to bidder homogeneity.

We are also able to obtain some results on bidder rents, two of which stand out. First, our model delivers an example in which a bidder can be made worse off by having more information. Second, we show that an "outside" bidder, for whose information the insider's information is a sufficient statistic with respect to the true value of the object, can nevertheless earn positive expected rent if his information is private. Such a possibility is suggested in Milgrom and Weber [8], but no specific example is provided there. Thus, our results will have implications both for how a seller should treat a situation in which there is a potential inside bidder, and for how bidders should react to opportunities to gain information.

We develop a simple two-bidder model of a pure common value first-price auction. Although special, its simplicity allows for closed-form solutions of equilibrium bidding behavior in all specifications of the bidders' information structure that are of interest. We do indeed find, for instance, that when a particular environment with an insider is compared to an environment in which bidders are homogeneous but have private information, revenues are higher with the insider.[1] We present the model and intuition for its results in what follows.

2. The Model

This section presents a two-bidder model of a pure common value first-price auction. In this environment there are three random variables of interest: V, the common value of the single object being auctioned, and two informative signals of V, X_1 and X_2. Each of the three variables takes on a realization of either 0 or 1. The two signals are independent conditional on the realization of V. The joint probability distribution function $\pi(V, X_1, X_2)$ is as follows:

$$\pi(0, 0, 0) = \pi(1, 1, 1) = \frac{\alpha^2}{2};$$

$$\pi(0, 0, 1) = \pi(0, 1, 0) = \pi(1, 0, 1) = \pi(1, 1, 0) = \frac{\alpha(1 - \alpha)}{2};$$

$$\pi(0, 1, 1) = \pi(1, 0, 0) = \frac{(1 - \alpha)^2}{2}.$$

α is a parameter lying in $[\frac{1}{2}, 1]$ that can be used as a measure of the degree of affiliation between the variables. For $\alpha = \frac{1}{2}$ the variables are independent of each other, while for $\alpha = 1$ they are perfectly correlated. For $\alpha \in (\frac{1}{2}, 1]$ they are strictly affiliated. Note that the expected value of V is $\frac{1}{2}$ regardless of α.

Our goal is to compare bidding behavior and expected seller revenue from a first-price auction across environments that differ in the observability of signals to the two bidders. Assuming that the bidders never observe V and that each observes at least one signal, there are four possible kinds of information a bidder could observe: the realization of X_1 only; the realization of X_2 only; the *unordered* realization of both X_1 and X_2 (i.e., the total number of signals realizing any given value, but not specifically which signals realize which values); and the *ordered* realization of both X_1 and X_2 (i.e., the exact mapping from signals into realizations). The distinction between the last two cases will be important because if one bidder observes an unordered realization of $\{0, 1\}$ and his rival observes the realization of only one signal, the bidder does not know which realization his rival has observed. Excluding redundancies due to the symmetry of bidders, there are 10 possible specifications ($\binom{4}{2}$) plus 4 in which the bidders learn the same information). Furthermore, since X_1 and X_2 have a symmetric joint distribution, three of these specifications are effectively redundant, reducing the total number that must be considered to 7. These are, without loss of generality: (1) both bidders observe the realization of X_1; (2) both bidders observe the unordered realization of X_1 and X_2, (3) both bidders observe the ordered realization of (X_1, X_2). (4) bidder 1 observes the unordered realization of X_1 and X_2, bidder 2 observes the ordered realization of (X_1, X_2). (5) bidder 1 observes the realization of X_1, bidder 2 observes the realization of X_2; (6) bidder 1 observes the realization of X_1, bidder 2 observes the ordered realization of (X_1, X_2). (7) bidder 1 observes the realization of X_1, bidder 2 observes the unordered realization of X_1 and X_2.

2.1 Environments of No Private Information

Environments (1), (2) and (3) above share the feature that each bidder's observed information is common knowledge. In these environments, the seller will extract all surplus from the bidders in any equilibrium: each bidder will bid the expected value of the object conditional on the public information, so the seller's expected revenue is the expected conditional expectation of V, which is the unconditional expected value of V. Similarly, in environment (4) the bidders always have the same posterior on the probability that $V = 1$, so both bidders bid the common expectation of V in the unique equilibrium.

These results are well-established in previous literature on first-price common-value auctions. The intuition for the results is clear, but it is worth emphasizing why these environments yield the same revenue prediction despite the fact that the bidders' (common) information varies. A bidder's ability to earn rent in a first-price auction depends on his ability to submit bids that win with positive probability and that yield a positive expected payoff conditional on winning. An important element of this ability is uncertainty on the part of his competitors about what the bidder is willing to bid: such uncertainty gives competitors an incentive to shade their bids below their valuations to try to profit when they win, which reinforces the bidder's incentive to shade himself. In these four cases the bidders have no uncertainty about each other's willingness-to-pay, so the best-reply to any shading strategy must ensure that shading yields zero rent. We will return to the issue of bidder uncertainty about each other's willingness-to-pay as we examine the other three environments.

2.2 Homogeneous Private Information

Environment (5) above is a standard case in the literature, in which bidders receive signals with ex-ante identical distributions. For continuous signals, Milgrom and Weber [9] demonstrate the existence of an equilibrium in which bidders use symmetric bidding strategies in such an environment. A symmetric equilibrium also exists in our discrete environment and is as follows. A bidder who receives a signal of 0 bids the expectation of V conditional on $X_1 = X_2 = 0$, or $(1 - \alpha)^2/(\alpha^2 + (1 - \alpha)^2)$. A bidder who receives a signal of 1 employs a mixed strategy. The strategy has support $[(1 - \alpha)^2/(\alpha^2 + (1 - \alpha)^2), \alpha^2 + 2\alpha(1 - \alpha)^3/(\alpha^2 + (1 - \alpha)^2)]$, with the distribution over bids in this support given by

$$F(b) = \frac{2\alpha(1 - \alpha)}{\alpha^2 + (1 - \alpha)^2} \frac{b - \dfrac{(1 - \alpha)^2}{\alpha^2 + (1 - \alpha)^2}}{\dfrac{\alpha^2}{\alpha^2 + (1 - \alpha)^2} - b}.$$

We note that as α approaches $\frac{1}{2}$ all bids approach $\frac{1}{2}$ with probability 1, and as α approaches 1 the bids by bidders receiving signals of 0 approach 0, while the bids by bidders receiving signals of 1 approach 1. These correspond to cases in which the bidders know each other's willingness-to-pay with a high degree of precision, leading to nearly degenerate equilibria that mirror the pure-strategy equilibria when there is no private information.

The calculation of seller revenues is made simple by the assumption of pure common values: since revenues and bidder rents must sum to the common value of the object in all plays of the game, expected revenues are simply the difference between the expected common value and expected bidder rents. A bidder who receives a signal of 0 earns no rent. In a mixed strategy equilibrium all pure strategies in the support of the mixture yield the same expected payoff, so the rents of a bidder receiving a signal of 1 can be calculated using an arbitrary bid in the specified support, yielding $2\alpha(1 - \alpha)(\frac{1}{2} - (1 - \alpha)^2/(\alpha^2 + (1 - \alpha)^2))$. Ex-ante bidder is equally likely to receive each of the signals, and there are two bidders, so $2\alpha(1 - \alpha)(\frac{1}{2} - (1 - \alpha)^2/(\alpha^2 + (1 - \alpha)^2))$ is also the total expected rent of the bidders, and expected revenue is $\frac{1}{2} - 2\alpha$ $(1 - \alpha)(\frac{1}{2} - (1 - \alpha)^2/(\alpha^2 + (1 - \alpha)^2))$. This function is convex in α (see Fig. 1). As expected, its value is $\frac{1}{2}$ for $\alpha = \frac{1}{2}$ and for $\alpha = 1$; in these polar cases the bidders effectively have no private information and the seller extracts full expected surplus in equilibrium.

2.3 Heterogeneous Bidders I: Partitioned Information

Here we examine environment (6), in which one bidder learns both signals and knows which is which. We characterize this environment by "partitioned information," since bidder 2's information is strictly more fine than his information in environment (5). Like environment (5), the (unique) equilibrium is in mixed strategies, described as follows, Bidder 1, who observes only X_1, employs a mixed strategy for both possible signal realizations. When $X_1 = 0$ he mixes over the support $[(1 - \alpha)^2/(\alpha^2 + (1 - \alpha)^2), 1 - \alpha]$ with distribution

$$F(b) = \frac{\alpha - \dfrac{1}{2}}{\dfrac{1}{2} - b}.$$

When $X_1 = 1$ bidder 1 mixes over the support $[\frac{1}{2}, \alpha]$ with distribution

$$F(b) = \frac{\dfrac{\alpha^2}{\alpha^2 + (1 - \alpha)^2} - \alpha}{\dfrac{\alpha^2}{\alpha^2 + (1 - \alpha)^2} - b}.$$

Bidder 2 bids $(1 - \alpha)^2/(\alpha^2 + (1 - \alpha)^2)$ if he observes $(0, 0)$. If he observes $(1, 0)$ he bids $\frac{1}{2}$. If he observes $(0, 1)$ he mixes over the support $[(1 - \alpha)^2/(\alpha^2 + (1 - \alpha)^2), 1 - \alpha]$ with distribution

$$F(b) = \frac{\alpha^2 + (1 - \alpha)^2}{2\alpha(1 - \alpha)} \cdot \frac{b - \dfrac{(1 - \alpha)^2}{\alpha^2 + (1 - \alpha)^2}}{\dfrac{1}{2} - b}.$$

If he observes $(1, 1)$ he mixes over the support $[\frac{1}{2}, \alpha]$ with distribution

$$F(b) = \frac{2\alpha(1 - \alpha)}{\alpha^2 + (1 - \alpha)^2} \frac{b - \dfrac{1}{2}}{\dfrac{\alpha^2}{\alpha^2 + (1 - \alpha)^2} - b}.$$

In this equilibrium bidder 1 earns zero expected rents. This is expected, as his beliefs about V are common knowledge. Bidder 2 earns positive expected rents equal to $\alpha(1 - \alpha)(\frac{1}{2} - (1 - \alpha)) + (\alpha^2 + (1 - \alpha)^2)(\alpha^2/(\alpha^2 + (1 - \alpha)^2) - \alpha)/2$. Expected seller revenues are therefore $\frac{1}{2} - \alpha(1 - \alpha)(\frac{1}{2} - (1 - \alpha)) - ((\alpha^2 + (1 - \alpha)^2)/2)(\alpha^2/(\alpha^2 + (1 - \alpha)^2) - \alpha)$. Again, these revenues are $\frac{1}{2}$ for $\alpha = \frac{1}{2}$ and for $\alpha = 1$.

2.4 Heterogeneous Bidders II: Nonpartitioned Information

Finally, we consider environment (7), in which bidder 2 learns signals X_1 and X_2, but is not able to identify which is which. We characterize this environment as "nonpartitioned information" because unlike in environment (6), bidder 2's information in environment (7) is not a partitioning of his information in environment (5): he cannot distinguish between the signal realizations $(0, 1)$ and $(1, 0)$. Nevertheless, like in environment (6) bidder 1's information is a statistical garbling of bidder 2's information with respect to V: the distribution of V conditional on just bidder 2's information is the same as the distribution of V conditional on both bidders' information,

The (unique) mixed-strategy equilibrium in environment (7) has the following characteristics. If bidder 1 receives a signal of 0, he mixes over the support $[(1 - \alpha)^2/(\alpha^2 + (1 - \alpha)^2), b_1]$, where b_1 is to be determined. If bidder 1 receives a signal of 1, he mixes over the support $[b_1, b_3]$. If bidder 2 receives a signal of $\{0, 0\}$ he bids $(1 - \alpha)^2/(\alpha^2 + (1 - \alpha)^2)$. If bidder 2 receives an (unordered) signal of $\{0, 1\}$ he mixes over the support $[(1 - \alpha)^2/(\alpha^2 + (1 - \alpha)^2), b_2]$. If bidder 2 receives a signal of $\{1, 1\}$ he mixes over the support $[b_2, b_3]$. b_1, b_2 and b_3 satisfy $b_1 \leq b_2 \leq b_3$ and can be solved for jointly with the mixed strategy distributions by imposing the condition that each type of bidder be indifferent over all the bids in his support. The algebra involved in this solution is tedious and unilluminating; we relegate the derivation to the appendix and note only that as α approaches $\frac{1}{2}$, b_1, b_2 and b_3 also approach $\frac{1}{2}$, while as α approaches 1, b_1 and b_2 approach 0, while b_3 approaches 1.

The seller's expected revenue can be expressed straightforwardly as a function of b_1 and b_3. Bidder 1 makes zero expected profit conditional on receiving a signal of 0. Conditional on receiving a signal of 1 bidder 1 earns an expected profit of $\alpha - b_3$, which is strictly positive for all $\alpha \in (\frac{1}{2}, 1)$. Bidder 1's ex-ante expected profit is therefore $\frac{1}{2}(\alpha - b_3)$. Bidder 2 makes zero profit conditional on receiving a signal of $\{0, 0\}$. Conditional on receiving a signal of $\{0, 1\}$ bidder 2 earns an expected profit of $\frac{1}{2}(\frac{1}{2} - b_1)$. Conditional on receiving a signal of $\{1, 1\}$ bidder 2 earns an expected profit of $\alpha^2/(\alpha^2 + (1 - \alpha)^2) - b_3$. Bidder 2's ex-ante expected profit is therefore $\alpha(1 - \alpha)(\frac{1}{2} - b_1) + (\alpha^2 + (1 - \alpha)^2)/2 \, (\alpha^2/(\alpha^2 + (1 - \alpha)^2) - b_3)$. The seller's expected revenue is thus $\frac{1}{2} - \frac{1}{2}(\alpha - b_3) - \alpha(1 - \alpha)(\frac{1}{2} - b_1) - (\alpha^2 + (1 - \alpha)^2)/2 \, (\alpha^2/(\alpha^2 + (1 - \alpha)^2) - b_3)$. Again, there is full extraction for $\alpha = \frac{1}{2}$ and for $\alpha = 1$.

2.5 Discussion

Figure 8.1 depicts the seller's expected revenues as a function of α for each of the three classes of environment we consider, excluding those in which there is no private information. We comment here on several features of these functions. First, our analysis replicates the result that if bidders have no private information then the seller extracts all surplus, but if *any* bidder has any private information then full extraction is impossible in a first-price auction. In particular, the comparison between the environments of no private information and environment (6), where exactly one bidder has private information, is the one made in the literature on asymmetric common-value auctions referenced in our introduction.

Of potentially more interest is the comparison between environments (5), (6) and (7). We interpret the strict dominance of environment (6) within this set as a validation of Milgrom and Weber's [9] result on the positive revenue effects of increased bidder information. Milgrom and Weber show that when bidders are ex-ante homogeneous and play a symmetric equilibrium, if their information is affiliated then a public release of information *that preserves bidder homogeneity* must raise expected revenues in the new symmetric equilibrium.[2] A change from environment (5) to environment (6) may be interpreted as a public release of information (viz., bidder 1's signal) that does not preserve bidder homogeneity; nevertheless, expected revenue increases as a result of the new information just as in the homogeneous environment. Similarly, a change from environment (7) to environment (6) may be interpreted as a public announcement of bidder 1's signal, but in this instance the environment is not homogeneous before or after the announcement; the salutary effect on revenue obtains here as well.

The exact source of increased revenues in environment (6) can be found in the revenue functions. Rearrangement of bidder rents in environment (6) shows that they are equal to $2\alpha(1 - \alpha)(\frac{1}{2} - (1 - \alpha))$. Thus, the ratio of bidder rents in environment (6) to bidder rents in environment (5) is

$$\frac{\dfrac{1}{2} - (1 - \alpha)}{\dfrac{1}{2} - \dfrac{(1 - \alpha)^2}{\alpha^2 + (1 - \alpha)^2}} = \alpha^2 + (1 - \alpha)^2.$$

Expressing the ratio this way shows that the entire discrepancy in bidder rents across the two environments can be attributed to the fact that when bidder 1

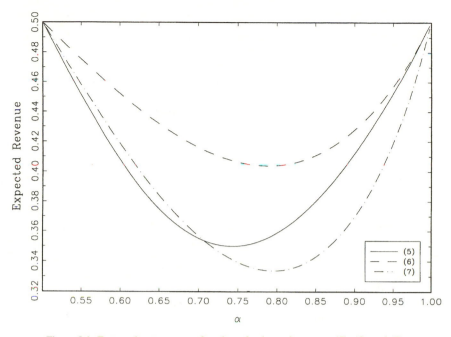

Figure 8.1. Expected revenue as a function of α in environments (5), (6), and (7).

receives a signal of 0, he bids more aggressively in environment (6) (up to $1 - \alpha$) than in environment (5) ($(1 - \alpha)^2/(\alpha^2 + (1 - \alpha)^2)$). The reason is that in environment (5) bidders receiving a signal of 1 compete vigorously because of the possibility that the other bidder has a signal of 1, making bids above $(1 - \alpha)^2/(\alpha^2 + (1 - \alpha)^2)$ unprofitable for a bidder receiving a signal of 0. However, when it is common knowledge that bidder 1 has a signal of 0, bidder 2 knows he can win with low bids, giving bidder 1 a weak incentive to compete where he has none in environment (5).

From the previous section, bidder rents in environment (7) can be written

$$\frac{1}{2}(\alpha - b_3) + \alpha(1 - \alpha)\left(\frac{1}{2} - b_1\right)$$
$$+ \frac{a^2 + (1 - \alpha)^2}{2}\left(\frac{\alpha^2}{\alpha^2 + (1 - \alpha)^2} - b_3\right).$$

It is readily verified that $b_1 \leq 1 - \alpha$ and that $b_3 \leq \alpha$, with equality only for $\alpha = \frac{1}{2}$ or $\alpha = 1$. Thus, bidder 2 makes greater rent in environment (7) than in environment (6) even though he has strictly less information in (7). We comment more on this below. Since bidder 1 also makes rent in environment (7) but not in (6), this proves that revenue is strictly greater in environment (6). Each type of bidder makes a lower maximum bid when bidder 1's signal is not common knowledge; because the equilibrium strategies are mixed, these maximum bids are accurate measures of bidder rents.

We believe that the forces behind these revenue rankings are essentially the same as those behind Milgrom and Weber's result for homogeneous environments. Uncertainty about opponents' willingnesses-to-pay creates a mutually enforced incentive to reduce bids in order to increase rents in the event that the object is won. An increased correlation in these willingnesses-to-pay thus leads to more aggressive bidding on average. Without providing any generally applicable conclusions, our results suggest that these factors have force even in environments with heterogeneous bidders.

We provide an additional remark on environments (5) and (6). The revenue dominance of environment (6) suggests that conclusions about the general revenue effects of heterogeneous bidder information are quite sensitive to the homogeneous benchmark used. Revenues in environment (6) are always lower than in the environments with no private information, but always higher than in environment (5) when bidders have identically distributed private information. Even as α approaches $\frac{1}{2}$ or 1, in which case environment (5) is converging to one of purely public information, revenue in environment (6) continues to lie strictly between revenues in the two homogeneous environments.

The final revenue comparison we make is between environments (5) and (7). Although bidder 2 has information in environment (7) that is strictly better than his information in environment (5) for the purpose of predicting V, environment (7) cannot be interpreted as the result of information release into environment (5), since there are states of the world in different elements of bidder 2's information partition in environment (5) ((1, 0) and (0, 1)) that he cannot distinguish between in environment (7). And indeed, the ranking of revenues across these two environments is seen to depend on α. Given that the revenue functions for environments (5) and (7) are both convex and cross exactly once for $\alpha \in (\frac{1}{2}, 1)$, the nature of their difference may be described in three equivalent ways: expected revenue is higher in environment (7) for small α and higher in environment (5) for large α; expected revenue achieves a minimum at a smaller α in environment (5) than in environment (7); and revenue in environment (5) is more sensitive to changes in α than is revenue in environment (7) for α near $\frac{1}{2}$, but less sensitive for α near 1. We focus on this last feature to provide intuition for the general shapes of the functions.

Recalling that the maximum bid in environment (5) is $\alpha^2 + 2\alpha(1 - \alpha)^3/(\alpha^2 + (1 - \alpha)^2)$, denote this function $\bar{b}(\alpha)$. Expected bidder rents in environment (5) can then simply be written as $\alpha - \bar{b}(\alpha)$, and the derivative of bidder rents with respect to α as $1 - \bar{b}'(\alpha)$. Bidder rents in environment (7), as before, are

$$\frac{1}{2}(\alpha - b_3(\alpha)) + \alpha(1 - \alpha)\left(\frac{1}{2} - b_1(\alpha)\right)$$

$$+ \frac{\alpha^2 + (1 - \alpha)^2}{2}\left(\frac{\alpha^2}{\alpha^2 + (1 - \alpha)^2} - b_3(\alpha)\right),$$

where bids b_1 and b_3 have been written explicitly as functions of α.

First, consider the behavior of these functions in the neighborhood of $\alpha = \frac{1}{2}$, at which both take on a value of 0. It is readily verified that $\overline{b}'(\frac{1}{2}) = 0$, so that the derivative of bidder rents with respect to α is 1 at $\alpha = \frac{1}{2}$. In other words, while the posterior probability that $V = 1$ of a bidder receiving a signal of 1 (i.e., α) changes at a rate of 1, the amount that bidder must bid to win undergoes no first order change for α near $\frac{1}{2}$. The derivative of bidder rents with respect to α in environment (7) can be verified to be $1 - \frac{1}{4} b_3'(\frac{1}{2})$ for $\alpha = \frac{1}{2}$. However, in this case, $b_3'(\frac{1}{2})$ is strictly positive (calculation shows it to be approximately .6). Thus, for small α, we may explain the discrepancy in revenues by two facts: that for all α, the highest bid submitted in environment (7) is greater than the highest bid submitted in environment (5), which is a consequence of the presence of a more optimistic bidder type in environment (7); and that for small α, this is the dominant effect.

For large α, we have that $\overline{b}'(1) = 2$, and that the derivative of bidder rents in environment (7) with respect to α at $\alpha = 1$ is $-b_3'(1)$. Since $b_3(\alpha) < \alpha$ for all $\alpha \in (\frac{1}{2}, 1)$ and $b_3(1) = 1$, we have that $b_3'(1) \geq 1$; exact calculation shows that it equals 2. Thus, the derivative of revenues with respect to α at $\alpha = 1$ is 1 in environment (5), 2 in environment (7). Here, the discrepancy has two sources. First, as α increases, the probability that bidder 2 receives the signal $\{0, 1\}$ diminishes, reducing his rent. This effect is second-order for small α, since for small α this type makes little rent, but is first-order when α is large. Second, the derivative with respect to α of $\alpha^2/(\alpha^2 + (1 - \alpha^2))$, which is bidder 2's posterior probability that $V = 1$ when he receives the signal $\{1, 1\}$, disappears as α approaches 1. So whereas bidder 2's loss of rent in environment (5) due to higher bids is mitigated by an improved assessment of the value of winning when α is large and increases, this mitigation is second order in environment (7) when bidder 2 gets the positive signal $\{1, 1\}$. To summarize, environment (7) yields greater revenues than environment (5) for small α because for small α all signals are similarly accurate and bidders with a given accuracy of signal bid more in environment (7) than in environment (5), while environment (5) yields greater revenues than environment (7) for large α because for large α bidder 2's signal is significantly more accurate in environment (7) than in environment (5), yielding him greater rent. Computer simulation demonstrates that in fact this tradeoff for the bidders between more aggressive bidding and better information is monotonic: the ratio of bidder rents in environment (7) to those in environment (5) is strictly increasing in α.

Aside from revenue implications, the equilibria of environments (6) and (7) provide two other notable results. First is the fact that bidder 2's expected rent is higher in environment (7), a result that may be somewhat surprising given that the only difference between the environments is that bidder 2 has strictly more information in environment (6). This occurs because of strategic interaction: when bidder 2 is uncertain about bidder 1's type, it gives him an incentive to gamble that bidder 1's type may be low and submit a low bid. This in turn promotes lower bidding by bidder 1, reinforcing the incentive for bidder

2 to reduce his bids, to the mutual benefit of the bidders. This result is in contrast to Theorem 4 in Milgrom and Weber [8], which says that starting from a situation in which only one bidder has private information, that bidder's rents must increase if he learns additional private information. The detrimental effect of improved information is obviously not universal, even within a first-price auction environment (e.g., bidder 2 earns a greater expected rent in environment (6) than in environment (5)), but the example emphasizes that the interaction between information and strategic play is not straightforward.[3]

The other result worth comment is that in the equilibrium of environment (7), bidder 1 earns a positive expected rent despite the fact that his information is a garbling of bidder 2's information with respect to V. This ability to earn rent stands in contrast to Milgrom and Weber's [9] result on second-price auctions in which a bidder has garbled information. They show that there is always an equilibrium in which a bidder with garbled information earns zero rent. The reason is that if each better-informed bidder use the strategy of bidding the expected common value conditional on the two highest signals being equal to his realized signal (or the expected common value given his own signal, if he is the only better-informed bidder), a bidder with garbled information would earn a negative expected profit by entering any winning bid. The only best response by such a bidder to said strategies by the better-informed bidders is therefore to enter a bid that wins with zero probability.

This result cannot hold in a first-price auction with only two bidders. The reason is that in order to earn rent, a well-informed bidder must bid below his expectation of the common value. This creates an opportunity for a less-informed bidder with private information to earn rent despite his informational disadvantage. The result holds even for more general signal structures. Suppose that the bidders receive signals x_1 and x_2 that lie in a continuum $[\underline{x}, \overline{x}]$, and that the signals and the common value are jointly affiliated, with x_1 a garbling of x_2 with respect to V; however, the distribution of x_1 conditional on x_2 is not degenerate, so that bidder 1 has some private information. It must be the case that bidder 2 earns positive rent in any equilibrium: for bidder 2 to be unable to earn positive rent playing a best reply it would have to be the case that all bids by bidder 2 less than $E[V \mid x_2]$ lose with probability 1. This would imply that bidder 1 must bid at least $E[V \mid x_2 = \overline{x}]$ for all x_1, a bid that would earn a negative expected payoff with probability 1. Thus, there is a positive probability that bidder 2 will submit a bid less than $E[V \mid x_2]$ for some positive measure of realizations of x_2. Choose a particular x_2 such that $b(x_2) < E[V \mid x_2]$. By affiliation, bidder 1's expected payoff from winning with a bid of $b(x_2)$ is strictly increasing in x_1. Thus, as long as $b(x_2)$ loses with positive probability in equilibrium, a positive measure of types of bidder 1 have a strategy that yields a positive expected payoff, since the type who bids $b(x_2)$ earns at least a payoff of zero. Thus, all types of bidder 1 who submit a winning bid with positive probability earn a positive expected rent.[4]

3. Conclusion

The revenue performance of standard auction rules when bidders are heterogeneous represents a relatively open topic in information economics. We have considered a very simple model of a first-price common-value auction with alternative information structures. The simplicity of the model allowed us to solve explicitly for equilibrium bidding under all possible information specifications. Our results are suggestive of several conclusions. First, there is no general relationship between seller revenues and whether bidders are homogeneously or heterogeneously informed. Even when the comparative static exercise is well defined (as in the comparison between environments (5) and (6), and between environment (6) and the public information environments in our model), we show that a given heterogeneous environment may yield more or less revenue than different homogeneous environments. Second, the basic forces that deliver Milgrom and Weber's [9] result on the beneficial revenue effects of more public information appear also to be present when heterogeneity between bidders is allowed for, yielding the same conclusion about revenues.

Our paper also clarifies some features of bidder rents in a heterogeneous common-value auction. First, because of the strategic interaction inherent in auctions, additional information may actually have negative value to an individual bidder. Second, in the benchmark first-price models, uninformed bidders earn zero expected rents in both the homogeneous and heterogeneous cases, a result consistent with previous results for second-price auctions when less informed bidders have private but "garbled" information. We show that the result does not extend generally to heterogeneous first-price auctions, even when garbling obtains. This occurs because in a first-price auction, a well-informed bidder has an incentive to shade his bid that is absent in second-price auctions.

Appendix

This appendix provides further detail on the equilibrium in environment (7). The values of b_1 and b_3, which are sufficient for the calculation of revenues, can be found as follows. Let $F_{0,\,1}(b_1)$ be the equilibrium probability that bidder 2 type $\{0,\,1\}$ bids less than b_1. Let $F_1(b_2)$ be the equilibrium probability that bidder 1 type 1 bids less than b_2. The following five equalities must hold in equilibrium:

$$(\alpha^2 + (1 - \alpha)^2)\left(\frac{(1 - \alpha)^2}{\alpha^2 + (1 - \alpha)^2} - b_1 \right)$$

$$+ 2\alpha(1 - \alpha)\, F_{0,\,1}(b_1)\left(\frac{1}{2} - b_1 \right) = 0$$

$$2\alpha(1 - \alpha)\, F_{0,1}(b_1)\left(\frac{1}{2} - b_1 \right) = 2\alpha(1 - \alpha)\left(\frac{1}{2} - b_2 \right)$$

$$2\alpha(1 - \alpha) \, F_{0,1}(b_1) \left(\frac{1}{2} - b_1 \right) = \alpha - b_3$$

$$\frac{1}{2}\left(\frac{1}{2} - b_1 \right) = \frac{1 + F_1(b_2)}{2} \left(\frac{1}{2} - b_2 \right)$$

$$F_1(b_2) \left(\frac{\alpha^2}{\alpha^2 + (1 - \alpha)^2} - b_2 \right) = \frac{\alpha^2}{\alpha^2 + (1 - \alpha^2)} - b_3$$

Successive substitution allows the five equations to be collapsed to a single quadratic equation in b_2, for which there is exactly one root between 0 and $\frac{1}{2}$. b_1 and b_3 are then easily solved for as functions of the derived b_2.

Notes

We are grateful to John Kagel for helpful discussions, to seminar participants at the University of Pittsburgh and an associate editor and referee for suggestions that improved the paper, and to Eric Tamashasky for valuable research assistance. Dan Levin thanks the National Science Foundation for financial support.

1. Kagel and Levin [6] observe this phenomenon in experimental data; Laskowski and Slonim [7] show that a similar revenue result must obtain in a limiting case of Kagel and Levin's experimental design.

2. Milgrom and Weber [8] show that this revenue result also obtains in heterogeneous environments when only one bidder has private information before the release of information.

3. Similarly, while bidder 1 earns a positive expected rent in environment (7) when he learns the realization of X_1 only and bidder 2 learns the unordered realization of both signals, he earns zero expected rent if he learns the unordered realization of both signals when bidder 2 does also. Engelbrecht-Wiggans [2] also notes this negative value of information to an initially less-informed bidder in examples similar to ours.

4. See Campbell and Levin [1] for a specific example with continuous signals.

References

1. C. M. Campbell and D. Levin, "Common-Value Auctions with Heterogeneous Information: Can the Seller Benefit from an Insider?," Ohio State University, mimeo, 1996.
2. R. Engelbrecht-Wiggans, "On the Value of Private Information in an Auction: Ignorance may be Bliss," University of Illinois, mimeo, 1986.
3. R. Engelbrecht-Wiggans, P. R. Milgrom, and R. J. Weber, Competitive bidding with proprietary information, *J. Math. Econ.* **11** (1983), 161–169.
4. K. Hendricks and R. H. Porter, An empirical study of an auction with asymmetric information, *Amer. Econ. Rev.* **78** (1988), 865–883.
5. K. Hendricks, R. H. Porter, and C. A. Wilson, Auctions for oil and gas leases with an informed bidder and a random reservation price, *Econometrica* **62** (1994), 1415–1444.

6. J. H. Kagel and D. Levin, Common value auctions with insider information, *Econometrica*, 1999, to appear.

7. M. C. Laskowski and R. L. Slonim, An asymptotic solution for sealed bid common-value auctions with bidders having asymmetric information, *Games Econ. Behav.* **28** (1999), 238–255.

8. P. R. Milgrom and R. J. Weber, The value of information in a sealed-bid auction, *J. Math. Econ.* **10** (1982), 105–114.

9. P. R. Milgrom and R. J. Weber, A theory of auctions and competitive bidding, *Econometrica* **50** (1982), 1089–1122.

10. R. B. Myerson, Optimal auction design, *Math. Operations Res.* **6** (1981), 58–73.

11. J. G. Riley and W. F. Samuelson, Optimal auctions, *Amer. Econ. Rev.* **71** (1981), 381–392.

12. M. Weverbergh, Competitive bidding with asymmetric information reanalyzed, *Manage. Sci.* **25** (1979), 291–294.

13. R. Wilson, Competitive bidding with asymmetric information, *Manage. Sci.* **13** (1967), 816–820.

9

Second-Price Auctions with Asymmetric Payoffs: An Experimental Investigation

—

Christopher Avery and John H. Kagel

1. Introduction

In the vast literature on auctions the effect of asymmetries between bidders has been little studied. Asymmetries are the norm and not the exception in many auctions. It is common for one bidder to be known to have a special interest beyond that of others in winning the auction. Some examples of this are an oil company bidding for a tract near its other properties, the current managers of a company bidding against outsiders for its, takeover, and the recent FCC broadband MTA auctions.[1]

In the important situation of common values and correlated information, asymmetries can lead to a reversal of the standard revenue ranking different auction rules.[2] For example, Milgrom and Weber (1982) prove that symmetric equilibrium bid functions produce (weakly) greater expected revenue in second-price than in first-price auctions, given the assumptions of affiliated information and risk-neutral bidders. In contrast, Bikhchandani (1988) shows that when one player is known to have a payoff advantage K in a second-price common-value auction then (1) the advantaged bidder must win the auction with certainty in any Nash equilibrium, no matter how small the size of K, and (2) the disadvantaged bidder reduces the bid drastically in response to the addition of K, causing a large decline in expected revenue compared to the symmetric payoff case.[3] This large loss in revenue holds for any value of K, no matter how small, so we say that the addition of the private value K has an *explosive* effect in reducing the theoretical expected revenue for the auction. However, the addition of the same asymmetry has little effect on the bids or the expected revenues in first-price auctions (see the Appendix). In view of recent debates over the format of government auctions (such as the treasury-bill auctions and the FCC auctions), studying the effect of asymmetries on bidding outcomes is of practical as well as theoretical importance.

This experiment studies the effects of asymmetries on bidding in common-value second-price auctions. The question of interest is "Can payoff perturbations have explosive effects on bidding functions as predicted by an equilibrium analysis of second-price auctions?" Past experiments indicate that even though the point predictions of Nash equilibrium bidding models are rarely satisfied, the comparative static implications of the theory are likely to be upheld (see, for example, Kagel and Levin, 1993). Therefore, we study behavior in both symmetric and asymmetric second-price auctions, concentrating on the prediction that disadvantaged bidders will reduce their bids explosively in asymmetric auctions relative to symmetric auctions.

Second-price asymmetric auctions are derived from symmetric second-price auctions by adding a separate private value component to the value of one bidder, giving that bidder a specialized, known advantage. We find evidence from the empirical bidding functions that disadvantaged bidders reduce their bids in response to the private-value advantage, but that the effect of the private-value advantage is proportional and not explosive. Thus, the expected revenue in second-price auctions is more robust to the addition of asymmetries than is predicted by equilibrium theory. The difference between the bids of advantaged and disadvantaged players is only slightly above the private-value advantage, rather than several times the private value as Nash equilibrium bidding theory predicts. Profits for advantaged bidders are held down from those of equilibrium by overly aggressive, bidding by disadvantaged bidders, who lose money on average as a result of their overly aggressive bidding. These losses by disadvantaged bidders can largely be attributed to a winner's curse. A comparison of the inexperienced and experienced cases suggests that bidders are moving in the direction of Nash equilibrium, but very slowly.

The paper proceeds as follows. Section 2 describes the formal of the two-bidder, second-price auctions utilized in the experiment arid derives the theoretical equilibrium bid functions for the participants. Section 3 explains the experimental design and gives, some particulars of the experimental sessions. Section 4 sets out the hypotheses to be tested, and Section 5 gives the main statistical results. Section 6 concludes.

2. The Base Model

We use the following general setting as the base case for experimental study. Two bidders participate in an auction for an object of value $\tilde{V}$, where $\tilde{V}$ is the sum of two independent symmetric random variables, X and Y, each uniform on the range (a, c). One bidder observes X, the other observes Y, and they compete in a sealed-bid second-price auction. Under these conditions a second-price auction is strategically equivalent to an English auction with fixed bidding increments.

One player may be known to have an additional private value of K for the object. When that is the case, we shall refer to that player as the advantaged bidder and to her opponent as the disadvantaged bidder. Then the advantaged bidder values the object at $\tilde{V} + K$, while her opponent continues to value it at $\tilde{V}$, which remains unknown. The value of K is common knowledge, as is the identity of the advantaged player. In the rest of the paper we refer to the case with no additional private value (i.e. $K = 0$) as a *standard second-price auction* and to the case with a positive value for K as a *private-value-advantage auction*.

2.1 Equilibrium Analysis

This subsection reviews the theoretical results that are relevant for our analysis. Although these results are not, for the most part, new, we record them as theorems to distinguish them from our experimental results, which we record as conclusions.

The standard second-price auction produces a class of equilibria as identified by Milgrom (1981) and Levin and Harstad (1986) among others. There is, however, just one equilibrium with symmetric bid functions for the bidders. Let $v(x, y) = E(\tilde{V} \mid X = x, Y = y) = x + y$. In the unique symmetric equilibrium of the standard second-price auction, both bidders follow the bidding function $B^*(x) = v(x,x) = 2x$, and the bidder with the higher private observation wins the auction.

Theorem 2.1. *There is no* ex post *regret in the symmetric equilibrium of the standard second-price auction. Even after learning the results of the auction, no bidder then wishes to change his bid.*

Proof. Suppose $x > y$. In equilibrium the winning bid, $2x$, falls above the true value $x + y$, which is in turn greater than the price set by the losing bid, $2y$. That is, the winning bidder is guaranteed a profit, while the loser could only lose money by raising his bid. The minimum price at which the loser can win the auction is $2x$, which is greater than the true value, $x + y$.

The no-regret property occurs regularly in private-value auctions but is rare in common-value auctions. In effect, the loser turns down a price that must be greater than the true value, although that price is never stated formally. The no-regret property is important for experimental purposes, because it means that the symmetric equilibrium is unaffected by risk aversion. It also implies that there is no possibility that limited liability for losses can be responsible for bidding above the Nash equilibrium. In equilibrium, profits are always non-negative. As in the Vickrey (private-value second-price) auction, each player achieves a profit in every instance in which it is available in equilibrium, and that profit does not depend on the winner's actual bid.

In addition to the symmetric equilibrium of the standard second-price auction, there are a continuum of asymmetric equilibria of the form $B_1(x) = v(x, f(x)) = x + f(x)$, $B_2(y) = y + f^{-1}(y)$. Any pair of functions $(B_1(x), B_2(y))$ constructed from an increasing function $f(\cdot)$ produces a bidding equilibrium. Each such pair has the same property as the symmetric equilibrium that the equilibrium bids are unaffected by risk aversion. It is possible to make a bid that falls above the upper bound for bids of one's opponent in a second-price equilibrium because that bid does not affect the price set in equilibrium.

We shall not be concerned with these asymmetric equilibria in the standard case, but they are vital in the private value advantage case. With $K > 0$, the discrepancy between the values for the two players invalidates most of the equilibria of the standard second-price auction. The following argument is based on related results from Bikhchandani (1988).[4] See Maskin and Riley (1996) for private value revenue comparisons between first-price and second-price asymmetric auctions.

Theorem 2.2. *In any second-price bidding equilibrium with continuous (and increasing) strategies in the private advantage case, one player must win the auction with probability 1.*

Proof. Suppose not. Then there is an equilibrium with continuous bidding functions $(B_1(x), B_2(y))$ such that each player wins the auction with positive probability. Since the bidding functions are continuous, there must then be values x^*, y^* such that $B_1(x^*) = B_2(y^*)$. Denote $b^* = B_1(x^*)$.

Suppose that $b^* < x^* + y^* + K$. Then player 1 prefers to win the auction if both players bid b^*. The value of the item to him is $x^* + y^* + K$, which is greater than his prospective price of b^*. Further, since the strategies are continuous, player 1 also prefers to win the auction if player 2's observation is in the neighborhood of x^* so that player 2's bid is just above b^*. Therefore, player 1 prefers to increase his bid from $B_1(x^*)$ and the proposed equilibrium fails. A similar argument would imply that player 2 should reduce his bid from $B_2(y^*)$ if $b^* \geq x^* + y^* + K$.

Ruling out the cases in which the advantaged player loses each auction, and restricting players to bid in the range of their own possible values conditional on their private signals, the natural set of remaining equilibria are those of the form $(B_A(x), B_a(y))$, where $B_A(x) \geq x + c$ is the bidding function for the advantaged player and $B_a(y) \leq y + a + K$ for the disadvantaged player and the bid functions satisfy $B_A(x) \geq B_a(y)$ for each (x,y). The advantaged player bids above the maximum value to her opponent, while the disadvantaged player bids below the minimum value to his opponent conditional on his private observation. These bid functions fulfill the conditions of equilibrium because of the implicit element of price discrimination in the auction. The relatively low bids of the disadvantaged player produce a low effective price for the advantaged player, which in turn give the advantaged player reason to set a high bid and thus a high effective price for the disadvantaged player. This same result does, not hold in a first-price auction, because the winner pays her own bid and thus cannot afford to make exorbitant bids.

While the conditions for a Nash equilibrium require the advantaged bidder to win every auction, there is some flexibility in the actual values of bids in equilibrium. In the most favorable outcome for the advantaged player, the equilibrium bid functions are $B_a(y) = y + a$ and $B_A(x) = x + c$ (or greater). In the least favorable outcome for the advantaged player, assuming that $K < (c - a)/2$, the equilibrium bid functions are $B_a(y) = y + a + K$ and $B_A(x) = x + c + K$. Although this flexibility produces a wider range of possible equilibria for larger values of K, it is important to remember that the equilibrium bid functions for advantaged and disadvantaged bidders are a matched pair. When the disadvantaged player bids more aggressively within the range of possible equilibria, the advantaged player increases her bids to compensate. Thus, the explosive effect of the private-value advantage holds in every equilibrium, and the privately advantaged player always wins the auction.

Since there are so many equilibria in the private-value-advantage auctions, it may seem desirable to allow for a failure of coordination in the players' actions. Thus, we consider the predictions of rationalizability, as well as those of Nash equilibrium. For two-player games, rationalizability is equivalent to solution by iterated strict dominance (Pearce, 1984). However, iterated strict dominance never eliminates any strategies in a second-price auction.

Conclusion 2.3. *All strategies are rationalizable in a second-price auction.*

Proof. Consider a strategy $\overline{B}_1$ in which player 1 bids above the maximum possible value for player 2. The best response for player 2 is to select any bid that will lose the auction. Thus, all strategies for player 2 are best responses to $\overline{B}_1$. Now consider a strategy for player 2, $\underline{B}_2$, in which player 2 bids 0. The best response for player 1 is to select any bid which will win the auction, meaning that $\overline{B}_1$ is a best response to $\underline{B}_2$ and vice versa. Both of these strategies will survive in each elimination of strictly dominated strategies, meaning that all other strategies survive as well.

Since all strategies are rationalizable in any second-price auction, to produce a prediction related to rationalizability, we strengthen the definition to consider the elimination of weakly dominant strategies: we call strategies which satisfy this requirement *weak-dominance rationalizable*.[5] For our case, the logic behind Nash equilibrium bidding is sufficiently close to iterated weak dominance that the two requirements nearly coincide.

Theorem 2.4. *All strategies that select bids in the range of conditional values (on observing one's signal) are weak-dominance rationalizable in the standard second-price auction. Any pair of strategies that are weak-dominance rationalizable in the private-advantage second-price auction cause the advantaged bidder to will the auction.*

Proof. See Appendix.

In the remainder of the paper, we distinguish between iterated weak dominance and Nash equilibrium by examining predictions suggested by the logic underlying iterated weak dominance.

2.2 Revenue Comparisons

Since the private observations are drawn independently, a standard second-price auction conforms to the requirements of the revenue equivalence theorem. Any auction rules and equilibrium strategies which give the same allocation of the good (and zero expected revenue to a player with the minimum observation) produce the same expected revenue to the auctioneer. In particular, since the symmetric equilibria of first- and second-price auctions allocate the good to the bidder with the highest observation, they must produce the same expected price.[6] The following theorem compares revenue between the standard and private value advantage second-price auctions.

Theorem 2.5. *The expected revenue from the symmetric equilibrium of the standard second-price auction is 2(2a + c)/3. The expected revenue for the private-value-advantage auction is no more than (3a + c)/2 + K.*

Proof. Calculating the revenue in the second-price symmetric equilibrium, we find that the expected price is $E(\min(B^*(x), B^*(y))) = E(\min(v(x, x), v(y, y))) = E(\min(2x, 2y)) = 2E(\min(x, y)) = 2(2a + c)/3$.

In the private-value-advantage case, the second-price equilibrium predetermines the advantaged player as the winner. Then the expected revenue to the auctioneer is simply the expectation of the disadvantaged player's bid. Since $B_a(y) \leq y + a + K$, expected revenue is bounded above by $E(y) + a + K = (3a + c)/2 + K$.

For K near zero, there is a drop in expected revenue of $(c - a)/6$ from the standard case to the private-value-advantage case. Ironically, a small increase in the value of the object to one of the bidders creates a significant decline in the seller's expected revenue in a second-price auction. For larger K, revenue can rise or fall depending on the choice of new equilibrium.

In contrast to these results for the second-price auction, the equilibrium of a first-price auction is relatively unchanged by the addition of a private value for one of the players.

Theorem 2.6. *In the private-value-advantage case, there is a first-price bidding equilibrium in which each player's bid is within K of the bid for the same observation in a standard first-price auction with no private value component for either player.*

The Appendix derives the first-price bidding equilibrium of the asymmetric case. See Klemperer (1997) for preliminary arguments towards generalizing this result beyond the specific case used in our experiments.

Theorems 2.5 and 2.6 imply that the theoretical revenue of the first-price auction dominates that of the second-price auction for the private-value-advantage case with K near zero. Our experiment is important for testing the relevance of this theoretical prediction. If equilibrium bidding is found in private-value-advantage second-price auctions, then sellers are likely to prefer a first-price auction when one bidder is known to have an unusual interest in the item up for auction.

3. Experimental Design

These experiments focus on comparing behavior for bidders in standard second-price auctions and private-value-advantage auctions. The base model was employed with the individual private observations X and Y independent and uniform on the range (1,4). Our choice of parameters was specifically designed to give bidders reasonable profit opportunities. In the standard case, the expected price is then $4, giving the bidders an aggregate expected profit of $1, or 50 cents each.

To study the private-value advantage, we chose $K = 1$, as we felt that a smaller value of K was unlikely to have much bite. Conditional on their observations, an advantaged bidder faced a uniform value on $(x + 2, x + 5)$ as opposed to $(y + 1, y + 4)$ for his opponent; on average, the increment is 20 percent of the common value. Then there is a range of Nash equilibria in which the advantaged bidder wins the auction and pays a minimum expected price of $3.50 against the bid function $B_a(x) = x + 1$ and a maximum expected price of $4.50 against the bid function $B_a(x) = x + 2$. Therefore, the choice $K = 1$ does not yield a sharp price prediction in comparison with the $4.00 expected price for the standard auction. The theory still makes a number of sharp predictions:

(N1) disadvantaged bidders should be reducing their bids on average compared to the symmetric auctions, with particularly sharp reductions in bids for higher values of x,

(N2) in equilibrium, for any given private information signal, the difference between bids of the advantaged and disadvantaged bidders should be at least $3.00, and

(N3) the advantaged bidders win all the auctions (or at least a vast majority of them).

We ran two sessions with inexperienced subjects for the standard case and two for the private-value-advantage case, as summarized in Table 9.1. After the sessions with inexperienced bidders, we brought back subsets of the individual groups to compete as experienced bidders under the same conditions. Participants began each session with a balance of $10 and accrued profits and losses over a series of periods of bidding. Bidders alternated roles as advantaged and disadvantaged in the private-value-advantage bidding sessions. Switching roles was intended to speed up any learning that might be going on in the auctions and to minimize rivalrous bidding that might result from "fairness" considerations.

TABLE 9.1
Experimental Sessions

Experimental Session	Subject Experience	Number of Players	Number of Auction Periods	Auction Type
1	Inexperienced	12	16	Private advantage
2	Inexperienced	10	16	Private advantage
3	Experienced[a]	10	24	Private advantage
4	Experienced[b]	8	22	Private advantage
5	Inexperienced	12	18	Standard
6	Inexperienced	11[c]	18	Standard
7	Experienced	14	24	Standard

[a]Advantaged/disadvantaged bidder positions maintained for five consecutive periods.

[b]Results of all auctions were publicly posted. Two players who participated in session 3 participated in this session as well.

[c]With an odd number of players, one player each round was unpaired, but that player did not know that until told the results of the auction. Subjects received a fixed payment of $1.00 for each such auction period.

For each experiment, the subjects drew their own observations from containers filled with random values.[7] In each round, subjects were paired anonymously for a second-price auction based on the values that they drew.[8] In the standard auctions there was no additional private value. In the private-value-advantage auctions it was known by both players that one bidder's value was $\tilde{V} + K$ and that the other's was $\tilde{V}$, where K was known to be 1 and $\tilde{V} + K$ unknown. Although the players did not know the identity of their opponent, they did know the value of K and whether they were advantaged or disadvantaged in a particular auction.

After each round, players learned the bid of their competitor and the value of the object, and in all but one session (see Table 9.1) did not learn the results of any other auction. Each session lasted two hours. Most of the participants were economics undergraduates recruited from advanced and introductory classes. To allow for some initial confusion, we began each session with inexperienced bidders with two practice rounds, and we discarded the first five periods of bidding. We also discarded the first few (four for asymmetric, two for symmetric) periods of bidding with experienced bidders.

The players were matched by prior assignment based on a round-robin format. Any pair of players were matched at most three times in a single session, and the players did not know the matching schedule. Since the players were matched so infrequently and there was no communication between rounds, it seems unlikely that there would be any incentive to alter one's strategy to attempt to create a bidding reputation.[9]

We changed formats slightly with experienced bidders in efforts to speed convergence to equilibrium. In the first experienced private-value-advantage session, bidders maintained an advantaged or disadvantaged position for sets of five periods in an effort to provide more time to adjust to the different circumstances of advantaged and disadvantaged bidders.[10] In the second experienced private-value-advantage bidders' session we employed a public information format in which players learned the results of the other auctions as well as their own. At the end of each round, the results of all the auctions were written on a blackboard rather than dispensed to each person privately. In addition, these outcomes were segregated so that cases where advantaged bidders won were posted separately from those where disadvantaged bidders won. Our purpose was to speed the transmission of information about the results of the game, since the disadvantaged players won relatively few auctions. Our conjecture was that a public information format would demonstrate that disadvantaged players tended to lose money when winning an auction, thus giving them additional incentive to adjust their bids towards the equilibrium where those players bid low enough to lose every auction.[11] As the analysis below indicates (see especially the support for Conclusion 5.3), these minor differences in treatment conditions had no material effect on behavior, so that we are fully justified in pooling the experienced subject data.

4. Experimental Hypotheses

The focus of the experiment was to test the Nash equilibrium prediction of Bikhchandani. For alternate hypotheses, we selected a number of other predictive models. While these alternate models predict disparate bidding results, Nash equilibrium is the only model that suggests that bidding should be systematically higher for bidders in the standard auction than for disadvantaged bidders in the private-value-advantage case. The other models (with the exception of the rivalrous model) conclude that since the distribution of individual signals and value are the same for symmetric and disadvantaged bidders, their bids should be the same in both cases. The expected-value model makes an explicit point prediction, while the other models merely make predictions for the general relationship between symmetric and asymmetric bids.
    The set of hypothesized models is as follows:

1. Nash equilibrium

There will be an explosive effect from the private-value advantage [prediction (N2)]. The advantaged bidder will win the vast majority of the auctions [prediction (N3)]. In comparison to the standard case, the disadvantaged ($K = 0$) bidder will reduce his bids while the advantaged player will increase her bids by more than the $1 K-value [prediction (N1)].

1a. Rationalizability and iterated weak dominance

Rationalizability makes no prediction whatsoever about the bidders' choice of strategies because of the infinite set of strategies available to them. The concept of iterated weak dominance makes almost the same prediction for behavior as the Nash equilibrium requirement for the private-value-advantage case. We distinguish between the two by the logic behind iterated weak dominance, which eliminates some bidding strategies prior to others. As shown by the analysis in the Appendix, the first serious requirement of iterated dominance is that advantaged bidders should bid at least $8.00 and win every auction with an observation above $3.00 and that disadvantaged bidders with observations in the range (1.00, 2.00) should lose every auction and bid no more than $3.00.

As noted above, iterated weak dominance makes no prediction about the comparison between standard and private-value-advantage auctions, because it does not eliminate any strategies in the standard second-price auction.

2. Expected value

Bidders will bid the expected value given their signal rather than the Nash equilibrium bid. In the standard case, that is the function $B_{EV}(x) = x + 2.5$. An advantaged bidder would add a dollar for the private-value-advantage case, while the disadvantaged bidder would not adjust at all. That is, the bid function for the disadvantaged bidders is the same as in the standard second-price auction.

Expected value is the classic example of bidders incurring a winner's curse. In the standard second-price auction, in a pure world of expected-value bidders, anyone with a private signal below the average value cannot win money in any auction: a bidder with a signal $x < 2.50$ wins the auction against a bidder with a signal $y \le x$, getting an asset of value $x + y$ for the price $2.5 + y$, resulting in a certain loss. In contrast, with expected-value bidding, bidders with signals $x > 2.50$ will make positive profits. Thus, bidding according to expected value, particularly for $x \le 2.50$, provides evidence of the winner's curse even when these bidders have the good fortune of not winning the auction. Judging from the results of earlier experiments (Kagel and Levin, 1986; Kagel et al., 1995), we expected that some form of winner's curse would prevail, at least in early bidding rounds.

Figure 9.1 depicts the expected value and Nash equilibrium bid functions for the standard case and for the advantaged bidders in the private-value-advantage case. For the standard auction, note that expected-value bids fall below equilibrium bids for the lowest private observations and then cross the equilibrium bidding curve exactly at $x = 2.5$. These relationships offer good possibilities for comparing the models in relation to the data.

3. Rivalrous bidding

The strong form of the rivalrous bidding model predicts that disadvantaged bidders will confuse the desire for profits with a desire to win the auction, bidding more aggressively than bidders in the standard-auction case to overcome their private-value disadvantages. An extreme version of the rivalrous

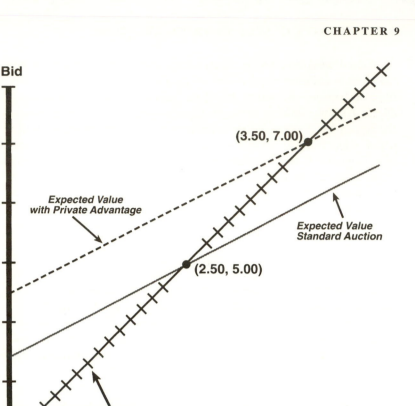

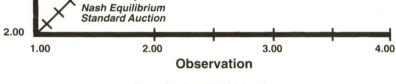

Figure 9.1. Possible bid functions.

bidding model predicts that the disadvantaged bidders will increase their bids sufficiently to completely offset the private-value advantage. In this case, the disadvantaged bidders will win 50% of the auctions, just as they would in the symmetric value case.

We will also consider a weaker version of the rivalrous bidding model in which disadvantaged bidders bid above equilibrium, not so much to win, but out of a rivalrous effort to deny large profits to the advantaged bidder.

4. Epsilon-equilibrium

Bidders will adjust to play approximate best responses to the aggregate set of strategies played by their opponents, but will not necessarily reach equilibrium. The ε-equilibrium calculations make no specific prediction about bidding strategies except that they will be close to (i.e. within ε of) best responses to rivals' play. Epsilon-equilibrium calculations provide measures of the (expected) cost of failing to respond optimally to the play of others.

In calculating best responses we constructed an empirical distribution of signals and bids from the experimental data and conducted an exhaustive Monte Carlo simulation for each combination of experimental conditions ({Experienced, Inexperienced} × {Standard, Private Value Advantage}). In effect, we calculated the average payoff for each bid in the sample when matched up with every other bid and x-value in the distribution, including that player's other bids. This procedure is consistent with that of Fudenberg and Levine (1997) for estimating deviations from best responses in normal-form, complete-information games. Our experiment is complicated by uncertainty and the vast number of possible x-values. We weight each empirical observation equally in our simulation, with the result that the x-values which were drawn more frequently in the experiments are also given more weight in the simulation.[12] The empirical bidding function underlying the simulations is equivalent to an explicit mixed strategy that replicates the randomness of the environment faced by bidders.[13]

5. Experimental Results

We now test the series of predictive models described in the previous section: Nash equilibrium [and the individual hypotheses (N1) to (N3)], weak-dominance rationalizability, expected-value bidding, rivalrous bidding (in two forms) and ε-equilibrium. We present our findings in the form of seven conclusions.

We begin by summarizing the bidding outcomes from the symmetric case in Conclusion 5.1 to set a baseline for comparison with the asymmetric auctions. Conclusion 5.2 rejects the strong version of the rivalrous bidding model. Conclusion 5.3 rejects the weak-dominance rationalizability model and hypothesis (N3) of the Nash model. Conclusion 5.4 rejects the remaining properties (N1) and (N2) of the Nash model, while providing support for the expected-value model. Conclusion 5.5 studies the ε-equilibrium predictions and shows that advantaged bidders are closer to using optimal strategies than are disadvantaged bidders. Conclusion 5.6 provides some counterevidence against the expected-value model and for prediction (N1) of the Nash model. Conclusion 5.7 rules out the weaker version of the rivalrous bidding model: that disadvantaged bidders increase their bids with the aim of reducing the profits of their opponents.

We now consider the results from the symmetric auctions. While we ran more sessions with the private-value advantage, we actually have a larger data set for standard auctions because bidders face the same game and the same situation in every period in that case. Further, the consistency of the standard auction format may also speed up learning (although we do not specifically test for this), since players do not have to learn how to play from the advantaged and disadvantaged positions. The equilibrium and expected-value predictions are the same in every period of the standard auction: $B^*(x) = 2x$, $B_{EV}(x) = x + 2.5$.

Conclusion 5.1. *There are strong traces of the winner's curse for the standard (control) case. Expected value is a better predictive model for the standard case* *than the Nash equilibrium prediction. Further, bidders almost invariably lose money, conditional on wining, for signal values of $2.50 or below, consistent with the presence of a winner's curse. However, what adjustments there are between experienced and inexperienced cases move bidding closer to the predictions of the Nash-equilibrium bidding model.*

The first evidence of the winner's curse is the simple fact that the winning bidder frequently lost money: 39.8%, of the auctions with inexperienced bidders and 29.2%, of the auctions with experienced bidders resulted in losses, despite the fact that the winning bidder always makes a profit in any Nash equilibrium. As a result, for inexperienced bidders profits averaged 18 cents per player and prices averaged $4.62 per auction period, while for experienced bidders profits averaged 23 cents per player and prices averaged $4.63 per auction period. This contrasts with equilibrium predictions of an average profit of 50 cents per player and an average price of $4.00 in each auction.

While there is an element of randomness in the players' bids, this set of results is much more consistent with the expected-value model than with the Nash model. Both models predict that the player with the higher draw will win the auction. But in contrast to the Nash prediction, expected-value bidding produces an expected profit of 25 cents to each bidder, an average price of $4.50, and losses in 25% of the auctions, quite close to the results for the experienced bidders. Further, consistent with the expected-value model's predictions, when bidders won the auction with signal values of $2.50 or less, they usually earned negative profits (66% of the time for inexperienced bidders and 65% of the time for experienced bidders), while with signal values above $2.50 they usually earned positive profits (83% and 76% of the time for inexperienced and experienced bidders, respectively). Average profits show an even more dramatic effect of winning with low compared to high signal values: for experienced bidders these average -36 cents conditional on winning with a signal value of $2.50 or less, compared to $+73$ cents conditional on winning with a signal value greater then $2,50.

The empirical bid distribution gives further support to the expected-value model, though it demonstrates that expected value does not fully describe the actions of the bidders. Bids fall almost exclusively above the equilibrium prediction for draws below $2.25, and almost exclusively below the equilibrium prediction for draws above $3.25. That bias in the residuals relative to the equilibrium fit indicates that the slope of the empirical bid function is much less than that of the Nash equilibrium, just as implied by expected-value bidding. However, bids also tend to be higher than the expected-value prediction for the highest signal values, though the bias is much less than for the Nash bidding model.

Table 9.2 reports error-components estimates of bid functions for the standard auctions which confirm these results. The estimated bid function is

$$B_{it} = \alpha_0 + \alpha_1 x_{it} + \varepsilon_{it}, \qquad i = 1, \ldots, N, t = 1, \ldots, T,$$

TABLE 9.2
Estimates of Error-Component Bid Functions for Standard Auctions

Bidders			R^2	F-Test Nash	F-Test Expected Value	Number of Observations
Inexperienced, $B_{it} =$	2.64	$+ 1.13x_{it}$	0.47	59.8	1.55	299
	$(0.68)^b$	$(0.08)^b$		(<0.01)	(0.21)	
Experienced, $B_{it} =$	1.99	$+ 1.34x_{it}$	0.75	80.9	22.6	308
	$(0.35)^b$	$(0.05)^b$		(<0.01)	(<0.01)	

[a]Standard errors in parentheses.
[b]Significantly different from 0 at the 0.01 level.

where the error term $\varepsilon_{it} = u_t + v_{it}$ is made up of a subject-specific error term u_i and an auction-period error term v_{it}.[14] This model can accommodate the Nash bidding hypothesis ($\alpha_0 = 0$, $\alpha_1 = 2$) and the expected-value hypothesis ($\alpha_0 = 2.5$, $\alpha_1 = 1$). F-tests of these two hypotheses are reported in Table II along with the coefficient estimates.

For inexperienced subjects, the F-statistic shows that we cannot reject expected-value bidding For experienced bidders, the results are sufficiently distinct from the two point predictions ($2x$ for Nash equilibrium, $x + 2.5$ for expected value) to reject them both immediately. Still, the results are closer to expected value thin to equilibrium. As with the profit data, what changes there are in going from inexperienced to experienced bidders show movement in the direction of the Nash equilibrium model's prediction, as the slope is increasing and the intercept is decreasing.[15]

The ε-equilibrium calculations measure the expected cost of deviating from a best response to the sample population's behavior. Overall, experienced bidders were within 7.1 cents of the optimal payoff against the empirical distribution, compared to 12.3 cents for inexperienced bidders.[16] Here too there are important differences in deviations from optimality for signal values of $2.50 or less compared to higher signal values, with the former showing losses of 12.4 cents for experienced subjects and 18.1 cents for inexperienced Subjects relative to the expected payoffs from optimal bidding.

We now consider the results for the private-value-advantage auctions. Most of our comparative statics results will rely on comparisons with the standard (control) auctions just discussed.

Conclusion 5.2. *There is little support for the strong form of the rivalrous bidding model: Although disadvantaged players consistently bid more than predicted in equilibrium, they bid consistently less then the advantaged bidders. Further, disadvantaged bidders bid the same or less than in the standard auctions in the range of the highest signal values, those signal values where they are most likely to win the auctions.*

There is no evidence that disadvantaged bidders are completely rivalrous, increasing their bids to win 50%, of the auctions. In fact, advantaged ($K = 1$) bidders win 62% of the auctions with inexperienced bidders and 71% of auctions with experienced bidders, both of which are significantly greater than 50%.

More generally, the rivalrous bidding model predicts that disadvantaged bidders will bid more than bidders in the standard second-price auctions. Tests of this hypothesis are offered in Table 9.3, where we pool the data from the standard auctions with bids of disadvantaged bidders and estimate the error-components bid function

$$B_{it} = \alpha_0 + \alpha_1 x_{it} + \alpha_2 D x_{it} + \alpha_3 D_i + \varepsilon_{it}.$$

In this equation, D is a dummy variable that takes on a value of 1 in the private advantage auctions and 0 in the standard auctions. An F-test of the joint hypothesis that α_2 and α_3 both equal 0 is reported in Table III along with the coefficient estimates.

For inexperienced bidders, the F-statistic indicates no significant differences between disadvantaged bidders and bidders in the standard auctions. This is, of course, inconsistent with the strong form of the rivalrous bidding hypothesis. For experienced bidders, the disadvantaged bidders bid more over lower signal values (the coefficient of the intercept dummy variable D_i is positive and statistically significant), but bid less over higher signal values (the coefficient for the slope dummy variable $D x_{it}$ is negative and statistically significant). The average disadvantaged bid is less than the average standard auction bid for signal values greater than $1.80. Given that disadvantaged bidders rarely win auctions with these lower signal values (experienced disadvantaged bidders *lose* 83% of all auctions for which they have signal values of $2.50 or less) and given that their bids are less over higher signal values, we do not count this as evidence for the strong form of the rivalrous bidding hypothesis. However, given that bidding is well above equilibrium in the standard auctions with lower signal values, the fact that bids of disadvantaged bidders are yet higher suggests the weaker form of rivalrous bidding—that disadvantaged bidders increase their bids to reduce the profits of their opponents. We discuss this possibility at the end of this section of the paper.

Conclusion 5.3. *We reject weak-dominance rationalizability and hypothesis (N3) of the Nash model. Advantaged bidders win more than 50% of the auctions, but far less than 100% as both Nash equilibrium bidding and weak-dominance rationalizability require. Further, there is little evidence for weak-dominance rationalizability, as both advantaged and disadvantaged bidders fail to satisfy the first serious requirements of iterated dominance.*

The advantaged bidders won 70.9% of the auctions for experienced bidders and 62.0% of the auctions for inexperienced bidders. Recall that weak-dominance-rationalizability requires that they will 100% of the auctions. Further, the first serious round of deletion of weakly dominated (rationalizable) strategies re-

TABLE 9.3

Bidding in Private-Advantage Auctions with $K = O$ Compared with Bidding in Standard Auctions[a]

Bidders		R^2	F-Test: No Difference[b] (prob F = 1.0)	Implied Bid Difference When D = 1		Number of Observations
				x = $1.00	$4.00	
Inexperienced, $B_{it} = 2.59 + 1.15x_{it} - 0.21Dx_{it} + 0.44D_i$ $(0.58)^c$ $(0.08)^c$ (0.15) (0.40)		0.45	1.34 (>0.25)	0.23	−0.40	419
Experienced, $B_{it} = 2.15 + 1.34x_{it} - .50Dx_{it} + 0.90D_i$ $(0.39)^c$ $(0.05)^c$ $(0.08)^d$ $(0.34)^c$		0.70	23.9 (<.001)	0.40	−1.10	483

[a]$D = 1$ in private advantage auctions; otherwise $D = 0$.

[b]Tests joint hypothesis that coefficients for Dx_{it} and D_i are both O.

[c]Significantly different from 0 at 1% level.

[d]Significantly different from 0 at 5% level.

quires that disadvantaged bidders with signal values of 2.00 or less never bid above 3.00 (see the Appendix). Nevertheless, this fails to be satisfied 86% of the time with inexperienced bidders and 83% of the time for experienced bidders. In addition, the first serious round of deletion of weakly dominated (rationalizable) strategies also requires that advantaged bidders with signal values of 3.00 or more should never bid below 8.00. Nevertheless, this fails to be satisfied 73% of the time for inexperienced bidders and 71% of the time for experienced bidders.

The next three conclusions relate to the comparative static implications of the Nash equilibrium bidding model resulting from the introduction of asymmetries.

Conclusion 5.4. *Contrary to hypotheses (N1) and (N2) of the Nash model, the effect of the private-value advantage on bid's and prices is proportional rather than explosive. The effect of the private-value advantage on bids and prices is closer to the predictions of the expected-value model than the Nash bidding model.*

Nash-equilibrium bidding theory requires advantaged bidders to bid $3.00 more than disadvantaged bidders with the same signal, compared to the expected-value model's prediction of a $1.00 difference in these bids. Table 9.4 tests this prediction through error-components estimates of the bid function for private-value-advantage auctions. Two alternative specifications are employed in the first specification we impose the restriction, implied by both the expected-value and Nash models, that the slope of the bid function does not vary as a function of being advantaged or disadvantaged. Instead, only the intercept changes in the equation

$$B_{it} = \alpha_0 + \alpha_1 x_{it} + \alpha_2 DK_{it} + \varepsilon_{it},$$

where $DK_{it} = 1$ when $K = 0$ and $DK_{it} = 0$ when $K = 1$. Under this specification the expected-value model predicts $\alpha_0 = 3.5$, $\alpha_1 = 1.0$, and $\alpha_1 = -1.0$. For both inexperienced and experienced bidders, this is very close to the estimated coefficient values. We are unable to reject a null hypothesis of the expected-value model at conventional significance levels for both inexperienced and experienced bidders. For the Nash bidding model, $\alpha_0 = 4.0$, $\alpha_1 = 1.0$, and $\alpha_2 = -3.0$. An F-test decisively rejects these restrictions for both inexperienced and experienced bidders, primarily because the coefficient α_2 is too small.

In the second specification, we drop the restriction that the slope coefficient is the same for advantaged and disadvantaged bidders, giving the equation

$$B_{it} = \alpha_0 + \alpha_1 x_{it} + \alpha_2 DK_{it} + \alpha_3 DKx_{it} + \varepsilon_{it},$$

where $DKx_{it} = x_{it}$, when $K = 0$ and $DKx_{it} = 0$ when $K = 1$. For inexperienced bidders, the value of α_3 is close to zero and not significant. For experienced bidders, α_3 is negative and statistically significant, while α_2 remains negative and statistically significant as well. So the difference between advantaged and disadvantaged bids grows with signal values. The minimum

TABLE 9.4

Estimates of Error-Component Bid Functions for Private-Advantage Auctions

Bidders	B_{it}[a]	R^2	F-test Nash	F-test Expected Value	Number of Observations
Inexperienced	3.82 $(0.80)^b$ $+$ $0.92x_{it}$ $(0.07)^b$ $-$ $0.73DK_{it}$ $(0.13)^b$	0.49	161.8 (<0.001)	1.85 (0.14)	242
	3.84 $(0.82)^c$ $+$ $0.91x_{it}$ $(0.10)^b$ $-$ $0.75DK_{it}$ $(0.38)^c$ $+$ $0.01DKx_{it}$ (0.14)	0.49	—	—	242
Experienced	3.94 $(0.51)^b$ $+$ $0.98x_{it}$ $(0.05)^b$ $-$ $1.18DK_{it}$ $(0.08)^b$	0.069	255.7 (<0.001)	1.98 (0.12)	344
	3.68 (0.51) $+$ $1.09x_{it}$ $(0.06)^b$ $-$ $0.64DK_{it}$ $(0.24)^b$ $-$ $0.22DKx_{it}$ $(0.09)^c$	0.69	—	—	344

[a] $DK_{it} = 1$ if $K = 0$, $= 0$ if $K = 1$; $DKx_{it} = x_{it}$ if $K = 0$, $= 0$ if $K = 1$.
[b] Significantly different from 0 at the 1% level or better.
[c] Significantly different from 0 at the 5% level or better.

difference between these predicted bids is $0.86 at the lowest signal value and the maximum difference is $1.52 at the highest signal value, $4.00. Thus, although there are significant differences in bids between advantaged and disadvantaged bidders, these differences are closer to the prediction of the expected-value model than to the prediction of the Nash model for almost the entire range of signal values. Finally, applying these regression specifications to individual subject data, only 1 of 16 experienced subjects consistently bid closer to the Nash than to the expected-value model's prediction.[17] Therefore, we conclude that the introduction of asymmetries does not produce anything approaching the explosive effect on bids and prices that the. Nash model predicts. In what follows, we try to understand the mechanism behind this outcome.

Conclusion 5.5. *The ε-equilibrium calculations show that the advantaged bidders are close to making optimal responses. In contrast, the disadvantaged bidders show the strongest deviations from optimal responses: they consistently bid too much, earning negative average profits and sharply reducing the profit opportunities for the advantaged bidders.*

The ε-equilibrium calculations show that experienced advantaged bidders were quite close to optimal best responses: they were bidding slightly below the optimum, averaging 5.4 cents below the maximum average return (bids averaged 11 cents below the optimum). In contrast, experienced disadvantaged bidders earned negative average profits (−12.6 cents; −40.0 cents conditional on winning) and were losing an average of 16.1 cents relative to optimal bidding. Further, their bids were a full $1.31 above the best response against the empirical distribution. For signal values below $3.00, most bids by disadvantaged players incurred average losses of 20 cents, or more in the simulation. Since they win only about 20% of the auctions for such observations, that implies an expected loss of $1 per auction conditional on winning. In this range of signals, bids by disadvantaged players are commonly $2 or more above the empirical best-response bid. But winning the auction for such observations may be a sufficiently rare event that there is little learning about the winner's curse. Finally, we see no noticeable differences in bidding with and without public information regarding auction outcomes. Either subjects did not notice or pay attention to the additional information, or they simply chose not to bid less when disadvantaged in spite of occasional losses.

A comparison between experienced and inexperienced bidders in the private-value-advantage auctions shows that experienced advantaged bidders increased their bids by 23 cents and experienced disadvantaged bidders reduced their bids by 16 cents on average. For the entire range of x-values, advantaged bidders won the auction more frequently in the experienced case than in the inexperienced case. For $x > 3.00$, the winning percentage increases from 79% to 98%. The increased bidding by experienced advantaged bidders moved them closer to optimal responses (inexperienced bidders averaged 11.2 cents below optimal earnings vs. 5.4 cents for the experienced case). In contrast, even though bidding less, the experienced disadvantaged bidders were worse off than in the inexperienced case (an average loss of 12.6 cents as opposed to 4.1 cents). The increased bidding by advantaged bidders simply provided many fewer profit opportunities than in the inexperienced case for disadvantaged bidders.

Conclusion 5.6. *Contrary to the expected-value model's prediction, there is a clear tendency for experienced disadvantaged bidders to bid less aggressively than in the standard auctions over higher signal values. This provides some weak support for hypothesis (N1) of the Nash model.*

With pure expected-value bidding, the disadvantaged bidders should bid no differently than in standard auctions. As the regression results in Table 9.4 show, a null hypothesis of expected-value bidding for inexperienced bidders would not be rejected at standard significance levels. However, for experienced disadvantaged bidders, there is reduced bidding over higher signal values compared to the standard auctions. That effect is inconsistent with pure expected-value bidding.

Trends within the experienced sessions reinforce the conclusion that experience leads to less aggressive bidding by disadvantaged players with high signals. We divided the experienced data into two subcategories of *early* and *late* in the session. The estimated bid function for the second half of the session gives bids of up to 70 cents more for disadvantaged bidders at low signal values than in the first half of the session, and tip to 35 cents less at high signal values than in the first half. In contrast, the standard auction bids seem to increase for all ranges of signals in the last half of the experienced session. One interpretation of the shift by disadvantaged bidders is that they learn to reduce their bids for high signals because that is the one situation where they most frequently win the auction and lose money. In contrast, the primary effect of higher bids by disadvantaged bidders with low signals is to reduce the profits of their advantaged opponents.

The question remains here as to what motivates these higher bids by disadvantaged bidders with lower signal values. One possibility that suggests itself is the weak rivalrous bidding hypothesis as described earlier in Section 4. It may be that disadvantaged bidders are reluctant to bid low enough that they will never win an auction, since such passive play would result in a very uneven distribution of earnings in favor of the advantaged bidder (minimum average profits of $1.50 in each auction for the advantaged bidder versus $0 for themselves). At least one player seems to have been motivated by this fact: paraphrasing the remarks of one subject on exiting the auction, "I know I should bid less with $K = 0$, but this just increases the profits of my opponent."

To examine this possibility, we looked at what disadvantaged bidders did following a failure to win the item when a winning bid would have earned negative profits [i.e., $x + y < B_A(x)$]. In general, disadvantaged bidders bid more aggressively following a failure to win the auction even when a winning bid would have lost money. This happened 63% of the time for inexperienced subjects and 56%, of the time for experienced subjects.[18] This tendency to bid more aggressively was *not* strongly conditioned on the disadvantaged bidder's signal value, *x*. Rather, it was strongly conditioned on whether or not the advantaged bidder earned positive or negative profits: Experienced bidders bid more aggressively 69%, of the time following the advantaged bidder winning and making a positive profit versus 20%, of the time following the advantaged bidder winning and making a negative profit ($Z = 3.63, p < .01$), even though a higher winning bid would have resulted in losses in both cases.[19] This would appear to be symptomatic of confusion (failure to think through the implications of winning with a higher bid) rather than rivalrous bidding designed to deny advantaged bidders high earnings.[20] This interpretation is reinforced by the fact that the same pattern prevailed in the standard auctions: Losing bids were followed by relatively more aggressive bids 56% of the time for inexperienced bidders and 63% of the time for experienced bidders even though the losing bidders would have lost money had they won. Here too, bidding was more aggressive when the winner made positive profits compared to when the winner made negative profits (77% vs. 36%, $Z = 4.98, p < .01$ for inexperienced bidders; 62% vs. 52%, $Z = 1.28, p < .10$, one-tailed test for experienced bidders). Finally, note that for both disadvantaged bidders and bidders in the standard auctions, winning and losing money typically resulted in less aggressive bidding in the next auction period (72% of the time for disadvantaged bidders; 70% of the time in the standard auctions).

Conclusion 5.7. *In both the standard and private-value-advantage auctions, winning the item and losing money tends to result in less aggressive bidding for the next auction period. This tends to correct for the winner's curse. However, in both auctions, failure to win the item when the winner made positive profits promotes more aggressive bidding ill the next auction period even in cases where the losing bidder would have succumbed to the winner's curse (lost money) had he won the item. The failure to fully appreciate the consequences of winning in the latter cases tends to perpetuate the winner's curse.*

The fact that the same phenomenon occurs in both the symmetric and asymmetric auctions leads us to reject the weaker form of the rivalrous bidding model in favor of a "confused bidder" model.

6. Summary and Conclusion

In our standard second-price common-value auctions, bidders suffer from a winner's curse, bidding closer to expected value than to the Nash equilibrium. Introduction of a private-value advantage generates changes in bidding. Among inexperienced bidders there are no significant differences between disadvantaged bidders and bidders in standard actions. Among experienced bidders, disadvantaged bidders bid less than standard-auction bidders over higher signal values, those for which they were most likely to win the auction. However, disadvantaged players still bid substantially more than in equilibrium, earning average profits of -40 cents conditional on winning for experienced bidders.

In contrast, experienced advantaged bidders, while not bidding as aggressively as the Nash model requires, are within 5 cents, on average, of maximum possible earnings, given the overly aggressive bidding of the disadvantaged bidders. The net result is that the existence of asymmetric valuations does not produce anything approaching the explosive change in bids, and reduction in revenues, that the Nash bidding model predicts, the primary impediment to this outcome being overly aggressive bidding by disadvantaged bidders.

Experienced subjects consistently bid closer to the Nash equilibrium than inexperienced bidders. But these changes are small and at times unsteady.[21] The introduction of a private-value advantage into the bidding might be expected to speed convergence to equilibrium (and elimination of the winner's curse), since the winner's curse will be exacerbated from the symmetric case unless disadvantaged players reduce their bids. However, a winner's curse remains, as disadvantaged bidders continue to lose money, primarily as a result of overly aggressive bidding with relatively low signal values.

Appendix

Proof of Iterated Weak-Dominance Results

Step one: Bidders must bid within the range of possible values conditional on their observations. This restricts the advantaged bidder to bids in the range $(x + 2, x + 5)$ given an observation of x, and the disadvantaged bidder to bids in the range $(y + 1, y + 4)$ given an observation of y.

Step two: Disadvantaged bidders with y less than \$2.00 cannot profit now from winning the auction. They face a price of at least $x + 2$ for an object whose value is $x + y < x + 2$ for $y < 2$. In this instance, they should bid no more than \$3.00 (the minimum advantaged bid retained from step one).

Similarly, advantaged bidders with observations greater than \$3.00 always profit from winning the auction. They face a price of at most $y + 4$ for an object whose value is $x + y + 1 > y + 4$ for $x > 3$. In this instance, they should bid at least \$8.00 (the maximum disadvantaged bid retained from step one).

Otherwise, bids may remain in the ranges $(y + 1, y + 4)$ for disadvantaged bidders with observations in $(2,4)$ and $(x + 2, x + 5)$ for advantaged bidders with observations in $(1,3)$.

Step three: The strategies remaining from step two yield competitive auctions for the cases where $x \in (1,3)$, $y \in (2,4)$. The minimum value for the advantaged bidder in these cases is $x + 3$, since $y \geq 2$, and the maximum value for the disadvantaged bidder in these cases is $y + 3$, since $x \leq 3$.

Therefore, the advantaged bidder must now bid in the range $(x + 3, x + 5)$ for observations in the range $(1,3)$, and the disadvantaged bidder must bid in the range $(y + 1, y + 3)$ for observations in the range $(2,4)$.

Step four: Consider the same range of observations (1,3) for the advantaged bidder and (2,4) for the disadvantaged bidder. Now advantaged bidders always prefer to win the auction with observations of at least $2.00, since the maximum price for them is $y + 3$ and the value is $x + y + 1$. Disadvantaged bidders always prefer to lose the auction with observations of $3.00 or less. As a result, the advantaged bidder should bid at least $7.00 for an observation in the range (2,3), and disadvantaged bidders should bid no more than $4.00 for any observation in the range (2,3).

Step five: Now the auction is competitive only if the advantaged bidder has an observation x, in the range (1, 2), bidding in the range $(x + 3, x + 5)$, and the disadvantaged bidder has an observation y, in the range (3,4), bidding in the range $(y + 1, y + 3)$.

The value for an advantaged bidder under these conditions is at least $x + 4$, and the value for a disadvantaged bidder is at most $y + 2$. Thus they should adjust their bidding ranges to $(x + 4, x + 5)$ and $(y + 1, y + 2)$, respectively.

Step six: The maximum bid by a disadvantaged bidder is now $y + 2$, and the minimum bid by an advantaged bidder is now $x + 4$. Therefore, advantaged bidders always wish to win the auction and should bid at least $6.00, while disadvantaged bidders always wish to lose the auction and should bid at most $5.00.

At this point, the advantaged bidders always win the auction, the disadvantaged bidders always lose the auction and the maximum expected price is $4.00 (with the disadvantaged bidders bidding no more than $3.00 with observations less than $2.00, no more than $4.00 with observations less than $3.00, and no more than $5.00 for any observation).

Proof of first-price auction result

We show that there is a first-price auction equilibrium for the asymmetric (perturbed) auction of the experiment with bids within ε of the bids for the symmetric game. For simplicity, we specialize to the case where each signal is $U(0,1)$, player 1's value is $x + y + \varepsilon$, and player 2's value is $x + y$.

Fix the strategy $b_2(y)$ for player 2, and consider player 1's best response for an arbitrary draw of x. With a bid of $b_1(x)$, player 1 wins the auction at price b_1 whenever player 2's observation is less than $b_2^{-1}(b_1)$. Therefore, player 1 chooses the bid b_1 to solve

$$\max_{b_1} \int_0^{b_2^{-1}(b_1)} \left(x + y + \varepsilon - b_1 \right) f(y)\, dy$$

$$\max_{b_1} \frac{y^2}{2} + y \left[x + \varepsilon - b_1 \right] \Bigg|_0^{b_2^{-1}(b_1)}$$

We look for an equilibrium with linear bidding strategies: $b_1(x) = a_1 x + c_1$, $b_2(y) = a_2 y + c_2$. Then $b_2^{-1}(b_1) = (b_1 - c_2)/a_2$, and player 1's maximization problem simplifies to

$$\max_{b_1} \frac{1}{2}\left(\frac{b_1 - c_2}{a_2}\right)^2 + \left(x + \varepsilon\right)\left(\frac{b_1 - c_2}{a_2}\right) - \frac{b_1(b_1 - c_2)}{a^2}$$

The first-order condition for this problem gives the outcome

$$b = \frac{a_2 x + a_2 \varepsilon + (a_2 - 1)c_2}{2a_2 - 1}.$$

Similarly, $b_2 = [a_1 y + (a_1 - 1)c_1]/(2a_1 - 1)$. For these to hold simultaneously, it must be that

$$a_1 = \frac{a_2}{2a_2 - 1'} \tag{1}$$

$$a_2 = \frac{a_1}{2a_1 - 1'} \tag{2}$$

$$c_1 = \frac{[(a_2 - 1)c_2 + a_2 \varepsilon]}{2a_2 - 1} \tag{3}$$

$$c_2 = \frac{[(a_1 - 1)c_1]}{2a_1 - 1} \tag{4}$$

Note that (1) implies (2) and vice versa. Substituting (1) and (2) into (3) and (4) gives

$$c_1 = (1 - a_1)c_2 + a_1 \varepsilon, \tag{3'}$$

$$c_2 = (1 - a_2)c_1. \tag{4'}$$

Putting all equations in terms of a_2 gives a set of three equations:

$$c_1 = \varepsilon/a_2, \tag{5}$$

$$c_2 = (1 - a_2)\varepsilon/a_2, \tag{6}$$

$$a_2 = \frac{a_2}{2a_2 - 1}. \tag{7}$$

At this point, the choice of a_2 is arbitrary, but there is also a boundary condition. In a first-price auction, the top possible bid by each side must be the same. Otherwise, one player should reduce the top bid, since it is possible to win with probability 1 with a lesser bid. This gives the further condition

$$a_1 + c_1 = a_2 + c_2. \tag{8}$$

The final set of equations (5)–(8) gives a quadratic equation for a_2 with the positive root $a_2 = (1 + \varepsilon) + \sqrt{1 + \varepsilon^2}/2$. The remaining parameters, a_1, c_1, c_2

are given by the appropriate equations in (5)–(8) and the value of a_2.[22] These values satisfy $1 - \varepsilon < a_1 < 1, 0 < c_1 < \varepsilon, - \varepsilon < c_2 < 0$. All bids by either player are within ε of the symmetric equilibrium bid functions $b^*(x) = x$.

Notes

We are grateful for comments from Sushil Bikhchandani, Peter Cramton, Glenn Ellison, Drew Fudenberg, David Laibson, Dan Levin, Al Roth, and Bob Wilson. Robert Avery, Alexis Miller, and Wei Lo assisted in conducting the experiments. Christopher Avery was supported by a State Farm Insurance Dissertation Fellowship and by the Stanford Center on Conflict and Negotiation; John Kagel received support from the National Science Foundation.

1. For example, in the FCC auctions it was well known that PacTel had a particular interest in acquiring licenses in Los Angeles and San Francisco (Cramton, 1997).

2. Maskin and Riley (1984) demonstrate the effect of asymmetries on first- and second-price auctions for bidders with asymmetric private values.

3. There is an alternative class (if equilibria in which the disadvantaged bidder wins each auction with certainty. Bikhchandani dismisses these equilibria because they rely on weakly dominated strategies.

4. In addition, the same qualitative results hold with a single advantaged bidder and more than one disadvantaged bidder. Thus, our use of only two bidders in the experiment should be viewed as a procedural modification.

5. The procedure of eliminating weakly dominated strategies may give different results depending on the order of the elimination of weakly dominated strategies. We follow the usual convention of eliminating all weakly dominated strategies at each stage (Fudenberg and Tirole, 1991, Sec. 11.3).

6. Note that only the symmetric equilibrium of a standard second-price auction produces the same expected revenue as that of a first-price auction. The asymmetric equilibria of second-price auctions produce much less revenue than the symmetric outcomes.

7. These experiments were conducted by hand. Copies of the instructions employed are available on request.

8. Theory predicts the same experimental results with a single advantaged bidder and more than one disadvantaged bidder, since Nash equilibrium predicts that an advantaged bidder must win every auction, regardless of how many disadvantaged bidders participate in the auction. Further, use of more than one disadvantaged bidder increases the costs of the experiments substantially.

9. Subjects were told that they were matched according to a random matching plan designed to minimize the chances of repeated interactions.

10. Player pairing continued to rotate between auction periods, so that the cost of this adjustment was that players could no longer be paired with all of the other participants evenly. To control for any confound this might have introduced, we used the same block-design with the experienced symmetric bidders.

11. Even when losing in auction, the players received enough information to figure out their profits had they bid high enough to win. However, it seems clear that not all players will bother with such calculations (see below) so that we thought that observing all of the actual losses and gains might speed up the learning process.

12. A Monte Carlo simulation which made all x-values equally likely would have to give more weight to the bids corresponding to less common x-values in the experiments.

13. In conducting the simulations it would be inappropriate to create a pure-strategy empirical bid function by averaging the set of bids for each observation, as this would disrupt the probabilities of winning and losing with a given bid. For example, the best response to a certain bid of $5.00 is likely to be much different than the best response to a bid of $8.00 with probability one-half and $2.00 with probability one-half.

14. Standard assumptions were employed: $u_i \sim (0, \sigma^2_{it})$ and $v_{it} \sim (0, \sigma^2_{it})$ where the u_i and the v_{it} are independent of each other and among themselves. Baltagi's (1986) weighted least-squares computational procedure was used to invert the variance-covariance matrix. A fixed-effects error specification generated similar coefficient estimates and standard errors.

15. A regression model restricted to returning bidders shows this same pattern, with the changes in coefficient values being jointly significantly different from zero at just above the 5% level. Thus, the movement towards Nash equilibrium, although small, does not reflect a self-selection effect.

16. Deviations from optimality are, of course, considerably larger in the choice space (bids) then in payoff space (costs), as the former average $0.52 mid $0.73 for inexperienced and experienced bidders respectively.

17. Applying the second regression specification to the individual subject data, we fail to reject the null hypothesis (at the .10 level or better) that $a_3 = 0$ for 12 of 16 subjects. For only one of these twelve subjects was a_2 less than $-$2, i.e., closer to the Nash equilibrium prediction. The remaining four bidders all had a's < 0, so that the difference between advantaged and disadvantaged bids grows with higher signal values. We then evaluated these four hill functions to find the value of x for which the slope coefficient declined to less than $-$2 (closer to Nash). In one case, there was no such x-value, while the average value in the other three cases was $2.67, just above the midpoint of the interval for which signal values were drawn.

18. Bidding more or less aggressively between auction periods was measured by comparing the bid less the signal value in auction t with the bid less the signal value in auction $t + 1$. The slope of the aggregate bid function with respect to own signal value is close to 1 under all treatments, which is necessary to justify this calculation. To control for the slope coefficient for own signal value differing from 1, we also measured relative aggressiveness by subtracting the hid implied by the aggregate bid function from the actual bid in each auction period and compared these differences. Our results are robust to this alternative measure. In both cases, calculations are restricted to auctions in which a player was a disadvantaged bidder.

19. Data for inexperienced bidders is too thin to reach conclusions on this score, as there were relatively few cases in which the advantaged bidder won and lost money.

20. Garvin and Kagel (1994) report similar results in first-price common-value auctions.

21. For example, a within-session analysis of bidding in the standard auctions shows that, on average, players *increased* their bids in the last half of the auction session, actually moving away from equilibrium rather than towards it.

22. With these values $c_1 > c_2$. Some of player 2's bids fall below the minimum possible bid by player 1. For those bids below c_1 to be optimal, the equilibrium bid functions must satisfy an additional boundary condition $b_2(c_1) = c_1$. But this new boundary condition is guaranteed by the first-order equations and satisfied algebraically by the given values.

References

Baltagi, B.H., 1986, "Pooling Cross-Sections with Unequal Time Lengths," *Economics Letters*, 18, 133–136.

Bikhchandani, S., 1988, "Reputations in Repeated Second-Price Auctions," *Journal of Economic Theory*, 46, 97–119.

Cramton, P., 1997, "The FCC Spectrum Auctions: An Early Assessment," *Journal of Economics and Management Strategy*, this issue.

Fudenberg, D. and D.K. Levine, 1997, "Measuring Players' Losses in Experimental Games," *Quarterly Journal of Economics*, 112, 507–536.

——— and J Tirole, 1991, *Game Theory*, Cambridge, MA: The MIT Press.

Garvin, S. and J.H. Kagel, 1994, "Learning in Common Value Auctions: Some Initial Observations," *Journal of Economic Behavior and Organization*, 25, 351–372.

Kagel, J.H. and D. Levin, 1986, "The Winner's Curse and Public Information in Common Value Auctions," *American Economic Review*, 76, 894–920.

——— and ——— 1993, "Independent Private Value Auctions: Bidder Behavior in First-, Second- and Third-Price Auctions with Varying Numbers of Bidders," *Economic Journal*, 103, 868–879.

———, ———, and R.M. Harstad, 1995, "Comparative Static Effects of Number of Bidders and Public Information on Behavior in Second-Price Common Value Auctions," *International Journal of Game Theory*, 24, 293–319.

Klemperer, P., 1997, "Almost Common Value Auctions: The 'Wallet' Game and Its Applications in Takeover Battles and PCS Actions," Mimeo, Nuffield College, Oxford University.

Levin, D. and R. Harstad, 1986, "Symmetric Bidding in Second-Price, Common-Value Auctions," *Economic Letters*, 20, 315–319.

Maskin, E.S. and J.G. Riley, 1996, "Auction Theory with Private Values," *American Economic Review*, 75, 150–155.

——— and ———, 1991, "Asymmetric Auctions," Mimeo, Harvard University.

Milgrom, P., 1981, "Rational Expectations, Information Acquisition and Competitive Bidding," *Econometrica*, 49, 921–943.

——— and R. Weber, 1982, "A Theory of Auction, and Competitive Bidding," *Econometrica*, 50, 1089–1122.

Pearce, D., 1984, "Rationalizable Strategic Behavior and the Problem of Perfection," *Econometrica*, 52, 1029–1050.

10

Learning in Common Value Auctions: Some Initial Observations

Susan Garvin and John H. Kagel

1. Introduction

Common value auctions are auctions in which the value of the item is the same to all bidders. However, bidders do not know the value of the item at the time they bid, basing their bids on private estimates (signals) related to the value. Assuming that each individual bidder's estimate of value is unbiased, and symmetry in bidding strategies (or some reasonable approximation thereof), winning bidders need to account for the adverse selection problem inherent in winning the item: the high bidder has an overly optimistic estimate of the item's value. Unless this adverse selection problem is accounted for, winning bids will result in below normal, or even negative, average profits. The systematic failure to account for the adverse selection problem is called the 'winner's curse.'

There have been numerous reports of a winner's curse in field data, particularly with respect to outer continental shelf (OCS) oil lease auctions (Capen, Clapp and Campbell, 1971; Lorenz and Dougherty, 1983). There is documentation of a strong winner's curse for inexperienced bidders in experimental auction markets (Kagel et al., 1989; Lind and Plott, 1991). However, work with experienced bidders in laboratory auction markets shows that bidders adapt, overcoming the worst effects of the winner's curse and consistently earning positive profits which average a respectable fifty percent or more of predicted (Nash equilibrium) profit (see Kagel and Levin, 1986 for auctions with small numbers of bidders, and Kagel and Levin, in preparation, for auctions with larger numbers of bidders).

The question addressed in this paper is what underlies the learning/adjustment process observed in these laboratory auction markets. To study this we mine the data from two series of laboratory auction markets. This data mining exercise not only generates insights into the learning/adjustment process for these auctions, but also generates insights relevant to other experimental settings and suggests additional experimental treatments. Learning/adjustment processes are endemic to much experimental research and are of growing importance in rationalizing the emergence of Nash equilibria (Fudenberg and Kreps, 1988; Kalai and Lehrer, 1990; Milgrom and Roberts, 1991 to cite a small part of the growing literature on this topic). This paper aims to better understand how these processes actually work.

The specific questions addressed in this paper are the following: Is the reduction in the severity of the winner's curse observed for experienced bidders simply a market selection effect whereby more aggressive bidders go bankrupt (or earn less money) and do not return for more auctions? If there is individual learning, what is the mechanism behind it? Is it strictly a school of hard knocks so that bidders only learn by winning and losing money? Is there a role for observational learning, seeing others bid and lose money and reducing bids in response to this?

The paper proceeds as follows. Sections 2 and 3 characterize the underlying structure of the experiment and the basic theoretical concepts employed in the analysis. Section 4 starts by reporting market data for inexperienced bidders, those participating in their first sealed bid auction session, compared to these same subjects participating in a second experimental session. Large differences in market outcomes between inexperienced and experienced bidders constitute the learning phenomena to be explained. The remaining parts of section 4 (i) compare bidding between returning and non-returning subjects to determine the extent to which more aggressive bidders self-select out of returning for further sessions (we find significant self-selection effects) and (ii) examine changes in bidding strategies in response to information feedback about auction outcomes, distinguishing between experiential and observational learning (both types of learning are present in the data). The concluding section of the paper summarizes our main results.

2. Experimental Design

Each experimental session consisted of a number of auction periods in which a single unit of a commodity was awarded to the high bidder in a first-price sealed bid auction. The high bidder earned a profit equal to the value of the item less his bid; all other bidders earned zero profits.

The value of the item, V, was not known at the time bids were placed and was randomly drawn each period from a uniform distribution on $(\underline{V}, \overline{V})$. Each auction period, each bidder received a private information signal, s, randomly drawn from a uniform distribution on $(V - \varepsilon, V + \varepsilon)$. $\underline{V}$, $\overline{V}$, ε and the number of bidders were common knowledge. Given s, ε, $\underline{V}$ and $\overline{V}$, the maximum and minimum possible values for the item were min $(s + \varepsilon, \overline{V})$ and max $(s - \varepsilon, \underline{V})$, respectively. These bounds were computed for each subject and reported along with s.

Examples of signal values relative to a given V were provided and discussed. Subjects were told that 'over a sufficiently long series of auctions, the differences between your private information signal and the value of the commodity will average out to zero (or very close to it); but for a given auction, your private signal can be above or below the value of the item. That's the nature of the random selection process generating the signals.'[1]

After all bids were tendered, V was announced, subjects' profits were calculated, and balances updated. All bids were posted, from highest to lowest, along with the corresponding private information signal and the winning bidder's profit (or loss). Bidder identification numbers were suppressed so that it was not possible to identify individual bidders.

To cover the possibility of losses, subjects were given starting cash balances. Positive profits were added to this balance and losses subtracted from it. If a balance dropped to zero or less, the subject was no longer permitted to bid, was paid a $4.00 participation fee and was free to leave the room. Auction survivors were paid their end-of-session balance along with the participation fee in cash.

The size of the adjustment bidders must make in response to adverse selection forces depends in large part on N, the number of bidders. Target values for N were 4 and 7. Given anticipated bankruptcies, extra subjects were recruited, with only a subset of subjects bidding at one time (a rotation rule was employed to determine who would bid in each period). Extra subjects who did not play in a period got to observe auction outcomes for that period. In addition, the size of the starting cash balance was increased in sessions with fewer extra subjects, since the larger the starting cash balance, the less likely any given bidder is to go bankrupt.

Subjects in the University of Houston sessions were recruited primarily from upper division undergraduate courses in economics, with some subjects from MBA classes. The University of Pittsburgh sessions used primarily MBA students, with some undergraduates and PhD candidates from economics and business. All subjects were invited back to participate in subsequent sessions.

Each experimental session started with several dry runs in which outcomes did not count toward players' final earnings. The analysis of the data begins with the first auction period involving cash payoffs.

Table 10.1 summarizes the experimental treatment conditions. There are several points worth clarifying with respect to Table 10.1. In each auction series we restrict our analysis to market periods where the number of bidders remains fixed throughout at 4 for 'small' markets and at 6 or 7 (mostly 7 bidders) for "large" markets. In some cases this means that we do not analyze data from later auction periods because excessive bankruptcies reduced the number of bidders below the targeted value (auction series 3, 5, and 6) or because there were planned changes in the number of competing bidders that subjects had no previous experience with (auction series 10 and 11). Variations in the number of auction periods in the remaining sessions reflect running up against a time constraint (subjects were recruited for 2 hour sessions), in conjunction with differences in the number of questions asked in the course of delivering the instructions and during dry runs. Auction series with inexperienced bidders all began with several periods of $\varepsilon = \$6$, to provide subjects with experience

TABLE 10.1
Experimental Conditions

Auction Series	Subject Population (no. starting session)	Auction Period[c]	ε	Number Active Bidders (auction period)	Experience	Number of Bankruptcies	Starting Cash Balance
1[a]	U. Houston (7)	1–5 6–15 16–23 24	$6 $12 $24 $12	4	None	1	$15
2[a]	U. Houston (8)	1–6 7–16 17–21	$6 $12 $24	4 (2 small markets 1–22) (1 small market 23)	None	1	$20
3[a]	U. Houston (4)	1–6 7–8[d]	$6 $12	4	None	1	$20
4[a]	U. Houston (10)	1–6 8–18 19–23	$6 $12 $24	7	None	2	$15
5[a]	U. Houston (8)	1–6 7–16 17–20[e]	$6 $12 $24	7 (1–17) 6 (18–20)	None	4	$20
6[a]	U. Houston (9)	1–6 7–17 18–20[e]	$6 $12 $24	7 (1–14) 6 (15–20)	None	4	$15
7[b]	U. Houston (6)	1–6 7–14 15–22	$6 $12 $24	4	None	2	$15
8[a]	U. Houston (9)	1–20 21–28 29–31	$12 $24 $12	4 (2 small markets)	Yes Sessions 1,3,7	1	$10
9[a]	U. Houston (9)	1–20 21–30 31–33	$12 $24 $12	4 (2 small markets 1–28) (1 small market 29–35)	Yes Sessions 2,3,7	2	$10
10[a]	U. Houston (10)	1–12[f]	$12	7	Yes Sessions 4,6	1	$10
11[a]	U. Houston (8)	1–9[f]	$12	7	Yes Sessions 5,6	3	$10
12[b]	U. Pittsburgh (9)	1–7 8–23	$6 $12	7	None	1	$20

TABLE 10.1
Continued

Auction Series	Subject Population (no. starting session)	Auction Period[c]	ε	Number Active Bidders (auction period)	Experience	Number of Bankruptcies	Starting Cash Balance
13[b]	U. Pittsburgh (8)	1–8 9–37	$6 $12	7	None	0	$20
14[a]	U. Pittsburgh (7)	1–26 27–38	$12 $24	7	Yes Sessions 12,13	3	$10

[a] $\underline{V} = \$50$; $\overline{V} = \$550$.
[b] $\underline{V}$ 25; $\overline{V} = \$225$.
[c] Starting from first period with cash payoffs.
[d] Play continued with three bidders through period 20.
[e] Play continued with less than six bidders through period 24 in sessions 5 and 6.
[f] Play continued with markets of size 4.
[g] Two inexperienced subjects participated.

while minimizing the potential for bankruptcy, before switching to larger values of ε where both potential profits and losses were more substantial. Changes in the value of ε and planned changes in the number of competing bidders were never announced in advance.

3. Theoretical Considerations: Measures of Learning and Adjustment

The equilibrium bidding concept of choice in the auction literature is that of a symmetric, risk-neutral, Nash equilibrium (RNNE), as found in Wilson (1977) and Milgrom and Weber (1982). Restricting the analysis to signal values in the interval

$$[\underline{V} + \varepsilon, \overline{V} - \varepsilon] \qquad (1)$$

yields the RNNE bid function

$$b(s) = s - \varepsilon + Y, \qquad (2)$$

where $Y = [2\varepsilon/(N + 1)]\exp\{-(N/2\varepsilon)[s - (\underline{V} + \varepsilon)]\}$.[2] Y contains a negative exponential which diminishes rapidly as s increases beyond $\underline{V} + \varepsilon$. In a Nash equilibrium bidders properly account for the adverse selection forces inherent in winning the auction and discount their bids (reduce their bids relative to their signal values) accordingly. In fact, in equilibrium, bidders discount their bids more than enough to avoid the 'winner's curse,' taking account of the strategic possibilities inherent in the situation, in addition to the adverse selection problem.

However, games in which learning plays an important role are, by definition, out-of-equilibrium. In this case we find it convenient to compare bids (b) with the expected value of V *conditional* on having the highest signal value. For signals in the interval (1) this is

$$E[V \mid S = s_1] = s - \varepsilon(N - 1)/(N + 1), \tag{3}$$

where s_1 refers to the highest ranked signal value from the set $\{s_i, i = 1,2, \ldots, N\}$ of signal values drawn. $E[V \mid S = s_1]$ provides a convenient measure of the extent to which bidders suffer from a winner's curse since in auctions in which the high signal holder always wins the item, bidding above $E[V \mid S = s_1]$ results in negative expected profit. Further, even with zero correlation between bids and signal values, if everyone else bids above $E[V \mid S = s_1]$, bids above $E[V \mid S = s_1]$ result in negative expected profit. As such, if the high signal holder frequently wins the auction, and a reasonably large number of rivals are bidding above $E[V \mid S = s_1]$, individuals bidding above $E[V \mid S = s_1]$ are likely to earn negative expected profit. As will be shown, both of these conditions characterize inexperienced bidders.

We also find it convenient to measure the discount rate, $(s - b)/\varepsilon$, the difference between a bidder's signal value and the amount bid divided by ε. Rather high discount rates are required to avoid bidding above $E[V \mid S = s_1]$. For example, with $N = 4$ the required discount rate is 0.60, while with $N = 7$ it is 0.75. In the analysis that follows the discount rate serves as an important measure of bidders adjustment to the winner's curse which normalizes for changes in ε. It also serves a pivotal role in our analysis of individual subject learning/adjustment mechanisms in section 4.3 below.

4. Experimental Results

4.1 The Data to Be Explained: Adjustments in Bidding over Time in First-Price Auctions

Conclusion 1: There is a marked reduction in the frequency and severity of the winner's curse for experienced compared to inexperienced bidders as measured by a marked reduction in the frequency of bids *greater* than $E[V \mid S = s_1]$ and substantial increases in the discount rate of the high bidder.

The evidence for this is reported in Tables 10.2 and 10.3 which report data separately for auctions with $N = 4$ and with $N = 6$ or 7. For example, looking at Table 10.2 with $\varepsilon = \$12$, the winning bid ($b_1$) is *greater* than $E[V \mid S = s_1]$ in 75.6% of all auctions with inexperienced bidders compared to 34.8% with experienced bidders ($Z = 4.86$, $p < 0.01$). Overly aggressive bidding for inexperienced bidders is not restricted to the high bidders, as 64.6% of all bids are greater than $E[V \mid S = s_1]$ with $\varepsilon = \$12$, compared to 29.5% for experienced subjects ($Z = 7.90$, $p < 0.01$). Or, looking at the same behavior from a different angle, for inexperienced bidders the average discount rate for the winner

TABLE 10.2
Effects of Experience on Bidding: Auctions with $N = 4$

ε	Percentage of Auctions Won with s_1 (raw data)	High Bidders Percentage of $b_1 > E[V \mid S = s_1]$ (raw data)	All Bidders Percentage of $b_i > E[V \mid S = s_1]$ (raw data)	Percentage of Auctions Positive Profit (raw data)	Average Actual Profit (S_m)	Average Predicted RNNE Profit (S_m)	Average Discount Rate[a] $= (s - b)/e$ (S_m)
Inexperienced Bidders							
6	58.6 (17/29)	82.8 (24/29)	68.1 (79/116)	20.7 (6/29)	−2.13 (0.52)	2.76 (0.38)	0.05 (0.08)
12	73.2 (30/41)	75.6 (31/41)	64.6 (106/164)	43.9 (18/41)	−1.32 (0.79)	5.01 (0.60)	0.38 (0.06)
24	72.0 (18/25)	36.0 (9/25)	29.0 (29/100)	64.0 (16/25)	1.20 (1.93)	9.83 (1.25)	0.58 (0.08)
Experienced Bidders							
12	66.3 (59/89)	34.8 (31/89)	29.5 (105/356)	58.4 (52/89)	1.37 (0.49)	4.32 (0.41)	0.67 (0.03)
24	90.0 (27/30)	13.3 (4/30)	6.7 (8/120)	66.7 (20/30)	2.68 (1.54)	7.45 (1.17)	0.78 (0.05)

[a]Data for $s \geq \overline{V} + \varepsilon$.

S_m = standard error of mean.

TABLE 10.3
Effects of Experience on Bidding: Auctions with N = 6 or 7

ε	Percentage of Auctions Won with s_1 (raw data)	High Bidders Percentage of $b_1 > s_1$ E$[V \mid S = s_1]$ (raw data)	All Bidders Percentage of $b_1 > s_1$ E$[V \mid S = s_1]$ (raw data)	Percentage of Auctions Positive Profit (raw data)	Average Actual Profit (S_m)	Average Predicted RNNE Profit (S_m)	Average Discount Rate[a] $= (s - b) / \varepsilon$ (S_m)
Inexperienced Bidders							
U of H							
6	50.0 (9/18)	88.9 (16/18)	75.4 (95/126)	11.1 (2/18)	−3.85 (0.71)	0.99 (0.19)	0.05 (0.10)
12	56.7 (17/30)	76.7 (23/30)	58.2 (121/208)	30.0 (9/30)	−3.75 (0.89)	2.76 (0.53)	0.30 (0.08)
24	50.0 (5/10)	70.0 (7/10)	33.8 (22/65)	20.0 (2/10)	−6.29 (2.51)	4.76 (1.06)	0.27 (0.19)
U of P							
6	66.7 (10/15)	80.0 (12/15)	61.0 (64/105)	13.3 (2/15)	−3.38 (0.91)	1.10 (0.21)	0.15 (0.13)
12	62.2 (28/45)	68.9 (31/45)	33.7 (106/315)	42.2 (19/45)	−0.80 (0.82)	3.59 (0.54)	0.56 (0.05)
Experienced Bidders							
U of H							
12	47.4 (9/19)	68.4 (13/19)	33.8 (45/133)	31.6 (6/19)	−0.32 (0.56)	2.93 (0.54)	0.46 (0.09)
U of P							
12	87.0 (20/23)	34.8 (8/23)	13.7 (22/161)	43.5 (10/23)	−1.35 (1.21)	2.25 (0.48)	0.68 (0.09)
24	100.0 (12/12)	8.3 (1/12)	1.3 (1/77)	66.7 (8/12)	3.47 (2.01)	6.82 (1.47)	0.86 (0.04)

[a]Data for $s \geq \underline{V} + \varepsilon$.

S_m = standard error of mean.

was 0.38, which is much too small to avoid the winner's curse (this requires a discount rate of 0.60). This compares to an average discount rate of 0.67 for experienced bidders, which is significantly higher than for inexperienced bidders (t = 4.32, p < 0.01 for a two-tailed t-test with unequal variances).

This aggressive bidding translates into negative average profits for inexperienced bidders of $1.32 per auction period and losses in over 50% of all auction periods. This compares with positive average profits of $1.37 per period for experienced bidders and positive profits in 58.4% of all auction periods, These profit differences are statistically significant as well (t = 2.89, p < 0.01 for a two-tailed t-test with unequal variances).

Holding ε constant, similar experience effects are reported for N = 4 and ε = $24 (Table 2) and with N = 6–7 and ε = $12 within both the Houston data and the Pittsburgh data in Table 10.3.[3]

Also shown in both tables is a tendency for the discount rate to increase with increases in ε for inexperienced bidders (with a corresponding reduction in the frequency of winning bids above $E[V \mid S = s_1]$). As will be shown in section 4.3, this reflects the effect of both changes in ε and within session learning/adjustments on bidders' part.

4.2 Market Adjustments: Self-Selection among Returning Bidders

Conclusion 2: One reason for the marked reduction in the frequency and severity of the winner's curse for experienced bidders is that more aggressive bidders are less likely to return. Surprisingly, the self-selection mechanism does not depend exclusively on more aggressive bidders earning lower than average profits. In addition, bidders who went bankrupt bid most aggressively and were less likely to return. Although this mechanism insures market learning in auctions with closed entry (as in our experiment), in auctions with open entry (as would be the case with field data) the market implications are somewhat problematical.

Tables 10.4 and 10.5 provide supporting evidence for this conclusion. Table 10.4 compares the discount rate [(s − b)/ε] and profits earned for inexperienced bidders who returned compared to those who did not (*all* subjects were invited to return with equal enthusiasm). Returning bidders had higher average discount rates than non-returners for all values of ε. Using a simple frequency count, the likelihood of this happening by chance is less then 0.05, given that it is equally likely that returning bidder's discount rates will be higher or lower than non-returner's.

Average profits were higher (losses were lower) for returning bidders in the Houston data. But, surprisingly, this pattern fails to hold for the Pittsburgh data. In this case, lower losses in the face of a higher discount rate are explained by the luck of the draw, as profits predicted at the RNNE were substantially higher for auctions non-returners won (Table 10.4).

Table 10.5 compares average discount rates between inexperienced bidders

TABLE 10.4

Average Discount Rates and Profits: Returning versus Nonreturning Bidders

	Discount Rate[a] Epsilon			Profit Epsilon		
	6	12	24	6	12	24
U of H **N = 4**						
Returning (S_m)	0.35 (0.02)	0.56 (0.04)	0.67 (0.36)	−1.94 (0.55)	−0.27 (0.81)	4.27 (1.88)
Nonreturning (S_m)	0.34 (0.08)	0.32 (0.09)	0.53 (0.11)	−2.48 (1.13)	−2.88 (1.64)	−5.19 (3.26)
Difference (t-stat)	0.01 (0.08)	0.24 (2.92)**	0.14 (0.80)	0.54 (0.48)	2.61 (1.60)	9.49 (2.46)**
U of H **N = 6 or 7**						
Returning (S_m)	0.46 (0.43)	0.60 (0.08)	0.76 (0.06)	−2.32 (0.79)	−3.07 (1.35)	−0.98 (3.37)
Nonreturning (S_m)	0.42 (0.20)	0.40 (0.08)	0.23 (0.32)	−6.23 (0.69)	−4.51 (1.14)	−6.68 (1.41)
Difference (t-stat)	0.04 (0.20)	0.20 (1.53)	0.53 (2.67)**	3.91 (3.44)**	1.44 (0.80)	5.70 (1.56)
U of P **N = 6 or 7**						
Returning (S_m)	0.85 (0.38)	0.81 (0.06)	—	−5.03 (1.92)	−2.86 (1.08)	—
Nonreturning (S_m)	0.40 (0.14)	0.60 (0.11)	—	−2.28 (0.72)	−0.25 (0.99)	—
Difference (t-stat)	0.45 (0.95)	0.21 (1.84)*	—	−2.75 (−1.34)	−2.61 (−1.73)*	—

S_m = standard error of mean.

[a] Values are means across subject means. Each subject contributes only one observation for each value of ε.

*Significantly different from 0, 10% level, 2-tailed t-test.

**Significantly different from 0, 5% level, 2-tailed t-test.

TABLE 10.5

Average Discount Rates and Frequency of Returning: Bankrupt versus Solvent Bidders[a]

	Discount Rate[b] Epsilon			Number of Bidders	
	6	12	24	Returned	Not-return
N = 4					
Solvent (S_m)	0.40 (0.08)	0.52 (0.05)	0.72 (0.06)	17	3
Bankrupt (S_m)	0.14 (0.16)	0.30 (0.12)	0.09 (0.40)	1	4
Difference (t-stat)	0.26 (1.50)	0.22 (2.02)*	0.63 (3.85)**		
N = 6 or 7					
Solvent (S_m)	0.64 (0.11)	0.69 (0.06)	0.78 (0.05)	15	2
Bankrupt (S_m)	0.11 (0.10)	0.26 (0.09)	−0.10 (0.22)	3	7
Difference (t-stat)	0.53 (3.20)**	0.43 (4.34)**	0.88 (5.91)**		

S_m = standard error of mean.

[a]U of H data only. Only one subject went bankrupt in U of P data. Note differences in starting cash balances between samples in Table 10.1.

[b]Values reported as means across subject means. Each subject contributes only one observation for each value of ε.

*Significantly different from 0, 10% level, 2-tailed t-test.

**Significantly different from 0, 5% level, 2-tailed t-test.

who went bankrupt versus those who remained solvent and the return rates for bankrupt versus solvent bidders. Discount rates were substantially smaller for bankrupt bidders for all values of ε, with statistically significant differences in several paired comparisons. Further, a chi-square test shows that bankrupt bidders were significantly less likely to return than those who remained solvent ($\chi^2 = 17.9$, 1 degree of freedom, p < 0.01).

The self-selection effects identified here are hardly surprising, but were nevertheless not obvious to us when conducting the auctions. The results are reported because this market selection effect underlies some of the "learning" reported for experienced subjects in common value auctions and because similar forces may underlie the jumps in learning often found between inexperienced and experienced bidders in other experiments. Our results are a clear indication of the need to check for such effects.[4]

The relevance of this market adjustment effect beyond laboratory markets is somewhat problematical. Entry conditions were closed in the experiment— subjects were recruited back exclusively from those who had participated in earlier auction market sessions. In field settings, open entry conditions permit new, inexperienced bidders (firms) to join the bidding. It is not clear if these new players must undergo their own self-selection process de novo or whether they can somehow benefit from the experience of their predecessors or surviving bidders who have learned to adjust. Further, if new bidders must learn from scratch, this would impose severe penalties on experienced bidders who had learned to adjust, as these inexperienced bidders are much more likely to win the auction with overly aggressive bids.

4.3 Learning/Adjustment Mechanisms for Individual Bidders

Tables 10.2 and 10.3 suggest individual bidder learning/adjustment effects. This section analyzes the mechanism(s) underlying this adjustment process; i.e., the 'learning' process. This section is broken into three parts. Part 1 outlines the logic underlying the analysis. Part 2 presents the regression results as they relate to learning processes. Part 3 briefly discusses control variables included in the regressions.

4.3.a Plan of Analysis

Our measure of adjustment is the discount rate and how it varies between auction periods. The analysis is restricted to inexperienced bidders, subjects participating in their first auction series. Regression models are run in which the change in the discount rate is the dependent variable, with information available to bidders serving as right hand side variables. An unusually large number of explanatory variables are included in the regression specifications. This results primarily from efforts to capture the nuances of observational learning: responses conditional on different types of information feedback when a bidder has not won the item. Separate fixed-effect regression models were fit to the Houston and Pittsburgh data, with subjects serving as the fixed-effect variable, allowing each subject to have a different intercept, or base discount rate.[5]

Information available to bidders can be divided into two broad categories: (i) Information about relevant strategic variables, such as N, the value of ε, the fact that $s \leq \underline{V} + \varepsilon$ which provides bidders with additional information about V, the bidder's cash balance, etc. and (ii) Information about the results of bidding in the previous auction period. The latter consisted of V, own earnings, the profit or loss of the high bidder, and the bids and corresponding signal values for each bidder in the market. These data provide two types of learning opportunities: experiential and observational (see Figure 10.1).

Experiential learning occurs as a result of gains or losses from being the high bidder. Experiential learning forces are represented by the variables AG (actual gains), AL (actual losses), and the amount of money left on the table ($LEFT) when a positive profit was earned (the difference between the high bid and the next highest bid). Given the general overbidding reported in Tables 10.2 and 10.3, we clearly expect the coefficient for the AL variable to be positive and relatively large in size, so that losses produce a higher discount rate in later

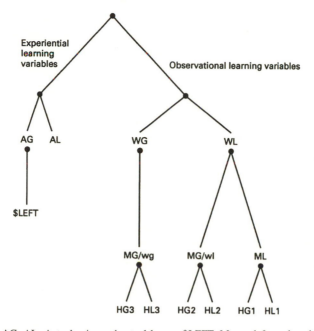

Figure 10.1. AG, AL: Actual gains and actual losses. $LEFT: Money left on the table (high bid less than second highest bid). WG, WL: Winner's gains and losses. MG/wg, MG/wl, ML: Gains and losses that losing bidders would have earned from winning the auction with the bid they submitted. HG1-HG3, HL1-HL3: Gains and losses that losing bidders would have earned from winning the auction with their discount rate applied to the high bidders signal value.

auction periods (all losses are measured in terms of their absolute value). This represents a kind of hot stove effect—the natural reaction to losing money is to bid less. The marginal impact of positive profits, by itself, is much more questionable. The marginal effect of money left on the table might be expected to promote a higher discount rate, as the more money left on the table, the more room there is to strategically bid less while still winning the auction.

Observational learning occurs as a result of information feedback when a bidder has *not* won the item. Our key measures of observational learning consist of gains and losses that a bidder would have earned had he applied his discount rate to the winning bidder's signal value and won the auction with this bid. In other words, in cases where a bidder fails to win the item, he can apply his discount rate to the high bidder's signal, calculate a bid, and determine the profits that would have been earned if he had won the item. This serves as a reasonable proxy for what would have happened if he had won the auction with his bidding strategy.[6] This is a fairly natural calculation to make, given that bids were listed from highest to lowest following each auction period, with the corresponding signal values listed next to each bid.

Figure 1 shows that these hypothetical loss and gain variables have been broken up into several different categories to capture responses conditional on the circumstances under which the gain or loss occurred. We employ three different hypothetical loss variables, HL1, HL2, and HL3, each of which measures the same thing, but under three different sets of circumstances.

HL1: The winning bidder lost money (the event WL occurred) and the bidder in question would have lost money had he actually won the auction with his bid (the event ML occurred).

HL2: The winning bidder lost money (the event WL occurred) and the bidder in question would have made money had he actually won the auction with his bid (the event MG | wl occurred).

HL3: The winning bidder made money (the event WG occurred) and the bidder in question would have made money had he actually won the auction with his bid (the event MG | wg occurred).

These three hypothetical loss variables are mutually exclusive and exhaustive.[7]

From a strategic point of view, or a pure informational point of view, the regression coefficients for HL1–HL3 should all be the same. This is because the information contained in these hypothetical loss measures, and the appropriate strategic response to these losses, is independent of the circumstances under which the losses occurred (events WL, WG, ML, etc.): in all cases, these hypothetical losses point to reducing bids in order to avoid losses when actually having the high signal value. Essentially what differentiates the three cases is the relationship of the losing bidders signal relative to the winner's signal, which with symmetry (or some reasonable approximation thereof) should have no impact on bidding strategies. For example, consider someone who bids his signal value, which is a strategy guaranteeing negative expected profit. Cases HL2 and HL3 will occur when this bidder has a relatively low signal value compared to his rivals. In contrast, case HL1 occurs when this bidder has a relatively high signal value, but it is not high enough to win the auction, given his strategy and his rivals' strategies.

In spite of the logic of the situation, the impact of these hypothetical losses might not be the same under all circumstances. Bidders might pay considerably more attention to hypothetical losses when the winner lost money and their bid would have lost money (HL1), compared to cases where the winner made money and their bid would have produced a profit (HL3). Alternatively, bidders might engage in a bit of wishful thinking and be much less responsive to hypothetical losses in the case of HL3 and/or overreact to the observed losses and discount their bids proportionately more in the case of HL1. As such, the size of the response to a hypothetical loss is likely to vary depending on the context in which it is realized.

In a similar fashion three different hypothetical gains variables are employed, HG1, HG2, and HG3, each of which measures hypothetical gains under different circumstances. However, in this case, the regression coefficients for the HG variables should differ, as the additional information underlying these different circumstances is essential to determining the appropriate strategic response. For example, HG1 takes on a non-zero value only when the winner suffered a loss and the losing bidder would have suffered a loss if he had won the item with his bid. As such the losing bidder's signal must be greater than the winner's signal, but his discount rate must be large enough that he would have earned a profit with the winner's signal. Under the circumstances, it is questionable whether this event offers the losing bidder encouragement to bid more and may well encourage him to bid less, as he may not want to beat such overly aggressive rivals. In contrast, HG3 takes on a non-zero value only when the winner earned a profit and the losing bidder would have earned a profit had he actually won the auction with his bid. In this case a lower bid would put the losing bidder further out of the money and a higher bid may well result in winning the auction and earning a positive profit.

In assuming that losing bidders will be responsive to these hypothetical gains and losses, HG1–HG3 and HL1–HL3, we may well be attributing too much reasoning and sophistication to the bidders. Bidders may simply ignore the information available from the posted bids and signal values. Alternatively, they may react naively to the winner's gains and losses, or to gains and losses had their bids actually won the auction, increasing their bids following gains and reducing them following losses, ignoring the additional information available in the hypothetical gains and loss calculations. The regressions specified permit us to test these propositions.

Two alternative regression specifications are reported. In the first specification, the individuating information variables—WL, WG and MG | wl, MG | wg and ML—are all included as continuous variables. In the second specification these variables are dropped. The primary results are robust to both data sets and both regression specifications employed.[8]

4.3.b Experiential and Observational Learning Effects

Conclusion 3: Actual losses are followed by large, statistically significant increases in the discount rate so that, as anticipated, these losses facilitate the adjustment process. Actual gains have no significant impact on bids.

The evidence for this conclusion rests on the regression estimates for the AL (actual loss) and AG (actual gain) variables reported in Table 10.6.

As anticipated, the coefficient for AL is positive and significant at better than the 1% level for both data sets and both specifications. Not surprisingly, actual losses have the largest marginal impact on reducing bids relative to signal values outside of the REG1 dummy control variable (see section 4.3.3 below). The coefficient for the AG variable is negative in all cases, meaning that there is some reduction in the discount rate (higher bids). But the effect is small and statistically insignificant as well.

The marginal effect of money left on the table ($LEFT) is to reduce the discount rate for the Houston data and to increase it for the Pittsburgh data. But neither effect is statistically significant or large in size. The net effect of money left on the table, in conjunction with the effect of the AG variable, evaluated at the mean of the variables in question, is not statistically significant either.

TABLE 10.6

Adjustment Mechanism Regression Results[a] (dependent variable—change in discount rate)

Variable	Specification 1		Specification 2	
	Houston	Pitt	Houston	Pitt
AL	0.072** (0.008)	0.087** (0.012)	0.081** (0.008)	0.090** (0.011)
AG	−0.003 (0.009)	−0.021 (0.022)	−0.005 (0.008)	−0.018 (0.022)
$LEFT	−0.004 (0.006)	0.010 (0.023)	−0.001 (0.006)	0.014 (0.023)
WL	−0.006 (0.004)	−0.002 (0.006)	—	—
WG	0.008 (0.007)	0.022* (0.012)	—	—
ML	0.012 (0.021)	−0.018 (0.044)	—	—
MG/wl	−0.006** (0.002)	−0.006 (0.004)	—	—
MG/wg	−0.007** (0.003)	−0.006 (0.005)	—	—
HL1	0.060** (0.010)	0.080** (0.024)	0.066** (0.007)	0.072** (0.016)
HL2	0.025** (0.006)	0.060** (0.010)	0.022** (0.005)	0.057** (0.010)
HL3	0.020* (0.012)	0.037 (0.032)	0.026** (0.012)	0.034 (0.030)
HG1	0.019 (0.025)	0.010 (0.047)	0.034 (0.024)	0.011 (0.046)
HG2	−0.006 (0.006)	−0.019** (0.008)	−0.009 (0.006)	−0.021** (0.007)
HG3	−0.007** (0.004)	−0.024** (0.008)	−0.006** (0.003)	−0.019** (0.005)
Reg1	−0.299** (0.077)	−0.510** (0.127)	−0.315** (0.078)	−0.516** (0.127)
EPS	0.008** (0.004)	−0.018* (0.010)	0.006 (0.004)	−0.016* (0.009)
N	−0.031 (0.031)	—	−0.030 (0.031)	—
BAL	−0.001 (0.003)	−0.008* (0.005)	−0.002 (0.003)	−0.008 (0.005)
PER	−0.004 (0.004)	0.006** (0.003)	−0.007* (0.004)	0.006** (0.003)
R^2	0.31	0.32	0.31	0.32
No. of Observations	653	401	653	401

[a]Standard errors in parentheses.
*Significantly different from 0, at 10% level, 2-tailed test.
**Significantly different from 0, at 5% level, 2-tailed test.

Conclusion 4. Hypothetical losses (HL1–HL3) increase the discount rate, so that observational learning contributes to bidders adjusting to the adverse selection forces. This effect is most pronounced in cases where the high bidder lost money and the bidder in question would have lost money had his bid actually won the item (case HL1).

The coefficient values for all three hypothetical loss variables (HL1–HL3) are positive, indicating that the marginal effect of these hypothetical losses is to increase the discount rate (lower bids relative to signal values). Further, these marginal responses are significantly different from zero, at the 1% level or better, with the exception of the HL3 variable. F-tests under the first specification show that we cannot reject a null hypothesis that HL1 = HL2 = HL3 for the Pittsburgh data (F = 0.43), but can reject this hypothesis for the Houston data (F = 5.87, significant at p < 0.01), as a result of the relatively low value of HL2 and HL3 compared to HL1. Similar results are reported for F-tests under specification 2.

To determine the net effect of these hypothetical losses on the discount rate requires accounting for the mediating variables—WL, WG, ML, etc.—in specification 1. For specification 2, which drops these variables, the regression coefficients record the net effects directly.

The net effect of the HL1 variable, measured at the mean value of the mediating variables WL and ML, is as large as the AL variable for the Houston data, and almost as large for the Pittsburgh data: HL1 results in an increase in the discount rate of 0.336 (0.043) versus an increase of 0.322 (0.035) following actual losses for the Houston data (standard errors are reported in parentheses) and 0.299 (0.069) for HL1 versus 0.377 (0.050) for AL for the Pittsburgh data. (Direct comparison of the coefficient values in specification 2 yields similar results.) Thus, there is a large observational learning effect associated with HL1 type hypothetical losses.

Considerably smaller net effects are reported for HL2 and HL3 type hypothetical losses, to the point that the net effect is negligible for the Houston data: the net effects, measured at the mean of the mediating variables and the variable in question are 0.016 (0.030) and -0.001 (0.054) for HL2 and HL3 type losses, respectively, for the Houston data and 0.124 (0.424) and 0.112 (0.105) for the Pittsburgh data (standard errors in parentheses). The smaller net effect of HL2 and HL3 results primarily from the sign and magnitude of the mediating variables MG | wl and MG | wg, as other things equal, losing bidders increase their bids when they would have earned a positive profit had their bid actually won the auction (a response, which by itself, is not particularly adaptive).

Conclusion 5: F-tests show that we cannot reject a null hypothesis that HG1 = HG2 = HG3 for either data set at conventional levels. However, measured at the mean value of the mediating variables, the net effect of HG2 and HG3 is a relatively large increase in bids. This retards convergence to the RNNE.

The coefficient for HG1 is positive, but far from significant, for both data sets, so that there is essentially no response, or a slight increase in the discount rate, from hypothetical gains of this sort. As already noted, this response is adaptive (or at least not maladaptive). In contrast, the coefficient for HG2 is negative for both data sets, and significant at the 1% level for the Pittsburgh data, so that hypothetical gains of this sort yield more aggressive bidding at the margin. Further, HG3 is negative and significant at the 1% level in both data sets, so that hypothetical gains conditional on the high bidder earning positive profits result in a reduction in the discount rate (more aggressive bidding). Although it is not possible to evaluate the adaptiveness of such a strategic response, it is certainly understandable.

Measured at the mean value of the relevant mediating variables, the net effect of HG2 and HG3 is a relatively large reduction in the discount rate for both data sets. For specification 1 these net effects result in reductions in the discount rate of 0.114 (0.033) and 0.137 (0,040) for HG2 and HG3 for the Houston data and 0.116 (0.406) and 0.161 (0.054) for the Pittsburgh data (standard error in parentheses). Given that virtually no one was bidding at the RNNE or less to begin with, these responses retard convergence to the RNNE. Further, the relatively large reductions in the discount rate for cases HG2 and HG3 may explain why there is no significant reaction of high bidders to money left on the table, as winning bidders may anticipate rivals bidding more aggressively in the next auction period.

For us, the most interesting results of this section are the identification of significant observational learning effects in the data. These results contradict Lind and Plott's (1991, p. 335) conjecture that in common value auctions ". . . the process of removing bankrupt subjects succeeded in removing subjects less prone to the (winner's) curse (i.e., those who had the experience of losing money and might adjust their behavior accordingly)." That is, Lind and Plott conjecture that the primary force underlying the elimination of the winner's curse is experiential learning. However, as shown here, the observational learning effect of HL1 is almost as great as experiential learning (AL) and, for the typical bidder, occurs with a much higher frequency.

The observational learning forces identified here involve losing bidders evaluating the impact of their bidding strategy in terms of the high bidder's signal value. The opportunity to make such calculations is unique to the informational structure of our auctions, which report all bids along with the underlying signal values and the value of the item. In contrast, in government mineral rights auctions only bids are announced. If we limited information feedback to bids and the value of the item, subjects could no longer perform the relevant HL and HG calculations.[9] Rather, they would be limited to responding to actual gains and losses, winners gains and losses, and what they might have earned if their bid had won, ignoring whether or not they had a high or low signal value.

Naive extrapolation of the regression results suggests that eliminating the informational basis to compute hypothetical losses would definitely retard adjustment to the winner's curse (as the marginal effect of the HL variables is always to reduce bids). In contrast, for hypothetical gains, extrapolation of the regression results implies that eliminating this feedback would result in a more rapid adjustment to the winner's curse, primarily as a result of HG2 and HG3 promoting more aggressive bidding. However, since events HG2 and HG3 occur with less frequency than events HL1–HL3, and since the size of the response to HL1 is substantially larger than to HG2 or HG3, the net effect is likely to be a slower adjustment to the winner's curse. This leads to the following conjecture:

Conjecture: Elimination of information feedback required to compute hypothetical losses (a feedback not available in field data), will retard both individual and market adjustments to the winner's curse.

The primary factors that might work against this effect are that (i) bidders deprived of the hypothetical loss information might learn to rely on other criteria that would promote the same, or more rapid, learning, or (ii) losses might be large enough that there would be a discrete jump in the individual learning/adjustment process. The obvious treatment effects required to explore this conjecture will be implemented in a future experiment.[10]

4.3.c Control Variables

The control variables included in the regressions all have sensible signs and interpretations. They are as follows:

REG1: This is a dummy variable that has a value of 1 when $s \leq \underline{V} + \varepsilon$. In this case bidders have additional (end-point) information which should result in a smaller discount rate. In all cases the regression coefficient is negative and significant, indicating that bidders employed a smaller discount rate, as they should.

EPS: This is a continuous variable explicitly accounting for changes in ε on the discount rate. Eyeballing the Houston data had suggested discrete increases in the discount rate as ε increased. This is captured in the positive regression coefficient reported, which is significant at the 5% level under the first specification offered. In contrast, the Pittsburgh data show the opposite effect, which is marginally significant under both specifications.

N: This is a continuous variable accounting for differences in the number of active bidders on the discount rate (present in the Houston data only). Note that with the inclusion of individual subject dummy variables in the regressions, N essentially measures the effect of going from six to seven bidders in auctions with larger numbers of bidders. As such it is no surprise that the coefficient for N is far from significant at conventional levels under both specifications.

BAL: This is a continuous variable accounting for the effects of beginning period cash balances on bidding.[11] The coefficient values are negative here, suggesting that larger cash balances are, if anything, associated with a lower discount rate (higher bids). Kagel et al. (1989) report the same pattern for inexperienced bidders in another series of common value auction experiments.

PER: This is a continuous time trend variable (the auction period number). The coefficient value is negative, but not significant in the Houston data. It is positive and significant in the Pittsburgh data indicating some increases in the discount rate (lower bids) independent of the information feedback variables employed.

5. Summary

We have examined learning/adjustment effects in a series of common value auction experiments. The object of this exercise has been to identify the mechanism(s) whereby inexperienced bidders who initially suffer from a strong winner's curse learn to overcome it. We report two major results: (1) there is an important market selection effect as the most aggressive bidders choose not to return for subsequent experimental sessions, and (2) individual bidders learn to adjust to the winner's curse through their own experiences (actual losses) and losses that might have been, had they been unfortunate enough to have won the auction with an overly aggressive bid (observational learning). In both cases we attempt to draw out the general implications of these results. The strong observational learning effect reported suggests additional experimental manipulations that will form the basis for future work.

Notes

Research support from the Social Science Division of the National Science Foundation and the Russell Sage Foundation is gratefully acknowledged. We thank Kamal Gular. Steve Kerman and Dan Levin for helpful discussions at an early point in the analysis and our colleague, Jack Ochs, and an anonymous referee for comments on an earlier draft. An earlier version of this paper was presented at the ESA meetings in Tucson, AZ and at the Economic Psychology and Experimental Economics conference in Frankfurt, Germany. We are grateful to our discussants and conference participants for helpful comments. Responsibility for errors is ours alone.

1. The instructions employed were virtually the same as those reported in Kagel and Levin (1986), with obvious adjustments for computerized bidding in the experiment reported here.

2. The RNNE bid function outside the interval $(\underline{V} + \varepsilon, -\varepsilon)$ is reported in Kagel and Levin (1986).

3. Experienced bidders do worse than inexperienced bidders only for average actual profit with $N = 6$–7 in the U of P data. This appears to be accounted for by the luck of the draw as average predicted profit under the RNNE is almost \$1.30 higher for inexperienced compared to experienced bidders.

4. It is clear that *not* all jumps in learning between inexperienced and experienced subjects result from such self-selection effects; see, for example, Forsythe and Lundholm (1990) and Jung, Kagel and Levin (in press).

5. The Houston regression excludes the data from session 4 since these data cannot be pooled with the other sessions. A separate fixed-effect regression for session 4 yields similar qualitative results to the pooled regressions reported. Those experimental sessions that are pooled readily pass formal statistical tests for pooling.

6. An alternative measure that recommends itself is to apply a losing bidder's discount rate to the high signal value, rather than the high bidder's signal value. Given the relatively high frequency with which the high signal holder won the auction (Tables 2 and 3), the two measures are closely related.

7. Given MG, ML cannot happen. That is, if the winning bidder earned a positive profit (event MG), a bidder who did not win the auction could not have lost money had his bid won. The mnemonic underlying the variable specifications is as follows: WG (winner gained), WL (winner lost), MG ('might' have gained), and ML ('might' have lost).

8. F-tests show that we cannot reject a null hypothesis, at conventional significance levels, that $WL = WG = ML = MG \mid w1 = MG \mid wg = 0$ for the Pittsburgh data ($F = 1.01$), but this null hypothesis can be rejected for the Houston data ($F = 2.88$, with 5 and 593 degrees of freedom, significant at $p = 0.05$ level).

9. Unless we change the reward structure for subjects, it is not clear how to eliminate reporting V. It is also clear that in field data, like off shore oil lease auctions or the commercial construction industry, bidders do not have access to the true value of the item until several years after bids have been accepted.

10. In bilateral bargaining experiments with asymmetric information there is virtually no within session adjustment to the winner's curse for inexperienced subjects over repeated trials (see Ball, Bazerman and Carroll, 1991 and Cifuentes and Sunder, 1991). In these experiments bidders only get to see their own outcomes, hence there is no room for observational learning, a result which is consistent with our conjecture.

11. See Hansen and Lott (1991), Kagel and Levin (1991) and Lind and Plott (1991) for arguments regarding the possible effects of changes in cash balances on bidding.

References

Ball, S.B., M.H. Bazerman, and J.S. Carroll, 1991, An evaluation of learning in the bilateral winner's curse, Organizational Behavior and Human Decision Processes 48, 1–22.

Capen, E. C., R.V. Clapp, and W.M. Campbell, 1971, Competitive bidding in high-risk situations, Journal of Petroleum Technology 23, 641–53.

Cifuentes, L. and S. Sunder, 1991, Some further evidence of the winner's curse, mimeographed, Carnegie-Mellon University.

Forsythe, R. and R. Lundholm, 1990, Information aggregation in an experimental market, Econometrica 58(2), 309–347.

Fudenberg, Drew and David M. Kreps, 1988, A theory of learning, experimentation, and equilibrium in games, unpublished monograph.

Hansen, Robert G. and John R. Lott, Jr., 1991, The winner's curse and public information in common value auctions: comment, American Economic Review 81, 347–61.

Jung, Y.J., J.H. Kagel, and D. Levin, 1994, On the existence of predatory pricing: an experimental study of reputation and entry deterrence in the chain-store game, RAND Journal of Economics 25, 72–93.

Kagel, John H. and Dan Levin, 1986, The winner's curse and public information in common value auctions, American Economic Review 76, 894–920.

Kagel, John H. and Dan Levin, 1991, The winner's curse and public information in common value auctions: reply, American Economic Review 81, 362–369.

Kagel, John H. and Dan Levin, in preparation, Common value auctions with asymmetrically informed bidders: an experimental evaluation.

Kagel, John H., Dan Levin, Raymond C. Battalio, and Donald Meyer, 1989, First-price common value auctions: bidder behavior and the winner's curse, Economic Inquiry 27, 241–258.

Kalai, Ehud and Ehud Lehrer, 1990, Rational learning leads to nash equilibrium, Discussion paper 895, Graduate School of Management, Northwestern University.

Lind, Barry and Charles R. Plott, 1991, The winner's curse: experiments with buyers and with sellers, American Economic Review 81, 335–46.

Lorenz, J. and E.L. Dougherty, 1983, Bonus bidding and bottom lines: federal off-shore oil and gas, SPE 12024, 58th Annual Fall Technical Conference.

Milgrom, Paul R. and Robert J. Weber, 1982, A theory of auctions and competitive bidding, Econometrica 50, 1089–1122.

Milgrom, Paul R. and John Roberts, 1991, Adaptive and sophisticated learning in normal form games, Games and Economic Behavior 3, 82–100.

Samuelson, William F. and Max H. Bazerman, 1985, The winner's curse in bilateral negotiations, in: V.L. Smith, ed., Research in Experimental Economics, Vol. 3, Greenwich, CT: JAI Press, 105–137.

Wilson, Robert, 1977, A bidding model of perfect competition, Review of Economic Studies 44, 511–518.

11

Cross-Game Learning: Experimental Evidence from First-Price and English Common Value Auctions

—

John H. Kagel

1. Introduction

There has been considerable interest among economists in learning models to explain how Nash equilibria might actually be achieved. In learning models equilibria emerge from an adaptive, dynamic adjustment process with players interacting repeatedly in exactly the same game. However, as Fudenberg and Kreps (1988) note, it seems unreasonable to expect to find many situations in which exactly the same game is repeated many times. As such, one would have considerably more faith in the ability of learning mechanisms to achieve equilibrium outcomes if agents were able to transfer their learning across 'similar' games.

Psychologists attribute cross-situation learning to individuals establishing a 'mental model' of one situation and applying it to a similar situation (Wickens, 1992, pp. 230–249). This results in positive learning transference when the mental model is accurate and relevant to the new application, as well as when the model is inaccurate but dictates actions which are reinforcing in the new situation. On the other hand, there may be no relationship between the mental model and the new situation, resulting in no cross-situation learning. And there might even be negative learning transference, when the mental model developed in one situation, while seemingly applicable to the new situation, is inaccurate and generates inaccurate responses to the new situation. Then behavior must be 'unlearned' before adaptation can begin.

This chapter investigates cross-game learning in common value (CV) auctions between first-price, sealed bid and irrevocable exit, English clock auctions. Obviously there are strong similarities as well as differences between these two auction games. Both involve auctions with strong adverse selection effects and bidding for an item of unknown (common) value based, in part, on private information signals affiliated with the CV. Furthermore, in our experiment the same information is available following each auction period, with all bids listed from highest to lowest along with the corresponding signal values, the true value of the item, and the profits of the winning bidder. However, the pricing rule differs between the two auctions. More importantly, drop-out prices in English auctions (EAs) generate substantial information about other bidders' signal values with no such 'public' information present in first-price auctions (FPAs). As such one would expect some, albeit incomplete, learning generalizability across games. What we find instead is a strong asymmetry in cross-game learning with experience in FPAs generalizing somewhat to EAs, but experience in EAs having *no* transfer value to FPAs.

2. Experimental Procedures and Performance Measures

Each experimental session consisted of a number of auction periods in which a single unit of a commodity was awarded to the high bidder. The value of the item, x_0 was randomly drawn each period from a uniform distribution on $(\underline{x}, \bar{x})$, with each bidder receiving a private information signal, x_i, randomly drawn from a uniform distribution on $(x_0 - \varepsilon, x_0 + \varepsilon)$. $\underline{x}$, $\bar{x}$, ε and the number of bidders, N, were common knowledge.

In each experimental session a single group of subjects participated in a number (20 or more) of auctions. In almost all cases there were more subjects (typically two or three more) than the number bidding (N) in which case group composition varied between auctions within a given session (inactive bidders observed the auction outcomes). In all sessions the value of ε varied within a session and/or the bid rule varied between FPA and EA.

Subjects had starting cash balances of between $10 and $20 with auction profits (losses) added to (subtracted from) this starting balance. If a subject's cash balance was non-positive they were no longer permitted to bid. Subjects were paid their end of session balances in cash along with a $4 participation fee. Subjects were primarily upper division undergraduate economics majors and MBA students at the University of Houston and the University of Pittsburgh. (See Levin et al., 1994, for additional details regarding experimental procedures.)

Inexperienced bidders in CV auctions suffer from a winner's curse, earning negative profits on average. This behavior is particularly pronounced in FPAs (see Kagel, in press, for a literature review). Actual and predicted profit under the symmetric, risk-neutral Nash equilibrium (RNNE) and bids relative to $E[x_0 \mid X_i = x_1]$ (the expected value conditional on having the high signal value) are reported for FPAs. In FPAs, with symmetry, or near symmetry, bidding above $E[x_0 \mid X_i = x_1]$ yields negative expected profit conditional on winning the auction, an appealing definition of the winner's curse.[1]

Unfortunately, there is no relatively unambiguous and simple measure of the winner's curse for EAs, since, assuming symmetry, the comparable order statistic is $(d_L + x_i)/2$, where d_L is the price at which the low signal holder drops out. In equilibrium, $d_L = x_L$ so that $(d_L + x_i)/2$ provides a sufficient statistic for $E[x_0 \mid X_i = x_1]$.[2] The problem with using $(d_L + x_i)/2$ to directly measure the winner's curse is that bidders often drop out at prices other than x_L, so that the EA comparisons are based strictly on average realized profit.

3. Experimental Results

Table 11.1 reports bidders with EA experience bidding in FPAs along with two control groups of FPAs. Although there is some variability between auction sessions holding experience level constant, the pooled data provide a reasonably accurate summary of the main effects and I concentrate on it.[3] Bidders with EA experience look no different than those with no auction experience: there is virtually no difference in the relative frequency with which high bidders (b_1) fell prey to the winner's curse $(b_1 > E[x_0 \mid X_i = x_1])$ or the extent to which all bidders fell prey to the winner's curse $(b_i > E[x_0 \mid X_i = x_1])$ between the two groups. Although average losses were greater and there were fewer auctions with positive profits for bidders with EA experience, this appears to be largely the luck of the draw as predicted RNNE profits are larger for bidders with no experience. This is confirmed by the fact that winning bidders reduced their bids relative to their signal values by roughly the same amount between the two groups (the last column in Table 11.1).

In contrast, bidders with EA experience do considerably worse when bidding in FPAs than bidders with FPA experience: high bidders with FPA experience tell prey to the winner's curse much less often than those with EA experience $(Z = 4.36, p < 0.01)$, as did all bidders $(Z = 6.02, p < 0.01)$. This less aggressive bidding paid off in terms of significantly higher profits for bidders with FPA experience compared with EA experience $(t = 4.23, p < 0.01)$.[4]

Table 11.2 reports bidders with FPA experience bidding in EAs, along with two control groups of EAs. Unfortunately the value of ε varies between comparison groups, although given the random draws actually realized, expected profits under the RNNE are quite similar. In contrast to Table 11.1, in this case bidders with cross-game experience do somewhat better than those with no experience (again, concentrating on the pooled data): average EA profits were $0.66 higher for bidders with FPA experience with $N = 4$ $(t = 0.38)$ and $2.36 higher with $N = 7$ $(t = 1.90, p < 0.10$, two-tailed t-test).[5] Furthermore, bidders with FPA experience do about as well in EAs as those with EA experience: for $N = 4$ their average profits were $0.48 less per auction period $(t = 0.27)$, whereas with $N = 7$ their average profits were $1.00 more per auction period $(t = 0.81)$.[6]

To summarize: for CV auctions, experience in FPAs improves performance in FPAs, but experience in EAs yields no benefits when bidding in FPAs. Although experience in EAs does not improve EA performance as dramatically as does same auction experience in FPAs, FPAs appear to have some positive transfer value to EAs.

TABLE 11.1
Bidding in First-Price Auctions: Cross-Game Experience Effects[a]

Prior Experience	Auction Session (no. auctions)	High Bidders: Percentage of $b_1 > E[x_0\|X_1 = x_1]$	All Bidders: Percentage of $b_1 > E[x_0\|X_1 = x_1]$ (raw data)	Average Actual Profit (S_m)	Average Predicted RNNE Profit (S_m)	Average Discount = $(x_i - b_1)$ (S_m)
English Auctions[b]	1 (13)	84.6 (11/13)	55.8 (29/52)	−3.50 (1.12)	3.59 (0.77)	4.44 (0.72)
	2 (11)	45.5 (5/11)	56.8 (25/44)	0.06 (1.64)	5.27 (1.15)	6.79 (0.69)
	3 (12)	91.7 (11/12)	58.3 (28/48)	−3.78 (1.32)	3.45 (0.78)	4.31 (0.94)
	Pooled (36)	77.8 (28/36)	58.3 (84/144)	−2.51 (0.81)	4.06 (0.52)	5.11 (0.48)
No Experience	1 (11)	54.6 (6/11)	52.3 (23/44)	−1.08 (1.51)	4.82 (1.02)	4.26 (1.87)
	2[c] (20)	80.0 (16/20)	73.8 (59/80)	−0.52 (0.84)	5.99 (0.86)	4.92 (0.66)
	3 (2)	100.0 (2/2)	62.3 (5/8)	−3.40 (7.02)	5.56 (4.07)	3.05 (2.96)
	4 (8)	87.5 (7/8)	47.5 (19/40)	−3.13 (2.55)	2.68 (1.31)	3.77 (1.91)
	Pooled (41)	75.6 (31/41)	64.6 (106/164)	−1.32 (0.79)	5.01 (0.60)	4.42 (0.69)
First-Price Auctions[d]	1[c] (46)	37.0 (17/46)	48.4 (89/184)	1.92 (0.66)	47.1 (0.50)	8.40 (0.52)
	2[c] (43)	34.9 (15/43)	26.7 (46/172)	0.78 (0.72)	3.90 (0.66)	6.42 (0.76)
	Pooled (89)	34.8 (31/89)	29.5 (105/356)	1.37 (0.49)	4.36 (0.41)	7.44 (0.46)

S_m = standard error of mean.

[a] ε = $12, N = 4 in all auctions.

[b] Subjects drawn from the "No experience" sessions with $N = 4$ in Table 11.2.

[c] Two groups of four bidders each bidding simultaneously. Subjects randomly allocated to a new bidding group in each auction period.

[d] Subjects drawn from the "No experience" sessions reported in this table.

TABLE 11.2
Bidding in English Auctions: Cross-Game Experience Effects

Conditions	Auction Session (no. auctions)	Average Actual Profit (S_m)	Average Predicted RNNE Profit (S_m)
First-Price Experience[a]	1	1.10	4.95
$N = 4$; $\varepsilon = 18$	(15)	(2.03)	(1.48)
	2	2.65	3.35
	(6)	(4.45)	(1.09)
	3	−1.86	1.07
	(20)	(2.22)	(1.15)
	Pooled	−0.12	2.82
	(41)	(1.46)	(0.80)
No Experience	1	0.38	4.09
$N = 4$; $\varepsilon = 12$	(10)	(1.52)	(1.17)
	2	−2.38	0.21
	(10)	(1.66)	(1.14)
	3	−1.43	1.57
	(12)	(1.93)	(1.50)
	4	0.17	3.03
	(13)	(2.25)	(1.43)
	Pooled	−0.78	2.25
	(45)	(0.95)	(0.69)
English Experience[b]	1	−0.64	2.02
$N = 4$; $\varepsilon = 12$	(10)	(1.31)	(0.93)
	2	−0.04	2.29
	(11)	(1.00)	(0.69)
	3	1.84	2.07
	(10)	(1.58)	(0.92)
	Pooled	0.37	2.13
	(3)	(0.75)	(0.47)
First-Price Experience[c]	1	−0.30	2.03
$N = 7$; $\varepsilon = 18$	(11)	(2.55)	(0.93)
	2	2.29	1.83
	(12)	(2.15)	(1.39)
	3	0.54	−1.12
	(14)	(1.02)	(0.89)
	4	−2.20	−0.27
	(4)	(2.24)	(2.42)
	Pooled	0.56	1.42
	(41)	(1.00)	(0.68)
No Experience	1	−1.45	1.84
$N = 7$; $\varepsilon = 12$	(16)	(1.41)	(0.61)
	2	−2.87	1.49
	(14)	(1.30)	(0.80)

TABLE 11.2

Continued

Conditions	Auction Session (no. auctions)	Average Actual Profit (S_m)	Average Predicted RNNE Profit (S_m)
	3	−1.06	1.68
	(13)	(1.30)	(0.73)
	Pooled	−1.84	1.73
	(43)	(0.77)	(0.40)
English Experience[b] $N = 4$; $\varepsilon = 12$ and 24	1	−2.76	2.39
	(19)	(1.30)	(0.78)
	2	0.97	2.00
	(28)	(1.22)	(0.60)
	Pooled	−0.54	2.16
	(47)	(0.93)	(0.47)

[a]Subjects participated in two prior auction sessions lasting over 20 auction periods. Subjects drawn from several first-price auction sessions.
[b]Subjects drawn from the "No experience" sessions with $N = 4$ in this table.
[c]Subjects drawn from the "No experience" sessions with $N = 7$ in this table.

4. Analysis and Conclusions

In FPAs bidders are forced to adjust to the winner's curse by reducing bids relative to their signal values. In contrast, in EAs, bidders can, and do, adjust to the winner's curse by using the information inherent in other bidders' drop-out prices (Levin et al., 1994). In EAs, higher valued signal holders learn to rely on lower signal holders' drop-out prices to correct for the overly optimistic estimate of item value inherent in their signal value. This crutch is removed in FPAs. As such, whatever learning occurs in EAs has little direct transfer value in FPAs.

The cross-game learning reported in going from FPAs to EAs is likely to rest on two factors. First, there is a strong tendency for overly aggressive bidders in FPAs to self-select out of returning for later auction sessions (Garvin and Kagel, in press). This is evidenced by bankrupt bidders being significantly less likely to return than those who did not go bankrupt.[7] Second, in terms of the mental model established as a result of bidding in FPAs, a key lesson learned is to sharply discount bids relative to signal values. And this FPA rule has some direct transfer value in EAs.

Situation-specific learning implies behavioral adaptation to a particular set of economic contingencies without any deep understanding of the optimal responses to these contingencies. Kagel and Levin (1986) reported situation-specific learning in CV FPAs: moderately experienced bidders who had learned to avoid the winner's curse in auctions with few ($N = 4$) bidders and earned positive average profits did not immediately adjust to the heightened adverse selection effect associated with larger numbers of bidders ($N = 7$), earning negative average profits. Situation-specific learning implies that games must be very similar in structure, or that the learning/adjustment effects developed in one game must be fortuitously advantageous in another game, before strong cross-game learning effects are likely to be observed. Whether this strong situation-specific learning is peculiar to CV auctions, which prove to be relatively complicated games to play, or is a more general feature of games is an empirical question that remains to be explored.

Notes

Research support from the National Science Foundation is gratefully acknowledged. I thank Ido Erev for helpful insights into the psychology literature on learning and Susan Garvin for research assistance. Responsibility for errors is mine alone.

1. For signals in the interval $\underline{x} + \varepsilon, \bar{x} - \varepsilon$, the RNNE bid function is $x - \varepsilon + h(x)$, where $h(x) = 2\varepsilon/(N + 1) \exp[- (N/2\varepsilon)(x - (\bar{x} + \varepsilon))]$. The bid function for signals outside this interval is characterized in Levin et al. (1994). Expected profit for the high bidder in this interval is approximately $2\varepsilon/(N + 1)$.

2. This is also a symmetric, RNNE bid function for signals in the interval $\underline{x} + \varepsilon$, $\bar{x} - \varepsilon$. The bid function for signals outside this interval is characterized in Levin et al. (1994). Expected profit for the high bidder in this interval is approximately $\varepsilon/(N + 1)$. There are multiple symmetric RNNE for this game, but expected profits are unique (Bikhchandani and Riley, 1991).

3. The alternative is to conduct t-tests treating each auction session as a *single* observation. Doing this does not alter the main conclusions drawn, as will be pointed out in footnotes along the way. Regressions were run to test for time trend effects within each auction session with realized profits as the dependent variable and right-hand-side variables RNNE profit, RNNE profit squared, and a linear (or a non-linear) time trend variable. The latter was usually not statistically significant and, when it was, varied in sign between auction sessions.

4. With each session a single observation for profits, $t = 2.35$, d.f. $= 3$, which barely misses statistical significance at the 10% level, (two-tailed test), and for the percentage of all bids falling prey to the winners curse ($t = 2.38$, d.f. $= 3$, $p < 0.10$) (two-tailed test).

5. With each auction session a single observation profits were $1.45 higher for bidders with FPA experience with $N = 4$ ($t = 1.07$, d.f. $= 5$, $p = 0.33$) and $1.88 higher with $N = 7$ ($t = 1.57$, d.f. $= 5$, $p = 0.18$) (two-tailed test in both cases). Combining these two independent tests (Maddala, 1977, pp. 47–48), we can reject a null hypothesis of no difference at $p = 0.23$.

6. With each auction session a single observation profits are marginally higher for those with FPA experience both for $N = 4$ ($0.23, $t = 0.16$) and $N = 7$ ($0.98, $t = 0.54$).

7. This factor is not present in going from EAs to FPAs as there are substantially fewer bankruptcies among inexperienced bidders in EAs (5%) than in FPAs (23%).

References

Bikhchandani, S. and J.G. Riley, 1991, Equilibria in open common value auctions, Journal of Economic Theory 53, 101–130.

Fudenberg, D. and D.M. Kreps, 1988, A theory of learning, experimentation, and equilibrium in games, mimeo, MIT.

Garvin, S. and J.H. Kagel, in press, Learning in common value auctions: Some initial observations, Journal of Economic Behavior and Organization.

Kagel, J.H., in press, Auctions: A survey of experimental research, in: J.H. Kagel and A.E. Roth, eds. Handbook of experimental economics (Princeton University Press, Princeton).

Kagel, J.H. and D. Levin, 1986, The winner's curse and public information in common value auctions, American Economic Review 76, 894–920.

Levin, D., J.H. Kagel and J.F. Richard, 1994, Revenue raising and information processing in English common value auctions, mimeo, University of Pittsburgh.

Maddala, G.S., 1977, Econometrics (McGraw-Hill, New York).

Wickens, C.D., 1992, Engineering psychology and human performance, 2nd edn. (Harper Collins, New York).

12

A Comparison of Naive and Experienced Bidders in Common Value Offer Auctions: A Laboratory Analysis

—

Douglas Dyer, John H. Kagel, and Dan Levin

Laboratory economics experiments typically use financially motivated students as subjects. An ongoing issue is whether this is an appropriate subject pool since the students are typically inexperienced in the types of decision-making required of them in the lab. This paper addresses this issue in the context of common value offer auctions as we compare the behaviour of experienced business executives in the construction contract industry ('experts') with that of ('naive') student subjects. Results of previous research of this sort have been equivocal; in some cases experts make the same errors as novices, in other cases they do not (Hogarth and Reder, 1987).

A series of sealed-bid, common value offer auctions in which bidders compete for the right to supply an item of unknown cost were conducted. Inherent to common value auctions (CVAs) is an adverse selection problem which may result in below normal or negative profits (the winner's curse). Experimental studies have documented the presence of the winner's curse with financially motivated student subjects in high price demand-side auctions (Kagel *et al.*, 1986; Kagel and Levin, 1986). The experiments reported here generalise these earlier studies from bid to offer auctions. Also, in employing offer auctions we establish a setting with which our 'experts' are familiar, thus allowing their experience the best chance to manifest itself.[1]

1. Structure of the Auctions

Experiments 1–3 employed University of Houston upper-level economics majors with no prior laboratory experience. Experiment 4 used executives from local construction companies with an average of over 20 years experience in the construction industry. All but one of these individuals had many years experience in the actual bid preparation process.

Each experiment consisted of a series of auction periods in which the right to supply a single unit of a commodity was awarded to the low bidder using a first-price, sealed-bid institution. The actual cost of producing the item, C, was unknown at the time bids were submitted. The low bidder earned a profit equal to the difference between his bid and the actual cost of supplying the item; all other bidders earned zero profits.

C was drawn randomly from a uniform distribution on [\$50.00, \$250.00]. Each bidder received a private information signal, c_i, randomly drawn from a uniform distribution on $[C - \varepsilon, C + \varepsilon]$. The distributions underlying both C and the private information signals were common knowledge as was ε and the number of bidders, N.

To cover the possibility of losses subjects were given starting capital credit balances of at least \$10.00. Losses were subtracted from this balance and profits added to it. Subjects were told that if this balance went to zero or less that they would no longer be allowed to participate. After all bids were submitted they were posted along with the corresponding signal values, and the low bid noted, C was announced and profits (or losses) were calculated and balances updated. Each period the profit or loss earned was announced, but not the identity of the low bidder.

Experiments 1–3 employed four active bidders throughout. Experiment 4 began with four active bidders; after 24 periods bidding was done in markets with $N = 7$ both with and without public information which consisted of announcing the highest cost estimate (C_H) received by an active bidder.[2] Profits were paid in only one of the two markets. The market paid was determined randomly.

2. Theoretical Considerations

Wilson (1977) was the first to develop a Nash equilibrium solution for first-price sealed-bid CVAs. In the interval $[\$50 + \varepsilon < c_i < \$250 - \varepsilon]$ the symmetric risk neutral Nash equilibrium (SRNNE) bid function is

$$b(c_i) = c_i + \varepsilon - Y \tag{1}$$

where $Y = [2\varepsilon/(N + 1)] \exp [- (N/2\varepsilon) (250 - \varepsilon - c_i)]$. The Y term contains a negative exponential and diminishes rapidly as c_i moves below $\$250 - \varepsilon$.

The SRNNE calls for signals to be "marked-up" by an amount approximately equal to ε.[3]

The winner's curse arises as the result of bidders failing to properly account for the adverse selection process at work in CVAs. Consider two alternative expectations of the actual cost, based on a given estimate. In the interval $[\$50 + \varepsilon < c_i < \$250 - \varepsilon]$ an unbiased estimate of C is:

$$E(C \mid C_i) = c_i. \tag{2}$$

However this expectation is naive in that it fails to account for the fact that the low bidder tends to have the lowest, or one of the lowest, private information signals. An estimator which takes this information into account would be the expected cost, conditional on having the lowest signal:

$$E(C \mid C_i = c_1) = c_i + [(N - 1)/(N + 1)]\varepsilon \tag{3}$$

where c_1 refers to the lowest signal. Given symmetry (or a high rank order correlation between bids and signals) in bidding, winning bids less than (3) will result in losses on average.

Note that there are two opposing forces at work when the number of bidders is increased in a CVA. There is a strategic force which tends to promote lower bidding as the number of bidders increases: With a greater number of rivals there is less room to markup bids relative to cost estimates and still win the auction. However item valuation considerations promote higher bidding: The adverse selection problem is greater the higher the number of bidders. Given the distributions in our design, the item valuation force dominates the strategic force, and the SRNNE requires that individual bids be constant or increasing as N increases (see (1)).

Milgrom and Weber (1982) extend the CVA model developed by Wilson. They show that in a high price auction, the release of public information regarding the true value of the item will raise seller's revenues on average. The analogous effect here is that the release of public information regarding the true cost of the item will lower the offer price, thus lowering bidder's profits.

Note that this is an equilibrium prediction. If the market is characterised by the winner's curse, i.e. below normal or negative profits, then the release of public information may have the effect of *increasing* the low bid, as bidders utilise the additional information to avoid the valuation errors which underlie the winner's curse.

3. Experimental Results

3.1 Experiments with N = 4

Figure 12.1 shows the market outcomes, by period, for experiment 4 (the executives). The actual profits earned along with the SRNNE predicted profits are shown for each period. Negative or near zero profits dominate; there appears to be little evidence of systematic learning over time within the experiment. A

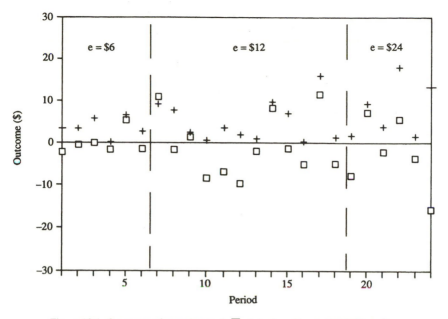

Figure 12.1. Outcomes of experiment 4. □, Actual profits; +, SRNNE profits.

similar absence of within experiment learning is reported for the student sub-jects (Dyer, 1987).

Table 12.1 begins our comparison of subject populations. The second column reports the percentage of auction periods in which the low bid was submitted by the lower signal holder. Columns 3 and 4 report average actual profits earned and average profits predicted by the SRNNE, respectively. The fifth and sixth columns report the percentage of times the low bid was less than (3), the ex-pected cost conditional on having received the lowest estimate and the percent-age of all bids that were less than this conditional expectation.

Regarding the comparison across subject populations, both groups commit the winner's curse as average profits are negative in three of the four experi-ments and are not statistically different from zero in the other experiment. We find no significant differences, at the 10% level or better, across populations in any of the following measures of market performance: the percentage of times the low bid was submitted by the low signal holder, average actual profits and the percentage of times the low bid was less than (3). Finally, at an individual level we find no difference in the percentage of all bids less than (3).

More detailed analysis of the data reveals some differences however. The student subject experiments show a pattern of decreasing losses as ε increases from 6 to 12, with positive profits as ε increases from 12 to 24. When ε is returned to 12 losses again dominate. The executives show a different pattern, with modest losses at ε = 6, which increases as ε increases.

Regression analysis on individual bid functions shows that the students em-

TABLE 12.1

Market Outcomes: N = 4

Experiment	Percentage of Auctions Won by the Low Signal Holder (no. times/no. per.)	Average Actual Profits (t-stat)	Average Profits under SRNNE	Percentage of Low Bids $b_i > E(C_0 \mid c_i = c_j)$ (no. times/no. per.)	Percentage of All Bids $b_i < E(C_0 \mid c_i = c_j)$ (no. times/no. per.)
1	70 (19/27)	−1.36 (−0.70)	6.03	85 (23/27)	67 (72/108)
2	65 (22/34)	0.18 (0.19)	4.43	53 (18/34)	45* (42/93)
3	77 (27/35)	−0.16 (−0.16)	4.83	66 (22/35)	52 (73/140)
Total (1–3)	71 (68/96)	−0.37	5.02	66 (63/96)	55 (187/341)
4 (execs)	79 (19/24)	−1.01 (0.74)	5.42	67 (16/24)	49 (47/96)

*All subjects had no prior laboratory experience except for two subjects in experiment 2 who had participated in experiment 1. Since there were seven subjects present for experiment 2 we believe any effects of these subjects' prior experience to be negligible.

†Experiments 1 and 2 began with two dry runs, experiment 3 with three dry runs, and Experiment 4 with one dry run. These periods are deleted from the analysis.

‡In Exp. 1 $\varepsilon = 6$ in periods 1–6, $\varepsilon = 12$ in 7–16 and 24–27, and $\varepsilon = 24$ in 17–23.
In Exp. 2 $\varepsilon = 6$ in periods 1–6, $\varepsilon = 12$ in 7–16 and 25–34, and $\varepsilon = 24$ in 17–24.
In Exp. 3 $\varepsilon = 6$ in periods 1–7, $\varepsilon = 12$ in 8–18 and 31–35, and $\varepsilon = 24$ in 19–30.
In Exp. 4 $\varepsilon = 6$ in periods 1–6, $\varepsilon = 12$ in 7–18 and 25–36, and $\varepsilon = 24$ in 19–24 and 37–40.

§The starting capital balance was $10.00 in Exp. 1 and 2 and $20.00 in Exp. 3. Exp. 4 began with a capital balance of $20.00. When N was increased from 4 to 7 each subject was given a new capital balance of $25.00, with the understanding that the ending balances from part one of the experiment would be added to the ending balances from part two and paid in cash at the end of the experiment.

ployed a larger fixed markdown and were more responsive to changes in ε than the executives. We believe these different bidding rules may be reflective of underlying differences in risk attitudes between the two groups, with the students exhibiting risk aversion and the executives risk neutrality. The latter argument is supported by the fact that with increases in ε, cost estimates are less precise, which, other things equal, is likely to be reflected in proportionately greater markups in bids relative to signal values for risk averse bidders. Further, it seems reasonable to assume that the executives would be closer to risk neutrality, especially over the sums at stake in these auctions, than the student subjects. In either case, we see a somewhat different pattern of bidding with changing ε across the two subject populations (see Dyer, 1987, for a more complete discussion).

The different pattern of profits/losses with changes in ε, and the differences in estimated bid functions, lead us to reject the maintained hypothesis that there

TABLE 12.2
Market Data with Changing N Experiment 4

	N = 4		N = 7	
ε	*Average Actual Profits*	*Average SRNNE Profits*	*Average Actual Profits*	*Average SRNNE Profits*
12	-0.57	5.08	-1.98	3.97
24	-2.77	7.94	-3.22	4.11

are *no* differences between the two subject pools; however, we feel that the similarities are much more striking than the differences.

3.2 Effects of Changing N and Public Information

Table 12.2 reports the results of changing N in experiment 4. Losses dominate with both $N = 4$ and $N = 7$ for both $\varepsilon = 12$ and $\varepsilon = 24$ and increase as N increases. Increasing losses with increased numbers of rivals implies that individual bidders are responding in the wrong direction, or are not responding sufficiently in the right direction, to overcome the increased adverse selection problem inherent in more bidders. Regression analysis shows the executives do bid slightly higher with $N = 7$. This response is qualitatively in the direction predicted by the SRNNE; however, the magnitude of the response is less than that needed to avoid larger losses with increased N.

The response to changing N is qualitatively different from results reported with student subjects in both low and high price experiments (Dyer, 1987 and Kagel and Levin, 1986) and may well represent a difference between the two subject pools. However this conclusion is not without qualification. The student experiments involved experienced subjects who were making relatively large positive average profits in markets with $N = 4$ when the number of bidders increased, while the executives were suffering losses when we increased market size from four to seven bidders. Coming from the domain of positive profits, the students may have been more sensitive to the strategic pressures of changing N than the item valuation forces, which would lead them to bid more aggressively when the number of rivals increased. The executives however, coming from the domain of negative profits, may have been more responsive to the item valuation forces. Given that they were already suffering from the winner's curse, when N increased simple survival pressures dictated bidding less aggressively to avoid bankruptcy, and exit from the market. These differences in context provide an alternative explanation to the observed behavioural differences than any fundamental difference between the two subject pools.

Table 3 reports the results of announcing C_H, the highest private information signal received by an active bidder, on the offer price. Pooled over the 11 observations, public information *raised* the offer price by \$2.91 ($t = 1.87$ sig-

TABLE 12.3
The Effects of Public Information on the Offer Price Experiment 4 $N = 7$

	Average Change in Offer Price		Results from Private Information Market		
ε (No. persons)	Actual (t-stat)	Predicted	Average Profits	SRNNE Profits	Percentage of Periods Won by Low Signal Holder
12	1.51	−3.34	−1.55	4.48	86
(7)	(1.60)				(6/7)
24	5.26	−0.52	−3.22	4.11	50
(4)	(1.35)				(2/4)
Combined	2.91	−1.60	−2.16	3.63	72
(11)	(1.87)				(8/11)

nificant at the 5% level, 2-tailed test). This is contrary to the theoretical prediction of a *decrease* in the offer price of $1.60 but is consistent with earlier findings with student subjects (Kagel and Levin, 1986). The perverse effects of public information relative to Nash equilibrium bidding theory generalise from students to the executives and from a bid to an offer auction institution.

4. Conclusion and Discussion

Our experiments show that the judgmental failure known as the winner's curse, which has been documented in laboratory high price auction experiments, extends to an offer auction institution. Further, results with inexperienced bidders in large markets extend to small markets, as a strong and persistent winner's curse was found when bidding was done in markets with only four bidders. Finally similar results are reported almost without exception across students and business executives. We conclude that the winner's curse phenomenon is robust across auction form, market size and subject population.

The results for the executives seem most surprising given their experience bidding in a market presumed to have a strong common value component. In reporting these surprising results two recurring issues have been raised: (1) the executives may not have been taking the experiment seriously, with bidding done more or less at random, and/or (2) there may be institutional factors which protect overly aggressive low price bidders from suffering losses in the field. We now address these two issues.

Regarding the attitude of the executives we emphatically reject the criticism that they did not take the experiment seriously. The group was attentive during the reading of the instructions, asked relevant questions, and in every way gave the impression of wanting to make as much money as possible. Although the amounts of money at stake were not large relative to their other earnings, predicted profits under the SRNNE approached $100.00 for the three hour experiment, not a trivial sum. Most important the data offer no support for the idea that the executives were not bidding seriously; regression analysis shows clearly that they were responsive to their private information signals, and that changes in N and ε had a statistically significant effect on behavior in the "right" direction.

The second criticism is more substantial. The executives *are* successful in their industry. If they made the same bidding errors consistently in the field, they could not remain in business. Instead recurring losses would necessitate a change in bidding strategy, or would result in bankruptcy and exit from the market. Why then are the executives successful in their field but suffer persistent losses in the lab? Several reasons suggest themselves. First, part of the dispersion of bids in the field reflects a strong private value component to bidding in the construction industry. This is reflected in one of the questions received following the reading of the instructions: "What is my overhead at this time?" This indicates that at any given time different firms have different opportunity costs of committing to a new project; part of the dispersion of bids in the field undoubtedly reflects different opportunity costs rather than different valuations.

Clearly however this is not the whole story. Here we rely on discussions with people in the industry, including the executive subjects. The response is always fundamentally the same—it definitely *is possible* to suffer losses (and large losses) on a given project.[4] While there are processes which may mitigate such losses, such as renegotiation or change orders, these losses are not eliminated altogether.

How then can we explain the divergence of behavior in the field and in the lab? We believe that the executives have learned a set of situation specific rules of thumb which permit them to avoid the winner's curse in the field but which could not be applied in the lab.[5] Success in the field is in part a function of detailed knowledge about a particular market environment; when removed from this environment the executives' behavior parallels that of "naive" subjects. Success in the field thus derives not from conformity to a narrow notion of rationality, but from acquiring and utilising detailed knowledge of a particular market environment.

This analysis implies that the winner's curse is likely to be strongest in the start-up phase of a market, in those markets which experience the greatest turnover of participants and in markets where large numbers of agents come in and out sporadically so as not to acquire any strong learning from experience. Further it has fundamental implications for how learning occurs in economic environments in general: Not through understanding and absorbing "the theory", but from rules of thumb that are likely to breakdown under extreme changes, or truly novel, economic conditions.

Notes

Financial support was received from the Information Science and Technology Division and the Economics Division of the NSF, the Sloan Foundation, and the Energy Laboratory of the University of Houston. We would like to thank Ron Harstad and Susan Garvin for comments and assistance. The paper has benefited from comments of discussants at the Winter 1987 Econometric Society meetings and the referee and editor of this JOURNAL. This is a shortened version of Dyer et al. (1987) which contains a complete description of the experimental design, including instructions. Interested readers should contact Douglas Dyer, Department of Economics, Memphis State University.

1. We do not claim that the laboratory setting we created is an exact replica of the commercial construction industry. However it captures many of the essential features and relevant economic considerations of that market. At the very least the executives are quite experienced in translating imprecise estimates into bids in competitive offer auctions.

2. Two experienced student subjects were added to the five executives to create a market with $N = 7$.

3. Unfortunately there is no clear cut prediction as to the effects of risk aversion on the equilibrium bid function. Depending on the nature and degree of the risk aversion, equilibrium bids could be greater than or less than the SRNNE.

4. Everyone we interviewed had stories of individual projects which resulted in large losses. These losses were attributed to a variety of factors, including poor take-offs, incorrect pricing formulas, and misforecast of such things as labor troubles, subcontractor reliability, and weather.

5. This learning may be the result of trial and error which through information feedback results in the adoption of rules which "work", or it may be the result of the market environment "selecting for" those agents whose behavior enables them to survive, with those agents using inappropriate rules not being viable (i.e. being forced out of the market). Kagel and Dyer (1987) and Kagel and Levin (1986) provide strong evidence that learning within the laboratory is situation specific as well.

References

Dyer, D. (1987). 'An experimental analysis of auction theory.' PhD Dissertation, University of Houston.

———— Kagel, J. and Levin, D. (1987). 'Common value offer auctions: bidding behavior of student subjects and construction contractors.' University of Houston, September.

Hogarth, R. M. and Reder, M. W. (1987). 'Perspectives from economics and psychology.' in *Rational Choice*, Chicago: University of Chicago Press.

Kagel, J. H. and Dyer, D. (1988). 'Learning in common value auctions.' *Experimental Games and Markets* (Reinhard Tietz, Wulf Albers and Reinhard Selten, eds.). Berlin: Springer-Verlag.

———— Levin, D., Battalio, R. C. and Meyer, D. J. (1989). 'First-price, sealed-bid, common value auctions bidder behavior and the "winner's curse".' *Economic Inquiry*, (forthcoming).

———— and Levin, D. (1986). 'The winner's curse and public information in common value auctions.' *American Economic Review*, Vol. 77, pp. 894–920.

Milgrom, P. and Weber, R. (1982). 'A theory of auctions and competitive bidding.' *Econometrica*, Vol. 50, pp. 1089–122.

Wilson, R. (1977) 'A bidding model of perfect competition.' *Review of Economic Studies*, Vol. 44, pp. 511–8.

13

Bidding in Common Value Auctions: How the Commercial Construction Industry Corrects for the Winner's Curse

—

Douglas Dyer and John H. Kagel

1. Introduction

Construction contract bidding is usually treated as a common value auction. In a pure common value auction the value of the item is the same to all bidders. What makes the auction interesting is that bidders have different estimates of the true value at the time they bid. Assuming that bids decrease with decreasing cost estimates, the low bidder faces an adverse selection problem, as he/she wins only when he or she has one of the lowest estimates of the cost of construction. Unless this adverse selection problem is accounted for in bidding, the low bidder is likely to stiffer from a "winner's curse," winning the item but making below normal or even negative profits.

Oil companies claim that they fell prey to the winner's, curse in early outer continental shelf (OCS) oil lease auctions (Capen et al., 1971; Mead et al., 1983; Gilley et al., 1986). Similar claims have been made in auctions for book publication rights (Dessauer, 1981), in professional baseball's free agency market (Cassing and Douglas, 1980), and in corporate takeover battles (Roll, 1986). The winner's curse has been shown to be a robust phenomenon in laboratory auction markets as well (Bazerman and Samuelson, 1983; Kagel and Levin, 1986; see Kagel 1995 for a review of laboratory research results).

"Sophisticated" bidders—executives drawn from the commercial construction industry—also suffer front a winner's curse in laboratory auction markets (Dyer et al., 1989). What is more remarkable yet is that these executives suffered from the winner's curse to the same extent as inexperienced student subjects: average losses per auction period were $1.01 for the executives versus losses of $0.37 per auction for the students (these differences are not statistically significant; predicted profits with risk-neutral Nash equilibrium bidding were over $5.00 per action in both cases). Further, losses in both cases were not simply a matter of bad luck, as over 65% of the *low* bids were below the expected value conditional on winning the auction for both subject populations, thereby ensuring negative expected profit in over 65% of all auction periods. Nor did these losses result from overly aggressive bidding on the part of one or two subjects, as 50% of *all* bids were below the expected value conditional on winning the auction, so that half of all bids resulted in negative expected profit for both subject populations.

How can experienced, seasoned executives fall prey to a winner's curse in the laboratory but compete successfully and prosper in substantially more complicated field settings? Or to phrase the question the way most biologists and a number of psychologists would: What are the essential differences between the theory underlying laboratory auction market experiments and the natural habitat (field environment) in which these expert bidders developed their skills ("evolved") that caused them to malfunction in the laboratory? We answer this question through follow-up interviews of these executives and others operating in the same market and the analysis of relevant field data.

Two broad conclusions are reached. One is that the executives have learned a set of situation-specific rules of thumb which help them to avoid the winner's curse in the field, but which could not be applied in the laboratory markets. The second is that the bidding environment created in the laboratory and the theory underlying it are not fully representative of the field environment. Rather, the latter has developed escape mechanisms for avoiding the winner's curse that are mutually beneficial to both buyers and sellers and which have not been incorporated into the standard one-shot auction theory literature. In the course of reporting these results we characterize and compare the distribution of bids in the commercial construction industry with outer continental shelf (OCS) oil lease sales, the other auction market commonly characterized as a pure common value auction.

The paper that is closest in spirit to this one is Burns (1985). Both papers share a common motivation: to explain the rather dismal performance of seasoned executives in laboratory auction markets. Both papers identify essential differences between field settings and the theory underlying the experiment that are of central importance to adaptation in the field. An important byproduct of this analysis is the identification of important modeling issues that have been overlooked in the theory. However, whereas Burns studied sequential, private value English auctions, our paper studies sealed bid, common value offer auctions. Thus, there are important differences between adaptive processes and institutional features of the two markets. In addition, we identify a number of interesting, industry-specific practices and show how modern auction theory literature can explain their evolution.

2. Bidding Structure, Industry Characteristics, and Sample Data

Competitive sealed-bid auctions are commonly used in the commercial construction industry. Bids are broken down into a basic bid and bids on alternate plan specifications. The winning bid is determined on the basis of the total bid, including the cost of the alternate conditions adopted. Bids must be submitted by a fixed deadline. The primary difference in bidding on private versus public construction is that there is no announcement of losing bids for private work. In addition, a considerable amount of private sector work, particularly for larger, more unusual jobs, is awarded through "negotiated" contracts.

Jobs that are up for competitive bid are listed in trade publications. These trade publications report the general contractors (GCs), by name, who have purchased the blueprints required to bid a job. Names of subcontractors (SCs) purchasing blueprints are also reported. In some cases bidding is restricted to an approved list of GCs (and sometimes to approved lists of SCs as well). These are contractors who have a track record for completing the work specified beyond satisfying the usual performance bond requirements.

GCs are primarily responsible for lining up SCs and general material supplies and for supervising and coordinating work on the job site. GCs provide minimal direct input into a job so that it is not unusual for SC and material expenses to total 90% of the price bid. SCs are responsible for the material expenses associated with their work and may employ other SCs as well.

Table 13.1 lists the GCs whose top executive officers were interviewed and/or provided us with extensive bid tab sheets (lists of the firm's bid and rivals' bids; bid tabs occasionally contain very illuminating written comments as well). Shown in the table are the gross value of construction contracts and the number of employees, along with the firm's primary activities (including SIC codes). Although there are no doubt some inconsistencies in the numbers reported, particularly in the relationship between sales and employment, the sales figures accurately capture the range of firm sizes, and the activity list is representative of the work performed. Two of the firms, Spaw-Glass and W. S. Bellows, consistently rank among the top 200 contractors in the United States (as measured by McGraw Hill's ENR reports).

3. Theoretical Considerations

The basic theory of discriminatory offer auctions assumes a buyer who purchases a single item from sellers in a one-shot auction. The number (n) of bidders and the probability distribution of bidders' private information are assumed to be common knowledge, with risk neutrality commonly assumed as well. Nature assigns each bidder i a pair of numbers (x_i, v_i), where x_i is a real valued "signal" observed before i submits a bid, and v_i is the construction cost

TABLE 13.1
Characteristics of Firms Included in Study

Company Name	Sales	Employment	Activities (SIC code)
Marshall Construction	10 MM	35	Commercial & office building, new construction (1542).
Basic Constructors, Inc.	13 MM	150	Waste water & sewage treatment plant construction (1629).
Paisan Construction Co.	13 MM	60	School building construction; religious building construction, hotel/motel & multi-family home renovation (1542, 1522).
Cahaba Construction Co.	70 MM	110	Commercial & office building, new construction, renovation and repair; school & hospital building construction (1542).
W. S. Bellows Construction	100 MM	300	Commercial & office building, new construction (1542).
Lott Group, Inc.	100 MM	200	Commercial & office building, new construction, renovation & repair; hotel/motel new construction (1542, 1522).
Spaw-Glass Construction, Inc.	262 MM	1200	Nonresidential construction; institutional building construction; industrial building & warehouses; hotel/motel, new construction; general contractor, highway & street construction (1542, 1541, 1522, 1611).

Data Source: The Million Dollar Directory Series (Year 1990).

of bidder i. If i wins the auction with offer o (x_i), profits are o $(x_i) - v_i$. In practice, x_i is interpreted as i's sample observation, which is used to establish an initial estimate, $E\{v_i \mid x_i\}$, of the cost of the item, with the true cost observed only after the auction.

In a pure common values model v_i is the same for all i. The main results for common value auctions are due to Milgrom (1979a, b) and Wilson (1977), who assume that signals are conditionally independent and identically distributed, given v, with positive density $f(\cdot \mid v)$ (each bidder's signal is an unbiased estimate of v). However, with symmetry, bidder i wins only when he has the lowest signal value, so that $E\{v \mid x_i\}$ is biased, conditional on the event of winning. This bias can be quite strong. Failure to account for this estimating bias is often referred to as the "winner's curse."

The characteristics of individual offer functions are sensitive to the distributions underlying the signal values and the marginal distribution of v. As n increases, two competing forces are at work-strategic factors promote lower offers, but the heightened adverse selection effect promotes higher offers. For a number of distributions the net effect is that the equilibrium bidding strategy first decreases in it and then increases (see Wilson, 1992 and Rothkopf, 1969). However, under assumptions that hold for most distributions, the expected winning offer decreases in n throughout.

"Money left on the table"—the difference between the low bid and the second lowest bid—is an important indicator of the variance underlying bidders' signal values. It also serves as an immediately available indicator that the winning bidder may have fallen prey to the winner's curse. It too varies with n, with the sign depending on the underlying distribution of signal values.

In the pure private values model $x_i \equiv v_i$. Here individual offer functions must be decreasing in n as there is no potential winner's curse promoting higher offers. As a consequence the winning offer will be decreasing in n as well. Here too the effect of n on money left on the table depends on the distribution function underlying the signal values.

Table 13.2 provides numerical illustrations of these effects, The common value auction calculations assume that v is uniformly distributed on the interval $[\underline{v}, \bar{v}]$, with individual bidder signal values, x_i, uniformly distributed on the interval $[v - \delta, v + \delta]$ (these distributions were used in Dyer et al., 1989). The private value calculations are for an affiliated private value auction in which the v_i are uniformly distributed on the interval $[v_o - \delta, v_o + \delta]$, with v_o uniformly distributed on the interval $[\underline{v}, \bar{v}]$ (the realization of v_o is unknown when bids are made). Players in this affiliated private value auction face essentially the same strategic considerations vis-a-vis other players' actions as in the common value auction, only there is no uncertainty about each player's "cost of construction."

The first row reports bid mark-ups as a percentage of δ required to avoid the winner's curse (these mark-ups are added to individual bidder's signal values). For the pure common value auction, to avoid the winner's curse (break even) requires a substantial mark-up of bids relative to signal values (60% with $n = 4$, 84.6% with $n = 12$). In contrast, with affiliated private values, as long as bidders do not bid below their private valuations, they cannot lose money. The second row reports bid mark-ups for the symmetric risk-neutral Nash equilibrium bid function (RNNE) (where, by symmetry, we assume that all bidders employ the same mark-up rule). In the case of common value auctions the two competing forces—bid more as a result of more competition, bid less on account of the winner's curse—just cancel each other out with bidders essentially

TABLE 13.2

Mark-up Factors, Winner's Expected Profit, and Money Left on the Table
(calculated as a percentage of δ)

			Auction Type			
		Common Value			*Affiliated Private Value*	
n:	4	7	12	4	7	12
Mark-up Needed to Prevent Winner's Curse	60%	75%	84.6%	0%	0%	0%
Equilibrium Bid Mark-up	100%	100%	100%	50%	28.6%	16.7%
Expected Profit	40%	25%	15.4%	50%	28.6%	16.7%
Money Left on Table	10%	3.6%	1.3%	10%	3.6%	1.3%

Equilibrium bid mark-up and expected profit are approximate as the bid function includes a negative exponential term that diminishes rapidly as x_i drops below $\bar{x} - \delta$ (see Dyer et al. 1989 for details).

adding a constant to their cost estimate independent of n. In contrast, with affiliated private values the mark-up is decreasing in n throughout, as there is no winner's curse to guard against. In both cases expected profit of the winning bidder is decreasing monotonically in n, as is money left on the table.

4. Bid Distribution Characteristics of Sample Data

Records of bid distributions on jobs were obtained directly from the firms interviewed. Our data consist of whatever bid tabs we could get from the firms (some firms did not maintain old records) and covers the years 1985–1990. Since only a single bid tab is needed to have complete information for a given job, and many of these firms compete regularly with each other, we also have considerable data for firms that did not maintain old records. Building activity in Houston peaked in the years 1984–85, with a sharp downturn from 1987–1990 (Smith, 1992). However, an interim analysis based on bid tabs for the years 1985–86 showed no major differences with our more complete six-year data analysis.

We've broken the bid tab data into the five categories in Table 13.3. Categories were determined on the basis of discussion with GCs indicating that remodeling work involved more uncertainty than new construction, and that remodeling for the Houston Public Housing Authority (HPHA) was subject to more than the usual sort of uncertainties, as they can be very hard to satisfy at times. Private construction is under-represented in the analysis as firms must call rivals to determine their bids or to get rough percentage figures for the distribution of bids from the owner or architect. We included those jobs for which we had reasonably complete bid tabs.

Summary statistics are in Table. 13.3. Listed first is the mean number of bidders by job category (with the standard deviation in parentheses). It averages

TABLE 13.3
Quantitative Analysis of Bid Tab Data (standard deviation in parentheses)

Job Categories	(1) Mean No. of Bidders	(2) Mean Bid	(3) Mean $(B_{L+1} - B_L)$	(4) Mean $\left[\dfrac{B_{L+1} - B_L}{B_L}\right]$	(5) Min $\left[\dfrac{B_{L+1} - B_L}{B_L}\right]$	(6) Max $\left[\dfrac{B_{L+1} - B_L}{B_L}\right]$	(7) No. of Jobs in Sample
Renovations and Remodeling: Public facilities	6.7 (3.2)	2,424,610 (3,328,764)	61,009 (100,499)	0.050 (0.081)	0.0003	0.497	53
Churches: New construction and additions	6.1 (1.9)	890,278 (714,324)	27,522 (22,667)	0.051 (0.056)	0.0070	0.261	29
Remodeling: Houston Housing Authority	3.2 (1.1)	2,565,176 (1,841,593)	218,939 (186,279)	0.157 (0.108)	0.0197	0.294	5
New Construction: Public schools and other public facilities	8.4 (3.4)	7,889,030 (8,035,336)	138,215 (247,007)	0.021 (0.027)	0.0000	0.222	176
Private construction: New and remodeling	6.0 (2.1)	1,928,710 (3,273,194)	59,449 (81,223)	0.070 (0.083)	0.0060	0.426	32

B_L = low bid; B_{L+1} = second-lowest bid.
All bid tab data included had two or more bids. We occasionally (1–2 times) came across a job with a single bid. These contracts were not awarded.

a high of 8.4 for new construction to a low of 3.2 for the HPHA, and averages between 6–7 in the other three job categories. In contrast, Hendricks et al. (1987) report an average of 3.5 bidders for wildcat OCS leases. Although the uncertainties encountered in bidding for OCS leases are typically orders of magnitude greater than those encountered in these construction contracts, both are commonly treated as canonical examples of common value auctions. As such it is worthwhile comparing the differences, as well as similarities, between bidding in the two markets (also see Keefer 1991 for discussion of standard assumptions underlying winner's curse models that are frequently violated in OCS bidding).

Mean bids are reported next. These range from a high of $7.9 million for new public construction to a low of $0.9 million in church construction.

Money left on the table is reported in both absolute dollar amount (column 3) and as a percentage of the low bid (columns 4–6). Mean money left on the table ranges from a high of 15.7% for the HPHA to a low of 2.1% for new construction in public schools and other public facilities. Note the latter is on jobs with the highest mean bid, $7.9 million. Outside of the HPHA, there is simply very little money left on the table as a percentage of the low bid, averaging 7% or less in all other categories. These data indicate that the underlying distribution of signal values, x_i, is quite compact, substantially more compact than in OCS leasing where money left on the table averages 50% of the winning bid for new leases (Hendricks et al., 1987). Only a very tiny part of this difference can be accounted for by the fact that there are fewer bidders, on average, in OCS auctions (on construction jobs with four bidders or less, the typical number in OCS leases, money left on the table averages 6.7%). Thus, even if commercial construction bidding were a pure common value auction, there is substantially less potential for a winner's curse than in OCS leasing.[1]

The top part of Table 13.4 reports partial correlation coefficients between major variables by job category. Column 1 shows that, with the exception of the HPHA, money left on the table is inversely related to the number of bidders, with statistical significance achieved in the new public construction job category. These negative correlations are consistent with a number of common distributions for the underlying signal values and the value of the item (recall Table 13.2). In contrast, for OCS leases, money left on the table is positively related to the number of bidders (Hendricks et al., 1987).

There is no consistent relationship across job categories between the size of the low bid and the number of bidders (column 2), so in general, larger jobs do not attract more bidders. Note the absence of a consistent positive correlation here may be artificial, resulting from more expensive jobs having more restrictive qualified bid lists.

With larger jobs there is more money left on the table, as indicated by the strong positive correlations between money left on the table and the mean bid in all job categories (column 3; statistical significance is achieved in all categories other than HPHA). However, there are consistent negative correlations between money left on the table as a percentage of the low bid and the mean bid

TABLE 13.4
Partial Correlation Coefficients (R): From Bid Tab Data (Prob $|R| = 0$ in parentheses)

Categories	(1) No. of Bidders and ($B_{L+1} - B_L$)	(2) B_L and No. of Bidders	(3) ($B_{L+1} - B_L$) and Mean Bid	(4) $\left[\dfrac{B_{L+1} - B_L}{B_L}\right]$ and Mean Bid
Renovations and Remodeling: Public facilities	−0.150 (0.285)	−0.167 (0.231)	0.903 (0.001)	−0.213 (0.126)
Churches: New construction and additions	−0.103 (0.595)	0.435 (0.018)	0.335 (0.075)	−0.407 (0.028)
Remodeling: Houston Housing Authority	0.059 (0.925)	−0.627 (0.258)	0.500 (0.391)	−0.923 (0.021)
New Construction: Public schools and other public facilities	−0.205 (0.006)	−0.164 (0.030)	0.562 (0.001)	−0.076 (0.314)
Private construction: New and remodeling	−0.063 (0.731)	0.272 (0.132)	0.777 (0.001)	−0.261 (0.149)

Regression Analysis: Bid Tab Data

Dependent Variable	Mean Bid[a] (standard error)	Number of Bidders (standard error)	Job Category Class Variable F-statistic (prob F = 1)	R^2
($B_{L+1} - B_L$)	0.018 (0.001)**	265,551 (123,870)*	0.63 (0.64)	0.390
($B_{L+1} - B_L$) / B_L	−8.00E−10 (0.0000)	0.101 (0.041)*	7.59 (<0.01)	0.196
B_L	0.948 (0.004)**	425,172 (367,038)	0.15 (0.96)	0.945
B_i	1.00 (0.002)**	$14730n - 628n^2$ (20973) (1027)	0.02 (0.999)	0.990

B_L = low bid; B_{L+1} = second-lowest bid.
*Significantly different from 0 at 5% level or better.
**Significantly different from 0 at 1% level or better.

(column 4). Similar negative correlations are found in OCS leases (Hendricks et al., 1987).

The bottom part of Table 13.4 reports several regressions. The first regression shows that money left on the table is positively related to the size of the project (mean bid) and inversely related to the number of bidders (the independent variable employed is $1/n$). The second regression shows that money left on the table as a percentage of the low bid is inversely related to the number of bidders ($1/n$) as well. Both these conclusions are robust to alternative (linear) specifications and reinforce those reached on the basis of the partial correlation coefficients reported in the top of the table.

The third regression relates the winning offer to the number of bidders ($1/n$), using the mean bid on the project as a proxy for the underlying true cost. Controlling for the underlying cost of the item, the *winning* offer is decreasing in n, although it fails to achieve statistical significance at conventional levels ($t = 1.16$, significant at the $p = 0.25$ level). Thus, the result is (weakly) consistent with one of the most basic predictions of the auction theory literature.

The last regression relates individual bids to the number of bidders, once again using the mean bid as a proxy for the common underlying cost component. The function is quadratic in n permitting offers to first decrease and then increase as n increases. Although neither coefficient is statistically significant, nor are they significant jointly ($F = 0.30$), the coefficient estimates show that individual bids are *increasing* for all values of n (through $n = 23$). Thus, the results are closer to the predictions of a common value auction, as private value auctions require *reductions* in individual bids as n increases.

5. Differences in Auction Structure between Theory and Practice

Although the adverse selection effect may be considerably weaker in the commercial construction industry than in OCS leasing, there is still room for a winner's curse; i.e., winning bidders reevaluating the expected cost of a job on the basis of rivals' bids and regretting winning (bids are announced almost immediately after the bid closing). No respondent used the term "winner's curse," but there are several indications that at least some of the GCs and SCs interviewed are aware of the potential for one. Clear examples of this come from written comments on the bid tabs. For example, one GC, on winning a bid, observed a 6.8% difference between his bid and the next closest bid on a new construction project, which is a relatively large difference (see Table 13.3). The GC notes:

> "Architect sent out addendum instructing all bidders to fill in calendar days at 180 [= 26 weeks]. We figured a job of this size shouldn't take more. than 19 weeks [this GC specialized in this type of work.] The others grabbed the 26 week time for general conditions [the GC is directly responsible for these costs]. This would have put us at about $K thousand dollars [a difference of 2% from the next lowest bidder, a difference much more in line with average money left on the table]."

This same GC, on winning a remodeling job, observed a 7.4% difference between his bid and the next lowest bid. This is not that unusual for a remodeling job, but still a relatively large difference. The GC notes:

"K. B. at firm C [the next lowest bidder] said he got greedy—could have been $K thousand dollars [meaning C could have bid as low as $K thousand, where $K was below this GC's winning bid]. We're OK."

As shown here and in the previous example, this GC focused on money left on the table as indicative of a potential bidding error. Although money left on the table has no necessary relationship to the existence of a winner's curse, and may simply reflect regret for not having bid higher and earning even more profit, the tone of these remarks clearly indicates concern about having bid too low and losing money as a consequence.

5.1 Mechanisms for Escaping the Winner's Curse

Simple survivorship principles suggest that we will not observe systematic overbidding by experienced GCs. However, as remarks on the bid tab sheets indicate (see below), experienced GCs nevertheless do, at times, fall prey to the winner's curse, bidding too little and immediately regretting their bid. In these cases there are at least three mechanisms at their disposal for escaping the winner's curse that are not accounted for in the standard one-shot auction theory literature.

One mechanism for escaping the winner's curse is that, by law, in most states and municipalities low bidders can withdraw bids on public projects without penalty when the bid contains "arithmetic errors." The interpretation of arithmetic errors is often quite broad. It covers clear arithmetic errors such as the obvious failure to total project costs in a computerized spread sheet program (to cite one example we found). However, it can also be used to permit withdrawal of bids (without loss of the bid bond) as a result of clear mistakes that are only identified after the bids are announced; for example, the failure to include $250,000 in required kitchen equipment in a school bid, the fact that a low SC withdrew his bid just after the bid closing, deducting "$40,000 too much" for an alternate condition specified in the bid plans (to cite three explanations of bid withdrawals found in the bid tabs). Interviews with GCs indicate that equally liberal interpretations of "arithmetic errors" are employed in the private sector as well. Of course, once a GC withdraws his bid he cannot submit a new, adjusted bid unless the job is rebid, thereby eliminating the obvious strategic advantage of possibly bidding too low.

One reason for buyers' liberal interpretation of arithmetic errors is that no buyer wants a GC working for them who has bid so low that they are bound to lose money on a job since there is an ongoing relationship between the owner and GC that is necessary for the job's completion. At worst, there is a real potential for the GC going bankrupt, which would have a radical impact on timely completion of the job, resulting in a number of uninsurable expenses. At a minimum, there is likely to be an impact on when the job is completed and the "headaches" associated with the construction. As a result, owners requiring that such bids be lived up to are likely to suffer from a winner's curse of their own. In contrast, these considerations play no role in OCS bidding where the winning bid is determined by the highest cash bonus bid. For an oil company deciding whether it is profitable to undertake the extensive development costs required to produce oil, this bonus bid is a true sunk cost and should have no impact on subsequent development decisions.

Buyers are reluctant to require performance bond forfeiture for bid with-drawals as it can adversely affect the number of bids submitted on subsequent jobs and/or the amount of profit/cost hedging built into these bids. This last consideration is but one of several ways in which repeated play/reputational elements, not considered in the one-shot auction games which theory typically deals with, impact on behavior in the industry. Indeed, these repeated play elements are, we believe, at the heart of the differences between actual behavior and the economic theory of auctions which the sociologist Smith (1989) cites, and which he attributes to fundamental differences in perspective between soci-ologists and economists.

A second mechanism for escaping the winner's curse involves the relation-ship between GCs and SCs. In cases where a GC has obviously bid too much, he can ask for "help" from his SCs. Help may be provided for two reasons: (1) an SC may not get the job at all if the GC withdraws his bid, as there is no guarantee that the SC is the low bidder for the second-lowest GC, and (2) GCs work repeatedly with the same SCs, so there is room for helping each other out on the basis of a long term relationship. Thus, one GC notes on his bid tab:

> "We busted this—left out $20,220 in storm sewers and force main. Have since negotiated price reductions [with SCs] of $82,757—should have picked up a good bit."

One may wonder why SCs would stay with GCs who bid poorly and try to pass their mistakes on to them. Clearly, if an SC is squeezed too hard he can walk away from the job. Further, as we argue below, the repeated play interaction between SCs and GCs results in each SC preferring to work with particular GCs and vice versa.

A third mechanism for escaping the winner's curse is found in change orders. Inevitably, situations arise which cause owners to deviate from the original scope of construction called for. The reasons for such changes maybe either aesthetic or structural in nature. The price of a change order is a matter of negotiation between the GC and the owner and the architect who acts as the owner's agent. If the GC realizes that he has underbid a job, he is now in a position to at least "cut his losses" through exceptionally tough negotiations. Although the GCs interviewed all agreed that no job should be bid low *expect-ing* to make money on change orders, they were frequently mentioned as being particularly profitable. However, this renegotiation process is clearly not an open-ended source of increased revenue, given the architect's role as the owner's agent. Finally, although it can be argued that GCs always have an incentive to make as much money as possible on change orders, regardless of the threat of losses, this argument ignores "fairness" considerations players are likely to bring to the game (see, for example, Rabin 1993).

The arithmetic errors and busted bids reported here do not involve the kind of repeated valuation errors by the *same* individual that economists usually refer to when discussing the winner's curse. As already noted, survivorship principles suggest that we will find few traces of systematic errors by individuals when tracking seasoned GCs. Nevertheless, the "mistakes" identified here are, apparently, endemic to the bidding process, and if not corrected, can wreak havoc on industry outcomes and the fortunes of individual bidders. They are representative of a market level winner's curse, as the competitive bidding process rewards low bidders, which involve proportionately greater numbers of busted bids.

5.2 Avoiding the Winner's Curse: Situation-Specific Learning

Dyer et al. (1989) conjectured that one reason the construction executives suffered from a winner's curse in laboratory bidding was that they had learned a set of situation-specific rules of thumb which helped them to avoid overbidding in the field, but which could not be applied in the laboratory. Evidence supporting this argument emerged from our interviews as well. An important determinant of the risk associated with bidding a job involves the architect/owner. The architect/owner's reputation for admitting mistakes or ambiguities in construction plans, and their willingness to implement functionally equivalent outcomes using alternative—and cheaper—construction techniques than originally specified, plays an important role in the cost estimates assigned to specific job components and the markup assigned to the total cost estimate (in the experiment, one of the executives jokingly inquired "Who is the architect associated with this job?").[2]

In addition, firms (or different estimators within a firm) tend to specialize in different types of construction projects. Experienced GCs pride themselves on their familiarity with building different types of structures and figure their estimates to lie within a rather narrow band of the true value. This familiarity is based on past experience. For example, in one bidding session we sat in on, the firm had just completed a similar building by the same architect. When in doubt on the cost estimate to assign to a particular job component, the GC pulled up records from the recently completed job and filled in the missing numbers? Finally, almost everyone we interviewed had stories about how GCs, unfamiliar with a particular owner or industry, suffered unanticipated losses. Experienced GCs tend to treat these costs as necessary start-up expenses associated with specializing in a new line of construction.

5.3 Private Value/Chance Elements in Bidding

Some of the dispersion in bids reported in Table 13.3 reflect strictly private, rather than common, value elements. It is widely acknowledged within the industry that the amount of profit and/or markup assigned to a bid reflects the opportunity cost of the job. For example, foremen are key personnel in any construction company so that firms are extremely reluctant to let good ones go for lack of work. As such, there is clearly some range of "below normal" profits at which it is better to keep a foreman active than have him stand idle or let go. Although profit and overhead are typically a small component of total cost, given the small spread between bids, small variations can make the difference between winning or losing a contract. Further, it's also possible that the "need" for work plays a role in determining the estimates assigned to different job tasks and the decision to take a chance with less experienced, or less reliable, low-cost SCs.

SC costs constitute the bulk of job expenses for a GC. Variations in SC bids can make the difference between winning or losing a contract. SC costs will differ across GCs for several distinct reasons: an SC may not bid all GCs, an SC may bid different GCs differently, or a GC may choose not to use a particular SC's bid.

The major source of variation in SCs' bids involves failure of a given SC to bid a GC. There are two possible explanations for this. One, which we often heard in interviews, is that SCs will not bid a GC because of past difficulties in working with the GC (reputation effects). This would involve a clear private value element (in addition to such obvious potential sources of friction as timely payment for work completed and the quality standards the SC will be held to, GCs have a large impact on the time it takes to complete a job as they coordinate the work of the SCs). On the other hand, failures to bid a GC may result from the chaotic, last minute submission of SCs' bids (and changes in these bids) that characterize the industry, so that an SC may not get through to all the GCs. To the extent this last element dominates, variation in SCs' bids might best be attributed to pure chance. What is likely is that both factors are at work, with SCs bidding their favorite GCs first and, if time permits, getting through to the rest.

GCs will sometimes not use a low SC's bid because of past difficulties in working with the SC or because the SC has no proven track record. Again quoting from the bid tabs:

> "We used subcontractors who were not low but who we considered to be better qualified for our team. This amounted to a penalty of approximately $23,000 [the GC was the second lowest bidder, by $10,000, on this $900,000 job]. The subs not used were considered either not sufficiently experienced or had performed poorly on previous jobs of ours."

GCs sometimes purchase performance bonds for their major SCs which provide some insurance. This insurance is incomplete, however, since nonperformance can result in major coordination problems on a job that increase the GC's costs substantially.

A brief appendix, available from the authors, illustrates variation in SCs' bids and their importance in determining the winning bid.

6. Industry-Specific Characteristics and Their Relationship to Auction Theory

Bids for a number of subcontracting tasks arrive in a flurry of activity immediately before the bid deadline. Right up until the moment bids are closed a GC will be working with SCs, confirming the scope of activity associated with the SCs' bids, and accepting/arguing for cuts in the SCs' bids (a member of the GC's bid team will be stationed at the bid site to fill in bid values moments before the bid closing). It is not uncommon for major SCs' bids to arrive within the last 10–20 minutes before the bid closing, resulting in chaotic last minute interactions with SCs.

There appear to be two primary reasons for this flurry of last minute bid activity. One is that SCs (and, in turn, their SCs and suppliers) often do not know the opportunity costs of their bids until bid day, as they are likely to have been bidding on a number of other jobs, and these costs are not fully determined until outcomes of previous bids are known (capacity constraints will affect the size of the mark-up to assign to a particular job). Second, SCs want to avoid having their bids broadcast to other SCs as a target for other SCs to beat. Such "bid shopping" on the part of GCs, although frowned on (particularly by SCs), is probably inherent in the bid process, as it converts a sealed bid auction into a quasiopen (English) auction. And since SCs' costs are affiliated, English auctions are likely to lower the buyer's costs relative to a sealed-bid auction (Milgrom and Weber, 1982). This bid shopping problem no doubt affects SCs' suppliers as well, contributing to the last minute flurry of activity. Given the deadline associated with submitting the final sealed bid, SCs have some control over bid shopping by submitting last minute bids.[4]

Negotiations between GCs and SCs often extend beyond the bid deadline as losing SCs contact the GC, or the GC may continue to negotiate with low or favored SCs. Almost everyone we spoke with had stories about how other (unnamed) GCs would bid shop SCs after the bid closing. Such bid shopping is generally considered to have crossed the line between ethical and unethical behavior. However, such bid shopping is likely to take place as the winning GC attempts to discover the overlap in different SC bids. In doing this the GC may find that the second- or third-lowest SC is indeed the lowest bidder, once the unnecessary duplication has been eliminated.

One particularly striking aspect of these last minute interactions is to observe a GC trying to convince an SC that their bid is too low, that something important has been overlooked in the building specifications. That is, a GC will often work quite hard to help an SC avoid the winner's curse. The incentive for the GC is quite straightforward. In using such a bid the GC faces the prospect of the SC withdrawing his bid after the bid closing, or trying to force an SC to live up to a bid he's very unhappy with, with the same problems an owner faces in forcing a GC to live up to a bid he wants to withdraw. Further, the GC has an interest in not having his rivals employ such a bid, as it may result in his losing the contract, with no assurance that his rival will withdraw his bid once the SC withdraws his bid.

The competitive bidding process, with GCs submitting sealed bids prior to a fixed deadline, is not the only procedure for awarding commercial construction contracts. A considerable amount of private sector work is awarded through negotiated contracts. The term "negotiated contract" covers a variety of practices with differing degrees of competition between rival GCs, but typically involves larger, more unusual jobs where the owner, the architect, and the GC are all involved in working out the scope of the project together (in effect, the GC provides construction engineering services in addition to his building services). There is definitely a competitive element to these contracts, as one respondent whose firm is heavily involved in negotiated work noted:

> "What the list [of negotiated jobs won] does not show are the negotiated type projects that we chased but failed to catch."

The more complete disclosure of unusual building characteristics inherent in the negotiated bid process reduces the contingency fees necessary to cover these risks, and results in lower expected costs to owners (see Rothkopf, 1969, p. 365).

One common characteristic of these negotiated contracts is that at some point the CC specifies a guaranteed maximum price (GMP), with some arrangement made for the owner and GC to share cost savings below the GMP.[5] Such cost savings might amount to as much as 5% of the GMP once the contract is completed. With the GC's involvement in the final building plan specifications and the GMP, negotiated contracts appear to provide a vehicle for risk sharing and quality control on more complicated and specialized building jobs, thereby reducing the scope for a winner's curse on jobs of this sort.

7. Summary and Conclusions

Construction contract bidding is usually treated as a common value auction. This paper has identified a number of differences between theoretical and experimental treatments of one-shot common value auctions and practices in the commercial construction industry. Adverse selection problems in the commercial construction industry are considerably smaller than those associated with OCS oil lease bids. Experienced GCs are unlikely to suffer from systematic valuation errors. Nevertheless, there is scope for a market level winner's curse as the competitive bidding process results in busted bids being over-represented among winning bids. Both owners and contractors have an interest in contractors escaping this market level winner's curse, as this can affect the timely delivery and headaches associated with the job (an owner's curse). The net result is that contractors are commonly permitted to withdraw unusually low winning bids without penalty. This mutual interest in escaping the winner's curse extends to SCs, resulting in GCs trying to convince unusually low SCs to withdraw their bids.

There are important repeated play elements to the commercial contracting game. Owners' stringent enforcement of bond forfeiture for withdrawing a winning bid can result in fewer interested bidders in subsequent jobs or in bidders who increase their mark-up to account for the added risk. There are private value elements to bidding, too, whose importance is exaggerated because of the compact distribution underlying bids.

At the same time modern auction theory helps explain some peculiar industry characteristics. The flurry of last minute SCs' bids (and cuts in bids) may be explained in part by GCs' efforts (and SCs' counter efforts) to turn a scaled-bid auction into an open (English) auction with its resultant reduction in GCs' costs. More complicated and specialized projects tend to involve negotiated contracts, which may be interpreted as a device for minimizing the risk of a winner's curse, for both owner and contractor, on jobs of this sort.

We draw several lessons from this study about the use of experimental techniques. First, in designing an experiment to test and modify a formal economic theory (which is what our original experiment was designed to do), it is important to recognize that the experimenter implements essential simplifications of the "real world" that are embodied in the theory. In doing this the experimenter may eliminate essential adjustment mechanisms and institutional factors that underlie behavior outside the laboratory. Consequently, to the extent that successful economic behavior involves learning and adaptation to economic contingencies, and learning is situation-specific, performance of economic agents may deteriorate substantially in laboratory compared to field settings (also see Hogarth, 1981). Further, to the extent that one discovers seemingly anomalous behavior of the kind that motivated this study, it is essential to look outside the laboratory to discover those institutional factors (if any) that help relieve the problem. For without this, we would not have dreamed of those elements which help relieve the winner's curse in the construction industry. Identifying these industry characteristics may also help pinpoint important modeling issues that have been previously overlooked (see, for example, Harstad and Rothkopf, 1992). Finally, in designing experiments intended to have a direct impact on policymaking, unlike experiments designed to test formal economic theories, it is essential for the experimenter to construct an accurate scale model of the target economy. This is, indeed, one of the central principles underlying the design of policy-making experiments in economics (Plott, 1987).[6]

Appendix
Variation in Subcontractor Bids to General Contractors

This appendix provides some more detailed data on the variation in subcontractors' bids across different general contractors. Tables 13.A.1 and 13.A.2 provide data on subcontractors' bids obtained from "top-sheets" (bid preparation forms) from several companies. Both jobs are new public schools bid in 1986. They were selected with a view to maximizing the number of firms we thought we could obtain top sheets from. The subcontracting categories are self-contained in the sense that they require minimal direct input from the general contractor or from other subcontractors. For both jobs the total of these subcontractors' bids was 45% of the general contractors' bid. All values are reported in terms

TABLE 13.A1

Differences in Low Subcontractors' Bids to General Contractors: Project 1 ($N = 14$; median general contractors bid = $4.36 million)
(All bids are measured in terms of deviations from low bid in a given category.)

Rank of General Contractor's Bid	General Contractor's Bid	Subcontractors' Bids						Sum of Subcontractor's Bid Deviations
		Structural Steel	Masonry	Drywall	Heating & AC	Electrical	Plumbing	
1	−30,000	5865[a]	1800	6908	0	5000	0	0
2[d]	0	241	1800	0	0	5000	43,473	30,941
3	32,000	1569	1800	6908	0	5000	58,130[e]	53,834
4	64,000	865	1800	6908	36,612[a]	5000	0	31,612
5	74,600	5620	1000[b]	6908	0	0[b]	40,583[f]	34,538
8	105,000	0[b]	1800	6908	0	30,000	58,130[a]	77,265
11	155,000	865	1800	8595	0	1,000	0	−7,313
14	564,000	5865[c]	0[b]	36,161[c]	36,612[a]	54,000[c]	58,130[a]	171,195

[a]Low subcontractor did not bid this general contractor.
[b]Variation in low subcontractor's bid to this general contractor.
[c]Did not use low subcontractor's bid.
[d]No listing of subcontractor's bids by name.
[e]Received withdrawn low bid but did not use.
[f]Low bid excluding withdrawn low bidder. Substantially lower price offered to this general contractor than to other general contractors.

TABLE 13.A2

Differences in Low Subcontractors' Bid to General Contractors: Project 2 ($N = 9$; median general contractor bid = $13.82 million)
(All bids are measured in terms of deviations from low bid in a given category.)

Rank of General Contractor's Bid	General Contractor's Bid	Structural Steel	Masonry	Drywall	Heating & AC	Electrical	Plumbing	Sum of Subcontractor's Bid Deviations
					Subcontractors' Bids			
1	0	6,613	0	0	0[e]	42,000	0	0
2	13,000	0[b]	0	0	1,415	3,000	24,584[a]	−6,632
4	168,800	10,730	12,668[d]	67,724[d]	95,000	0[e]	37,600	175,091
8	620,000	30,730[c]	0	9,730[b]	20,000	15,300	0	27,129
9	1,320,000	6,613	12,668[a]	0	184,716	0	68,600[a]	223,966

[a] Low subcontractor did not bid this general contractor.
[b] Variation in low subcontractor's bid to this general contractor.
[c] Did not use low subcontractor's bid.
[d] Rejected low subcontractor's bid in favor of subcontractor with enhanced design characteristics.
[e] No subcontractor listed.

of deviations from the low bid in a category. Shown along with the subcontractors' bids are deviations in the general contractors' bids. The low bid for the job in Table 13.A.1 was withdrawn.

Notes

1. We focus on money left on the table to measure bid dispersion primarily for ease of comparison with published data from OCS leases. It might be argued that our construction industry measure is biased downward since GCs account for only around 10% of job cost. However, the GC is fully responsible for SCs completing their work at or below bid.

2. Owners and architects also carry reputations for making change orders, which experienced GCs will use in determining their markup.

3. It's our understanding that oil companies specialize in different geological formations so that they can better apply accumulated past knowledge to interpret seismic records.

4. In response to bid shopping, SCs sometimes form bid depositories, where SCs' bids must be placed several hours before the bid deadline. Sanctions are imposed on GCs and SCs for adjusting these bids. Both the FTC and several (but not all) court cases have declared bid depositories as violations of anti-trust laws (FTC docket #9183, November, 1985). Although bid depositories primarily involve surplus transfers between GCs and SCs, and between contractors and owners, they also prohibit the winning GC from negotiating with SCs to eliminate duplication in construction activities, This prohibition is likely to reduce economic efficiency.

5. Interestingly, most negotiated contracts have an important asymmetry with the GC covering all costs above the GMP. Presumably, GCs are more knowledgeable than owners regarding costs, and bear this risk, while owners have assurance regarding the financing costs of the job.

6. This research was supported by the Sloan Foundation, the Russell Sage Foundation, and the National Science Foundation. We thank the many people in the Houston construction industry who helped with this project: Bill Bain, Bill Baxter, Paul Bell, Ted Connor, Hortense Dyer, George Gillis, Jessie Gonzales, Jeff Holstein, Al Jensen, Dick Lewis, Gene Liggan, Walter Murphy, Jack Marshall, Johnny Meyer, George Miner, John Pollack, Jim Roach, and Cecil Windsor. We thank Susan Garvin and Martha Charepoo for valuable research assistance. We have benefitted from discussions with Doug Davis, Dan Levin, Al Roth, Reinhard Selten, and Jim Smith, from comments on an earlier version of this paper presented at the ESA meetings and the Federal Trade Commission, and the comments of an associate editor of this journal and two referees.

References

Bazerman, M. H. and W. F. Samuelson, "I Won the Auction But Don't Want the Prize," *J. Conflict Resolution*, 27 (1983), 618–634.

Burns, P., "Experience and Decision Making: A Comparison of Students and Businessmen in a Simulated Progressive Auction," in V. L. Smith (Ed.), *Research in Experimental Economics*, Volume 3, JAI Press, Greenwich, CT, 1985.

Capen, E. C., R. V. Clapp, and W. M. Campbell, "Competitive Bidding in High-Risk Situations," *J. Petrol. Technology*, 23 (1971), 641–653.

Cassing, J. and R. W. Douglas, "Implications of the Auction Mechanism in Baseballs' Free Agent Draft," *Southern Economic J.*, 47 (1980), 110–121.

Dessauer, J. P., *Book Publishing*, Bowker, New York, 1981.

Dyer, D., J. H. Kagel, and D. Levin, "A Comparison of Naive and Experienced Bidders in Common Value Offer Auctions: Laboratory Analysis," *Economic J.*, 99 (1989), 108–115.

FTC, Docket Number 9183, "The Electrical Bid Registration Service of Memphis, Inc.," November 21, 1985.

Harstad, R. M. and M. H. Rothkopf, "Withdrawable Bids as Winner's Curse Insurance," *Oper. Res.*, 43 (1995), 983–994.

Hendricks, K., R. H. Porter, and B. Boudreau, "Information, Returns, and Bidding Behavior in OCS Auctions: 1954-1969," *J. Industrial Econ.*, 35 (1987), 517–542.

Hogarth, R. M., "Beyond Discrete Biases: Functional and Dysfunctional Aspects of Judgmental Heuristics," *Psychology Bulletin*, 90 (1981), 197–217.

Kagel, J. H., "Auctions: A Survey of Experimental Research," in J. H. Kagel and A. E. Roth (Eds.), *The Handbook of Experimental Economics*, Princeton University Press, New Jersey, 1995.

——— and D. Levin, "The Winner's Curse and Public Information in Common Value Auctions," *American Economic Review*, 76 (1986), 894–920.

Keefer, D. L., "Resource Allocation Models with Risk Aversion and Probabilistic Dependence: Offshore Oil and Gas Bidding," *Management Sci.*, 37 (1991), 377–395.

Mead, W. J., A. Moseidjord, and P. E. Sorensen, "The Rate of Return Earned by Leases Under Cash Bonus Bidding in OCS Oil and Gas Leases," *Energy J.*, 4 (1983), 37–52.

Milgrom, P. R., *The Structure of Information in Competitive Bidding*, Garland Publishing, New York, 1979 (a).

Milgrom, P. R., "A Convergence Theorem for Competitive Bidding with Differential Information," *Econometrica*, 49 (1979b), 921–943.

——— and R. J. Weber, "A Theory of Auctions and Competitive Bidding," *Econometrica*, 50 (1982), 1485–1527.

Plott, C. R., "Dimensions of Parallelism; Some Policy Applications of Experimental Methods" in A. E. Roth (Ed.), *Laboratory Experimentation in Economics: Six Points of View*, Cambridge University Press, 1987.

Rabin, M., "Incorporating Fairness into Game Theory and Economics," *American Econ. Rev.*, 83 (1993), 1281–1303.

Roll, R., "The Hubris Hypothesis of Corporate Takeovers," *J. Business*, 59 (1986), 197–216.

Rothkopf, M. A., "A Model of Rational Competitive Bidding," *Management Sci.*, 15 (1969), 362–373.

Smith, B. A., "The Fall and Rise of the Houston Real Estate Market," Publication 92–04, Center for Public Policy, University of Houston, Houston, Tx, May 1992.

Smith, C. W., *Auctions: The Social Construction of Value*, Free Press, New York, 1989.

Wilson, R., "A Bidding Model of Perfect Competition," *Rev. Econ. Studies*, 44 (1977), 511–518.

———, "Strategic Analysis of Auctions," in R. J. Aumann and S. Hart (Eds.), *The Handbook of Game Theory with Economic Applications*, Volume 1, Elsevier Science Publishers, Amsterdam, 1992.

═══ **Instructions** ═══

We provide a collection of instructions from the experiments. We provide here:

1. Instructions for common value auctions with and without public information (chapter 3).
2. The parallel set of instructions for second-price common value auctions with and without public information (chapter 4).
3. Instructions for the affiliated private value auctions for all three institutions: first-price, second-price, and English-clock auctions (chapter 5).
4. Cross-over instructions for the English-clock common value auctions and for the first-price auctions with insider information (chapters 6 and 7).
5. Instructions for second-price auctions with private value advantage (chapter 9).
6. Instructions for the low price offer auctions (chapter 12).
7. Summary instructions for experienced bidders. These would have been read prior to the start of any given experimental session.

Instructions for Chapter 3

This is an experiment in the economics of market decision making. The National Science Foundation has provided funds for conducting this research. The instructions are simple, and if you follow them carefully and make good decisions you may earn a CONSIDERABLE AMOUNT OF MONEY which will be PAID TO YOU IN CASH at the end of the experiment.

1. In this experiment we will create a market in which you will act as buyers of a fictitious commodity in a sequence of trading periods. A single unit of the commodity will be auctioned off in each trading period. There will be several trading periods.

2. Your task is to submit written bids for the commodity in competition with other buyers. The precise value of the commodity at the time you make your bids will be unknown to you. Instead, each of you will receive information as to the value of the item which you should find useful in determining your bid. The process of determining the value of the commodity and the information you will receive will be described in Sections 6 and 7 below.

3. The high bidder gets the item and makes a profit equal to the difference between the value of the commodity and the amount they bid. That is,

$$(\text{VALUE OF ITEM}) - (\text{HIGHEST BID}) = \text{PROFITS}$$

for the high bidder. If this difference is negative, it represents a loss.

If you do not make the high bid on the item, you will earn zero profits. In this case, you neither gain nor lose money from bidding on the item.

4. You will be given a starting capital credit balance of $100.00. Any profit earned by you in the experiment will be added to this sum, and any losses incurred will be subtracted from this sum. The net balance of these transactions will be calculated and paid to you in CASH at the end of the experiment.

The starting capital credit balance, and whatever subsequent profits you earn, permit you to suffer losses in one auction to be recouped in part or in total in later auctions. However, should your net balance at any time during the experiment drop to zero (or less), you will no longer be permitted to participate. Instead we will give you your participation fee and you'll be free to leave the auction.

You *are* permitted to bid in excess of your capital credit balance in any given period.

5. During each trading period you will be bidding in a market in which *all* the other participants are also bidding. After all bids have been handed in they will be posted on the blackboard. We will circle the high bid and note the second high bid, and post the value of the item. We will also indicate whether a profit or loss was earned by the high bidder.

6. The value of the auctioned commodity (V^*) will be assigned randomly and will lie between $25.00 and $225.00 inclusively. For each auction, *any value within this interval has an equally likely chance* of being drawn. The value of the item can never be less than $25.00 or more than $225.00. The V^* values are determined randomly and independently from auction to auction. As such a high V^* in one period tells you nothing about the likely value in the next period—whether it will be high or low. It doesn't even preclude drawing the same V^* value in later periods.

7. Private Information Signals:

Although you do not know the precise value of the item in any particular trading period, you will receive information which will narrow down the range of possible values. This will consist of a private information signal which is selected randomly from an interval whose lower bound is V^* minus epsilon (ε), and whose upper bound is V^* plus epsilon. *Any value* within this interval has an *equally likely* chance of being drawn and being assigned to one of you as your private information signal. You will always know what the value of epsilon is.

For example, suppose that the value of the auctioned item is $128.16 and that epsilon is $6.00, Then each of you will receive a private information signal which will consist of a randomly drawn number that will be between $122.16 ($V^* - \varepsilon = \$128.16 - \$6.00$) and $134.16 ($V^* + \varepsilon = \$128.16 + \$6.00$). Any number in this interval has an equally likely chance of being drawn.

The line diagram below shows what's going on in this example.

$V^* - \varepsilon = \$122.16$ $V^* = \$128.16$ $V^* + \varepsilon = \$134.16$ $\varepsilon = \$6.00$

$\vdash$————————$($————————$\mid$————————$)$————————$\dashv$

$\$25.00$ Signal values may be $\$225.00$
                                          anywhere in this interval

The data below show the entire set of signals the computer generated for our sample bag. (Note we've ordered these signal values from lowest to highest.)

$V^* = \$128.16$; $\varepsilon = \$6.00$. Signal values: $122.57
                                                      124.14
                                                      124.68
                                                      126.76
                                                      128.84
                                                      129.51
                                                      129.96
                                                      129.98
                                                      132.07

You will note that some signal values were above the value of the auctioned item, and some were below the value of the item. Over a sufficiently long series of auctions, the differences between your private information signal and the value of the item will average out to zero (or very close to it). For any given auction, however, your private information signal can be above or below the value of the item. That's the nature of the random selection process generating the signals.

You will also note that V^* must always be greater than or equal to your signal value $- \varepsilon$. The computer calculates this for you and notes it. Further, V^* must always be less than or equal to your sample value $+ \varepsilon$. The computer calculates this for you and notes it.

Finally, you may receive a signal value below $\$25.00$ (or above $\$225.00$). There is nothing strange about this, it just indicates V^* is close to $\$25.00$ (or $\$225.00$) relative to the size of epsilon.

8. Your signal values are strictly private information and are not to be revealed to anyone else prior to opening the bids.

You will be told the value of ε prior to bidding and it will be posted on the blackboard. However, you will not be told the value of V^* until after the bids have been posted. Finally, we will post all of the signal values drawn along with the bids.

9. No one may bid less than $\$0.00$ for the item. Nor may anyone bid more than their signal value $+ \varepsilon$. Any bid in between these two values is acceptable.

Bids must be rounded to the nearest penny to be accepted.

In case of ties for the high bid, we will flip a coin to determine who will earn the item.

10. You are not to reveal your bids, or profits, nor are you to speak to any other subject while the experiment is in progress.

11. As promised, everyone will receive $4 irrespective of their earnings for participating in the experiment.

Let's summarize the main points: (1) High bidder earns the item and earns a profit = value of item − high bid price. (2) Profits will be added to your starting balance of $10.00, losses subtracted from it. Your balance at the end of experiment will be paid in cash. If balance turns negative you're no longer allowed to bid. (3) Your private information signal is randomly drawn from the interval $V^* − \varepsilon$, $V^* + \varepsilon$. The value of the item can never be more than your signal value $+ \varepsilon$, or less than your signal value $− \varepsilon$. (4) The value of the item will always be between $25.00 and $225.00.

Are there any questions?

Additional Instructions: Periods with Public Information

1. From now on bidding will be done twice during each trading period, once under each of two different information conditions. First, you will bid on the basis of your private information signals, just as you have been doing. After these bids have been made and collected, but before they are opened, you will be provided with additional information (to be described shortly) concerning the value of the item *and be asked to bid again on the commodity*. This additional information will be posted on the blackboard for everyone to see and will be referred to as a public information signal.

2. The public information signal will consist of posting on the blackboard the *lowest* of the private information signals any of you received. Note we will not reveal the bid of the player with the lowest information signal, just the signal value.

3. Note that V^* does *not* change between auctions, Your private information signals do *not* change between auctions either. However, what the public information signal does do is provide *everyone* with additional information about the possible value of V^*.

4. After both sets of bids have been collected they will be opened and the bids posted in each market and the high bid noted. We will also post the value of the item and compute profits and/or losses in the two markets as before:

$$\text{PROFITS} = (\text{VALUE OF ITEM}) − (\text{HIGH BID PRICE})$$

Finally, to speed things up a bit we will no longer post all of the signal values drawn along with the bids.

5. However, we will only actually pay profits (or hold you accountable for losses) in one of the two markets. We will flip a coin to decide which market to pay off in. Heads we pay off in the market with private information values only, tails we pay off in the market with private and public information.

6. There is no obligation to make the same bid, or to bid differently in the two markets. This is strictly up to you to decide what to do in terms of what you think will generate the greatest profits.

Are there any questions?

Instructions for Second-Price Auctions (Chapter 4)

This is an experiment in the economics of market decision making. The National Science Foundation has provided funds for conducting this research. The instructions are simple, and if you follow them carefully and make good decisions you may earn a CONSIDERABLE AMOUNT OF MONEY which will be PAID TO YOU IN CASH at the end of the experiment.

1. In this experiment we will create a market in which you will act as buyers of a fictitious commodity in a sequence of trading periods. A single unit of the commodity will be auctioned off in each trading period. There will be several trading periods.

2. Your task is to submit written bids for the commodity in competition with other buyers. The precise value of the commodity at the time you make your bids will be unknown to you. Instead, each of you will receive information as to the value of the item which you should find useful in determining your bid. The process of determining the value of the commodity and the information you will receive will be described in Sections 6 and 7 below.

3. The high bidder gets the item and makes a profit equal to the difference between the value of the commodity and the *second highest bid price*. That is

(VALUE OF ITEM) − (2ND HIGHEST BID) = PROFITS

for the high bidder. If this difference is negative, it represents a loss.

If you do not make the high bid on the item, you will earn zero profits. In this case, you neither gain nor lose money from bidding on the item.

4. You will be given a starting capital credit balance of $10.00. Any profit earned by you in the experiment will be added to this sum, and any losses incurred will be subtracted from this sum. The net balance of these transactions will be calculated and paid to you in CASH at the end of the experiment.

The starting capital credit balance, and whatever subsequent profits you earn, permit you to suffer losses in one auction to be recouped in part or in total in later auctions. However, should your net balance at any time during the experiment drop to zero (or less), you will no longer be permitted to participate. Instead we will give you your participation fee and you'll be free to leave the auction.

You *are* permitted to bid in excess of your capital credit balance in any given period.

5. During each trading period you will be bidding in a market in which *all* the other participants are also bidding. After all bids have been handed in they will be posted on the blackboard. We will circle the high bid and note the second high bid, and post the value of the item. We will also indicate whether a profit or loss was earned by the high bidder.

6. The value of the auctioned commodity (V^*) will be assigned randomly and will lie between $25.00 and $225.00 inclusively. For each auction, *any value* within this interval has an *equally likely chance* of being drawn. The value of the item can never be less than $25.00 or more than $225.00. The V^* values are determined randomly and independently from auction to auction. As such a high V^* in one period tells you nothing about the likely value in the next period—whether it will be high or low. It doesn't even preclude drawing the same V^* value in later periods.

7. Private Information Signals:

Although you do not know the precise value of the item in any particular trading period, you will receive information which will narrow down the range of possible values. This will consist of a private information signal which is selected randomly from an interval whose lower bound is V^* minus epsilon (ε), and whose upper bound is V^* plus epsilon. *Any value* within this interval has an *equally likely* chance of being drawn and being assigned to one of you as your private information signal. You will always know what the value of epsilon is.

For example, suppose that the value of the auctioned item is $128.16 and that epsilon is $6.00. Then each of you will receive a private information signal which will consist of a randomly drawn number that will be between $122.16 ($V^* - \varepsilon = \$128.16 - \$6.00$) and $134.16 ($V^* + \varepsilon = \$128.16 + \$6.00$). Any number in this interval has an equally likely chance of being drawn.

The line diagram below shows what's going on in this example.

The data below show the entire set of signals the computer generated for our sample bag. (Note we've ordered these signal values from lowest to highest.)

$$V^* = \$128.16; \ \varepsilon = \$6.00. \text{ Signal values: } \$122.57$$

124.14
124.68
126.76
128.84
129.51
129.96
129.98
132.07

You will note that some signal values were above the value of the auctioned item, and some were below the value of the item. Over a sufficiently long series of auctions, the differences between your private information signal and the value of the item will average out to zero (or very close to it). For any given auction, however, your private information signal can be above or below the value of the item. That's the nature of the random selection process generating the signals.

You will also note that V^* must always be greater than or equal to your signal value $- \varepsilon$. The computer calculates this for you and notes it. Further, V^* must always be less than or equal to your sample value $+ \varepsilon$. The computer calculates this for you and notes it.

Finally, you may receive a signal value below \$25.00 (or above \$225.00). There is nothing strange about this, it just indicates V^* is close to \$25.00 (or \$225.00) relative to the size of epsilon.

9. Your signal values are strictly private information and are not to be revealed to anyone else prior to opening the bids.

You will be told the value of ε prior to bidding and it will be posted on the blackboard. However, you will not be told the value of V^* until after the bids have been posted. Finally, we will post all of the signal values drawn along with the bids.

10. No one may bid less than \$0.00 for the item. Nor may anyone bid more than their signal value $+ 2\varepsilon$. Any bid in between these two values is acceptable.

Bids must be rounded to the nearest penny to be accepted.

In case of ties for the high bid, we will flip a coin to determine who will earn the item. Since the high bidder pays the second high bid price, in case of ties the high bidder would pay the price bid.

11. You are not to reveal your bids, or profits, nor are you to speak to any other subject while the experiment is in progress. This is important to the validity of the study and will not be tolerated.

12. As promised, everyone will receive \$4 irrespective of their earnings for participating in the experiment.

Let's summarize the main points: (1) High bidder earns the item and earns a profit = value of item $-$ second high bid price. (2) Profits will be added to your starting balance of \$10.00, losses subtracted from it. Your balance at the end of experiment will be paid in cash. If balance turns negative you're no longer allowed to bid. (3) Your private information signal is randomly drawn from the interval $V^* - \varepsilon$, $V^* + \varepsilon$. The value of the item can never be more than your signal value $+ \varepsilon$, or less than your signal value $- \varepsilon$. (4) The value of the item will always be between \$25.00 and \$225.00.

Are there any questions?

Additional Instructions

1. From now on bidding will be done twice during each trading period, once under each of two different information conditions. First, you will bid on the basis of your private information signals, just as you have been doing. After these bids have been made and collected, but before they are opened, you will be provided with additional information (to be described shortly) concerning the value of the item *and be asked to bid again on the commodity*. This additional information will be posted on the blackboard for everyone to see and will be referred to as a public information signal.

2. The public information signal will consist of posting on the blackboard the *lowest* of the private information signals any of you received. Note we will not reveal the bid of the player with the lowest information signal, just the signal value.

3. Note that V^* does *not* change between auctions. Your private information signals do *not* change between auctions either. However, what the public information signal does do is provide *everyone* with additional information about the possible value of V^*.

4. After both sets of bids have been collected they will be opened and the bids posted in each market and the high bid noted. We will also post the value of the item and compute profits and/or losses in the two markets continuing to use the second price bid rule:

Profits = (Value of Item) − (Second High Bid Price)

Finally, to speed things up a bit we will no longer post all of the signal values drawn along with the bids.

5. However, we will only actually pay profits (or hold you accountable for losses) in one of the two markets. We will flip a coin to decide which market to pay off in. Heads we pay off in the market with private information values only, tails we pay off in the market with private and public information.

6. There is no obligation to make the same bid, or to bid differently in the two markets. This is strictly up to you to decide what to do in terms of what you think will generate the greatest profits.

Are there any questions?

Instructions for First-Price Affiliated Private Values (Chapter 5)

This is an experiment in the economics of market decision making. The National Science Foundation has provided funds for conducting this research. The instructions are simple, and if you follow them carefully and make good decisions you may earn a CONSIDERABLE AMOUNT OF MONEY which will be PAID TO YOU IN CASH at the end of the experiment.

1. In this experiment we will create a market in which you will act as buyers of a fictitious commodity in a sequence of trading periods. A single unit of the commodity will be auctioned off in each trading period. There will be several trading periods.

2. Your task is to submit written bids for the commodity in competition with other buyers. In each trading period you will be assigned a RESALE VALUE for the item. This indicates the value to you of purchasing the item. This value may be thought of as the amount you would receive if you were to resell the unit. The process of determining resale values will be described in Sections 6 and 7 below.

3. The high bidder obtains the item and earns a profit equal to the difference between his/her resale value and the high bid. That is

$$\text{(Resale Value)} - \text{(High Bid)} = \text{Profit}$$

for the high bidder. If you do not make the high bid, you earn zero profits for the trading period.

Note that your cash profits depend upon your ability to buy a unit at a price below the resale value assigned. Also note that if you buy a unit at a price equal to its resale value, your profit will be zero. Bids in excess of your resale value will not be accepted.

4. The sum total of your profits across trading periods will be calculated and paid to you in CASH at the end of the experiment. In addition you will receive $4.00, as promised, for participating in the study.

5. During each trading period you will be bidding in a market in which *all* the other participants are also bidding. After all bids have been handed in, they will all be posted on the blackboard. We will circle the high bid and note the second high bid.

6. Resale values will be assigned as follows. First, we will randomly draw a number between $25 and $125 inclusively. Call this number D^*. For each auction, *any value* between $25 and $125 has *an equally likely* chance of being drawn.

7. Once D^* is determined, resale values will be assigned randomly and will be selected from an interval whose lower bound is D^* minus epsilon (ε), and whose upper bound is D^* plus epsilon (ε). *Any value* within this interval has *an equally likely* chance of being drawn and being assigned to one of you as your resale value. For example, suppose that D^* is $35.50 and that epsilon ($\varepsilon$) is $6.00. Then each of you will receive a resale value which will consist of a randomly drawn number that will be between $29.50 ($D^* - \varepsilon = \$35.50 -$

$6.00) and $41.50 ($D^* + \varepsilon = \$35.50 + \$6.00$). Any number in this interval has an equally likely chance of being drawn.

The line diagram below shows what's going on in this example.

$D^* - \varepsilon = \$29.50$ $D^* = \$35.50$ $D^* + \varepsilon = \$41.50$ $\varepsilon = \$6.00$

```
├────────────(──────────┼──────────)──────────────────────────────────┤
$25.00          Resale values may be                                         $125
              anywhere in this interval
```

8. Your resale values are strictly private information and are not to be revealed to anyone else.

You will be told the value of ε prior to bidding and it will be posted on the blackboard. However, you will not be told the value of D^*.

The following data are typical of the resale values you are likely to receive in the case where $D^* = \$35.50$ and $\varepsilon = \$6.00$ and 12.00, respectively. (Note we've ordered these resale values from highest to lowest for the case of six bidders.)

$$D^* = \$35.50$$

$\varepsilon = \$6.00$	$\varepsilon = \$12.00$
$31.58	$24.08
$33.12	$27.65
$35.67	$30.73
$37.35	$39.20
$38.42	$41.35
$39.54	$43.58

Note the larger ε is, the more spread out resale values are likely to be. Also you may receive a resale value below $25.00 (or above $125.00). There is nothing strange about this, it just indicates D^* is close to the $25.00 (or $125.00) relative to the size of epsilon.

Finally, as already noted, your cash profits depend upon your ability to buy a unit at a price below your resale value. As the tabulated resale values indicate, there are clear trade-offs in deciding what to bid: the lower your bid relative to your resale value, the higher your profits should you be the high bidder, but the lower your chances are of being the high bidder. Further, the exact nature of this trade-off depends on what other bidders are doing in terms of these trade-offs also.

9. The D^* values are determined randomly and independently from auction to auction. As such, a high value in one period tells you nothing about the likely value in the next period—whether it will be high or low. It doesn't even preclude drawing the same D^* value in later periods. Since a similar random, independent determination process underlies the resale values, the same holds true here too.

10. No one may bid less than $0.00 for the commodity. Nor may anyone bid more than their resale value.

Bids must be rounded to the nearest penny to be accepted.

In case of ties for the high bid, we will flip a coin to determine who will earn the item.

11. You are not to reveal your bids, or profits, nor are you to speak to any other subject while the experiment is in process. This is important to the validity of the study and will not be tolerated.

Are there any questions?

Additional Instructions

1. From now on bidding will be done twice during each trading period, once under each of two different information conditions. First, you will bid on the basis of your private resale values, just as you have been doing. After these bids have been submitted, but before they are opened, you will be provided with additional information (to be described shortly) and asked to bid again on the commodity.

2. This additional information will consist of posting the value of D^* on the blackboard along with $D^* - \varepsilon$, $D^* + \varepsilon$. That is, we will provide you with information indicating exactly the interval from which your private resale values were drawn.

3. After both sets of bids have been collected, they will be opened and all bids posted in each market and the high bid noted.

4. We will then flip a coin to decide which market to pay off in. Heads we pay off in the market where D^* is not known, tails we pay off in the market where D^* is known. The high bidder in the market we pay off in will earn profits equal to

$$\text{(Resale Value)} - \text{(High Bid)} = \text{Profits}$$

All other bids earn zero profits, including the high bid in the other market.

6. There is no obligation to bid the same, or to bid differently, in the two markets. This is strictly up to you to decide what to do in terms of what you think will generate the greatest profits.

Are there any questions!

Instructions for Second-Price Affiliated Private Values (Chapter 5)

This is an experiment in the economics of market decision making. The National Science Foundation has provided funds for conducting this research. The instructions are simple, and if you follow them carefully and make good decisions you may earn a CONSIDERABLE AMOUNT OF MONEY which will be PAID TO YOU IN CASH at the end of the experiment.

1. In this experiment we will create a market in which you will act as buyers of a fictitious commodity in a sequence of trading periods. A single unit of the commodity will be auctioned off in each trading period. There will be several trading periods.

2. Your task is to submit written bids for the commodity in competition with other buyers. In each trading period you will be assigned a RESALE VALUE for the item. This indicates the value to you of purchasing the item. This value may be thought of as the amount you would receive if you were to resell the unit. The process of determining resale values will be described in Sections 6 and 7 below.

3. The high bidder obtains the item and earns a profit equal to the difference between his/her resale value and the *second highest bid price*. That is,

Profit $=$ (resale value of the high bidder) $-$ (2nd highest bid)

for the high bidder. If you do not make the high bid, you earn zero profits for the trading period.

4. You will each be given a $5.00 starting capital balance to guard against the possibility of losses and to provide a minimum level of compensation for participating in the experiment. Profits earned during trading periods will be added to this balance, losses subtracted from it. Your net balance will be paid to you in cash at the end of the experiment. If your net balance goes negative, you will no longer be permitted to bid.

5. During each trading period you will be bidding in a market in which six (6) other participants are also bidding. After all bids have been entered, the computer will sort them, determine the high bidder and his/her profits, and post all bids in descending order on your terminal screens. Since the terminal screens can only display a limited amount of information, we've got pencils and paper available for you to keep supplementary records if you wish.

6. Resale values will be assigned as follows. First we will randomly draw a number between $25 and $125 inclusively. Call this number D^*. For each auction *any value* between $25 and $125 has *an equally likely* chance of being drawn.

7. Once D^* is determined, resale values will be assigned randomly and will be selected from an interval whose lower bound is D^* minus epsilon (ε), and whose upper bound is D^* plus epsilon (ε). *Any value* within this interval has *an equally likely* chance of being drawn and being assigned to one of you as your resale value. For example, suppose that D^* is $35.50 and that epsilon ($\varepsilon$) is $6.00. Then each of you will receive a resale value which will consist of a randomly drawn number that will be between $29.50 ($D^* - \varepsilon = \$35.50 - \$6.00$) and $41.50 ($D^* + \varepsilon = \$35.50 + \$6.00$). Any number in this interval has an equally likely chance of being drawn.

The line diagram below shows what's going on in this example.

$D^* - \varepsilon = \$29.50$ $D^* = \$35.50$ $D^* + \varepsilon = \$41.50$ $\varepsilon = \$6.00$

```
 |————————(————————|————————)——————————————————————————————————|
$25.00              Resale values may be                                          $125
                    anywhere in this interval
```

8. Your resale values are strictly private information and are not to be revealed to anyone else.

You will be told the value of ε prior to bidding and it will be posted on your terminal screens. However, you will not be told the value of D^*.

The following data are typical of the resale values you are likely to receive in the case where $D^* = \$35.50$ and $\varepsilon = \$6.00$ and $\$12.00$, respectively. (Note we've ordered these resale values from highest to lowest for the case of six bidders.)

$D^* = \$35.50$

$\varepsilon = \$6.00$	$\varepsilon = \$12.00$
$31.58	$24.08
$33.12	$27.65
$35.67	$30.73
$37.35	$39.20
$38.42	$41.35
$39.54	$43.58

Note the larger ε is, the more spread out resale values are likely to be. Also you may receive a resale value below $25.00 (or above $125.00). There is nothing strange about this, it just indicates D^* is close to the $25.00 (or $125.00) relative to the size of epsilon.

9. The D^* values are determined randomly and independently from auction to auction. As such, a high value in one period tells you nothing about the likely value in the next period—whether it will be high or low. It doesn't even preclude drawing the same D^* value in later periods. Since a similar random, independent determination process underlies the resale values, the same holds true here too.

10. No one may bid less than $0.00 for the commodity. Nor may anyone bid more than their resale value plus 2ε.

Bids must be rounded to the nearest penny to be accepted.

In case of ties for the high bid, the computer will randomly determine who will earn the item.

11. You are not to reveal your bids, or profits, nor are you to speak to any other subject while the experiment is in process. This is important to the validity of the study.

Are there any questions?

Instructions for English Auctions: Affiliated Private Values (Chapter 5)

This is an experiment in the economics of market decision making. The National Science Foundation has provided funds for conducting this research. The instructions are simple, and if you follow them carefully and make good decisions you may earn a CONSIDERABLE AMOUNT OF MONEY which will be PAID TO YOU IN CASH at the end of the experiment.

1. In this experiment we create a market in which you will act as buyers of a fictitious commodity in a sequence of trading periods. A single unit of the commodity will be auctioned off in each trading period. There will be several trading periods.

2. Your task is to bid for the commodity in competition with other buyers. In each trading period you will be assigned a RESALE VALUE for the item. This indicates the value to you of purchasing the item. This value may be thought of as the amount you would receive if you were to resell the unit. The process of determining resale values will be described in Sections 7 and 8 below.

3. Prices will be called out in ascending order. So long as you are willing to buy at the current price, continue to hold up your "active" signal. Just as soon as the current price rises above what you are willing to pay, set down your "active" signal, to indicate that you are dropping out of competition for the commodity in this trading period.

Once you set down your "active" signal, you *cannot* re-enter the auction until the next trading period.

4. The auction stops as soon as only one bidder is holding up his/her "active" signal. This last active bidder obtains the commodity and earns a profit equal to the difference between his/her resale value and the current price (that is, the price at which the next-to-last active bidder set down his/her signal). That is,

Profit = (his/her resale value) − (current price)

for the last active bidder. Each bidder who drops out of the auction earns zero profit for that trading period.

5. You will each be given a $5.00 starting capital balance to provide a minimum level of compensation for participating in the experiment. Profits earned during trading periods will be added to this balance, losses subtracted from it. Your net balance will be paid to you in cash at the end of the experiment.

6. Each period, six bidders will compete for the item, others sitting out that period. Everyone will take turns sitting out of the auction.

7. Resale values will be assigned as follows. First, we will randomly draw a number between $25 and $125 inclusively. Call this number D^*. For each auction, *any value* between $25 and $125 has *an equally likely* chance of being drawn.

8. Once D^* is determined, resale values will be assigned randomly and will be selected from an interval whose lower bound is. D^* minus epsilon (ε), and whose upper bound is D^* plus epsilon (ε). *Any value* within this interval has *an equally likely* chance of being drawn and being assigned to one of you as your resale value. For example, suppose that D^* is $35.50 and that epsilon ($\varepsilon$) is $6.00. Then each of you will receive a resale value which will consist of a randomly drawn number that will be between $29.50 ($D^* - \varepsilon = \$35.50 - \$6.00$) and $41.50 ($D^* + \varepsilon = \$35.50 + \$6.00$). Any number in this interval has an equally likely chance of being drawn.

The line diagram below shows what's going on in this example.

$D^* - \varepsilon = \$29.50$ $D^* = \$35.50$ $D^* + \varepsilon = \$41.50$ $\varepsilon = \$6.00$

$\vdash$————————$($————————$\vert$————————$)$————————————————————————$\dashv$

$25.00   Resale values may be $125
                    anywhere in this interval

9. Your resale values are strictly private information and are not to be revealed to anyone else.

You will be told the value of ε prior to bidding. However, you will not be told the value of D^*.

The following data are typical of the resale values you are likely to receive in the case where $D^* = \$35.50$ and $\varepsilon = \$6.00$ and $12.00, respectively. (Note we've ordered these resale values from highest to lowest for the case of six bidders.)

$$D^* = \$35.50$$

$\varepsilon = \$6.00$	$\varepsilon = \$12.00$
$31.58	$24.08
$33.12	$27.65
$35.67	$30.73
$37.35	$39.20
$38.42	$41.35
$39.54	$43.58

Note the larger ε is, the more spread out resale values are likely to be. Also you may receive a resale value below $25.00 (or above $125.00). There is nothing strange about this, it just indicates D^* is close to the $25.00 (or $125.00) relative to the size of epsilon.

10. The D^* values are determined randomly and independently from auction to auction. As such, a high value in one period tells you nothing about the likely value in the next period—whether it will be high or low. It doesn't even preclude drawing the same D^* value in later periods. Since a similar random, independent determination process underlies the resale values, the same holds true here too.

11. The price will rise by smaller increments as fewer bidders are actively competing. If the last two bidders drop out of the auction at the same time, a coin flip will determine which of the two obtains the commodity.

12. Please fill in your resale value, the current price when you dropped out, the market price, and your profit each period on your record sheet. The other columns on the record sheet are optional—you can fill in any information you find helpful.

13. If you drop out of the auction, you are not to reveal your resale value, nor are you to speak to any other subject while the experiment is in progress. This is important to the validity of the study.

Are there any questions?

Instructions for English Auctions (Chapter 6)

1. We will continue auctioning off a single unit of the commodity in each trading period as we have been doing, only the auction rules have changed. You will no longer enter a bid at your computer terminals for the item. Instead, several seconds after receiving your private information signals, a price will automatically be displayed on your terminal screen, where your bid would have been displayed had you entered it. The starting price will be $50.00, the lowest possible value for the item, and will increase *rapidly* at increments of $1.00.

2. As long as you are willing to buy at the current price, you do nothing. As soon as the price on the screen rises to the maximum amount you are willing to pay, hit any terminal key. This will automatically drop you out of the bidding for the commodity in this trading period. Once you have dropped out of the bidding for a period, you *cannot* re-enter the auction until the next trading period.

3. The auction stops as soon as there is only one active bidder. This last bidder earns the item and makes a profit equal to the value of the item less the price at which the next-to-last active bidder dropped out. That is,

Profit = (Value of the item) − (price at which the next-to-last active bidder dropped)

All other bidders earn zero profits.

In case the last two bidders drop out at the same price, the computer will randomly decide who earned the item. In this case, the price paid will be the dropout price.

4. The number of active bidders remaining in the auction will always be displayed just below the bid price on the terminal screen.

5. Once the first bidder drops out, there will be a pause of several seconds, before prices start increasing again. The price at which the first bidder dropped out will be frozen on your terminal screens during this period. Prices will increase a little slower after this, and the size of the increments will start to decrease as more people drop out of the bidding (however, there will no longer be any extra-long pauses in between price increments). Once there are only two active bidders remaining, price increases will be $0.20 with epsilon equal to $18.

6. Once the bidding is completed for a period, profits for the high bidder will be calculated and balances updated. We will also report back on your terminal screens the value of the item, the private information signals received, and the prices at which the bidder holding each signal dropped out of the bidding.

Are there any questions?

Additional Instructions for Insider Auctions (Chapter 7)

1. From now on bidding will be done twice during each market period, once under each of two different information conditions.

First, you will bid on the basis of your private information signals, just as you have been doing.

After these bids have been made and collected, but before they are announced, *one* of the *active* bidders will be told the true value of the item, and *all* of you will be asked to bid again on the commodity. The computer will randomly determine, from period to period, the bidder who is told the true value of the item. The value of the item will be highlighted on the right-hand side of this bidder's screen, just above the bid enter/confirmation position. The rest of you will receive no additional information.

2. After both sets of bids have been entered and sorted, they will be posted on your terminal screens, along with the private information signals underlying them, with the high bid noted. We will post the value of the item and compute profits and/or losses separately in each of the two markets.

Profits will be equal to the value of the item less the high bid price in *that market* (note the value of the item is the same in both markets).

However, we will only pay profits, or hold you accountable for losses, in one of the two markets. The computer will randomly determine the market we pay off in.

3. There is no obligation to make the same bid, or to bid differently in the two markets. This is strictly up to you to decide what to do in terms of what you think will generate the most profits.

Are there any questions?

Instructions for Second-Price Auctions with Asymmetric Payoffs (Chapter 9)

This is an experiment in the economics of market decision making. The National Science Foundation has provided funds for conducting this research. The instructions are simple, and if you follow them carefully and make good decisions, you may earn a CONSIDERABLE AMOUNT OF MONEY which will be PAID TO YOU IN CASH at the end of the experiment.

1. In this experiment we will create a market in which you will act as buyers of a fictitious commodity in a sequence of trading periods. In each trading period, you will be paired randomly with another participant. A single unit of the commodity will be auctioned with the two of you as bidders. Your pairings will vary over a series of trading periods and will remain anonymous.

2. The common value V^* of an item is determined randomly in each trading period as the sum of two independent component values, X and Y. X and Y are assigned randomly and will lie between $1.00 and $4.00. Each value within this interval has an equally likely chance of being drawn, and the value of X has no bearing on the value of Y. No matter what the value of X, *every value* between $1.00 and $4.00 is equally likely to be the value of Y.

Prior to bidding in each trading period, you will learn one, and only one, of the two component values. The bidder you are paired with will learn the other value (but *not* your value).

Example 1: Suppose you learn that $X = \$3.00$ and the bidder you are paired with learns that $Y = \$1.50$. Then the common value $V^* = \$4.50$.

Example 2: Suppose you learn that $X = \$1.25$ and the bidder you are paired with learns that $Y = \$3.75$. Then the common value $V^* = \$5.00$.

Note that the values of X and Y are determined randomly and independently from auction to auction. As such, a high V^* in one period tells you nothing about the likely value in the next period—whether it will be high or low. It doesn't even preclude drawing the same V^* value in later periods.

3. There will also be a private value element for the item—K_i (where i stands for bidder i). In each period, one bidder (either you or the bidder you are paired with) will have K_i fixed at $1.00. The other member of the pair will have K_i fixed at $0.00. The value of the item to bidder i will be $V^* + K_i$. In other words, in each trading period one bidder will value the item at V^* and the other bidder will value it at $V^* + \$1.00$.

The bidder with the positive value of K_i will be determined randomly for each pair of bidders and for each trading period. You will always know your own value of K and therefore the value of K for the bidder you are paired with as well.

Example 1: Suppose you learn that $X = \$3.00$ and that your value of $K = 0$ (so that the other bidder's value of K is $1.00), and that the other bidder learns that $Y = \$1.50$. Then the value of the item to you is $4.50 and the value to the other bidder is $5.50.

Example 2: Suppose you learn that $X = \$1.25$, your value of K is $1.00 (so that the other bidder's value of K is 0), and that the other bidder learns that $Y = \$3.75$. Then the value of the item to you is $6.00 and the value to the other bidder is $5.00.

Note that the bidder with the positive value of K is chosen independently of the values of X and Y. So if you learn X, your value of K tells you nothing about the possible value of Y.

4. Market Organization:

In each period you will submit a scaled bid for the item. The high bidder earns the item and makes a profit equal to the difference between the value of the commodity to him and the *second highest bid price*. That is,

$$V^* + K_i - (\text{2ND HIGHEST BID}) = \text{PROFITS}$$

for the high bidder. If this difference is negative, it represents a loss.

If you do not make the high bid, you will earn zero profits. In this case, you neither gain nor lose money from bidding on the item.

5. You will be given a starting capital credit balance of $10.00, which includes your $5.00 participation fee. Any profit you earn in the experiment will be added to this sum and any losses you incur will be subtracted from it. The net balance of these transactions will be calculated and paid to you in CASH at the end of the experiment.

The starting capital credit balance and whatever subsequent profits you earn permit you to recoup losses in one auction in part or in total in later auctions. Should your net balance drop to zero (or less) at any time during the experiment, however, you will no longer be permitted to participate. Note that your participation fee was included in the $10.00 starting balance.

6. All participants will be competing in pairs in each trading period. We will record the results for your auction after all bids have been handed in and return them to you individually. We will list the signals and the bids, then circle the high bid and post the value of each item. We will also indicate whether a profit or loss was earned by the high bidder.

7. No one may bid less than $0.00 for the item, and bids must be rounded to the nearest penny. In case of a tie for the high bid, we will flip a coin to determine the winner and assess the 2nd highest bid, which is the same as the high bid, as the price.

8. Your signals are strictly private information and are not to be revealed to anyone else. You will be told your value of K prior to bidding, but you will not be told the value of V^* until after the bids have been posted.

You are not to reveal your bids or profits, nor are you to speak with other subjects while the experiment is in progress. This is important to the validity of the study and will not be tolerated.

Let's summarize the main points: (1) High bidder wins the item and earns a profit = personal value for the item − second high bid price. (2) Profits will be added to your starting balance of $10.00, losses subtracted from it. Your balance at the end of the experiment will be paid in cash. (3) Your private information signal is one of the two component values of V^*, where $V^* = X + Y$. (4) One bidder values the item at V^* and the other at $V^* + \$1.00$. (5) V^* always falls between $2.00 and $8.00.

Instructions for First-Price Offer Auctions (Chapter 12)

This is an experiment in the economics of market decision making. The National Science Foundation has provided funds for conducting this research. The instructions are simple, and if you follow them carefully and make good decisions you may earn a CONSIDERABLE AMOUNT OF MONEY which will be PAID TO YOU IN CASH at the end of the experiment.

1. In this experiment we will create a market in which you will act as suppliers of a commodity in a sequence of trading periods. A single unit of the commodity will be sold in each trading period. There will be several trading periods.

2. Your task is to submit written bids for the right to supply the commodity in competition with other sellers. The precise cost of production at the time you bid will be unknown to you. Instead, each of you will receive information about costs which you should find useful in determining your bid. The process of determining costs and the information you will receive will be described in Sections 6 and 7 below.

3. The low bidder sells the item and makes a profit equal to the difference between the amount that they bid and the actual cost of the commodity. That is,

LOWEST BID − COST OF THE ITEM = PROFITS

for the low bidder. If this difference is negative, it represents a loss. In other words, to make a profit you must sell the item at a price higher than its cost to you. If the item's cost is greater than what you agree to sell it for, you earn losses that period.

If you do not make the low bid on the item, you will earn zero profits. In this case, you neither gain nor lose money from bidding on the item.

4. You will be given a starting capital credit balance of $10.00. Any profit earned by you in the experiment will be added to this sum, and any losses incurred will be subtracted from it. The net balance of these transactions will be calculated and paid to you in CASH at the end of the experiment.

The starting capital credit balance, and whatever subsequent profits you earn, permit you to suffer losses in one auction, to be recouped in part or in total in later auctions. However, should your net balance at any time during the experiment drop to zero (or less), you will no longer be permitted to participate. Instead, we will give you your participation fee and you'll be free to leave the auction.

You *are* permitted to bid in excess of your capital credit balance in any given period.

5. Each period, you will know exactly how many bidders are participating. After all bids have been received, they will be displayed on your terminal. We will note the low bid and the actual cost of the item, and indicate whether a profit or a loss was earned by the low bidder.

6. The cost of the item (C^*) will be assigned randomly and will lie between \$50.00 and \$250.00 inclusively. For each auction, *any cost* within this interval has an *equally likely chance* of being drawn. The cost of the item can never be less than \$50.00 or more than \$250.00. The C^* values are determined randomly and independently from auction to auction. As such, a high C^* in one period tells you nothing about the likely cost in the next period—whether it will be high or low. It doesn't even preclude drawing the same C^* value in later periods.

7. Private Information Signals:

Although you do not know the precise cost of the item in any particular trading period, you will receive information which will narrow down the range of possible costs. This will consist of a private information signal which is selected randomly from an interval whose lower bound is C^* minus epsilon (ε), and whose upper bound is C^* plus epsilon. *Any cost* within this interval has an *equally likely* chance of being drawn and being assigned to one of you as your private information signal. You will always know what the value of epsilon is.

For example, suppose that the cost of the auctioned item is \$128.16 and that epsilon is \$6.00. Then each of you will receive a private information signal which will consist of a randomly drawn number that will be between \$122.16 ($C^* - \varepsilon = \$128.16 - \$6.00$) and \$134.16 ($C^* + \varepsilon = \$128.16 + \$6.00$). Any number in this interval has an equally likely chance of being drawn.

The line diagram below shows what's going on in this example.

$$C^* - \varepsilon = \$122.16 \qquad C^* = \$128.16 \qquad C^* + \varepsilon = \$134.16 \qquad \varepsilon = \$6.00$$

```
├─────────────────(───────────────────┼──────────────────)─────────────────┤
$50.00                          Signals may be                        $250.00
                              anywhere in this interval
```

The data below show the entire set of signals the computer generated for our sample. (Note we've ordered these signals from lowest to highest.)

$$C^* = \$128.16; \ \varepsilon = \$6.00. \text{ Signal values: } \$122.57$$

$$124.14$$
$$124.68$$
$$126.76$$
$$128.84$$
$$129.51$$
$$129.96$$
$$129.98$$
$$132.07$$

You will note that some signals were above the cost of the auctioned item, and some were below it. Over a sufficiently long series of auctions, the differences between your private information signal and the cost of the item will average out to zero (or very close to it). For any given auction, however, your private information signal can be above or below the cost of the item. That's the nature of the random selection process generating the signals.

You will also note that C^* must always be greater than or equal to your signal $- \ \varepsilon$. The computer calculates this for you and notes it. Further, C^* must always be less than or equal to your signal $+ \ \varepsilon$. The computer calculates this for you and notes it as well.

Finally, you may receive a signal below \$50.00 (or above \$250.00). There is nothing strange about this, it just indicates C^* is close to \$50.00 (or \$250.00) relative to the size of epsilon.

9. Your signals are strictly private information and are not to be revealed to anyone else.

You will be told the value of ε prior to bidding and it will be posted on your terminal. However, you will not be told the value of C^* until after the bids have been posted. Finally, we will post all of the signals drawn along with the bids.

10. No one may offer to sell the item for more than \$250.00 $+ \ \varepsilon$. You may bid as low as you wish, but note that bidding below your signal value $- \ \varepsilon$ will insure losses should you be the low bidder.

Bids must be rounded to the nearest penny to be accepted.

In case of ties for the low bid, we will flip a coin to determine who will earn the item.

11. You are not to reveal your bids, or profits, nor are you to speak to any other subject while the experiment is in progress.

12. As promised, everyone will receive \$4 irrespective of their earnings for participating in the experiment.

Let's summarize the main points: (1) low bidder sells the item and earns a profit = low bid price $-$ cost of item. (2) Profits will be added to your starting balance of \$10.00, losses subtracted from it. Your balance at the end of the experiment will be paid in cash. If your balance turns negative, you're no longer allowed to bid. (3) Your private information signal is randomly drawn from the interval $C^* - \varepsilon$, $C^* + \varepsilon$. The cost of the item can never be more than your signal $+ \varepsilon$, or less than your signal $- \varepsilon$. (4) The cost of the item will always be between $50.00 and $250.00.

Are there any questions?

Summary of Instructions

Experienced Bidders: First-Price Common Value Auctions

All of you will participate in a single-market bidding for one unit of a commodity of unknown value each market period.

The value of the auctioned item (V^*) will be randomly selected in each period from an interval whose lower bound is $50 and whose upper bound is $550.

Your private information signal is randomly drawn from the interval $V^* - \varepsilon$, $V^* + \varepsilon$. The value of the item can never be more than your signal value $+ \varepsilon$, or less than your signal value $- \varepsilon$.

High bidder earns the item and makes a profit of

VALUE OF ITEM − *HIGH* BID PRICE.

Profits will be added to your starting balance of $10.00, losses subtracted from it. Your balance at the end of the experiment will be paid in cash. If your balance turns negative, you're no longer allowed to bid.

Remember you may *not* communicate with each other until the end of the experiment.

Experienced Bidders: English Auctions

Seven of you will participate in a single-market bidding for one unit of a commodity of unknown value each period.

The value of the auctioned item (V^*) will be randomly selected from the interval whose lower bound is $50 and whose upper bound is $250.

Your private information signal is randomly drawn from the interval V^* − eps, V^* + eps. The value of the item can never be more than your signal value + eps, or less than your signal value − eps.

You will not enter bids. Instead, the computer will increase prices automatically, beginning with a starting price of $50. Once the price gets to a value at which you no longer want to bid, hit any key, and you will automatically be dropped from the bidding.

The high bidder earns the item and makes a profit equal to the value of the item less the price at which the next-to-last active bidder dropped out.

Profits will be added to your starting balance of $10, losses subtracted from it. Your balance at the end of the experiment will be paid in cash. If your balance turns negative, you're no longer allowed to bid.

Remember, you may *not* communicate with each other until the end of the experiment.

All bids are binding. So be careful to avoid mistakes. We can't forgive any bids.

Index

adverse selection effect, 7, 22, 36, 149, 192, 311; adjustment to, 86; in common-value auctions, 151; in the construction industry, 358; in early auctions, 37; institutional remedies for, 39; and number of bidders, 11, 123, 162, 165, 169; and the RNEE, 115
affiliation, 11, 149, 158; strict positive, 109, 177
airwave rights auctions, 65–66, 240n.1; and British "third-generation" mobile phone licenses, 65; irrevocable exit element in, 241n.6; and Major Trader Area (MTA), 63; narrow-band spectrum license sales, 63. *See also* Federal Communications Commission broad band auctions
Andreoni, J., 266n.3
Armantier, O., 53
auctions, 1; and asymmetries, 284; common-value elements, 149, 210; comparison of large- and small-group auctions, 11, 12; economic analysis of, 1; with endogenous participation, 64–65; and experience, 77n.71; government, 1–2; irrevocable exit auctions, 212; and low-quality products, 76n.51; multiauction settings, 16; private-sector, 1; and public information, 12; and safe havens, 64, 73n.73; "shoebox," 69–70. *See also* auctions, common-value; auctions, common-value, and comparison of naive and experienced bidders; auctions, common-value with insider information; auctions, English; auctions, first-price common-value; auctions, first-price sealed-bid; auctions, sealed-bid; auctions, second-price common-value; auctions, second-price sealed-bid
auctions, common-value, 1, 2, 107–8, 210; and adjustments in bidding over time, 316, 319; and basic auction structure, 108–9; and bidding patterns with private information, 119–20, 122–23, 126–27, 270–71; and calculation of revenue differences, 74–75n.37; complexity of, 171; and design of learning experiments, 312–13, 315; and effects of public information on seller's revenues, 127–31; and the experience factor, 113–14; learning in, 311–12, 329; learning/adjustment mechanisms for individual bidders in, 322–29; and measures of learning

and adjustment, 315–16; and mineral-rights auctions, 2; with public information, 112–13; and research questions of primary interest, 118–19; self-selection among returning bidders in, 319, 321–22; and varying number of bidders, 113. *See also* auctions, common-value, and comparison of naive and experienced bidders; auctions, common-value with insider information; construction contract bidding; outer continental shelf (OCS) oil-lease auctions and sales
auctions, common-value, and comparison of naive and experienced bidders, 340; experimental results of, 342–45; structure of, 341; theoretical considerations of, 341–42
auctions, common-value with insider information, 27–29, 31, 276–81; auctions with asymmetric information structure (AIS), 75n.41, 245, 249–51, 263–64; auctions with symmetric information structure (SIS), 245, 249, 263–64; basic auction structure, 246–47; and environments with no private information, 272–73; and homogeneous private information, 273–74; and increases in expected revenue, 264–65; and inexperienced bidders, 100, 251, 254, 256; and learning and adjustments over time, 261–62; and super-experienced bidders, 256–57, 261; and the winner's curse, 248–49
auctions, Dutch, 209n.25
auctions, English, 1, 20, 24–27, 57, 177, 211–12; basic auction structure, 181; best approximations, 241n.6; bidding behavior in, 26–27, 221–23; bid patterns over time, 197–98, 200; clock auction, 200, 206n.8; derivation of equilibrium bid functions, 234–35; econometric analysis, 222–23; effect of auction institution on revenue, 200–202; effect of bidding errors on other observable quantities, 230, 232; and experienced bidders, 25–26; factors inhibiting revenue raising, 216–17; factors promoting revenue raising, 213–16; full information analysis, 229–30; increase in revenue in, 26; and inexperienced bidders, 217–19; with insider information, 23–27; and the irrevocable exit procedure, 24, 241n.6; in Japan, 24; "Japa-